Churchill, Roosevelt & Company

ALSO BY LEWIS E. LEHRMAN

Lincoln at Peoria: The Turning Point
Lincoln "by littles"
Money, Gold, and History

Churchill, Roosevelt & Company

Studies in Character and Statecraft

Lewis E. Lehrman

Published by Stackpole Books
An imprint of Globe Pequot

Distributed by
NATIONAL BOOK NETWORK
800-462-6420

British Library Cataloguing in Publication Information Available

Library of Congress Cataloging-in-Publication Data is available.

ISBN 978-0-8117-1898-1 (hardcover)
ISBN 978-0-8117-6547-3 (e-book)

∞™ The paper used in this publication meets the minimum requirements of American National Standard for Information Sciences—Permanence of Paper for Printed Library Materials, ANSI/NISO Z39.48-1992.

Printed in the United States of America

Always for Louise.

For Peter and Eve, Eliza and Filip, Thomas and Mara,
John and Jenifer, Leland and Vera.

For my grandchildren: Sadie Louise, Caroline, Reed, Lawrence, Eleanor, Forest,
James, Jasmine, Isabel, Rose, Peter Lewis, Berenika, Kestrel, and Cree.

Contents

Winston Churchill and Franklin D. Roosevelt in Casablanca, January 1943.
FRANKLIN D. ROOSEVELT PRESIDENTIAL LIBRARY

Preface

At the onset of World War II, Anglophobia was commonplace among civilian and military leaders in Washington. Mutual distrust had resulted from decades of Anglo-American competition. Bad blood had followed World War I, not least because of Britain's failure to pay its debts to the United States. In Britain, condescension prevailed among the British elite, toward the "backward," self-centered, disorganized ways of the American government. Appeasement and isolationism characterized both countries. National and personal pride inhibited effective collaboration. Indeed, in Britain and America there existed a widely held opinion that Soviet Russia might prove an equally desirable partner. Some American leaders in Washington harbored a suspicion that sophisticated and experienced British leaders, such as Winston S. Churchill and John Maynard Keynes, might be a slippery bunch that would fleece America to keep the British Empire intact. The rules by which America gave critical Lend-Lease aid to Russia were for many reasons much looser than the very strict requirements imposed on Britain.

To defeat Nazi Germany and imperial Japan, the leaders of the United Kingdom and the United States had to overcome widespread distrust in the ranks. Within each government, jealousy among civilian departments and the military services was everywhere apparent. Churchill never doubted that he required the full support of the United States to defeat Adolf Hitler. President Franklin D. Roosevelt would become both a willing and a reluctant partner for Churchill—waiting until Pearl Harbor, nearly 18 months after the fall of France, to join Britain in war against the Nazis and Japan. During those months, FDR did establish the basis for U.S. military cooperation with Great Britain.

Working under Churchill and Roosevelt were several tiers of military and civilian leaders, many of whom did embrace the team spirit needed by the Anglo-American alliance. On neither side of the Atlantic, however, was the team spirit pervasive. In Washington, Secretary of State Cordell Hull, Secretary of the Treasury Henry Morgenthau, and their subordinates, among others, shed their Anglophobia reluctantly. U.S. Army Chief of Staff George C. Marshall and Supreme Commander in Europe Dwight D. Eisenhower supervised many officers who made the alliance work, but others regularly impeded its effectiveness. Among the most important officials who usually aimed at cooperation were Harry Hopkins, Averell Harriman, Max Beaverbrook, and Anthony Eden. Scores of less prominent individuals played key roles critical to Anglo-American success.

The Soviet Union became an ally, but an altogether different kind of ally, as this book tries to make clear. Even as the Anglo-American alliance led to teamwork on civil and military matters, the British and the Americans would differ on postwar cooperation, trade and monetary policy, and policy toward the Soviet Union. Imperfect men—they were almost all men—worked together, negotiated together, fought together, smoked together, ate and drank together. They shared their frustrations with their colleagues, their wives, and their diaries. President Roosevelt and the United States increasingly flexed their military and economic muscle, wounding British pride and undermining British political influence. American officials continued to impose on Britain economic and procedural restrictions that they did not impose on aid to Soviet Russia. Having failed to establish strict limits on their accommodation of Soviet aggression in the Baltic and Eastern Europe during the conflict, the Roosevelt and the Churchill administrations, and later the Truman administration, found it very hard to negotiate fairly and effectively with Moscow as the war came to a close. Huge Soviet armies occupied the territory of Central and Eastern Europe at war's end.

World War II concluded with FDR dead, Churchill out of office, and Joseph Stalin in control of virtually all Eastern Europe. Churchill, Roosevelt, and company had won the war in the West and in the Pacific, but the Soviet army had destroyed the bulk of the Nazi army in the East. With the development of Cold War tensions, the Anglo-American alliance would fail to win the peace.

Churchill, Roosevelt & Company is a book about some of the principal actors and events in the most massive global war of history.

* * *

This book's purposes are *strictly limited* to exploring some of the diplomatic, political, war-making, and peacemaking efforts of Churchill, Roosevelt, and several of their key civilian and military teammates. This book does not pretend to be a history of World War II, nor a history of the peacemaking efforts. Instead, by rigorous selection from among the principals, it attempts to cast a singular spotlight on specific people, decisions, and events during this extraordinary war, narrowing the focus of what I have called *Churchill, Roosevelt & Company.*

President Roosevelt, Prime Minister Churchill, and Prime Minister Mackenzie King of Canada at the Second Quebec Conference, September 1944.
FRANKLIN D. ROOSEVELT PRESIDENTIAL LIBRARY

The Historical Record

> So I derive confidence that the will-power of the British nation, expressing itself through a stern, steadfast, unyielding House of Commons, once again will perform its liberating function and humbly exercise and execute a high purpose among men; and I say this with the more confidence because we are no longer a small Island lost in the Northern mists, but around us gather in proud array all the free nations of the British Empire, and this time from across the Atlantic Ocean the mighty Republic of the United States proclaims itself on our side, or at our side, or, at any rate, near our side.[1]
>
> ***Winston S. Churchill**, speech to House of Commons, May 7, 1941.*

> We have faith that future generations will know that here, in the middle of the twentieth century, there came a time when men of good will found a way to unite, and produce, and fight to destroy the forces of ignorance, and intolerance, and slavery, and war.[2]
>
> ***Franklin D. Roosevelt**, speech to White House Correspondents' Association, Washington, D.C., February 12, 1943.*

The World War II generation has been called America's greatest generation. True or not, World War II did produce great civilian and military leaders, who led the Anglo-American campaign to destroy Nazi Germany and war-making Japan, then to rebuild democracy and prosperity in both countries. In April 1945, U.S. General George C. Marshall wrote British Prime Minister Winston S. Churchill, "Our greatest triumph lies in the fact that we achieved the impossible, Allied military unity of action."[3] Prime Minister Churchill wrote in his memoirs, "Till the arrival in Normandy in the autumn of 1944 of the great mass of the American Army, we had always the right to speak at least as an equal and usually as the predominant partner in every theatre of war except the Pacific and the Australasian; and this remains also true, up to the time mentioned, of the aggregation of all divisions in all theatres for any given month."[4] The nature of this Anglo-American alliance was repeatedly tested as the Americans mobilized in the West, the Russians in the East. Churchill, Roosevelt, Marshall, and a host of other Anglo-American leaders adapted to the rapidly changing circumstances of the German-Japanese threat.

The military and political leaders on both sides of the Atlantic had to overcome mutual mistrust at all levels of society. From the moment that Nazi Germany began its invasion of Belgium, Holland, Luxembourg, and France, on May 10, 1940, doubts about motives threatened to poison the Anglo-American relationship. Churchill biographer Martin Gilbert wrote: "At the end of the War Cabinet [on May 27, 1940] there was some discussion on the attitude of President Roosevelt, who seemed, the minutes noted, 'to be taking the view that it would be very nice of him to pick up the bits of the British Empire if this country was overrun.' It was important, declared [Air Secretary Archibald] Sinclair, to get it realised in the United States that we mean to fight on."[5]

Over the next five years, the Anglo-American relationship matured, but doubts persisted. One British officer commented in 1943, "Some Americans are curiously liable to suspect that they are going to be 'outsmarted' by the subtle British, perhaps because we sometimes do such stupid things that they cannot take them at face value but suspect them of being part of some dark design."[6] In early 1943, even General Dwight D. Eisenhower asserted: "I am not so incredibly naive that I do not realize that Britishers instinctively approach every military problem from the viewpoint of Empire." However, he emphasized that "one of the constant sources of danger to us in this war is the temptation to regard as our first enemy the partner that must work with us in defeating the real enemy."[7] Eisenhower's insight, common sense, and discriminating judgment proved vital to the alliance and thence to victory.

In the seven decades since World War II, the Anglo-American leaders have inspired many biographers and historians. In 2012, British historian David Dilks published *Churchill and Company*, which focused on the relations between Winston S. Churchill and contemporary allies and leaders, primarily those in Europe and the Commonwealth. Indeed, Dilks's work suggested the title for this book. No study of Churchill should proceed without considering the work of Richard Langworth and Martin Gilbert. Other studies focus on the relationship between Prime Minister Churchill and President Franklin D. Roosevelt—among the most recent being Warren F. Kimball's *Forged in War: Roosevelt, Churchill, and the Second World War* (1997); Jon Meacham's *Franklin and Winston: An Intimate Portrait of an Epic Friendship* (2004); Andrew Roberts's *Masters and Commanders: How Four Titans Won the War in the West, 1941–1945* (2008); David Stafford's *Roosevelt & Churchill: Men of Secrets* (2011); and Simon Berthon's *Allies at War: Churchill v Roosevelt v De Gaulle* (2013). Each has its own theme; each illuminates the historic Churchill-Roosevelt alliance. For example, Roberts's *Masters and Commanders* explored the Allied military strategy fought out among Roosevelt, Churchill, and their army chiefs—Generals George C. Marshall and Alan Brooke. Jonathan W. Jordan's *American Warlords* (2015) explored the intricate relationships among American civilian and military leaders.

Unlike Churchill, President Roosevelt was not a writer, but many of the key Anglo-American leaders were dedicated diarists in war, or later became accomplished authors.[8] Some American cabinet members dictated their memoirs to their secretaries.[9] These leaders produced a mountain of material for historians to review. British economist and financial ambassador John Maynard Keynes produced papers that run to 13,500 pages in their printed form.[10] Winston Churchill's writings were even more prodigious, 15 million words according to one estimate.[11] The prime minister was scrupulous in maintaining, indeed insisting on, a written record of his own and his government's actions—believing as he did that written orders focused unequivocal responsibility for execution. Although Churchill's eye was not only on the present, but also on the future, the prime minister kept no diary.[12] After First Lord of the Admiralty Churchill's first meeting with Prime Minister Neville Chamberlain's cabinet in September 1939, one colleague observed that Churchill "is writing his new memoirs."[13] After World War I, he published five volumes of *The World Crisis, 1911–1918*. Even in April 1940, he found some time to work on *A History of the English Speaking Peoples*.[14] In December 1940, the prime minister told an aide that after the war, he intended to "retire to Chartwell and write a book on the war, which he already had mapped out in his mind chapter by chapter."[15] He did write the book, but he did not retire. Philosopher Isaiah Berlin noted an important difference between the prime minister and FDR: "Roosevelt had not left us his own account of his world as he saw it; and perhaps he lived too much from day to day to be temperamentally attracted to the performance of such a task. But both [Roosevelt and Churchill] were thoroughly aware of their commanding position in the history of the modern world, and Churchill's account of his stewardship is written in full consciousness of this responsibility."[16]

British and American leaders wrote countless memos daily about events and decisions, and then at night filled their diaries with more intimate observations. Marshall kept no diary as a matter of principle, believing them to be self-serving.[17] Contrary to the British Official Secrets Act, some British leaders—General Brooke, Foreign Secretary Eden, Permanent Under-Secretary for Foreign Affairs Alexander Cadogan, and Principal Private Secretary to the Foreign Secretary Oliver Harvey, as well as Churchill's own physician, Dr. Charles Wilson—kept diaries and made biting comments about people and circumstances. Cadogan understood the uneven nature of his diary entries, writing in September 1941: "I keep it scrappily and simply haven't the time to indicate what interviews are about, or to relate one thing to another."[18] David Dilks, editor of Cadogan's diaries, noted: "As terse on paper as in speech, he enjoyed the luxury of saying in private what he could not utter elsewhere," such as, "I think he's got something pressing on his brain," "a nasty mind but a nice wit," "he has a soul above that sort of thing," and simply, "wish she'd go home."[19] At the 1945 Yalta Summit, Cadogan's impatience with the tired prime minister boiled over: "*How* have we conducted this war, with the PM spending *hours* of his own and other people's time simply drivelling, welcoming every red herring so as only to have the pleasure of more irrelevant, redundant talk?"[20] As is always the case in this form of writing, some diary entries are reliable, some implausible, and still others self-centered. Some authors later altered or enlarged their diary entries, one of the many criticisms made of Dr. Wilson's published diary. Brooke took a more transparent approach, writing supplemental notes to his original diary, which Alex Danchev and Daniel Todman included in *Lord Alanbrooke's War Diaries, 1939–1945*.

The diaries of Anglo-American leaders reflect the ebb and flow of the developing alliance. In editing U.S. General Raymond Lee's journals, James Leutze wrote of the summer of 1941: "American progress toward entry into the war now seems like a steady, inexorable movement. At the time there was great uncertainty and much hesitation, and each forward step was taken only after some measure of procrastination."[21] Many critical judgments about what leaders on the other side of the Atlantic were doing wrong were expressed early in the war. Talking to a top British official just back from America in July 1941, General Lee, head of American military intelligence in London, wrote that his impression was that "the War Department is working long hours and desperately, but with no clear objective. This has not yet been handed down by the highest political authorities," meaning that FDR had not made up his mind.[22]

For some British and American officials, the diary was a form of emotional release as well as their personal historical record—records that the British officials were prohibited from keeping during wartime. (Americans were under no such prohibition.) Eden aide and diarist Oliver Harvey wrote of Churchill, who himself kept no diary: "If allowed to, he will win the war and lose the peace as certain. A.E. [Anthony Eden] can't possibly acquiesce in such policies. He is the second man in the Government and with him [Eden] on postwar [planning] is the bulk of the country."[23] As outspoken as Harvey could be in his diary, he held a dim view of the liberties that British Ambassador Archibald Clark Kerr held in his formal reports to the Foreign Office. Clark Kerr had a sardonic view of the world. When Churchill arrived in Moscow in August 1942, Clark Kerr reported to the Foreign Office: "The first glimpse I had of the PM was a pair of stout legs dangling from the belly of the plane and feeling for terra firma. They found it, and then came the plump trunk and finally the round football head, and quite a normal hat."[24] Pictures of Churchill alighting from airplanes confirm this description.

Americans such as Secretary of State Edward Stettinius tended to be more circumspect in their diaries. Exceptions were the diaries of Secretary of War Henry Stimson, who freely expressed his frustrations with FDR, and those of Secretary of the Interior Harold Ickes, whose unvarnished observations about colleagues were salted with severe commentary from his meetings with Ambassador William C. Bullitt.[25] Those that Treasury Secretary Henry J. Morgenthau Jr. dictated now fill 860 volumes and 285,000 pages at the Franklin D. Roosevelt Presidential Library in Hyde Park, New York.[26] FDR's first secretary of state, Cordell Hull, composed two well-written but not entirely reliable volumes of memoirs that made the case for his point of view. (To read Hull's more pungent observations, it is necessary to consult the diaries of Assistant Secretary of State Breckinridge Long.[27]) As Army chief George Marshall believed, diaries and memoirs are full of special pleading and self-justification.

Seldom do they represent a broader perspective and the full context of facts and circumstances. The memoirs of some World War II leaders tiptoed around the personal conflicts they had endured during the war. Some were self-serving while critical of others. Historian Fraser J. Harbutt wrote that cabinet diaries "suggest a remarkable self-preoccupation. The diaries of Henry Wallace, in particular, are a strong corrective to anyone in thrall to the romantic conception of statesmanship. The well-intentioned vice president, almost totally obsessed with Washington intrigue and his own declining political prospects, appears . . . almost unaware of the great world events through which he was passing."[28]

Numerous American military leaders did publish memoirs, including General Dwight D. Eisenhower, General Omar Bradley, and Admiral William D. Leahy. Memory is imperfect, even for those skilled at reporting events they observe. In *Hinge of Fate*, Churchill admitted his own faulty memory regarding the history of the Allied policy of unconditional surrender. Churchill concluded: "I am reminded of the professor who in his declining hours was asked by his devoted pupils for his final counsel. He replied: 'Verify your quotations.'"[29] The diarist labors under no such injunction. Truth is elusive. In *Their Finest Hour,* Churchill acknowledged: "The reader of these pages in future years should realise how dense and baffling is the veil of the Unknown. Now in the full light of the after-time it is easy to see where we were ignorant and too much alarmed, where we were careless or clumsy. Twice in two months we had been taken completely by surprise. The overrunning of Norway and the break-through at Sedan, with all that followed from these proved the deadly power of the German initiative."[30]

The Russian viewpoint has been harder to fathom, because Russian archives have remained largely closed, except for a short period after the collapse of the Soviet Union. Moreover, few early Soviet leaders survived Joseph Stalin's ruthless dictatorship, nor did most survivors dare to write down their recollections. Foreign Minister V. M. Molotov, who outlived Stalin and died at 96, was a remarkable exception. Molotov recounted his memories to journalist Felix Chuev, published in English translation as *Molotov Remembers*. In one conversation, Molotov expressed qualified admiration of Churchill's writings, but he emphasized that Churchill "never forgot to write things down. Keep in mind that he stated the facts in his own way. You need to check them against other sources. He stated them very artfully. He was an imperialist to the core."[31] The Soviet communist system, equally imperial, was a murderous regime under Stalin, and became even worse in war. For example, capture by the Germans was a mark for soldiers and their families of perpetual dishonor, from which Stalin's own son and daughter-in-law did not escape. "Stalin was the greatest tactician," contended the loyal Molotov. Implausibly, he rationalized that the stunning 1939 pact with Hitler was strategically necessary as a means to delay war: "Stalin saw through it all. Stalin trusted Hitler? He didn't trust all his own people!"[32] Stalin's dismissal of all warnings of the Nazi invasion led to a near total disaster for the Russian people. His jealousy undermined relationships with his military leaders, like the tireless Marshall Georgy Zhukov, the Russian general who bravely clashed with Stalin on military decisions, but in the end loyally declared: "He is the greatest and wisest military genius who ever lived."[33]

General Aleksandr Vasilevsky, chief of the General Staff of the Soviet Armed Forces during World War II, was one of the few senior Russian generals who lived to write his memoirs, *The Matter of My Whole Life*. Vasilevsky survived not only Stalin, but also the de-Stalinization of Russia under Nikita Khrushchev in 1956. "Stalin was unjustifiably self-confident, headstrong, unwilling to listen to others; he overestimated his own knowledge and ability to guide the conduct of the war directly," wrote Vasilevsky, who also served as a frontline commander. Stalin "relied very little on the General Staff and made no adequate use of the skills and experience of its personnel. Often for no reason at all, he would make hasty changes in the top military leadership." With regard to strategy, the general observed: "Stalin quite rightly insisted that the military must abandon outdated strategic concepts, but he was unfortunately rather slow to do this himself. He tended to favour head-on confrontations . . . Stalin did not fully master the new forms and methods of armed combat until the battle of Kursk" in the summer of 1943.[34] This characterization of Stalin resembles that of Hitler at war.[35] Allied generals, and King George VI in one case, had to restrain Churchill, a brave former cavalry officer, from getting too close to war zones. Stalin avoided personal contact with the vast Russian war front.[36] Marshal S. S. Biryunov observed that Stalin "was the supreme commander in chief, but the troops never saw him at the front, and not once did his eyes behold a soldier in combat."[37]

Diplomat Ivan Maisky survived the hothouse of Stalin's wartime diplomacy, including tours of duty at the Yalta and Potsdam summits. He also served as the Russian ambassador in London from 1932 to 1943. Some of Maisky's work focused on postwar policy, a centerpiece of discussions at Yalta. Maisky retired at war's end. His 1965 memoirs were critical of Stalin, confirming that the Russian dictator contemplated domination of Russia's western neighbors as early as 1941.[38] After his London service, Maisky served as deputy commissar for foreign affairs with Maxim Litvinov, Russia's former ambassador in Washington, who would die in 1951, partly as a result of a Stalin-inspired assassination attempt. In his memoirs, Molotov suggested that Litvinov was a good diplomat but an untrustworthy politician, who had "remained among the living only by chance."[39] Roy Medvedev was one of the first Russian intellectuals to criticize Stalin's wartime leadership. Medvedev argued "that had there been a more competent supreme command, a different kind of preparation for the war, a more intelligent assessment of the danger of war in June 1941—above all, if the [Soviet] military commanders and cadres killed in the purges of 1937–1938 had been preserved—the victory over Nazi Germany would have come much sooner and at much less cost."[40] Responsibility must rest on Joseph Stalin, under whom Russian diplomats and bureaucrats, and even generals and military intelligence officers, had little discretion. "Stalin and I kept a tight hold on everything—we couldn't do it any other way at the time," recalled Molotov. "On the whole we quite confidently directed our centralized diplomacy."[41] In Stalin's case, this was generally true of economic, political, and military strategy as well.

Public complaints about Stalin did not surface among Soviet leaders during World War II. Russian officials and army officers dared not make a move without his approval, especially after the bloodthirsty and intimidating purges of the late 1930s. Colleagues of Churchill and Roosevelt, however, did complain about the prime minister and the president. Churchill was most exposed to criticism because he was confident and quick to try out his ideas and military proposals in discussion. Though he did not override his military chiefs, he surely agitated those around him who wanted him to be more deliberate, less opportunistic. By contrast, Roosevelt's style was oblique. He was devious with his comments and opinions, changing them, even denying them, with different people and in different circumstances. FDR aggravated subordinates, whom he allowed to work at cross-purposes because he had failed to declare his policy, if in fact he had formulated one. Churchill had the advantage over Roosevelt, in that he lived to tell (in six volumes) his side of *The Second World War*, especially on critical points where the Anglo-American leaders differed, such as at the 1945 Yalta summit.[42] Even if FDR had lived, he probably would not have labored over memoirs. He did not like to write, nor had he developed the discipline to do so.

Churchill, Roosevelt & Company focuses on some of the most prominent Anglo-American leaders who had gained the trust of Churchill or Roosevelt—directly or indirectly. Some books—like Lynne Olson's *Citizens of London: The Americans Who Stood with Britain in Its Darkest, Finest Hour* or Thomas Parrish's *To Keep the British Isles Afloat*—dwell on that small group of key Americans who worked in London, especially Harry Hopkins, Ambassador John G. Winant, and W. Averell Harriman. Other books have a different story to tell. Michael Beschloss's *The Conquerors* covered the conflicts within the Roosevelt and Truman administrations concerning postwar policy toward Germany. John Lewis Gaddis's *The Cold War* and *George F. Kennan* explored the origins of the Cold War between the United States and Russia.[43] Other works have emphasized the confused and disappointing results of the 1945 Yalta summit; these include Fraser J. Harbutt's *Yalta 1945: Europe and America at the Crossroads* and S. M. Plokhy's *Yalta: The Price of Peace*. These authors built on the 1957 work of erstwhile State Department advisor Herbert Feis in *Churchill-Roosevelt-Stalin: The War They Waged and the Peace They Sought*.

Harbutt argued that before World War II, few Americans or Europeans knew a great deal about each other. He observed that "very few leaders of the wartime generation had any first-hand knowledge. Stalin, Hitler and Mussolini never crossed the Atlantic. Churchill made several pre-1939 trips, but this was exceptional among the British elite."[44] Leaders from the wealthy and hereditary American elite, like Franklin D. Roosevelt, visited Europe, giving FDR an exaggerated belief in his own geopolitical knowledge of the continent. Harbutt wrote: "Doubtless Americans knew more about Europe than vice versa. There was a widespread if thin awareness of some element of the British past, less so of continental history." There were Anglo-skeptics and America-skeptics on both sides of the Atlantic; the First World War had reinforced this skepticism.[45] Historian Warren Kimball wrote that Roosevelt and

Churchill, like most people, held strong opinions not always based upon fact. Kimball wrote of the "remarkable ignorance each displayed about the political system in the other's country," each overestimating freedom of action in the other's country.[46] For everyone on both sides of the Atlantic, World War II would be a painful, but successful, learning experience in forming the transatlantic alliance and agreeing on military-political strategy in the war against the Axis powers.

Considerations of Churchill and Roosevelt have spawned endless comparisons. Roosevelt reveled in his disorganized government, which required his intervention to settle disputes even when he was not ready to do so. Roosevelt's cabinet colleagues found it hard to get him to make up his mind, even to decide on an urgent policy. Churchill's cabinet colleagues fought to dissuade the prime minister from pursuing policies he had decided too quickly. Churchill's physician, Dr. Charles Wilson, observed that "no one could stand up to him, either in the Cabinet or in the House of Commons. Once he had made up his mind, nobody could make him change it."[47] This was not the case in military operations. The prime minister always sought the approval of the military chiefs of staff and, despite much aggravation, did not overrule their final decisions. He had learned much from his leadership experience in World War I, as had FDR.

Churchill was a stickler for precision and for written records. In this, he was very unlike Roosevelt, who "did not like to keep records," as State Department official Charles E. Bohlen noted.[48] The president wanted to be free to change his mind, even to be unaccountable for previous opinions and decisions. With no formal records of meetings, FDR maintained deniability. The president did record, secretly, meetings held in his office. Churchill was different. His cabinet-level authority in World War I had taught him that without written orders and written records of decisions made, generals and political authorities would evade responsibility, even deny agreed-upon decisions. Thus, in July 1940, the prime minister wrote to his aides, Cabinet Secretary Edward Bridges and General Hastings Ismay: "Let it be very clearly understood that all directions emanating from me are made in writing, or should be immediately afterwards confirmed in writing, and that I do not accept any responsibility for matters relating to national defence on which I am alleged to have given decisions unless they are recorded in writing."[49] Defending his government before the House of Commons in July 1942, Churchill declared: "Nearly all my work has been done in writing, and a complete record exists of all the directions I have given, the inquiries I have made, and the telegrams I have drafted. I shall be perfectly content to be judged by them."[50]

At war, words were a vital resource for the prime minister, a matter of life and death. Words and instructions had to be clear and authoritative, the essence of effective decision-making. The scholar Isaiah Berlin wrote: "Churchill's language is a medium which he invented because he needed it. It has a bold, ponderous, fairly uniform, easily recognizable rhythm which lends itself to parody (including his own) like all strongly individual styles. . . . The origins, the constituents, the classical echoes which can be found in Mr. Churchill's prose are obvious enough; the product is, however, unique."[51] More important, the prime minister generally accepted responsibility for his decisions, as they were recorded in writing. FDR did not want to be similarly pinned down.

Churchill made history and wrote history. He understood, however, the limits of historical judgments. "In one phase men seem to have been right, in another they seem to have been wrong," the prime minister told the House of Commons in November 1940. "Then again, a few years later, when the perspective of time has lengthened, all stands in a different setting. There is a new proportion. There is another scale of values. History with its flickering lamp stumbles along the trail of the past, trying to reconstruct its scenes, to revive its echoes, and kindle with pale gleams the passion of former days."[52]

Churchill was a master of persuasive argument, a special virtue of his leadership in war. Historian Walter Reid wrote that his "communications, like his speeches, did not consist simply of magnificent and memorable phrases. The bravura climaxes followed on detailed, supremely well-argued and logical forensic analyses. The Secret Session speeches [in Parliament] are particularly worth studying. They are almost completely free from oratorical flourishes, but rather consist of the logical deployment of substantial data, skilfully set out in a persuasive argument of which a distinguished member of the Bar would be proud."[53] His memoirs could be defensive, but very direct in confronting and attempting to refute competing narratives. When his books about World War II began to appear, South African Field Marshal Jan Smuts complained that "you, more than anybody in the world could have written as no one else could have written, the true history of the war, and instead of that you have produced these books." Churchill replied: "This is my story. If someone else likes to write his story, let him."[54] The prime minister, for example, did not accept Eisenhower's version of his attempt, in June 1944, to accompany the D-Day invasion of Normandy. He went to great lengths to refute Eisenhower's narrative. Like all memoirs, Churchill's were not and could not be always accurate. He writes of his first meeting with FDR envoy Harry Hopkins in January 1941: "I therefore arranged that he should be met by Mr. Brendan Bracken on his arrival at Poole airport, and that we should lunch together alone the next day."[55] His secretary, John Martin, recorded a different story: "The significance of this visitor did not seem to be immediately realised by the Foreign Office, but it was by Brendan Bracken, who alerted the Prime Minister and welcomed Hopkins with red-carpet treatment at Bournemouth."[56]

More than Roosevelt, the prime minister enjoyed being surrounded by interesting people. His country weekends were populated with official guests, many of them Americans. By comparison, FDR was a loner. Although Roosevelt exuded charm when on display, he escaped Washington for the seclusion of Hyde Park as often as possible. Roosevelt's self-imposed isolation was one reason the presence of Harry Hopkins, who lived at the White House, proved so important. Hopkins became the liaison who connected key people on both sides of the Atlantic. Moreover, the president cultivated a false, first-name intimacy with people, whereas Churchill was more reserved with strangers. With a smile, a tilt of his cigarette holder or a wave of his hand, and a few charming words, Roosevelt contrived to keep people at a distance. A comment by FDR's daughter, Anna, found its way into Vice President Henry Wallace's diary. Roosevelt, Anna had said, "doesn't know any man and no man knows him. Even his own family doesn't know anything about him." She confirmed this analysis three decades later. A secretive FDR compartmentalized his life, even meeting with his former mistress Lucy Mercer Rutherford in Georgia on the day of his death.[57] As the chief executive and commander in chief for twelve years, the president made many crucial, winning decisions that have survived the test of time, despite the fact he failed to organize and integrate his own administration. Nor did FDR communicate as the team leader, in the way the prime minister did. In 1945, President Roosevelt, sick unto death, did not keep Vice President Harry Truman informed of important developments in military and diplomatic policy, such as the development of the atomic bomb.

During his entire life, Churchill was a leader of boundless energy, always launching entrepreneurial, risky actions, no less so in war. John Colville, the most prolific diarist among Churchill's wartime aides, recalled: "Churchill was constantly on the move, visiting defences, new weapon displays, bombed cities and military formations or, as the war expanded, Washington, Moscow and the theatres of war. FDR, Stalin and Hitler were reluctant to travel. Wherever the British Prime Minister might be, he expected to carry on his normal business precisely as if he were sitting in the Cabinet Room in Downing Street." The prime minister insisted on preparing himself, wherever he was, whatever the issue. The president was not so thorough, too often willing to proceed without thorough preparation. The personalities of the two could be uneven, as the diary entries of Chief of the Imperial General Staff Alan Brooke revealed, when Arthur Bryant excerpted them in 1957. Historian David Reynolds noted: "Privately, several of Churchill's wartime contemporaries believed that the portrait in [Bryant's] *Turn of the Tide* was apt and essentially fair. [His successor] Clement Attlee told Bryant, 'We who worked with him know how quickly he could change from the great man to the naughty child.'"[58]

On balance and with the benefit of hindsight, the prime minister and the president exercised good judgment in major decisions, often encouraging those they trusted to carry on without constant consultation. Leaders that they were, they possessed the vision, the character, and the persistence to carry on the war with Nazi Germany and Japan to the successful bitter end. However imperfect their decisions might occasionally have been, they never gave up. Despite the catastrophic defeats Britain experienced in early 1942 at the hands of the Nazis and the Japanese, Churchill acted the part of the invincible leader in public, imparting inspiration to his beleaguered countrymen. Few witnessed his private disappointments. Paralyzed by polio and less mobile, FDR relied more on the radio to impart his optimism to the home front, to his administration, and to his armed forces.

"I told you hard things at the beginning of these last five years," Churchill said to Londoners on VE Day, May 9, 1945. "[Y]ou did not shrink, and I should be unworthy of your confidence and generosity if I did not still cry: Forward, unflinching, unswerving, indomitable, till the whole task is done and the whole world is safe and clean."[59] VJ Day would come four months later.

NAMES AND TITLES

If a British public official had been elevated to the peerage before World War II, as were Lord Beaverbrook, Lord Halifax, and Lord Lothian, he is generally referred to in this book by that honorific. If British officials were raised to the peerage during or after the war (Dr. Charles Wilson became Lord Moran in 1943, and John Maynard Keynes became Lord Keynes in 1942), the style in *Churchill, Roosevelt & Company* is generally to refer to them by their pre-peerage name. Similarly, many top British soldiers were named field marshals during and after World War II, among them Harold Alexander (1944), Claude Auchinleck (1946), Alan Brooke (1944), John Dill (1941), Bernard Montgomery (1944), Archibald Wavell (1943), and Henry Maitland Wilson (1944); but they are generally not referred to by that title. For simplicity's sake, the honorific of knighthood is generally omitted; "Sir" Winston Churchill was not knighted until 1953.

NOTES

Endnotes numbered at the back of the book are an integral part of this volume, in many cases containing important information and interpretation.

People and Events in *Churchill, Roosevelt & Company*

Note: The individuals listed in the following chronology are those who appear regularly in the text of this book. This list is not comprehensive and some individuals have not been mentioned. For example, First Sea Lord Dudley Pound attended many important meetings, but he did not play a central role in the development of the Anglo-American relationship. By comparison, Pound's successor, Andrew B. Cunningham, played a more critical role, even though he was not as close to Prime Minister Churchill as Pound had been.

January 17, 1938	Joseph P. Kennedy assumes duties as U.S. Ambassador to the United Kingdom.
August 11, 1939	Laurence Steinhardt assumes duties as U.S. Ambassador to Moscow.
August 23, 1939	Molotov-Ribbentrop nonaggression pact is signed in Moscow between communist Russia and fascist Germany.
September 1, 1939	Germany invades Poland.
September 3, 1939	Britain and France declare war on Germany.
	Winston Churchill is appointed First Lord of the Admiralty.
September 1939	Lord Lothian (Philip Kerr) takes up post as British ambassador in Washington.
September 11, 1939	President Franklin D. Roosevelt initiates correspondence with fellow "former naval person," Churchill.
September 17, 1939	Russia invades Poland.

May 2, 1940	British troops withdraw from Norway after successful German invasion of the country.
May 9, 1940	Confidence vote on government of Neville Chamberlain, triggered by humiliation in Norway, for which Churchill was partly responsible.
May 10, 1940	Germany overruns Belgium, Holland, and Luxembourg.
	Winston Churchill named prime minister.
	Harry Hopkins, FDR confidant, moves into the White House.
May 20, 1940	U.S. Ambassador Joseph Kennedy reports to President Roosevelt, "Democracy in Britain is finished."
May 26–June 4, 1940	Operation DYNAMO (1940): Dunkirk evacuation rescues most of the British Army and many French soldiers.
	Paris falls to Germany.
June 10, 1940	Italy declares war on France and Britain.
June 22, 1940	Marshal Philippe Pétain, new French chief of state, signs armistice with Germany.
June 28, 1940	Churchill government recognizes General Charles de Gaulle as the leader of the Free French.
July 1940	Russia annexes Latvia, Lithuania, and Estonia.
July 10, 1940	Republicans Henry L. Stimson (secretary of war) and Frank Knox (secretary of the navy) take office.
July–August 1940	Attorney William Donovan, future head of American spy agency, visits Britain, meeting with Churchill and other officials.
August 10, 1940	Battle of Britain begins with German Luftwaffe bombing British cities.
Fall 1940	Operation Seelöwe ("Sealion"): planned German invasion of Britain, is anticipated.
September 3, 1940	Destroyers-for-Bases deal agreed to by the United States and the United Kingdom. Britain is effectively insolvent.
September 18, 1940	Harry Hopkins resigns as U.S. secretary of commerce.
October 27, 1940	Ambassador Joseph Kennedy returns to the United States, meets with President Roosevelt and James F. Byrnes.
November 5, 1940	President Roosevelt reelected to third term promising no Americans will go to war.
November 23, 1940	Admiral William D. Leahy is appointed U.S. Ambassador to the Vichy government in France, replacing William C. Bullitt.
December 1940	Ambassador Joseph P. Kennedy announces resignation.

December 9, 1940	Operation COMPASS, British counteroffensive in North Africa against Italian troops, begins.
December 12, 1940	British Ambassador to Washington, Lord Lothian, dies.
December 15, 1940	Lord Halifax appointed British Ambassador to the United States to replace Lord Lothian. Anthony Eden appointed British foreign secretary to replace Halifax.
January 1941	Hopkins visits London, meeting with Churchill, Eden, and Foreign Office Permanent Under Secretary Alexander Cadogan.
January 26, 1941	Former Republican presidential candidate Wendell Willkie arrives in London on mission for Roosevelt.
January–March 1941	William Donovan tours Europe and North Africa for President Roosevelt, meets in Cairo with British officials about aid to Greece.
January 29– March 27, 1941	ABC (American-British-Canadian) talks in Washington establish the Atlantic and Europe military theater as primary, with the Pacific theater secondary. FDR still pleads neutrality.
February 1941	John Gilbert Winant arrives in London as U.S. ambassador.
March–April, 1941	British reinforce Greece to meet German invasion.
March 11, 1941	U.S. Congress passes Lend-Lease Act to supply Britain on credit.
March 1941	W. Averell Harriman arrives in London to supervise Lend-Lease program.
March 19, 1941	William Donovan reports to Roosevelt on foreign tour.
April 6, 1941	Yugoslavia and Greece are invaded by Germany, along with bad weather, delaying Hitler's invasion of Russia.
April 13, 1941	Japan and Russia sign nonaggression pact.
April 1941	U.S. Army Air Corps Chief Henry H. Arnold visits Britain.
April 24, 1941	Operation DEMON: Allied troops evacuated from Greece.
June 15–17, 1941	Operation BATTLEAXE: unsuccessful British attack on Axis forces in North Africa, to relieve Tobruk.
June 22, 1941	Operation Barbarossa: Germany invades Russia, believing quick victory possible before deadly Russian winter sets in.
July 11, 1941	Roosevelt establishes Office of the Coordinator of Information (forerunner of OSS and CIA), and appoints William Donovan to head the espionage agency. Donovan works closely with British intelligence.

July 1941	Harry Hopkins visits Britain, followed by a trip to Moscow.
	General Claude Auchinleck replaces General Archibald Wavell as British commander in North Africa.
August 1941	Averell Harriman, Lend-Lease coordinator, returns to United States for consultations.
August 9–12, 1941	Arcadia Conference of Roosevelt and Churchill in Placentia Bay, Newfoundland, attended by Lord Beaverbrook, W. Averell Harriman, Harry Hopkins, Sumner Welles, Alexander Cadogan; Generals George C. Marshall and John Dill; Admirals Ernest King and Harold Stark; Vice Chief of Air Staff Wilfrid Freeman; and First Sea Lord Dudley Pound.
September 24, 1941	Signing of the Atlantic Charter by Belgium, Czechoslovakia, Greece, Luxembourg, the Netherlands, Norway, Poland, and Yugoslavia, as well as by the Soviet Union.
September 27, 1941	Germany, Italy, and Japan sign Tripartite Pact.
September 29–October 1, 1941	Averell Harriman and Lord Beaverbrook visit Stalin and Molotov in Moscow, about Anglo-American military assistance. In the delegation were Admiral William Standley and Generals Stanley Embick, James Burns, and Hastings Ismay.
October 16, 1941	Japanese Cabinet of Prince Fumimaro Konoe resigns, replaced by expansionist Admiral Hideki Tojo.
December 6, 1941	German troops, who had come within sight of Moscow on December 2, are thrown into retreat by a Russian assault and temperatures that fell below –30°C. German soldiers not properly clothed.
December 7, 1941	Japanese aircraft carriers attack Pearl Harbor.
December 8, 1941	United States and Britain declare war on Japan. Japan sinks British battleship HMS *Prince of Wales* and battlecruiser HMS *Repulse* near Singapore.
December 11, 1941	Germany and Italy, joining Japan, declare war on the United States.
December 15–22, 1941	Anthony Eden and Alexander Cadogan visit Stalin and Molotov in Russia.
December 1941–January 1942	Arcadia Conference held in Washington between Roosevelt and Churchill, who is accompanied aboard the HMS *Duke of York* by Averell Harriman. Attendees include Marshall, Stimson, Hull, Hopkins, and Beaverbrook.
December 25, 1941	General Alan Brooke becomes Chief of the Imperial General Staff, replacing John Dill, who becomes Chief of the British Joint Staff Mission in Washington.

January 27, 1942	Churchill endorsed in vote of confidence in House of Commons, 464–1.
February 15, 1942	British garrison at Singapore surrenders. Churchill stunned.
February 1942	British Cabinet shakeup; Lord Beaverbrook resigns.
February 1942	Archibald Clark Kerr replaces Stafford Cripps as British Ambassador to Moscow.
March 1942	Beaverbrook campaigns for Anglo-American second front in France to help Russia.
March 1942	Beaverbrook visits Washington and meets with Roosevelt.
March 1942	General Dwight D. Eisenhower, guided by General Marshall, produces preliminary plans for Operation BOLERO, a buildup of American forces in Britain, and Operation ROUND-UP, a cross-channel invasion of France later in 1942.
April 1942	Harry Hopkins, General Marshall, and U.S. military planners visit Britain, where they meet with General Brooke and British military planners to discuss military plans for European theater.
April 18, 1942	Air raid on Japan led by General James Doolittle.
May 1942	Russian Foreign Minister Vyacheslav Molotov visits London and Washington.
May 1942	British economist John Maynard Keynes visits Washington to confer with Treasury officials on British credit.
May 26, 1942	Britain and Soviet Union sign Twenty-Year Mutual Assistance Agreement.
June 2, 1942	General Arnold returns from London with Air Marshal Charles Portal and Admiral Mountbatten.
June 4–7, 1942	Crucial Battle of Midway won by U.S. Navy. The Japanese lose four carriers, a cruiser, and 292 airplanes; a turning point in Pacific war.
June 19–25, 1942	Conferences held between Roosevelt and Churchill in Hyde Park and Washington. Attendees included Harry Hopkins; Generals Alan Brooke, Hastings Ismay, John Dill, George Marshall; and Admiral Ernest King. Secretary of State Cordell Hull and Lord Halifax participate.
June 21, 1942	British garrison at Tobruk in North Africa surrenders.
June 22, 1942	Harry Hopkins introduces Eisenhower to Churchill at the White House.
July 2, 1942	Churchill easily survives parliamentary vote of confidence, 475–25.
Summer 1942	John Maynard Keynes visits Washington.

July 1–27, 1942	First Battle of Alamein. Germans under Erwin Rommel prevail.
July 1942	Harry Hopkins and General Marshall visit Britain.
July 30, 1942	Harry Hopkins marries Louise Macy at the White House.
August 1942	Churchill flies to Cairo to review Middle East strategy. Averell Harriman joins him there.
August 8, 1942	British Mideast Commander Claude Auchinleck replaced by General Harold Alexander.
August 12–17, 1942	Churchill, Averell Harriman, Alexander Cadogan, Archibald Wavell, Arthur Tedder, and Alan Brooke meet with Stalin and Molotov in Moscow. U.S. Ambassador William H. Standley is not invited.
August 19, 1942	Failed British-Canadian invasion of Dieppe, France, suggests difficulty of cross-channel invasion.
August 1942– February 1943	Battle of Stalingrad.
September 1942	Former Republican presidential candidate Wendell Willkie meets with Stalin in Moscow, and tours Russia.
October 15–27, 1942	Henry Morgenthau Jr. and Harry Dexter White visit Britain and North Africa.
October 23– November 5, 1942	Operation SUPERCHARGE: British and Commonwealth armies under General Bernard Montgomery attack at El Alamein, Egypt.
October 23– November 15, 1942	Eleanor Roosevelt visits Britain.
November 5–16, 1942	Operation TORCH (early name was Operation GYMNAST): Anglo-American landings in Morocco and Algeria.
November 22, 1942	Signing of Allied Agreement with Admiral François Darlan.
January 14–24 1943	Summit held between Roosevelt and Churchill at Casablanca, Morocco. Attendees included Harry Hopkins, Averell Harriman, Robert Murphy, Harold Macmillan, and Generals Marshall, Eisenhower, Alexander; Hastings Ismay, John Dill, Alan Brooke, Albert Wedemeyer, Henri Giraud, and Charles de Gaulle; Admirals Ernest King and Charles Cunningham; Air Marshal Arthur Tedder.
February 2, 1943	Surrender of German forces near Stalingrad.
March 1943	Anthony Eden visits President Roosevelt in Washington. At White House meeting with

	Halifax, Hopkins, Hull, and Welles on March 27, formation of United Nations is discussed.
April 22–May 13, 1943	Operation VULCAN: Final Allied assault on Axis forces trapped around Tunis.
May 1943	Admiral William H. Standley resigns as U.S. Ambassador to Moscow, effective in September.
May 12–25, 1943	Summit conference between Roosevelt and Churchill in Washington. Traveling across Atlantic on *Queen Mary*, Churchill is accompanied by Averell Harriman, Lord Beaverbrook, and Generals Alan Brooke, Archibald Wavell, and Hastings Ismay. In Washington, Harry Hopkins, Generals George Marshall and John Dill, and Admirals Ernest King and William Leahy join them.
May 29, 1943	Talks begin in North Africa with Churchill; Generals Marshall, Eisenhower, Brooke, Ismay, Alexander, Montgomery; Air Marshall Arthur Tedder; Admiral Andrew Cunningham.
July 5–August 23, 1943	Russians defeat Germans during Battle of Kursk, generally considered the largest tank battle in history. A turning point.
July 10, 1943	Operation HUSKY: Allied invasion of Sicily.
July 1943	Churchill flies with General Marshall to North Africa, for talks with General Eisenhower.
July 15–19, 1943	Secretary of War Henry Stimson visits London, where he meets with Churchill and Winant, and later North Africa, where he meets with Eisenhower.
August 1943	Sumner Welles is removed as under secretary of state.
August 14–24, 1943	Roosevelt-Churchill summit held at Quebec. Attendees include Cordell Hull, Anthony Eden, Harry Hopkins, Averell Harriman, Alexander Cadogan; American Generals George C. Marshall, John Deane, and Albert C. Wedemeyer; British Generals Alan Brooke, Hastings Ismay, and John Dill; American Admirals William Leahy and Ernest King. Churchill tells Brooke that an American will command OVERLORD, the cross-channel invasion.
September 3, 1943	Operation AVALANCHE: Allied invasion of Italy.
September 1943	Churchill visits Roosevelt in Hyde Park and Washington. On September 6, Churchill delivers speech at Harvard.
September 8–November 22, 1943	Britain unsuccessfully campaigns to capture Dodecanese islands off Turkey.

October 1943	W. Averell Harriman takes over as U.S. Ambassador to Moscow with General John R. Deane as the new head of the U.S. military mission.
October 18–November 1, 1943	Foreign Ministers Conference in Moscow, attended by Cordell Hull, Anthony Eden, and V. Molotov. Others participating in the 12-day meeting include diplomats Averell Harriman, Charles Bohlen, James C. Dunn, Archibald Clark Kerr, and Oliver Harvey, as well as Generals John Deane and Hastings Ismay.
1943–1944	Operation BOLERO: buildup of American forces in Britain for Allied invasion of France.
November 23–26, 1943	Churchill-Roosevelt summit in Cairo, attended by China President Chiang Kai-shek. Also participating are Harry Hopkins, Anthony Eden, Alexander Cadogan, Averell Harriman, John Gilbert Winant, Harold Macmillan, John McCloy, Lewis Douglas, Charles Bohlen, John Deane, Archibald Clark Kerr; Generals George C. Marshall, Alan Brooke, Hastings Ismay, John Deane, Joseph Stilwell, Albert Wedemeyer, and Henry Arnold; Admirals William Leahy, Ernest King, and Andrew Cunningham; Air Marshal Charles Portal.
November 28–December 1, 1943	Teheran summit conference held with Churchill, Roosevelt, and Stalin. Also attending are Harry Hopkins, Averell Harriman, John G. Winant, Anthony Eden, Archibald Clark Kerr, former U.S. Ambassador to Moscow Joseph E. Davies, V. M. Molotov; Generals Alan Brooke, John Dill, Hastings Ismay, George C. Marshall, Klimenti Voroshilov, John R. Deane; Admirals William Leahy and Ernest King.
December 4–6, 1943	Second Cairo Conference between Churchill and Roosevelt.
December 1943	General Eisenhower appointed to command Operation OVERLORD. William J. Donovan, chief of the Office of Strategic Services, visits Moscow.
December 1943	On the way home from Teheran summit, Churchill stops in Tunisia, stricken with pneumonia; visited by Anthony Eden and Dwight Eisenhower.
January 26, 1944	Operation SHINGLE: Allied landings at Anzio, Italy.
April 1944	Under Secretary of State Edward Stettinius visits Britain.
April 28, 1944	Secretary of the Navy Frank Knox dies and is succeeded by James Forrestal.

June 4, 1944	Allies capture Rome, Italy.
June 6, 1944	D-Day; Operation OVERLORD: invasion of Normandy, France, begins.
June 1944	Generals George Marshall and Henry H. Arnold and Admiral Ernest King visit Britain and France to confer with British counterparts and Churchill.
July 1–22, 1944	Bretton Woods Conference on international trade and finance held in New Hampshire. Secretary of the Treasury Henry Morgenthau Jr. is president of meeting attended by Fred Vinson, Harry Dexter White, Assistant Secretary of State Dean Acheson, John Maynard Keynes, and U.S. Treasury staffers Frank Coe, William Ludwig Ullmann, Nathan Gregory Silvermaster.
July 6–8, 1944	General Charles de Gaulle visits Washington and Roosevelt.
July 11, 1944	Roosevelt administration recognizes the Free French.
July 19–21, 1944	Democratic National Convention renominates Roosevelt for president.
August 1944	Secretary of the Treasury Morgenthau and Harry Dexter White visit Britain and France. They begin to develop the "Morgenthau Plan" for postwar German deindustrialization.
August 15, 1944	Operation DRAGOON (initially named Operation ANVIL): Allied invasion of southern France. Churchill witnesses landing.
August 21–October 7, 1944	Dumbarton Oaks Conference held to plan for United Nations. Attendees included Edward Stettinius, Alexander Cadogan, Lord Halifax, and Russian Ambassador to the United States Andrei Gromyko.
August 24, 1944	Romanian coup d'état reverses the country's allegiance from the Axis to the Allies.
August 25, 1944	Paris liberated.
September 12–16, 1944	Summit between Roosevelt and Churchill held at Quebec; attended by Anthony Eden, Alexander Cadogan, George Marshall, William Leahy, Alan Brooke, Henry Morgenthau, and Harry Dexter White. On September 15, Roosevelt and Churchill initial a memo in general support of the "Morgenthau Plan." Harry Hopkins does not attend conference.
September 17–25, 1944	Operation MARKET GARDEN: unsuccessful Allied attempt to secure bridges over the main rivers of the Netherlands.

September 18–20, 1944	Roosevelt and Churchill meet at Hyde Park; Eleanor Roosevelt and Harry Hopkins in attendance; Clementine Churchill meets FDR for the first time. (She is not charmed.)
September 23, 1944	Averell Harriman and Archibald Clark Kerr report to Stalin on the Quebec conference.
October 3, 1944	Surrender of the rebels in Warsaw after two months of fighting.
October 9–17, 1944	Churchill, Eden, Brooke, and Ismay visit Stalin in Moscow. Averell Harriman acts as an American "observer" along with General Deane.
November 4, 1944	John Dill, British liaison to the U.S. Joint Chiefs, dies and is replaced in Washington by General Henry W. Maitland.
November 7, 1944	Roosevelt reelected to fourth term.
November 11, 1944	Churchill visits Paris, celebrating Armistice Day (from World War I) with General Charles de Gaulle. Anthony Eden, Alexander Cadogan, and Generals Alan Brooke and Hastings Ismay accompany Churchill.
December 1944	Edward Stettinius Jr. succeeds Cordell Hull as secretary of state, shaking up State Department hierarchy.
December 16, 1944	Battle of the Bulge in the Ardennes forest begins.
December 25, 1944	Churchill and Anthony Eden fly to Athens to stop Greek civil war. Churchill initiative succeeds against the odds. Communist coup avoided.
January 17, 1945	Russians capture Warsaw after letting Germans destroy Warsaw uprising.
January 20, 1945	Roosevelt inaugurated for fourth term.
January 30–February 3, 1945	Roosevelt and Churchill and their military staffs meet at Malta, on the way to Yalta.
February 4–11, 1945	Yalta Conference includes Roosevelt, Churchill, and Stalin. Attended by Harry Hopkins, Averell Harriman, Edward Stettinius, James Byrnes, Charles Bohlen, Alger Hiss, Anthony Eden, Alexander Cadogan, Clark Kerr, V. M. Molotov, former Russian Ambassador to Britain Ivan Maisky; Generals John R. Deane, George C. Marshall, Harold Alexander, Alan Brooke, Hastings Ismay, Henry M. Wilson; Admirals Ernest King and William D. Leahy.
February 23, 1945	U.S. first firebombs Tokyo.
March 1945	Operation PLUNDER launched. Allied crossing of the Rhine; Churchill observes on March 24–25.

April 12, 1945	President Roosevelt dies.
April 1945	Harry Hopkins, sick and exhausted, resigns from government. Averell Harriman returns to Washington to confer with President Truman.
April 23, 1945	Foreign Secretary V. M. Molotov meets with President Truman, Edward Stettinius, Averell Harriman, and Charles Bohlen. Truman criticizes Molotov regarding dishonorable Russian policy toward Poland.
April 23, 1945	Russian army enters Berlin.
April 25–June 26, 1945	United Nations Conference in San Francisco is attended by Anthony Eden, Edward Stettinius, V. M. Molotov, Cordell Hull, Lord Halifax, and Harry Dexter White.
April 28, 1945	Benito Mussolini killed by Italian partisans.
April 30, 1945	Adolph Hitler commits suicide in Berlin.
May 8, 1945	Victory in Europe (VE) Day.
May 1945	Harry Hopkins visits Stalin, and Joseph Davies visits Churchill on behalf of President Truman.
May 23, 1945	British war coalition government breaks up. Churchill forms temporary Conservative government.
June 27, 1945,	James F. Byrnes succeeds Edward Stettinius as secretary of state.
July 5, 1945	British election for House of Commons takes place.
July 6, 1945	Henry Morgenthau Jr. resigns as secretary of the Treasury.
July 17–25, 1945	Churchill, Stalin, Truman, Eden, James Byrnes, and Molotov attend Potsdam summit. Attendees included Clement Attlee, Henry Stimson, Joseph Davies, Charles Bohlen, and Averell Harriman, as well as Generals Alan Brooke, George Marshall, Bernard Montgomery, and Harold Alexander, and Russian Field Marshal Georgy V. Zhukov.
July 26, 1945	Results of British election show Churchill soundly defeated by Labour Party. He resigns. New Prime Minister Clement Attlee takes Churchill's place at Potsdam conference.
August 6, 1945	United States drops atomic bomb on Hiroshima.
August 8, 1945	Russia declares war on Japan.
August 9, 1945	United States drops atomic bomb on Nagasaki.
August 15, 1945	Victory over Japan (VJ) Day.

Winston Churchill and Franklin Roosevelt (supported by his son Elliott) at the Atlantic Conference, August 1941. Ensign Franklin D. Roosevelt Jr. is on the left.
FRANKLIN D. ROOSEVELT PRESIDENTIAL LIBRARY

Former Naval Persons: Winston and Franklin

Upon this battle depends the survival of Christian civilisation. Upon it depends our own British life and the long continuity of our institutions and our Empire. The whole fury and might of the enemy must very soon be turned on us. Hitler knows that he will have to break us in this island or lose the war. If we can stand up to him, all Europe may be free and the life of the world may move forward into broad, sunlit uplands. But if we fail, then the whole world, including the United States, including all that we have known and cared for, will sink into the abyss of a new Dark Age, made more sinister, and perhaps more protracted, by the lights of perverted science.[1]

Winston S. Churchill *(1874–1965), speech on June 18, 1940. Churchill had been First Lord of the Admiralty during the first two years of World War I, brigade commander at the front in France, and minister of munitions. From 1924 to 1929, he was chancellor of the exchequer. He had followed his father into politics after a brief but notable career in the British cavalry, but his chief financial support was his work as an author and journalist. Churchill was again named First Lord of the Admiralty in September 1939, before being named prime minister in May 1940.*

Some indeed still hold to the now somewhat obvious delusion that we of the United States can safely permit the United States to become a lone island, a lone island in a world dominated by the philosophy of force. Such an island may be the dream of those who still talk and vote as isolationists. Such an island represents to me and to the overwhelming majority of Americans today a helpless nightmare of a people without freedom—the nightmare of a people lodged in prison, handcuffed, hungry, and fed through the bars from day to day by the contemptuous, unpitying masters of other continents. It is natural also that we should ask ourselves how now we can prevent the building of that prison and the placing of ourselves in the midst of it.[2]

Franklin D. Roosevelt *(1882–1945), speech at University of Virginia, June 10, 1940. Roosevelt had been assistant secretary of the navy during World War I, and* *the unsuccessful Democratic candidate for vice president in 1920. After a long period of recovery and rehabilitation from polio, Roosevelt reentered politics in 1924, with a rousing convention speech nominating New York Governor Al Smith. In 1928, Roosevelt succeeded Smith as governor. FDR prevailed over Smith for the 1932 presidential nomination.*

Americans, observed a British diplomat, were "extraordinary people—quite charming and kind to an extraordinary degree." Alexander Cadogan added that Americans "in some ways [were] rather like ourselves but . . . so utterly different."[3] Bridging Anglo-American differences challenged American and British leaders in World War II. British envoy Harold Macmillan observed haughtily that the British "are like the Greeks in the later Roman Empire. They ran it, because they were so much cleverer than the Romans, but they never told the Romans this. That must be our relation to the Americans."[4] Early in the war, President Franklin D. Roosevelt spoke patronizingly about what he thought was Britain's failure to adopt an appropriately stiff upper lip. In 1939, the president had quipped: "What the British need is a good stiff grog, inducing not only the desire to save civilisation but the continued belief that they can do it. In such an event they will have a lot more support for Britain from their American cousins."[5] Full American support would come only after the bombing of Pearl Harbor on December 7, 1941, and Hitler's declaration of war on the United States on December 11.

FDR notwithstanding, Prime Minister Winston S. Churchill and the British people had drunk the stiff grog in 1940 and 1941. While the British Empire and Commonwealth fought Hitler alone, FDR waited, hesitant to lead public opinion toward the war he was expecting. In 1940, the president's priority was to win a third presidential term in November. Alone, facing an anticipated Nazi invasion, the prime minister would inspire in the British people the necessary confidence to carry on the fight.[6] In July 1942, a British general told an American advisor that in working with Churchill, "I had learned that it was important to realize that he hated looking on the worst side of things; he felt that even to speak of failure was half-way to bringing it about."[7] But a gap persisted in Anglo-American thinking. In January 1942, shortly after the United States entered the war, FDR told Yugoslav intellectual Louis Adamic at a White House dinner: "You know, my friend over there," referring to Churchill, "doesn't understand how most of our people feel about Britain and her role in the life of other peoples. . . . It's in the American tradition, this distrust, this dislike and even hatred of Britain—the Revolution, you know, and 1812; and India and the Boer War, and all that. There are many kinds of Americans of course, but as a people, as a country, we're opposed to imperialism—we can't stomach it."[8] FDR conveniently overlooked the Mexican-American War of the 1840s, the imperialist tendencies of his cousin Teddy, the Spanish-American War of 1898, and the American colonial war in the Philippines. But pulling the lion's tail was an old American habit. Roosevelt was perhaps a bit jealous of the already outsized reputation of the prime minister.

Winston Churchill was half-American. His strategy for defeating Nazi Germany included his determination to persuade America to enter World War II. An Anglo-American alliance, he believed, was the decisive way to defeat Germany. Some British officials were dubious about Churchill's split heritage. The Tories that he had abandoned for the Liberals in 1904, returning in 1924, did not trust him. Shortly after Churchill became prime minister on May 10, 1940, an aide described him as a "half-breed American whose main support was that of inefficient but talkative people of a similar type."[9] Historian David Dilks got it right when he wrote that Churchill "might have described himself as half-American, half-cosmopolitan, and wholly English."[10] Dilks might have added that Churchill was also a lifelong Francophile.

From the moment he received the seals of office from King George VI, the prime minister had no alternative but to focus on the survival of Britain. After the evacuation of Dunkirk and the fall of France in June 1940, Russian Ambassador Ivan Maisky met with Churchill, and inquired about the prime minister's "major strategy." He responded: "*Major strategy?* First of all, to survive the next three months, and then we shall see."[11] The prime minister hoped, charmed, and worked to recruit America as an ally in the war against the Nazis. In May, Churchill's son Randolph heard the prime minister say as he shaved: "I shall drag the United States in."[12] In his stoical self-confidence of 1940 and 1941, the prime minister wooed FDR like a mistress. He even experienced bouts of naive optimism that the United States would soon enter the war.[13] The prime minister, though one-half American, failed to understand the pervasive isolationist sentiment of the United States in 1940. Historian John Lukacs wrote of Churchill's "overestimation of the extent and influence of Americans who were, by origin or inclination, Anglophiles."[14] Churchill did not tire of finding or creating Anglophiles in Anglophobic America. One could find them among the Protestant elites, especially in the East. But their influence was weak in the governing Democratic Party of the 1930s, home of the anti-English Irish and other immigrant groups, and indifferent to the prime minister's conception of English-speaking peoples.

Churchill was a self-confident product of the British aristocracy, notorious for his blunt honesty. To build the Anglo-American alliance, he would make a special effort to charm, even defer to, American leaders from 1940 to 1945. He partly succeeded with FDR. Encouraged by his success, he persisted in his charm crusade. U.S. Secretary of War Henry Stimson visited Britain in the summer of 1943. Stimson reported to President Roosevelt: "Although I have known the P.M. for many years and had talked freely with him, I have never had such a series of important and confidential discussions as this time. He was extremely kind and, although we discussed subjects on which we differed with extreme frankness, I think the result was to achieve a relation between us of greater mutual respect and friendship than ever before. . . . Although I differed with him with the utmost freedom and outspokenness, he never took offense and seemed to respect my position."[15] Stimson was part of the eastern Protestant elite, and an Anglophile to some extent, a perfect target for the prime minister's charm offensive. When Churchill entertained important

American visitors, he "was the most generous and flattering of hosts and one of the most persuasive of propagandists," noted biographer Paul Addison.[16] The British prime minister did feel genuine affection for Americans, even when he disagreed with them. He never tired of trying to convert them to his view of the world. Most informed Americans learned that it was his persuasive powers that inspired the Allied war effort. The Churchill government was not always transparent in Allied negotiations, but compared to the disorganization and internal disputes within the Roosevelt administration, the prime minister's policies, his resolve, and that of his government, were clear and compelling. In February 1942, two months after Pearl Harbor, Washington journalist David Lawrence wrote in his diary: "The American people are indebted to Prime Minister Churchill for having told them the essential facts about the present-day war situation which previously had been denied them by the American Government."[17]

FDR was the first, and always the ultimate, target for Churchill's American charm campaign. The prime minister treasured the relationship between the "former naval persons"—a phrase that President Franklin Roosevelt used when he wrote to First Lord of the Admiralty Churchill, after Britain declared war on Germany in September 1939 after the Nazis invaded Poland.[18] In 1934, Churchill had written a flattering portrait of FDR, later included in his very successful book, *Great Contemporaries*.[19] Both men self-consciously embraced their primary roles in the unfolding drama of history.[20] The prime minister and the president considered themselves charismatic storytellers.[21] They tended to control conversations with anecdotes. FDR's "mind does not follow easily a consecutive train of thought," wrote Stimson in his diary, "but he is full of stories and incidents and hops about in his discussions from suggestion to suggestion and it is very much like chasing a vagrant beam of sunlight around a vacant room."[22] Stimson deplored this Roosevelt characteristic.

Roosevelt "was an expert at dividing his day into periods of work and play, of excitement and relaxation, of importance and minutiae," wrote an aide.[23] In Churchill's memoirs, he described FDR's fishing at Camp Shangri-la: "No fish were caught, but he seemed to enjoy it very much, and was in great spirits for the rest of the day. Evidently he had the first quality of an angler, which is not to measure the pleasure by the catch."[24] The same could not be said of the prime minister. Churchill himself was all-war-all-the-time. There was a breezy charm and superficiality to FDR, but an unmistakable intensity and earnestness to the prime minister. In different ways, they inspired loyalty and affection.[25] During 1940–1942, they worked hard to bridge their differences and to establish common ground and strategy for the alliance. When the prime minister wished Roosevelt happy birthday in January 1942, FDR responded: "It is fun to be in the same decade with you."[26] These were the honeymoon years. In 1943, their relationship would change.

All recognized Churchill as a bulldog. He never gave up. His work at war was his life's fulfillment. FDR would compare himself to "a cat. I make a quick stroke, and then I relax."[27] Churchill was the more tenacious, better prepared by study and attention to detail. He was generally more forthcoming than the enigmatic, catlike

Roosevelt. On some occasions, FDR compared himself to the Sphinx.[28] The prime minister was a goad for work—in formal argument blunt, abrupt, and prepared to make his case—often emotional. But he could be ingratiating, writing FDR in December 1940, after the president had explained Lend-Lease to Americans in a fireside chat: "I thank you for testifying before all the world that the future safety and greatness of the American Union are intimately concerned with the upholding and the effective arming of that indomitable spirit."[29] Churchill's rhetoric in parliamentary debate often rose to the level of the sublime, whereas the American system never tested Roosevelt the same way. FDR's rhetoric was honed for speeches and "fireside chats" on the radio.

As global-war leaders, both had equipped themselves with extraordinary knowledge of global geography. Labor Secretary Frances Perkins recalled that Roosevelt had "an amazing amount of information about the height of mountains and the depth of oceans, the rivers and their sources and the plains they watered."[30] (FDR followed Churchill's example of establishing permanent and traveling map rooms, first in the West Wing and then on the ground floor of the White House.[31]) The president had traveled frequently to Europe as a boy and as a young man; he had more exposure to Europe than Churchill had to America.[32] Churchill's infrequent visits to North America had usually been moneymaking lecture tours. Roosevelt's talented, ambitious, and well-connected parents had attended to his formal and informal education, and thus gave their only child exposure to leading figures in Britain and Europe.[33]

The prime minister and the president could be impulsive tactical improvisers, reacting to circumstance and opportunity. But they were confident statesmen at war, each with a strategic vision, flawed to some extent by misunderstanding the new impact on war of air power. Both suffered respiratory problems that sometimes immobilized them. Both were world-class flatterers—FDR by habit, and Churchill by practice, with a purpose. After President Roosevelt's reelection in November 1940, Churchill wrote him in exalted tones, emphasizing the historic nature of their partnership: "Things are afoot which will be remembered as long as the English language is spoken in any quarter of the globe, and in expressing the comfort I feel that the people of the United States have once again cast these great burdens upon you I must avow my sure faith that the lights by which we steer will bring us all safely to anchor."[34] The prime minister and the president were devoted cheerleaders for their countrymen and their allies. Churchill radiated confidence and energy; Roosevelt, confidence and calm. FDR's decision-making process was more opaque and manipulative than Churchill's. "By allowing his subordinates to argue both with him and with each other until a decision became necessary," wrote historian David Kaiser, "Captain Roosevelt made sure that he could draw on a well-thought-out plan for any course of action he eventually chose."[35] But other high officials thought FDR a disorganized procrastinator, often unwilling to make decisions.

The prime minister and the president were patricians of great ambition, inspired not least by their elite families and famous forebears. Churchill, often overconfident in his personal analysis of issues, was the more impatient of the two. Roosevelt was cautious by temperament. Both valued every minute of their time. Historian James Leasor wrote of their conversations on a secure phone: "Roosevelt, while willing to speak to Mr. Churchill, was not at all eager to come to the telephone until he knew for certain that the Prime Minister was actually waiting for him at the other end. Churchill was also reluctant to be closeted in the tiny, airless telephone room, wasting time, while the President was being wheeled to the telephone in the White House."[36]

Roosevelt proved the better grassroots politician, having built a political organization in the Republican stronghold of New York's Hudson Valley, enabled by inherited wealth and the family presidential legacy of his Republican cousin, Theodore. When FDR entered New York politics, TR was probably the most famous American in the world. The Democratic Party, understanding the power of the progressive Republican's reputation, nominated FDR, who had never held statewide political office, for vice president in 1920. It was different for Churchill. His heart beat to the rhythms of debate in Parliament, not to the noise of grassroots politics. He lost his first race for Parliament and two elections to the House of Commons in the 1920s. Historian Ronald Lewin noted, "Outside Westminister . . . Churchill had no roots. Of course he had a constituency; but during his long political career he had held several, he was not a true constituency M.P."[37] Political itinerancy, however, was customary in British politics. Roosevelt was much more attuned to, and even governed by, public opinion. In 1941, after three presidential victories, Roosevelt still lacked a decisive congressional majority to support his policies, thereby reinforcing his natural caution. Churchill presided over a large coalition government throughout the war. Thus, he seldom had to worry about serious parliamentary revolt. During the war, Roosevelt fought two campaigns for the presidency, in 1940 and 1944. Prime Minister Churchill faced no parliamentary election until war's end in 1945.

Churchill's character and temperament made him more straightforward than Roosevelt. FDR was practiced at deception, as he himself readily acknowledged. He told Secretary of the Treasury Henry Morgenthau: "You know I am a juggler, and I never let my left hand know what my right hand does." He added: "I may have one policy for Europe and one diametrically opposite for North and South America. I may be entirely inconsistent and furthermore I am perfectly willing to mislead and tell untruths if it will help win the war."[38] He once wrote that the Washington-based Pacific War Council "serves primarily to disseminate information as to the progress of operations in the Pacific—and secondly, to give me a chance to keep everybody happy by telling stories and doing most of the talking!"[39] Secretary of the Interior Harold Ickes once complained to Roosevelt, "You won't talk frankly even with people who are loyal to you and of whose loyalty you are fully convinced. You keep your cards close up against your belly. You never put them on the table."[40] British Foreign Secretary Anthony Eden took a similar view of the president, recalling FDR's "grace" after meetings in March 1943, but describing him as "a conjuror, skilfully [*sic*] juggling with balls of dynamite, whose nature he failed to understand.'"[41] Even Roosevelt loyalist Robert E. Sherwood, comparing Churchill to Roosevelt, wrote: "If either of them could be called a student of Machiavelli, it was Roosevelt." The British Ambassador to Washington recalled that Roosevelt was "a very astute politician. But what he did was to split the American people" politically.[42]

Churchill and Roosevelt perplexed their appointees. Sympathetic biographer James MacGregor Burns wrote that Roosevelt "could be bold or cautious, informal or dignified, cruel or kind, intolerant or long-suffering, urbane or almost rustic, impetuous or temporizing, Machiavellian or moralistic."[43] The prime minister could alternate between charmer and curmudgeon. Churchill's true feelings tended to show through; he rarely bothered to hide them. More tightly wound, more focused on the war alone, more intense than Roosevelt, he would indulge in his love of painting only once during World War II, and that while convalescing from pneumonia in Morocco. He would not rest from prosecuting the war. FDR's beloved stamp collection, however, was seldom far from his wheelchair. With it, he found peace of mind. British academic Isaiah Berlin wrote:

> The differences between the President and the Prime Minister were at least in one respect something more than the obvious differences of national character, education, and even temperament. For all his sense of history, his large, untroubled, easygoing style of life, his unshakable feeling of personal security, his natural assumption of being at home in the great world far beyond the confines of his own country, Mr. Roosevelt was a typical child of the twentieth century and of the New World; while Mr. Churchill, for all his love of the present hour, his unquenchable appetite for new knowledge, his sense of the technological possibilities of our time, and the restless roaming of his fancy in considering how they might be most imaginatively applied, despite his enthusiasm for Basic English, or the siren suit which so upset his hosts in Moscow—despite all this, Mr. Churchill remains a European of the nineteenth century.[44]

A Victorian, an Edwardian, and a parliamentary (democratic) monarchist.[45]

The president and the prime minister treasured the secrets and secret intelligence of war. Their self-confidence embraced outsized personalities such as American financier Bernard Baruch, American businessman Vincent Astor, and Canadian-born tycoon Max Beaverbrook, and the information and influence these international men of affairs could share with them.[46] FDR tended to use unconventional, *ad hoc* methods for gathering intelligence. Roosevelt chronicler Joseph Persico noted: "Spying in the mold of an E. Phillips Oppenheim thriller excited his imagination, but the technical world of radio wave interception, mathematical analysis, permutations, combinations, and gadgetry to break codes bored him"—symptoms of the amateur.[47] Characteristic of the gifted professional, Churchill plumbed the technical questions of war, and employed a close friend, "Prof" Frederick Lindemann of Oxford University, to make sure he understood them.[48] With the help of scientist Lindemann, he pushed the development of innovative and scientific approaches to warfare. He quickly promoted nascent technologies, such as radar.[49] He worked harder than FDR to master the new tools of war and to prepare himself for the momentous decisions in war—a habit of intense, independent study carried on from his early mature years.

Churchill talked through his thoughts and strategies openly with experts he trusted. "Roosevelt was more a person of things," observed historian Warren Kimball, "someone who kept his own counsel and solved, dismissed, or ignored a problem."[50] He was intuitive, often impulsive in decision-making. The president was a more elusive personality than Churchill, though both delighted in subterfuge. FDR reveled in the tactical maneuvers required to evade reporters while traveling to the 1941 Placentia Bay meeting with the prime minister. Elliott Roosevelt recalled that his father "was delighted as a kid, boasting of how he had thrown the newspapermen off the scent by going as far as Augusta, Maine, on the presidential yacht *Potomac*" before transferring to an American cruiser, the USS *Augusta.*[51] The president happily kept key personnel in the dark. He regularly disappeared into the isolation of a Caribbean cruise or his Hyde Park estate. There, he ate better food than at Eleanor Roosevelt's White House. There too, he found rest and privacy.

Secrets were part of FDR's way of life. Eleanor Roosevelt recalled that even before Pearl Harbor, "People naturally wanted to listen to what he had to say. But the fact that he carried so many secrets in his head made it necessary for him to watch everything he said, which in itself was exhausting."[52] In October 1942, the president embarked on a tour of American military production facilities. Reporters accompanied him, but were forbidden to write about his speeches. "You know, you know I am not supposed to be here today," he said at one stop in Portland, Oregon. He impishly declared: "You are the possessors of a secret which even the newspapers of the United States don't know."[53] Indeed, journalist Merriman Smith noted that one of FDR's "great talents was his ability to put over sheer, unadulterated hokum."[54]

Harry Hopkins acted as a "confidential contact man between Roosevelt and private citizens who were advocating some policy of which the President approved but which he did not want to advocate publicly for political reasons at the time," wrote White House aide Robert E. Sherwood. "There was more than one occasion when Roosevelt wanted to be 'attacked' for inactivity and thus 'goaded' into action by public demand."[55] The president rarely took the lead much in advance of public opinion. He became the first poll-driven president.[56] On at least two occasions during World War II, the American president turned the White House over to the British prime minister and secretly took the presidential train home to Hyde Park, New York. Of one such occasion at the White House in September 1943, Churchill wrote: "It was an honour to me to preside over this conference of the Combined Chiefs of Staff and of American and British authorities in the Council Room of the White House, and it seemed to be an event in Anglo-American history."[57]

General Hastings "Pug" Ismay, Churchill's patient senior military aide and liaison to the British Chiefs of Staff, once joked: "Churchill is the great military genius in history. He can use one division on three fronts at the same time."[58] The prime minister's imagination occasionally overcame his grasp of reality. Roosevelt vainly imagined that Americans would be welcome in places such as Vichy-governed North Africa, because the president supposed the British to be anathema to the French but the Americans welcome. The prime minister and the president cherished the new and bold. "Roosevelt liked novel ideas, bold courses, and dramatic actions, and he liked the sort of men who could come up with such suggestions," recalled Attorney General Robert H. Jackson. "Some associates had influence in the sense that many of their suggestions bore fruit. . . . The man who influenced Roosevelt most . . . was the one who would marshal him the way that he was going, would provide reasons and arguments for doing what he wanted to do."[59] FDR's vanity made him susceptible to yes-men. Biographer James MacGregor Burns thought Roosevelt a risk-taker: "As war administrator, as businessman, as president, he liked to try new things, to take a dare, to bring something off with a flourish."[60] U.S. General Joseph Stilwell was immune to FDR's charm and critical of the president as decision maker: "Besides being a rank amateur in all military matters, F.D.R. is apt to act on sudden impulses."[61] General Marshall proved himself unreceptive to FDR's charm and subtle flattery; Marshall disdained to laugh at the president's jokes.[62] Nor did General Marshall encourage the use of his first name by FDR, seeing through the false intimacy it implied.

From his earliest years as an only child, FDR's inherited wealth underwrote his impulsiveness, just as Churchill's overweening self-assurance stemmed in part from his ducal lineage, of which he was very proud. In an interview with a University of Michigan law student in 1901, Churchill observed: "I was lucky enough to start with a name very well known in England, and as you know, a name counts a great deal with us [the British]. In your country it is somewhat of a handicap to have a great father—few of your great men have had great sons."[63] Winston Churchill, belittled as a boy by his father, Lord Randolph, aimed in his late teens to be a great man. The son would surpass the father, who died at 45 on January 24, 1895; Sir Winston Churchill died at 90 on the same day 70 years later. The prime minister's only son, Randolph Churchill, died an alcoholic at the age of 57, having labored under the handicap of a great father.[64]

The prime minister and the president were masters of language. FDR's usage was often colloquial, but Churchill's was more formal—sometimes terse, other times ornate. They were adept at using language to humor others and to defuse confrontations. FDR resorted to humor to deflect journalists' questions he did not intend to answer. Churchill's humor was witty, subtle, ironic, a key to his effectiveness as a leader of Parliament. The prime minister appreciated clever people. Aide John Colville recalled: "A gift which captivated even his opponents was his gaiety. He employed it as an art of government, for if ever he was in a tight corner in Parliament he would make the House laugh, and laughter disarms opposition."[65] Most important for the alliance, noted Isaiah Berlin, the prime minister and the president charmed each other: "The relationship was made genuine by something more than even the solid community of interest or personal and official respect or admiration—namely, by the peculiar degree to which they liked each other's delight in the oddities and humors of life and their own active part in it."[66] Despite mutual interests, neither could always be frank with the other. National interest came first. Churchill, for example, did not divulge to American officials his view of the much diminished threat of a German invasion of England in late 1940 and early 1941. Similarly, only in December 1940, after reelection, did FDR propose the controversial Lend-Lease program, enacted by Congress in March 1941.

Both men endured periods of mild depression before they rose to their nation's highest office. Once in power, their basic character traits gave rise to different leadership styles. Roosevelt was a man of intuition and impulse, and the harder man to understand, even for those who worked closely with him. "I tried continually to study him, to try to look beyond his charming and amusing and warmly affectionate surface into his heavily forested interior," wrote speechwriter Robert E. Sherwood. "He was hard and he was soft. At times he displayed a capacity for vindictiveness which could be described as petty, and at other times he demonstrated the Christian spirit of forgiveness and charity in its purest form."[67] Churchill was the more honest and forthright with others—sometimes brutally so. Not religious in any orthodox sense, the prime minister's motives and ideas were seldom hidden, often high-minded. He informed himself better than the president did. He was relentless and less accommodating than FDR, more on-the-job in the way he drove subordinates. As the king's first minister in a democratic political environment, he was a superb parliamentarian, a confident chief executive and war leader. But his generals and admirals found him maddening. A storm of Churchill's anger could quickly be followed by the sunlight of Churchill's generosity.

The prime minister and the president would spar with barbed jokes when jousting with others. Churchill's anger was usually direct, Roosevelt's feline. FDR could deliver put-downs behind his target's back.[68] Alan Brooke noted that Churchill "could drive you to complete desperation and the brink of despair for weeks on end, and then would ask you to spend a couple of hours alone with him and would produce the most homely and attractive personality."[69] The public and the elites at the beginning of World War II viewed the prime minister's personality negatively. Historian John Lukacs wrote that, before May 1940, "people in Britain thought Churchill to be impulsive, erratic, wordy, unduly combative, a maverick, perhaps a publicity hound; in one word, unsteady."[70] This opinion was especially true of the prime minister's Tories. But Churchill as prime minister became the embodiment of Britain's tough character in war. The British people admired the virtues of their supreme warlord resisting the Nazis. He was still the fighter he had proved himself to be as a young cavalry officer. His bravery, force of personality, self-confidence, and defiance of a powerful enemy emboldened the people of the United Kingdom during its most desperate hours.

Churchill and Roosevelt were not modest. Neither suffered fools gladly. Churchill was more hands-on as prime minister than FDR was as president. The prime minister was the more organized, the more conscious of organization and efficiency—even as he interfered regularly with Whitehall, the British government bureaucracy. Historian Richard Holmes wrote that the prime minister "could see no reason why a man or woman engaged in anything quite so important and interesting as a war should want to take leave, spend an evening at home or even go to bed early."[71] Churchill did have a grand strategy and vision, but he micromanaged tirelessly, generally to good effect. Roosevelt was a big-picture man, even a bit disengaged, who left much presidential business to his subordinates. Some, like Generals Marshall and Eisenhower, were wisely chosen, as were the senior admirals. But Roosevelt was much less detail-oriented than Churchill. Historian Warren Kimball noted that the president "dismissed detail with a cavalier wave of the hand. With the possible exception of the promotion lists for the U.S. Navy, which he monitored painstakingly, Roosevelt focused on ends, not means."[72] Churchill had learned from hard experience in World War I that means and ends were inseparable, coordination of both being the business of the supreme warlord. FDR did choose his own senior warlords well: Marshall, Eisenhower, Leahy, King, and Nimitz. The president's strategic decisions were generally shrewd and successful.

Roosevelt encouraged, often perversely, competition as well as conflict among officials of his administration. As unprepared as the British government may have been in 1939–1940 for a war of survival, it was better organized under Neville Chamberlain and Winston Churchill than the American government was under Franklin Roosevelt, even though FDR, expecting war as he did, had until December 7, 1941, to get ready. By then, he had been in office for almost nine years. Churchill knew the kind of organization needed to lead and to manage a far-flung war machine, from his experience in World War I, during which he had witnessed the struggle between the "frockcoats" (politicians) and "brasshats" (generals). The prime minister would tolerate no such conflict. On the other hand, in peace and war, FDR was the supreme improviser. "All of the aides on the White House staff were, in effect, officials of the President's 'household' and not officers in any chain of administrative command," wrote Robert Sherwood. "Thus, the President before 1939 had no real executive organization of his own."[73] Roosevelt's sympathetic biographer, Arthur M. Schlesinger Jr., wrote that FDR's "favorite technique was to keep grants of authority incomplete, jurisdictions uncertain, charters overlapping. The result of this competitive theory of administration was often confusion and exasperation on the operating level."[74]

This was the way FDR did business. New York Democratic leader Edward J. Flynn, a close Roosevelt ally, observed: "The Boss either appoints four men to do the job of one man, or one man to do the job of four." Flynn added, "Often none of the four knew what the other three were doing."[75] British economist John Maynard Keynes, frequently engaged in economic negotiations in Washington, observed: "There is a perpetual internecine warfare between prominent personalities. Individuals rise and fall in general esteem with bewildering rapidity."[76] Oliver Harvey wrote in his diary on August 15, 1941: "Keynes just back from America. He gave most amusing description of chaotic conditions of work of U.S. Government departments—each department letting down the other—no coordination and no over-riding authority—no records or written decisions are kept of anything—all oral and all that can be repudiated—not because of trickery but simply because in view of above conditions no Government department felt able honestly to bind itself to deliver the goods."[77]

Gradually, the Roosevelt administration, especially the military, developed a more effective structure. Alan Brooke and George C. Marshall were decisive, well-organized military leaders, willing to challenge civilian judgments. One of Churchill's military aides, General Leslie Hollis, recalled that Brooke was "resolute, volatile, vibrant, versatile and sharp tempered." He was a match for Churchill in their frequent arguments.[78] The prime minister happily wrote of a June 1942 conference at Hyde Park: "The President was very glad to hear I had brought the C.I.G.S. with me. His field of interest was always brightened by recollections of his youth. It had happened that the president's father had entertained, at Hyde Park, the father of General Brooke. Mr. Roosevelt therefore expressed keen interest to meet the son, who had reached such a high position. When they met two days later he received him with the utmost cordiality, and General Brooke's personality and charm created an almost immediate intimacy which greatly helped the course of business."[79]

The testimony of colleagues suggests that Franklin Roosevelt was a subtle juggler and manipulator of men. Winston Churchill was often overbearing, bold, and blunt with other men. FDR tended to govern by dissimulation and surprise. In his diary, Secretary of War Stimson called the president "the poorest administrator I have ever worked under in respect to the orderly procedure and routine of his performance."[80] FDR interfered less than the prime minister with the bureaucracy; instead, Roosevelt ignored it or worked around it. This conduct demoralized the leaders of key departments of government. Biographer James MacGregor Burns wrote that Roosevelt "conducted business in a flurry of telephone calls, personal conferences, formal correspondence cleared with appropriate agencies, informal letters cleared with no one, chits to secretaries and cabinet officers, evening conferences."[81] The president and the prime minister had to make the best use of a limited set of civilian and military leaders at the onset of war. Labor Secretary Perkins recalled that as time went by in FDR's administration, his "cabinet administration came to be like most previous ones—a direct relationship between a particular cabinet officer and the President in regard to his special field, with little or no participation or even information from other cabinet members. Certainly almost no 'cabinet agreements' were reached. Something about our governmental form and tensions between the legislative and executive functions seems to make fully responsible cabinet action unlikely."[82] Such an arrangement was unthinkable for the prime minister, who was bound by parliamentary and cabinet government procedures, enshrined in the British political tradition and the unwritten British constitution.

Churchill did respect protocol, not least because he respected the constitutional traditions of the Parliament and of cabinet government.[83] In June 1943, Harold Macmillan cabled the British prime minister about FDR's interventions in French affairs in North Africa—especially FDR's efforts on behalf of opponents to General Charles de Gaulle, the leader of the Free French. "For your private information which should of course be kept very secret, Generals Eisenhower and [Walter] Bedell-Smith are getting more and more concerned about the President's autocratic instructions." Churchill responded: "Strictly personal and secret. I am shocked to hear that

Generals Eisenhower and Bedell-Smith should have communicated to you their differences from their own President and Commander-in-Chief. You may be sure I shall not allow this to become known."[84] To get America into the life-and-death struggle against Hitler, against whom the British Empire and Commonwealth fought alone in 1940–1941, the prime minister had made FDR his principal diplomatic target. In the following three years, Churchill's energy, integrity, and willingness to do exhausting travel reinforced the alliance not only with Roosevelt, but with Stalin too.

The prime minister and the president had different personal habits. Roosevelt loved martinis (very American), and turned them into an early evening ritual called the "children's hour." Churchill the aristocrat detested them as a vulgar innovation, preferring simply whisky very diluted with soda, wine, or champagne served at any time of day. Both men started their working day in bed, awakening after 8 AM. After a mid-afternoon nap of deep sleep, the prime minister could generally begin about 5 PM, and then work most of the night, putting in longer work hours than the younger Roosevelt. (The president tired more easily from many afflictions, including polio.) FDR usually went to bed by 11 PM. Churchill often worked or talked to colleagues until 3 AM—sometimes later. FDR complained that Churchill "gets bright ideas in the middle of the night and comes puttering down to my bedroom. They are probably good ideas. But I need my sleep."[85] Lord Halifax later recalled that General Marshall "told me that the President would not look forward to Winston's visits. He knew too much about military matters, he kept such shocking hours."[86] Churchill, fortified by a late afternoon nap and a tireless constitution, set a challenging example of long hours and hard work. However, many of his colleagues complained of the prime minister's hours, believing them exhausting and unproductive, especially because most military and civilian officials had to rise in the early morning and could not take afternoon naps.

The prime minister and the president socialized with their deputies. Attorney General Robert Jackson wrote that FDR "liked to have about him in his moments of relaxation those with whom he worked."[87] Churchill would play bezique using two decks of cards.[88] Roosevelt's game was poker.[89] Both enjoyed movies. The president, a patrician but a grassroots politician, was superficially more sociable than the prime minister, a parliamentary politician not always comfortable working with new people.[90] Churchill's friendships were few but deep—Max Beaverbrook, Brendan Bracken, F. E. Smith. Labor Secretary Frances Perkins recalled: "Roosevelt's principal social talent lay in making people feel at ease in his society and in getting them to talk about the things they knew."[91] With the conspicuous exception of General Marshall, who did not yield to his flattery, Roosevelt addressed most people by their first name after meeting them. This affected intimacy was one of FDR's manipulative tools. Winston Churchill, on the other hand, could dominate conversations, talking nonstop; at other times, he could become lost in silence. The problem for the prime minister's associates was that Churchill's monologues were generally interesting. Despite their differences, until 1943 the president and the prime minister reciprocated the direct, even intimate, relationship each desired. "My relations with the President gradually became so close that the chief business between our two countries was virtually conducted by . . . interchanges between him and me," recalled Churchill with some exaggeration. "As Head of State as well as Head of the Government, Roosevelt spoke and acted with authority in every sphere; and, carrying the War Cabinet with me, I represented Great Britain with almost equal latitude."[92] By tradition and necessity, Churchill had to "carry" the War Cabinet with him on policy; Roosevelt could be indifferent to his cabinet, and he was. But for the prime minister to carry the cabinet, he had to persuade, a rhetorical art he had worked at from boyhood. His ability to persuade with evidence, argument, and humor marked his leadership in Parliament and in Allied councils of war, especially from 1940 to 1943.

For information and decision, both war leaders deployed back channels in addition to normal diplomacy, and neither was aware of all such channels. Both men harbored a disdain for unimaginative diplomatic and military bureaucracy. Historian David Dilks noted that the prime minister "counted a number of diplomats as friends. For the Foreign Office itself he had a lesser respect, believing it so well attuned to the needs and cultures of other countries that it was institutionally inclined to give way."[93] On the day Roosevelt died in April 1945, he signed a State Department letter that he complained, "Said nothing at all."[94] FDR's disdain for the State Department was reflected in a conversation about a phrase in one of his speeches. The State Department had objected to a proposed FDR sentence: "There are also American citizens, *many of them in high places*, who, unwittingly in most cases, are aiding and abetting the work of [fifth column] agents." When Roosevelt was told of the State Department's objections, he responded, "Very well. We'll change it to read—'there are also American citizens, many of them in high places—*especially in the State Department*'—and so forth."[95] In this example, there is an inescapable irony, as FDR's own lack of interest in Soviet spying in Washington allowed "a fifth column of agents" to penetrate high levels of the State, War, and Treasury departments.

Anglo-American relations in normal diplomatic channels atrophied during World War II. They often were superseded by the *ad hoc* operations of men such as Harry Hopkins, Averell Harriman, and Max Beaverbrook. For more than two years beginning in March 1940, no high-ranking official of the State Department visited London, although personal representatives of the president, such as Hopkins and Harriman, made the trip. The U.S. State Department was divided organizationally between Secretary of State Cordell Hull, a popular former Tennessee congressman and senator, and Under Secretary of State Sumner Welles, a career diplomat who had old school ties to President Roosevelt dating back to prep school.[96] Welles came from the same cultural background as FDR, but the icy Welles was more aloof and polished than the president.[97] Roosevelt preferred Welles's pliability on policy to the principled rigidity often displayed by Hull. While the president was preparing to fight World War II in 1941, Hull was focused on the historic Democratic Party fight for global trade liberalization. State Department official Dean Acheson later wrote that Hull "looked like a statesman in the classic American tradition." But the slow-moving Hull was easily irritated. Acheson wrote: "Suspicious by nature, he [Hull] brooded over what he thought were slights and grievances, which more forthright handling might have set straight. His brooding led, in accordance with Tennessee-mountain tradition, to feuds." In Acheson's opinion, Hull became "one of the least influential [cabinet] members at the White House."[98] Acheson would patronize Hull, as he too had grown up in the same social world as Welles and FDR.

Hull feuded repeatedly with Welles, whom "Roosevelt valued . . . as a reflection of the idealism in the country about world affairs," wrote historian Robert Dallek.[99] In early 1940, Welles had been dispatched to tour Western Europe, especially to size up Adolf Hitler for FDR.[100] In March, Welles had visited First Lord of the Admiralty Winston Churchill. The under secretary of state reported his description of the future prime minister as "sitting in front of the fire, smoking a 24-inch cigar, and drinking a whiskey and soda. It was quite obvious that he had consumed a good many whiskeys before I arrived."[101] From Welles's exaggerations (there was no 24-inch cigar), FDR inferred incorrectly that the prime minister drank excessively. Indeed, in May 1940, Welles told Assistant Secretary of State Adolf Berle that Churchill was "tired" and perhaps not up to the task of leading Britain as prime minister. (Ironically, it would be Welles's drinking and other excesses that would eventually force him from office.) In his memoirs, Welles wrote: "In July of 1940 very few of us in Washington believed that Britain, even under Winston Churchill's inspired leadership, could long hold out against Nazi Germany. The entire Atlantic coast as far as the Spanish frontier was in Hitler's hands. We knew that Hitler would try to make a deal with Franco. If he succeeded, Hitler would seize Gibraltar, close the western entrance to the Mediterranean, and extend his control to North Africa. If Britain fell, all the vast resources of Western Europe would be in Nazi hands. The threat to the safety of the United States was acute."[102] Nevertheless, FDR would wait to act until Hitler declared war on America in December 1941, following Pearl Harbor. There was irony in Hitler's declaration of war against America. He was not obliged by treaty with Japan to make it. In that sense, Hitler's declaration of war was gratuitous, making inevitable America's prompt, defensive declaration of war against not only Japan, but Nazi Germany as well. Churchill's courtship of FDR and America finally had brought about engagement, if not full marriage.

The prime minister skillfully used rhetoric to influence public opinion. He knew that when he spoke to Parliament in the dark days of 1940, he reached far wider audiences—not least of which was the American public. On June 4, he addressed the Commons: "The House should prepare itself for hard and heavy tidings. I have only to add that nothing which may happen in this battle can in any way relieve us of our duty to defend the world cause to which we have vowed ourselves; nor should it destroy our confidence in our power to make our way, as on former occasions in our history, through disaster and through grief to the ultimate defeat of our enemies."[103] Although disappointed that the U.S. government had failed to respond more aggressively in 1940–1941 to the Nazi peril facing Britain and America, Churchill persisted in patiently building the alliance foundation. By argument and action, the prime minister would inspire Americans in the period before the congressional declaration of war on December 8, 1941. "We shall go on to the end," Churchill declared to the House of Commons on June 4, 1940.

> We shall fight in France, we shall fight on the seas and oceans, we shall fight with growing confidence and growing strength in the air, we shall defend our island, whatever the cost may be. We shall fight on the beaches, we shall fight on the landing grounds, we shall fight in the fields and in the streets, we shall fight in the hills; we shall never surrender, and even if, which I do not for a moment believe, this island or a large part of it were subjugated and starving, then our Empire beyond the seas, armed and guarded by the British Fleet, would carry on the struggle, until, in God's good time, the New World, with all its power and might, steps forth to the rescue and the liberation of the Old.[104]

One day later, Churchill lamented: "Although President is our best friend, no practical help has [reached us] from the United States as yet."[105] The president was preoccupied by his election prospects for an unprecedented third term.

At war, the president and the prime minister practiced the art of the plausible—FDR more in virtue of his natural caution, Churchill hardened and disciplined by his leadership experience and disappointment in World War I. "They were two men in the same line of business—politico-military leadership on a global scale—and theirs was a very limited field and the few who achieve it seldom have opportunities for getting together with fellow craftsmen in the same trade to compare notes and talk shop," wrote FDR aide Robert Sherwood. "They appraised each other through the practiced eyes of professionals and from this appraisal resulted a degree of admiration and sympathetic understanding of each other's professional problems that lesser craftsmen could not have achieved."[106] At war, they surely believed their roles, as prime minister of the British Empire and president of the American republic, to be different, even if their national interests intersected for several years of total war. In planning for peace, each held to divergent plans for the postwar world. FDR took a more abstract, Wilsonian global view, anchored by a new United Nations. The equally idealistic but more traditional Churchill, as the king's first minister, focused on Europe and the Empire. "Roosevelt and Churchill did not march to the same drumbeat," recalled W. Averell Harriman. "Roosevelt enjoyed thinking aloud on the tremendous changes he saw ahead—the end of colonial empires and the rise of newly independent nations across the sweep of Africa."[107] FDR did not foresee the intractable problems of newly independent nations, which in many cases would lead to civil war and lower standards of living. Churchill, a former colonial secretary, was skeptical that potential new nations were fully prepared for independence, especially members of the British Empire.

As ever in human affairs, rumors, jealousies, misunderstandings, and bureaucratic rigidity affected relations between the United States and Britain during World War II. Problems of course surfaced at the outset of war, exemplified by Joseph P. Kennedy, U.S. Ambassador to the Court of St. James, who repeatedly announced that Britain was "finished." Sincere differences over strategy and tactics caused other difficulties in the Alliance during the war. Alone among the Big Three—Churchill,

Roosevelt, and Stalin—the prime minister undertook exhausting travel at great personal risk, seeking to reduce misunderstandings by speaking directly with American and Russian allies. President Franklin D. Roosevelt and Russian dictator Joseph Stalin limited their travel for health reasons, inconvenience, and unwillingness to travel far away from their nation's political centers.[108] The prime minister was the oldest of the three, and his health was at times fragile, but Churchill's will did not falter. Stalin hugged Kremlin security because he feared flying, and did not trust ambitious party leaders who might try a coup. Indeed, the Soviet leader's first-ever airplane flight was to meet Roosevelt and Churchill at Teheran in November 1943. FDR preferred the comfort of trains and ships, along with the secrecy they provided for his movements. His first flight as president took him to Casablanca in January 1943.

At times, the president (a happy warrior) and the irrepressible prime minister insisted on playing tour guide for each other. After the Casablanca Conference, Churchill implored FDR to visit Marrakesh: "You cannot come all this way to North Africa without seeing Marrakesh. Let us spend two days there. I must be with you when you see the sunset on the snows of the Atlas Mountains."[109] Casablanca may have been the high point of their relationship. The president "is in great form, and we have never been so close," Churchill wrote Anthony Eden.[110] At their final dinner, Churchill recalled, "we all sang songs. I sang and the President joined in the choruses, and at one moment was about to try a solo. However, someone interrupted and I never heard this."[111]

Despite polio paralysis and other afflictions, FDR's few trips abroad still appealed to his sense of adventure. At the Casablanca summit, FDR aide Harry Hopkins told Churchill's physician: "The President came here because he wanted to make the trip; he is tired of sending me to London and Moscow. He loves the drama of a journey like this. They are always telling him that the President must not fly; it is too dangerous. This is his answer."[112] Despite frequent sickness, minor strokes and heart attacks, and the danger of accidents or attack from enemy ships and planes, Churchill traveled tirelessly. His trips were complicated by security plans to prevent leaks or enemy attack. Churchill's pilots did not always know where they were going until the last minute. Often, they improvised navigation plans, flying at low altitudes required to evade enemy fire and high mountains. Dr. Charles Wilson observed: "As for the P.M. when he gets away from his red boxes and leaves London, he puts his cares behind him. It's not only that he loves adventure; he feels, too, at times that he must 'let up'; even a week or two away from the unending grind helps." Wilson even suggested that neither Churchill nor Roosevelt had "ever grown up."[113]

Joseph P. Kennedy (right) on the day he was sworn in as U.S. Ambassador to the United Kingdom, February 1938. He is pictured with his aide, former New York Times *correspondent Harold Hinton.*
LIBRARY OF CONGRESS

I

The Joseph Kennedy Conundrum

[First Lord of the Admiralty Winston Churchill] kept smiling when he talked of "neutrality" and "keeping the war away from the U.S.A." I can't help feeling he's not on the level. He is just an actor and a politician. He always impressed me that he'd blow up the American Embassy and say it was the Germans if it would get the U.S. in [the war]. Maybe I do him an injustice but I just don't trust him.[1]

Joseph P. Kennedy Sr. *(1888–1969), diary entry, October 5, 1939. Kennedy was a Massachusetts political power whose economic interests included real estate, Wall Street, liquor, and the movies. He maneuvered to become the first chairman of the Securities and Exchange Commission in 1934, and the chairman of the Maritime Commission in 1936. Harboring aspirations to be president, Kennedy was named ambassador to Great Britain in 1938.*

Kennedy told me Hitler had twice sent him a message asking him to go to Germany for a conference—which he of course refused. Hitler must have got the impression Kennedy had views which Hitler might use as an approach to us. As a matter of fact Kennedy thinks we ought to lay the basis for some cooperation. He does not go to the extent of appeasing—but the extent to which he would go is undefined.[2]

Breckinridge Long *(1881–1958), diary entry, November 7, 1940. Assistant Secretary of State Long was an unsuccessful Missouri politician and lawyer who had previously served as ambassador to Italy. Long came to know Assistant Secretary of the Navy Roosevelt during World War I, when Long first served as assistant secretary of state. During World War II, Long was a confidant of Secretary of State Cordell Hull, and responsible for the majority of the department's operations. His reputation suffered from his adamant stance against allowing immigration of desperate European refugees (including Jews, escaping the Holocaust).*

At the outset of the war, the British had in Lord Lothian an effective ambassador in Washington. The U.S. Ambassador to the Court of St. James was not so well chosen. Joseph P. Kennedy had arrived in London in 1938, with isolationist views and vague presidential ambitions.[3] Denied the position he wanted as secretary of the Treasury, the socially and politically ambitious Kennedy, a Democratic Party power, had begged to be the first Irish-American ambassador to Britain. The incumbent secretary of the Treasury, Henry Morgenthau, wrote in his diary that FDR told him: "I have made arrangements to have Joe Kennedy watched hourly, and the first time he opens his mouth and criticizes me, I will fire him," adding that "Kennedy is too dangerous to have around here."[4] Once in London, Kennedy's freewheeling habits clashed with the buttoned-up men at the State Department. FDR's "appointment was woefully shortsighted; indeed, in 1940 it came close to being disastrous," observed historian John Lukacs. "That Kennedy was a new-rich millionaire, with a strong streak of vulgarity running through his mind and character; moreover, a man with an enduring chip on his shoulder, resentful of the older, Anglo-Saxon American elite of the Eastern Seaboard, did not matter much in London, not until the function of an American ambassador there would become much more than largely ceremonial."[5]

Kennedy was a fierce anticommunist who viewed the anti-Bolshevik Hitler as a relatively benign dictator. Kennedy thought Churchill a force for disaster. Problems in Anglo-American relations at the beginning of World War II were complicated by Kennedy's egotistical tendency to pursue diplomatic policies at odds with the State Department and the president—never forcefully brought back into line by either Secretary of State Hull or even a cautious Roosevelt.[6] Before the German invasion of Poland in September 1939, Kennedy publicly doubted British success in a conflict with Germany. "Hitler has every reason to go to war and is able," Kennedy told the famous columnist Walter Lippmann. "All the English in their hearts *know* this to be true, but a small group of brilliant people [e.g., Churchill] has created a public feeling which makes it impossible for the government to take a sensible course"—namely appeasement. At a dinner party attended by Kennedy and Churchill, the future prime minister confronted Kennedy, saying that he would "willingly lay down my life in combat, rather than, in fear of defeat, surrender to the menaces of these most sinister men [Nazis]."[7]

The U.S. ambassador had first met Churchill in 1933, when, as a businessman, he and FDR's son James came to England to secure a liquor deal. Kennedy knew how to ingratiate the president with favors for his son. The prime minister invited Kennedy and young Roosevelt to Chartwell.[8] Once Kennedy became ambassador in 1938, Churchill attempted to maintain friendly relations with him. The prime minister and Kennedy were linked by the simultaneous affairs carried on by journalist Claire Booth Luce with Kennedy and Churchill's son Randolph.[9] On May 14, 1940, Kennedy met with the prime minister at the Admiralty, where Churchill temporarily maintained his office. Kennedy wrote in his diary: "I couldn't help but think as I sat there talking to Churchill how ill-conditioned he looked and the fact that there was a tray with plenty of liquor on it alongside him and he was drinking a scotch highball, which I felt was indeed not the first one he had drunk that night, that, after all, the affairs of Great Britain might be in the hands of the most dynamic individual in Great Britain but certainly not in the hands of the best judgment in Great Britain."[10] After the meeting, Kennedy wired the White House that Churchill had said: "Regardless of what Germany does to England and France . . . England will never give up as long as he remains a power in public life even if England is burnt to the ground. Why, said he, the government will move to Canada and take the fleet and fight on.'"[11] This was what the prime minister wanted Kennedy to say to FDR and what the prime minister wanted FDR to hear. On this point, Churchill was consistent. On May 15, 1940, only five days after he became prime minister and one day after his meeting with Kennedy, Churchill wrote directly to President Roosevelt: "As you are no doubt aware, the scene had darkened swiftly. If necessary, we shall continue the war alone and we are not afraid of that. But I trust you realize, Mr. President, that the voice and the force of the United States may count for nothing if they are withheld too long. You may have a completely subjugated, Nazified Europe established with astonishing swiftness, and the weight may be more than we can bear."[12]

"Secretly, surreptitiously working through his confidant ambassadors (foremost among them William C. Bullitt, in Paris), Roosevelt began to intimate his support of politicians in Paris and London who were willing to stand up to Hitler," wrote historian John Lukacs.[13] During this period, Bullitt made himself a crucial source of information for Roosevelt.[14] On May 15, after meeting with French Premier Paul Reynaud, Bullitt wrote to FDR and Secretary of State Cordell Hull: "Churchill, Reynaud said, had screamed at him that there was no chance of the war being lost and he, Reynaud, had replied that Churchill knew as well as he knew him that so long as he, Reynaud, should remain Prime Minister France would fight to the bitter end. It was his duty however to tell Churchill the facts. Churchill thereupon promised . . . to persuade the War Cabinet to promise to send the British pursuit planes . . . to join in the battle of the Meuse."[15] Bullitt grew ever more pessimistic the next day, writing FDR that "in order to excape [sic] from the ultimate consequences of absolute defeat, the British may install a government of [British Fascist] Oswald Mosley and the union of British fascists which would cooperate fully with Hitler. That would mean that the British navy would be against us."[16] Secretary of State Cordell Hull recalled: "In response to Reynaud's almost pitiful pleas for backing, the President urged Mr. Churchill to send planes to France; but the Prime Minister refused. Bullitt, outraged by this decision, communicated to the President and me on June 5 his fear that the British might be conserving their air force and fleet so as to use them as bargaining points in negotiations with Hitler."[17]

Bullitt deceived himself. The prime minister held back the planes to defend England to the bitter end; he was right to do so, because France surrendered shortly thereafter.[18] Although Bullitt was anti-Hitler, he was skeptical of Churchill's abilities and angered by his unwillingness fully to commit British airplanes to the defense of

France.[19] Bullitt did not appreciate that the planes would be indispensable for the defense of England. The prime minister's decision not to dispatch the planes to France, where many would have been lost with the French surrender, was soon vindicated in the Battle of Britain that began in August. The British Royal Air Force (RAF) prevailed by a narrow margin over the Luftwaffe in the summer and fall of 1940.

The U.S. ambassador in London was not as well positioned as Bullitt in Paris to receive intelligence from either France or Britain. In his memoirs, Kennedy admitted: "My contacts with the Churchill cabinet were certainly far less friendly than with the old government" of Neville Chamberlain and its policy of appeasement.[20] Kennedy became increasingly frustrated at being on the outside of both the Churchill and Roosevelt governments. Not unlike other American officials, the ambassador, despite his attitude, got more information from the prime minister than from his own president. Kennedy diaried: "It is of course apparent that we are being kept completely in ignorance of what Roosevelt is doing. . . . I am interested to find out, and I will if possible, just why it is Churchill sees any reason at all for keeping me advised; because if he didn't send me these cables occasionally I would have no conception whatsoever of what is going on. I am at a loss however to understand why he wants to keep me posted."[21] The prime minister knew Kennedy was an appeaser, but Churchill could still use him for information and communication.

On May 27, 1940, as the evacuation of Dunkirk was beginning, Kennedy informed the Roosevelt administration: "My impression of the situation here is that it could not be worse. Only a miracle can save the B.E.F. [British Expeditionary Force] from being wiped out or as I saw yesterday, surrender. I suspect that the Germans would be willing to make peace with both the French and British now—of course on their own terms, but on terms that would be a great deal better than they would be if the war continues." Kennedy added: "Churchill, Attlee and others will want to fight to the death, but there will be other members who realize that physical destruction of men and property in England will not be a proper offset to a loss of pride. In addition to that, the English people, while they suspect a terrible situation, really do not realize how bad it is. When they do, I don't know which group they will follow—the do or die, or the group that want a settlement."[22] To the American president, the British prime minister now wrote bluntly:

> If members of the present [Churchill] administration were finished and others came into parley amid the ruins, you must not be blind to the fact that the sole remaining bargaining counter with Germany would be the Fleet, and, if this country was left by the United States to its fate, no one would have the right to blame those then responsible if they made the best terms they could for the surviving inhabitants. Excuse me, Mr. President, putting this nightmare bluntly. Evidently I could not answer for my successors who in utter despair and helplessness might well have to accommodate themselves to the German will.[23]

Churchill himself would never seriously consider accommodation to the Nazis. Roosevelt's confidant Robert Jackson, then U.S. attorney general, remembered that

Churchill "made valiant efforts at once to convey the strongest impression of Britain's desperate need while at the same time stopping short of confirming any sense of hopelessness."[24] The prime minister's reference to the British fleet falling into Nazi hands was a cleverly masked threat. The president held the view that seapower would be decisive in world affairs. Thus, he would be alarmed if the British fleet fell to the Germans. If the German, Italian, and French fleets were combined, the Nazis might command the seas. With the Royal Navy added, they undoubtedly would.

Kennedy's defeatism permeated his public and private comments. "For the first time this morning," observed Kennedy on June 14, "many people realize that they are in for a terrible time . . . they are beginning to say we have everything to lose and nothing to gain, and what is the use of fighting. If the English people thought there was a chance of peace on any decent terms, an upheaval against the government might come."[25] Eleven days later, Churchill wrote the British ambassador in Washington: "Never cease to impress on President and others that if this country were successfully invaded and largely occupied . . . some Quisling government would be formed to make peace on the basis of our becoming a German protectorate. In this case the British Fleet would be the solid contribution with which this Peace Government would buy terms. Feeling in England against the United States would be similar to French bitterness against us now. We have really not had any help worth speaking of from the United States so far."[26] Still, Churchill would make no deal with the Nazis. Kennedy, the deal maker from Wall Street, was incredulous.

"If Germany bombs Great Britain into a state of subjection," the British prime minister had warned Ambassador Kennedy in October 1939, "one of their terms would certainly be to hand over the Fleet. . . . If they got the British Fleet, they would have immediate superiority over the United States and then your trouble would begin."[27] In Washington, FDR, assistant secretary of the navy under President Woodrow Wilson, increasingly worried about the possibility of both the British and French navies falling under German control. It was in the fall of 1939 that the president and First Lord of the Admiralty Churchill had begun to exchange messages between "former Naval Persons." A new code clerk at the U.S. embassy in London passed these letters along to a German operative until British authorities arrested the clerk on May 18, 1940—eight days after Churchill took over as prime minister. The clerk was denied diplomatic immunity by the United States, quickly tried, and imprisoned under British law.[28]

After his nomination for a third term in July 1940, Roosevelt phoned Kennedy to keep him in London—and out of domestic politics. After indicating that Democratic leaders wanted Kennedy to run the presidential campaign, FDR stroked Kennedy's ego by dissimulating that the State Department "is very much against your leaving England." Roosevelt said the Democratic leaders "were very anxious to have you and you know how happy I would be to have you in charge, but the general impression is that it would do the cause of England a great deal of harm if you left there at this time and I didn't want you to hear that you had been named and your name had been turned down by me." Kennedy responded: "I am seriously considering going home: that, as far as I can see, I am not doing a damn thing here that amounts to anything and my services, if they are needed, could be used to much better advantage if I were home."[29]

During that summer, the relationship between Kennedy and Churchill grew increasingly adversarial, as Churchill sought to ingratiate himself with the American president, while the ambassador sought to distance the United States from Britain. "At this early stage of the war, to be well informed on England's weaknesses was to be pessimistic," wrote Kennedy biographer Richard J. Whalen. "But few Britons went as far as Kennedy in the direction of defeatism."[30] When he resigned officially in December 1940, Kennedy issued a statement: "Today the President was good enough to express regret over my decision, but to say that, not yet being prepared to appoint my successor, he wishes me to retain my designation as ambassador until he is prepared. But I shall not return to London in that capacity. My plan is, after a short holiday, to devote my efforts to what seems to me the great cause in the world today—and means, if successful, the preservation of the American form of democracy. That cause is to help the President keep the United States out of war." Kennedy's critics, like Interior Secretary Harold Ickes and columnist Joseph Alsop, saw through Kennedy's statement as a potential vehicle for the launch of a campaign to support isolationism.[31]

Most Roosevelt administration officials in Washington in 1940 developed war strategy unlike those of the defeatist ambassador in London. Hull recalled: "The President and I . . . reached a different conclusion from Kennedy's. It seemed to us we should do better to keep fighting away from our own back yard. This we could do by helping Britain and France remain on their feet." He added that "the President and I had not the slightest doubt; namely, that an Allied victory was essential to the security of the United States."[32] And so it was that the Roosevelt government slowly moved to help the United Kingdom.

Lord Lothian, the British ambassador in Washington, carried on negotiations for the Destroyers-for-Bases agreement in the summer of 1940.[33] Kennedy protested to FDR that he had been left in the dark: "I would have no knowledge whatsoever of the situation had it not been for the fact that the Prime Minister had seen fit to send some cables back through me and has also furnished me with supplemental facts."[34] A devious Roosevelt was more than a match for the proud and clever Kennedy. FDR responded evasively: "There is no thought of embarrassing you and only a practical necessity for personal conversations makes it easier to handle details here."[35] During the five months after Churchill took over as prime minister, Kennedy became increasingly pessimistic in his communications to Washington about the future of Britain. He put the worst possible gloss on what was happening in London.

That summer, Kennedy wrote Hull: "There is constant agitation here in the newspapers alleging that the Allies have asked for help from the United States; planes are mentioned most often and destroyers occasionally. I think it is important that some kind of statement should be made over there by some important person or over here after the policy has been decided explaining just why the United States is limited as to what she can give the Allies."[36] Kennedy's cable probably referred to the restrictions imposed by the U.S. Neutrality Acts and isolationist public opinion. Roosevelt did not heed the ambassador's recommendation to make such a statement. Outmaneuvered by the president, Kennedy was out of office by December 1940, though he had long been on the outside with FDR.

William J. Donovan (right), seen here with George Wadsworth, the U.S. consul general in Jerusalem.
LIBRARY OF CONGRESS

II

William J. Donovan and William Stephenson: Master Secret Agents

I have been given an opportunity to study at first hand these great battles going on in the Atlantic and in the Mediterranean, in Africa, in Greece and in Albania. . . . From my observations I have been able to form my conclusions . . . [which] I will submit to my country for its use in furtherance of our national defence, an essential part of which is our policy of aid to Great Britain. . . . And I say to you, my fellow citizens, all that Mr. Churchill has told you on the resolution & determination and valour and confidence of his people, is true.[1]

William J. Donovan *(1883–1959), radio broadcast, March 25, 1941. Donovan headed the Office of Strategic Services, the U.S. spy agency during World War II, and the predecessor of the CIA. Donovan was first appointed by FDR in 1941, as "Coordinator of Information," a misleading title cloaking his role as the top American spy. FDR and Donovan had been in the same class at Columbia Law School, but had never been friendly. The World War I hero and Justice Department veteran had strong political ambitions and excellent international contacts, but as a Republican, he had to navigate bureaucratic jealousies in the Roosevelt administration.*

The procurement of certain supplies for Britain was high on my priority list and it was the burning urgency of this requirement that made me instinctively concentrate on the single individual who could help me. I turned to Bill Donovan.[2]

William Stephenson *(1897–1989) headed British Security Coordination in the United States during World War II. The Canadian-born industrialist had worldwide contacts. He was effectively Britain's top spy in the United States, in charge of coordinating espionage efforts with the United States, changing American opinion toward Britain, and spying on the American government. He was successful at all three.*

Like Prime Minister Winston Churchill, President Franklin D. Roosevelt had an insatiable appetite for political and military intelligence, though typically in a less organized and focused way than Churchill preferred. The manipulative and secretive president was a natural spymaster. "Roosevelt was never content with official channels alone," historian David Stafford wrote. "He also developed personal contacts as alternative sources of information. One of the most prolific was the syndicated Washington journalist John Franklin Carter, who had easy access to the NBC shortwave radio network. . . . Roosevelt used him for private investigative work and paid him generously from his Presidential Emergency Fund."[3] During the 1920s, merchant marine scion Vincent Astor had developed a relationship with FDR that deepened in the early 1930s, when Astor invited FDR to cruise aboard Astor's yacht. The well-traveled Astor, who had served in the navy during World War I, maintained a strong interest in naval intelligence. Along with well-connected friends, Astor formed an organization of like-minded New Yorkers named "The ROOM." As tensions in the Pacific heated up, the members, renaming themselves "The CLUB," undertook to monitor banking and shipping data gleaned from bank sources and British intelligence. Astor's influence peaked in mid-1940, and declined after he sought an official appointment in early 1941. He was named area controller for the New York area for the Office of Naval Intelligence, to which Astor had long provided information.[4] By then, Roosevelt had better operatives in place, and Astor began to fade from FDR's intelligence network.[5]

British and American spymasters proved themselves a powerful team. In June 1940, under the direction of the Churchill administration, Canadian-born industrialist William Stephenson had launched British Security Coordination (BSC) in New York City. BSC was the successor to a less ambitious operation named the British Passport Office. Stephenson's connections in Britain, Canada, and the United States proved invaluable to his new operation. The spy chief would emerge from the shadows of espionage only in November 1946, when he received the U.S. Medal for Merit for his wartime work in "intelligence and special operations."[6] Although he served as Britain's top American spymaster throughout war, controversy has lingered over his role for decades—especially the nature and closeness of his relationship with Winston Churchill. After World War II, Stephenson became famous through publication of two biographies—*The Quiet Canadian* by H. Montgomery Hyde, and *A Man Called Intrepid* by William Stevenson.[7] The publicity-shy Stephenson alternately cooperated with and impeded publication of the biographies, and apparently contributed to inaccuracies about his life story, and to what critics called an inflation of his importance.[8] Historians Hugh Trevor-Roper and David Stafford attacked errors in both books.[9] Spies do not often maintain the best records, but Stephenson had an official history of the BSC compiled after the war, before destroying all of the BSC records. The official history, however, remained a closely held document, and many of those employed by BSC were Canadians who followed Stephenson's example of maintaining a quiet profile.[10] The record of British activities was further muddled by the treachery of British agents, such as Kim Philby, and men who were stationed in the United States but worked for the Russians. Stephenson's first top deputy was C. R. "Dick" Ellis, an Australian veteran of the British spy agency, who later filled a similar role for the Americans. Ellis was subsequently suspected of being a secret German agent, and later perhaps a secret Russian agent as well. Constrained by British secrecy rules, Ellis tried to write about Stephenson without ever getting his work into publication.[11]

Although Stephenson's importance diminished over time as the network of Anglo-American cooperation deepened, he played a crucial role in 1940–1941.[12] As Keith Jeffery concluded in *The Secret History of MI6,* under Stephenson, "BSC developed with astounding speed into an impressively wide-ranging organisation."[13] The Canadian came to America with strong contacts on both sides of the Atlantic. His initial residence was at the St. Regis Hotel, owned by his friend Vincent Astor, who reportedly arranged for Stephenson to meet FDR at Hyde Park.[14] Stephenson established a relationship with FBI Director J. Edgar Hoover, through boxer Gene Tunney.[15] White House aide Robert Sherwood dubbed Stephenson the "quiet Canadian," for his work in coordinating Anglo-American espionage.[16] In Britain, Stephenson's close contacts included Churchill aides Desmond Morton and British General Hastings Ismay.[17] In the early summer of 1940, Stephenson worked with newly appointed Navy Secretary Frank Knox to arrange a fact-finding mission to Britain by William J. Donovan, then working at a prestigious Wall Street law firm.[18] Confusion surrounds the origins of the Stephenson-Donovan relationship, but its development is unquestioned. Stephenson worked closely with the British ambassador in Washington, Lord Lothian, and with the director of MI6 in London, Stewart Menzies, to promote the work of Donovan. American "Big Bill" and Canadian "Little Bill" became key links in the Anglo-American war team. Stephenson's job required perseverance and a low profile, because he needed to lobby for military assistance to the United Kingdom and to promote pro-British media coverage, without obviously violating American laws or stoking anti-British, isolationist resentment. According to Stephenson, he had been delegated by Churchill to "assure sufficient aid for Britain, to counter the enemy's subversive plans throughout the western Hemisphere . . . and eventually to bring the United States into the war."[19]

With FDR's approval, Knox dispatched Donovan as his special representative to England.[20] Donovan had traveled through Europe in the 1930s, to meet with key leaders like Benito Mussolini. He had run unsuccessfully as a Republican for governor of New York in 1932. He had hopes of becoming secretary of war under Democrat Roosevelt, just as he had earlier expected to get the job of attorney general under Republican Herbert Hoover. Neither cabinet job materialized—even though FDR wanted to broaden the bipartisan appeal of his administration as he prepared to campaign for a third term. The European challenge came at the right time (Donovan's daughter had died in a car crash in the spring of 1940). Thus, Roosevelt selected a rising Irish-American Republican, Donovan, to counterbalance an unreliable Irish-American Democrat, Kennedy. Ahead of Donovan's visit as FDR's representative, Stephenson bluntly cabled the British government in London: "UNITED STATES EMBASSY NOT BEING INFORMED." The U.S. embassy had in fact been informed by the State Department. In response to a message from Secretary of State Cordell Hull about Donovan's mission, an unhappy Kennedy wrote: "I will render any service I can to Colonel Donovan whom I know and like. Our staff I think is getting all the information that possibly can be gathered and to send a new man in here at this time, with all due respect to Colonel Knox, is to me the height of nonsense and a definite blow to good organization."[21]

Over the next two weeks, Churchill overcame his suspicions about the Irish-Catholic Donovan's loyalties, giving him full access to Britain's logistical and military strengths and weaknesses. A European correspondent for the *Chicago Daily News*, partly owned by Knox, enhanced the productivity of Donovan's whirlwind visit. Journalist Edgar Ansel Mowrer agreed to help Donovan in his research and to brief him on what he learned.[22] One of Donovan's first meetings was with King George VI.[23] A British naval official who conferred with Donovan reported that he favored a new American ambassador and new American military aid to Britain: "It was obvious that we had a good friend in Donovan and one who had the ear of the President and knew how to work with the British."[24] His biographer Douglas Waller observed that Donovan got "secret briefings on ships and planes in her arsenal, on output by her industry, and on food supplies from her farms. He inspected a fighter squadron at Essex and a naval officers training camp in Portsmouth. Churchill had to assign seven men working overtime to prepare answers to all the questions Donovan left behind from each visit."[25]

Still, Churchill was cautious about sharing all of Britain's secrets with American counterparts, writing Hastings Ismay on July 17, 1940, that he was "not in a hurry to give out secrets until the United States is much nearer war than she is now."[26] Another 17 months would pass before America went to war. Thus, both nations hesitated to give out all their own deep secrets without getting the deepest secrets of the other in return. But, the growing personal relationship between Roosevelt and Churchill allowed information to flow. Historian David Stafford wrote: "Any of the intelligence quarrels simmering beneath the surface could have exploded into open conflict had either leader behaved differently."[27] As early as 1940, therefore, the Nazis had reason and evidence to expect a British-American alliance. FDR maintained the conceit of neutrality, which did not fool the Nazis, who anticipated war with the United States.

Ambassador Kennedy resented the outside interference posed by his visitor, impetuously telling Donovan that England's defeat was certain. Donovan's mission, and the decision of the Roosevelt administration not to include the ambassador in discussions about aid to Britain, had upset Kennedy. He complained to Washington that he had been treated as a "dummy."[28] FDR nevertheless tried to charm and deceive the ambassador with flattery, writing: "Don't forget that you are not only not a dummy but are essential to all of us both in the Government and in the Nation."[29] In London, Kennedy undermined Donovan's activities, expressing discontent about his thin journalistic cover.[30] But Churchill well understood his secret mission and gave him full access to the British war effort.[31] The British gave him frank but upbeat answers to his questions, and unprecedented access to secret military and espionage activities.

When Donovan came back to the United States in August 1940, he briefed FDR on a train ride through New England, and gave President Roosevelt a very different message than Kennedy had. After Donovan's return from Britain, Arthur Purvis, the top British purchasing agent in Washington, wrote to London: "Colonel Donovan was working with great energy in our interest. We now had a firm friend in the Republican camp and this was proving of immense value."[32] Eventually, Roosevelt would call Donovan "my secret legs."[33] Donovan was capable of impressing even the dour secretary of the Treasury, Henry Morgenthau, who commented: "I think he knows more about the [European] situation than anybody I have talked to by about a thousand percent."[34] Foreign Minister Halifax and Ambassador Kennedy, both appeasers, did not cooperate that summer with Donovan, who nonetheless earned the respect of the president and the prime minister.

Throughout 1940, Roosevelt cautiously considered how to aid the British war effort—even while masquerading at U.S. neutrality in the middle of a difficult presidential campaign. At one point in the preelection discussions over a potential Destroyers-for-Bases deal, he sought a public guarantee that, in the event of a British defeat, the United Kingdom would turn over their blue-water fleet to the United States. Churchill refused, writing Lord Halifax: "We have no intention of surrendering the British fleet or sinking it voluntarily. Indeed, such a fate is more likely to overtake the German Fleet or what is left of it. The nation would not tolerate such a discussion of what we should do if our island were overrun. Such a discussion, perhaps on the eve of an invasion, would be injurious to public morale, now so high."[35] The same day, the prime minister wrote the British ambassador in Washington: "I have already several weeks ago told you that there is no warrant for discussing any question of the transference of the Fleet to American or Canadian shores."[36] Churchill desperately longed for American help, but he would not countenance talk of defeat, even from the U.S. president.[37]

Kennedy continued to peddle his defeatist line, especially after the vaunted German air force began the Battle of Britain in August 1940. In late September, he wrote the State Department:

> I cannot impress upon you strongly enough my complete lack of confidence in the entire conduct of this war. I was delighted to see that the President said he was not going to enter the war, because to enter this war, imagining for a minute that the English have anything to offer in the line of leadership or productive capacity in industry that could be of the slightest value to us, would be a complete misapprehension. . . . If by any chance we should ever come to the point of getting into the war we can make up our minds that it will be the United States against Germany, Italy and Japan, aided by a badly shot to pieces country which in the last analysis can give little, if any, assistance to the cause.[38]

The German government had obtained its version of this Kennedy message through its own channels in Washington. A Nazi diplomat there had informed Berlin that

Kennedy "warned the President urgently not to take irreparable steps. England was finished (completely through) and the U.S.A. would have to pay the bill."[39]

England would prove much sturdier than Kennedy's prophecy had suggested. New men appeared on both sides of the Atlantic to foster Anglo-American relations. Donovan was a key player. In November 1940, Stephenson reported that Donovan was "the *strongest* friend whom we have here."[40] In December, Menzies and Stephenson, with the determined support of Churchill's government, arranged for Donovan to conduct a second fact-finding trip, this time of Britain, Europe, and the Middle East. Meanwhile, British intelligence became one of FDR's best sources of military and diplomatic secrets, supplied through British intercepts of German communications. Early in the war, a top British official acknowledged "that to all intents and purposes U.S. security is being run for them at the President's request by the British. . . . It is of course essential that this fact should not be known in view of the furious uproar it would cause if known to the isolationists."[41] Stephenson's mission was to bring the United States into the war on the side of Britain, while undermining any isolationist or pro-German activities.

In the spring of 1941, Stephenson and Admiral John Henry Godfrey, chief of British naval intelligence, would encourage the selection of Donovan as an American intelligence chief. From his headquarters on the 36th floor of Rockefeller Center, Stephenson knew he needed a high-level American counterpart—preferably someone who, like him, had traveled widely in Europe in the prewar years. Like Stephenson, Donovan was a self-made man who had risen from humble roots, entrepreneurial, eclectic, and well connected.[42] By reason of his wife's wealth, Donovan was financially independent.

Bill Donovan was anything but a government bureaucrat. He was an entrepreneur who lacked the bureaucrat's requisite patience for rules and procedures. Roosevelt recognized a fellow nonconformist, and reached an agreement with Donovan to become "Coordinator of Information," in command of his own budget and personnel. Bill Stephenson reported to his London bosses on June 18, 1941: "Donovan saw President today and after long discussion where in all points were agreed, he accepted the appointment. He will be coordinator of all forms [of] intelligence including offensive operations."[43] Many in the Roosevelt administration were less pleased than Stephenson that this independent Republican would compete for espionage resources.[44] At the OSS, Donovan would develop his own team—through which Stephenson sometimes funneled British intelligence directly to the White House. It was through such back channels that Anglo-American relations were frequently conducted, whereby British influence was sanitized through a powerful American conduit.

Donovan annoyed military officials by operating outside their structure. He aggravated FBI Director J. Edgar Hoover by setting up a competing intelligence network. But Donovan knew how to get things done on behalf of Anglo-American interests. The FBI and other agencies, opposed to an Anglo-American spy alliance, or jealous of their own turf, were persistent critics, even an occasional threat to the Donovan-Stephenson operations. Hoover spread his criticism to friendly bureaucratic ears such as those in the State Department, saying that "a good many things being done are probably in violation of our espionage acts."[45] On this allegation, Hoover was correct, but espionage implies a violation of domestic laws and procedures, especially in wartime.

FDR orchestrated America's unconventional diplomacy, partly through Wild Bill Donovan, surely an unconventional personality. Like the president, Donovan could be Machiavellian and a careless administrator. Historian Arthur Schlesinger Sr., who worked under Donovan, called him "exasperating but adorable," adding, "He was generally forgiven and adored." Schlesinger wrote that he was "a winning combination of charm, audacity, imagination, optimism and energy," a description that could apply as well to FDR.[46] Douglas Waller wrote: "The president and his spy chief had developed their own, somewhat peculiar rapport. Donovan sent Roosevelt documents from France in their original French, knowing FDR liked to exercise his fluency in the language. Roosevelt was as open to strange ideas as Donovan."[47] Later in the war, Donovan did not fully appreciate Churchill, but in early 1942, he understood Churchill's Mediterranean strategy far better than most American military strategists. During this time, the British had nothing but respect for Donovan. "[T]o all intents and purposes US [intelligence] security is being run for them at the President's request by the British," observed Churchill colleague Desmond Morton, of Donovan's appointment as national intelligence coordinator.[48] He meant that Stephenson and Donovan acted together. Almost a year after the opaquely named "Office of Coordinator of Information" was established, the equally opaque Office of Strategic Services (OSS) replaced it.

Relations between British and American intelligence services were often complicated by envy and suspicion. David Stafford wrote that British spy chief "Menzies jealously resisted American efforts to launch intelligence operations into Europe from British soil. One result was to make the OSS station in [Bern] Switzerland Donovan's most important European base—and to launch its head, Allen Dulles, on the track that within a decade made him President Eisenhower's Director of Central Intelligence."[49] Churchill had cultivated his own back channels to American leaders, using such men as Gerald Wilkinson, a British businessman stationed in the Philippines during 1941. Wilkinson became a confidant of Douglas MacArthur. He reported to London on MacArthur's actions, ruminations, and political ambitions.[50] Wilkinson, however, developed an American enemy—General Charles Willoughby, who succeeded in poisoning MacArthur's mind about Wilkinson, and eventually succeeded in barring the Brit from the Pacific theater. Wilkinson was subsequently posted to the United States to head up British intelligence efforts focused on the Pacific region. Historian David Stafford wrote: "American Far Eastern intelligence as well as Japanese military information was now Wilkinson's target, and for the next two years he reported regularly on American challenges to British interests in the region."[51]

Churchill was not without friends in the State Department. The ambitious Nelson Rockefeller, who later became assistant secretary of state for Latin America, had arranged cheap Manhattan offices for Stephenson at Rockefeller Center. However, some important American officials with close ties to Roosevelt were not friendly to Britain. One was Adolf Berle, a member of the original Roosevelt "brain trusters." In addition to his duties as assistant secretary of state for Latin American affairs, Berle served as an informal advisor and speechwriter for FDR, and chairman of the State Department's Interdepartmental Committee on Intelligence and Security. Berle was a stickler for the proprieties of American law, which he correctly believed British agents (and Americans such as Donovan) repeatedly violated.[52] The level of intrigue sometimes aggravated tempers in Washington. David Stafford wrote that in 1942, the president's "patience with Donovan's empire-building and the Washington turf wars they provoked was also running thin, and to Berle . . . he confessed that he was thinking of putting Donovan on 'some nice, quiet, isolated island, where he could have a scrap with some Japs every morning before breakfast.'"[53]

Berle and Assistant Secretary of State Breckinridge Long "were noted for their Anglophobia and antiwar attitudes," wrote historian Lynne Olson. "Indeed, Long, who did his best to prevent Jewish refugees from entering the United States in the late 1930s and early 1940s, was labeled a 'fascist' by Eleanor Roosevelt."[54] A so-called gentleman-diplomat, Long enjoyed the confidence of Secretary Hull.[55] In 1940, Long observed that Hull's estrangement from Under Secretary of State Welles came about because Welles "thinks so fast and moves so rapidly that he gets way out in front and leaves no trace of positions taken or commitments made."[56] Harvard-educated Berle had early gained the confidence of Harvard-educated President Roosevelt, who never finished his law degree at Columbia, where Berle became a professor.

Among Berle's responsibilities at the State Department were security issues.[57] Berle believed the British were manufacturing intelligence in order to influence the American government. "You are familiar with the fact that we recently took up with the British Government the fact that British Intelligence had given us documents which they had forged; and on one occasion had approached our people to collaborate with them in certain other forgeries. The FBI, therefore, has regarded all British Intelligence information of this kind as subject to check," Berle wrote Hull in July 1941. "Without going into a long mess of detail, I believe that the British Intelligence probably has been giving attention to creating as many 'incidents' as possible to affect public opinion here."[58] In the tangled world of Anglo-American relations, Berle was close to Ernest Cuneo, a Washington–New York lawyer and journalist, who in turn was close to Bill Stephenson and FDR.[59]

What Berle did not know was that British intelligence was providing Roosevelt with top-secret information from the "Ultra" decryption of German "Enigma" scrambled communications—Churchill's best-kept wartime secret, not officially disclosed until 1974. Berle's opposition to British intelligence efforts within U.S. borders continued even after the United States entered the war. In January 1942, after Pearl Harbor, Congress passed legislation that would have outlawed any foreign spying in the United States. The British sought and got FDR's veto of the bill—with the help of Donovan and presidential aide Robert Sherwood. Berle wrote in his diary that "British Intelligence who maintain a lively and not too creditable spy system . . . don't want any such act because they don't want their spy system interrupted. They intervened with the [British] Embassy but the Embassy said they could do nothing about it. Thereupon they intervened with Bill Donovan, who promptly put in a memorandum to the President asking him to veto the bill which was on his desk. I am impressed by Donovan's courage though I don't think much of it in terms of national wisdom."[60] The buccaneering Donovan, a decorated soldier and entrepreneurial lawyer, prevailed over Berle, a professor-bureaucrat.

Secretary of State Cordell Hull receives a report from Under Secretary Sumner Welles, January 1939.
LIBRARY OF CONGRESS

III

Roosevelt: His Own Secretary of State

> When I accepted this office, I knew that I would be misrepresented, lied about, let down, and that there would be humiliations that no man in private life could accept and keep his self-respect. But I made up my mind in advance that I would accept all these things and just do my job.[1]
>
> ***Cordell Hull*** *(1871–1955) was appointed secretary of state at the outset of President Franklin Roosevelt's first administration in 1933, and served until he resigned for reasons of bad health and frustration in 1944. The courtly, old-fashioned, former Tennessee congressman and senator was a fervent proponent of free trade, the economic policy hallmark of southern Democrats.*

Before President Roosevelt named him to create what became the Office of Strategic Services (OSS), William J. Donovan had acquired many critics inside and outside of government.[2] In December 1940, when Donovan left for Europe for a second time on behalf of the Roosevelt administration, *New York Times* columnist Arthur Krock, a supporter of ex-Ambassador Joseph P. Kennedy, wrote: "Donovan is the kind of foreign emissary who causes difficulties for the foreign service."[3] But neither Roosevelt nor Churchill worried much about creating difficulties for diplomats. They focused on creating difficulties for Hitler, no matter the protocol. FDR himself was an unconventional and disorganized administrator. "Roosevelt's personality and administrative methods encouraged . . . turbulence. He delegated power so loosely that bureaucrats found themselves entangled in lines of authority and stepping on one another's toes," wrote biographer James MacGregor Burns. "Despite his public disapproval of open brawls, Roosevelt actually tolerated them and sometimes even seemed to enjoy them." He often used one set of players to get another set of players to do what he wanted. He was adept at perversely manipulating officials against each other. Burns noted: "Again and again Roosevelt put into the same office or job men who differed from each other in temperament and viewpoint." The president was determined that he himself would remain the center of political decision-making. Both Churchill and Roosevelt opposed those who set themselves up as competing power centers, especially those with whom they disagreed, cutting down to size those who overreached their authority. "By establishing in an agency one power center that counteracted another, [Roosevelt] made each official more dependent on White House support; the President in effect became the necessary ally and partner of each."[4] By contrast, the prime minister described his own approach to lines of authority when he wrote of his government's crisis in January–February 1942: "My personal authority even seemed to be enhanced by the uncertainties affecting several of my colleagues or would-be colleagues. I did not suffer from any desire to be relieved of my responsibilities. All I wanted was compliance with my wishes after reasonable discussion."[5] Churchill generally encouraged intense discussion, logical arguments based on evidence, and then firm decisions on policy.

"The President of the United States is his own Secretary of State to the extent he wishes to be," noted Arthur Krock. "The consequences of limiting the role of the Secretary of State, if the President chooses, to a mere supervisor of the conduct of his foreign policy adversely affects the international relations of the United States and internal Administration morale, especially in the State Department."[6] But Dean Acheson, who would later serve as secretary of state himself, explained the situation differently: "The President cannot be Secretary of State; it is inherently impossible in the nature of both positions. What he can do, and often has done with unhappy results, is to prevent anyone else from being Secretary of State."[7] This Roosevelt did with profound effect. Charles E. Bohlen—an experienced, respected diplomat—observed that White House disdain for the State Department "was destructive of morale for many of us in the department, and we were most unhappy about it."[8] Bohlen wrote: "Roosevelt and his chief assistant, Harry Hopkins, were concerned mostly with the present. That meant that they focused on military decisions, because the immediate problem was turning back the Nazis. Eager to prove to the Soviets that the United States was a true ally, the White House [FDR] thought the State Department's worry about political problems smacked of foot-dragging."[9]

Under President Roosevelt, the State Department was administered primarily by Under Secretary Sumner Welles, a Harvard graduate, fluent in French and Spanish. French diplomat Raoul Aglion observed: "The President trusted him and charged him, as Undersecretary of State, with European Affairs and especially with the thorny French problem. Everyone was aware of the personal rivalry between Welles and Cordell Hull."[10] As businessman W. Averell Harriman prepared himself to take up an important post in London in early 1943, he met with State Department officials. Newly appointed Assistant Secretary of State for Economic Affairs Acheson told Harriman "that he was still in the dark as to the State Department's policy on just about every important question on the international agenda."[11] FDR kept the answers close to his chest.

The president could be a mercurial political creature; Hull was a careful man of the legislature. Labor Secretary Frances Perkins recalled: "Hull was different from Roosevelt—more deliberate, more thoughtful perhaps, more cautious."[12] Bohlen wrote that Hull was "too rambling, too imprecise" for FDR, a rambler himself.[13] The cautious Hull and the impulsive Roosevelt came from different worlds. Welles and Roosevelt—with clever, quicker minds—came from the same elite social circle in the Northeast. Hull was born in a Tennessee log cabin. Though Hull was the secretary of state, Welles effectively ran the department and managed relations with the president. Nevertheless, FDR appreciated Hull's reputation and reportedly considered him as a running mate in 1940, because Hull had the look of a statesman.[14] Hull expected the president to reach out to him: "If the President wishes to speak to me, all he has to do is pick up that telephone, and I'll come running. It is not for me to bother the President of the United States."[15] Acheson later observed that "Hull rankled under what he believed to be Welles's disloyalty and the President's neglect." Acheson emphasized that the State Department became divided between Hull loyalists and Welles loyalists.[16] When British Foreign Secretary Anthony Eden visited Washington in March 1943, he observed of the State Department's top officials: "Their relations were vinegar, although the Secretary of State when speaking of his Under-Secretary in his absence was acidly correct, to foreigners at least."[17]

Roosevelt believed the State Department ineffective. He told Berle: "Hull was magnificent on principle but timid; Sumner [Welles] was fundamentally a 'career man.'"[18] But Welles had the access—and the willingness—to appeal directly to FDR. Circumvention of Hull's authority infuriated the secretary of state, especially when Welles got the president to support his actions. Hull's diffidence toward the president enabled the ambitious activist Welles.[19] At the 1942 Rio de Janeiro conference of Western Hemisphere nations, Welles organized united opposition to the Axis.[20] Hull later wrote of Welles: "From our earliest association I had sought to give him reasonable latitude in carrying on his work. I had asked him to go directly to the President with matters on which he was working, especially when I was closely engaged at the Department. . . . I found, however, that Welles abused this privilege by going to the President at times without my knowledge, and even attempting to secure a decision, again without my knowledge."[21] Hull believed Welles was making new policy through speeches. When confronted in 1942, "Welles replied that he was not aware that he had been defining new foreign policy in his speeches," wrote Hull. "He then said that, in view of what I had said, he would cease making speeches altogether."[22]

In the 1930s, Hull had been a leading advocate for global trade liberalization. In his second volume of memoirs, Welles summarized what he saw as Hull's defects.

> Secretary Hull's discourses to the foreign diplomats whom he received and to his associates in the State Department always reminded me irresistibly of the story of the Civil War politician whose speeches—more notable for their length than for their content—were once likened to a train with twenty cars from which emerged but a single passenger. In Mr. Hull's trains the passenger was always the same—the Trade Agreements

> Programme. . . . But no matter how beneficial a liberal economic regime might have been in more normal times, after 1936 no economic remedy could have dissipated the political and military threats that confronted all the democracies. This Mr. Hull seemed unable to understand.[23]

In his memoirs, Hull attempted to place himself at the center of American foreign policy decision-making, which in reality was conducted at the White House. Hull wrote: "I was in constant contact with Mr. Churchill's thought by reason of the fact that the President was, in general, accustomed to sending me the telegrams and messages he received from the Prime Minister on subjects involving foreign relations rather than military affairs. He asked me to prepare and recommend to him suitable replies, or to reply direct for him. This he did at almost all times in case of messages to him from the chiefs of other governments as well, or when he wished to originate a message to a foreign statesman."[24] This curious passage belies the observations of colleagues in FDR's government. Hull was often the odd man out in the formulation of foreign policy. Nevertheless, in 1944, he told Arthur Krock that Roosevelt "was basing his hope for re-election on a foreign-policy record which I personally made—often after talking the President out of 'some folly.'"[25]

As the sickly Hull came to despise Welles, the secretary of state used any method, including the FBI, to force Welles from office. "The State Department in 1940 was overwhelmed by intrigue and fatigue," wrote historian Jordan A. Schwarz. "Hull was then sixty-nine and . . . [he] may not have known the intricacies of foreign policy, but he certainly knew the levers of power better than any member of Roosevelt's cabinet and his high esteem in Congress made him valuable to the president. He was determined to outlast and destroy Welles, Berle or any other man who may have coveted his portfolio."[26] Historian Irwin Gellman wrote that Hull "launched a concerted attack against his chief assistant [Welles] on three grounds; first, he was a homosexual and therefore an embarrassment (or worse) to the State Department; second, he acted irresponsibly in making foreign policy decisions; and third, he had proven disloyal. Hull became particularly upset with Welles' encouragement of postwar planning."[27] The conflict between the contemplative Hull and the action-oriented Welles created an open wound in the Roosevelt administration. FDR tolerated or encouraged other personnel conflicts, but this one he tried to ignore. Hull's intrigue against Welles gained the support of erstwhile U.S. Ambassador to France William C. Bullitt Jr., who had neither office nor authority in the State Department after he fled Paris in June 1940.[28] Bullitt used his free time to disseminate evidence that in 1939, a drunken Welles had made homosexual propositions to two black railroad porters on the way home from the funeral of House Speaker William B. Bankhead in Alabama.[29]

For more than two years, former FDR confidant Bullitt crusaded for Welles's dismissal. The White House and the FBI had investigated Welles's personal behavior in early 1941, with the conclusion by the president that Welles needed to be monitored, not dismissed.[30] Roosevelt was quick to forgive incidents that he believed resulted from excessive consumption of alcohol.[31] On April 23, 1941, Bullitt confronted

FDR with a report of the incident. Roosevelt acknowledged he knew about the report and the "truth in the allegations." The president rebuffed Bullitt's demand to dismiss Welles, explaining that the bodyguard assigned to Welles would prevent any recurrence of the incident, and there was no possibility of publication of the news. The president insisted he needed Welles, the most congenial State Department official with whom he could work. Bullitt refused to drop his campaign against Welles—despite the president's personal request.[32] Historian H. W. Brands summarized the president's dilemma: "He considered Welles something of a protégé, and he enjoyed Welles's company more than that of Hull. He also considered Welles far more capable than Hull. As for Bullitt, he had never trusted him though he sometimes found him useful." On one occasion when Bullitt called at the White House in 1943, FDR allegedly declared: "You've tried to destroy a fellow human being; get out of here and never come back."[33]

Roosevelt's distant relative Margaret "Daisy" Suckley stayed at the White House in July 1943, and wrote that the president was bedeviled by "Cordell Hull's feelings! Mr. Hull is somehow jealous of Sumner Welles, who is a very useful man. Every time Mr. Welles has a talk with the P., Mr. Hull imagines they talk about all sorts of things besides the subject Mr. Hull knows about."[34] In August, Hull finally pushed Welles out, just before the Anglo-American summit at Quebec. Welles's formal resignation lingered for a month while he abruptly left the capital for his Maine home.[35] FDR complained about Hull's sensitivity to criticism, telling Suckley that Hull "was so upset over being criticized in the papers during the past year; also the differences over Sumner Welles, etc. Finally, the P. just reminded him that for the past 10 yrs. the P. himself has been attacked constantly & has been able to survive it & still smile."[36] Welles wrote that FDR told him "that he had never been angrier in his life at the situation in the State Department, which has now reached an impossible climax. . . . 'I need you for the country. After all, whom have I got. Harry Hopkins is a sick man. I thought he would die when he joined me last week.'"[37] After a month of speculation, Welles officially resigned on September 26, 1943, and was replaced as under secretary by Edward Stettinius, an ally of Harry Hopkins. A former steel executive, Stettinius had served as Washington administrator of Lend-Lease.

Stettinius joined a State Department deeply split over postwar planning—Adolf Berle on one side and Dean Acheson on the other. Bullitt argued that there were actually four State Departments—led by Hull, Welles, Berle, and Acheson, respectively.[38] Not unlike the feuding Hull and Welles, Berle and Acheson despised each other.[39] Berle worried that influential Supreme Court Justice Felix Frankfurter was angling to put Acheson into Hull's position.[40] Washington gossip and intrigue was, as always, Machiavellian during World War II and contributed to the divisions. Columnists Drew Pearson and Walter Winchell used and were used by British and American sources to spice up their columns.[41] Thomas E. Mahl contended that famous columnist Walter Lippmann "was both giving and receiving advice from the British."[42] British agents, such as Stephenson, found ways to bend journalists to their purposes. Americans like Washington insider Ernest Cuneo, a former football player, played politics and press relations as a contact sport. Decades later, Cuneo wrote: "My relationships with BSC [British Security Coordination, run by Stephenson] was one of the many source-relationships I maintained as part of my de facto editorship of Winchell's policies. . . . We 'moved' about 1,200 words a day, six days a week and had also to prepare a Sunday broadcast. For years I did this as a service to FDR." Cuneo maintained that Winchell was not a British agent.[43]

When Secretary of State Hull wanted to undermine Welles in 1943, he commissioned a *New York Times* article by compliant bureau chief Arthur Krock, an occasional thorn in FDR's side.[44] Welles was a close friend of columnist Drew Pearson, himself a political operator acting as a journalist. Welles consulted Pearson during his resignation crisis, and some of Pearson's subsequent columns contributed to Hull's hatred of Welles.[45] One column called Hull "anti-Russian" and prompted Roosevelt to angrily declare at a press conference: "I don't hesitate to say that the whole statement from beginning to end was a lie, but there is nothing new in it, because the man [Pearson] is a chronic liar in his columns."[46] Pearson had launched a vituperative campaign against Hull, charging that "the exit of one of the few liberals in the State Department, leaving a battery of Soviet-haters behind, is not going to help things at a time when Russian relations remain on tenterhooks."[47]

Welles declined FDR's repeated requests to undertake an important mission to Moscow in the fall of 1943. The president insisted that Welles would be a better representative of the Roosevelt administration at Moscow, arguing that Hull would "mess things up."[48] Welles contended that Hull would undermine any such mission, and declined to go. When *Times* columnist James Reston wrote a pro-Welles column, Hull summoned Reston to his office to give the journalist an anti-Welles file from the FBI. In a final parting shot at Welles, Hull flew to Moscow for a conference of the Big Three foreign secretaries, including Vyacheslav Molotov and Anthony Eden. The conference aimed to be a planning session for a summit of Roosevelt, Churchill, and Stalin, in late November. In mid-October, Hull met up in Teheran with the new U.S. Ambassador to Russia, Averell Harriman, and they proceeded together to the Russian capital. Moscow was a brief moment in the diplomatic sun for Hull, who soon thereafter was again shut out of important foreign-policy decisions while he suffered debilitating bouts of sickness. Welles meanwhile devoted himself to a book, *The Time for Decision*, about his years at the State Department and the need for a United Nations organization. Welles elaborated on the theme that he and President Roosevelt had directed foreign policy, not Secretary Hull.[49]

In fact, Roosevelt acted as his own secretary of state—especially with Britain. He often did so with a blatant disregard for bureaucratic lines of authority.[50] "In foreign affairs, Roosevelt did his job only moderately well. The methods and techniques that he usually used with consummate skill in domestic politics did not fit well in foreign affairs. He relied on his instinctive grasp of the subject, which was good, and his genius for improvisation to find solutions to problems," wrote State Department expert Charles Bohlen. "In foreign affairs, particularly when dealing with Soviet leaders, this style meant a lack of precision."[51] FDR's instinct for flattery would not work with Stalin.[52]

"The State Department, which should have been the vital instrument of our most important national policy," wrote FDR aide Robert E. Sherwood, was "relegated to the status of the querulous maiden aunt whose sole function is to do all the worrying for the prosperous family over the endless importunities of the numerous poor relations living on the other side of the tracks."[53] Hull became frustrated that "the President is running foreign affairs and I know the President will not let me help him anymore." In a conversation with Morgenthau in early 1943, he said: "What is it we can do to improve the situation? . . . The President runs foreign affairs. I don't know what's going on. . . . I asked to see the political part of the cables between the President and Churchill, because I have to find out from Ambassador Halifax what's going on between the President and Churchill." Roosevelt said "he would give it to me and three hours later, I got a message that the President had decided he would not do it."[54] Historian H. W. Brands summarized the results of the president's leadership style: "His habit of employing personal envoys irritated Hull, even insulted him. The secretary of state tolerated Hopkins, but only barely, and that because Hopkins worked for the president rather than for the State Department and because Hopkins seemed likely to die any day."[55] For his part, Hopkins waited for Hull to follow through on one of his repeated threats to resign.

Suspicion, jealousy, and bitterness crippled much of the talent at the State Department. FDR cannot escape responsibility for its demoralization, confusion, and immobility—even though he did find options to the traditional channels of foreign relations.

At the Yalta Conference. Left to right: Secretary of State Edward Stettinius, Major General L. S. Kuter, Admiral E. J. King, General George C. Marshall, Ambassador Averell Harriman, Admiral William Leahy, and President Roosevelt.

LIBRARY OF CONGRESS

IV

Roosevelt as Commander in Chief

I can't help feeling a little bit uneasy about the influence of the Prime Minister on him at this time. . . . The trouble is WC and FDR are too much alike in their strong points and in their weak points. They are both penetrating in their thoughts but they lack the steadiness of balance that has got to go along with warfare.[1]

Henry L. Stimson *(1867–1950), diary, June 20, 1942. In an attempt to add a bipartisan flavor to his administration, President Roosevelt appointed Stimson, then 72, as U.S. secretary of war (1940–1945). Republican Stimson had previously served both as secretary of war and secretary of state. Stimson supported early American entry into the war, but opposed harsh postwar treatment of Germany.*

Churchill, I thought, was at his best at Yalta. He was completely and wholeheartedly devoted to the interests of the British Empire. I could take no exception to that attitude, even when his proposals were not in full accord with what I believed to be the best interests of my own country. He was a great Englishman, as Roosevelt was a great American.[2]

William D. Leahy *(1875–1959), in his memoirs. A former chief of naval operations, Admiral Leahy in late 1940 became U.S. Ambassador to the Vichy French government of Marshal Henri Philippe Pétain. In the summer of 1942, Leahy returned to the United States and was appointed to the dual role of chief of staff to President Roosevelt and the first chairman of the Joint Chiefs of Staff.*

Anglo-American victory celebrations disguised the relative unimportance of many of the high-ranking decision makers on both sides of the Atlantic, often excluded from the inner circle of policy making. Some, like Secretary of State Cordell Hull, were deliberately kept poorly informed by President Roosevelt. It was FDR who prevented Hull from attending the key Casablanca summit in January 1943. The president pressed Churchill successfully to exclude Foreign Secretary Anthony Eden from this meeting as well. In the fall of 1940, Roosevelt had instructed Robert Murphy, the American chargé to the Vichy government, to strike up a relationship with French General Maxime Weygand. "Don't bother going through the State Department," FDR instructed Murphy.[3] Hull resented Roosevelt's high-handed treatment—left out of major conferences as he was, even excluded from important channels of information.

Churchill dispatched Lord Halifax, British foreign secretary under Prime Minister Neville Chamberlain, to the British embassy in Washington, in January 1941. Anthony Eden then took over the Foreign Office. Presidential aide Harry Hopkins tried to keep Halifax informed of military and diplomatic developments. "There were few people I genuinely admired more, and whose good opinion I thought more flattering to have," Halifax wrote of Hopkins. The American ambassador in London, John "Gil" Winant, was not always included in top Anglo-American meetings. But early in the war, Winant had direct and frequent contact with Prime Minister Churchill, especially on weekends at the prime minister's Chequers estate, where Winant developed his own channels of communication.

Roosevelt failed to keep U.S. military chiefs always informed of important strategic and tactical discussions with the prime minister.[4] This profound defect, even negligence, in presidential leadership was remedied by the head of the British military mission to Washington, General John Dill, who received regular reports from the British War Cabinet and British Chiefs of Staff. Surreptitiously, Dill passed them on to Army Chief of Staff George C. Marshall, to keep him informed. "Britain," wrote historian Andrew Roberts, "was fortunate that, despite the undoubted presence of some Anglophobes in the higher reaches of the American Army and Navy Departments, the President and US Army Chief were not of their number."[5] Dill, who had been Chief of the Imperial General Staff (CIGS) until Churchill sacked him in December 1941, was a crucial information link between the British and American military leadership in Washington. The prime minister did not fully appreciate the talents of the man he called "Dilly-Dally," but Marshall clearly did. So did Marshall's British counterpart, Alan Brooke, who described Dill as "the most invaluable link between Marshall and me."[6] Brooke had been the one to persuade Churchill to send Dill to America. After his appointment, Dill admitted: "It is odd that Winston should want me to represent him here when he clearly was glad of an excuse to get me out of the CIGS job."[7] Brooke recalled: "From the very start he built up a deep friendship with Marshall. It is unfortunate that Winston never gave him the credit that was due him."[8] In Churchill's desperate hour of 1940, Dill had not been aggressive enough to suit the prime minister, whose impatience intensified as losses to the Germans focused responsibility on the CIGS.

Arriving in Washington in late 1941, after Pearl Harbor, Dill saw clearly that America was not ready for conflict. "[T]he ordinary American firmly believes that they can finish off the war quite quickly—and without too much disturbance," Dill reported to Brooke. "Never have I seen a country so utterly unprepared for war and so soft."[9] Like many World War II leaders, the grind of war took its toll on Dill's health, and by late 1944, he had slowed considerably. On November 4, Dill died of aplastic anemia.[10] Dill's death diminished British influence at a time when the Americans had become the dominant force in the Anglo-American alliance. As Churchill himself later admitted: "No British officer we sent across the Atlantic during the war ever acquired American esteem and confidence in an equal degree. His personality, discretion, and tact gained him almost at once the confidence of the President. At the same time he established a true comradeship and private friendship with General Marshall."[11] Churchill embraced Dill's work in Washington, but he never knew the full scope of Dill's collaboration with Marshall.[12]

Roosevelt's relationship with top American generals and admirals was more formal, distant, and infrequent. Thus, American military leadership was less informed and coordinated by the commander in chief than were the top military leaders organized by the prime minister. Churchill worked day and night with his military staff; FDR did not. Robert H. Jackson, who served as attorney general in 1940–1941, recalled: "Roosevelt was not over-awed by military or naval rank and did not feel any sense of inferiority in the presence of a general or an admiral. He knew that the winning of a war is not all seamanship or generalship but in large part politics and economics. He often repeated that war is too important a matter to be left to the generals."[13] The prime minister was neither awed by military rank nor was he oblivious to the need for close coordination with military leaders. As a former assistant secretary of the navy, Roosevelt was more confident about seaborne affairs than land operations. He did not micromanage well-chosen admirals or generals. As commander in chief, however, he was inclined to reserve key strategic decisions for himself. There were at least two Roosevelts: the cagey politician, slow to action and carefully following public opinion; and the war strategist, ready and able to make big and wise decisions, such as the invasion of North Africa in 1942 and upholding Churchill and overruling Marshall on the timing of the cross-channel invasion of France. During 1941–1943, FDR often deferred to the charismatic persuasion and war experience of Churchill. In the last two years of the war, after America and Russia came to dominate the alliance, Roosevelt no longer did so.

* * *

Following the French collapse in June 1940, U.S. Ambassador Bullitt left France. On November 7, he resigned. Two days later, President Roosevelt rejected the resignation. Over the next few days, a decision on Bullitt's successor was made. When the president met with Bullitt on November 16, he failed to tell Bullitt about his replacement. When Bullitt learned about it a few hours later, he was furious. "I forgot about the whole business completely!" explained FDR, who asked Bullitt's forgiveness.[14] FDR could repeatedly forget inconvenient decisions that might lead him into confrontations he sought to avoid. Under Secretary Sumner Welles recalled the deliberations within the Roosevelt administration to find a successor to Bullitt, who had alienated FDR when he disobeyed his orders the previous summer.[15] "It seemed to us that Marshal Pétain would probably be favourably impressed by the appointment of a very high-ranking officer of the American armed services."[16] Welles and Roosevelt discussed several names that were rejected.

The next day, Welles arrived at the White House while the president was having breakfast in bed. "When I suggested Admiral Leahy, the President's face immediately lit up as it always did when a new idea appealed to him. Without further ado he seized the telephone at his bedside and asked the operator to get the Admiral on the long-distance telephone." Leahy's relationship with Roosevelt dated back to World War I; in 1939, FDR had appointed Leahy as governor of Puerto Rico, after the admiral finished a term as chief of naval operations. FDR informed Leahy: "I feel that you are the best man available for this mission. . . . [T]he position which you have held in our own Navy would undoubtedly give you great influence with the higher officers of the French Navy who are openly hostile to Great Britain." Appointment of the balding, outspoken, emotionally reserved admiral aimed to keep the French fleet out of Nazi hands.[17] The German ambassador in Washington accurately reported to Berlin: "Ambassador Leahy's task will consist in intervening wherever possible and obstructing cooperation between Germany and France." Roosevelt had indeed instructed Leahy that "United States Policy [was] to give Britain all possible assistance short of war."[18] Churchill approved, saying that FDR had appointed an ambassador "of so much influence and character as Admiral Leahy, who was himself so close to the President."[19] FDR's instructions to Leahy show that the president, reelected to a third term, had privately abandoned masquerades at neutrality, despite the restrictions of the Neutrality Acts of the 1930s and his own campaign promises of 1940.[20]

American war policy toward Vichy began with accommodation to Hitler's victory over France. The policy attracted much criticism in the United States and United Kingdom, including that of Churchill. Sumner Welles wrote of Hull's sensitivity to such attacks: "As long as he was Secretary of State he regarded any public criticism of his department or of a policy for which he assumed responsibility as a personal affront, and an affront that he would not forgive." Welles argued that "it was perhaps not unnatural that the Secretary came to believe that the increasingly sharp attacks upon the Department of State as the Vichy policy was continued were instigated chiefly by the more liberal advisers in the White House, with at least the tacit, if not open, approval of the President himself."[21] The Americans and the British had embraced conflicting positions regarding the Vichy government. Churchill backed the anti-Vichy, Free French movement led by General Charles de Gaulle, who at the beginning of the war had little support either in France or among French citizens living in the United States. "We could understand the British were righteously indignant at the role played by the [pro-German] Vichy regime; we conceded the logic of their desire to build up de Gaulle so that he would be more likely to gain the adherence of France's possessions overseas," maintained Welles in his memoirs. "Still it was often highly difficult for us to understand how Mr. Churchill himself could urge us to stretch our diplomatic influence in Vichy to the fullest possible extent in Britain's behalf, while at the same time agencies of the British Government, over which he possesses full authority, used every propaganda weapon at their command to convince both the British and the American people that our Vichy policy was one of contemptible appeasement, and that in Britain's best interest we should withdraw our Ambassador and sever all relations with the regime."[22] Ambassador Leahy's responsibility was to put pressure on Admiral François Darlan to keep France's military resources, especially its navy, out of German hands. On December 22, 1941, in the wake of Pearl Harbor, Leahy wrote Roosevelt that "French opinion has reacted with a leaning over toward our side of the question but with reservations and with preparations to jump back on a moment's notice."[23]

As the Anglo-American conflict over policy toward the Vichy French government demonstrated, U.S. entry into World War II would require much tighter Allied coordination of strategy, including the use of U.S. armed forces. The American military hierarchy had long been less integrated than its British counterpart—opening the way for the far-seeing General Marshall to urge adoption of the British chiefs of staff system. He knew that an institutional reform of the armed forces was necessary, once war was declared in December 1941. According to Andrew Roberts: "Part of the reason Marshall wanted to institute a Joint Chiefs of Staff Committee to mirror the British Chiefs of Staff Committee was his recognition that the way the British High Command had been organized since the early 1920s gave them an undoubted edge in military planning."[24] Churchill's hands-on leadership as prime minister and minister of defence enhanced the advantage.

Admiral Leahy's long relationship with Roosevelt became an important factor in his eventual appointment as chairman of the Joint Chiefs of Staff. In the spring of 1942, Marshall had proposed the creation of a new post: chairman of the Joint Chiefs of Staff (JCS). He then proposed Admiral Leahy as the ideal chairman. Marshall pressed his case to FDR: "I explained to him in great frankness that it was impossible to conceive of one man with all of his duties as president being also, in effect, the chief of staff of all the military services."[25] Marshall shrewdly overcame the opposition to the joint chiefs system by Chief of Naval Operations (CNO) Ernest King—by proposing an admiral rather than a general to take the position of chairman. Marshall also sidestepped FDR's jealous aversion to competitive centers of power in the White House; the president liked Leahy and, in early July 1942, met with him about the idea. On July 21, while Marshall was out of the country, Roosevelt acted on the proposal and named Leahy as his chief of staff. (The retired admiral was seven years older than the president; he would outlive FDR and outlast him in office, working under President Harry Truman until 1949.[26]) The responsibilities and power of the new position were unclear; historian Mark A. Stoler noted that "as Roosevelt defined his [Leahy's] task he was to represent the president's position to the JCS rather than vice versa."[27]

Leahy had to improvise on his authority as he went along. His job had three clear duties. First, he was the president's chief of staff, handling a variety of issues and complaints that came to the White House and filtering those that should reach Roosevelt. Leahy recalled: "Almost immediately it developed that there were matters to take up with the President every day, so I made arrangements to meet him every morning at about a quarter of ten. I usually arrived at the office between 8:30 and 8:45." Leahy went through the dispatches and reports that had been received overnight, and brought the most important to Roosevelt, sometimes while Roosevelt was shaving in his bathroom.[28] Second, Leahy was chairman of the Joint Chiefs. Third, he was the president's chief military aide. Leahy wrote: "The most important function of the Chief of Staff was the maintaining of daily liaison between the President and the Joint Chiefs of Staff. It was my job to pass on to the Joint Chiefs of Staff the basic thinking of the President on all war plans and strategy. In turn I brought back from the Joints Chiefs a consensus of their thinking."[29] Leahy had an aversion to any involvement by the JCS in "political matters," and rejected any discussion of "grand strategy" by the JCS.[30] Unlike Churchill's relations with the British Chiefs of Staff, little was committed to written records by FDR and his staff. [31] Such was the Roosevelt preference.

Although Leahy's importance to FDR grew with time, the president self-consciously prevented Leahy from developing a competing power center. Stoler wrote of Leahy: "FDR insisted on using him primarily as a 'legman' and messenger to the chiefs, not a JCS chairman and personal strategic adviser representing them [the Joint Chiefs] as Marshall had desired when he first proposed the appointment."[32] Nevertheless, observed historian S. M. Plokhy, Leahy's "discretion, loyalty, and ability to get along with people made him indispensable to Roosevelt. He successfully competed for the president's ear with his more liberal advisers and allies."[33]

The Leahy-Marshall relationship became crucial to Anglo-American prosecution of the war. Marshall diplomatically guided Leahy into his new role as chairman of the nation's highest military team.[34] As Leahy noted, the duties of the JCS "never were defined precisely. I have heard that in some file there is a chit or memorandum from Roosevelt, setting up the Joint Chiefs, but I never saw it."[35] Although Leahy was chairman of the JCS, the diplomatic but decisive Marshall remained the real leader of the group, working carefully to develop a consensus with the crusty Admiral King. "Everybody knows who runs the Joint Chiefs of Staff," observed a leading Republican.[36] Still, Leahy exercised a quiet influence. As JCS chairman, Leahy exhibited a calm, down-home demeanor. Addressing Marshall, he might say: "Well George, I'm just a simple old sailor. Would you please back up and start from the beginning and make it simple, just tell me step one, two and three, and so on." One aide to the Joint Chiefs recalled that Marshall "kept falling for this thing, and they would back up and explain to this 'simple old sailor.' And as they did it—which is what Leahy knew damned well would happen—and went through these various steps, they themselves would find out the weakness of misconception or that there was something wrong with it. So he [Leahy] didn't have to start out by saying, 'This is a stupid idea and it won't work.'"[37] Marshall was himself without excessive pride. Prudent and flexible, he could give up pet ideas when persuaded. General Marshall's self-confidence and self-discipline regulated his temper and his willingness to listen. Widespread respect for Marshall set him apart from other leading generals and admirals.

President Roosevelt remained protective of his prerogatives as the nation's commander in chief. When he appointed Leahy, he told the press that Leahy was *not* the nation's commander in chief—that as president, he was—a gratuitous remark in light of his constitutional responsibilities.[38] In making the appointment, FDR was deliberately vague on any specifics, thus preserving his maneuverability.[39] Nevertheless, as Secretary of War Stimson recalled, the Joint Chiefs had "a most salutary effect on the President's weakness for snap decisions; it thus offset a characteristic which might otherwise have been a serious handicap to his basically sound strategic instincts."[40] With proximity to President Roosevelt, Leahy's influence steadily increased, especially in 1944, as Harry Hopkins's sickness and absence from the White House left a vacuum in foreign-policy affairs. Leahy had strong conservative convictions and connections; he met with conservative politicians of both parties. "When possible, I would tell Roosevelt about these and similar conversations I heard from time to time. If there was opportunity, I would tell the President in advance of my acceptance of invitations of this nature to be sure that he had no objection—not from the political angle—but because the conversation might turn to military matters. The President never objected, as he knew I wasn't going to divulge any secrets." The admiral recalled: "I followed a fixed policy of not becoming involved in any domestic partisan politics." Leahy's political leanings were not hidden, however, and he affably called Harry Hopkins "Pinko" and "Do-Gooder."[41]

Contrary to Churchill's transparent policy of command through written orders and records, the president followed a fixed policy of keeping his meetings with the JCS off the record. FDR explicitly overruled Marshall's request, in November 1942, that minutes be kept of his meetings with the JCS.[42] FDR's decision to prevent meetings of the JCS from being recorded stemmed from the president's determination to preserve his flexibility to change his mind and reject or deny positions or decisions previously taken. Despite his great talents, this trait of FDR was a character defect and a hindrance to accountability, war planning, written communication, and decision-making. It was this very defect, which Churchill had witnessed at the highest level among the British war planners of World War I, that led him to insist on the written record of decisions and orders. Thus, he held himself and his officials responsible in writing for their actions and their orders to generals and admirals in the field.

As at the State Department, officials in the Departments of the Army and the Navy, early in the war, fretted that Churchill's global reputation, ingenious mind, military experience, prolific pen, and persuasive mastery of history and the facts too easily influenced Roosevelt. Secretary of War Henry Stimson had been a strong advocate in private and public for entering the war against Germany, but he nevertheless opposed FDR's early assistance to Britain.[43] "Aid to Britain remained at least as controversial at the War Department, where Stimson became almost apoplectic over yet another allocation of heavy bombers to the British in September [1941]," wrote historian David Kaiser.[44] Those in the Roosevelt cabinet who were the strongest supporters of war with Germany—Stimson, Frank Knox, Henry Morgenthau, and Secretary of the Interior Harold Ickes—were neither Anglophiles nor inclined to give Britain war materials that the United States might need in the future. In mid-October 1941, Stimson complained that FDR was "entirely in the hands of people who see only the side of the other nations and who are wedded to the idea that with our weapons they can win the war. I am perfectly certain that they cannot, and perfectly certain that eventually we will have to fight and this method of nibbling away at our store of weapons is reducing our weapons down to what I fear is a dangerous thing."[45] Stimson, a former New York lawyer who had served for nearly two years as secretary of war under President William Howard Taft, argued persistently that the United States should retain American-produced armaments. Like General Marshall, Stimson worried that Churchill exercised excessive influence over FDR. This observation was generally true of FDR from 1940 until early 1943—whereupon, with the huge American army and navy soon to dominate the western front and the Pacific, the president would turn on his charm campaign to impress Joseph Stalin. By late 1943, American and Russian power would lead the war against Hitler.

By 1941, key American cabinet members explicitly favored U.S. entry into the war. Navy Secretary Knox and Secretary of War Stimson advocated a stronger response to the Germans. They were ahead of public opinion—to which FDR was acutely sensitive. Politically cautious, Roosevelt was reluctant to lead despite his reelection. Stimson persistently pressed Roosevelt to take stronger action against the Germans, believing that the U.S. help to Britain might be *casus belli* to the Germans and Japanese.[46] After Roosevelt described American patrols in the Atlantic as a step forward, Secretary of War Stimson responded, "Well, I hope you will keep on walking, Mr. President."[47] Even among loyalists, there was impatience with the president's failure to lead after his landslide victory in the 1940 election. Ickes and other war hawks, like Stimson and Knox, worked to get FDR to act in the spring of 1941. "I find a growing discontent with the President's lack of leadership," wrote Ickes. "He still has the country if he will take it and lead it. But he won't have it very much longer unless he does something. It won't be sufficient for him to make another speech and then go into a state of innocuous desuetude again. People are begging him to say, 'I am tired of words; I want action.'"[48]

Roosevelt did keep raising the temperature of American belligerence, but he still worried about his imprudent 1940 campaign pledge to American mothers not to send their sons to war.[49] Warning of Nazi aggression, FDR declared in a fireside chat at the end of 1940: "Our national policy is not directed toward war. Its sole purpose is to keep war away from our country." The commander in chief aimed to arm the anti-Axis combatants, without sufficiently arming Americans to defend themselves if the war came—thus, America's lack of readiness for war when it arrived at Pearl Harbor. Still, Roosevelt did argue "that there is a far less chance of the United States getting into war, if we do all we can now to support the nations defending themselves against attack by the Axis than if we acquiesce in their defeat, submit tamely to an Axis victory, and wait our turn to be the object of attack in another war later on."[50] Of this outcome, the prime minister had warned the president. FDR was no appeaser, but he was not yet a warrior, denying as he did that U.S. military help to Britain made war inevitable. As Stimson implied, it is hard not to infer that somehow the president believed he would deceive Hitler into believing that U.S. aid to Britain was consistent with U.S. neutrality. American aid to the United Kingdom, he thought, was similar to neutral Sweden's sale of iron ore to Germany.

However, with Roosevelt's approval, U.S. military authorities had begun actively planning for war—after Admiral Harold "Betty" Stark produced the "Dog Memo" on strategy in November 1940. That led to the ABC (America-Britain-Canada) conference in early 1941 in Washington. The conference confirmed a Germany-first strategy in the event of war. After Pearl Harbor, Churchill and General Alan Brooke sought explicit American agreement that war in Europe was a higher priority than the Pacific war against Japan. The prime minister then pressed American leaders to commit to war in the Mediterranean and North Africa, as a prelude to a later cross-channel invasion of northwest Europe from Britain. After Germany declared war on the United States, Stimson and Marshall opposed FDR's mid-1942 agreement with Churchill to attack North Africa before northern France. They energetically fought the North African initiative when Churchill visited Washington and Hyde Park in June 1942. "It looked like [FDR] was going to jump the traces over all that we have been doing in regard to BOLERO [the code name for the troop buildup in Britain] and to imperil really our strategy of the whole situation," wrote Stimson as Churchill flew to Washington. Roosevelt "wants to take up the case of GYMNAST [attack on North Africa] again, thinking he can bring additional pressure to save Russia. The only hope I have about it at all is that I think he may be doing it in his foxy way to forestall trouble that is now on the ocean coming towards us in the shape of a new British visitor."[51]

In his diary, Stimson confided: "I can't help feeling a little bit uneasy about the influence of the Prime Minister on him at this time." He added: "The trouble is Churchill and Roosevelt are too much alike in their strong points and in their weak points. They are both brilliant. They are both penetrating in their thoughts, but they lack the steadiness of balance that has got to go along with warfare."[52] Stimson biographer McGeorge Bundy wrote: "Stimson's disapproval of TORCH [formerly called GYMNAST] was fully shared by the War Department staff, but after a final protest to the President on July 24, during which the two men offered to bet each other about the wisdom of the operation, Stimson limited himself to extracting a promise from Marshall that he would make a stand against the final execution of the operation if at any time 'it seemed clearly headed for disaster.'"[53] Collectively, their opposition to the attack in North Africa was well intentioned, but after FDR's decision had been made, their continued opposition bordered on insubordination.

The president supported Churchill's persuasive and well-reasoned strategy for an attack on North Africa. Still, if the British would not agree to an invasion of France instead of North Africa, American military leaders, led by Anglophobe Admiral King, threatened to switch U.S. military priorities to the Pacific.[54] U.S. military authorities were playing two games of chicken: one with the British, the other with the president. "After the war, Marshall, King and Stimson insisted that this proposal [to focus on the Pacific] had been a bluff designed to scare the British into agreeing to SLEDGEHAMMER [a limited cross-channel invasion], and there is no question that the July 10 memorandum [suggesting a switch to a Pacific strategy] did contain an *element* of bluff," wrote Mark A. Stoler. "Marshall and King were more than willing to use their proposal as a threat to scare Britain into a reconsideration of SLEDGEHAMMER, but they were equally disposed to make good on the threat if London remained adamant."[55] FDR cleverly called their bluff when he asked for the plan for a Pacific initiative—which they had not prepared.

Forthwith, FDR sent General Marshall to Britain, to prepare military plans for Europe. Marshall and Harry Hopkins emplaned for London in July 1942. Churchill put a full-court press on Hopkins. "The Prime Minister threw the British Constitution at me with some vehemence," wrote Hopkins to the president. "As you know, it is an unwritten document, so no serious damage was done."[56] Roosevelt ultimately chose Operation TORCH, the invasion of North Africa through Morocco and Algeria, but his military chiefs continued to fight for alternatives.[57] Hopkins undercut their efforts when he asked FDR to set a date to launch TORCH. FDR did so on July 25, 1942. Then, on July 30, at a White House conference to which he had summoned General Marshall and Admiral King, Roosevelt ordered that "TORCH would be undertaken at the earliest possible date. He considered that this operation was now our principal objective and the assembling of means to carry it out should take precedence over other operations."[58] The president did not equivocate. Admiral King acquiesced, but he still prepared for war against Japan in the Pacific.[59]

By issuing the clear order that Operation TORCH should begin by October 30, Roosevelt finally set the North African attack in motion, but U.S. military planners continued to balk and plan their options.[60] General John Dill wrote Marshall in August to complain: "I am just a little disturbed about TORCH. . . . For good or for ill it has been accepted [as joint Anglo-American policy] and therefore I feel that we should go at it with all possible enthusiasm and give it absolute priority. If we don't, it won't succeed," wrote Dill. "From what our Planners tell me, there are some of your people who feel that TORCH is not a good operation. That, of course, must be a matter of opinion but those who are playing a part in mounting the operation must be entirely whole-hearted about it, or they cannot give it all the help it should have and overcome all the difficulties that will arise." Marshall responded: "You may feel sure . . . U. S. Planners will enthusiastically and effectively support decisions made by the Commander-in-Chief."[61] The army chief had been given support from the newly appointed JCS chairman, Admiral Leahy, who had been concerned about the war in the Pacific.[62] Despite the difficulties, TORCH did become the next Anglo-American military priority.

Unfortunately for amicable Anglo-American military relations, Churchill had produced plans not only for North Africa, but also for a second attack on Norway. Americans like Stimson and Marshall were single-minded hedgehogs, determined to open a second front in France. They were appalled by the fox-like tendency of the prime minister to devise many different tactics for attacking Hitler. And now he had a plan to attack Norway, a diversion from the main goal of a cross-channel assault on the German army in France. In an attempt to derail Operation TORCH, Marshall had argued to FDR: "The advantages and disadvantages of implementing the Gymnast plan as compared to other operations, particularly 1942 emergency Bolero operations [building up American troop strength in Britain], lead to the conclusion that the occupation of Northwest Africa this summer should not be attempted."[63] Marshall believed correctly that successful British and American support for TORCH and its execution would delay D-Day until the spring of 1944. Given the immense preparations D-Day required, and the strength of crack German troops in France, Churchill and British Army chief Alan Brooke argued for delay. They believed that the Allies were not yet ready for the colossal cross-channel invasion. They proved correct.[64]

As usual, President Roosevelt did not run a straight course. He tacked and trimmed with the political winds. Before December 7, 1941, Roosevelt anticipated war, but by arming Britain and Russia, he might avoid or delay American formal entry into the conflict. Historian Walter Reid wrote: "It is very difficult to be clear about Roosevelt's deepest beliefs. He may have had few. He was essentially a political and pragmatic creature, reactive in instinct, seeking to achieve practical ends. General Douglas MacArthur typified some of FDR's critics when he described the president as 'A man who never told the truth when a lie would serve him just as well'. But his reputation for unreliability largely came from his desire to avoid making enemies unnecessarily."[65] FDR wanted to be liked. This characteristic surely helped with politicians and voters, but in the end, it would not serve him well in his negotiations with Joseph Stalin.

Lunch at Casablanca, January 1943. Left to right: Elliott Roosevelt, Harry Hopkins, Franklin Roosevelt Jr., George Durno, and President Roosevelt.
FRANKLIN D. ROOSEVELT PRESIDENTIAL LIBRARY

V

Harry Hopkins

> You know as well as I that we do not have the chance to get a genuinely good peace unless Russia, Great Britain and the United States can see eye to eye and this means far more than the narrow confines of government in the Foreign Offices. . . . The more I see of the problems and conflicts engendered by the kind of thing that you have written me about, the more I realize how essential it is for us to have men managing our affairs who have a deep and profound conviction not only about world peace and the harnessing of Japan and Germany, but about the bold moves which must be made if a world economy is to be developed which can provide the environment without which our goals can never be attained.[1]
>
> ***Harry Hopkins** (1890–1946), letter to Ambassador John G. Winant, September 4, 1944. Hopkins was a former social worker who served as director of the Federal Emergency Relief Administration and the Works Progress Administration, as well as commerce secretary before World War II. Hopkins became President Roosevelt's closest foreign policy advisor, trusted confidant of Prime Minister Churchill, and designated troubleshooter until he was overcome by sickness.*

Americans Harry Hopkins and W. Averell Harriman as well as Great Britain's Anthony Eden and Max Beaverbrook (Canadian by birth) bore much of the burden of senior Allied communications during World War II. Each of these four envoys—essential partners of Churchill, Roosevelt, and company—held the attention of both FDR and the prime minister. They became well known to Stalin, whose paranoia and suspicions were a constant threat not only to his Soviet colleagues, but also to the alliance itself. Three of the four—Hopkins, Eden, and Beaverbrook—had serious health problems, but, like Churchill, they still undertook punishing and perilous trips. Perhaps the most important, as well as the most unlikely nontraditional diplomat, was Hopkins—a one-time social worker and man of the left who became FDR's most trusted advisor. Hopkins was shrewd, perceptive, and direct.

"FDR enjoyed Harry's company," recalled one Roosevelt grandson. "He was funny, always had a flip remark. He shared with the president this capacity to make anything amusing, rather than serious, unlike my grandmother [Eleanor Roosevelt]."[2] Hopkins, who understood how to manage the complicated president, became his intimate sounding board at home; then his foreign emissary abroad. Roosevelt had even considered him a possible successor.

Before World War II, Hopkins nursed a strong anti-British attitude that faded abruptly with the visit of King George and Queen Elizabeth to the White House in 1939. The recently widowed Hopkins and his daughter, Diana, were staying there. Little Diana was excited at the opportunity to meet royalty. But on the night of Queen Elizabeth's appearance at a state banquet, six-year-old Diana was bedridden with a fever. Hopkins later told the story to Churchill aide John Colville: "[S]omebody (though not her aloof father, who would have died rather than ask a favour of British royalty) told of the tears she was shedding. So when the Queen was dressed for the banquet, wearing a beautiful crinoline dress, the Order of the Garter, a blazing array of jewels and a splendid tiara, she went upstairs to the sickroom and the child did see a real Queen, adorned as she imagined Queens always were." Diana was bewitched. "And that," said Hopkins, "is how I first came to think you people must have some good in you after all," said Hopkins. Colville added: "And that also illustrated how a small act of kindness, undertaken without any calculation of policy, can have an indirect effect on the affairs of nations; for in those days Harry Hopkins had a great, if unpublicised influence."[3] Through Eleanor Roosevelt's simple request to Queen Elizabeth to visit Diana, the Queen had helped set the stage for a wartime alliance.

The divorced and widowed Hopkins had moved into the White House at FDR's insistence while he was still secretary of commerce. Hopkins's first night, on May 10, 1940, coincided with the German invasion of the Low Countries and Churchill becoming prime minister. Hopkins's bedroom on the second floor of the White House was just a wheelchair ride away from the president's. Unschooled in foreign affairs or diplomacy, the gifted Hopkins essentially turned himself into Roosevelt's national security advisor, long before such a post existed. Hopkins's influence was partly determined by his sheer proximity to the commander in chief. With Hopkins living down the hall, Eleanor Roosevelt acknowledged that the president "doesn't ask my advice any more. . . . Harry tells him everything he needs to know."[4] The very earnest First Lady did not always approve of the more frivolous activities engaged in by her husband and his friend.[5] Hopkins's unique living arrangements made him conveniently available and useful to FDR, especially from late 1941 to 1943. When Churchill visited the White House, the three or any two could speak at any moment from morning to night.

From 1940 to 1943, Hopkins became in effect the "listener in chief" to the commander in chief. "Hopkins did not originate policy and then convince Roosevelt it was right," wrote Hopkins biographer Robert E. Sherwood. "He had too much intelligence as well as respect for his Chief to attempt the role of mastermind. He made it his job to provide a sounding board for discussions of the best means of attaining the goals that the President set for himself. Roosevelt liked to think out loud, but his greatest difficulty was finding a listener who was both understanding and entirely trustworthy."[6] Hopkins did more than listen. Historian Fraser Harbutt wrote that Churchill "could deal directly and eloquently with Roosevelt on the profound and large policy issues (and also smaller matters when appropriate), though even here he was frequently dealing in a sense with Hopkins, who drafted an indeterminate number of the president's letters. At the same time the Prime Minister could conduct with Hopkins most of his practical American business—which included a wide range of political, supply, strategic, military, and other problems—through telephone calls of which little record remains, and through cables, and letters."[7] British officials were amazed by the multiple roles Hopkins played. A top Foreign Office diplomat, Oliver Harvey, visiting Washington in March 1943, wrote that Hopkins "does everything here. He is like the secretary to the Cabinet, the private secretary to the President and general coordinator all in one. He has this unique position because there is literally no contact between different departments or ministers and no Cabinet control as we have it. He is a most helpful and admirable man and knows exactly how to handle the President."[8] FDR's disorganized administration had made Harry Hopkins desirable, even indispensable.

In January 1941, Hopkins visited Britain on the president's behalf to assess the support of the British people for the war, and the ability of Britain to withstand the Nazi attack. Roosevelt announced that the trip was "just to maintain—I suppose that is the word for it—personal relations between me and the British Government." Roosevelt downplayed Hopkins's mission to the press: "He's just going over to say 'How do you do?' to a lot of my friends!"[9] Although he himself had suggested it in December 1940, Hopkins learned of his assignment to London when FDR's press secretary, Steve Early, called him shortly after the president had made the announcement at a press conference. "Just think about it for a minute," responded Hopkins. "I was a social worker. My father was a harness maker and my mother was a schoolteacher. And I'm going over to talk to Winston Churchill and the men who run the British government. If that isn't democracy, I don't know what is."[10] Hopkins arranged to leave Washington immediately—avoiding briefings from the State Department, but well informed by a long talk with FDR himself. French businessman Jean Monnet, who would later become the father of the European Common Market in the mid-1950s, advised Hopkins: "I've seen how things work in Britain. Believe me, don't look for authority there except in Churchill. Churchill *is* the War Cabinet. Everything will be simpler if you can establish a close link between Roosevelt and him."[11] Hopkins's commission from the president read simply: "Reposing special faith and confidence in you, I am asking you to proceed at your early convenience to Great Britain, there to act as my personal representative."[12]

W. Averell Harriman, the well-travelled, well-connected, and opportunistic heir to a great fortune, asked to accompany Hopkins. Harriman knew the British scene, but Hopkins declined his assistance, perhaps perceiving Harriman's grasping ambition, or understanding that there would be another, larger role for Harriman.[13] The Hopkins-Harriman friendship had developed steadily during the 1930s, as Harriman sought to expand his government contacts and influence. In 1938, the heir to the Union Pacific Railroad had provided critical support for Hopkins's confirmation as secretary of commerce. They were an odd pair—Harriman, the debonair, well-dressed son of privilege, and Hopkins, the rumpled, baggy-suited expert on poverty, seen around the White House halls in his bathrobe. (A *New Yorker* profile described Hopkins as "an animated piece of shredded wheat."[14]) Harriman sensed that the route to power and influence would go through Hopkins. The solicitous Harriman would be waiting for Hopkins at the airport in New York, to greet FDR's envoy on his return several weeks later.

On his first night in London, Hopkins was briefed by the accomplished American chargé d'affaires, Herschel Johnson. On his second day in London, Brendan Bracken greeted Hopkins at 10 Downing Street; then gave him a tour of the building before lunch with Churchill, who took personal responsibility for arranging Hopkins's afternoon. The prime minister would recall: "Thus I met Harry Hopkins, that extraordinary man, who played, and was to play, a sometimes decisive part in the whole movement of the war. . . . He was a crumbling lighthouse from which there shone the beams that led great fleets to harbour. He had also a gift of sardonic humour. I always enjoyed his company, especially when things went ill. He could also be very disagreeable and say hard and sour things."[15] Of his first meeting with Churchill at 10 Downing Street in January 1941, Hopkins wrote President Roosevelt: "A rotund—smiling—red faced, gentleman appeared—extended a fat but none the less convincing hand and wished me welcome to England." (In fact, photographs showed that Churchill's hands were not fat, but fine and elegant.) Theirs was an instant bond, cemented during their first three-hour meal. Later that day, Hopkins declared: "God, what a force that man has!" He wrote Roosevelt: "*Churchill* is the gov't in every sense of the word—he controls the grand strategy and often the details—labor trusts him—the army, navy, air force are behind him to a man."[16]

Asked by CBS newsman Edward R. Murrow why he had come to London, Hopkins replied: "I suppose you could say that I've come here to try to find a way to be a catalytic agent between two prima donnas."[17] Churchill aide John Martin wrote after the initial meeting with Hopkins: "In the next few weeks—including a stay at Chequers, where he suffered severely from the cold, later vowing that his victory present would be to install adequate central heating—he had many talks with Churchill and a warm personal friendship grew up between them."[18] General Hastings Ismay, the prime minister's military chief of staff, wrote: "Hopkins had no authority to negotiate, and no instructions except to talk with everyone who mattered, to see everything that he could, and to report back to his chief. . . . He played his part to perfection." According to Ismay, "Churchill was attracted to Hopkins at once and scarcely let him out of his sight."[19] The prime minister charmed and persuaded Hopkins, as he would FDR. Churchill's strategy was a deliberate, sustained effort to co-opt Hopkins—and all influential Americans—in order to bring America into the war against the Nazis.

The Hopkins-Churchill relationship became one foundation stone upon which was built the Anglo-American alliance. Hopkins "was the most faithful and perfect channel of communication between the President and me," wrote the prime minister. "But far more than that, he was for several years the main prop and animator of Roosevelt himself. Together these two men, the one a subordinate without public office, the other commanding the mighty Republic, were capable of taking decisions of the highest consequence over the whole area of the English-speaking world."[20] If Hopkins were the animator of FDR, Churchill was surely a prominent animator of Hopkins. In Hopkins, the prime minister had found the perfect channel for direct influence on the American president.

Hopkins quickly ingratiated himself with his hosts. From the British point of view, noted General Ismay, Hopkins "got right inside Churchill's mind, and gained his complete confidence; he had won the hearts of us all, from the highest to the lowest; he had seen everything. We felt sure that he would report to his chief that we were worth backing to the limit. Henceforward he was not only Roosevelt's principal adviser, but also a 'precious link' between his chief and Churchill."[21] Hopkins, an ardent gambler on horse races, had decided to bet on Britain.[22] "I shall never forget these days with you—your supreme confidence and will to victory—Britain I have ever liked—I like it the more," wrote Hopkins to the prime minister before departing. "As I leave for America tonight I wish you great and good luck—confusion to your enemies—victory for Britain."[23]

Roosevelt was very proud of his decision to send Hopkins to Britain, and gloated about it in a February 7 meeting of his cabinet. Harold Ickes reported that FDR "had worked it out in his mind that his friend from Iowa was just the right kind of human being who would make the greatest impression on Winston Churchill, son of a duke, English gentleman, etc. And, according to the President, the deeply laid plot had worked out even better than he had anticipated."[24] White House aide Robert Sherwood recalled that "Beaverbrook told me years later that Hopkins's warm-hearted sympathy at this time and his confidence and the conviction that went with it provided more tangible aid for Britain than had all the destroyers and guns and rifles and ammunition that had been sent previously."[25] Churchill too believed that the American war materiel amounted to little effective help, only a tiny fraction of the United Kingdom's production, when the British Empire stood alone to face the Nazi continental war machine. Hopkins, the protagonist in Roosevelt's plot, soon became a protagonist in Churchill's plot to forge the Anglo-American alliance.

With Hopkins, Churchill had created his own back channel to Roosevelt, which he often used to press sensitive matters in an indelicate way. On February 28, 1941, Churchill telegraphed Hopkins regarding what the prime minister called the Battle of the Atlantic: "I am . . . increasingly anxious about the high rate of shipping losses in North-western Approaches and the shrinkage in tonnage entering Britain. This has darkened since I saw you. Let me know when the [Lend-Lease] Bill will be through. The strain is growing here."[26] The battle with the German U-boats for supremacy in the Atlantic could starve Britain of essential food and equipment. Thus it was in early 1941 that Hopkins helped to shepherd Lend-Lease legislation through a lengthy congressional approval process. He then was appointed by Roosevelt to oversee the dispatch of shipments to Britain—with W. Averell Harriman going to England to supervise the London receipts. During difficult times, Hopkins knew how to bolster Churchill's mood. "Action of House of Commons today delighted me," wrote Hopkins to Churchill in July 1942, after a difficult but overwhelmingly positive vote on parliamentary confidence in the prime minister. "These have been some of the bad days. No doubt there will be others," commiserated Hopkins.[27] Even top British military officials realized "that, in him, we had a good and powerful friend."[28] Churchill's active strategy to use all means to co-opt FDR into the war against Hitler moved relentlessly forward.

In 1937, before Hopkins had been appointed secretary of commerce, much of his cancerous stomach had been removed—a problem which was publicly described as ulcers.[29] His subsequent difficulty in digesting food put Hopkins in a recurrent state of near collapse, especially because he undertook strenuous airborne global missions. After leaving his Commerce post in September 1940, Hopkins continued to hold some governmental titles, including membership on the War Production Board and the Pacific War Council. Of course Hopkins's real power came from his personal relationship with FDR, magnified by his daily proximity to the president on the second floor of the White House. Hopkins also accompanied the president on his frequent trips to Hyde Park. As a result of this intimacy with FDR, Hopkins developed many enemies in Washington. He "had a reputation for being irritable, and he was," noted Charles Bohlen, who observed Hopkins's suspicions of anti-Soviet bias in the State Department. "He was said to be arrogant, which he was not."[30] Even Churchill acknowledged that Hopkins was "jealous about his personal influence with his Chief and did not encourage American competitors."[31]

On Hopkins's return from Britain in late January 1941, he had been greeted on his arrival by Averell Harriman, a future ambassador to Russia in 1943, and John G. Winant, ambassador-designate to Britain. Harriman wrote that Hopkins "was impressed by the determination of the British to resist, but appalled by their lack of means to do so and the need for immediate American help—on a scale we had not till then imagined."[32] This was precisely what Churchill hoped Hopkins might say. Fortunate it was that Hopkins and Harriman were already friends. Together, they helped to mold both Anglo-American and Russo-American alliances during World War II. Although the prime minister would be a one-man minister of British morale, he would himself need and take great comfort from words that Hopkins uttered at the end of his three-week, fact-finding visit to Britain. These words had such a powerful effect on the prime minister that he repeated them to the new American ambassador when he arrived in February. At a small dinner in Glasgow with British government officials, Hopkins had said: "I suppose you wish to know what I am going to say to President Roosevelt on my return. Well, I'm going to quote you one verse from that Book of Books in the truth of which Mr. [Tom] Johnston's mother and my own Scottish mother were brought up: 'Whither thou goest, I will go, and where thou lodgest, I will lodge; thy people shall be my people, and thy God my God.'" In a softer voice, Hopkins added dramatically: "Even to the end." As Ambassador Winant recalled: "It was hard for Mr. Churchill to speak of this incident without being overcome with emotion."[33] The prime minister could cry unself-consciously when overcome by powerful feelings. General Hastings Ismay recorded that Hopkins's words "moved us all deeply. It was a small party, and the story never leaked."[34] If the president had in Hopkins his trusted emissary, now too the prime minister did.

In July 1941, Hopkins again visited London to discuss Lend-Lease arrangements, now that the dissipating threat of Nazi invasion of Britain had been ended by the decisive British air victory over the Luftwaffe in the Battle of Britain. Instead, on June 22, Hitler unleashed Operation Barbarossa—historically unparalleled in scale—a colossal three-million-man invasion of Russia.[35] As usual, Hopkins's job was to collect information that could allay concerns about Britain's ability to continue the fight against Germany. Hopkins told Churchill "that the men in the United States who held the principal places and took decisions on defence matters" thought the Middle East was no longer defensible, but that the president disagreed with them.[36] In this judgment, the president and the prime minister concurred. Operation TORCH in North Africa would be the result.

Before Hopkins returned to the United States in late July, he briefed Ambassador Winant at the U.S. embassy. Previously, Hopkins and Winant had lunch with the Russian ambassador in London, Ivan Maisky, after the German invasion of Russia. Maisky demanded an immediate second front in Western Europe. Hopkins had responded: "We in the USA are a non-belligerent country now, and cannot do anything to help you in regard to a second front."[37] But at the U.S. embassy, Winant now argued that "we had to do something for Russia. He [Hopkins] answered that he realized the need, but that we had no authority to move. I [Winant] said that even a generous gesture would mean something in the desperate fight that was being carried on with such gallantry and sacrifice on the Eastern Front. I asked him [Hopkins] if he thought it would help if the President would allow me to fly to Russia in order to carry some message of encouragement. He said he thought it would, and then, after a moment of silence, he [Hopkins] said, 'What would you think of my going from here?' I said that it would mean much more because I was certain that Stalin knew of his relationship with the President and the part he had played in getting Lend-Lease materials to Great Britain. We worked out together a telegram to the President."[38] Ambassador Maisky had already suggested a similar mission. On July 25, Hopkins wired FDR. "I am wondering whether you would think it important and useful for me to go to Moscow. . . . If Stalin could in any way be influenced at a critical time I think it would be worth doing by a direct communication from you through a personal envoy. I think the stakes are so great that it should be done. Stalin would then know in an unmistakable way that we mean business on a long term supply job."[39]

Two days later, FDR approved the trip, the danger of which Hopkins had downplayed. Although reluctant to see such a valuable Anglo-American friend take such a dangerous trip, Churchill gave Hopkins a message for Stalin: "Tell him that Britain has but one ambition today, but one desire—to crush Hitler. Tell him that he can depend on us. . . . God bless you, Harry."[40] Before Hopkins departed for Russia, he delivered an address on the BBC. Hopkins told Britain: "I have been with the President when messages came to him telling him of the bombing of workers' flats in East End of London. I was with him when the news first came of the tragic bombing of Coventry and later of Plymouth. I heard the words which came not from his lips but from his heart. I watched the stern development of his determination to defeat Hitler. The President is one with your Prime Minister in his determination to break the ruthless power of that sinful psychopath of Berlin."[41] All this spoken by Harry Hopkins, the president's emissary to England, almost six months before America and Germany were at war. The conceit of American neutrality had vanished with events.

To go to Russia, Hopkins needed a visa, usually approved in Moscow. As a substitute, Winant convinced Ambassador Maisky to return to London and issue the document in his own hand. The American ambassador then rushed to the railroad station. As the train began to pull out, Winant ran alongside and thrust the Russian visa into Hopkins's waiting hand. Hopkins took the train north to Scotland, embarking there in an unheated flying boat for Archangel, where he switched planes for Moscow, arriving on July 30. "Perhaps because he had known," wrote historian David Kaiser, "that he might die of his digestive problems at any moment, Hopkins acted fearlessly throughout the war, and to reach the Soviet Union he had to fly around Norway in a PBY seaplane in the midst of nearly twenty-four-hour arctic daylight, knowing that the plane would be doomed if German aircraft based in Norway should encounter it."[42]

In Moscow, Stalin dictated a list of armaments he needed to hold off the Nazi onslaught. Despite having ignored American and British warnings about an imminent German invasion in June, and despite his cowardly retreat to his Kremlin hideaway, Stalin had recovered and quickly turned demanding in talks with Hopkins. In a private memo to FDR, Hopkins wrote that Stalin had declared that "the one thing that could defeat Hitler" was American entry into the war. "I told Stalin that my mission related entirely to matters of supply and that the matter of our joining in the war would be decided largely by Hitler himself and his encroachment upon our fundamental interests. I told him that I doubted our Government, in event of war would want an American army in Russia but that I would give his message to the President."[43] Hopkins biographer David Roll noted that although Hopkins nicknamed Stalin "Uncle Joe," the American troubleshooter "understood that the marshal was no one's lovable uncle. There was an aura of power and menace about him that set him apart from any of the formidable leaders Hopkins had thus far confronted."[44] Still, Hopkins was able to convince the president that Stalin was worth the bet of substantial American aid—even though Churchill believed Russia's defeat likely.[45]

American diplomats subsequently acknowledged the Russian dictator's special affinity for Hopkins. Russian-speaking diplomat Charles Bohlen, who accompanied Hopkins to his later meetings with Stalin, recalled that Stalin once said in his presence that Hopkins was "the first American to whom he had spoken '*po dushe*'—from the soul." Still, noted Bohlen, "[N]o personal feeling which may have been felt by the Soviets ever affected their single-minded pursuit of their objectives."[46] Averell Harriman, who was present at the 1943 Teheran summit, observed that "Stalin in greeting Hopkins displayed more open and warm cordiality than he had been known to show to any foreigner; evidently the Marshal saw in Hopkins one who had made promises and done his level best to keep them."[47] Both Churchill and Stalin desperately wanted America in the war; thus, the need to please FDR and also Harry Hopkins. On that first visit in July 1941, Hopkins found Stalin brusque and straightforward. But Stalin knew "what he wanted, knew what Russia wanted, and he assumed that you knew," wrote Hopkins. Stalin could ingratiate himself when necessary. Hopkins reported to the president: "He repeatedly said that the President of the United States had more influence with the common people of the world today than any other force."[48] FDR liked to hear this. Hopkins "learned more about Russian requirements in three days than could have been ascertained through more conventional channels in three years," noted British General Hastings Ismay.[49] On his return from Russia, Hopkins inspired the confidence of the president, who told his son Elliott: "I know already how much faith the P.M. has in Russia's ability to stay in the war." The president gestured zero. "I take it you have more faith than that," said Elliott. FDR answered: "Harry Hopkins has more. He's able to convince me."[50]

By the time Hopkins departed Moscow, he was completely exhausted. Facing strong headwinds, his 24-hour trip to Scotland further debilitated him. When Hopkins's plane reached the British naval base at Scapa Flow to transfer him to HMS *Prince of Wales*, he appeared to be on death's door, virtually prostrate because he had neglected to bring his stomach medicines from Moscow. In Scotland, he was given blood transfusions, as he awaited Churchill's arrival for a voyage across the Atlantic to the Canadian coast to meet FDR. When Churchill boarded the ship, he greeted Hopkins: "Hello, Harry! How is our friend Joe?" Hopkins replied: "Joe is looking very well, Winston, and is sorry he didn't take your advice" about the pending German invasion. The prime minister responded: "He should have taken my advice. *Everybody* should take my advice. At all times."[51] The prime minister telegraphed the president: "Harry returned dead beat from Russia but is lively again now. We shall get him in fine trim on the voyage. We are just off. It is 27 years ago today that the Huns began their last war. We all must make good job of it this time."[52]

As Churchill and companions crossed the Atlantic in August 1941, Hopkins wrote Ambassador Winant: "I do hope you take care of yourself. It seems to me you all work too hard. That is very absurd advice coming from me; hence, I withdraw it."[53] Hopkins recovered his health while his British shipmates feasted on the caviar he had brought back from Russia. Churchill aide John Martin wrote that prior to the transatlantic trip to visit President Roosevelt, the prime minister had been "as excited as a boy, planning all the details of the entertainment of the other fellow—ordering grouse, ordering turtle and ordering a band" for his meeting with FDR.[54] Hopkins biographer Robert E. Sherwood wrote that during the voyage, Hopkins "told Churchill all the points from his talks with Stalin which touched on Russia's military situation and her needs, and the Prime Minister, as he listened, understood all the better why Hopkins was of such value to the President, for he had never before heard harshly objective and salty reporting quite like this."[55]

Hopkins and Churchill had developed so strong a bond that Hopkins could occasionally tease the prime minister. At the Quebec summit in August 1943, Churchill drank some iced water before commenting: "This water tastes very funny." Hopkins responded: "Of course, it does. It's got no whisky in it. Fancy you a judge of water." The same day, the prime minister was in the midst of one of his monologues on the future of the world, when Hopkins interrupted him: "Now I'll tell *you*, Mr PM, what's going to happen." When Churchill asked him to explain, Hopkins responded: "Your pants is coming down."[56] At the Teheran summit conference in November 1943, Hopkins cheekily toasted Churchill's 69th birthday, saying that after "a long and thorough study of the British Constitution, which is unwritten, and of the War Cabinet, whose authority and composition are not specifically defined . . . I have learnt that the provisions of the British Constitution and the powers of the War Cabinet are just whatever Winston Churchill wants them to be at any given moment."[57]

Both the president and the prime minister eagerly awaited their shipboard summit—just as they enjoyed the cloak-and-dagger trappings of the planning. Churchill and Roosevelt had met briefly at the end of World War I, but the prime minister had forgotten that meeting. To FDR's chagrin and annoyance at the time, Churchill had not paid much attention to the then assistant secretary of the navy. This time would be different. The prime minister was both a hero and a supplicant. From August 9–12, 1941, anchored off Newfoundland at Placentia Bay, the two national leaders had their first substantive meeting of World War II. Churchill was nervous aboard the HMS *Prince of Wales* as he approached Canada. In his disarming way, he had earlier asked Averell Harriman about Roosevelt: "I wonder if he will like me?" The Anglo-American leaders developed an instant, if wary, positive chemistry. "The President is intrigued and likes him enormously," noted Harriman, who had flown in for the meeting with Sumner Welles.[58] From the USS *Augusta* on August 8, FDR wrote his distant cousin and close friend Margaret Suckley that Sumner Welles and Harriman "came by plane this P.M. & we had a 'dress rehearsal' conference including Gen. Marshall, Gen. Arnold, Ad. Stark, Ad. King. All set for the Big Day tomorrow."

After Churchill arrived the next day, the president wrote that the prime minister "is a tremendously vital person & in many ways is an English Mayor LaGuardia! Don't say I said so. I like him—& lunching alone broke the ice both ways."[59] Elliott Roosevelt recalled that by the second day of the conference, his father and Churchill "had sparred, had felt each other out, and were now readying themselves for outright challenge, each of the other."[60] Churchill tried to inspire Roosevelt and to scare him into war. After Placentia Bay, he remarked that he told the president that he "would not answer for the consequences if Russia was compelled to sue for peace and, say, by the Spring of next year, hope died in Britain."[61] The leaders differed over British colonies and trade preferences.[62] The prime minister loyally defended the British

Empire to FDR, an anti-imperialist. Their strategies on the postwar world would increasingly differ as the war moved toward Allied victory in 1945. Before the end, they would meet seven times, in addition to the three-party summits at Teheran in November 1943, and Yalta in February 1945. Churchill twice travelled alone to Moscow to meet with Stalin. In sum, Churchill and Roosevelt would spend about 17 weeks together.[63]

To Placentia Bay, Churchill brought Chief of the Imperial General Staff John Dill, First Sea Lord Dudley Pound, and Vice Chief of Air Staff Wilfrid Freeman, as well as Permanent Under-Secretary of State for Foreign Affairs Alexander Cadogan and military aides Leslie Hollis and Ian Jacob. FDR had invited Under Secretary of State Welles, but not Secretary of State Cordell Hull.[64] American military chiefs were used more as decoration than for negotiation, but they did begin to know their British counterparts. The main product of the conference was the "Atlantic Charter" and its eight principles during a war in which the United States was not officially engaged.[65] British historian John Charmley observed: "The Atlantic Charter was designed to meet the fears of those many Americans like Berle and Winant who were afraid that America was underwriting British war aims."[66]

At Placentia Bay, Churchill did not persuade FDR to enter the war, but the prime minister wired Labour leader Clement Attlee from the Placentia conference: "I have established warm and deep personal relations with our great friend."[67] The president was also pleased. "Look after the Prime Minister," said Roosevelt to Churchill's bodyguard. "He is one of the greatest men in the world. In fact he may very likely be *the* greatest."[68] When the prime minister returned to London, Ambassador Winant greeted him, and Churchill said: "I like your President." Winant recalled that Churchill "never changed—he liked him to the end. Whenever I talked with the President, I felt the same sense of caring on his part."[69]

During the Placentia Bay conference, Harry Hopkins never strayed far from Roosevelt's side, having briefed FDR before the president and the prime minister got a chance to meet. Hopkins's proximity and influence often led to criticism from outside the Roosevelt administration, and jealousy within it. Hopkins had become a rival to Secretary of the Interior Ickes, Secretary of State Hull, and Treasury Secretary Morgenthau, a longtime FDR confidant. After meeting with FDR in late August 1944, Morgenthau wrote in his diary: "I couldn't help but flash through my mind to how, a couple of years ago, the President said, 'You and I will run this war together,' and then it was . . . Hopkins and himself, and me out on my ear."[70] Ickes wrote of Hopkins in his diary, after taking a March 1941 cruise aboard the presidential yacht: "I do not like him, and I do not like the influence that he has with the president."[71] Erstwhile Attorney General Robert Jackson observed that Roosevelt's "disposition was to let" Ickes and Hopkins "fight it out." The president sometimes invited both to accompany him on trips, despite their disagreements.[72]

Some Washington officials, jealous of Hopkins's relationship with FDR, nevertheless recognized his value as an advisor and troubleshooter. Secretary of War Henry Stimson observed: "The more I think of it, the more I think it is a Godsend that he should be at the White House."[73] Hopkins's understanding of the president's thinking was without peer. British Army chief Alan Brooke recalled a White House meeting in June 1942, at which the fall of the British garrison at Tobruk was announced: "As I was walking out of the President's room, Hopkins said: 'Would you care to come round to my room for a few moments' talk? I could give you some of the background which influenced the President in the statements he has just made and the opinions he has expressed.' I went with him expecting to be taken to his office. Instead we went to his bedroom where we sat on the edge of his bed looking at his shaving brush and tooth brush, whilst he let me into some of the President's inner thoughts!" Brooke added that this meeting was "so typical of" the "man who played a great and nebulous part in the war as the President's right hand man."[74] Secretary of State Edward R. Stettinius would observe that Hopkins "had an uncanny knowledge of the President's moods. He knew when to suggest a given policy and when to remain quiet."[75]

By March 1943, presidential aide William D. Hassett confirmed "Harry Hopkins' decline in popular favor. Poor Harry, the public is done with him; he is a heavy liability to the President, emeralds, bride in the White House, and the rest of it, a sorry mess."[76] Historian David Stafford noted that Hopkins's "detractors, many of whom were Roosevelt-haters, seized on Hopkins as a convenient symbol of all they loathed and resented about the New Deal. By mid-1943 criticism became virulent and personal with wild Republican allegations in Congress. . . . The nadir came when the *Chicago Tribune* likened the former social worker and WPA Administrator to the sinister Russian mystic Rasputin, whose influence over the last of the czars had been so mysterious and malevolent."[77] In his memoirs, Churchill acknowledged Hopkins's detractors: Hopkins "in some ways bore out the poet Gray's line, 'A favourite has no friend'. But this was not my affair. There he sat slim, frail, ill, but absolutely glowing with refined comprehension of the Cause. It was to be the defeat, ruin, and slaughter of Hitler, to the exclusion of all other purposes, loyalties, or aims. In the history of the United States few brighter flames have burned."[78] Charles Bohlen observed: "Hopkins was shrewd, pragmatic, and cynical in his judgments. He made mistakes, especially in his view of Soviet policy. However, more than any other public official I ever met, he was ready to admit his errors."[79]

Hopkins's political problems became magnified in 1942, when he met and fell in love with former magazine editor Louise Macy—and sanctified his third marriage in the Oval Study on the second floor of the White House in July 1943. In the aftermath of Hopkins's marriage, he "was less immediately available for consultation" with the president, wrote historian Kenneth Davis. Hopkins "was less exclusively *his*—than formerly he had been. His fiancée had become a frequent overnight guest at the White House and Hyde Park, and always, during these visits, she was the main focus of his attention."[80] In late 1943, the newlyweds moved out of the White House to their own Georgetown home. In December, FDR's daughter, Anna Roosevelt Boettiger, moved into the Lincoln suite that Hopkins had occupied. Hopkins spent much of the first part of 1944 in hospitals or convalescent facilities around the country. When a Chinese official pressed for his intervention on an issue, Hopkins wrote: "I can't do this sort of thing out here. Tell them I'm *sick*." In July 1944, Hopkins finally left a hospital in White Sulphur Springs, West Virginia, for Washington. He began occasionally to visit the White House that summer, but still was too weak for regular work.[81]

The Roosevelt-Hopkins relationship had changed. Historian Warren Kimball observed that "Hopkins's influence had depended on two factors; his remarkably close personal relationship with the President, and his overall awareness of almost everything that went on in the White House, something that was still possible in the Roosevelt era."[82] It was true, too, that FDR, from 1943 to 1945, would cultivate Stalin more, Churchill less. Hopkins made up an essential part of the alliance with the prime minister. He was not so crucial a link with Stalin and Moscow.

On the return trip from Yalta in February 1945, Roosevelt stopped at Cairo to meet with the region's leaders. Seen here aboard the president's ship are Ambassador John Gilbert Winant, the president's daughter, Anna, and Harry Hopkins.
FRANKLIN D. ROOSEVELT PRESIDENTIAL LIBRARY

VI

John Gilbert Winant

> We must always remember that it is the things of the spirit that in the end prevail. That caring counts. That where there is no vision, people perish. That hope and faith count, and that without charity there can be nothing good. That by daring to live dangerously, we are learning to live generously. And that by believing in the inherent goodness of man, we may meet the call of your great Prime Minister and "stride forward into the unknown with growing confidence."[1]
>
> ***John Gilbert Winant** (1889–1947), speech to British coal miners whose strike he had helped end, June 6, 1942. Winant served as U.S. Ambassador to the United Kingdom from 1941 to 1946. A Republican, he had served three terms as governor of New Hampshire, before President Roosevelt named him as the first chairman of the Social Security Board in 1935.*

British leaders celebrated in early 1941, when the United States sent a new ambassador to London to replace Joseph P. Kennedy. Like William Donovan, John Gilbert Winant was a Republican; but the former New Hampshire governor had better relations with the American president than did the Wall Street attorney. Once in Britain, "Gil" Winant occasionally accompanied the media-wise prime minister on his trips to bombed-out communities. Churchill knew the political value of exposing American visitors to the results of German bombing by visiting hard-hit cities, or taking them to the roof of the Downing Street Annexe to view bombing raids.[2] The prime minister made certain that American visitors understood the depth and breadth of British suffering. As the U.S. ambassador wrote President Roosevelt:

> The Prime Minister's method of conducting a campaign on what one might call a morale front is unique. He arrives at a town unannounced, is taken to the most seriously bombed area, leaves his automobile and starts walking through the streets without guards. The news of his presence spreads rapidly by word of mouth, and before he has

> gone far, crowds flock about him and people call out to him, "Hallo, Winnie," "Good old Winnie," "You will never let us down," "That's a man." I was interested to note that his "Cheerio" in our earlier visits changed to "God bless you" when we reached Bristol where people were still shaken by the bombing. The whole town was back on its feet again and cheering within two hours of his arrival, although no one had got any sleep during the night.[3]

The reserved, intense Yankee diplomat found a kindred British soul in Alan Brooke. U.S. General Omar N. Bradley recalled Brooke as "soft-spoken, retiring, self effacing, a British version of George Marshall. Excluding Churchill, Brooke was the principal architect of British war strategy."[4] The prime minister's physician noted that the shy Winant "has wrestled with the world and has hidden, like Brooke, behind a curtain of his own making. It appeared to lift a little when the two men came together."[5] Churchill aide John Colville remembered:

> Winant was self-effacing, though proud that he was generally said to look like Abraham Lincoln. His modesty disguised the courage of a lion, physical as well as moral. One night in February 1941 Churchill sent me in an armored car to the American Embassy with a draft on which he wanted Winant's comments. The [German air] raid that night was heavy. While I sat with Winant upstairs at Number 1 Grosvenor Square, the earth shook. I counted the whistles of four bombs which seemed to fall close and, though I hesitated to say so, I felt that the basement would provide a more convenient working place. Winant did not lift his eyes from the document he was studying.[6]

Several weeks later, Colville took a speech on which Churchill was working "to the American embassy to show Winant. He made four pertinent observations in respect to the effect on U.S. opinion and I was deeply impressed by his unassertive shrewdness and wisdom. I afterwards explained these points to the P.M. who accepted them."[7]

The traditional welcome of the new U.S. ambassador took place at a meeting of the Pilgrims Society in March 1941. Churchill declared: "Mr. Ambassador, you share our purpose, you will share our dangers, you will share our anxieties, you shall share our secrets, and the day will come when the British Empire and the United States will share together the solemn but splendid duties which are the crown of victory."[8] In his response, Winant reaffirmed Britain's purpose: "Today it is the honor and destiny of the British people to man the bridgehead of humanity's hopes. It is your privilege to stand against ruthless and powerful dictators who would destroy the lessons of two thousand years of history. It is your destiny to say to them: 'Here you shall not pass.'"[9]

Winant's presence reassured Britain in 1941, during the anxious year before Japan forced FDR and Congress to declare war on December 8. Churchill himself told a London conference in March 1941: "It is a great pleasure to see Mr. Winant among us. He gives us the feeling that President Roosevelt's men give me, that they would be shot stone dead rather than see this cause let down."[10] Winant was not a great speaker, but he made up for that deficiency with the decency and sincerity with which he embodied Lincolnesque appearance, ideals, and rhetoric. When Winant was called upon to talk at the inauguration of the Lord Mayor of Plymouth, he ended his speech by quoting "from Franklin K. Lane's great soliloquy as he stood before [Augustus] Saint-Gaudens' statue of Abraham Lincoln in Chicago." As Winant wrote in his memoirs: "I tried to help the British see America through Lincoln's eyes by reciting Lane's words." Lane had written:

> It [the Lincoln statue] is to me all that America is, physically and spiritually. I look at those long arms and long legs, large hands and feet, and I think that they represent the physical strength of this country, its power and its youthful awkwardness. Then I look up at the head and see qualities which have made the American—the strong chin, the noble brow, those sober and steadfast eyes. They were the eyes of one who saw with sympathy and interpreted with common sense; they were the eyes of earnest idealism limited and checked by the possible and the practicable. They were the eyes of a truly humble spirit, whose ambition was not a love for power, but a desire to be supremely useful. They were the eyes of compassion and mercy and a deep understanding. They saw far more than they looked at. They believed in far more than they saw. They loved men, not for what they were but for what they might become. They were patient eyes, eyes that could wait and wait and live on in the faith that right would win. They were eyes which challenged the nobler things in men and brought out hidden largeness. They were humorous eyes that saw things in their true proportions and in their real relationships. They looked through cant and pretense and the great and little vanities of great and little men. They were the eyes of unflinching courage and an unfaltering faith rising out of a sincere dependence upon the Master of the Universe.[11]

Winant worked hard to solidify his favorable public opinion among British citizens. R. A. Butler, who served as British under secretary of foreign affairs at the beginning of the war, wrote: "Despite his great difficulty in expressing himself, it was impossible to be with Winant and not to feel his genius. He forecast to me that England would go socialist after the war: I knew no one else whose instinct was then so sure."[12] Winant developed a genuine affection for Britain and Churchill. In his diary, Dr. Charles Wilson described Winant aboard ship, on the way to the Teheran conference in November 1943: "Before he utters a syllable people want to see more of him. He has the rapt gaze of a monk; the big dark eyes, buried in his head, look beyond you." Wilson quoted an interchange between Churchill and Winant about France, ending with the prime minister's comment: "The ambassador always stands out for the larger view, and he is, of course, right."[13]

Colville wrote that Winant's "popularity with Churchill did nothing to prevent his [Winant's] fight for the American point of view when it conflicted with British intentions."[14] In his memoirs, Colville noted: "With his quiet voice, his courtesy, his liking for people and willingness to concentrate on their interests, he became and remained a personal friend of the Churchills, their children and their whole entourage. Nobody maligned Winant, but he, if he thought his own Government at fault, was outspoken in his criticisms of and to them. In his loyalties he bestrode the Atlantic."[15] The sharp pen of Dr. Wilson made a practical point: "The P.M. is attracted by Winant's optimism, but it is not to him that he turns for advice. He prefers the tart cleverness of Harry Hopkins, for the same reason that he is drawn to Max Beaverbrook."[16] To advocate for his interests with FDR, Churchill needed not only Ambassador Winant, but also Lend-Lease facilitator Averell Harriman, especially in the months before the United States officially entered World War II. The prime minister's aide Colville wrote: "During 1941 it was rare for one of them not to be found at Chequers at the week-end. Often both would be invited, as much for the pleasure of their company as for the business to be done."[17] Winant and Harriman walked a fine line in their official duties. "They were, in effect, serving two governments: they were their country's top representatives in Britain while acting as Churchill's agents for conveying Britain's needs to the United States," wrote historian Lynne Olson. "But, as they made clear to British officials, their primary duty was to their own chief executive and country."[18] Colville recalled one Chequers weekend in April 1941, after Winant and the prime minister had just visited bombed-out Bristol: "That evening . . . Winant received a message from Roosevelt announcing America's intention to extend her naval patrol area as far west as the 25th meridian [virtually all of the western Atlantic]. I asked Winant and Harriman if that might not mean war between the United States and Germany. 'That's what I hope', said Harriman. Winant smiled his assent."[19] FDR was in no such hurry.

There was an unspoken rivalry between Winant and Harriman. "Averell not only took the glamour out of Winant's job," journalist Harrison Salisbury remembered, "he substantially undercut his relationship with Churchill."[20] In July 1941, Hopkins told the top American military official in London: "I have given Harriman the most strict and explicit instructions not to touch anything which is in any way political. That is the Ambassador's business, and his alone. I also told Churchill that we had at the moment in England the best, the finest, and most highly qualified man for ambassador that we have had for twenty-five years, and a man who is the sincere friend of Great Britain, and therefore that he must deal with Winant direct and fully in all matters which had any political aspect whatever."[21] No matter, Harriman's ambition would not be contained.

First Lady Eleanor Roosevelt made it clear which American envoy she preferred when she visited Britain in October 1942.[22] Although she had known Harriman for decades, Mrs. Roosevelt "also greatly respected the abilities of Winant, to whose moral character she was much more closely attuned, and her sense of fairness had been outraged by the written terms under which her husband had dispatched Harriman to London as lend-lease administrator, terms that undercut Winant's authority," wrote historian Kenneth S. Davis. Mrs. Roosevelt deliberately ignored the advice of Harry Hopkins "not to bother with Winant" and to work exclusively with Harriman.[23] Indeed, she did the reverse.

Colville noted that the quietly competent and intrepid "Winant stayed in London throughout the war, never losing Churchill's affection and confidence."[24] However, General Leslie Hollis observed that Winant "never gave decisive advice if he could help it, and . . . generally spoke in such a low voice that people could hardly hear what advice he did give."[25] Over time, Winant realized that he had lost his original utility and had been superseded by FDR's unorthodox diplomacy. Winant complained to Hopkins in 1943:

> During the past six months a situation has developed which has cut down my usefulness. I have had no business delegated to me as Ambassador that could not have been done by an efficient Foreign Service officer. I have been by-passed continuously. I have had no contacts with the Prime Minister except on two occasions when he invited me to meet with him so that he could bring me up to date on Anglo-American Relations. Nine-tenths of the information I receive comes from British sources. Matters of serious importance relating to our foreign policy go to Mr. Churchill or Mr. Eden through other channels. Officials of the British Government have been friendly and frank with me but they are quick to appreciate when one in my position has been deprived of his authority.

Hopkins responded sympathetically: "I know exactly how you feel about it and if I were in your shoes I would feel just the same."[26]

Lord Beaverbrook discusses British military and civilian needs with representatives of the Office of Production Management in Washington, August 19, 1941. Left to right: Sidney Hillman, associate director, OPM; John Lord O'Brian, general counsel, OPM; Edward R. Stettinius Jr., director of priorities, OPM; Lord Beaverbrook, British minister of supply; William S. Knudsen, director-general, OPM.
LIBRARY OF CONGRESS

VII

Lord Beaverbrook

> Churchill remains predominant. He has no rivals. And his critics serve only, in the main, to fortify him in the affection of the public. For when the people compare the critics with the object of their criticism they have no doubt which they prefer.[1]
>
> ***Max Aitken, Lord Beaverbrook** (1879–1964), letter to Paul Patterson, September 29, 1942. Beaverbrook was an industrialist and newspaper baron who, by World War II, was Churchill's oldest political ally. Beaverbrook's wealth allowed him to come to Churchill's aid with independent means, and his pugnacity made him an effective, if controversial, emissary. As minister of aircraft production in 1940, he proved remarkably able, vindicating the prime minister's decision to appoint him to the post. Beaverbrook's success in augmenting aircraft production was one key to the 1940 air victory over the Luftwaffe in the Battle of Britain.*

Canadian-born Max Aitken and half-American Winston Churchill were the only two men to serve in the British war cabinets of both World War I and World War II. Lord Beaverbrook had a long personal and political relationship with Churchill, but the two strong-willed men had differed in the late 1930s, over British appeasement policy toward Hitler—Churchill implacably opposed, Beaverbrook vacillating but, in the end, an appeaser. After the Second World War, Churchill wrote of Beaverbrook: "People who did not know the services he had rendered during his tenure of office or his force, driving power, and judgment, as I did, often wondered why his influence with me stood so high. . . . Often we had been on different sides in the crises and quarrels of those former days; sometimes we had even been fiercely opposed; yet on the whole a relationship had been maintained which was a part of the continuity of my public life, and this was cemented by warm personal friendship."[2]

The prime minister possessed the rare virtue of separating his appreciation of Beaverbrook's talents from the many political disagreements with his friend. Churchill exhibited this mark of self-confidence not only with friends, but also with political enemies. "Churchill had been aware of Beaverbrook's capacities for a quarter of a century: his power to inspire and drive, his ability to get at the heart of a problem at speed, his refusal to despair or admit defeat," wrote Beaverbrook biographers Anne Chisholm and Michael Davie. "Their relationship had never depended on shared political convictions; it had survived in spite of politics, not because of them. . . . In war, Churchill knew, Beaverbrook's sustaining strengths would outweigh his weaknesses; in a context of supreme national danger, his previous views and conduct, however deplorable and ill-advised, did not matter."[3] The prime minister wrote in his memoirs that Beaverbrook's appointment to the cabinet in 1940 caused "[t]he greatest difficulty." After mentioning the sources of opposition to Beaverbrook, he observed: "I felt sure . . . that our life depended upon the flow of new aircraft; I needed his vital and vibrant energy, and I persisted in my view."[4] Beaverbrook served as minister of aircraft production for nearly a year—the decisive year when the RAF triumphed over the Luftwaffe in the Battle of Britain. He understood the nature of opposition to his appointment and frequently used it as an excuse for resignation.[5] Despite the dramatic jump in aircraft production that he engineered, the fiercely independent Beaverbrook locked horns with Churchill, military officers, other ministers, and officials.[6] Churchill's insight, that the critical path in 1940 was through aircraft production, and his judgment that "the Beaver" was the man for the job, helped save England from a potential German invasion. British victory in the air battle over Britain turned Hitler away from Operation Sea Lion, the anticipated cross-channel invasion of the United Kingdom, toward a ground invasion of Russia. Total air superiority would prove crucial to the Allies in the D-Day invasion of Normandy in June 1944.

The diminutive Beaverbrook had important detractors on both sides of the Atlantic. His assertive ways did not endear him to other officials. Shortly after Churchill was named prime minister in 1940, King George had written him: "I have been thinking over the names you suggested to me this evening in forming your government, which I think are very good, but I would like to warn you of the repercussions, which I am sure will occur, especially in Canada, at the inclusion of the name of the Lord Beaverbrook for air production in the Air Ministry. You are no doubt aware that the Canadians do not appreciate him, & I feel that as the Air Training Scheme for pilots & aircraft is in Canada, I must tell you this fact. I wonder if you would not reconsider your intention of selecting Lord Beaverbrook for this post. I am sending this round to you at once, as I fear that this appointment might be misconstrued." The king added: "I hoped you will understand why I am doing this, as I want to be a help to you in the very important & onerous office which you have just accepted at my hands."[7]

The prime minister admired the king, but he would keep his own counsel on this occasion.

British cabinet member Oliver Lyttelton recalled:

> Winston had a deep, almost an emotional friendship for Max Beaverbrook. The causes were manifold. Max was the only leading member of his government near him in age who had shared experiences in the First World War and in politics outside the span of the rest of us. His support had been powerful: his achievements at the Ministry of

> Aircraft Production during the deadly days of the Battle of Britain need no telling. He added the gift of being able to amuse and entertain the Prime Minister: his talk had a zest, a mixture of enthusiasm and cynicism, of kindness and harshness, but above all an original twist which makes it astringent and exhilarating.[8]

The Beaverbrook-Churchill friendship had endured frequent strains, especially in the decade before World War II. Historian Robert Rhodes James wrote that during the 1930s, Beaverbrook thought Churchill a "busted flush." Rhodes argued: "Churchill was not enthusiastic about Beaverbrook's darling, the Empire Free Trade movement—a protectionist program for free trade within the British Empire. The Prime Minister had been a global free trader, only reluctantly accepting Tory protectionism in the 1930s. Beaverbrook did not share Churchill's black estimates of Russian and German ambitions."[9] As two of the British Empire's most dynamic personalities, it was perhaps inevitable that in crisis, they would be drawn back together. Before World War II broke out, one of Beaverbrook's young *Express* reporters, Patrick Campbell, spoke with Beaverbrook in his garden. Beaverbrook "said, without warning, 'This man Churchill is the enemy of the British Empire.' I was so astonished, and alarmed, that I stepped backwards into a wet flowerbed, covering my shoe with mud." Beaverbrook then called Churchill "a warmonger. He is turning the thoughts of the people of the British Empire to war. He must be stopped. Go get him."[10] Beaverbrook's negative judgment of Churchill seemed plausible before 1939. Then, in fact, it was the conventional British elite opinion. Beaverbrook declared in November 1938: "This man of brilliant talent, splendid abilities, magnificent power of speech, and fine stylist, has ceased to influence the British public."[11] Within a year, the tide of opinion on the German threat would begin to rise in favor of Churchill.

Beaverbrook was known for his eccentric behavior, but Churchill harnessed the press lord's energy behind the war effort. The prime minister often brought him along on key wartime trips. Beaverbrook's decisiveness was contagious. His impatience and self-confidence rivaled Churchill's. He and the prime minister enjoyed arguing almost as much as they enjoyed working with each other. British Ambassador to Spain Samuel Hoare wrote Beaverbrook that Churchill "needs someone like yourself constantly at his side to discuss with him the really big issues that are now more than ever emerging in the war. . . . You and he are on such intimate terms together that he will always however listen to you."[12] Biographer Kenneth Young concluded: "Churchill, in addition to his other great gifts, was a remarkable manager of men. With Beaverbrook, he was also the most understanding of masters."[13] Mastering Beaverbrook took time, observed Churchill's colleagues; Minister of Information Brendan Bracken quipped "that he takes up more of P.M.'s time than Hitler."[14]

When Prime Minister Chamberlain's government fell in early May 1940, Beaverbrook understood then that Churchill's moment had arrived. On May 10, 1940, Winston Churchill became prime minister. In June 1940, as France was collapsing, Beaverbrook wrote: "Winston is standing up to the strain very well, he is the Atlas with two worlds to carry. With one hand he bears up the British Empire, with the other he sustains the French Republic. And the French Republic takes a bit of supporting, let me tell you."[15] Observing the failing French army and the faltering

French government, the dynamic Beaverbrook told the prime minister: "There is nothing to do but to repeat what you have already said, Winston. Telegraph to Roosevelt [for help] and await the answer. Tell [French Premier Paul] Reynaud that we have nothing to say or discuss until Roosevelt's answer is received. Don't commit yourself to anything. We shall gain a little time and see how those Frenchmen sort themselves out. We are doing no good here. In fact, listening to these declarations of Reynaud's only does harm. Let's get along home."[16] Secretary of State Hull wrote in his memoirs that FDR appreciated Churchill's realism regarding France in 1940: "[W]e were convinced that Britain, under Churchill's indomitable leadership, intended to fight on. There would be no negotiations between London and Berlin."[17]

As a cabinet member in the summer of 1940, Beaverbrook saw one of his early tasks as helping to control Ambassador Kennedy, with whom he had established a friendship before the war.[18] "My son was shooting down Germans in the air," Beaverbrook recalled. "I was obliged to be ruthless on the ground."[19] Kennedy, an isolationist, opposed aid to Britain; FDR feared the politically influential Kennedy might campaign against him on this very issue before November 1940. Back in New York, Stephenson was provided with reports on Kennedy's outrageous comments, which were turned over to FDR. Kennedy was cabled to return to the United States. Delicate timing, however, was critical, because the unpredictable Kennedy could damage Roosevelt's reelection chances.

Kennedy threatened to publish an "indictment of President Roosevelt's administration" if he were not permitted leave to return to the United States.[20] In October, Kennedy, anxious to go home, finally was recalled by Roosevelt in a note: "Dear Joe: I know what an increasingly severe strain you have been under during the past weeks and I think it is altogether owing to you that you get a chance to get away and get some relief. The State Department has consequently telegraphed you my desire to come back for consultation during the week commencing October 21."[21] Presidential politics, as well as Kennedy's negative diplomacy, was at stake. Beaverbrook and Halifax worried that Kennedy might switch his allegiance away from Roosevelt and support Republican presidential candidate Wendell Willkie. FDR had similar worries, telling Under Secretary Welles to get Kennedy to the White House "before anyone else got at him to talk."[22]

Kennedy understood that his usefulness in London had come to an end, and that the State Department had leaked his dispatches to undermine him. The ambassador wanted to get away from the Battle of Britain and to return to the United States, but the president did not want Kennedy to become an independent force in the presidential race, perhaps siding with isolationist Republicans. FDR proved more than a match for Kennedy. The president contrived to have Kennedy remain quiet, until the ambassador had visited the White House. There, he could be brought under FDR's legendary charm and control. Roosevelt in person was very persuasive. Kennedy himself admitted he could "say no to that fellow on the telephone but face to face he gets me."[23] Leaving Britain for the United States on October 22, Kennedy received several messages from President Roosevelt, asking him to make no statements to the press.[24] As troublesome as Kennedy had been for FDR when in London, the Irish-American speculator had a following that could still help FDR win an unprecedented third term.

The president invited Kennedy and his wife to the White House for an intimate and carefully planned dinner, during which South Carolina Senator James F. Byrnes pressed Kennedy to make a radio address in support of FDR's reelection.[25] Although Kennedy told the president that he was "damn sore at the way I have been treated," the grumpy envoy announced he would make the speech and "will pay for it myself."[26] Publicly, Kennedy refused to reveal immediately his support for FDR; indeed, he deliberately cultivated suspense about what he intended to say. On October 29, Kennedy delivered his radio address—helping to shore up Roosevelt's noninterventionist credentials, especially with Irish-Americans. First, however, Kennedy declared his political independence in the speech: "I sent reports to the President and the Secretary of State which were my best judgment about the forces that were moving, the developments that were likely and the course best suited to protect America."[27] A grateful president telegraphed Kennedy that it was "a great speech." Kennedy himself would later declare the unstated reason behind his address: "I simply made a deal with Roosevelt. We agreed that if I endorsed him for President in 1940, then he would support my son Joe for governor of Massachusetts in 1942."[28] The night after Kennedy's speech on CBS radio, FDR spoke in Boston and welcomed the return of "that Boston boy, beloved by all of Boston, and a lot of other places, my ambassador to the Court of St. James's, Joe Kennedy."[29] Kennedy's son Joe would die in August 1944, when his B-24 Liberator blew up. The "robot" bomb in the plane young Kennedy was piloting to France detonated prematurely over England. The explosion killed Kennedy before he and his copilot could bail out. His death further embittered Joseph Kennedy.

In some quarters, Lord Beaverbrook was as controversial as Kennedy. Averell Harriman's daughter, Kathleen, described Beaverbrook in 1941 as "small, baldish, big stomach and from there he tapers down to two very shiny yellow shoes. His idea of sport is to surround himself with intelligent men, then egg them on to argue and fight among themselves."[30] Kathleen Harriman did not appreciate Beaverbrook, comparing him to Churchill: "One's a gentleman and the other is a ruffian. Ave [Harriman], luckily, can talk both languages."[31] General Brooke had a similar opinion of Beaverbrook and his manners—recalling a Chequers weekend where "after dinner he sat at the writing table, pouring himself out one strong whisky after another, and I was revolted by his having monkey-like hands as they stretched out to grab ice cubes out of the bowl. The more I saw of him throughout the war, the more I disliked and mistrusted him. An evil genius who exercised the very worst of influence on Winston."[32] Alan Brooke was a member of an aristocratic Ulster military family, generations of which had served the British Empire with distinction.[33]

Beaverbrook, however, had an avuncular side to him. He took a paternal interest in the problems of Churchill's young daughter-in-law, Pamela Digby Churchill, married to Churchill's erratic son Randolph. Pamela became a close friend of Kathleen

Harriman on the way to becoming her father's mistress. Beaverbrook provided a home for Pamela's baby at Beaverbrook's Cherkley estate, and money to relieve Pamela of husband Randolph's gambling debts.[34] Eventually, Averell Harriman rented a small cottage for the weekend use of Kathleen and Pamela. In London, the three lived together at the Dorchester Hotel, where the prime minister's daughter-in-law and Harriman carried on their affair. According to Pamela's biographer: "[S]he frequently passed along reports of their conversations to Beaverbrook and her father-in-law."[35] Harriman himself was drawn to Beaverbrook's social circle, often visiting Cherkley where Pamela learned much from Beaverbrook's handling of guests, conversation, and information.[36] When in July 1942, Harriman fell ill with paratyphoid, he was treated by Beaverbrook's physician and fed by Beaverbrook's chef.[37]

As his enemies predicted, Beaverbrook's consuming drive to increase airplane production brought him into conflict with other officials. General Leslie Hollis recalled that at meetings with Churchill, Beaverbrook was like "an old eagle perched high on some rocky crag, surveying the scene beneath him, ready to swoop on the instant one of his projects became involved."[38] Hollis recalled that "Churchill gave him complete and virtually dictatorial powers [to increase aircraft production], and protected him from the anger of other less forceful Ministers who complained that he was 'interfering' with what had hitherto been their concern." Beaverbrook "never carried an oil can. He did as he liked, when he liked."[39] Beaverbrook's office displayed three signs that summed up his entrepreneurial, administrative principles:

> Organization is the enemy of improvisation.
> It is a long jump from knowing to doing.
> Committees take the punch out of war.[40]

Beaverbrook and Churchill shared not only friendship, but also energy, enthusiasm, and enemies. Combativeness marked their personalities. Each in his own way was a gifted entrepreneur. Beaverbrook resisted rules and restrictions. Both insisted on control, not least because each thought he knew best. Each was a hands-on leader-manager. American Air Corps Chief Henry "Hap" Arnold visited Beaverbrook in April 1941: "Beaverbrook struck me then—and I have never changed my opinion of him—as a most capable, far-seeing man, with tremendous executive powers."[41]

Beaverbrook made sure he was at important events. For example, he demanded to be included on the roster of British officials assigned to the flying boat that took Churchill back to Britain from Washington in January 1942. Temperamentally, Beaverbrook and the prime minister could be mercurial. One day in March 1944, Churchill, in bed, told Beaverbrook: "I'm through. I cannot carry the burdens any longer. . . . I have done my job. The Americans are in and we cannot lose. Anthony can carry on. I must get out." At that very moment, the prime minister received word by phone that the House of Commons had defeated his government's education bill. Ignoring what he had just said, Churchill jumped from bed, proclaiming to Beaverbrook: "I need a life of action!"[42]

Beaverbrook could match Churchill with strange ideas, such as his suggestion in May 1943 that the prime minister should disembark in New York from the *Queen Mary* in a small boat, and then parade through Manhattan.[43] Disputes between the two British leaders had long characterized their relationship. Aboard ship on the way to Washington in May 1943, the garrulous Beaverbrook grew annoyed and critical of the prime minister. At one point, recalled Harriman, Churchill "put his hand on Beaverbrook's knee . . . and softly said, 'you don't talk any more.' Beaverbrook later complained to Harriman, 'I don't talk because the P.M. talks all the time.'"[44] Even with the choleric Beaverbrook, the irrepressible Churchill dominated the conversation, as he did with almost all men and women, with the exception of Frederick E. Smith. Elevated to the peerage as the first Earl Birkenhead, Smith was a brilliant lawyer, a compelling speaker, and a Tory through and through. A devoted Churchill friend, he died in 1931.[45]

There was at least one striking difference between Beaverbrook and Churchill's other longtime confidant, Brendan Bracken, who moved tirelessly among opinion leaders in search of useful information. Beaverbrook expected others to come to him at one of his British residences. Moreover, he possessed a rare talent for feuds and conflict. British journalist Woodrow Wyatt wrote: "When one of Lord Beaverbrook's feuds is in full swing nothing is too petty or unscrupulous for him." Wyatt concluded that one of Beaverbrook's "motivating forces" was envy. "He cannot bear to think that other men should be accounted great when he is not quite certain that he will be. . . . Often this envy provokes him into feuds in which he persecutes the object of his hate vigorously and unfairly through his newspapers. . . . Often it is smaller people who are the subject of attack, people who have annoyed or riled him in some way."[46]

In reply to Beaverbrook's first resignation threat in late June 1940, Churchill answered: "I have received your letter of June 30, and hasten to say that at a moment like this when an invasion is reported to be imminent there can be no question of any Ministerial resignations being accepted. I require you, therefore, to dismiss this matter from your mind, and to continue the magnificent work you are doing on which to a large extent our safety depends."[47] Doubts continued to plague Beaverbrook. "I am not now the man for the job," Beaverbrook wrote in another resignation letter of December 1940. "I will not get the necessary support." Churchill responded: "There is no question of my accepting your resignation. I told you, you are in the galleys and will have to row to the end."[48] In this very personal relationship, the prime minister knew what to say in order to disarm his independent colleague.

As difficult and egotistical as Beaverbrook could be, Churchill had the self-confidence to use him to manage important problems. After working with Americans in Washington on war production, Beaverbrook joined Churchill at the Placentia Bay conference in August 1941. Elliott Roosevelt recalled that at the end of the conference, he was placed in charge of making arrangements for Beaverbrook's return from Placentia Bay to Washington. "Beaverbrook and I were set ashore, forced to take a train back up to my base, where I would get him a seat on a plane bound for Washington and further conferences with our Lend-Lease officials." The train was uncomfortable, annoying "my astonishing little companion. When an inoffensive trainman made an understandable error, and misdirected us, the Beaver let him have it for nearly three minutes in a wonderfully shrill voice, interlarding his choicer comments with some of the more pungent Anglo-Saxon four-letter words."[49] Given the deepening Anglo-American relations and Britain's urgent needs, Beaverbrook got on well with American procurement officials, especially Harry Hopkins. He well understood the prime minister's priorities, namely, bringing America into the war, and making the United States the arsenal of the British war effort.

Hopkins enjoyed the presence of Beaverbrook, with whom he continued to exchange letters and opinions, even when Hopkins was hospitalized. In July 1944, Hopkins wrote Churchill: "I am remaining here in Washington and not going with the President [to a military conference in Hawaii]. I am able to work only two or three hours a day. . . . I look forward to Beaverbrook's arrival which will assure a big breeze here in Washington."[50] With Hopkins, the Beaver could drop diplomatic niceties. Both men indulged in a salty vocabulary.

Meeting with Beaverbrook, shortly after the Bretton Woods monetary conference had concluded in the summer of 1944, Hopkins wrote to FDR about "how difficult it is to hold a formal economic conference with Great Britain on any single subject at this particular time. Max, himself, was quite unhappy, not so much because he did not have his way about the [Bretton Woods] agreement but because he claims he senses a good deal of hostility there. One of our present difficulties is that everybody thinks the war is over. I hope if you decide to speak on the radio from Seattle, that you will scotch this."[51] In one letter to Hopkins in October 1944, Beaverbrook wrote: "Here in Britain we are passing through a strange phase in public life. For the first time, the English are not absolutely sure of themselves. They are anxious about their future. And this in some measure is due to the extent to which they have had to rely on outside assistance in the war. Without your friendship we would never have got it. We know that you came with a discerning eye. You saw the prospect of defeat and the possibility of resistance and you decided to back the resistance. But having come so far with the assistance for which you were primarily responsible, the British must very soon go forward under their own power."[52] Beaverbrook's anxiety was justified. As early as 1941, Great Britain was insolvent, a military and economic dependent of America, unable to fight a war of national survival out of its own resources.[53]

Beaverbrook's enthusiasms reinforced his strengths and his weaknesses. In September 1941, after the Placentia Bay summit, Beaverbrook was dispatched to Moscow with an equally ambitious Averell Harriman.[54] (Despite a disappointing manganese business deal in the Soviet Union in the 1920s, Harriman had remained a modest and privileged investor in Russia.) Churchill wrote in his memoirs: "Lord Beaverbrook returned from the United States having stimulated the already powerful forces making for a stupendous increase in production. He now became the champion in the War Cabinet of Aid to Russia. In this he rendered valuable service."[55] Harriman and Beaverbrook had three days of productive meetings with Stalin. "Beaverbrook has been a great salesman," wrote Harriman. "His personal sincerity was convincing. His genius never worked more effectively."[56] Hopkins biographer Robert E.

Sherwood wrote that Harriman observed "friction between Beaverbrook and the military members of the British Mission. Beaverbrook had by then become, as he was to continue, a vociferous advocate of the second front in the West. He was forever opposing any diversion from this fixed purpose." He wrote in October 1941: "There is today only one military problem—how to help Russia. Yet on that issue the Chiefs of Staff content themselves with saying that nothing can be done. They point out the difficulties but make no suggestions for overcoming them. It is nonsense to say that we can do nothing for Russia."[57] But at that time, the British consensus held that superior German arms would prevail over Russian resistance. Even more important, the British military chiefs and the prime minister held that a second front in the West was premature, and that the Americans and British were not yet militarily prepared for the monumental cross-channel invasion, not to mention the fact that America was not officially at war with Germany in October 1941.

The British and American envoys to Russia reported directly to Churchill upon their return to Britain.[58] As often occurred when Beaverbrook was present, a circus of recriminations ensued. Harriman recalled: "As soon as we sat down to dinner, Beaverbrook began to berate the prime minister. It was intolerable, he said, for Churchill to accuse him of embarrassing the government by importing illicit caviar from Russia. Churchill protested that he had made no such accusation. By way of changing the subject, I accused Eden of trying to run the American delegation when he and [Stafford] Cripps had objected to my bringing [journalist] Quentin Reynolds to Moscow as my press officer. Eden attempted to shift the responsibility to Cripps." Harriman added: "Beaverbrook, as always, enjoyed this kind of contretemps, and the argument raged through much of the dinner."[59] Beaverbrook did not readily yield to Churchill, nor did the prime minister yield to the Beaver's improbable demand for an immediate second front in Europe.

About three months later, in December 1941, he accompanied the prime minister to Washington after the Japanese attack on Pearl Harbor. Beaverbrook took an active part in pressing for expedited American production and shipping, writing FDR on December 27: "It is my hope that you will permit Mr. Hopkins to take charge of a committee of production with full powers and entire authority. Such a committee would not only dispose of the production requirements but would also be responsible for mobilising and distributing the necessary raw materials."[60] Churchill's personal physician thought Beaverbrook unhelpful. "He has not much for our sailors and soldiers, and likes showing off to the Americans his influence with the P.M."[61] Nevertheless, in a telegram to the War Cabinet in London, Churchill called Beaverbrook's performance "magnificent."[62]

Several weeks later, Beaverbrook resigned from the War Cabinet in one of his regular disputes with Churchill. Beaverbrook later admitted that resignations were "a deliberate act of promotion. The object was 'urgency and speed.'"[63] Beaverbrook's ego and ambition could get the better of him. In February 1942—after major naval and ground defeats of the British by the Germans and the Japanese—Beaverbrook, Eden, and former ambassador to Russia Stafford Cripps thought they might succeed an embattled prime minister in the near future. The humiliating military defeats in

Southeast Asia and the Middle East forced Churchill to reorganize his administration. Churchill wrote Beaverbrook on February 10, 1942, urging him to accept the post of minister of production: "If, after all else has been settled, you break on this point, or indeed on any other in connection with the great office I have shaped for you, I feel bound to say that you will be harshly judged by the nation and in the United States, having regard to the extreme emergency in which we stand and the immense scale of the interests which are involved. I therefore hope that you will not fall below the high level of events and strike so wounding a blow at your country, at your friend, and above all at your reputation."[64] Beaverbrook vacillated. On February 17, he responded in writing to Churchill:

> What can be done, by means of changes in the structure of the Administration, to give the people what they want?
>
> 1. The addition of Sir Stafford Cripps to the Government? But the desire of the public for Cripps is a fleeting passion. Already it is on the wane.
> 2. The appointment of a Minister of Defence, or perhaps a Deputy Minister of Defence? But no one can be found for this post who will at once give satisfaction to the public and to you, under whom he would serve. . . .
> 3. The setting up of a War Cabinet composed of a few Ministers, each of whom would preside over groups of departments and would be free from departments and would be free from departmental duties. This plan should be adopted. . . .
> 4. Lastly, some of the Government are looked on by the public as unsatisfactory Ministers. Their names are well known to you.[65]

By the end of February, Beaverbrook had resigned again, this time allegedly because of chronic asthma. Businessman Oliver Lyttelton was appointed to the post. Churchill wrote in his memoirs: "But now that all appeared settled Lord Beaverbrook resigned. His health had completely broken down, and he did not feel he could face the new and great responsibilities he had assumed. I did my utmost to dissuade him, but the long and harassing discussions which took place in my presence between him and other principal ministers convinced me that it was better to press no further."[66] Although loyal to the prime minister in tough times, Beaverbrook anticipated that Churchill might be forced to resign: "At the time he left the government and for some time thereafter [he] felt that the days of Churchill's Government were numbered and that there was a possibility, if he got out, that he would be called [to replace Churchill]," wrote Averell Harriman. "He believed, I think, that the situation would get so bad the public would call for him. Still, he personally made no public move to injure Churchill at any time. He based his hopes largely on the demand of the people for a man who would be sympathetic to Russia and had shown aggressive tendencies."[67] Harriman admired the mercurial Beaverbrook, and noted: "Since Beaverbrook left the Government there is no one who has the aggressiveness to get things done in the same manner and I would personally welcome his return."[68] Beaverbrook was a master at gamesmanship. Harriman wrote one night, after a game of poker with Beaverbrook and Churchill: "The PM considers that Beaverbrook can do a lot of things which he cannot, such as building up his successful newspapers, financial acquisitiveness, successful gambling, etc., and he does not understand what is back of them. Beaverbrook realizes this and never gives himself away. Winning from the PM at poker is an essential part of their relationship."[69]

In March 1942, after Beaverbrook's resignation, Churchill packed him off on a mission to Washington. "Max is off tomorrow and I should be grateful if you will impress upon the President that though he is for the time being out of office at his own wish, we remain close friends and intimate political associates," Churchill wrote Hopkins. Beaverbrook's cover on this trip was rest and recuperation, but he conducted talks with Roosevelt and Hopkins, to whom he preached the necessity of a second front to help Russia.[70] The Americans were aware of a possible move to have Beaverbrook take up permanent residence as the British ambassador. Hopkins was told that "Churchill was considering the possibility of calling Lord Halifax back to London for service in the War Cabinet and as Leader of the House of Lords. His place as British Ambassador would be taken by Lord Beaverbrook." Nothing came of this idea, although Hopkins wired Churchill: "The idea of Max coming is of course agreeable and it is believed here that he could be extremely useful in the light of the problems which confront our two countries."[71] Beaverbrook in America continued his relentless drive for a second front in Europe to help Russia. He found a few receptive ears in America. But it was senior British military authorities—especially the prime minister and General Brooke—who argued that an invasion of France, in 1942, would end in failure. The evidence suggests that General Marshall's early push for the very risky cross-channel invasion in 1942 was premature. Churchill and British Army chief Alan Brooke got it right; neither Britain nor the United States was yet ready. Operation TORCH in North Africa, Operation HUSKY in Sicily, and Operation AVALANCHE in Italy—all from the sea—would prepare them for the immense waterborne invasion of France.

By February 1943, Beaverbrook complained that his relationship with Churchill had cooled: "I see Churchill seldom. I say that it is Churchill's fault, but Bracken says it is my fault. For my part I don't feel it is a good thing for me to be in close contact with him at present. It seems better that I should look on him as the peasants of Savoy look on Mont Blanc, with astonishment and admiration."[72] His reticence lasted two months. In May 1943, he would again accompany Churchill to New York aboard the *Queen Mary*—breaking a period of relative estrangement between the two men. When FDR invited Beaverbrook to join them at Camp Shangri-la for the weekend, Beaverbrook declined, writing back that "some of the [British] newspapers seek to associate me with the Prime Minister. And that always leads to complications for him in the British Parliament." Harry Hopkins called Beaverbrook and said: "The President of the United States is not in the habit of selecting his guests in deference to the sentiment of the British press or any other press."[73] In truth, he disagreed with Churchill at the time because he favored a speedy cross-channel invasion of France—and a second front to relieve Russia. The prime minister and General Alan Brooke at that moment advocated military operations in Italy. Beaverbrook reluctantly went to Camp Shangri-la—knowing that his support for the American position would infuriate the prime minister. He was right. Churchill was infuriated, but Beaverbrook, who had long favored opening a second front, was not intimidated by such disagreements.[74]

Lord Lothian, British ambassador, deposits the Magna Carta at the Library of Congress for safekeeping during the war, November 1939. Accepting the document, which was displayed opposite the Declaration of Independence and Constitution, is Librarian of Congress Archibald MacLeish.
LIBRARY OF CONGRESS

British Ambassador to the United States Lord Halifax (left) talks with Russian Ambassador Maxim Litvinov at a garden party in Washington, 1942.
LIBRARY OF CONGRESS

VIII

Lord Lothian and Lord Halifax

[T]here is a wave of pessimism passing over this country [the United States] to the effect that Great Britain must now inevitably be defeated, and that there is no use in the United States doing anything more to help it and thereby getting entangled in Europe. . . .There is some evidence that it is beginning to affect the President.[1]

***Philip Henry Kerr, Lord Lothian** (1882–1940), report to the Foreign Office, June 27, 1940. Prior to World War II, Lord Lothian had served in a variety of posts in government, journalism, and public affairs. He was appointed British Ambassador to the United States in 1939, in part because he was already well known among prominent Americans such as President Franklin Roosevelt. In the mid-1930s, Lothian had been a supporter of appeasement of Hitler. As ambassador, he became a key advocate for American military assistance to Britain, until he died suddenly in December 1940.*

It may well be that instead of studying closer union with France, we shall find ourselves contemplating the possibility of some sort of special association with the U.S.A.[2]

***Edward F. L. Wood, Earl of Halifax** (1881–1959), letter to Maurice Hanky, July 15, 1940. Halifax had been appointed foreign secretary in February 1938, after Anthony Eden resigned in a dispute with Prime Minister Neville Chamberlain over appeasement and negotiations with Italy. Halifax had supported Chamberlain's policy of accommodating Nazi Germany's territorial expansion. When the Chamberlain government fell in May 1940, Halifax remained the logical successor for most Tories and for King George VI. Halifax deferred to Winston Churchill, who kept him in his post until December, when he appointed Halifax to replace Lord Lothian as the ambassador to the United States. Eden, admired by Churchill, then returned to his old job as foreign secretary.*

Many British officials did not greet with approval Lord Lothian's original appointment, in 1939, as British ambassador to the United States, especially those in the

British Foreign Office. Lothian, however, had been a longtime friend of Foreign Minister Halifax, who thought Britain needed a higher profile in Washington.[3] Lothian had another influential supporter—the U.S. president, who did not want another colorless career diplomat to hold the post. Roosevelt knew and liked Lothian, even though he did not always agree with him. Lothian also had many friends in American academic and journalist circles.[4] Lothian, an aristocrat, had a common touch. The new ambassador "grasped that Americans were much taken with bluebloods exhibiting a just-plain-folks demeanor," wrote historian Joseph Persico. "Thus he wore a battered gray fedora, drove his own car, and bought his own train tickets when traveling in the United States."[5] Lothian also possessed a wry sense of humor. When American congressmen visited the British embassy, the ambassador would point to a painting on the stairs and announce that it was of "the Founder of the American Republic." Only after their quizzical looks appeared did Lothian add: "King George III."[6]

Lothian's shy and retiring predecessor, Ronald Lindsay, had held the post nearly a decade. In contrast to Lindsay, Lothian would practice public diplomacy—which he called "mutual education"—even though the British Foreign Office preferred private diplomacy. Historian David Reynolds noted that Lothian was well suited for his post; he "knew America and Americans as well as any living Briton in public life."[7] Lothian decided to open Anglo-American relations to frank discussion of the problems of Britain at war. Although not an inspiring speaker, he gave speeches designed to be reprinted, and thus to influence a wider audience.[8] Lothian could be erratic. The British ambassador could also be clear eyed; unlike other British officials, including Churchill, Lothian had no illusions that FDR's November 1940 reelection would free the president to enter the war at Britain's side.[9]

Lothian preferred an attention-grabbing style to safe, private diplomacy. Officials on both sides of the Atlantic worried about the consequences. Occasionally, his forthright style could be counterproductive—as it was in a speech at Yale University in mid-June 1940, in which he frankly warned that the United States should not expect to inherit the British fleet if Britain were defeated by Germany. Roosevelt wanted to buck up British morale and resolve, without getting America into the war. FDR wanted an America-first insurance policy, without having to pay high premiums with the lives of American soldiers. During the summer of 1940, an indecisive president doubted Britain's will and ability to withstand Hitler. He needed reports from agents like William Donovan to sustain his confidence. By August 1940, he decided that after victory in the air battle with the Luftwaffe, Britain had the will to fight and survive.[10] Mutual suspicions, however, continued to influence policy on both sides of the Atlantic. FDR weighed the political ramifications, with American isolationists, of a Destroyers-for-Bases deal that might appear overly generous to Britain. Still, Lothian pushed relentlessly ahead in negotiations. He was a marriage broker who worked hard to persuade the prospective bride and groom to agree to a transatlantic engagement.[11]

Lothian had suggested a Destroyers-for-Bases deal in late May 1940. At the time, Churchill did not embrace the proposal. In the summer of 1940, U.S. assumption of British bases in the Western Hemisphere came up again, in a conversation between Secretary of the Navy Henry Knox and Ambassador Lothian.[12] The prime minister, at one time wary of Lothian, became an admirer as he advanced the Destroyers-for-Bases negotiations and sought equipment to be built in America for the British military, on terms that would not bankrupt Britain. "Airy, viewy, aloof, dignified, censorious, yet in a light and gay manner, [Lothian] had always been good company," recalled Churchill. "Now, under the same hammer that smote upon us all, I found an earnest, deeply-stirred man. He was primed with every aspect and detail of the American attitude. He had won nothing but goodwill and confidence in Washington by his handling of the Destroyer-cum-Bases negotiations. He was fresh from intimate contact with the President, with whom he had established a warm personal friendship."[13]

During the summer of 1940, Lothian was the principal British negotiator with the Roosevelt administration. Several factors complicated the negotiations. FDR was timid, always rationalizing inaction by references to the Constitution, Congress, or American public opinion—worrying also that an arrangement that helped Britain, but did not provide a commensurate improvement in American security, would not be popular.[14] Furthermore, the Roosevelt administration—warned by Churchill—fretted about the future disposition of the British fleet in the event of a British defeat by Germany. In early June 1940, the British prime minister wrote Canadian Prime Minister Mackenzie King, who was close to the American president: "We must be careful not to let Americans view too complacently the prospect of a British collapse out of which they would get the British fleet and the guardianship of the British Empire, minus Great Britain."[15] The prime minister emphasized the danger to the United States if the British fleet fell into enemy hands, but he refused to make any agreement that might pledge the fleet to the United States *in extremis*. He then sent a series of instructions to Lord Lothian, designed to persuade the United States to act quickly. On June 6, a tough-minded Churchill wrote:

> If Great Britain broke under invasion, a pro-German Government might obtain far easier terms from Germany by surrendering the Fleet, thus making Germany and Japan masters of the New World. This dastard deed would not be done by His Majesty's present advisers, but if some Quisling Government were set up it is exactly what they would do, and perhaps the only thing they could do, and the President should bear this very clearly in mind. You should talk to him in this sense and thus discourage any complacent assumption on United States' part that they will pick up the *débris* of the British Empire by their present policy. On the contrary, they run the terrible risk that their sea-power will be completely over-matched.[16]

During these negotiations, the prime minister and the president had similar political problems. They had to get the best deal possible, while accommodating mutual self-interest. Churchill believed "that the survival of Britain is bound up with the survival of the United States."[17] He wrote that in early August, FDR pressed "to be assured that if Britain were overrun the Fleet would continue to fight for the Empire overseas and would not either be surrendered or sunk. This was, it was said, the argument which would have the most effect on Congress in the question of destroyers."[18] The prime minister was concerned about the impact of such a discussion on British public opinion. He wrote Foreign Secretary Halifax: "We have no intention of surrendering the British Fleet, or of sinking it voluntarily. . . . The nation would not tolerate any discussion of what we should do if our Island were overrun. Such a discussion, perhaps on the eve of an invasion, would be injurious to public morale, now so high."[19] Churchill meanwhile continued to flatter and press FDR directly to send Britain fifty old destroyers, in exchange for the lease of strategic British bases in the Western Hemisphere. At the end of August, he wrote to the president: "You ask, Mr. President, whether my statement in Parliament on June 4, 1940 about Great Britain never surrendering or scuttling her Fleet 'represents the settled policy of His Majesty's Government'. It certainly does."[20]

Unfortunately for Anglo-American relations, Britain lost an effective ambassador when Lord Lothian died suddenly on December 12, 1940. A devout Christian Scientist, Lothian declined to seek medical help for his health problems, which turned out to be uremia. The ambassador died after only 15 months in his post, and a few weeks after conferring in England with the prime minister at Chequers. Churchill would describe Lothian as a "singularly gifted and influential" diplomat whose death was "a personal shock."[21] Lothian was unusually forthright for a diplomat. Returning from England to LaGuardia Airport on November 23, 1940, Lothian is said to have told reporters bluntly and provocatively: "Britain's broke, it's your money we want."[22] Historian David Reynolds has doubted that Lothian ever stated those exact words, noting that press accounts quote him as saying "England will be grateful for any help. England needs planes, munitions, ships and perhaps a little financial help."[23] What is not in doubt is that Lothian aimed to remake the Anglo-American relationship. Churchill remonstrated with his ambassador: "I do not think it was wise to touch on very serious matters to reporters on the landing stage. It is safer to utter a few heartening generalities and leave the grave matters to be raised formally with the President or his chief lieutenants."[24] Lothian did not agree, writing Lord Halifax: "In this as in every other question the ultimate determinant is public opinion."[25] The straightforward Lothian never forgot that knowledgeable popular support must inform good public policy. President Roosevelt preferred to manipulate public opinion. He would stonewall any comment on further aid. After meeting with Lothian, the president was asked at a press conference on November 26 whether "the British Ambassador present[ed] any specific requests for additional help?" FDR replied: "I am sorry, I shall have to disappoint quite a number of papers; nothing was mentioned in that regard at all, not one single thing—ships or sealing wax or anything else."[26] The Americans and the British were on the cusp of an agreement.

Lothian's final contribution to the war effort was to persuade Churchill to write out a detailed picture of Britain's problems for FDR's consideration; Churchill would call it "one of the most important [letters] I ever wrote."[27] The missive was delivered to FDR in early December, while the president cruised the Caribbean aboard a U.S. warship—just days before Lothian's death. Churchill had labored long and hard to argue the case for American aid to Britain. Lothian had urged him to include more detail, but the prime minister resisted. The timing was important; Lothian wanted FDR to get the letter so he could read it on the leisurely cruise. FDR did linger over Churchill's memo, which spelled out how Britain could be helped. On December 16, after his return to Washington, FDR announced to the press: "Suppose my neighbour's house catches fire and I have a length of garden hose four or five hundred feet away. If he can take my garden hose and connect it up with his hydrant, I may help him to put out the fire. Now what do I do? I don't say to him before that operation, 'Neighbour, my garden hose cost me fifteen dollars; you have to pay me fifteen dollars for it.' No! What is the transaction that goes on? I don't want fifteen dollars—I want my garden hose back after the fire is over."[28] FDR had decided that Lend-Lease legislation would expand U.S. assistance to an insolvent Britain, on credit!

The president meanwhile wired King George VI his regrets on Lothian's death. The ambassador had been "well qualified to talk Roosevelt's language and, in turn, to interpret Roosevelt to Churchill," wrote FDR staffer Robert E. Sherwood. "He had been able to understand, as a less flexible Briton might have failed to do, the manifold domestic obstacles that beset Roosevelt's path and he most scrupulously avoided adding to the president's embarrassments by making excessive, impatient demands."[29] Until his death, Lothian had been a crucial advocate for expanding Anglo-American cooperation. Churchill now cast around for a new ambassador with the requisite status. The prime minister toyed with the potentially disastrous idea of drafting David Lloyd George.[30] The former prime minister, almost 78, had been an accommodationist toward Hitler in the mid-1930s, even considering negotiations with Hitler after the fall of France.

Eventually, the prime minister decided that Foreign Secretary Halifax, a holdover from the appeasement government of Neville Chamberlain, should go to Washington. Halifax had been Churchill's major rival to succeed Chamberlain. Historian John Lukacs wrote that in late May 1940, as France was collapsing, "Halifax chose to confront Churchill, whose single-minded combativeness he thought disastrous. He also knew that in thinking this he was not alone. There is no evidence that Halifax acted as leader of some kind of cabal, ready and willing to oust Churchill. But he thought that Churchill had to be curbed, to say the least—or, more precisely, diverted from a disastrous course."[31] After seven months working with Halifax at the Foreign Office, the prime minister decided he preferred Halifax in Washington to Halifax in London.[32] He rationalized his tactical move in his most artful prose: "For a Foreign Secretary to become an Ambassador marks in a unique manner the importance of the mission. His high character was everywhere respected, yet at the same time his record in the years before the war and the way in which events had moved left him exposed to much disapprobation and even hostility from the Labour side of our National coalition."[33] Churchill then chose Anthony Eden as foreign secretary.

Before Halifax departed for Washington, the prime minister praised him in a speech before the Pilgrims Society: "In Edward Halifax we have a man of light and leading, whose company is a treat and whose friendship it is an honour to enjoy. I have often disagreed with him in the twenty years I have known him in the rough and tumble of British politics, but I have always respected him and his actions because I know that courage and fidelity are the essence of his being."[34] Halifax, the "Holy Fox," was very cautious—a characteristic that he brought along to Washington. After Pearl Harbor, Churchill asked for an immediate visit to Washington in December 1941; FDR balked and Halifax counseled caution. After meeting with Roosevelt, Halifax wrote Churchill that FDR "was not quite sure if your coming here might not be rather too strong medicine in the immediate future for some of his public opinion that he still feels he has to educate up to the complete conviction of the oneness of the struggle against both Germany and Japan."[35]

Halifax had been reluctant to move to Washington. His wife was even more agitated about the move and the obvious demotion of her husband.[36] Churchill put the best gloss on the appointment when he wrote Roosevelt that the "relationship between our two countries, and also the contact with you, Mr. President, are of such supreme consequence to the outcome of the war that it is my duty to place at your side the most eminent of my colleagues, and one who knows the whole story as it unfolds at the summit."[37] When Halifax arrived in the United States aboard the battleship *King George V*, President Roosevelt went to Annapolis to greet the British diplomat.[38] "[T]he selection did not appear to be inspired," recalled British embassy official John Wheeler-Bennett. "To send to the United States at this juncture a great patrician, noted as a Master of Foxhounds, who in his political career had been closely identified with the expediency of Appeasement—even though, as Roy Jenkins has written, 'he lent dignity to a squalid policy'—did not at first glance seem to bristle with wisdom, more especially since he was to succeed the democratic, easygoing, informal and ever-accessible Lord Lothian."[39]

After some initial awkward moves, Halifax settled into his job—more effectively because the courtly ambassador was "congenial to both Roosevelt and Hopkins."[40] Halifax had difficulty understanding the loose and disorganized decision-making at the Roosevelt White House, and the intrapersonnel conflicts that split the U.S. government. "Their Government seems to me quite baffling," observed the aristocratic ambassador. "I suppose it is rather like a disorderly line of beaters out shooting; they do put the rabbits out of the bracken, but they don't come out where you expect."[41] Historian J. Garry Clifford noted that Halifax was confounded by the American government: "He expressed amazement at the deference President Franklin D. Roosevelt seemed to pay to every ripple of public opinion. He was aghast at the distance and suspicion that separated the White House and Congress along Pennsylvania Avenue.

Nor could he make sense of the institutional crosscurrents and personal rivalries among the various executive departments."[42] In April 1941, the British ambassador wrote the prime minister: "The President seems to me all out to be helpful, and I thought it was friendly of him the other night to ring me himself to tell me that they could take the ships you wanted them to repair. But every day that I am here makes me see more and more how terribly disjointed is the whole machine of government. I don't think the President ties up awfully well; I am quite sure Harry Hopkins doesn't."[43] Halifax did not change his opinion 16 years later, calling Roosevelt "a very adroit manipulator, without doubt a very astute politician." FDR was not, in Halifax's opinion, "a very great man."[44]

Embassy aide John Wheeler-Bennett observed that "Halifax came at a moment when . . . the status of ambassador was on the wane" because of the direct relationship that Roosevelt and Churchill established, bypassing usual diplomatic channels. Wheeler-Bennett noted that the Placentia Bay conference, in August 1941, "ushered a new and far more personal element into the conduct of Anglo-American relations. From thenceforward the President and Prime Minister pursued the course of their policies for the prosecution of the war on terms of close intimacy; an intimacy which sometimes resulted in cabinet colleagues, Chiefs of Staff and ambassadors being informed rather than consulted. Philip Lothian could not, I believe, have tolerated such a situation; Lord Halifax accommodated himself to it with facility."[45] Still, Halifax was a key player in Churchill's efforts to stage-manage America's entry into the war. After meeting with FDR in September 1941, Halifax recorded that the president's "perpetual problem was to steer a course between . . . (1) the wish of 70% of Americans to keep out of war; (2) the wish of 70% of Americans to do everything to break Hitler, even if it means war. He said that if he asked for a declaration of war he wouldn't get it, and opinion would swing against him. He therefore intended to go on doing whatever he best could do to help us, and declarations of war were out of fashion."[46]

Because Halifax was not among those whom Roosevelt invited to share his mini-vacations at Camp Shangri-la in Maryland, or at Springwood, the Roosevelt home in Hyde Park, the ambassador was at a disadvantage when it came to personal interactions with the American president. This reality became clear when Churchill came to Washington after Pearl Harbor. The first substantive meeting of the new allies took place in late December 1941, when the prime minister took up temporary residence at the White House. Historian Andrew Roberts wrote that "on New Year's Day 1942, Halifax recorded that Roosevelt and Churchill were consulting in Churchill's bedroom, while he and Beaverbrook were waiting on a box in the corridor and Harry Hopkins was 'floating past in a dressing-gown'. The Ambassador can be forgiven for thinking it 'the oddest ménage anybody has ever seen'."[47] The persuasive power of the prime minister—in private and public—was recognized by Washington journalist David Lawrence, who wrote in his diary of Churchill's first visit to Washington: "Mr. Churchill has impressed official Washington, and this goes for all parties and factions. He has been a morale builder of incalculable value to the whole war cause.

His long experience with the war itself, his calmness and confidence in the future are a needed tonic at this stage of the game as America sees herself defeated in the Far East for the time being." He added: "Mr. Roosevelt sees eye to eye with Churchill that the big chance to crack Hitler lies in Europe and that, if Germany cracks, Japan will be easy picking for the combined British and American naval and air forces."[48]

Like his American counterparts, Halifax could be exhausted by the demands of a Churchill visit to America. The ambassador wrote of Churchill in Washington on June 18, 1942: "Winston arrived at 8 P.M., and I brought him to dine and sleep at the Embassy. He was rather put out at the President being away, and inclined to be annoyed that he hadn't been diverted to New York. . . . He got into a better temper when he had had some champagne, and we sat and talked, he doing as usual most of it, until 1.30 A.M." Generals Brooke and Ismay nodded off on the porch of the embassy as Churchill pontificated.[49] Similarly, Halifax wrote of Churchill's May 1943 visit: "Winston came to dine last night, having proposed himself with a party of Averells, Hopkinses and sisters etc., and sat drinking whiskeys and sodas and jawing, sometimes quite well, but at the end not at all, til 1.30 A.M. Isn't that pretty criminal? . . . I am sure his being here is immensely valuable for the war and for his getting to know the President so well, and all that. And I am fond of him; but I shall be glad when the visit comes to an end and we can settle down to work again!"[50]

The prime minister had developed consistent habits of official work during decades of holding high office. "When Churchill visited Washington his practice of holding private conferences with the President, sometimes late at night, when matters of high policy were decided, was liable to make the Ambassador's position an unenviable one," wrote one Halifax biographer. "As Roosevelt did not want the informality of these meetings to be impaired by the presence of members of the State Department, the Ambassador was also often excluded from them. . . . [I]t was Edward's [Lord Halifax's] misfortune that this necessity should weaken his own position as the local representative. This exclusion was in itself a matter of small concern as he greatly disliked late nights, but he was sometimes mortified by the fact that the major decisions were made about which he had not been consulted, and the nature of which he only later discovered."[51] Even Army Chief of Staff Marshall was often left in the dark. He had to rely on the British military liaison in Washington, John Dill, to keep him up to date by way of dispatches that Dill received from London.

The pragmatic Halifax accepted the good with the bad. After the prime minister's visits to Washington in May 1943, Halifax wrote that Churchill "was in good shape here, and with all his fault of egocentricity—and total lack of the right sort of humility—and utter inconsiderateness for anybody but himself, I do take off my hat to the sheer confidence, vitality and vision of the man. It's that that gives him his strength, and that has really impressed people here. The force of it just wells up. There is nothing artificial about it, and the stream seems quite inexhaustible."[52] Halifax remained ever cautious, Churchill ever impish. When Halifax warned Churchill that he might encounter questions about repayment of Lend-Lease when he appeared on Capitol Hill before the joint congressional foreign relations committees, Churchill responded: "Oh, I shall like that one. I shall say, yes by all means let us have an account if we can get it reasonably accurate, but I shall have my account to put in too, and my account is for holding the baby [Hitler] alone for eighteen months, and it was a very rough brutal baby I had to hold. I don't quite know what I shall have to charge for it."[53]

Observing Lord Halifax, Lord Beaverbrook was envious of his position. His ambitions turned repeatedly to a post in Washington. Biographer Kenneth Young wrote: "Lothian, to Beaverbrook's way of thinking, had never had a proper appreciation of the American dilemma nor an understanding of Americans. Now that he was dead, there was, he believed, a chance to remedy this; and it is not surprising to find Beaverbrook himself among the names . . . being bandied about in the newspapers as possible successors."[54] Instead, it was Beaverbrook himself—at Churchill's request—who on December 17, 1940, had informed Lord Halifax of the proposal for Halifax to succeed Lord Lothian. That did not stop Beaverbrook, a few months later, from believing that he himself should succeed Halifax in Washington. Even after he lost his personal ambition for the post, Beaverbrook persisted in his criticism of Halifax, writing Churchill in July 1943: "The American Presidential Election depends largely on the good opinion there of Britain. Lord Halifax is incapable in disposition of bringing any influence to bear on the American newspapers."[55] Beaverbrook then pushed Brendan Bracken, a Churchill intimate and former newspaperman, as the proper replacement. Bracken, however, remained as Churchill's minister of information until after the German surrender. Halifax would remain in Washington until 1946. Beaverbrook would get other assignments.

Prime Minister Churchill and President Roosevelt at a joint press conference in the Oval Office sixteen days after Pearl Harbor.
FRANKLIN D. ROOSEVELT PRESIDENTIAL LIBRARY

IX

Pearl Harbor

Hostilities exist. There is no blinking at the fact that our people, our territory and our interests are in grave danger. With confidence in our armed forces, with the unbounding determination of our people, we will gain the inevitable triumph, so help us God. I ask that the Congress declare that since the unprovoked and dastardly attack by Japan on Sunday, December 7, 1941, a state of war has existed between the United States and the Japanese Empire.[1]

***Franklin D. Roosevelt**, speech to Congress, December 8, 1941.*

We are at the turning point now. The German army is tired out. Its commanders had hoped to end the war before winter and did not make the necessary preparations for the winter campaign. The German army today is poorly dressed, poorly led and losing morale. Meanwhile, the USSR has prepared large reinforcements and put them into action in recent weeks. . . . We are advancing and will continue to advance on all fronts.[2]

***Joseph Stalin**, conversation with Anthony Eden, December 16, 1941. From 1922 until a few months before his death in March 1953, Stalin was general secretary of the Central Committee of the Communist Party of the Soviet Union. After the death in 1924 of Vladimir Lenin (from whom Stalin had become increasingly alienated), Stalin consolidated his hold on the Communist Party and the Soviet Union. A series of purges in the 1930s exterminated his opposition and much of the Soviet officer corps. In August 1939, Stalin approved a Soviet-German non-aggression pact. Despite repeated warnings from the United States and Britain, Stalin ignored signs of the impending Nazi invasion that took place in June 1941. At first poorly led by a politicized officer corps, the Soviet army suffered immense casualties during the German invasion. From 1941 until his death, Stalin was chairman of the Council of Ministers. From 1941 until 1946, he was also people's commissar for defense. The consensus of scholars is that Stalin was a totalitarian dictator, every bit as ruthless as Hitler, who learned much from Stalin's methods of the 1920s and 1930s.*

Ambassador John Winant went to Anthony Eden's country home late on Saturday, December 6. "He [Eden] was to leave for Moscow on Sunday morning, taking with him a memorandum for Marshal Stalin which he hoped might be the basis of a joint statement on war aims and plans for post-war organization of peace." Winant recalled: "This [joint statement] conformed with the fundamental principles of the Atlantic Charter to which the Russians had agreed at the Inter-Allied Conference on September 24, 1941. Mr. Eden had shown this memorandum to me in its original form in order to get a judgment on the reactions in the United States. Since then the Cabinet had made certain changes which he wanted me to know about." Ambassador Winant arrived at Eden's house, ate, then discussed the foreign secretary's trip to Moscow. Rather than accept his invitation to stay while Eden departed for Moscow, Winant said he wanted to visit Churchill in case the Japanese attacked the United States. On Sunday, the foreign secretary left for Russia, and the ambassador drove to Chequers, where he found the prime minister pacing outside the house. Churchill asked Winant if there would be war between the United States and Japan. When Winant replied in the affirmative, the prime minister erupted: "If they declare war on you, we shall declare war on them within the hour." The more cautious American replied: "I understand, Prime Minister. You have stated that publicly."[3]

Winant remained at Chequers, along with Averell Harriman and his daughter Kathleen. On Sunday night, recalled Winant:

> It was a few minutes before nine o'clock when we went into the dining room. The Prime Minister looked very grim and sat in complete silence. It was his custom to listen to the nine o'clock broadcast which usually gave the fullest summary of the day's news. Just before the hour struck, he roused himself and called out to [valet Frank] Sawyers, the butler, to put the radio on the table. It was a small fifteen-dollar portable set that Harry Hopkins had sent him after his return to the United States. The Prime Minister reached out his hand and raised the lid that set it going. For a moment there was a jangle of music, and then suddenly, from the little black box, a voice announced that Japan had attacked our fleet at Pearl Harbor.

The BBC reported: "The news has just been given that Japanese aircraft have raided Pearl Harbor, the American naval base at Hawaii. The announcement of the attack was made in a brief statement by President Roosevelt. Naval and military targets on the principal Hawaiian island of Oahu have been attacked. No further details are yet available."[4] Churchill himself recalled that he had "lifted the lid of the pocket wireless which Harriman gave me. The nine o'clock news had started. At the end there was something about the Japanese attacking American shipping. It wasn't very clear, and I didn't realize what had happened when Sawyers came into the room. He said: 'It's quite true. We heard it ourselves outside. The Japs have attacked the Americans.'"[5] Winant wrote:

> Even allowing for the difference in time, it meant that the radio had got the momentous news to the Prime Minister of Great Britain two hours later, but before the intelligence services of either country had been able to inform the British High Command.

> We looked at one another incredulously. Then Churchill jumped to his feet and started for the door with the announcement, "We shall declare war on Japan." There is nothing half-hearted or unpositive about Churchill—certainly not when he is on the move. Without ceremony I, too, left the table and followed him out of the room. "Good God," I said, "you can't declare war on a radio announcement."[6]

Ambassador Winant called President Roosevelt and put Prime Minister Churchill on the phone, telling FDR that he had "a friend" with him who wanted to speak with the president. A little later, Foreign Minister Eden called the prime minister to ask if he should postpone his trip to Russia. Churchill urged Eden to continue to board the destroyer and sail to Murmansk.[7] Drafting his memoirs, Churchill wrote: "No American will think it wrong of me if I proclaim that to have the United States at our side was to me the greatest joy." He recalled: "I went to bed and slept the sleep of the saved and thankful."[8] Churchill's draft recollections did not make it into print. Instead, Churchill wrote in *The Grand Alliance* that after he had hung up with FDR, "We then went back into the hall and tried to adjust our thoughts to the supreme world event which had occurred, which was of so startling a nature as to make even those who were near centre gasp. My two American friends took the shock with admirable fortitude. We had no idea that any serious losses had been inflicted on the United States Navy. They did not wail or lament that their country was at war. They wasted no words in reproach or sorrow. In fact, one might almost have thought they had been delivered from a long pain."[9]

In Washington, Harry Hopkins had been sitting with the president on the evening of December 6, when Roosevelt received an intercept of a message to Japan's Washington embassy. "This means war," FDR told Hopkins, after reading the transcript regarding the Japanese termination of settlement negotiations in the United States. Hopkins himself had only recently come back to his White House work after one of his periodic hospital stays. The next day, Hopkins was taking lunch with Roosevelt in the Oval Room on the second floor of the White House, when word of the attack on Pearl Harbor reached them. "We were talking about things far removed from war when at about 1:40 Secretary Knox called and said that they had picked up a radio from Honolulu from the Commander-in-Chief of our forces there advising all our stations that an air raid attack was on and that it was 'no drill.' I expressed the belief that there must be some mistake and that surely Japan would not attack Honolulu," wrote Hopkins, who had just been released from a month-long stay in a military hospital. For the next 11 hours, the White House was a whirl of activity, as President Roosevelt prepared to appear before Congress the following day to ask for a declaration of war against Japan. Japanese aircraft had destroyed four battleships and 188 planes at Pearl Harbor. FDR was determined, according to Hopkins, "to submit a precise message and had in mind submitting a longer message later."[10] Roosevelt rejected suggestions from the cabinet, led by Secretary Hull, that he submit a more detailed explanation of events.[11]

"The President, stunned and incredulous at first, quickly regained the poise that always marked him in moments of crisis," recalled FDR's physician, Ross T. McIntire.[12] The president had clearly been shocked by the attack, as well as by the extent of the devastation. Robert Jackson, by then a Supreme Court Justice, recalled "that with all the war talk there had been, he [FDR] did not believe Japan would make a surprise attack. Of course it was a great embarrassment to him. . . . Here, on an exposed perimeter of the country, nobody apparently was anticipating any difficulty. I think it was a great jolt to him."[13] But historians William L. Langer and S. Everett Gleason wrote that "the President, Secretary Hull, and their associates were all acutely aware of the probability of a surprise attack. However, none of them expected it at Pearl Harbor."[14] Neither did FDR's top spy, Bill Donovan, who had to be recalled from a New York football game to meet with the president, and admit that he too was clueless.[15]

There were, however, confused signals within the Roosevelt cabinet. Secretary of State Hull complained to Arthur Krock of the *New York Times* that Interior Secretary Ickes had inspired "newspapermen to write that Ickes had seen the Japanese threat from the beginning, had urged total embargoes and other forceful acts, but was opposed by [Hull], who had hoped to appease the unappeasable."[16] Pearl Harbor had embarrassingly revealed the failure of the country's commander in chief and the Roosevelt administration, despite anticipating war with Japan, to gear up adequately for the conflict.[17] "If the Army and Navy were unprepared for war, the State Department was no less so," observed Dean Acheson. He politely wrote after the war that the State Department "did not chart a course to be furthered by the success of our arms, or to aid or guide our arms. Rather it seems to have been adrift, carried hither and yon by the currents of war or pushed about by collisions with more purposeful craft."[18]

For much of 1941, Roosevelt and Hull had tried to avert the outbreak of hostilities with Japan, even while embargoing Japanese access to necessary imports such as oil, needed to fuel their defense industry and well-known war preparations. The Japanese government may have perceived the U.S. oil embargo, among other restrictions, as *casus belli* at a time and place of their choosing. FDR believed that the United States was not prepared for a two-ocean navy and that time was necessary to ramp up a planned two-ocean navy and American opinion. Indeed, America was not yet prepared for a one-ocean war. Although the president had made decisions in violation of the spirit and the letter of the Neutrality Acts, which clearly indicated that Japan and Germany were enemies, FDR perhaps deceived himself that his belligerent initiatives were not occasions for war. "Let us make no move of ill will," the president belatedly told the secretary of state in early November 1941. "Let us do nothing to precipitate a crisis."[19] Still, the *de facto* oil embargo, imposed on Japan in August, had intensified the developing war crisis with Japan. It is true that the Navy and War Departments warned commanders in Pearl Harbor and the Philippines on

November 27 of a Japanese attack. When the Japanese attacked shortly before 8 A.M. Sunday morning, December 7, they not only caught American military personnel in Hawaii unprepared, despite warnings, but they also caught the American government by surprise. FDR was highly distressed, perhaps shamed by the events. "It was obvious to me that Roosevelt was having a dreadful time just accepting the idea," wrote Secretary of Labor Frances Perkins.[20] For months, Roosevelt had avoided making provocative armed defensive moves despite what he believed to be an inevitable conflict with Japan. He had told Hopkins on December 6, as he had earlier ruled out an American preemptive first strike: "We are a democracy and a peaceful people."[21] But American public opinion had become increasingly belligerent toward Japan amid its ruthless aggression against China and Southeast Asia. Furthermore, FDR had promised Ambassador Halifax a few days earlier that in the event of a Japanese attack in Southeast Asia, Britain could count on American support.[22] "All of us believed that in the last analysis the enemy was Hitler," wrote Hopkins defensively after the Pearl Harbor attack, "and that he could never be defeated without force of arms; that sooner or later we were bound to be in the war and that Japan had given us an opportunity."[23] This may have been Hopkins's rationalization for a bad outcome for which FDR, Hopkins, and the American government, with the knowledge they had, might have been better prepared.

All the Allies—Britain, Russia, and the United States—at different times had been unprepared for war, despite clear warnings they had received. The British and the French, already at war since September 1939, had been caught relatively unprepared for the Blitzkrieg in May 1940. Stalin and therefore Russia had been caught unprepared for the German invasion in June 1941. The U.S. government was unprepared for a war FDR had expected. Though Roosevelt was shocked and embarrassed, he was resolute. "In the days that followed Pearl Harbor," recalled Roosevelt's physician, "he was by far and away the least emotional of all those who gathered in the White House for consultation."[24] Knowing all he knew in advance, FDR may not have been so surprised. Thus, he was emotionally ready for the conflict. "At 8:30 P.M. that fateful Pearl Harbor Sunday, members of Roosevelt's Cabinet began to gather in his White House study," wrote World War II intelligence expert David Stafford. "Normally he greeted them warmly, deploying his legendary charm and friendliness. Tonight he was withdrawn and silent, hardly noticing them at all."[25]

Like Churchill, the president did benefit from having the right people in the right place to reinforce the Anglo-American relationship and to smooth difficulties between the two countries. For example, CBS London bureau chief Edward R. Murrow waited at the White House on December 7, 1941, for an informal dinner with the Roosevelts, while the president managed the Pearl Harbor crisis. Murrow's *This Is London* broadcasts to the United States had been unapologetically pro-British. Murrow "was concerned, very concerned that his own country wasn't aware of the facts of life," recalled a friend. "And that if Hitler & Co. were not stopped here, the next stop was Manhattan."[26] After dining with the First Lady over scrambled eggs, Murrow finally got in to see the president and spy chief Donovan after midnight. To the broadcaster, Roosevelt expressed his anger that American planes had been destroyed "on the ground" at Pearl Harbor.[27] To Donovan, Roosevelt said: "They caught our ships like lame ducks! Lame ducks, Bill!"[28] Some ships and planes at Pearl Harbor and bombers in the Philippines were destroyed. It is unfair to blame FDR for not anticipating the Japanese attack precisely at Pearl Harbor. Indeed, Pearl Harbor and the Philippines should have been prepared by the Navy and War Department warnings. But it is implausible to believe that FDR did not feel embarrassed and thus a certain responsibility for the dead soldiers and sailors at Pearl Harbor.[29]

The historian can never penetrate FDR's inner thoughts, even if he can know the facts and circumstances of the Japanese-American rivalry and the imminent threat of war in the Pacific in December 1941. But if war were to come at the initiative of Japan, all knew it must come by sea or air in the Pacific. All knew the Pacific fleet had been moved from protected San Diego to exposed Hawaii. Would not a former, highly competent, well-informed assistant secretary of the navy instinctively avoid such a strategic danger in advance? Clio, the muse of history, cannot answer this question. But she must surely ask it.

"Thinking of you much at this historic moment," Churchill and Harriman cabled Hopkins shortly after they received the news of Pearl Harbor. In subsequent days, the prime minister pressed FDR to allow him to come to the United States for consultations. Initially reluctant, Roosevelt relented. Churchill, accompanied by Harriman and Beaverbrook, crossed the Atlantic by battleship to America. On December 22, FDR's press secretary told the White House press corps: "Gentlemen, the Prime Minister of Great Britain, Mr. Churchill, is now with Mr. Roosevelt in the White House. He arrived by air, and the President met him at an airport near Washington."[30] Many of the key decision makers of the Anglo-American alliance had gathered at the White House shortly before Christmas. "The President punctiliously made the preliminary cocktails himself," recalled the prime minister, "and I wheeled him in his chair from the drawing room as a mark of respect."[31]

At a White House meeting on December 22, Churchill and Roosevelt were joined by Beaverbrook, Halifax, Hopkins, Hull, and Welles. Military leaders, who were not present, subsequently learned that Churchill and Roosevelt had supposedly decided that reinforcements for the Philippines might be diverted to Singapore. Historian Kenneth S. Davis wrote that Marshall and Eisenhower "saw this as a yielding by Roosevelt to the British willingness to sacrifice the Philippines to the defense of Singapore. They went at once in high dudgeon to Secretary Stimson. Stimson at once phoned Harry Hopkins to say that if the President persisted in this kind of decision-making, he would have to find a new secretary of war. Hopkins, shortly thereafter, when he, Churchill, and FDR were alone together, told the two heads of government what Stimson had said. Roosevelt and the prime minister then flatly denied that they had made any agreement on this matter."[32]

At the end of this ARCADIA conference in Washington, Hopkins wrote Clementine Churchill: "You would have been quite proud of your husband on this trip. First because he was ever so good-natured. I didn't see him take anybody's head off and he eats and drinks with his customary vigor, and still dislikes the same people. If he had half as good a time here as the President did having him about the White House he surely will carry pleasant memories of the past three weeks."[33]

British Foreign Secretary Anthony Eden talks with U.S. Secretary of State Cordell Hull at the Moscow summit, October 1943.
U.S. DEPARTMENT OF STATE

X

Anthony Eden

Mr. Churchill did not like to give his time to anything not exclusively concerned with the conduct of the war. This seemed to be a deep instinct in him and, even though it was part of his strength as a war leader, it could also be an embarrassment.[1]

Anthony Eden *(1897–1977), in his memoirs. After distinguished service in the British Army during World War I, Eden began a career in Conservative Party politics and government. In 1935, he was named foreign secretary in the government of Prime Minister Neville Chamberlain. He resigned in a policy dispute in 1938, as he became more opposed to Chamberlain's policy of appeasement of Fascist Italy. When Winston Churchill became prime minister in May 1940, Eden was named secretary of war. When Lord Halifax was moved to the British embassy in Washington at the end of 1940, Eden returned as foreign secretary. He was generally considered Churchill's heir apparent.*

Winston Churchill's strength lay in his vigorous sense of purpose and courage, which carried him undismayed over obstacles daunting to lesser men. He was also generous and impulsive, but this could be a handicap at the conference table. Churchill liked to talk, he did not like to listen, and he found it difficult to wait for, and seldom let pass, his turn to speak. The spoils in the diplomatic game do not necessarily go to the man most eager to debate.[2]

Anthony Eden *(1897–1977) in his memoirs.*

Winston Churchill's partner in foreign policy was Anthony Eden, a traditional diplomat who had resigned in 1938, in a dispute with Prime Minister Chamberlain over policy toward Mussolini. Had Eden stayed as foreign secretary, he might have been the logical Tory, instead of Churchill, to replace Chamberlain in 1940. Eden was well respected by the Conservative Party; Churchill was not. Churchill entered Parliament in 1900, as a Tory. In 1904, he crossed over to the Liberal Party, subsequently indicting the Conservative Party in every significant respect. In 1924, he crossed over again to the Tories. Staunch Conservatives thought him an opportunistic renegade. They still did not trust him in 1940.[3]

Although the prime minister and Eden would have disagreements—especially over relations with French General Charles de Gaulle—they worked well together. Churchill kept Eden far better informed of his initiatives than FDR did the State Department. The prime minister wrote of his diplomatic correspondence: "Having obtained from the Cabinet any specific decisions required on policy. . . . I was of course hand-in-glove with the Foreign Secretary and his department, and any differences of view were settled together."[4] He would make the decorous, tall diplomat his right hand and frequent troubleshooter—especially in representing Britain's interests on crucial trips that the prime minister could not make.[5]

On February 21, 1941, Churchill dispatched newly appointed Foreign Secretary Eden to Cairo: "During his visit to the Mediterranean theatre the Foreign Secretary will represent His Majesty's Government in all matters diplomatic and military."[6] When Eden was away or sick, the prime minister assumed Eden's duties in addition to his own. Such a wartime burden had no precedent, but he soldiered on. In 1942, Churchill told King George that Eden was his designated replacement, should the prime minister die or become incapacitated. The prime minister considered his relationship with Eden to be paternal. Eden aide Oliver Harvey wrote in his diary on October 9, 1941: "A.E. dined with P.M. last night. They had a long and intimate evening. 'I regard you as my son' Winston said—'I do not get in your way nor you in mine'."[7] Harvey wrote in his diary on July 24, 1942: "The relation of P.M. to A.E. is father to son and heir, but the others are left out in the cold and there is risk of A.E. becoming himself isolated from his own age group of colleagues."[8] Eden wrote that Churchill told him, in April 1943: "I was his chief lieutenant and only really intimate friend among his colleagues and that, though he would hate to lose me, etc., etc. In short Winston's imagination has clearly caught fire, encouraged no doubt by the difficulty of finding anybody else and by the fun of reconstructing his government which he proceeded to do straight away!"[9]

At the outset of his government in May 1940, Churchill as prime minister had thought it inexpedient to remove Lord Halifax as foreign secretary. He thus appointed Eden as secretary of state for war, rather than return him to the Foreign Office, where Eden had served from 1935 to 1938. When Eden became foreign secretary in December 1940, the prime minister cross-examined him in order to be sure he had the right man. As secretary of war, Eden had traveled at Churchill's request to the Middle East in October 1940, to review the political and military situation, just as Italy was preparing to attack Greece. Before Eden departed, Churchill instructed him on the efficient use of British military personnel:

> Please examine in detail the field state of the Middle Eastern Army in order to secure the largest proportion of fighting men and units for the great numbers on our ration strength. . . . All British battalions should be mobile and capable of taking part in battle. I fear that the proportion of fighting compared with ration strength is worse in the Middle East than anywhere else. Please do not be content with stock answers. Even Army Ordnance and Service Corps depots and other technical details can all help in

keeping order where they are, and should be organized for use in an emergency. Not only the best, but the second and third best, must be made to play their part.[10]

Here, Churchill attended to the details of full mobilization of fighting men in the Middle East. The prime minister believed in the doctrine of every soldier a fighting man, equipped to engage the enemy. From his experience in World War I, Churchill well understood modern warfare, even total war. He nevertheless had difficulty adjusting to the scale of manpower needed for logistical support in World War II.

Eden returned to London at the beginning of November 1940, bringing with him news of British plans by General Archibald Wavell for a bold and preemptive attack on Italian divisions massing for an onslaught on the British in Egypt. Churchill was clearly delighted by news of the proposed Operation COMPASS. Churchill recalled: "Here, then, was the deadly secret which the Generals had talked over with their Secretary of State. This was what they had not wished to telegraph. We were delighted. I purred like six cats."[11] General Wavell got enthusiastic permission to proceed with the attack, which would become one of the very rare British successes in the first two years of World War II. But victory over the Italian troops was a different matter from the coming struggles with superior German forces that Britain would face in 1941 and 1942.

Anthony Eden seemed prepared by central casting to represent his country in diplomatic affairs. "Eden was the very image of a British gentleman in appearance, speech and manners," wrote historian S. M. Plokhy.[12] Eden grew close to U.S. Ambassador Winant, the Lincoln look-alike. They developed an excellent working relationship in early 1941, soon after they assumed their respective offices. "We used to go down occasionally on a Sunday to his country house in Sussex," noted Winant. "It was not different from London as far as the work load was concerned, and we had the same long hours hooked up to a 'scrambler' telephone, but instead of a room and a desk we used to go out into the garden." Winant argued that Eden's "entire foreign policy was based upon a high conception of moral right."[13] In wartime, Eden would be called upon to do things that diminished his self-esteem and his high-minded values.

The Eden-Churchill relationship itself was not without strains. Eden aide Oliver Harvey wrote in his diary, on August 4, 1941: "A.E. told me today that he had been over to Chequers on Saturday—as I had expected—P.M. was most penitent, apologising for having kept him so long and even saying 'Yes, I'm afraid sometimes I do talk rather a lot. I'm quite ashamed of myself!'"[14] Five months later, Harvey wrote in his diary that Eden was "perturbed at P.M. himself who is again showing increasing signs of weary and dictatorial behaviour."[15] But there were warm, intimate moments as well. Eden wrote Churchill on his birthday in November 1940: "Very few men in all history have had to bear such a burden as you have carried in the last six months. It is really wonderful that at the end of it you are fitter & more vigorous, and better able than ever to guide & inspire us all."[16]

More than most cabinet colleagues, Eden could stand up to Churchill. Historian David Dilks noted that the World War I veteran stood out in London, "which abounded in people who were on the point of waxing valiant before the Prime Minister but was less full of those who had actually steeled themselves to this feat, which did require no mean degree of courage."[17] On one occasion in February 1943, Private Secretary John Martin conspired with Foreign Secretary Eden to delay a Churchill telegram to Harold Macmillan, then minister resident in Northwest Africa. When Eden talked to Churchill about it the next day, Churchill was incensed: "By what right do you interfere with my private correspondence?" Eden recalled in his memoirs that Churchill asserted "that he was not dead yet and would send any telegrams he chose." Eden was concerned that Churchill's pneumonia was affecting his thinking. Later that day, Eden returned to see the bedridden Churchill. "Oh, by the way," said Churchill after dealing with other topics, "you remember that message I intended to send? Perhaps we had better not send it."[18] Eden aide Harvey wrote in his diary, on July 14, 1943, of the frequent arguments that characterized the Eden-Churchill relationship: "A reconciliation! I'm beginning to know the form now. Frightful rows, nervous exhaustion on both sides, then next day a rather contrite P.M. seeking to make up, like a schoolboy who knows he's been naughty, rather shamefaced, needing much face-saving."[19]

Eden travelled much more than his American counterparts.[20] He was a frequent traveling partner of Churchill, but he often travelled solo. When Roosevelt made his plans for the Casablanca Conference of January 1943, FDR made clear that he did not intend to bring Secretary of State Hull: "My thought would be that each of us could be accompanied by a very small staff made up of our top Army, Air, and Naval Chiefs of Staff. I could bring Harry [Hopkins] and Averell [Harriman] but no State Department representative, although I believe we should arrive at tentative procedures to be adopted in event of a German collapse."[21] German collapse would not come until two long years in the future. A few days later, FDR added: "In view of Stalin's absence, I think you and I need no Foreign Affairs people with us, for our work will be essentially military."[22] FDR told Averell Harriman that "Hull was forceful, stubborn, difficult to handle. He had some rigid ideas and Roosevelt felt he would be a nuisance at the conference."[23] As a result, Eden was left in London to handle de Gaulle and manage de Gaulle's visit to Casablanca. There, during the summit, in an effort to unite the French opposition to Vichy and the Nazis, the prime minister and the president brought about a "marriage" between de Gaulle and General Henri Giraud.

"Soviet policy is amoral; United States policy is exaggeratedly moral, at least where non-American interests are concerned," Eden wrote in January 1942.[24] The foreign secretary was more focused on relations with Russia than Churchill, but the key Russians did not respect him. Years later, Russian Foreign Minister Vyacheslav Molotov would describe Eden as "spineless, too delicate, quite helpless," but "I could deal with him."[25] In December 1941, Stalin had pressed Eden for British recognition of Russia's borders, including the Baltic states established after the 1939 Molotov-Ribbentrop agreement. Eden demurred; Churchill balked. The Americans were highly reluctant to make any such commitment, but were also unwilling to act decisively to block Stalin. After a March 1942 meeting at the White House, Halifax reported to Eden that FDR "proposed to tell Stalin that, while everyone recognized Russia's need for security, it was too dangerous to put anything on paper, now. But there was no need to worry about the Baltic states since their future clearly depended on Russian military progress and, if Russia reoccupied them, neither the United

States, nor Britain, could or would turn her out."[26] The president had given Stalin the green light. At the end of the war, both Britain and the United States recognized the Baltic takeover by the Soviet Union as a *fait accompli*.[27]

In early February 1943, Churchill suggested that Eden visit Washington, a trip that had been under discussion in London since the previous summer. FDR, who had met Eden when he was foreign secretary under Neville Chamberlain, replied: "This is an excellent thought about Anthony Eden. Delighted to have him. The sooner the better."[28] Eden visited the United States in March, and initially impressed President Roosevelt with the "progressive" nature of his worldview.[29] FDR wrote Churchill: "Anthony has spent three evenings with me. He is a grand fellow, and we are talking everything, from Ruthenia to the production of peanuts!" He added: "It is an interesting fact that we seem to agree on about 95 per cent of all the subjects—not a bad average."[30] Roosevelt thought Eden "the nicest type of Englishman, very clever. He thinks he sees the future as F.D.R. sees it, but is not sure that he has the strength to go against conservatives in England," reported FDR companion Margaret Suckley. "Winston Churchill of course would not ever 'see' much beyond the British Empire. A.E. told the P. that the P. will have to run for a 4th term—'We need you in the peace conference.'"[31] Talking to Hopkins in Washington in March 1943, Eden recognized that FDR "loves Winston as a man for the war, but is horrified at his reactionary attitude for after the war."[32] A few months later, Suckley wrote that the president had changed his mind about Eden, writing that the president "had great hopes that Anthony Eden would be a progressive and helpful in the post-war world, [but] after seeing A.E. in Canada, he feels he is no more progressive than W.S.C. and he will be 'difficult to get on with.'"[33]

Eden was consistently skeptical of American actions and more willing to disagree with the Roosevelt administration than Churchill.[34] On July 25, 1942, Eden wrote the prime minister: "American views are of interest, but ours are even more important where Europe is concerned. . . . As regards America, we should always consult U.S. Government, but our object should be to bring them along with us. They know very little of Europe and it would be unfortunate for the future of the world if U.S. uninstructed views were to decide the future of the European continent."[35] Over a year later, Eden wrote on September 10, 1943, after the Quebec summit: "Roosevelt has had his way again and agreed to Moscow for the Foreign Secretaries' conference with alacrity. His determination not to agree to a London meeting for any purpose, which he says is for electoral reasons, is almost insulting considering the number of times we have been to Washington. I am most anxious for good relations with U.S. but I don't like subservience to them."[36] It was in 1943 that FDR would edge toward Stalin, away from Churchill.

"Roosevelt was, above all else, a consummate politician," wrote Eden in his memoirs. "Few men could see more clearly their immediate objective, or show greater artistry in obtaining it. As a price of these gifts, his long-range vision was not quite so sure. The President shared a widespread American suspicion of the British Empire as it had once been and, despite his knowledge of world affairs, he was always anxious to make it plain to Stalin that the United States was not 'ganging up' with Britain against Russia. The outcome of this was some confusion in Anglo-American relations which profited the Soviets."[37] Historian Fraser J. Harbutt argued that the

British government was more Eurocentric than America, and that Eden was even more Eurocentric than the prime minister. "While Churchill was typically furthering the war effort by spending weekends entertaining United States Ambassador John Winant and other American visitors at Chequers . . . Eden was just as vigorously trying to shape the future by lunching with and otherwise cultivating the leaders of the exile of European governments."[38]

A major source of conflict between Eden and the Americans was diplomatic recognition of Charles de Gaulle and the French Committee of National Liberation. American leaders disdained de Gaulle, who in turn held them in contempt. The general was a hair shirt of frustration for Churchill. At the beginning of World War II, the American government, as a neutral power, was intent on maintaining good relations with the Vichy government of France. After America entered the war, they were affronted by de Gaulle and reluctant to give him a formal status. De Gaulle's brusque and arrogant manner, and his devotion to French grandeur and retention of French colonies, did not help. FDR objected to French colonial policy more than to British policy. He seemed intent on breaking up the weakened French colonial empire, especially in Indochina and West Africa, where Roosevelt coveted Dakar as a U.S. air base, administered by his new United Nations.[39] The president's animus to de Gaulle ran deep, and his annoyance with de Gaulle's public statements frequently surfaced in comments he made to Churchill: "The bride evidently forgets that there is still a war in progress over here. . . . Best of luck in getting rid of our mutual headache."[40]

Secretary of State Hull could nurture a grudge. He reinforced Roosevelt's dislike of the Free French leader. Hull wrote that at the August 1943 summit in Quebec, "Eden thereupon said he felt that Mr. Churchill could not accept any formula with regard to the French Committee of National Liberation which did not contain the word 'recognition.' My advisers and I argued that 'recognition' was given only to a government or some form of government, where in this case we understood that both the British and the United States Governments had no intention whatever of considering the French Committee as a government. . . . Eden remarked that the British public was against our view, and that this fact required consideration."[41] On August 20, Eden wrote in his diary: "More work after luncheon and then talk for more than two hours with old Hull. Most of it was about recognition of French Committee. . . . I like the old man but he has an obsession against Free French which nothing can cure. I eventually suggested we each take our own course."[42]

Ten months later, Eden clashed with General Marshall over General de Gaulle's uncooperative attitude regarding Operation OVERLORD. According to Army Secretary Stimson, Marshall erupted at Eden during a London meeting, and Eden walked out.[43] The foreign secretary and the prime minister often differed on de Gaulle, whose arrogance infuriated Churchill. Eden consistently supported de Gaulle, and he advocated recognizing the French National Liberation Committee. At one point in August 1942, Churchill and de Gaulle had a furious argument. "You claim to be France!" exclaimed Churchill. "You are not France! I do not recognise you as France."[44]

After the Roosevelt-Churchill summit at Quebec in August 1943, it was decided to seek a preliminary meeting of foreign secretaries—which the Russians insisted must be held in Moscow. General Hastings Ismay, whom Eden asked to accompany him, noted that Secretary of State Hull, then 72, "was very aged and had never flown before." Once in Moscow, noted Ismay, Eden's "hours of work were phenomenal, and he was extremely thorough. Nothing was too much trouble and he never went to a meeting without making sure he had every aspect of the problem at his finger tips. He could be tough when necessary, but he could also give way gracefully if the situation demanded it. He had a pretty wit, and transparent integrity."[45]

The Moscow meeting produced the first big tripartite agreements—less than a month before the Allied Big Three were to gather at Teheran. "Simultaneously in Washington, Moscow, and London announcement was made of five documents agreed upon in Moscow by Secretary Hull, Russian Foreign Minister [Vyacheslav] Molotov, and British Foreign Minister Eden, providing close co-operation of the signatory powers in war and postwar operations," wrote presidential aide William D. Hassett.[46] The next day, FDR claimed that his contribution had been to insist on the inclusion of China—against the wishes of Russia and Britain, whose governments dismissed the importance of the Chiang Kai-shek government. Churchill wrote of the importance of a secret protocol that the Allied foreign ministers signed "to establish a European Advisory Committee in London to begin work on the problems which would arise in Germany and the Continent when the Hitler régime neared collapse." Unlike the dissonance that sometimes characterized Allied meetings in Moscow, Churchill explained: "There had been a smoothing of many points of friction, practical steps for further co-operation had been taken, the way had been prepared for an early meeting of the heads of the three major Allied Governments, and the mounting deadlock in our working with the Soviet Union had in part been removed."[47]

Churchill and Eden could disagree in the presence of U.S. officials. At Yalta in February 1945, Edward Stettinius recorded a major disagreement between them over the necessity for "unanimity" of the Big Three powers. Eden said that the prime minister had declaimed vigorously against a report from foreign secretaries on territorial trusteeship, whose target was Japanese possessions, but which Churchill feared might be applied to the British Empire. Eden wrote: "Though the Prime Minister's vehemence was a warning signal to the Americans it appeared to give most pleasure to Stalin."[48]

Eden's immense labors imposed a heavy burden on the foreign secretary during the war. For two years, he also served as leader of the House of Commons, itself a very demanding and time-consuming duty. Churchill had told King George VI that Eden was his choice *in extremis* to take his place as prime minister. Churchill occasionally had doubts about Eden's readiness to succeed him, but the prime minister praised Eden in speaking to the House of Commons in February 1945: "I cannot describe to the House the aid and comfort he has been to me in all our difficulties. His hard life when quite young in the infantry in the last war, his constant self-preparation for the tasks which have fallen to him, his unequalled experience as a minister at the Foreign Office, his knowledge of foreign affairs and their past history, his experience of conferences of all kinds, his breadth of view, his powers of exposition, his moral courage, have gained for him a position second to none among the Foreign Secretaries of the Grand Alliance."[49]

The often-disappointed Eden would have to wait another ten years until 1955, when Churchill, then 80, made way for Eden to succeed him.

General Dwight D. Eisenhower (left) and General George C. Marshall wave to a crowd in Washington, D.C., June 1945.
NATIONAL ARCHIVES

XI

George C. Marshall and Dwight D. Eisenhower

We are determined that before the sun sets on this terrible struggle, Our Flag will be recognized throughout the World as a symbol of Freedom on the one hand and of overwhelming force on the other.

George C. Marshall *(1880–1959), West Point Commencement Address, May 29, 1942. President Roosevelt appointed Marshall as army chief of staff in September 1939. He took office the day that Hitler invaded Poland. He supervised the military preparations for World War II and the expansion of the U.S. Army from fewer than 200,000 soldiers to more than 8 million. Although he was the leading candidate to command the D-Day invasion, FDR decided Marshall was needed at his side in Washington.*

London's hospitality to the Americans, her good-humored acceptance of the added inconvenience we brought, her example of fortitude and quiet confidence in the final outcome—all these helped to make the Supreme Headquarters of the two Allied expeditions the smooth-working organizations they became.[1]

Dwight D. Eisenhower *(1890–1969), Guildhall Address, June 12, 1945. Before World War II, Eisenhower had served as an aide to two army chiefs of staff, Douglas MacArthur and George C. Marshall, as well as serving under MacArthur in the Philippines. He rose to chief of the War Plans Division after the United States was attacked at Pearl Harbor. He was then chosen to command the Allied landings in North Africa (1942) and France (1944). The latter was the largest seaborne invasion of history.*

Appointed army chief of staff in September 1939, General George C. Marshall "established a reputation as a straight-talking Army chief," wrote historian Andrew Roberts. "Despite being, in the words of one of Roosevelt's biographers, 'a courtly and reserved Pennsylvanian', he could be exceedingly blunt when necessary."[2] In a 1938 meeting at the White House, Marshall had opposed the president's plan to build thousands of new airplanes without providing for the training of thousands of new pilots. After FDR had made some self-serving remarks, he asked rhetorically: "Don't you think so, George?" Marshall replied: "Mr. President, I am sorry but I don't agree with that at all." A few months later, Roosevelt named him chief of staff of the army.[3] To FDR's credit, he recognized a general with impeccable integrity. The independent Marshall avoided Roosevelt's easily recognized charm offensive by not visiting the president at Hyde Park. Marshall kept his distance from Roosevelt, who, unlike Churchill, limited his formal contact with the Joint Chiefs of Staff. Marshall noted: "Informal conversation with the president could get you into trouble. He would talk over something informally at the dinner table and you had trouble disagreeing without embarrassment. So I never went."[4] Similarly, Marshall tried to evade Winston Churchill's strategic courtship by avoiding casual military conversations with him, but the general always made himself available for the business of war.

The Churchill-Marshall relationship endured many disagreements. The prime minister in the end thought Marshall the "greatest Roman of them all."[5] In his memoirs, Churchill wrote: "Hitherto I had thought of Marshall as a rugged soldier and a magnificent organiser and builder of armies—the American [Lazare] Carnot," the great organizer of the French Revolutionary Army in 1793–1794. "But now I saw he was a statesman with a penetrating and commanding view of the whole scene."[6] Marshall was a "reserved and dignified" figure whose warmth was hidden by a generally austere exterior.[7] Churchill's opinion of Marshall's strength, partly formed at the Placentia Bay conference, was reaffirmed in December 1941, when the prime minister visited Washington. Churchill's doctor wrote in his diary: "Marshall remains the key to the situation. The PM has a feeling that in his quiet, unprovocative way he means business, and that if we are too obstinate he might take a strong line. And neither the PM nor the President can contemplate going forward without Marshall."[8]

Speaking in Virginia after the war, Churchill declared that Marshall and Dwight D. Eisenhower had "that character, that quality of selflessness [that] has been a bond uniting all Allied Armies and the key to the victory which we have had together."[9] The prime minister devoted intense efforts to cultivating both men. Of August 1942, Churchill wrote in his memoirs: "I was at this time in very close and agreeable contact with these American officers. From the moment they arrived in June, I had arranged a weekly luncheon at Number 10 on Tuesdays. These meetings seemed to be a success. I was nearly always alone with them, and we talked all our affairs over, back and forth, as if we were all of one country. I set great value on these personal contacts. Irish stew turned out to be very popular with my American guests, and especially with General Eisenhower."[10]

Marshall worried—as did other American officials—that Churchill would outtalk and out-argue Americans, and thus shift strategy in ways the Americans opposed. Historian Elisabeth Barker observed that "Marshall and the U.S. Chiefs of Staff were deeply suspicious of Churchill's apparent switches and swerves in strategic thinking, and also his influence over Roosevelt in strategic matters."[11] Marshall had disagreements with both the prime minister and the president, as he sought to direct

Anglo-American efforts to prepare for a cross-channel invasion. Historian Walter Reid wrote: "From the point of view of the United States, they could rely on Marshall to not be pushed around by the British: Roosevelt was firmly of the view that Churchill did not greatly like Marshall because the latter could always get the better of him."[12] Marshall biographer Forrest C. Pogue wrote of a White House meeting on March 25, 1942, attended by Henry C. Stimson, Frank Knox, Hap Arnold, Ernest King, and Harry Hopkins:

> The President proved difficult. "Roosevelt had a habit of tossing out new operations," General Marshall once declared. "I called it his cigarette-holder gesture." Stimson on this occasion called it "a dispersion debauch in which Roosevelt toyed with possible operations in the Middle East and the Mediterranean. Only by strenuous exertions did the Army leaders steer him [FDR] back to the Atlantic. In "a very fine presentation" Marshall won the President's backing for a cross-Channel effort. Finally Roosevelt asked that a detailed plan be prepared for his examination. Hopkins, who wanted prompt action by the British, recommended that as soon as the plan was made and approved, someone take it directly to London, bypassing the British Mission in Washington.[13]

In April 1942, with his cross-channel invasion plan uppermost in his mind, Marshall left for London to meet with Churchill. There, the Americans and their British counterparts tried to work out a common strategy. Pogue wrote that Marshall

> worked with Churchill more closely and over a longer period of time than on any other occasion during the war. Attempting to win the fight for his [Marshall's] strategy, he was able to observe the master of the Allied cause at close range. Marshall admired his gift for language, his knowledge and his sense of history, his splendid contempt for the enemy, his capacity for boldness. He was appalled by swift changes of plans, a flexibility that brought chaos in planning, a daring that brushed aside careful details. Most of all he dreaded the Churchillian influence on Roosevelt, who also delighted in the dramatic and the unexpected and who was determined, now that he was in the war, to strike a sudden and vital blow at the Nazis.[14]

The American president had decided that American troops and American leadership would strike such a blow.

Despite his courtliness, Marshall was not only tenacious, but he also had a temper that he generally controlled.[15] Even his British friend John Dill noted: "It is odd how that charming person Marshall can fly off the handle and be so infernally rude. Also he gets fixed ideas about things and people which it is almost impossible to argue."[16] British General Hastings Ismay recalled meeting with the U.S. Chiefs of Staff in June 1942. Marshall, Ismay wrote: "was a big man in every sense of the word, and utterly selfless. It was impossible to imagine his doing anything petty or mean, or shrinking from any duty, however distasteful. He carried himself with great dignity."[17] American General Omar N. Bradley wrote that "if ever a man was indispensable in a time of national crisis, he [Marshall] was that man.[18] Churchill, who understood American suspicions about his persuasive opposition to a premature cross-channel invasion, had taken Marshall along to North Africa on his return from Washington in May 1943, in order to disarm any suggestion that the prime minister was going to exert undue influence on Eisenhower regarding future strategy. But in this case, both Churchill and Roosevelt had already embraced the North African assault, Operation TORCH, which would precede D-Day by 19 months. The path of future operations remained in doubt.[19] General Marshall did give way reluctantly to the combined decision of the president and the prime minister to delay the cross-channel invasion until the spring of 1944.

American and British generals differed often, but George Marshall always commanded their respect, although his British counterpart, Alan Brooke, had serious doubts about Marshall's strategic vision. Brooke had first met Marshall in 1942, when Marshall and Hopkins came to London to discuss war strategy, especially the possibility of the cross-channel invasion that year. "I liked what I saw of Marshall, a pleasant and easy man to get on with, rather over-filled with his own importance," wrote Brooke in his diary.[20] Brooke was not impressed with Marshall's strategic thinking and premature schedule for what would become the cross-channel invasion, Operation OVERLORD. "I discovered that he had not studied any of the strategic implications of a cross Channel operation. He argued that the main difficulty would be to achieve a landing. I granted this would certainly present great difficulties, but that our real troubles would start after the landing. . . . I saw a great deal of him throughout the rest of the war, and the more I saw of him the more clearly I appreciated that his strategic ability was of the poorest. A great man, a great gentleman and great organizer, but definitely not a strategist."[21] The patronizing Brooke put down almost everyone's strategic competence, holding a very high opinion of his own. Marshall did not claim to have a complete plan for D-Day in 1942. He expected careful consideration of necessary Anglo-American preparation. The 1942 date was ultimately rejected by the prime minister and the president.

Brooke, like Marshall, aspired to command the Allied invasion of France, which Churchill had promised him more than once. When Stalin queried Roosevelt about the OVERLORD supreme command at Teheran in November 1943, FDR said he had not yet made up his mind. Hopkins biographer Robert E. Sherwood wrote: "Stalin thereupon made it clear that until a supreme commander were named he could not believe in the reality of the operation."[22] The view, generally expressed at that time by political leaders, was that General Marshall would get the plum assignment. "The appointment of Marshall to the supreme command of OVERLORD was vehemently opposed by Admiral [Ernest] King and General [Henry] Arnold on the ground that Marshall could not be spared from his position as their colleague and, indeed, acknowledged leader of the Joint Chiefs of Staff," wrote Robert Sherwood. "Admiral Leahy, titular leader of the Joint Chiefs, agreed with them and said so when Roosevelt asked for his opinion, but Leahy otherwise made no positive attempts to influence the President's decision. King, however, was by no means diffident in stating his opinion. He said, 'We have the winning combination here in Washington. Why break it up?'"[23]

However, Churchill did object to giving an American overall control of the entire European theater, the command of which, until December 1941, the British had shouldered alone. American generals thought memories of the enormous casualties and emotional baggage of World War I hobbled the British. However, the British views about the risks and challenges entailed in a cross-channel invasion were more realistic. American military leadership decided that the European theater should have but one commander. Collectively they wrote FDR: "The necessity for unified command, in our opinion, is so urgent and compelling that, in spite of the fact that the bulk of the forces, both ground and air, will ultimately be American, we are willing to accept a British officer as over-all commander for European operations provided the man named is Sir John Dill."[24] It was not to be. Churchill doubted Dill's ability. Americans like Secretary of War Stimson thought that a British general could not be trusted to lead Operation OVERLORD because "[t]he shadows of Passchendaele [World War I] and Dunkerque [World War II] still hang too heavily over these leaders of [Churchill's] government. Though they have rendered lip service to the [cross-channel] operation, their hearts are not in it," Stimson wrote FDR.[25] Stimson's opinion correctly recognized the impact of World War I manpower losses on British military thinking. The Americans were ever optimistic about a cross-channel invasion, but Churchill was ever optimistic about the timeliness and wisdom of his Mediterranean strategy to precede the cross-channel invasion.

Marshall's self-assurance grew as he directed the Anglo-American military effort during World War II, more so as he handled interservice rivalries and intra-Allied differences.[26] Military historian Mark A. Stoler wrote: "For two years after Pearl Harbor, one . . . issue would dominate Marshall's time and energies: the search for a unified global strategy for the United States and its allies. To arrive at such a strategy was no simple task. Never before had a war been fought on so many fronts and over such large areas. The battlefield was the entire globe and the problems of organization and coordination unprecedented."[27] Fortunately, Marshall had matured into a great leader-manager. Equally important, American production and manpower was up to the task. General Marshall shrewdly delegated and confidently reinforced the authority he gave to his subordinates. He mastered both his temper and difficult colleagues like Admiral King, even insubordinate senior commanders like General Douglas MacArthur. Although Chief of Staff Marshall continued to rankle his British counterpart, CIGS Brooke, First Sea Lord Andrew Cunningham became a fan: "One did not need to be long in his company before recognizing his sincerity and honesty of purpose. He could be obstinate enough; but would always listen to another point of view."[28]

Marshall's persistent but premature advocacy of an invasion of northwestern France in 1942 and 1943—and his stubborn opposition to military operations in the Mediterranean—gave rise to informal opposition among British civil and military leaders. "There was a deep difference of opinion over the American and Communist demand for a second front [in France] in 1942, which General Marshall ill-advisedly recommended, Harry Hopkins doubted and Lord Beaverbrook mischievously promoted," noted John Colville.[29] Brooke and Churchill opposed Marshall's drive for a second front in France. In early 1942, Generals Marshall and Eisenhower held clear views of taking the pressure off Russia through Operation SLEDGEHAMMER—a direct cross-channel invasion of France from a base in Britain. On January 27, 1942, Ike had written: "We must win in Europe. It's going to be one h— of a job, but, so what? We can't win by sitting on our fannies giving our stuff in driblets all over the world, with no theater getting enough."[30] Churchill and Brooke would argue that the Allied target in 1942 should be North Africa, for which they believed the Anglo-American forces could be made ready in time.

Ultimately, Operation OVERLORD would succeed in June 1944. Still, the logistical challenges were so immense that not even Eisenhower, the invasion's commander and advocate, would be confident of success. When the Allies landed in Normandy in June 1944, after months of meticulous preparation, Allied soldiers would quickly bog down in the unique German-occupied French terrain—as General Brooke had foreseen. Allied forces experienced great difficulty advancing out of Normandy in the summer of 1944. Breaking through the cordon of disciplined and brave German troops, well generalled and battle hardened, proved much tougher than the Americans expected. Prime Minister Churchill and General Brooke were not surprised.

Churchill had promised command of the Normandy invasion to General Brooke, who, in 1942, had turned down the job of leading British forces in Egypt. But in the summer of 1943, the prime minister deferred to FDR on the choice of OVERLORD's supreme commander. Secretary Stimson strongly backed Marshall for the command, writing that "General Marshall already has a towering eminence of reputation as a tried soldier and as a broad-minded and skillful administrator."[31] In December 1943, after considering the available candidates, FDR decided that he could not do without Marshall's leadership in Washington. Marshall had provided the detailed organization and management of the entire American war effort, compensating for FDR's inability to do the same. Meeting with Roosevelt, after the decision for Eisenhower had been made, Stimson "said that I knew that in the bottom of his heart it was Marshall's secret desire above all things to command this invasion force into Europe; that I had had very hard work to wring out of Marshall that this was so, but I had done so finally beyond the possibility of misunderstanding."[32]

Under the American conception, OVERLORD command would include supreme command for both the cross-channel invasion and the Mediterranean operations—indeed, a European theater supreme commander. Admiral Leahy, chairman of the Joint Chiefs of Staff, recalled that Americans "assumed that Roosevelt would name Marshall as Supreme Commander. There was vehement objection to such a move in the Press. Opponents charged that Marshall was being given a 'Dutch promotion'; that Roosevelt planned to take him out of a big job and put him into a small job; that it was a plot against Marshall. At the other extreme, there were reports that the Joint Chiefs considered the post of supreme command a promotion and were jealous of Marshall."[33] John S. D. Eisenhower wrote that on November 20, 1943, at Tunis, General Eisenhower met with Marshall and King for a drink. King dominated the conversation about the OVERLORD command and the possibility that Eisenhower might become the army chief of staff:

> King then made a bow in Eisenhower's direction. If all this came to pass, he said, he would afford Ike the same cooperation as he had given to Marshall. And the prospect of Eisenhower's coming as Army Chief of Staff was all that prevented Marshall's departure from being unbearable. Having said that, however, King pressed his main point. "We now have a winning combination," he exclaimed. "Why do we want to make a radical change? Each of us knows his own role; each of us has learned how to work with the others. Why doesn't the President send you [Eisenhower] up to OVERLORD and keep General Marshall in Washington? Marshall is the truly indispensable man of this war: Congress and the public trust him; the President trusts him; his associates in the Combined Staff trust him; and the commanders in the field trust him. Why do we change?"[34]

Marshall recalled that Harry Hopkins, FDR's herald, had visited him in Cairo in early December 1943, after the Teheran summit. Hopkins "told me the President was in some concern of mind over my appointment as Supreme Commander. I could not tell from the Hopkins' statement just what the President's point of view was and in my reply I merely endeavored to make it clear that I would go along wholeheartedly with whatever decision the President made. He need have no fears regarding my personal reaction. I declined to state my opinion." The following day, Marshall met with FDR, who announced: "I feel I could not sleep at night with you out of the country."[35] Roosevelt knew he needed an experienced, trusted steady hand at the wheel in Washington, on duty full-time, in order to compensate for the president's physical limitations and long absences from Washington.[36]

General Eisenhower was a protégé of Marshall, dating to the early days of the war when Eisenhower was Marshall's chief of planning. Like Marshall, Eisenhower was very shrewd and sensitive to political questions. Marshall told Brooke that Churchill exerted more pressure on Eisenhower than did Roosevelt: "The President practically never sees General Eisenhower and never writes to him—that is on my advice—because he is an *Allied* commander."[37] British diplomat John Wheeler-Bennett, who served at the S.H.A.E.F. headquarters preparing for D-Day, observed that Eisenhower was

> absolutely ideal for the highly unusual job he held. S.H.A.E.F. was not only an allied military headquarters but also a kind of joint stock company of allied activities. The success of both was dependent on the new formula of 'integration', which did not come entirely easily to many British and to many Americans. General Eisenhower, however, not only understood its vital importance but was the personification of its principle. He seemed to have deliberately thought himself into a state of mind in which he literally did not know the difference between the two major allies under his command and woe betide the offender, be he American or British, who transgressed the spirit of co-operation.[38]

In his diary, General Brooke was less complimentary of Eisenhower: "There is no doubt that Ike is all out to do all he can to maintain the best relations between British and Americans, but it is equally clear that Ike knows nothing about strategy and is *quite* unsuited to the post of Supreme Commander as far as running the strategy of the war is concerned!"[39] As his diaries make clear, Brooke thought himself an accomplished strategist.

Anglo-American military strategy in Europe had combined British insistence on the invasion of North Africa in 1942, then Sicily and Italy in 1943, then the delayed cross-channel invasion of France in 1944. Tension persisted between Marshall and Brooke over strategy, especially the timing of Operation OVERLORD. Both generals believed they must also bring their civilian chiefs to focus on their version of military reality. "The President had no military knowledge," recalled Brooke, "and was aware of this fact and consequently relied on Marshall and listened to Marshall's advice. Marshall never seemed to have any difficulty in countering any wildish plans which the President might put forward. My position was very different." The Sandhurst-trained Churchill was a historian of war and military strategy. In the summer of 1942, FDR had deliberately shelved the cross-channel strategy pushed by Stimson and Marshall, opting instead for Churchill's North Africa strategy, Operation TORCH. The Marshall-Brooke relationship exhibited a surface correctness, perhaps concealing an undercurrent of distrust—particularly in mid-1942, when Marshall believed that the British, led by General Brooke and the prime minister, had reneged on a pledge to support his cross-channel invasion plans of 1942. But in fact, it was FDR who had been persuaded, primarily by Churchill, to put off the cross-channel invasion and to invade North Africa first.[40]

The prime minister and General Eisenhower worked well together. Eisenhower's driver and purported lover, Kay Summersby, recalled that "Churchill's fondness for the American commander was best revealed at the dinner parties. Although Eisenhower normally was the lowest-ranking general present, and in spite of the rigid protocol which rules Government and military circles in England, the P.M. invariably placed General Eisenhower in the highest chair of honor, to his immediate right." She noted that "it was plain they shared a mutual respect and sincere natural friendliness despite many arguments on a military plane."[41] Eisenhower aide Harry Butcher reported a visit to 10 Downing Street that Eisenhower made in April 1945: "When the meeting finished, the Prime Minister walked with General Ike to the car. They were as homey as neighbors on adjoining Iowa farms."[42] After Churchill visited North Africa in February 1943, Butcher

> asked Ike what had been gained by the visit. Ike thought it was the fact that the PM had come to learn, see, and feel the situation at first hand. Then there was the opportunity afforded for complete discussion of problems. The PM had told Ike he must take care of himself, that he was doing a magnificent job, that he should be careful that nothing should happen to him, all because the PM didn't see a man [a substitute for Eisenhower]

> in sight, except General Marshall, and he couldn't be spared from his present job, to be Allied Commander. He emphasized that the Allied Command was held together by dint of personality of the Commander-in-Chief, that he was very happy with Ike, etc., etc.[43]

Eisenhower was a good writer. He had once turned down an offer as a military correspondent that would have earned him nearly seven times his army salary.[44] Like Marshall, Eisenhower shared Churchill's love of history. On his first visit to Chequers, Eisenhower wrote in his diary: "Upon going to bed at 2:30, I found in my room a book that dealt exclusively with the history of Chequers, together with the furniture and objects of art all over the place. I could not go to sleep without reading that part applying to my own room."[45] During his visit to North Africa in 1943, Churchill engaged Eisenhower in exhausting conversation late into the night. Sometimes, Churchill would soak in the hot tub while he invited Eisenhower to perch on the nearby toilet. Summersby claimed that the general needed to "change into a fresh uniform afterwards, because the steam was murder on trouser creases." She wrote in her memoirs: "Ike really liked Churchill. They disagreed on a number of things, matters of strategy and military priorities, and had some very spirited arguments, but this did not affect their relationship. The only thing that Ike really deplored about the P.M. was his habit of staying up until all hours. By nature Ike was an early-to-bed, early-to-rise man; the P.M. was the opposite."[46]

Like Churchill, Eisenhower became an inspiration, a morale booster for the Allied cause. Eisenhower wrote his wife in the summer of 1942: "In a place like this the D.G. [Commanding General] . . . must be a bit of a diplomat-lawyer-promoter-salesman-social hound-liar (at least to get out of social affairs)-mountebank-actor-Simon Legree-humanitarian-orator and incidentally (sometimes I think most damnably incidentally) a soldier!"[47] Eisenhower was astute enough to ingratiate himself with FDR-insider George Allen, who angled to be perceived as an insider in London as well. Allen, who had never met Eisenhower, wanted to be seen as the general's friend. Ike agreed to a bit of theater in which they would run into each other in a hotel restaurant: "George, I haven't been to the Savoy for lunch for six months. You get there at one o'clock. I'll arrive at one fifteen. As soon as I walk into the Grill Room, I'm going to yell at the top of my voice, 'Hello, George,' and you'll yell back, 'Hello, Ike.'" Allen and Eisenhower would later become golfing buddies.[48] Eisenhower understood the importance of the personal touch, even in minor matters.

Churchill did not fear to challenge Eisenhower's authority, his plans, and his command structure. In early 1945, Brooke and the prime minister urged the appointment of a British ground commander for the European continent to serve under Eisenhower. General Marshall first argued against the British proposal, writing Eisenhower that with any such appointee, "being who he is and our experience being what it has been, you would have great difficulty in offsetting the direct influence of the P.M."[49] The British then got Marshall's support. Still, Eisenhower refused to yield to Churchill's desire to appoint his favorite, British General Harold Alexander, as the deputy Allied commander in Europe. "Ike first got Monty on his side, then forthrightly faced down Churchill and Alan Brooke," recalled General Omar N. Bradley. "It was the most emphatic demonstration yet that Ike had taken full command of the war on the Continent."[50] Not only did Eisenhower experience the hard challenge of managing the private egos of American and British leaders; he also had to anticipate the public reaction in both countries for blame or credit in the failure and success of military operations. Circumstances forced Eisenhower to be a political general, and he proved he had the talent for the task.[51] In supreme command of an integrated Anglo-American army, a "political general" was not a pejorative, but a necessity.

Years later, after Eisenhower had been elected president in 1952, Churchill worried that criticism by him, in his writings, of the general's wartime decisions might hurt Anglo-American cooperation—Churchill's strategic postwar priority. During his second stint (1951–1955) as prime minister, Churchill wrote President Eisenhower in April 1953: "Now that you have assumed supreme political office in your country, I am most anxious that nothing should be published which might seem to others to threaten our current relations in our public duties or to impair the sympathy and understanding which exist between our two countries." Churchill added: "There was in fact little controversy in those years; but I have been careful to ensure that the few differences of opinion which arose are so described that even ill-disposed people will be unable now to turn them to mischievous account."[52] Churchill wrote in his World War II memoirs: "In him [Eisenhower] we have had a man who set the unity of the Allied Armies above all nationalistic thoughts. In his headquarters unity and strategy were the only reigning spirits. The unity reached such a point that British and American troops could be mixed in the line of battle, and that large masses could be transferred from one command to the other without the slightest difficulty. At no time has the principle of alliance between noble races been carried and maintained at so high a pitch."[53]

British military leaders liked Eisenhower personally, but they did not trust his strategic judgment. General Leslie Hollis wrote: "I remember him, not as a strategic man, or as a planner, not as one who could initiate strategy, but as a very able conciliator."[54] General Brooke grudgingly recalled: "We were pushing Eisenhower up into the stratosphere and rarified atmosphere of a Supreme Commander, where he would be free to devote his time to the political and inter-allied problems, whilst we inserted under him one of our own commanders to deal with the military situations."[55] Brooke had expected to be named Allied commander for the invasion. He was very disappointed when told by Churchill that an American would get the job. FDR's selection of Eisenhower over Marshall annoyed the officious British even more, since top-ranking British generals already held higher military ranks than their American counterparts, including Eisenhower and Marshall.[56]

Before and after D-Day, Churchill's remarkable stamina was the source both of aggravation and admiration among Allied generals. The prime minister was almost 70 years of age. General Bradley recalled Churchill's inspection of an American unit in late March 1944:

> Churchill was recovering from a recent and severe illness, but you would never have known it. [General] Joe Collins, who joined us on the second day, recalled: "Churchill had had two strenuous days of inspections and had ridden for miles perched on the tonneau of an open car so that he could better see and be seen by the troops. . . . He had insisted on getting out of the car to walk around the honor guards and examine the weapons displayed. That day he had stood through a review of our regiments and delivered a stirring address to the men. In one of the towns through which we had passed he had gotten out of the car to walk with General Eisenhower for a couple of blocks through throngs of cheering townspeople, who pressed about him in their enthusiasm, many with tears streaming down their cheeks."

Collins recalled the prime minister's energy, even at the end of the second day: "Churchill was fresh as we were and held forth after dinner until eleven o'clock, dominating the conversation, alternately regaling us with stories or stirring us as he spoke feelingly of our common ideals and endeavors."[57] Churchill's energy was internally generated, but it was intensified by cheering crowds and dinners with major leaders whose conversation he dominated.

Socially, the British and the Americans mixed well, but strategic differences could not be papered over. Bradley later wrote: "Generally, the British leaned toward what we called an 'indirect' or 'peripheral' strategy. They argued that while Hitler exhausted Germany in his vast land war with Russia, the United States and Britain should defeat Hitler's U-boats [the Battle of the Atlantic], which had almost paralyzed the Allies; smash the German war production base to smithereens with massive air bombardments; and chip away at the periphery of the Axis empire in the Middle East, the Balkans and the Mediterranean—Churchill's famous 'soft underbelly' approach."[58] However, Bradley noted that the American military leaders preferred a more direct attack—an early invasion across the English Channel into France and Germany, striking straight at the heart of the German empire. This underlying difference in strategic thinking would keep the American and British staffs at loggerheads for nearly three years. He added: "The indirect strategy had led the British into a deep and costly involvement in the Mediterranean–North African theater of war."[59] Strangely, Bradley did not emphasize nor celebrate the success of Operation TORCH in North Africa, especially the fact that TORCH diverted crack German troops from the Russian front, just as Russian arms neared a successful turning point against the Nazis on a long line from Leningrad to Moscow to Stalingrad. The integrated Anglo-American command under Eisenhower gained indispensable experience in the waterborne North African invasion. It was perhaps the best real-time preparation for the cross-channel invasion on D-Day.

Not everyone on the American and British sides contributed to harmonious Allied relationships. Among the leaders of the British and American air forces, there were hard factions. On land, the vainglorious British General Bernard Montgomery was a hard nut to crack. Eisenhower met him in the summer of 1942 in England, whereupon Eisenhower lit up a cigarette. Montgomery imperiously ordered him to extinguish it. "[T]hat son of a bitch!" said Eisenhower in leaving Monty's office.[60]

The British general later admitted that he was "a very difficult subordinate."[61] Indeed, Montgomery had spent several decades alienating his superiors in the British Army.[62] In the spring of 1943, British Air Marshal Arthur Tedder suggested that Montgomery was "a little fellow of average ability who has had such a build-up that he thinks of himself as Napoleon—he is not."[63] Montgomery was not merely anti-American; he aggravated very able British colleagues, such as Tedder and Admiral Andrew B. Cunningham.[64] As Winston Churchill observed: "If he is disagreeable to those about him he is also disagreeable to the enemy."[65] The mercurial and arrogant British general often quarreled with American military leaders, and Brooke generally backed him. Montgomery had established his reputation as a field general with his defeat of German forces at El Alamein in the Libyan desert, in late 1942. He did help Eisenhower in the planning for Operation OVERLORD, but his outsized ego often got in the way. Historian Max Hastings wrote of Montgomery that "throughout his military career, a worm of self-destruction in the austere, awkward little man in the beret caused him to disparage the contribution of his peers, shamelessly to seize the credit for the achievements of others, and rewrite the history of his own battlefield planning to conform with the reality of what took place."[66] Hastings added that Montgomery was not without an inspiring human touch, which he displayed when he met the U.S. 2nd Armored Division. He ordered the Americans to take off their helmets: "All right, put them back on. Now next time I see you, I shall know you."[67]

On French soil after D-Day, Montgomery's forces quickly bogged down against better-equipped and more effective German soldiers. Montgomery often predicted Allied advances, but brave German soldiers repulsed them during the critical first two months of the invasion. Even Prime Minister Churchill lost patience with Montgomery's lack of progress against tenacious German forces.[68] Montgomery resented Eisenhower as a staff officer, not the field commander Montgomery considered himself to be. Monty's disdain for Eisenhower boiled over upon his arrival in France, to take overall command of the ground forces in Europe. At one meeting in September, Montgomery was so insubordinate in his language to Eisenhower that the Allied commander patiently placed his hand on Montgomery's knee: "Steady, Monty! You can't speak to me like that. I'm your boss."[69] In his memoirs, Montgomery summed up: "I would not class Ike as a great soldier in the true sense of the word. He might have become one if he had ever had the experience of exercising direct command of a division, corps, and army—which unfortunately for him did not come his way." Montgomery ungenerously ignored Eisenhower's successful command of Operations TORCH and HUSKY. "But he was a great Supreme Commander—a military statesman. I know of no other person who could have welded the Allied forces into such a fine fighting machine in the way he did, and kept a balance among the many conflicting and disturbing elements which threatened at times to wreck the ship."[70] Belated recognition of true statesmanship had finally led the prickly British general to acknowledge General Eisenhower's remarkable achievement.

Churchill too mitigated his criticism, writing in his memoirs: "Eisenhower was a broad-minded man, practical, serviceable, dealing with events as they came in cool selflessness."[71] Time and distance mellowed wartime controversies. As historian Andrew Roberts has noted, private dyspepsia during the war gave way to public praise after the war: "Anyone who was shocked by the attacks on Churchill contained in Brooke's unexpurgated diaries that were published in 2001 . . . ought to read the journals of the equally peppery Admiral Lord Cunningham in the British Library. . . . Yet in Cunningham's 710-page autobiography, *A Sailor's Odyssey,* it is hard to spot a sentence of criticism of Churchill."[72]

For every British Montgomery, there was an American counterpart. In his memoirs, British General Hastings "Pug" Ismay noted that American Admiral Ernest King "was blunt and stand-offish, almost to the point of rudeness."[73] King's crusty British counterpart, First Sea Lord Cunningham, recalled of King: "A man of immense capacity and ability, quite ruthless in his methods, he was not an easy person to get on with. He was tough and liked to be considered tough, and at times became rude and overbearing." Cunningham added: "I think Ernest King was the right man in the right place, though one could hardly call him a good co-operator."[74] King's American colleagues knew that the U.S. chief of naval operations (CNO) was smart, tough, effective, and undiplomatic. In March 1942, Eisenhower suggested in his diary: "One thing that might help win this war is to get someone to shoot King. He's the antithesis of cooperation, a deliberately rude person, which means he's a mental bully."[75] Eisenhower observed: "At the start [of the war], King was intolerant and suspicious of all things British, especially the Royal Navy; but he was almost equally intolerant and suspicious of the American Army. War against Japan was the problem to which he had devoted the study of a lifetime, and he resented the idea of American resources being used for any other purpose than to destroy the Japanese. He mistrusted Churchill's powers of advocacy, and was apprehensive that he would wheedle President Roosevelt into neglecting the war in the Pacific."[76] In this conclusion, King was correct about the early influence of the prime minister on the president. King, one of several American military leaders who thought the Pacific theater should have taken precedence over the European theater in war planning, was not shy in voicing his opinions. At the 1943 conference in Cairo, before the Teheran summit, Britain's Alan "Brooke got nasty and King got good and sore," reported General Joseph Stilwell, who was himself both cantankerous and anti-British. "King almost climbed over the table at Brooke. God, he was mad. I wish he had socked him."[77] General Brooke observed in his diary that King was "a shrewd and somewhat swollen headed individual. His vision is mainly limited to the Pacific."[78] The anti-English enmity of Admiral King was so great that at the Quebec conference in September 1944, he strongly objected even to participation of the British fleet in the Pacific theater.[79] The American navy could do it—all by itself—and then get the credit it deserved.

Although Admiral King preferred a Pacific-first strategy, it was ironic that his predecessor as CNO, Admiral Harold "Betty" Stark, had established in 1940 that Germany-first must be the U.S. priority, and he made that priority American policy. When King replaced Stark in 1942, Stark was ordered to London to organize Atlantic naval operations. Stark, though a mentor for King, was temperamentally very different from him.[80] Stark's diplomatic demeanor was a godsend for British-American coordination of antisubmarine warfare and preparations for D-Day. Stark had developed good relations down the line of command, starting with Churchill and King George VI. Stark's tasks were made considerably easier by the appointment of a well-connected British admiral, Geoffrey Blake, to Stark's staff.[81] Stark not only developed good relationships with First Sea Lord Dudley Pound and his successor, Admiral Andrew B. Cunningham; he also proved an important bridge to General Charles de Gaulle, especially in 1942–1943.[82] Stark's decades-long relationship with Roosevelt and King meant that he could communicate effectively with Washington.

Military planners in Washington were obsessed with keeping Russia in the war against Germany, and also getting Russia's assistance in what they thought would be a bloody conclusion to the war with Japan. So, too, thought FDR. The planners also sought to translate Roosevelt's vague pro-Russian ideas and dreams for postwar cooperation into concrete military plans. Anti-British, anti-imperial, and anti-Churchill suspicions were a commonplace in Roosevelt's Washington. Mark A. Stoler wrote that the anti-British military clique in Washington "came to recognize the importance of Western Europe to U.S. security, but their concern over British manipulation, belief in the limited and defensive nature of Soviet postwar goals, and fear of the catastrophic effects of another world war led them to perceive Soviet-American collaboration as an alternative approach, one that mirrored Roosevelt's own views and hopes." Stoler noted: "It is no accident that Marshall, [General Stanley D.] Embick and Stimson were three of the strongest and longest-lasting supporters of the cooperative policy vis-à-vis the Soviets, for it was the army that would have to take the bulk of the additional casualties in any extended war against Germany and Japan without Soviet participation and in any future war against the USSR."[83]

In many ways, the military planners in Washington, responsive to FDR, were more active in setting international political policy than their civilian counterparts in the State Department. They had better access to FDR and had the advantage of accompanying FDR to international summits. After their failures in the summer of 1942 to prevent TORCH, American military planners were consistently vigilant to blunt any Churchillian idea that deviated from their priorities. Moreover, the military planners led by Marshall had determined to work *with* FDR, rather than *against* him as they had in 1942. FDR's most expansive version of postwar policy was delivered in an offhand manner to the Joint Chiefs of Staff aboard the U.S.S. *Iowa* on November 15 and 19, 1943, on the way to the Teheran summit. The president communicated his prejudices, his thoughts on strategy, and his notions about postwar Germany. "As their position emerged from their talks, the JCS would support OVERLORD as scheduled, a campaign in Burma, and getting on with the Pacific War, but no Eastern Mediterranean–Balkan operation," wrote Maurice Matloff in the Army's official history of its strategic planning. "Never since the United States had entered the war had he [FDR] given them [the JCS] a glimpse of his reflections on the political problems that were bound up with the war and its outcome."[84] By 1943, Churchill and the British-American military planners grew more apprehensive about the long-term postwar military threat posed by the Soviet Union. They would try to use Russia to their short-term advantage. Eisenhower and other senior war leaders were anxious, for example, in January 1945, to determine when Russia would launch its next eastern offensive against Germany, a massive attack that would relieve German pressure on the Allied western front. British Air Marshal Tedder, Eisenhower's deputy, was dispatched to Moscow to confer with Stalin about joint Russian and Anglo-American strategy for the final months of the war. British interpreter A. H. Birse wrote of Tedder's visit that he "penetrated the inscrutable façade and left an impression of reliability and resolution. It was all accomplished without any high-sounding words or embellishments, but by a plain statement of the facts, delivered in an unambiguous way in his quiet voice."[85]

At the Cairo Conference, November 1943. Front: President Chiang Kai-shek of China, President Roosevelt, and Prime Minister Churchill. Back, left to right: General Henry "Hap" Arnold; Lt. General Brehon B. Somervell; General George C. Marshall, U.S. Army chief of staff; unknown; Field Marshall Sir John Dill; Air Chief Marshall Sir Charles Portal; Admiral William D. Leahy, Roosevelt's chief of staff; Admiral Ernest J. King, commander in chief, U.S. Navy; Admiral Sir Andrew Cunningham, commander of the British Fleet; General Sir Alan Brooke, British general chief of staff; Admiral Louis Mountbatten; General Sheng Chen, Chinese army; U.S. Lt. General Joseph W. Stillwell; Lt. General Ling Wol, Chinese army; and Major General Adrian Carton de Wiart of the British general staff.

FRANKLIN D. ROOSEVELT PRESIDENTIAL LIBRARY

XII

Unsung Stalwarts of the Alliance

The only times I ever quarrel with the Americans are when they fail to give us a fair share of opportunity to win glory. Undoubtedly I feel much pain when I see our armies so much smaller than theirs. It has always been my wish to keep equal, but how can you do that against so mighty a nation and a population nearly three times your own?[1]

***Winston S. Churchill**, letter to Clementine Churchill, April 6, 1945.*

The British seem to favor what might be called "an opportunist war," that is striking where and when the circumstances seem to dictate at a given moment. Americans, on the other hand, like to plan and fight by that plan and not run a hit or miss war.[2]

***Admiral Ernest King** to reporters, September 1943. From 1941 to 1945, King served as chief of naval operations, replacing Admiral Harold Stark. In 1940, Stark had promoted King to commander in chief, Atlantic Fleet, in which job King got to work with President Roosevelt. King deferred to FDR, but often clashed with other military leaders in the United States and Britain.*

World War II opened a new chapter in the complicated relations between the British Empire and its offspring, the United States of America. Protected, even isolated politically, by the Atlantic and Pacific Oceans, and the British Navy after the Napoleonic Wars, isolationism dominated America during the 1920s and 1930s. During this period, isolationism intensified because of America's bitter experience during and after World War I. Anti-British sentiments, exemplified by the socially ambitious U.S. Ambassador to Britain, Joseph P. Kennedy, were commonplace. Churchill aide John Colville wrote that the Anglo-American relationship changed markedly after Churchill became prime minister in May 1940. "[T]he main channel of business was direct from No. 10 to the White House. . . . On 27 May [1940], Lord Lothian, the British

Ambassador in Washington, reported a conversation with the President from which he deduced that if Britain really was *in extremis* the United States would enter the war. Kennedy for his part, assuming the role of Cassandra, sent home nothing but prophecies of woe; but fortunately his second-in-command at the embassy, the steadfast, loveable and unpretentious Herschel Johnson, was unrattled by the crescendo of disaster to the allied cause and maintained an attitude of commendable firmness."[3]

When General Raymond E. Lee arrived in London in early July 1940, to lead the American military intelligence mission, he came into conflict with Kennedy's chronic pessimism about Britain's future, compounded by the ambassador's sympathy for Hitler's Germany. After his first dinner at the prime minister's residence, Lee jotted: "10 Downing Street = powerhouse. Churchill knows people better than Chamberlain. Tells them facts: trouble, work, anguish. After nothing but defeat they are in better spirit."[4] From London, General Lee, privately skeptical of the leadership in both Britain and the United States, collected and transmitted information to Washington on the war effort, providing the raw data for serious American-British collaboration.

American aid to Britain depended on an accurate picture of British war mobilization, a briefing few British bureaucrats were anxious to provide. When Lee complained to Lord Beaverbrook in mid-December 1940 about problems in the free flow of information, Beaverbrook said he "had been accustomed to furnishing much valuable information direct to Morgenthau on Morgenthau's request. This is another piece of the damned foolishness which mixes everything up because there is information going to the President direct, information going to Morgenthau direct, information going through the Embassy, and probably a good deal of it does not agree with the rest of it, particularly the stuff that comes from Beaverbrook, who is not at all accurate about what he says."[5] Beaverbrook was as controversial in Britain as Hopkins was in the United States, but the key diplomatic roles played by both in developing Allied relationships were based on the trust between the president and the prime minister.

General Lee did not get on well with Beaverbrook, but he did so with General John Kennedy, Churchill's chief of military planning, and then-CIGS, John Dill. Early in the war, the cultured, well-read Lee, diplomat Herschel Johnson, Generals James Chaney and James McNarmey of the air corps, and Admiral Robert L. Ghormley were among the nearly invisible but able American representatives in London. They were key but quiet leaders who developed Anglo-American relationships by careful information sharing in the year before Pearl Harbor.[6] They did their best to implement American policy (not always clear to them) with British officials who were not always forthcoming. Such dedicated men, lower on the chain of command, helped to cement the victorious Anglo-American alliance. In a conversation with General Lee in July 1941, his English driver suggested that "there is a little more bonhomie about" in London. Lee agreed but added: "[D]on't you think, that for $7,000,000,000 [in American aid] . . . we ought to be entitled to a little bonhomie!"[7]

Lee was correct. Anglo-American bonhomie was often in short supply, even after years of cooperation. "The Arnold-King-Marshall combination is one of the stupidest strategic teams ever seen," an annoyed Churchill wrote in a memo to General Ismay on July 6, 1944, just a month after D-Day.[8] In Churchill's case, such sentiments occurred at moments of frustration but rarely in public. In Washington, serious divisions and lack of coordination persisted within and among key U.S. departments, like War and State. Some officials and officers of the Navy, War, and State Departments did work hard at coordination among the departments. Still, the roadblocks, conscious and otherwise, set up by President Roosevelt, Secretary of State Hull, and others, persisted because FDR and senior officials tended to delegate titles of authority without delegation of full power.[9] The sharing of intelligence among national agencies was often more difficult than between governments. War tends to engender confusion and chaos, notably on the battlefield, but off the battlefield, too, through competition for authority and suspicion of espionage. Harry Dexter White, the high-ranking deputy to Treasury Secretary Morgenthau, and a Soviet agent, arranged for interchange of information among the Departments of State, Treasury, and War, and diverted data to Soviet espionage channels. Through other American and British spies for the Soviet Union, Allied sources kept Moscow well informed.[10]

In 1940–1941, the Americans had trouble coordinating departmental preparations for war. In coordinating with the United Kingdom, they ran into internal conflicts among the British over issues such as the use of RAF bombers to hunt German U-boats, instead of bombing Germany itself.[11] In London, in May 1941, General Lee wrote in his diary that "[i]t has come to a pretty pass when the American Navy can come to an agreement with the British Navy, and the American Army can come to an agreement with the British Army, more easily than the American Army can come to an agreement with the American Navy."[12] Lee had proposed the creation of a Joint Intelligence Committee, but learned a few days later that FDR had rejected the idea, "saying he had no man who was capable of doing the work. He [FDR] cannot seem to understand that this is not a matter of personality so much as it is a matter of an organization. It only confirms what I have always heard, which is that Roosevelt knows practically nothing, and cares less, about administration."[13] General Lee's judgment of the president, also among friends and foes, was virtually universal. Many hollow rationalizations have been developed by FDR loyalists to justify Roosevelt's impulsive, disorganized administration, but none is convincing in the face of the hard evidence and testimony of so many who loyally worked for the president. Did the president's disorganization hinder the Allied war effort? The answer must be yes; but the vast industrial resources and manpower depth of the United States and Russia absorbed and mitigated Allied mistakes, even covered them up. Their resources and reserves dwarfed German, Italian, and Japanese reserves, armed manpower, and productive capacity. Moreover, Hitler and the Axis powers made even more mistakes than the Allies. The limited manpower and industrial depth of Hitler's Germany could not absorb major strategic errors with indifference, such as its invasion of Eastern Europe and the Soviet Union. Indeed, the Axis powers never coordinated war campaigns against the Allies.

Fortunately, Allied collaboration on the delivery of supplies, troops, munitions, and food was moved along by able executives such as Lewis W. Douglas, deputy chairman of the U.S. War Shipping Administration (WSA), and Beaverbrook's successor, Oliver Lyttelton, the British minister of production from 1942 to 1945. They collaborated with Hopkins and his team to move needed goods across the Atlantic. Historian George McJimsey wrote: "Gracious and good-natured when he held the upper hand, Douglas was a sarcastic, plain-speaking combatant in an administrative tussle. He was also wise enough to stay near the source of his power, and he cooperated with Hopkins and his network throughout his tenure with the WSA."[14] Lyttelton had met Hopkins when he had first visited Britain in January 1941, but he came to appreciate Hopkins's political talents when he visited Washington in June 1942. "At times, when the [American military] Services had reached some deadlock, I had to invoke the aid of Harry Hopkins," wrote Lyttelton in his memoirs. "If the President himself was the greatest maker of bottle-necks, Harry was the main force in breaking them down. He had an uncanny instinct for the essential. He added to this gift a great influence with the President, and a considerable hold over Generals Marshall and Arnold and Admiral King."[15] For his part, Hopkins wrote Churchill: "Oliver is here and getting about his business quietly but effectively."[16]

Methods of military management in Britain and the United States differed too. The British coordination of military services at the top was superior, although interservice problems naturally persisted lower down the chain of command. The British exercised more direct control of the line of command. They thought their organizational structure preferable to the American style. General Eisenhower recalled: "The American doctrine has always been to assign a theater commander a mission, to provide him with a definite amount of force, and then to interfere as little as possible in the execution of his plans." In contrast, Eisenhower observed that "the British Chiefs in London maintained throughout the war the closest kind of daily contact with their own commanders in the field and insisted upon being constantly informed as to details of strength, plans, and situation."[17] To launch and manage an operation as complicated as the D-Day invasion required a joint Allied command structure under Eisenhower, detached from the usual British chain of command—but clearly modeled on the more integrated British command system.

To Eisenhower's credit, he was able to create and maintain the unified joint Allied command structure and to administer it effectively. Eisenhower not only became the leading exponent of Anglo-American unity; he became its embodiment. As General Hastings Ismay observed, Eisenhower "regarded Anglo-American friendship almost as a religion."[18] The bloody, bruising success of D-Day was a living monument to the Combined Chiefs of Staff, and the tight relationship that American and British leaders had built up over four years. Statistics confirm the genius of their well-organized, if tense, partnership: over two million men and over three million tons of supplies had been landed in France, in but two months after the invasion.[19] On May 9, 1945, the day following VE-Day, Prime Minister Churchill wrote President Truman: "Let me tell you what General Eisenhower has meant to us. In him we have had a man who set the unity of the Allied Armies above all nationalistic thoughts. In his headquarters unity and strategy were the only reigning spirits. . . . At no time has the principle of alliance between noble races been carried and maintained at so high a pitch. In the name of the British Empire and Commonwealth I express to you our admiration of the firm, far-sighted, and illuminating character and qualities of General of the Armies Eisenhower."[20] In the glow of victory, the prime minister overlooked his former criticisms of General Eisenhower. These very criticisms would reemerge in his postwar writing, as well as during his second government as prime minister (1951–1955).

The entire, complicated British-American relationship was held together by much more than the mutual respect of the prime minister and the president. During World War II, Roosevelt and Churchill appointed envoys and military leaders who worked at close quarters with one another in unprecedented harmony, despite suspicions and prejudices that some colleagues and countrymen harbored about each other. The Anglo-American relationship was inspired and reinforced by strong entrepreneurial envoys such as William Donovan, Harry Hopkins, Averell Harriman, and Max Beaverbrook, all of whom operated confidently with the delegated authority of the president and the prime minister. Not all envoys were created equal, and there were outliers from the best alliance model. Former Moscow Ambassador Joseph Davies, who remained close to FDR, was considered a joke as an envoy to Moscow; even the Russians made fun of his sycophantic film *Mission to Moscow.* Roosevelt nevertheless valued the views of the bumptious Davies, who reflected FDR's consistent desire to do whatever necessary to please Stalin. Because the president and the State Department thought Ambassador William H. Standley's candor had unnecessarily alienated Stalin, the president sent Davies to Moscow in April 1943 to arrange a summit between the Russian and American leaders.[21]

Such special envoys could and did undermine the authority and influence of respected, credentialed ambassadors abroad, emasculating the role of the State Department at home. During a White House meeting in December 1942, Ambassador Standley emphasized to FDR that visits by 1940 Republican presidential candidate Wendell Willkie and similar dignitaries made very difficult the performance of his duties. Roosevelt "ignored my statement about Willkie and turned to Bill Leahy with some offhand remarks. As we rose to go, my last words to the President were, 'Chief, you got your fingers burnt once, with Mr. Willkie. Don't do it again.'" Indeed, when Vice President Henry Wallace toured Russia and China in 1944, he was kept far away from Moscow, forestalling any potentially embarrassing comments the Soviet sympathizer might make there. The course of the war showed that strong leaders such as Roosevelt and Churchill needed subordinates willing to challenge them. As Andrew Roberts showed in *Masters and Commanders,* the prime minister and the president needed each other and their military chiefs, to avoid any one of them creating strategic errors. Useful to this purpose was the fact that a military leader like General Alan Brooke was not intimidated by the prime minister; nor was General George C. Marshall cowed or charmed by FDR.

The British and the Americans did harbor many suspicions about each other, and about their conflicting strategic objectives in the war. Many American officials believed British strategy aimed to preserve its empire. The British suspected that

American claims of high-minded idealism masked a desire to wrest trade advantages from a disassembled British Empire.[22] FDR and those he influenced spent too much time doubting their British ally and its fading empire, instead of focusing on the Soviet Union and the Russian bear's transparent, imperial appetite during and after the war. For example, disagreements mounted over the amount of German reparations at Yalta in February 1945. Hopkins wrote FDR a note: "The Russians have given us so much at this conference that I don't think we should let them down. Let the British disagree if they want to, and continue their disagreement at Moscow."[23] Roosevelt and Hopkins, in some ways more sympathetic to the Soviets than to the British, were too ready to believe Hopkins's mistaken view that the Russians gave much at Yalta.

In a war environment, just as in any competitive circumstances, building bridges of trust is hard, but essential. Building bridges did not come naturally for many self-centered military officers—for some of whom condescension came more naturally. John S. D. Eisenhower, who was a West Point cadet for much of World War II, wrote of "the remarkable dislike for everything British held by many of the senior American officers. Some of it doubtless originated in resentment of the condescension exhibited by the British military toward Americans in general. This national dislike, so prevalent west of the Alleghenies, was exacerbated by a feeling of professional inferiority, a realization that the British chiefs had been lieutenant generals when most of the Americans had been lieutenant colonels."[24] Historically, British military officers came from the aristocracy of a class-ridden society; whereas American officers were primarily middle-class, in a society with no aristocracy based on heredity.

Soon after General Eisenhower arrived in Britain in the summer of 1942, he told British General Ismay, Churchill's top military aide: "If we are not going to be frank with each other, however delicate the topic, we will never win this war."[25] Meetings, formal and informal, were critical. "British and Americans met round the bar, went for walks down to the beach together, and sat around in each other's rooms in the evenings," wrote a top British military officer of the Casablanca summit in January 1943. "Mutual respect and understanding ripen in such surroundings, especially when the weather is lovely, the accommodation is good, and food and drink and smokes are unlimited and free."[26] At formal sessions, tensions returned—even after the pleasant tour of Virginia's colonial Williamsburg arranged by Marshall in May 1943. Tensions also returned after a tour of Quebec's Plains of Abraham in August 1943, the better to understand the heroic confrontation there between British and French soldiers in 1759.[27] They were, after all, fighting men; they fought, but then they made peace.

Sometimes the most effective intermediaries among the Allies were the least likely. Lord Beaverbrook was widely considered impossible by many of his British cabinet colleagues, but he operated effectively with Hopkins and Harriman, even with Stalin. Like Hopkins, Beaverbrook could advise about how the two national leaders might better achieve their objectives. When Marshall proposed a unified command for Southeast Asia in early 1942, Churchill balked. Beaverbrook wrote a note to Hopkins: "You should work on Churchill. . . . He is open-minded and needs discussion."[28] Always suspicious of American economic motives, Beaverbrook still kept open the lines of communication to the White House.[29]

Even good men who were demoted proved useful. Churchill grew tired of the prudent, quiet British General John Dill, replacing him as Chief of the Imperial General Staff with General Brooke. The prime minister sent Dill to the United States, where he became the indispensable link between the American chiefs of staff and their British counterparts. Brooke and his American counterpart, George C. Marshall, both admired and trusted Dill. "Marshall had to create an American army from an even more complete state of unpreparedness, and no praise can be too great for what he achieved," wrote Lord Halifax, the former foreign secretary who was the British ambassador in Washington from 1941 to 1946. Marshall and Dill "were entirely devoid of any thought of self-seeking and were heart and soul devoted to the achievement of Allied Victory. With complete confidence in each other's motives, they could examine every case without risk of the conclusion being affected by any consideration smaller than the merits of it."[30] Thus, Marshall learned from Dill much of what the British were thinking, and Dill learned from Marshall what the American chiefs of staff thought. This back-channel flow of information enabled the Allied Combined Chiefs of Staff to keep well informed of the thoughts of the prime minister and the president. For example, Dill could tell Marshall what FDR told Churchill but failed to tell his own army chief of staff, Marshall. Dill's appointment to Washington was matched by the appointment of former Chief of Naval Operations Harold Stark to London in 1942. Dill and Stark had the diplomatic skills, the institutional knowledge, and access to information so needed by the Anglo-American military alliance.[31]

American General Tom Handy observed that American "military people were at a marked disadvantage compared with the British. You see, Mr. Churchill was not only the prime minister, but also he was minister of defense, and, as you know, he was in intimate touch with his staff officers at all hours of the day and night. And he was vitally interested. But the prime minister of England is not the same as the President of the United States. You don't just casually see the President—it isn't that kind of thing. The British knew what was on Churchill's mind. We didn't know what was on the President's. So at times the only way we could find out what the prime minister and the President were up to was through Sir John [Dill]."[32] He and Marshall worked in tandem to prevent disagreements between Britain and America from stalling joint action. Dill, never able to master his relationship with Churchill in London, proved a particularly skillful military diplomat in Washington—mastering and fostering Anglo-American relations as he did.[33] The institutional comparison by General Handy of a distant presidency and hands-on prime ministership was not in principle correct, even if true in practice. FDR, as commander in chief, was at liberty to be as hands-on as Churchill. (For example, President Abraham Lincoln at war was even more hands-on than the prime minister.) In fact, FDR preferred a detached distance, not engagement with line responsibility. But the high quality of his military appointments, as well as the depth of American manpower and production capacity, compensated for his disorganized habits.

Harry Hopkins understood and encouraged the importance of mutual respect and friendship between the commanders in chief. In July 1941, General Lee wrote that

Hopkins "said he was not at all qualified to make decisions on large matters of military supply, and he is apprehensive lest great events might turn upon the decisions which he makes without any real military knowledge. He said that he would really like to manage matters so that the thing [Lend-Lease] would run smoothly and he could unload it." Furthermore, Hopkins emphasized: "The only thing I really want to do as my contribution to the success of this was to arrange for General Marshall to establish and maintain complete free access to the President." Because Roosevelt desired some involvement in strategic military decisions, "I think a close relationship between Marshall and [then Chief of Naval Operations] Stark on the one hand and the President on the other is absolutely essential."[34] Such a relationship with the top military brass was critical, because FDR did not embrace close, daily links with his military leaders that Churchill strived to maintain.

Active cooperation between Britain and the United States—beyond Lend-Lease supplies and military equipment going from the United States to the United Kingdom and Russia—began during the Battle of the Atlantic in 1941, long before Pearl Harbor. For example, the United States extended its military sphere in the Atlantic, farther east, in order to reduce the convoy protection burden undertaken by an overstretched Britain. Churchill had concluded prematurely that the Battle of the Atlantic had been nearly won in mid-1941, but the effectiveness of U-boat attacks on U.S. convoys to the United Kingdom intensified in the second half of the year, threatening the British naval lifeline of food and war supplies. When the British "Ultra" decrypts of the Nazi signals from "Enigma" were working, the British Navy and RAF destroyed U-boats. When the Nazis added a fourth wheel to Enigma, the British decrypts failed, and the U-boats could again torpedo convoys with impunity. Ultimately, the U-boat menace was overcome, and the convoys became indispensable in moving supplies and manpower across the Atlantic to prepare for D-Day.

Early in 1941, British naval officials had pressed the United States to send its fleet to Singapore, to deter a Japanese attack. In February, Churchill rebuked the Admiralty: "Anyone could have seen that the United States would not base a battle-fleet on Singapore and divide their naval forces."[35] But the prime minister overrated air power. He had written to the War Cabinet on September 3, 1940: "The Navy can lose us the war, but only the Air Force can win it."[36] That summer, Churchill had declared that "only one thing" would "bring [Hitler] down," and that is an absolutely devastating, exterminating attack by very heavy bombers from this country upon the Nazi homeland. We must be able to overwhelm them by this means, *without which I do not see a way through.*"[37] Churchill thought such a tactic was in part retaliation for Nazi bombing of English cities. Thus, until D-Day in June 1944, area bomber attacks on Germany and its cities became a primary Allied attack strategy. Cooperation between British and American naval and air forces had become effective in 1941 and 1942, but cooperation among officers of the Allied land forces designated for a cross-channel invasion required much more planning. The first major test of a sea-based invasion came in November 1942, with the launch of Operation TORCH in North Africa. TORCH was successful. The major errors and omissions in the planning and execution of TORCH prepared the Allies for the infinitely more complex cross-channel invasion on D-Day.

As in all human affairs, military and political egos could be impediments to Allied victory—as they surely were between the "frock coats" (politicians) and "brass hats" (generals) in World War I, a conflict Churchill would not permit as prime minister and minister of defence in World War II. On the military side, American General Eisenhower and British Air Marshal Arthur Tedder led the coordination of air and ground forces necessary for success in the invasions of North Africa and France.[38] There were many Anglo-American officers who lacked their vision and steady temperament. Because he needed Marshall at home, FDR had selected Eisenhower for overall D-Day command. It was a wise choice. "Sometimes when I get tired of trying to arrange the blankets smoothly over several prima donnas in the same bed I think that no one person in the world can have so many illogical problems," Eisenhower confided to Marshall in March 1945, before he acknowledged that the problems of the army chief of staff were even worse than his.[39] Eisenhower's extraordinary diplomacy even extended to his relations with testy General Charles de Gaulle. Anthony Eden noted that Eisenhower smoothed the transition to an important role for de Gaulle after D-Day, writing that "the Supreme Commander had never failed to practise patient diplomacy."[40]

Churchill supported Air Marshal Tedder, over less astute and less cooperative officials in the Air Ministry. His decision was a key to D-Day success. But Tedder had his hands full dealing with the obstinate leaders of the American and British air forces.[41] "Now, listen, Arthur," an exasperated Eisenhower told Tedder by telephone on March 6, 1944. "I am tired of dealing with a lot of prima donnas. By God, you tell that bunch that if they can't get together and stop quarreling like children, I will tell the Prime Minister to get someone else to run this damn war."[42] Among the most difficult British officers in the D-Day planning was Air Marshal Arthur Harris, who considered Operation OVERLORD a diversion from his cherished bombing of German cities. Harris declared: "If we attempt to substitute for this process [German city bombing] attacks on gun emplacements, beach defences, communications or [ammunition] dumps in occupied territory [France], we shall commit the irremediable error of diverting our best weapons from the military function, for which it has been equipped and trained, to tasks which it cannot effectively carry out."[43] "Bomber Harris" did not weaken over the following months. "He complained what a nuisance this Overlord operation was," recalled Admiral Cunningham of a May 1944 meeting of the top commanders, "and how it interfered with the right way to defeat Germany, i.e., by bombing."[44]

In the end, Harris cooperated with Eisenhower. The notoriously independent Harris subordinated himself to Tedder and the goals of OVERLORD. Biographer Henry Probert wrote: "The great variety of operations Harris and his men were now being called on to undertake marked a major turning point in Bomber Command's war. No more—at least for the present—were they concentrating mainly on large-scale attacks on relatively distant targets. Instead they were often being required to divide their forces so as to attack simultaneously objectives of many different types, such as railways, aircraft factories, airfield, military depots and coastal batteries." Harris even obeyed directions to concentrate against V-1 sites. Eisenhower wrote Marshall on September 25, 1944: "In view of earlier expressed fears that Harris would not willingly devote his Command to the support of ground operations, he actually proved to be one of the most effective and co-operative members of this team. Not only did he meet every request I ever made of him, but he actually took the lead in discovering new ways and means for his particular types of planes to be of use in the battlefield." Harris himself later paid tribute to "one period of calm sailing . . . when all went well, when all pulled together, when there was at last continuity of contact between the compass course required and the lubber line—and that was during the all too short period when Eisenhower was Admiral and Tedder the Captain on the bridge."[45]

Fortuitous events also played a part in the selection of Allied officers for key positions. In 1942, Admiral Stark was appointed commander of Naval Forces Europe. Previously, as chief of naval operations (CNO), Stark had played a key role in pushing for a Europe-first strategy, even before the United States entered the war.[46] In November 1940, Stark had been the leading proponent of Plan Dog, emphasizing the priority of Germany over Japan as the top military target in the event of war. Churchill remarked: "In my view Admiral Stark is right, and Plan D is strategically sound and also most highly adapted to our interests. We should therefore, so far as opportunity serves, in every way contribute to strengthen the policy of Admiral Stark, and should not use arguments inconsistent with it."[47] Stark may not have been the tough, nail-chewing battle chief that his successor Ernest King typified, but Stark proved the kind of low-key planner who made Anglo-American strategic cooperation possible.[48]

Stark's reputation had been deeply wounded by the Pearl Harbor disaster. A Naval Court of Inquiry in 1944 found Stark and Admiral Husband E. Kimmel responsible for Pearl Harbor. CNO King initially endorsed the findings, but in 1948, he reversed himself and withdrew his endorsement: "Considering that Admiral Stark had occupied the most important post in European waters, by order of President Roosevelt, for the better part of three years immediately preceding the date of the endorsement, that he remained in that post during the entire war and until he was ordered to duty in the Navy Department in late 1945, and that his performance of duty in high office during that period was in all respects outstanding, the suggestion that he be relegated to a subordinate position in which superior judgment would not be required seems to me now to have been singularly inappropriate."[49]

Admiral King, the noisiest "Pacific First" official in Washington, helped push Stark out as the navy's chief in early 1941. In his London-based role, Stark presided over the American contribution to the Battle of the Atlantic and the naval buildup to D-Day. "More than 4,000 naval ships and craft and over 100,000 naval officers and men were used in the D Day assault. The fact that these ships and men were available is directly attributable to the efforts of Admiral Stark," declared Eisenhower in July 1944. "Planning for the assault was complete in the smallest detail, and served to make the combined naval and ground forces of the United States an integrated unit. The results so far accomplished in this assault on the Fortress of Europe would have been impossible without the complete and wholehearted support on the part of the Navy."[50] Stark was exactly the kind of team player that D-Day required.

So was British Vice Admiral Bertram Ramsay, the unflappable Allied commander of naval forces for D-Day, who had superintended the evacuation of Dunkirk in 1940, as well as the naval effort of Operations TORCH and HUSKY. Ramsay's attention to detailed instructions for naval units on D-Day annoyed his American counterpart, Admiral Alan Kirk, who was both anti-British and insubordinate.[51] Historian Correlli Barnett wrote that Ramsay "combined austere personal integrity, high professionalism and a personal warmth which won the enthusiastic loyalty of his subordinates."[52] Admiral Cunningham, who succeeded First Sea Lord Dudley Pound in late 1943, likewise provided a model for Anglo-American cooperation not always found in top officers of the air and ground commands. Eisenhower developed good relations with Cunningham, writing in his diary after Operation TORCH: "He remains in my opinion at the top of my subordinates in absolute selflessness, energy, devotion to duty, knowledge of his task, and in understanding of the requirements of allied operations. My opinions as to his superior qualifications have never wavered for a second."[53]

Allied military and civilian authorities did not always evaluate data or forecasts the same way. In 1944, British authorities, backed by dubious statistics produced by "The Prof" Lindemann, Churchill's science advisor, raised serious objections to Air Marshal Tedder's plan to bomb German transportation junctions prior to D-Day. Churchill feared that heavy French civilian casualties would destroy French morale and support for the invasion. Eisenhower and FDR backed Tedder's bombing plan, which proved indispensable to Allied success. Eisenhower responded to British criticism of the plan: "The French people are slaves [of the Nazis]. Only a successful OVERLORD can free them." To Washington, Eisenhower wrote of Tedder's Transportation Plan: "There is no other way in which this tremendous air force can help us, during the preparatory phase, to get ashore and stay there."[54] Tedder even proved an effective emissary when he was detailed to meet in Moscow with Stalin in August 1942, and again in January 1945. When Stalin was given two boxes of cigars on the second visit, the dictator coarsely asked: "When do they go off?" The British officer looked at his watch and replied: "[N]ot until after I've gone."[55]

Marshall, the principled, disciplined organizer of America's overall war effort, might have clashed more with Brooke and Churchill, had Marshall been named OVERLORD commander. Eisenhower could on occasion be tough *and* diplomatic. Marshall could let his temper get away from him. On November 25, 1943, during a military chiefs meeting in Cairo, Churchill grandly told Marshall: "His Majesty's Government can't have its troops standing idle. Muskets must flame" in a British invasion of the island of Rhodes. The prime minister's preoccupation with the capture of the Dodecanese islands annoyed the top American commanders. But his declining influence on the Roosevelt administration in 1943 hardened the American military attitude toward Churchill. In the case of the proposed invasion of Rhodes, Marshall responded: "God forbid if I should try to dictate but . . . not one American soldier is going to die on [that] goddamned beach." Marshall added: "Churchill never held this against me, but Ismay had to stay up with him all night."[56] Marshall's demeanor and constrained temper were enough to discipline an overbearing and stubborn prime minister.

From left to right, U.S. Secretary of State Edward Stettinius, British Permanent Under-Secretary for Foreign Affairs Sir Alexander Cadogan, and U.S. Ambassador to the Soviet Union Averell Harriman, pictured in February 1945.
FRANKLIN D. ROOSEVELT PRESIDENTIAL LIBRARY

XIII

W. Averell Harriman

> As you know, I am a confirmed optimist in our relations with Russia because of my conviction that Stalin wants, if obtainable, a firm understanding with you [FDR] and America more than anything else—after the destruction of Hitler. He sees Russia's reconstruction and security more soundly based on it than on any alternative. He is a man of simple purposes and, although he may use devious means in attempting to accomplish them, he does not deviate from his long-run objectives.[1]
>
> ***W. Averell Harriman*** *(1891–1986), letter to Franklin D. Roosevelt, July 5, 1943. Harriman was the son of E. Roland Harriman, the Union Pacific Railroad tycoon. Harriman founded his own Wall Street investment firm in the 1920s. He allied himself with President Franklin D. Roosevelt and his associate Harry Hopkins. In World War II, Harriman maneuvered to be named to a key post. He was first named Lend-Lease administrator in Britain, and later U.S. Ambassador to Moscow.*

> This war is not as in the past; whoever occupies a territory also imposes on it his own social system. Everyone imposes his own system as far as his army can reach. It cannot be otherwise.[2]
>
> ***Joseph Stalin*** *(1878–1953) in an April 1945 interview with Milovan Djilas. Born Iosif Vissarionovich Dzhugashvili in Georgia, Stalin became a Bolshevik revolutionary. After the death of Lenin, he rose to the top of the Bolshevik party through maneuver and bloody purges. Stalin became the unchallenged dictator of the Soviet Union, every bit as powerful in the Soviet Union as Adolf Hitler in Germany.*

After Harry Hopkins had returned from his first trip to Britain in early 1941, President Roosevelt chose W. Averell Harriman to "go over to London and recommend everything that we can do, short of war, to keep the British Isles afloat."[3] As was often the case with FDR's diplomacy, Harriman's appointment and his work coordinating war assistance, including Lend-Lease, occurred outside the usual diplomatic channels.

Secretary of State Cordell Hull supported the Harriman initiative, despite his "mission's independence of the State Department."[4] In March 1941, the new envoy took up his duties in London as FDR's designated "expediter" of economic and supply matters.

Upon arrival in Britain on March 15, Harriman went directly to Chequers to meet with Churchill. "You shall be kept informed," the prime minister told Harriman. "We accept you as a friend. Nothing will be kept from you."[5] Harriman became fully integrated into Churchill's household. "Harriman, hardworking, well informed and cosmopolitan in experience, may have been daunted by his first invitation to dine at 10 Downing Street," recalled John Colville. "After dinner he was given a steel helmet and bidden to follow the Prime Minister onto the Air Ministry roof to watch a sharp and noisy air raid. His face was long, handsome, but rather heavy and the general impression was one of almost uniform grayness. He spoke, like Hopkins, slowly and deliberately. He was serious and his smile was the more attractive for being comparatively rare. Everything he did he did well, and he found the second best intolerable."[6] Like Hopkins, Harriman was quickly brought into the Churchill social circle—visiting Chequers or Ditchley Park on weekends, bonding with Clementine Churchill over croquet and backgammon games.[7]

The self-reliant and aggressive Harriman soon invaded the territory and authority of Ambassador Winant. Harriman observed in his memoirs that the London assignment "was another of Roosevelt's improvisations, designed in part to keep Cordell Hull and the State Department at arm's length while he and Churchill, using the Harriman channel, worked out their strategic decisions."[8] Once installed in London, Harriman "involv[ed] himself more and more in matters that had nothing to do with Lend-Lease," wrote historian Lynne Olson. "As a businessman and sportsman, he had long been known for his sharp-edged, elbows-out tactics."[9] As he had with Hopkins, Churchill took Harriman with him on trips around Britain to survey the impact of Nazi bombing. At Chequers on Easter Sunday, 1941, Colville "asked Harriman if he did not think last night's news from the U.S. might mean war with Germany." The night before, FDR had announced that U.S. naval patrols in the Atlantic would be extended eastward toward Europe, thus relieving the British Navy of the duty. Harriman responded: "That's what I hope."[10]

Roosevelt resisted being drawn into the war. A few weeks later, Churchill "dictated a telegram to the President drawing a sombre picture of what a [British] collapse in the Middle East would entail. Then he sketched to Harriman, Pug [Ismay] and me a world in which Hitler dominated all of Europe, Asia and Africa and left the U.S. and ourselves no option but an unwilling peace."[11] (Both Winant and Harriman would develop other relationships with the Churchills. Harriman had an affair with the prime minister's ambitious daughter-in-law Pamela, whose marriage to his son had just begun; Winant became involved with his daughter, Sarah, whose marriage was dissolving.[12])

Hopkins and Harriman created and reinforced vital links between FDR and Churchill—particularly in the critical year of 1941. Historian Fraser Harbutt observed that the prime minister "took the Americans to high-level meetings where secret matters were discussed; he encouraged them to criticize the British effort; and he corresponded with them regularly—often in a more frank and pragmatic manner than one reads in the Churchill-Roosevelt letters of 1941—on a variety of practical issues, from Lend-Lease supply to the state of American opinion."[13] Ambassador Winant would occasionally travel to the United States, to confer with FDR; Harriman would return more frequently from Europe to report to the president, especially in the early years of the war. Harriman ranged far and wide, relentlessly extending his authority, based on his relationship with not only FDR, but also the prime minister. He had first met Churchill in early 1927, when he was returning from a business trip to Russia. Harriman made a detour to Cannes, to consult him when he was chancellor of the exchequer. In June 1941, when Harriman visited Cairo, he took with him a letter from Churchill to General Wavell: "Mr. Harriman enjoys my complete confidence and is in the most intimate relations with the President and with Mr. Harry Hopkins. No one can do more for you."[14] In between his foreign sojourns, Harriman sometimes went directly to Hyde Park, where the Roosevelts collected an odd assortment of family, aides, friends, and exiled royalty at their Springwood estate.[15]

While in New York during the summer of 1941, Harriman lobbied FDR to attend the upcoming Placentia Bay conference with the British.[16] After the summit in Canada, the prime minister decided that Harriman and Beaverbrook—already working on Anglo-American war production problems—should consult with the Russians in Moscow. Over the opposition of military leaders, Churchill proposed to divert to Russia some American aid meant for Britain. "I brought the proposal to send Lord Beaverbrook to Moscow before my colleagues on August 28," wrote Churchill in his memoirs. "The Cabinet were very willing that he should present the case to Stalin, and the President felt himself well represented by Harriman."[17] The prime minister noted that the demanding Stalin was not realistic about Anglo-American aid. After an exchange of messages early in September, the Russian leader wrote his British counterpart in mid-month: "It seems to me that Great Britain could without risk land in Archangel twenty-five to thirty divisions, or transport them across Iran to the southern regions of the U.S.S.R." In his memoirs, Churchill commented: "It is almost incredible that the head of the Russian Government with all the advice of their military experts could have committed himself to such absurdities."[18] But Stalin was desperate as German armies advanced toward Moscow.

Beaverbrook, once a supporter of Chamberlain's appeasement policies, had become what the prime minister called "the champion in the War Cabinet of Aid to Russia."[19] Harriman himself was surprised to be chosen as the U.S. representative on the Moscow mission, since both Secretary of the Treasury Henry Morgenthau and Secretary of the Navy Frank Knox wanted the job. Harriman's relationship with Churchill and Beaverbrook prevailed. Beaverbrook, angling at that moment to replace Lord Halifax as ambassador in Washington, argued that Eden and Hopkins should lead the mission to Moscow. The prime minister could not be moved, writing Beaverbrook: "I wish you to go to Moscow with Mr. Harriman in order to arrange the long-term supply of the Russian armies. This can only be achieved almost entirely from American resources, though we have rubber, boots, etc. . . . Your function will be not only to aid in the forming of the plans to help Russia, but to make sure we are not bled white in the process, and even if you find yourself affected by the Russian atmosphere, I shall be quite stiff about it here. I am sure, however, you are the man for the job, and the public instinct has endorsed it." Churchill added: "The decision to send Harriman means that Hopkins does not feel well enough to go himself."[20]

Beaverbrook, Ismay, and Harriman flew from the Scapa Flow naval base in Scotland to Russia on September 22, 1941. Ismay recalled: "Immediately on arrival we had a meeting amongst ourselves in Beaverbrook's room. It was impossible to talk freely, owing to the fact that microphones were almost certainly installed everywhere." They found Stalin's mood could shift abruptly in dealing with his Anglo-American allies. The first meeting at the Kremlin went well, but "Beaverbrook and Harriman returned from their second meeting at the Kremlin in the depths of depression. For some unknown reason the atmosphere had been very different from that of the previous evening. Stalin had been unmannerly and apparently uninterested."[21] Beaverbrook had gone to Moscow with a unique negotiating strategy—whatever the Russians wanted, they should have. Harriman told his fellow Americans upon arrival: "To give and give and give, with no expectation of any return, with no thought of a quid pro quo."[22] As usual, the British press lord wanted his mission to make a big splash. "Whenever the technical committees reached deadlock, Beaverbrook and Harriman saw Stalin on their own and met his demands," wrote Beaverbrook biographer A. J. P. Taylor. "Time and again, Beaverbrook gave up Great Britain's share of American supplies so that it could be allotted to Russia. As the list rolled on, [Russian Foreign Ministry official Maxim] Litvinov, who was interpreting, bounded from his seat and cried: 'Now we shall win the war'. Stalin, although less demonstrative, was also impressed."[23] Churchill himself believed Russia indispensable to the defeat of Hitler's armies. For Russia, the war would be catastrophic. By 1946, 27 million Soviet soldiers and citizens had died in the war against the Nazis.[24] Stalin's murderous dictatorship had been saved by the bravery of his people, his soldiers, and American equipment. The Russians won the ground war against the Germans in Europe, though the Allied cross-channel invasion surely helped to deliver the *coup de grace*.

General Hastings Ismay, who served as military chief of staff to Defence Minister Churchill, often took part in missions to North America or Russia. He traveled to Moscow with Averell Harriman and Max Beaverbrook in the fall of 1941, again with the prime minister in August 1942, and a third time in October 1944. Strange things would happen on these trips. For example, on the final trip, the British delegation was ready to depart when "two large crates of vodka and caviare . . . [were] loaded into our aircraft without a word of explanation." After they had been distributed in London to friends and family, the diplomats learned that the vodka had been intended for the Russian embassy, specifically for Russian military officers.[25]

Like Beaverbrook, Harriman intrigued to be present when major Anglo-American and Anglo-American-Russian conferences took place. Historians Walter Isaacson and Evan Thomas wrote: "Harriman was the type of busy man who took pride in always being busy."[26] General Alan Brooke acknowledged that he disliked Harriman, "who annoys me intensely."[27] Harriman was not an easy businessman to work with. American diplomat Charles Bohlen wrote of Harriman: "One thing he does not like is too much contradiction although he enjoys a good discussion."[28] Bohlen doubted that Harriman "ever fully understood the nature of the Soviet system. Reading ideological books was not his forte. He had an enormous capacity for assessing the tactical nature of the problem and for understanding what the Soviets were after in a specific situation. But he did not take the indispensable step of relating his keen observations to the over-all Soviet ideological attitude toward the world and the capitalist nations."[29] His were the tactical insights of a commercial man. It should not be forgotten that Harriman was born to one of the great American fortunes; his family was a major influence in American politics. From birth, he was accustomed to getting his way. He became a shrewd, second-generation man of affairs.

Whenever there was a major summit, Harriman was usually there. In August 1942, Harriman flew with Churchill to Moscow. (Roosevelt had refused Harriman permission to go to Moscow with Churchill in August 1942, but Harriman prevailed on the prime minister to persuade the president to change his mind.[30]) Harriman described the airplane: "It was converted for passengers in the most primitive manner, without insulation, and with two rows of hard benches facing each other. The noise was so great it made conversation impossible."[31] Conversations with Stalin proved even more difficult, especially when the topic of the delayed Anglo-American second front came up. Despite Stalin's demands, the second front would be postponed.

Harriman ingratiated himself with Churchill at cards.[32] (Hopkins used backgammon.[33]) In April 1943, the prime minister decided to travel to the United States aboard the *Queen Mary*—along with 5,000 German prisoners below decks. He invited Beaverbrook and Harriman to go with him—giving plenty of time for Harriman and Churchill to play bézique, a two-pack game of cards he enjoyed. Harriman recalled that Churchill "talked a lot during bézique and afterward, when we went along to the War Room, about the amount of effort that was being put into protecting this ship. He spoke of the tremendous courage and risks of the merchant seamen." Harriman took this intimate opportunity to caution the prime minister about criticizing the very aggressive U.S. bombing strategy: "I said that the anti-British and anti-Atlantic group were always ready to explain how wise the British were when it was [in] their interest to do so. This seemed to amuse him and later on in the evening, he said: 'Don't worry, I won't express my views about bombing; but it is a tragedy that your brave men are taking such risks in order to prove a theory when they could be more effectively employed—and at less risk.'"[34] The prime minister made a valid point about the U.S. continental bombing raids conducted in broad daylight. More than half of American airmen who flew on those raids would perish.

On this trip to the United States, Churchill told Harriman what Churchill intimates knew well: "I won't be captured. The finest way to die is in the excitement of fighting the enemy." He acknowledged: "[I]t might not to be so nice if one were in the water and they tried to pick me up." Harriman responded: "Prime Minister, this is all very disquieting to me. I thought you told me that the worst a torpedo could do to this ship, because of its compartments, was to knock out one engine room, leaving sufficient power to steam at twenty knots." Churchill responded: "Ah, but they might put two torpedoes in us. You must come with me in the [life]boat and see the fun."[35] It was such cavalier, *sang-froid* moments that Churchill enjoyed with noncabinet emissaries of Roosevelt, but rarely with cabinet-level or subcabinet officials. As prime minister, he generally respected British protocol. Fraser Harbutt wrote that "Churchill drew a sharp distinction between presidential agents and department heads. Thus, in a crucial moment during the 1941 Lend-Lease negotiations, he resisted Whitehall's efforts to involve him directly with the United States secretary of the Treasury, Henry Morgenthau Jr., minuting, 'I do not think it would be a good thing for me to try to deal either directly or indirectly with one of the President's Departmental Chiefs.'" Clearly, he thought it desirable and appropriate to maintain his relationship with the United States through two primary channels—the president himself and persons he viewed as the president's confidants.[36] The prime minister well understood that in war, the president was the commander in chief, endowed with full executive power. To deal with the president's envoys was to deal with the decision maker.

In June 1943, Harriman and Max Beaverbrook travelled together from the United States to Moscow, at a time when Russian relationships with the United States and Britain had frayed because of the postponement of the second front, the Allied invasion of France. In Moscow, Harriman "was to deliver the message that the President proposed to meet privately with Stalin prior to any formal conference of the Big Three. The objective, as expressed by Secretary of State Hull, was "to talk Mr. Stalin out of his shell, so to speak, away from his aloofness, secretiveness and suspiciousness until he broadens his views, visualizes a more practical international cooperation in the West. . . . Roosevelt believed that he would get along better with Stalin in Churchill's absence." (This particular conceit FDR would nurse until his death.)

Harriman reported to President Roosevelt on the Moscow meeting: "Max and I arrived [in Moscow] late Wednesday afternoon after two nights on the plane with little sleep to find an invitation to dine with the Prime Minister that evening. Max was tired and would have preferred to go to bed. He was not, therefore, in too good a mood." Beaverbrook and Churchill argued, and Harriman waited until after Max departed "to give the Prime Minister alone your several messages. The talk, which started with the proposed [Roosevelt-Stalin] meeting, developed into a two-hour discussion of every subject—from de Gaulle to China to India to Poland, etc., coming back throughout the talk to Russia and the question of the meeting." Harriman frankly admitted that Roosevelt—for domestic considerations—wished to avoid a meeting in Britain with Churchill as host. Parts of the FDR political coalition strongly opposed the British Empire. The prime minister later opposed a separate Roosevelt-Stalin meeting for the same reason that Roosevelt proposed it—domestic political considerations. Both leaders understood their national politics; each nurtured an unrealistic belief in his ability to handle Stalin.[37] However, by June 1943, Churchill, unlike Roosevelt, began to understand Stalin's territorial ambitions in Eastern Europe.

The post of U.S. Ambassador to the Russian capital was hard to fill. Lawyer Joseph E. Davies had been the U.S. Ambassador to Moscow from 1936 to 1938, and unlike most American envoys, he never lost his affinity for the Soviet government or his attachment to the high life.[38] At FDR's request, he turned his diplomatic service in Russia into a book, *Mission to Moscow*, which was then made into a pro-Russian movie.[39] Davies's solicitude for the Soviet Union was not inconsistent with FDR's pro-Russian policy. The president periodically used Davies as a special envoy during World War II. When Davies visited Moscow in May 1943, he carried a special message to the Soviet leader from FDR, which he declined to deliver in the presence of U.S. Ambassador William Standley, a former chief of naval operations who had been appointed to his diplomatic job in February 1942.[40]

The forthright Standley, who succeeded the ineffective Ambassador Laurence Steinhardt, was especially critical of the Russian government's ingratitude for and suppression of news about America's immense aid.[41] In the fall of 1942, Standley had met with Roosevelt in Washington, and declared he would not go back to his post if he continued to be ignored. "If I were to return to my post in Moscow, it would have to be with positive evidence of continued confidence in me and increased prestige."[42] Standley complained that he "saw Special Representative after Big Dignitary [come] to Russia, leapfrog over my top-hatted head, and follow out the Rooseveltian policy" that Standley summarized as "do not antagonize the Russians, give them everything they want, for, after all, they are killing Germans, they are fighting our battles for us."[43] Standley, already alienated from the Soviet government and increasingly isolated from his own government, resigned in 1943. "Harriman himself contributed substantially to Standley's personal dissatisfaction," wrote biographer Rudy Abramson. "He regularly involved himself in U.S.-Soviet affairs, communicating directly with Stalin without consulting Standley and urging the Soviet boss to deal directly with Roosevelt."[44]

Desperate for a replacement when Davies's poor health prevented a second tour in Moscow, FDR recruited a reluctant Harriman himself to be the next U.S. ambassador to Russia. "Having undermined both Winant and the two previous American ambassadors in Moscow," wrote Lynne Olson, "Harriman knew how precarious and difficult an ambassador's position could be, especially in the Soviet Union."[45] Harriman called the ambassadorial post "an intolerable existence for anyone with an active mind."[46] He told the president that if he failed in his Russian endeavor, he wanted to return to his work in London. Before assuming his new post, Harriman accompanied Churchill aboard the *Queen Mary* to the Anglo-American summit in Quebec. In advance of his departure for Moscow, Harriman visited in Washington with his predecessor, Ambassador Standley, whom he told: "I know it will be difficult, but they're only human, those Russians. Stalin can be handled."[47] Harriman indulged himself in Roosevelt's vain conceit.

FDR frequently undermined his envoys, setting a confusing example for Harriman to follow. Ambassador Harriman continued to circumvent diplomatic channels. Walter Isaacson and Evan Thomas wrote that Secretary of State Edward Stettinius "was disturbed at the ambassador's presumption." When Harriman came up with a postwar plan for aid to Russia, the annoyed Stettinius declared: "It is not something for an ambassador to run to daddy with." But Harriman was not to be kept away from "daddy."[48] Harriman knew how to ingratiate himself with the president. In the 1944 election, Ambassador Harriman played a role similar to that of Ambassador Kennedy in 1940.[49] The immensely rich Harriman paid for radio time to endorse

Roosevelt's tough reelection: "Never in the history of the world has a nation had so great an opportunity to play such a vital role in affecting the course of history."[50] With those who worked under him, Harriman had little patience. Harriman "was not inconsiderate," remembered one longtime aide. "He was just no good at human relations—naturally aloof."[51]

Initially warm and positive toward Stalin, Harriman grew increasingly frustrated with Russian intransigence after he became ambassador, a job that had worn out and alienated the previous two men to hold it.[52] Harriman himself said: "A large number of important people in the West including the Prime Minister and the President, as well as some lesser lights, had the idea that they knew how to get along with Stalin. I confess that I was not entirely immune to that infectious idea. Having been to Moscow in 1941 and again in 1942, having been through those tough talks with Stalin, and having come out of those tough sessions with some sort of agreement, I was quite hopeful of accomplishing significant results."[53] Harriman's job was not made easier by the enmity of FDR's chief of staff, the prickly Admiral Leahy, who blamed Harriman for the difficulties that fellow Admiral Standley had encountered in the job.[54] Nor did his friend Harry Hopkins, sick and isolated from FDR in 1944, ease his work. Hopkins could not intervene for the new ambassador in Moscow.

Furthermore, Harriman had a high opinion of his own knowledge and skills. As ambassador, Harriman felt reduced to the level of a mere diplomatic messenger—the kind Stalin was inclined to ignore. "The essential quality of our relations with the Russians is still patience and forbearance," wrote Harriman to Churchill in November 1943. Harriman "felt that he could learn more that was important in one interview with Stalin than the rest of us could learn in months of pedestrian study of Soviet publications," observed American diplomat George Kennan, who served under Harriman and who developed a skeptical attitude toward Russian intentions in Eastern Europe much earlier than Harriman.[55]

Kennan in Moscow was instinctively and intellectually a hard-liner.[56] Harriman became a hard-liner through experience in Moscow. General John R. Deane, who served as secretary of the Combined Joint Chiefs of Staff at the beginning of the war, was named chief military liaison in the Moscow embassy in late 1943. Deane would also become a harsh critic of Russian intransigence, but Marshall and the JCS ignored his memos urging retaliation against Russia.[57] Ambassador Harriman and General Deane understood the brutality and rigidity of Stalin, and the repressive Soviet political system, in ways that their colleagues in Washington did not.[58] In one memo, Deane protested that the desperate situation that had justified unlimited aid to Russia had changed, "but our policy has not."[59] This strange fact can be explained by FDR's sustained accommodation of "Uncle Joe," not least because FDR wanted Stalin in the war against Japan. Moreover, the president believed that the Soviet Union and the United States could preside amicably over the United Nations and world peace, even as the British Empire fell apart. FDR's views permeated his civilian and military hierarchy.

In Washington, Secretary of the Navy James Forrestal was perhaps the first to distill the strategic notion that Russia would be America's prime postwar enemy.[60] Sooner rather than later, some Roosevelt appointees generally came to see Stalin as a potential enemy. Historian S. M. Plokhy wrote that "more often than not, the president would find himself in a state of undeclared war with his ambassadors to Moscow and Soviet experts in the State Department, [FDR] trying to root out opposition to his generally friendly policy toward the Soviet Union. He regularly shuffled diplomatic personnel and circumvented government bodies, but each new shift eventually went the way of its predecessors, repulsed by the culture of secrecy, suspicion, and duplicity that characterized Soviet dealings with the West."[61] Harriman himself wrote: "General Deane and I, particularly, had seen for ourselves how deeply suspicious Stalin could be. We had been through the long and painful negotiations over shuttle-bombing, the exchange of weather and intelligence information, the fruitless attempt to get bases in the Maritime Provinces for our bombers in the Far East. Stalin's suspicion of our motives always stood in the way of our getting things done."[62]

Both Harry Hopkins and FDR objected to anti-Russian sentiment at the State Department. One night at a dinner, Hopkins inquired of Russian expert Charles Bohlen if he were part of an anti-Russian cabal of State Department officials. Walter Isaacson and Evan Thomas wrote that "despite his love for the occasional good argument among friends, it was not Bohlen's style to challenge (at least with any fervor) Washington's prevailing pro-Soviet attitude nor to tangle with the exemplar of that attitude, Hopkins. He replied that he knew of no such anti-Soviet cabal in the State Department. Hopkins then launched into a discourse about how great the Russians were acting in the war. Yes, Bohlen agreed, that is perfectly true, but there were other aspects of the Soviet Union that should not be forgotten, especially their opposition to freedom."[63] Bohlen was surely correct that Russian heroism in war was separate from Soviet ideological and territorial ambition. Soviet brutality and cynicism, mixed with territorial ambition, showed itself when Russian armies, very near Warsaw, failed to assist the Polish uprising against the Nazis in August–September 1944. The Nazis then mercilessly crushed the Poles, making Poland easy prey for Soviet Russia.[64]

Stalin was not only cruel and murderous, but he also proved a stubborn and crafty negotiator. When an Anglo-American delegation visited Moscow, a relatively pleasant first meeting was usually followed by a nasty second meeting with Stalin—then by a more conciliatory third meeting. He could be charming and quick-witted; then, he could be demanding and insulting. The Soviet leader was remarkably well prepared about military and international affairs, often much better informed than the prime minister and the president. Admiral King commented of the Teheran summit in November 1943: "Stalin knew just what he wanted when he came to Teheran and he got it. Stalin is a stark realist, and there is no foolishness about him. He speaks briefly and directly to the point—not a wasted word."[65] General Brooke wrote of Teheran: "We were reaching a very dangerous point where Stalin's shrewdness, assisted by American shortsightedness, might lead us anywhere."[66] Indeed, FDR declared in a radio address to America nearly a month later on December 24: "I may say that I 'got along fine' with Marshall Stalin . . . and I believe that we are going to get along very well with him and the Russian people—very well indeed."[67] British

Foreign Under-Secretary Alexander Cadogan, who had a harsh word in his diary for almost everyone, confided during the Yalta summit: "I think Uncle Joe much the most impressive of the three men. He is very quiet and restrained. . . . When he did chip in, he never used a superfluous word, and spoke very much to the point."[68] At Yalta, FDR did not let go of his vain delusion that "Uncle Joe" was his friend and that he could charm Stalin by presidential power and sweet talk. He would try to use the same devious techniques he affected with naive visitors to the White House. Stalin listened, and then did what he wanted.

At conferences with American or British leaders, Stalin would bully the principals to test their character. In his memoirs, Churchill wrote that at the 1943 Teheran summit, British Chief of Staff Brooke showed his true grit when he responded to a tough allegation made by Stalin that "I [Brooke] had failed to show real feelings of friendship towards the Red Army, that I was lacking in a true appreciation of its fine qualities, and that he hoped in future I should be able to show greater comradeship towards the soldiers of the Red Army!" Brooke decided that if he did not respond, "I should lose any respect he [Stalin] might ever have had for me, and that he would continue such attacks in the future." Brooke concluded his response: "Well, Marshal, you have been misled by dummy tanks and dummy aeroplanes, and you have failed to observe those feelings of true friendship which I have for the Red Army, nor have you seen the feelings of genuine comradeship which I bear towards all its members." After Brooke's words were translated, Stalin turned to Churchill and said: "I like that man. He rings true. I must have a talk with him afterwards."[69]

When Churchill decided to go to Moscow without Roosevelt in October 1944, FDR declined to send either Stettinius or Marshall to accompany him, writing Churchill: "I have . . . instructed Harriman to stand by and to participate as my observer, if agreeable to you and Uncle Joe, and I have so informed Stalin. While naturally Averell will not be in a position to commit the United States—I could not permit anyone to commit me in advance—he will be able to keep me fully informed, and I have told him to return and report to me as soon as the conference is over."[70] The prime minister wrote that it was "vital to get there [Moscow] now and certainly Uncle Joe has shown himself more forthcoming than ever before. We must strike while the iron is hot."[71] Harriman, however, would be excluded from key meetings. This Moscow summit revived Churchill's optimism about Stalin. (It would not last.) "Eden and I have come away from the Soviet Union refreshed and fortified by the discussion which we had with you, Marshal Stalin, and with your colleagues," wrote the prime minister to Stalin on his return. "This memorable meeting in Moscow has shown that there are no matters that cannot be adjusted between us when we meet together in frank and intimate discussion."[72] From this high point in his personal relations with the Soviet dictator, Churchill's increasing fear of Russia's territorial ambition revived. In Eastern Europe and Germany, the prime minister anticipated the advance of Russian arms toward Berlin. He became alarmed again.

Stalin had the shrewd and cynical ability to adapt dramatically during meetings in ways that increased his negotiating power. Anthony Eden noted that "if I had to pick a team for going into a conference room, Stalin would be my first choice. Of course the man was ruthless and of course he knew his purpose. He never wasted a word. He never stormed, he was seldom even irritated. Hooded, calm, never raising his voice, he avoided the repeated negatives of Molotov which were so exasperating to listen to. By more subtle methods he got what he wanted without having seemed so obdurate."[73] Stalin *could* be obdurate, but he could also be well behaved, even generous, when it worked to his advantage. British General Ismay noted that on October 14, 1944, "Stalin attended a special command performance which had been arranged in our honour in the Bolshoi Theatre. He sat in the centre of the royal box, with Churchill on his right hand and Harriman on his left. During the first interval he asked Churchill to stand up at the front of the box alone in full view of the audience, and the cheering was tumultuous. Many of us were astonished that such a ruthless man of steel as Stalin should be capable of such old-world courtesy."[74]

Secretary of State Edward Stettinius wrote that Harriman's ambassadorial position was unique. "His task was totally different from that of a mere ambassador. He was the over-all co-ordinator of both civilian and military matters in Moscow." All Americans posted there reported to him directly.[75] Roosevelt divided American policy making into sectors, sometimes blocking one sector from knowledge about important issues, such as negotiations with Russia to enter the war against Japan. "President Roosevelt and the War Department had assigned Harriman the task of discovering what was necessary to bring Russia into the Far Eastern war. By the time Harriman reached Yalta, I [Stettinius] have understood, he [Harriman] already had some idea of what was necessary to bring the Russians into the Japanese conflict."[76] When Stettinius asked FDR whether he wanted the secretary of state to become involved, Roosevelt said "he thought it had best remain on a purely military level."[77]

Harriman's British counterpart was Ambassador Archibald Clark Kerr who, in early 1942, replaced the ineffective Ambassador Stafford Cripps.[78] In January, Cripps had returned to London at a Churchill low point, with nebulous ambitions to become prime minister. Churchill wrote in his memoirs: "Cripps had long wished to end his mission in Russia. The post of Ambassador to the Soviets had been found extremely unattractive by all British and Americans who have been called upon to fill it, both during and after the war. During the period before Hitler's attack ranged Russia with us our envoy had been almost entirely ignored in Moscow. He had hardly ever had access to Stalin, and Molotov held him and all other Allied Ambassadors at a frigid arm's length." After Russia had been attacked, the situation changed: "When so much was being done by direct communication between me and Stalin and now between the president and Stalin, the functions of the Ambassador became increasingly separated from the scene of decisive business."[79] Clark Kerr had a long and distinguished diplomatic career, having previously been posted as the British ambassador to China. The prime minister once responded to the ambassador, who had sought guidance from him: "You want a directive? All right. I don't mind kissing Stalin's bum, but I'm damned if I'll lick his boots."[80]

An experienced diplomat, Clark Kerr had longed for an appointment to Moscow since 1934. Married to a Chilean three decades younger than himself, he had served as ambassador in Chile, Sweden, Iran, and China, before he was named to Russia in

March 1942. Stalin, with whom he could exchange blunt comments and crude jokes, sometimes appreciated his irreverent attitude.[81] At the Teheran summit, Clark Kerr joked about a colleague's flatulence, and the ambassador was sharply rebuked by a note from the prime minister: "Do not let the heat imparted by someone else's buttocks detract [sic] you from the discipline of a solemn matter."[82] Clark Kerr could be "eccentric," according to Charles Bohlen; at Yalta, he offered a toast to the Russian who "looked after our bodies," meaning the head of the Soviet secret police, Lavrenti Beria.[83]

A useful, if not dynamic, presence in Anglo-Russian relations, Ambassador Clark Kerr was described by Churchill's doctor as "an earthy creature, with his feet planted firmly on the ground."[84] The British ambassador was a natural optimist, one more diplomat who sought accommodation with Russia. Biographer Donald Gillies wrote: "If Clark Kerr did have a failing, it was his tendency to give opponents the benefit of the doubt, to believe the best of them. For years he had been preaching the need to treat the Soviet Union as an equal, to trust her."[85] The British ambassador had a disdainful opinion of the American ambassador, once describing him, after Harriman's 1942 visit to Moscow, as "no more than a kindly ass" and "a champion bum sucker."[86] Harriman proudly recorded Churchill telling him at one point during the 1942 trip that "no Prime Minister has been better supported by a representative of another country."[87] In his diary, Clark Kerr observed: "Every now and then he [Churchill] would . . . take Harriman by the hand, making remarks like 'I am so glad, Averell, that you're here with me. You are a tower of strength.'"[88]

Many Americans and Englishmen in Moscow thought they could manage Stalin. The Soviet dictator more often managed the Anglo-Americans. "There was a cult of personality about Stalin among Western strategists almost as powerful as the one that his propagandists had ordained for him back in the USSR," noted historian Andrew Roberts.[89] Ruthless, knowledgeable, well prepared, Stalin in discussion could be alternately aloof and pleasant. At the Yalta Conference, his mental faculties and preparation were clearly sharper than those of either Roosevelt or Churchill. Early in the war, the president and the prime minister had embraced the fantasy that they could handle the Russian dictator, especially one on one. Indeed, FDR angled to develop his own bilateral relationship with Stalin. Roosevelt had a self-absorbed faith in his own charm. Clementine perceived this at her first meeting with FDR, telling the prime minister that FDR's "personal vanity was inordinate."[90] In March 1942, Roosevelt had written Churchill: "I think I can personally handle Stalin better than either your Foreign Office or my State Department. Stalin hates the guts of all your top people. He thinks he likes me better, and I hope he will continue to do so."[91] Stalin certainly did like the enormous war resources FDR poured into the Soviet Union. Still, he remained suspicious of the Anglo-American alliance. But the president would be solicitous of Stalin's goodwill, ingratiating in the presence of the Russian dictator. Stalin was a shrewd and cynical judge of character. FDR's vanity, combined with his ever-present desire to be liked, enabled Stalin to take advantage of the American president.

By 1945, Ambassador Harriman had become increasingly disenchanted with the Russian government as the Allies headed toward a conclusive victory. "His [Harriman's] melancholia had turned into something like hate," wrote Ambassador Kerr, "and he was determined to advise his government to waste no more time on the effort to understand and to cooperate with the Russians."[92] Harriman came to believe a tough negotiating stance with Russia was necessary. Stalin was not to be trusted. FDR died in April 1945, never knowing the irony that it was he who had been charmed and manipulated by Stalin. After FDR's death, Harriman rushed back to the United States to confer with President Truman, who he feared "did not understand, as I had seen Roosevelt understand, that Stalin is breaking his agreements."[93]

Stalin was not the only Soviet leader who engaged the vanity of Roosevelt. Soviet Foreign Minister Vyacheslav Molotov was as much an enigma as Stalin. FDR cousin Margaret Suckley wrote of a Hyde Park lunch in June 1942: "It was a fascinating lunch." Churchill and Roosevelt "were both in fine form, rested & playing on & with each other. . . . Both like Molotov; both think he understands English, though they conversed only through interpreters. W.C. thinks Molotov was persuaded that F.D.R. & W.C. are sincere in wishing to bring a better world out of the present chaos—F.D.R. said he was warned that he would find Molotov 'frozen.' He *was* frozen, until after dinner, when F.D.R. says he said something humorous & Molotov smiled! After that he was 'quite human.' I would call that a real victory for F.D.R.!" She added: "Mr. Churchill said he *almost* got to the point of saying to Molotov: 'I wish I understood Russian as well as you understand English.' But *not quite*."[94]

Churchill could even make fun of Molotov in Stalin's presence. Visiting Stalin in August 1942, the prime minister asked: "Was the Marshal aware that his Foreign Secretary on his recent visit to Washington had said he was determined to pay a visit to New York entirely by himself, and that the delay in his return was not due to any defect in the aeroplane, but because he was off on his own?" Stalin responded: "It was not to New York he went. He went to Chicago, where the other gangsters live."[95] This was not mere tongue-in-cheek humor. Stalin himself had been a ruthless gangster and bank robber in the pre-Revolution Bolshevik Party. Molotov and Stalin each knew the criminal Bolshevik background of the other. One night before Churchill departed Moscow, Stalin invited Churchill for drinks in his Kremlin apartment. Almost as an afterthought, Stalin asked Churchill: "Do you mind if we have Molotov as well?" The Russian dictator quipped: "There is one thing you can say in defence of Molotov: he can drink."[96] Eden observed "a confidence, even an intimacy, between Stalin and Molotov such as I have never seen between any other two Soviet leaders, as if Stalin knew that he had a valuable henchman and Molotov was confident because he was so regarded. Stalin might tease Molotov occasionally, but he was careful to uphold his authority."[97]

The normally imperturbable Molotov appeared shaken by Roosevelt's death in April 1945, and insisted on paying his respects immediately to Harriman, even though it was the middle of the night. "I have never heard Molotov talk so earnestly," Harriman wired home.[98] Molotov had reason to be shaken. The passing of Roosevelt meant a new president and a new era, which the Soviet Union, Stalin, and Molotov would not find so accommodating as FDR had been, before and at the Yalta summit of February 1945.

At the Yalta Conference from left to right: Andrey Vyshinsky, F. T. Gousev, U.S. Ambassador to the Soviet Union W. Averell Harriman, Soviet Foreign Minister Vyacheslav Molotov, British Foreign Secretary Anthony Eden, U.S. Secretary of State Edward Stettinius, British Permanent Under-Secretary at the Foreign Office Alexander Cadogan, Russian Deputy Foreign Minister Ivan Maisky, Ambassador Archibald Clark Kerr, Director of the Office of European Affairs Freeman Matthews, and U.S. Director of the Office of Special Political Affairs Alger Hiss.

FRANKLIN D. ROOSEVELT PRESIDENTIAL LIBRARY

XIV

Edward Stettinius Jr.

I believe that the whole discussion that evening as well as the spirit of most of the [Yalta] Conference, furnishes a genuine example to the world that, where objective conditions exist, people with different backgrounds and training can find a basis of understanding.[1]

Edward Stettinius Jr. *(1900–1949). Stettinius was an able business executive with General Motors and U.S. Steel, two crucial industries in World War II. He began serving in advisory posts in the Roosevelt administration in the 1930s. In 1941, he was named administrator of the Lend-Lease Program. In the fall of 1943, he was named under secretary of state to succeed Sumner Welles. A year later, he was named secretary of state to succeed Cordell Hull. He was replaced in July 1945 by former Senator James F. Byrnes.*

The Stettinius quote above suggests he had not grasped the true consequences of Yalta.

So far as I could see, the President had made little preparation for the Yalta Conference. His inauguration had taken place the Saturday before we left and for ten days preceding that he had been overwhelmed with engagements. On the cruiser, the President, Admiral Leahy and I, on four or five occasions, usually after dinner, discussed some of the questions to be considered, particularly the proposal for the United Nations. But not until the day before we landed at Malta did I learn that we had on board a very complete file of studies and recommendations prepared by the State Department. . . . I am sure the failure to study them while en route was due to the President's illness.[2]

James F. Byrnes *(1882–1972), memoirs. Byrnes served as a South Carolina congressman and senator before World War II. He served briefly on the U.S. Supreme Court before he was named director of the Office of Economic Stabilization in 1942, and director of the Office of War Mobilization in 1943. Although he longed to be named secretary of state by President Roosevelt, it was not until July 1945 that President Truman appointed him to that post.*

In November 1944, President Roosevelt appointed Edward Stettinius Jr. to succeed an exhausted and sick Cordell Hull as secretary of state. The leading alternative to Stettinius had been former South Carolina Senator James F. Byrnes, a Roosevelt intimate who had clashed with Harry Hopkins in the past.[3] "When it was finally decided that Stettinius should be promoted from Under Secretary to the senior Cabinet post there was no doubt in anyone's mind that Hopkins was largely responsible," wrote FDR aide Robert E. Sherwood.[4] In August 1941, the president had appointed the former executive of General Motors and U.S. Steel as Lend-Lease administrator, in which role Stettinius had demonstrated his administrative talents. Although FDR permitted, even encouraged, bureaucratic conflicts of epic proportions, Stettinius proved he could be the rare pacifist among bureaucrats at war. Stettinius was a quick study, but he was not always politically deft. Anti-Roosevelt business executives classified Stettinius as one of Hopkins's "tame millionaires."[5] On the other hand, intellectual snobs at the State Department tended to look down on businessmen as tradesmen. For example, the imperious Dean Acheson acerbically suggested: "Before arriving in Washington at the age of thirty-eight, Stettinius had gone far with comparatively modest equipment."[6] With his prematurely white hair and dark black eyebrows, Stettinius cut a distinguished figure in Washington. When he attained the top spot at the State Department, the press described him and his subordinates as "Snow White and the seven dwarfs."[7]

The rise of Stettinius began in the late summer of 1943. Under Secretary Sumner Welles had already been forced out, and Stettinius had emerged as the compromise choice for the post. One of his primary backers had been Byrnes, who called Stettinius in San Francisco to prepare him to accept the post: "I've engineered around for you," claimed Byrnes, who said Hull and Roosevelt had both pushed other candidates, "but now all agree on you for undersecretary of state."[8] From Hull's standpoint, Stettinius was someone who would not compete with him for policy leadership. For Byrnes, Stettinius was someone who lacked the experience to contest him for Hull's job, should the ever-sickly Hull resign.[9] Hull quit after he was hospitalized in late October 1944. The reason for his resignation was not entirely bad health, Hull told Assistant Secretary Breckinridge Long, who confided to his diary that Hull was fed up with Roosevelt: "He was tired of intrigue . . . tired of being relied upon in public and ignored in private . . . tired of fighting battles which were not appreciated."[10] Hull's wife told journalist Arthur Krock that the Morgenthau Plan (which would have made Germany primarily an agricultural country), presented at the Quebec summit in September 1944, had been "the final blow" and an "inconceivable intrusion in a desperate and delicate affair." The State Department had been joined by the War Department in opposition to the Treasury Department's pastoral plan for Germany. Mrs. Hull said her husband "could not understand how the President could conduct matters of such grave import, and foreign affairs in particular, with such irresponsibility and deviousness."[11] In this particular case, Hull was not exaggerating FDR's cavalier conduct.

In Stettinius, Hopkins appeared to have his own man who might counter State Department Anglophobes like Adolf Berle.[12] In 1940, Berle had symbolized State Department antipathy to Great Britain: "The history of our past English 'interpretations' was a history of half truths, broken faith, intrigue behind the back of the State Department, and even the President, and everything which goes with it."[13] Berle's disdain toward British diplomacy was typical of State Department colleagues. British academic Isaiah Berlin, at the British embassy in Washington, held Berle in contempt. Berle "is a very clever man with a very torturous mind, whose early academic success went to his head," wrote Berlin. "He is very vain, likes elaborately constructed intellectual patterns which he weaves ingeniously and falls easily for the flattery of foreigners, for whose intellect he has respect. . . . He is in fact a megalomaniac who has to be humored."[14] Fortunately for Anglo-American diplomacy, Berle was appointed U.S. Ambassador to Brazil in 1944, shortly after Hull resigned.

Winston Churchill had reason to be grateful to Stettinius, who as Lend-Lease administrator worked successfully to expedite the shipment of war materials to Britain. In January 1942, Stettinius had loaned his beachfront Florida home to the prime minister for a short vacation. Because Stettinius's knowledge of State Department affairs was limited and his link to FDR was through Bohlen, the State Department became somewhat marginalized after the departure of Sumner Welles, upon whom the president had relied. Hopkins became very sick at the beginning of 1944, so he could not assist his friend Stettinius in his new role of under secretary of state. Stettinius did work harder than Welles to assure Hull of his preeminence, but he could not alter Hull's insecurity in dealing with the news media.

Upon becoming under secretary, Stettinius reorganized the leadership and personnel of the State Department, and did so again when he became secretary.[15] In December 1944, Assistant Secretary Acheson wrote his son that "at Ed's request, Berle, Long and Shaw resigned. . . . The President nominated Joe Grew to be Under Secretary; Jimmy Dunn to be Assistant Secretary in charge of geographical areas other than the Western Hemisphere."[16] Eleanor Roosevelt worried that Dunn, a top European affairs official, might be taking the State Department in conservative directions. "I realize very well that I do not know the reasons why certain things may be necessary nor whether you intend them or do not intend to do them," Eleanor wrote her husband in December 1944. "It does, however, make me rather nervous to hear you say that you do not care what Jimmy Dunne [sic] thinks because he will do what you tell him to do and that for three years you have carried the State Department and you expect to go on doing it. I am quite sure that Jimmy Dunne is clever enough to tell you that he will do what you want and to allow his subordinates to accomplish things which will get by and which will pretty well come up in the long-time results to what he actually wants to do."[17] Eleanor Roosevelt was both a liberal and also a shrewd observer.

In March 1944, Under Secretary Stettinius had been dispatched on a mission to London, to consult on "a very wide range of subjects of current mutual interest to our two governments." As Stettinius was the highest-ranking State Department official to visit London during the war, suspicion about the trip abounded in Washington. "You know," said the president, "that the senators and congressmen, the newspapers and everyone else will immediately accuse me and the secretary and all of you going to London of making all sorts of secret deals with the British. They are sure to say that it is all underhanded and illegal and even unconstitutional."[18] One of the key issues at the London conference was future American economic support for Britain. The British presented a plan that showed that "we will come out of this war with debts of fifteen billion and assets of one billion."[19] Great Britain had been *de facto* insolvent and sought continued financial help, but Churchill opposed discussions of postwar organization and planning as distractions from winning the war. Foreign Secretary Eden supported such postwar efforts as necessary business. Stettinius wrote in his daily calendar notes that there is "a fundamental difference between the prime minister and Eden." When Stettinius brought up the issue with Churchill, "The prime minister's reaction was negative. . . . People are thinking about fighting now, and he thought it would be bad to interrupt the psychological trend of war and start thinking abut the future peace of the world."[20]

British ability to mold the plans for the postwar world paled in comparison to the power of the United States and the Soviet Union. By late 1944, American and Soviet armies dominated the war against the Nazis and imperial Japan. Therefore, why rush with peace negotiations when winning the war was the immediate problem? Churchill knew he was losing stature. Stettinius explained that Secretary "Hull had informed us that it would be fatal both domestically and in our relations with the Soviets if there were any intimation whatsoever that we had discussed the world security organization while in London."[21] Stalin's sensitivities about Anglo-American conspiracies were well known, as was the likelihood that FDR and his administration would defer to the Russians. Americans themselves remained reluctant to give any real authority to the tripartite European Advisory Commission that met in London with Ambassador Winant as the official American representative, and diplomat William Strang as the British representative. Stettinius was permitted to make a short speech to the House of Commons. "We have all learned the bitter lesson of disunity," he said. "Henceforth, we know that only by working together can we maintain our freedom and progress toward great horizons of opportunity for all men."[22] With this bromide, the under secretary headed home.

"Despite Stettinius's attempts to refurbish its image, the State Department continued to suffer a bad press during much of 1944," wrote historians Thomas M. Campbell and George C. Herring. "The columnist Drew Pearson, a long-time adversary of Hull, was particularly critical, and in a column of May 12, he revived old charges of dissension among the department's top officials." Stettinius wanted to confront the problem, but Hull restrained him.[23] For much of the rest of 1944, Stettinius persisted in trying to defuse prominent critics like Pearson, Walter Lippmann, and James Reston of the *New York Times.* At the Dumbarton Oaks estate in late summer, the Big Three—represented by Stettinius, Under-Secretary Alexander Cadogan, and Andrei Gromyko, the Russian ambassador to the United States—discussed postwar world organization.[24] Secrecy about the conference infuriated American newsmen.

On November 27, 1944, several weeks after the conclusion of the Dumbarton Oaks conference, FDR summoned Stettinius to his office to discuss Hull's replacement: "I had three [names] under consideration—Henry Wallace, Jimmy Byrnes and yours. It would have killed the secretary [Cordell Hull] to have Henry. As for Jimmy, he has no understanding of geography. Of course in this whole foreign situation I am going to have to work awfully intimately with Stalin and Churchill. Jimmy has always been on his own in the Senate and elsewhere and I am not sure that he and I could act harmoniously as a team." FDR added: "You and I could have a perfect understanding and complete harmony and work as a team, you recognizing the big things I would have to handle, at your suggestion." Stettinius responded: "In other words, Jimmy might question who was boss." Roosevelt said: "That's exactly it. As far as you and I are concerned we will never have any misunderstanding on who carries what and we will work things out so that everything will fit in properly between the White House and the department."[25] (In January 1947, Secretary of State Byrnes, having been appointed by President Truman, would himself be eased out of the State Department by his longtime friend Truman, after Byrnes once too often thought he was the boss of American foreign policy. In FDR's case, however, he knew a useful Irish-American when he saw one, and so he took Byrnes to Yalta. Roosevelt deployed Byrnes to explain the controversial decisions at Yalta to the American public.[26]) Stettinius remarked to the president that the State Department needed to be kept in the loop about plans and actions: "The past record had not been good."[27] FDR acknowledged that improvement was necessary.[28] Unlike Hull, Stettinius was a firm proponent of interdepartmental cooperation. Hull had angered Secretary Stimson by communicating directly with the JCS, rather than through Stimson. Stettinius, Stimson, and Secretary of the Navy James Forrestal agreed to cooperate more closely—in part to avoid being shut out of policy making by FDR.[29]

Anglo-American differences could be negotiated early in World War II, but they became very difficult issues in 1943–1944. For example, as civil war threatened in Greece in 1944, Churchill believed that Great Britain had a special responsibility for the nation—which he had persuaded Stalin to recognize at the October 1944 summit in Moscow. In June 1944, the prime minister had written President

Roosevelt: "We are an old ally of Greece. We had 40,000 casualties in trying to defend Greece against Hitler, not counting Crete. The Greek King and the Greek Government have placed themselves under our protection."[30] The Greek communists, strongly opposed to the monarchy, had taken the lead in partisan fighting against the Germans. Now they threatened street fighting and civil war in a contest for government power. Churchill restlessly watched the disorder from afar. At the request of the Greek government in exile, without consulting any other ally, Churchill ordered British troops into Athens to help restore order, after Germany began an evacuation in September and October 1944. The future form of government, its alliances, and the leadership in Greece remained in doubt. Greek King George II remained the country's nominal leader, with Georgios Papandreou as prime minister. Roosevelt thought the king "a charming fellow, considering what an empty head."[31] George II was unacceptable to Greek communists—composed of the National Liberation Front (EAM) and National Popular Liberation Army (ELAS). Greek Orthodox Archbishop Damaskinos Papandreou was put forward as a compromise regent but the king rejected that proposal for both political and legal reasons. He did not trust the archbishop nor did the king believe he had constitutional authority to accept the proposal.

This debate was not the only one about monarchy in Europe. Secretary Stettinius soon disagreed with Churchill about whether to restore monarchies in both Italy and Greece. A top British diplomat was dispatched to protest the secretary's high-minded and unrealistic comments that American policy opposed interference in the domestic politics of other nations. The British envoy remarked that the State Department statement "had caused great embarrassment and that the Prime Minister and Mr. Eden were aroused." In response to the visit, the secretary of state arranged for a reporter to ask him a question the next day at a press conference. With Greek communists in the streets of Athens aiming to seize governmental control, the secretary's obtuse response, emphasizing Greek self-determination, further inflamed Anglo-American relations.[32] The Roosevelt administration's self-destructive position, opposing British intervention in Greece, was not unlike FDR's hands-off position to total Soviet subjugation of Poland, and the unwillingness of the president to intervene in support of the Warsaw uprising the previous August. Churchill complained to Hopkins: "The reference in the last sentence of Mr. Stettinius's Press release has of course been taken all over the world and in Greece as a suggestion that the United States is against the action we have taken in Greece, and this undoubtedly makes our task more difficult and costly in British and Greek life."[33]

Much of American public opinion, encouraged by Secretary of State Stettinius and the press, disapproved of British intervention in Greece—even though the British intended to establish an interim government until a referendum could decide the form of a future Greek government. In his memoirs, Churchill lamented: "The vast majority of the American Press violently condemned our action, which they declared falsified the cause for which they had gone to war."[34] American anti-imperial opinion was a national reflex. Defending his government's intervention before Parliament, Churchill declared: "One must have some respect for democracy and not use the word too lightly. The last thing which resembles democracy is mob law, with bands of gangsters, armed with deadly weapons, forcing their way into great cities, seizing the police stations and key points of government, endeavouring to introduce a totalitarian regime with an iron hand."[35] Hopkins telephoned support for Churchill's speech, but FDR and his administration remained hostile to the prime minister's decisive and successful action in Greece. Churchill tried to rally Hopkins to his side: "I hope you will tell our great friend that the establishment of law and order in and around Athens is essential to all future measures of magnanimity and consolation towards Greece. After this has been established will be the time for talking. My guiding principle is 'No peace without victory'."[36]

The United States stayed aloof from the Greek crisis, partly for political reasons that Roosevelt laid out in a telegram on December 13: "As anxious as I am to be of the greatest help to you in this trying situation, there are limitations, imposed in part by the traditional [anti-imperial] policies of the United States and in part by the mounting adverse reaction of public opinion in this country. No one will understand better than yourself that I, both personally and as Head of State, am necessarily responsive to the state of public opinion."[37] Churchill tried to explain the rationale for his actions and the difficulties to which all the Greek parties contributed. In a telegram to FDR on December 14, the prime minister complained: "Stern fighting lies ahead, and even danger to our troops in the centre of Athens. The fact that you are supposed to be against us, in accordance with the last sentence of Stettinius's Press release, has added, as I feared, to our difficulties and burdens. I think it probable that I shall broadcast to the world on Sunday night and make manifest the purity and disinterestedness of our motives throughout, and also of our resolves."[38] The British argued that they only aimed to prevent the communists seizing power.

On December 16, Hopkins wired Churchill: "Public opinion here is deteriorating rapidly because of Greek situation and your statement in Parliament about the United States and Poland." One paragraph from Hopkins concerned Churchill: "I do not know what the President or Stettinius may have to say publicly, but it may well be that one or both of them must state in unequivocal terms our determination to do all that we can to seek a free and secure world."[39] The prime minister responded to Hopkins: "Naturally I should welcome any public statements in America which set forth the aims stated in your last sentence. These are also ours."[40] The British leader could be forgiven his impatience, as it was he and the British Empire in 1940–1941 who battled alone for a free and secure world. Meanwhile, Stettinius had come under pressure regarding the future of Poland and the provisions for free elections there. The secretary of state issued a statement that seemed to pacify public opinion, but did not pacify the British. On December 20, Lord Halifax wrote Churchill about Roosevelt administration officials: "Our friends still cling to their old preference for dodging breathlessly round the field a few feet ahead of the bull rather than make up their minds to seize it boldly by at least one horn. In the end I fear with you that they may find themselves pinned in an uncomfortable position."[41]

On Christmas Eve 1944, Churchill (then seventy years old), at great personal risk, abruptly flew off with Eden to Greece, there to push Greek factions to work together rather than to fight one another. The prime minister wired Roosevelt: "Anthony and I are going out to see what we can do to square this Greek entanglement."[42] He had decided to act, on the ground in Athens, flying off to help solve the crucial problem of the future of Greece. Characteristically, the prime minister insisted on being directly on the spot in a messy and dangerous situation, while the American government unctuously implied moral superiority by abstaining from involvement in a situation that could produce a totalitarian Soviet satellite. After the prime minister's dramatic and successful personal effort in Athens to bring order out of chaos, Hopkins wrote him: "No one knows better than I what a gallant role you are playing. . . . I am proud to be known and even to be attacked by some of my countrymen as your good friend."[43] Despite FDR's equivocations, Hopkins recognized heroic statecraft when he saw it—especially after it was a success. During the crisis in Greece, the nominees for top posts in the State Department ran into confirmation trouble in the Senate. It required the personal intervention of FDR to break the congressional logjam. The issue between Stettinius and Churchill was resolved before the Yalta summit. Stettinius wrote that the prime minister "was rather outspoken to me regarding Greece and Italy. . . . However, he warmed up and was more cordial than he has ever been."[44]

At Yalta, for the first time, all three Allied foreign ministers attended the summit. And for the first time, their input was very important to Allied decision-making. A weakened, unprepared, ailing Roosevelt allowed Secretary of State Stettinius to play a key role on issues ranging from France and Poland, to reparations and the United Nations—but not on Far East policy and Russia's entry into the war against Japan.[45] FDR would agree to almost anything Stalin demanded in order to get the Russians into the war against Japan. In the end, the Soviet Union did virtually nothing to help the Americans and British as they brought imperial Japan to its knees—Stalin having declared war on Japan just one week before its surrender. FDR biographer Conrad Black emphasized that at Yalta, "[t]he Foreign ministers" had "large numbers of complex issues dumped in their laps at the end of each plenary session, so for the balance of the meetings at Yalta their proceedings assumed more importance than usual for foreign ministers."[46]

Stettinius would serve as secretary of state until July 1945, when President Harry Truman replaced him with James Byrnes, the man Stettinius had edged out for the post in 1944. Truman appointed Stettinius as the first American Ambassador to the United Nations, in which post his superiors regularly ignored him. Stettinius held office as United Nations ambassador for less than a year. He resigned in June 1946.

Stalin, Roosevelt, and Churchill pose for the cameras at the end of the Teheran conference, December 1943. Visible behind them are General Henry "Hap" Arnold, commanding general of the U.S. Army Air Forces; General Alan Brooke, Chief of the Imperial General Staff; Admiral Andrew "ABC" Cunningham, British First Sea Lord and Chief of the Naval Staff; and Admiral William Leahy, Roosevelt's chief of staff.
LIBRARY OF CONGRESS

XV

Churchill and Roosevelt: Increasingly Suspicious

> It appears that both of us have inadvertently taken unilateral action in a direction that we both now agree to have been expedient for the time being. It is essential that we should always be in agreement in matters bearing on our Allied war effort.[1]
>
> ***Franklin D. Roosevelt*** *to Winston S. Churchill, June 26, 1944.*

Margaret Suckley wrote of Churchill's visit to Hyde Park in August 1943, that she had "the impression that Churchill *adores* the P., loves him, as a man, looks up to him, defers to him, leans on him."[2] The impressionable Suckley surely adored her distant Roosevelt cousin, loved his importance, exaggerated his virtues, and ignored his defects. She worked to depressurize FDR's environment in a way that she felt the intense and earnest First Lady could not or would not.[3] After observing Churchill at the White House in early September 1943, Suckley contrasted the president and the prime minister. She judged Churchill to be harsher than Roosevelt. The prime minister "snaps out his disapproval. They say he fights with everyone, jumps all over them. One person alone he doesn't jump on, & that is the P.! The P. laughs about it: he says that if the P.M. ever *did* jump on him, he would just laugh at him!'" In fact, Churchill was more candid, FDR more devious. Indeed, FDR increasingly was ready to have laughs at Churchill's expense.[4]

Weekends at Chequers were different from FDR's escapes to Hyde Park. At Chequers, the prime minister created opportunities for Anglo-American discussions, not least for Churchill to wear down opposition to his ideas. On those weekends, he sought to charm and to persuade visiting American leaders. FDR speechwriter Samuel I. Rosenman recalled his stay at Chequers in March 1944. Rosenman had been appalled to learn at 10:30 at night that, in a freezing cold room, he was expected to watch a movie that turned out to be "long and dull and very badly acted." At 12:30, Churchill, who could endure the cold without complaint, began what was essentially a long monologue. "The P.M. really was very entertaining. He held the floor, reciting poetry and talking generally until 2:15 A.M., when he suddenly turned to me and wanted to know what I was putting in my food report and whether I was going to take any British food away from them." Rosenman added: "Thereupon followed serious discussion. . . . At 3:00 A.M. someone (bless his soul) suggested bed. The P.M. displayed surprise at the lateness of the hour, but I knew that he was not surprised."[5]

Churchill's stamina exhausted the younger Roosevelt, as well as many officials on both sides of the Atlantic. Americans, including FDR, breathed in relief when the prime minister departed Washington. Thereafter, the president needed several days to catch up on his sleep, often at Hyde Park. During his presidency, FDR regularly took his private train to Springwood, in order to rest at his father's Hudson River estate. On May 27, 1943, presidential aide William D. Hassett reported in his diary, after the British prime minister had departed America for North Africa: "Must be a relief to the Boss, for Churchill is a trying guest—drinks like a fish and smokes like a chimney, irregular routine, works nights, sleeps days, turns the clock upside down." Two days later, Hassett wrote: "The President greatly refreshed, as he said, after a ten hours' sleep which he much needed after the irregular hours he had kept with Churchill; said he would repeat this sleep marathon three nights more." The condescending Hassett observed: "The difference between the President and the Prime Minister is this: the P.M. has nothing on his mind but the war. The President, besides planning war strategy with the P.M., must also conduct the Government of the United States and cope with the coal-mine strike, Ruml Plan tax bill, and the rest of it."[6] In fact, Churchill's role as prime minister and minister of defense was considerably more demanding than FDR's routine as head of state and chief executive. The prime minister actually administered his government and the military, reporting regularly to cabinet and Parliament; the president kept more aloof. As the Hassett diary detailed, FDR's frequent trips to Hyde Park were marked with such diversions as taking exiled European royalty house hunting in New England. Historian Elisabeth Barker wrote that "the republican Roosevelt, who, though he might think it politically convenient that Washington should on occasion publicly deplore Churchill's monarchist leanings, himself enjoyed foreign royalty as a pleasing pastime."[7]

During World War II, the Americans and their British counterparts sustained suspicions of the other's motives. Americans worried about British intentions to restore and preserve the war-torn British Empire. Once the United States entered the war in 1941, the conflict between historical American anticolonialism and British imperial policy occasionally imperiled the alliance. In 1942, the empire in the Pacific was struck full force by the brutal onslaught of Japanese armies; Southeast Asia, Hong Kong, and Singapore fell to the merciless and well-trained Japanese conquerors; British control of India was suddenly threatened. The Atlantic Charter of August 1941 had been deliberately designed by FDR and the Americans to prepare the way for a postcolonial world. In 1940 and early 1941, Churchill, alone fighting the Nazis, desperately needed reluctant American help. So the prime minister let the president have his charter. However, Churchill did insert a short, simple clause into the charter, which he believed protected the integrity of the British Empire and the Commonwealth. (As amended, the charter read: "Fourth, they will endeavor, with due respect for their existing obligations, to further the enjoyment by all States, great or small, victor or vanquished, of access, on equal terms, to the trade and to the raw materials of the world which are needed for their economic prosperity."[8]) Roosevelt, in March–April 1942, urged Britain to make moves toward independence for India. In Parliament in the 1930s, Churchill had resisted Indian self-government; in the 1940s, he resisted again. In March 1942, Churchill sent Stafford Cripps to India, to seek resolution of a political crisis in India, but he kept very tight rein on Cripps. FDR sent Colonel Louis Johnson to Delhi to encourage negotiations for Indian self-government. British and Indian leaders failed to reach an acceptable compromise. Churchill critics, such as historian Nigel Hamilton, argued that "the saga of the Cripps mission—and the President's role in it—marked in truth the end of Britain's colonial empire, as Churchill willfully surrendered Britain's moral leadership of the democracies in World War II."[9] The prime minister held that British leadership and its long and relatively successful rule of India prevented the mutual slaughter of Hindus and Moslems that had characterized India in the millennium before British rule. Subsequently, the hurried and violent independence of India in August 1947, under the Labor government of Clement Attlee, vindicated Churchill's contention that thousands, even millions, of Hindus and Moslems would perish or be displaced in civil war and resettlement, if India received independence prematurely.[10]

In Churchill's view, the American position on colonies was incoherent, even self-contradictory, given America's own strategic outposts, among them Puerto Rico, Hawaii, and the Philippines. Ironically, FDR's high-minded anticolonial policy ran into military reality in 1945, when the strategic islands of the Pacific, coveted by American military officials, became American postwar military bases.[11] At a meeting with the American diplomatic team leaving for London in March 1944, the president was asked if he wished to bring up the colonialism issue with the British: "Yes, by all means, it is something I think we should discuss with them at every opportunity."[12] Anthony Eden observed that "Roosevelt did not confine his dislike of colonialism to the British Empire alone, for it was a principle with him, not the less cherished for its possible advantages. He hoped that former colonial territories, once free of their masters, would become politically and economically dependent upon the United States, and had no fear that other powers might fill that role."[13] In this view, Eden was proved correct, as the United States gradually assumed in the postwar era not only the peacekeeping role of the British Empire, but also Britain's mastery of world trade. FDR never tired of raising the colonialism issue—but he did so carefully, in a way that would not undermine the war effort.

Despite the prime minister's need for American support, Churchill had the grit to draw clear lines against U.S. interference in the British Empire. He expressed his view forcefully to Harry Hopkins, declaring he would resign before he dismantled the empire. Robert Sherwood wrote that India was "one subject on which the normal, broad-minded, good-humored, give-and-take attitude which prevailed between the two statesmen was stopped cold."[14] Churchill had pledged in November 1943: "I have not become the King's First Minister in order to preside over the liquidation of the British Empire."[15] Not unlike the presidential oath prescribed by the U.S. Constitution, the duty of the prime minister of the United Kingdom and of the British Empire and Commonwealth was implicitly to preserve and protect the constitutional monarchy and the authority of Parliament. In December 1944, the prime minister wrote Foreign Secretary Eden: "There must be no question of our being hustled or seduced into declarations affecting British sovereignty in any of the Dominions or Colonies."[16] After the war, Cordell Hull wrote of the American position: "We had definite ideas with respect to the future of the British colonial empire, on which we differed with the British. It might be said that the future of that Empire was no business of ours; but we felt that unless dependent peoples were assisted toward ultimate self-government and were given it when, as we said, they were 'worthy of it and ready for it,' they would provide kernels of conflict."[17] The future of British colonies caused recurring disputes between the United States and Great Britain. As Hull observed in his memoirs: "we wished to dissociate ourselves from British colonial policy as much as we could."[18] In addition, he wrote: "The American Government advocated the eventual self-government of all colonial peoples. Both the President and I repeatedly said we considered the Atlantic Charter applicable to all such peoples throughout the world."[19] Churchill disagreed. In Churchill's judgment, the integrity of the British Empire was made exempt in the Atlantic Charter.

The policy conflict with the United States over the future of British colonies began with the Anglo-American alliance itself. Indeed, it might be said that the conflict began with the American Revolution of 1776. The loyal Elliott Roosevelt maintained that in the middle of a Churchill monologue at the Placentia Bay conference in August 1941, the prime minister had "brandished a stubby forefinger under Father's nose. 'Mr. President,' he cried, 'I believe you are trying to do away with the British Empire. Every idea you entertain about the structure of the postwar world demonstrates it. But in spite of that'—and his forefinger waved—'in spite of that, we know that you constitute our only hope. And'—his voice sank dramatically—'*you* know that *we* know it. *You* know that *we* know that without America, the Empire won't stand.'"[20] Before the conference, FDR had told his son: "America won't help England in this war simply so that she will be able to continue to ride roughshod over colonial peoples."[21] Scholars have questioned the authenticity of some of Elliott Roosevelt's memories, but the dispute between Churchill and FDR on the future of the British Empire was very real.

During 1944, the prime minister "continued to be the standard bearer of an Anglo-American conception of British destiny rather than the empire-oriented future envisaged by Beaverbrook, the European option increasingly favoured by Eden and the foreign office, or indeed, the various universalist models emanating from the Roosevelt administration," observed historian Fraser Harbutt.[22] Hopkins foretold a potential split between the prime minister and the president when, prior to the 1944 elections, Hopkins said to Lord Halifax that the Republican Party might treat Britain more favorably than would FDR in a fourth administration. The GOP, said Hopkins, might "give you a free hand in India, in Europe and in the Middle East. You will have no embarrassing insistence on this or that in Saudi Arabia and all the other places where you have been accustomed to having your own way. It won't be like that with Roosevelt after the elections."[23]

The president and the prime minister differed about the role of constitutional monarchies in providing the symbol of institutional stability in historic Europe. In his memoirs, Churchill argued plausibly: "The prejudice of the Americans against monarchy, which Mr. Lloyd George made no attempt to counteract, had made it clear to the beaten [German] Empire [after World War I] that it would have better treatment from the Allies as a Republic than as a monarchy. Wise policy would have crowned and fortified the Weimar Republic with a constitutional sovereign in the person of an infant grandson of the Kaiser, under a Council of Regency. Instead, a gaping void was opened in the national life of the German people. All the strong elements, military and feudal, which might have rallied to a constitutional monarchy and for its sake respected and sustained the new democratic and Parliamentary processes, were for the time being unhinged. The Weimar Republic, with all its liberal trappings and blessings, was regarded as an imposition of the enemy."[24]

On one crucial fact, Roosevelt and Churchill decorously avoided frank discussion: Britain was broke, financially insolvent, and economically on life support from the United States. By this measure, Great Britain was no longer independent, nor was it a Great Power—for it could not defend itself out of its own resources, the essence of Great Power status. When Treasury Secretary Henry Morgenthau returned from an August 1944 trip to Britain, he reported to FDR that Churchill told him Britain "was broke. The President said, 'What does he mean by that?' I said, 'Yes, England really is broke.' That seemed to surprise the President, and he kept coming back to it. . . . He said, 'This is very interesting. I had no idea that England was broke.'" With tongue in cheek, Roosevelt said: "I will go over there and make a couple of talks and take over the British Empire.'"[25]

It was no joke. Britain had scarce financial reserves, depleted as they were during World War I, then exhausted preparing for and fighting alone, early in World War II, after the French surrender. Like a skeptical commercial creditor, FDR had insisted on sending a warship to South Africa, to collect British gold bullion there as security against present and future British debts to the United States.[26] Churchill drafted a delicate note to Roosevelt: "I am much puzzled and even perturbed by the proposal now made to send the United States battleship to collect whatever gold there may be in Cape Town. . . . It is not fitting that any nation should put itself in the hands of another, least of all a nation which is fighting under increasingly severe conditions for what is proclaimed to be a cause of general concern."[27] The prime minister did not send this complaint, but Churchill's government believed the Roosevelt administration inappropriately coveted British gold, the financial reserve of last resort for an insolvent but heroic nation. The prime minister believed the United Kingdom was fighting not only for its survival, but also indirectly for America. On the issue of Lend-Lease debts, he was forthright. "I must make it clear to you, as I have to the president, that we aren't going to repay the Lend-Lease debts," he told Stettinius in April 1944. "That will have to be adjusted someplace else along the lines of utilizing bases, Empire preferences, tariffs, etc."[28]

In March 1941, the U.S. Lend-Lease Act to supply Britain on credit became effective—despite the U.S. Neutrality Acts of the 1930s. In subsequent negotiations, it became apparent that the free-trade State Department aimed to undermine the imperial preference system of British tariff and trade policy, thus to encourage American exports and world free trade.[29] The Democratic Party and Secretary of State Hull, a dedicated free trader, opposed preferential tariffs. For a decade, Hull had focused on economic and trade policies, which FDR had left in Hull's hands.[30] Dean Acheson noted that every Hull speech tended "to turn into a dissertation on the benefits of unhampered international trade and the true road to it through agreements reducing tariffs."[31] American officials believed that policies that opened up international trade would help the United States and impact the British Empire.[32] American free-trade ideology, a dogma of the Democratic Party, and British intransigence on the issue of Commonwealth trade preferences, did hinder negotiations. Historian Warren Kimball wrote that "the determinants of American policy during negotiations of the Lend-Lease Master Agreement were the American vision of British opulence, the persistence of the Wilsonian concept of the interdependence of peace and liberal economic systems, and the political necessity of striking a good bargain."[33] Still, the Americans knew there was little opulence in Britain, that Britain was *de facto* insolvent.

FDR would not be constrained by Churchill's worldview, nor by the British imperial trade system, which encompassed almost one-quarter of the land mass of the globe and almost one-quarter of its population. From the British point of view, Americans were putting their prospects for future profits ahead of the agreed priority of defeating Hitler. Although Treasury Secretary Morgenthau was often less Anglophobic than Secretary of State Hull, he too got in on the act. In early 1944, "Roosevelt suddenly asked Churchill to reduce British dollar reserves to the very modest sum of $1 billion," noted Fraser Harbutt. Churchill responded that "reducing our dollar balances, which constitute our sole liquid reserve, to one billion dollars would not really be consistent with equal treatment of Allies or with any conception of equal sacrifice or pooling of resources."[34] One billion in reserves was less than the contingent reserves required for necessary imports—in wartime tantamount to insolvency. "The prime minister protested this squeeze on Great Britain's 'last reserves,' which emanated from the secretary of the treasury, Henry Morgenthau Jr., and pointed out that his people had 'already spent practically all our convertible foreign investments in the struggle.'" In 1944, Americans pressed for repayment arrangements, which Churchill would stubbornly resist.[35]

A naturally generous man, Churchill could not understand what he viewed as penny-pinching by the United States, ignoring as he did the indignation of American officials burned by numerous unpaid loans from World War I.[36] British officials thought America greedy and ungrateful for the sacrifices that Britain had made in World Wars I and II, from which the United States had waxed rich. Max Beaverbrook, very close to Churchill, resented American motives and greed. "It would appear that the United States are demanding our South African gold and proposing to collect and carry it away," Beaverbrook complained to Churchill on December 26, 1940. "That is a decision which I would resist very strongly and seek to destroy with means in my power." Beaverbrook added that the Americans "have conceded nothing. They have exacted payment to the uttermost for all they have done for us. They have taken our bases without valuable compensation [the Destroyers-for-Bases deal]. They have taken our gold. They have been given our secrets and offered us a thoroughly inadequate service in return."[37]

Throughout the war, U.S. negotiators drove a hard bargain, leading the British to believe that Americans aimed not only to win the war, but also to leave Britain beleaguered and bankrupt, in effect pauperized. Even Assistant Secretary of State Acheson complained that the Treasury Department "envisag[ed] a victory where both enemies and allies were prostrate—enemies by military action, allies by bankruptcy."[38] Beaverbrook remained a leading critic of American economic aggrandizement, and prepared to counter U.S. Treasury strategy. "That we should pursue friendship and collaboration with the United States is an unchallengeable principle. But in seeking that friendship we should aim, with an equal constancy, at maintaining and strengthening our own position as a world power," wrote Beaverbrook to Churchill in February 1944. "The two objectives are not irreconcilable. Indeed, we shall approach the nearer to a sound and lasting relationship with the United States insofar as we are able to build up our own prestige and safeguard our own inherited interests in the economic as well as the political and military spheres."[39] The principal British negotiator in Washington was often the brilliant and arrogant John Maynard Keynes—whose financial strategy aimed always at sustaining British solvency. Eventually in July 1944, he led the British delegation to the Bretton Woods Conference in New Hampshire, a conference that established the postwar monetary and financial system. Americans disliked dealing with Keynes, whom one State Department official characterized by his "well-known obstinacy."[40] The obstinacy and cleverness of Keynes was one diplomatic bulwark against British bankruptcy. "He sort of assumes that we don't give a damn" about Britain, observed Harry Hopkins, "and it just—it irritates me."[41]

Despite many disagreements and divergent national interests, Churchill and FDR carefully nurtured the Anglo-American relationship during the war years. Each knew of the other's compromised health, Roosevelt younger but in worse shape than Churchill. At key moments in his relationship with the president, the prime minister would behave with restraint, even deference to the failing and crippled FDR. "Though the role of attendant listener was uncongenial to him, the Prime Minister played faultlessly all these days, so that we came through without loss of any feathers, if not with our tails up," wrote Anthony Eden at the Cairo conference preceding the Teheran summit of November 1943.[42] During that same trip, in which FDR intentionally ignored and offended him, Churchill would play the role of dutiful Egyptian tour guide, taking FDR to see the Pyramids. At one point in the tour, as the weakened FDR struggled to get up before sinking back, the prime minister's eyes filled with tears. He told his daughter: "I love that man."[43] Dr. Charles Wilson remembered a similar, earlier moment in January, at Marrakesh, when Churchill had said the same thing.[44]

To the chagrin of the prime minister and other British leaders, FDR too often slavishly followed American public opinion, more rarely leading it. Churchill never fully understood FDR's need to gauge the impact of his actions on the run-up to the wartime elections of 1940, 1942, and 1944. FDR the politician was exquisitely sensitive to the need not to get too far ahead of public opinion, whereas the British leader often campaigned well ahead of or against public opinion. Historian James MacGregor Burns argued that Roosevelt "believed in moving on a wide, short front, pushing ahead here, retreating there, temporizing elsewhere. . . . To gain power meant winning elections; and to win elections required endless concessions to expediency and compromises with his own ideals."[45]

Especially before America was forced into the war by the Japanese attack on Pearl Harbor, the prime minister had been frustrated by Roosevelt's failure to lead public opinion rather than to follow it. Churchill's character, and his long and controversial political career, had fortified his natural courage. "There is in Winston the old aristocratic contempt for consequences," observed Brendan Bracken.[46] "Nothing is more dangerous in wartime than to live in the temperamental atmosphere of a Gallup poll, always feeling one's pulse and taking one's temperature," Churchill had told Parliament in September 1941. "I see that a speaker at the weekend said that this was a time when leaders should keep their ears to the ground. All I can say is that the British nation will find it very hard to look up to leaders who are detected in that somewhat ungainly posture. If today I am very kindly treated by the mass of the people of this country, it is certainly not because I have followed public opinion in recent years. There is only one duty, only one safe course, and that is to try to be right and not to fear to do or say what you believe to be right. That is the only way to deserve and to win the confidence of our great people in these days of trouble."[47] Churchill had a major political advantage over FDR. The prime minister was insulated from electoral defeat so long as he maintained the support of the House of Commons for his coalition government. A new election would await the end of the war, unless there were a vote in Parliament of no confidence. In fact, there was no general election in Britain from 1935 to 1945, because Churchill successfully led and maintained his large but contentious coalition in Parliament. "You must remember," Churchill observed in 1941, "that unlike the president I have to appear continuously before the legislature. Indeed I have had to give much more time to the House of Commons than I bargained for when the Ministry was formed."[48] John Colville noted that Churchill "was always prepared to fight for his convictions without the least regard to his personal popularity or political advantage."[49] However, FDR had to deal not only with general elections, but with fractious and self-important southern Democrats and Republicans, every bit as difficult as dissident Tory, Liberal, and Labour MPs.

Other issues divided the Allies. British policy focused on the reestablishment of a strong French nation, one of the world's leading colonial powers before the war. FDR focused on propping up the corrupt government of Chiang Kai-shek. The British objected to the venality and ineffectiveness of China. Churchill "felt that any policy based on confidence in China was a 'great illusion.'"[50] General Charles de Gaulle of the Free French pledged to uphold French glory and to retain France's colonial empire. FDR and the Americans thought the stubborn self-importance of de Gaulle obnoxious. The general radiated self-appointed authority, but he represented no legitimate democratic power. The Germans had divided France into Nazi-occupied France in the north and the Vichy government in the south. The pro-Vichy State Department objected in December 1941, when the Free French forces of de Gaulle abruptly commandeered Vichy-ruled French islands off the Canadian coast. Cordell Hull was astonished by the adverse press reaction to the secretary of state's criticism of the Free French seizure of St. Pierre and Miquelon. President Roosevelt brushed off the takeover, which had the useful effect of eliminating a potential Nazi spy and radio center in North America. Hull could not let the incident go.[51]

Hull was further infuriated by Churchill's speech to the Canadian Parliament on December 30, 1941, in which the prime minister strongly attacked the Vichy government. Hopkins wrote: "I think Hull . . . believes that the British have turned their press agents loose on him. He is obviously very sensitive of the criticism he is receiving, and blames it on the British and particularly on Churchill."[52] Hull recalled that "the refusal of the President to bring more pressure on Mr. Churchill to clarify the relations between Great Britain and the United States with regard to de Gaulle and Vichy was one of several factors that almost caused me to resign as Secretary of State in January, 1942."[53] Hull's reaction to a relatively minor incident signaled his inability to see the larger wartime diplomatic and political picture, but de Gaulle's Free French invasion did cost it some of the Roosevelt administration's goodwill.[54] Admiral Leahy, FDR's chief of staff, could be particularly vehement in his denunciation of de Gaulle, "sulking" in London. Stettinius recalled a June 1944 meeting with Free French diplomat Jean Monnet, at which "Admiral Leahy went into great detail reviewing the history of our relationship with the French committee over the past two years. He stated with great force that from the start they had hampered our war effort, and had caused us difficulty and embarrassment at every turn."[55] Military success in Europe exposed the divergent national interests of the English-speaking allies. "Washington and London are not as close as they were," wrote British Mediterranean overseer Harold Macmillan in June 1944. "The honeymoon stage between the President and the Prime Minister is over, and the normal difficulties and divergencies, inseparable from staid married life, are beginning to develop."[56]

By early 1942, American leaders, including FDR, had developed a visceral dislike of de Gaulle. After the North African invasion in late 1942, the Roosevelt administration had preferred General Henri Honoré Giraud to command French soldiers there. Reluctantly, both generals were coerced to become copresidents of the Comité Français de la Libération Nationale. Outmaneuvered by de Gaulle, Giraud resigned. Americans hoped for a more tractable alternative to de Gaulle, because the insufferably arrogant general stuck to narrow French national interests. Indeed, he could even be contemptuous of the Allies, who held the general's fate in their hands. To many French, English, and especially Americans, de Gaulle had no official standing other than his own pretensions. In addition, de Gaulle would not compromise.[57] Fueled by the opposition of many pro-Vichy French residing in the United States, the president's dislike of de Gaulle ran deep. At one point in June 1943, FDR wrote Churchill: "I am absolutely convinced that he has been and is now injuring our war effort and that he is a very dangerous threat to us. I agree with you that he likes neither the British nor the Americans and he would doublecross both of us at the first opportunity."[58] Roosevelt thought de Gaulle "a narrow-minded French zealot with too much ambition for his own good and some rather dubious views on democracy."[59] The French leader showed little interest in mitigating FDR's distrust or Churchill's annoyance.[60] De Gaulle's intransigence and his demands in the tense days before the D-Day invasion maddened Churchill. Foreign Secretary Eden defended de Gaulle as necessary to Allied invasion policy, even at his most difficult. At one point, Churchill ordered Eden to have de Gaulle returned to Algiers, "in chains if necessary. He must not be allowed to enter France." Eden got Churchill to countermand the order.[61] Only after the Allies had invaded France in June 1944 did de Gaulle visit the president in Washington. Despite the provocations, Churchill managed to avoid a complete break with the general, who in August 1944 became president of the Provisional Government of the French Republic.

The prime minister and the president fish at the presidential retreat at Shangri-La (later Camp David) in Maryland, May 1943.
FRANKLIN D. ROOSEVELT PRESIDENTIAL LIBRARY

XVIA

Churchill and Roosevelt: Increasingly Exhausted

> I realised at Teheran for the 1st time what a very *small country* this is. On one hand the big Russian bear with its paws outstretched—on the other side the great American Elephant & between them the poor little English donkey—who was the only one that knows the right way home.[1]
>
> ***Winston S. Churchill**, August 1, 1944, conversation with Lady Violet Bonham Carter.*

> I have a feeling this is a time for an intense new impulse, both of friendship and exertion, to be drawn from our bosoms and to the last scrap of our resources. Do not hesitate to tell me of anything you think we can do.[2]
>
> ***Winston S. Churchill**, memo to Franklin D. Roosevelt, January 6, 1945.*[3]

Sickness frequently waylaid the prime minister and the president—the flu and colds for Roosevelt, pneumonia and colds for Churchill—especially after strenuous trips. Rest was always elusive—particularly for Roosevelt, who needed more than Churchill.[4] Still, Churchill treasured closing his eyes, saying on one train trip: "What a blessing is the gift of sleep!"[5] After the Casablanca summit in January 1943, both men sickened with serious respiratory problems. "I think I picked up sleeping sickness or Gambia fever or some kindred bug in that hell-hole of your so called Bathurst," complained Roosevelt to Churchill of his stopover in Africa.[6] "Roosevelt suffered from a number of maladies, serious and less so," wrote historian Warren Kimball. "He experienced intermittent bouts of forgetfulness because of an insufficient blood supply to the brain . . . caused by a combination of high blood pressure, congestive heart failure, anemia, and congestion in his lungs."[7] FDR had to cope with the symptoms of an enlarged heart. He suffered repeated attacks of bronchitis. Thus, the president had little stamina; accordingly, his doctors and his daughter tried to restrict his work schedule.[8] Kimball noted: "Many of Roosevelt's health problems were either caused by his paralysis [polio] or accentuated by that condition. His anemia stemmed from bleeding hemorrhoids, made chronic by his inability to walk or stand."[9] Roosevelt's physician, Rear Admiral Ross McIntire, viewed Churchill "as Public Enemy Number One," talking with the president well past his bedtime. The prime minister "was a tremendously stimulating companion whom the President liked and enjoyed, and although I always asked that eleven o'clock be set as a dead line, it was rarely observed."[10]

Roosevelt's doctors, led by McIntire, were less aggressive on FDR's behalf than Dr. Charles Wilson was for Churchill. McIntire did not explicitly tell Roosevelt of his multiple problems despite the obvious physical symptoms—shaking hands, shrunken body, sleepless nights. In his White House memoirs, McIntire suggested that the death in February 1945 of General Edwin "Pa" Watson, FDR's folksy appointments secretary, came as a "terrible shock to the President. Up to that moment I do not think that the thought of death had ever entered his mind. Aside from natural buoyancy and sanguine temperament, there was his absorption in the job and the immediacy of the tasks that lay before him." McIntire contended that Roosevelt overworked on his return from Yalta. Roosevelt "would not take his afternoon rest, skipped his daily rub, and worked far into the night. Checkups continued to be satisfactory, showing no evidence of organic ailment, but each new day added to signs of fatigue."[11] Photographs of FDR contradicted McIntire's benign evaluation of Roosevelt—pictures suggesting rapidly deteriorating health. At one point in the summer of 1944, the perceptive Hopkins wired FDR: "The underground is working overtime here in regard to your health."[12]

The president and the prime minister warned the other to take care of his health. "Please, please for the sake of the world, don't overdo it these days," FDR wrote Churchill in March 1943. "You must remember that it takes about a month of occasional let-ups to get back your full strength."[13] In one note to Churchill in December 1943, when the prime minister was recovering from pneumonia, Roosevelt advised tongue in cheek: "The Bible says you must do what [physician] Moran orders but at this moment I cannot put my finger on the verse and chapter."[14] High fever was a frequent traveling companion of the prime minister. Dr. Wilson, who took these fevers in stride, wrote in his diary before the Yalta Conference: "Surely this bout of fever should put sense into his head. But Winston is a gambler, and gamblers do not count the coins in their pockets. He will not give a thought to nursing his waning powers. And now, when it was nearly midnight, he demanded cards and began to play bezique with Harriman."[15]

Medicines were available for many of the prime minister's problems. Dr. Wilson made sure that Churchill took them, even though some had adverse side effects.[16] No medicine was available at that time to treat one of FDR's core problems—high blood pressure. In February 1944, he had a cyst removed from his neck, and possibly another from above his eyebrow.[17] Only after the president suffered a serious attack of the flu in March 1944 was he treated for his heart problems.[18] Cardiologist Howard Bruenn, over the objections of McIntire and many of the top doctors at Bethesda, insisted on prescribing digitalis for FDR.[19] In May 1944, Roosevelt had gall bladder attacks. His gastrointestinal problems led to rumors of stomach cancer.[20] During trips later in 1944, Roosevelt suffered severe attacks of angina. His lapses of memory became more frequent. His secretary, Grace Tully, recalled that he sometimes fell asleep while dictating correspondence.[21] By 1944, "like hell" or "rotten" became FDR's stock answers to inquiries about how he was feeling.[22] The president spent nearly the whole month of April 1944 recuperating at Bernard Baruch's South Carolina estate. The degree of FDR's physical incapacitation seemed obvious to everyone except his own physician.[23] Surely, there was a desire not to reveal to the press FDR's serious health problems before the November 1944 presidential vote, perhaps not even to the president himself.

At Yalta in February 1945, the evidence of FDR's physical and mental deterioration was obvious to all. Churchill's physician wrote: "To a doctor's eye, the President appears a very sick man. He has all the symptoms of hardening of the arteries of the brain in an advanced stage, so that I give him only a few months to live."[24] At Yalta, FDR suffered from an irregular heartbeat. FDR's daughter, Anna Boettinger, wrote home to her husband: "Just between you and me, we are having to watch OM [the old man, her father] very carefully from the physical standpoint. He gets all wound up, seems to thoroughly enjoy it all, but wants too many people around, and then won't go to bed early enough. The result is that he doesn't sleep well. [Doctors] Ross and Bruenn are both worried because of the old 'ticker' trouble—which, of course, no one knows about but those two and me. . . . I have found out thru Bruenn (who won't let me tell Ross that I know) that this 'ticker' situation is far more serious than I ever knew. And the biggest difficulty in handling the situation here is that we can, of course, tell no one of the 'ticker' trouble. It's truly worrisome—and there's not a heluva lot anyone can do about it."[25] Charles Bohlen wrote that by March 1945, FDR's "hands shook so that he had difficulty in holding a telegram. His weariness and general lassitude were apparent to all, although he could call on reserves of strength whenever he had to meet with congressional leaders or other public figures." Roosevelt "was forced to rely more than he would have normally on the good faith and judgment of his advisers. Some persons took advantage of his condition."[26] Certainly, the State Department did so in early March, when Under Secretary of State James Dunn got Roosevelt to initial a German reconstruction plan, which FDR later claimed not to have read and which conflicted with plans from the War and Treasury Departments.[27]

To ease his mood in the last years of his life, FDR sought the company of women with whom he could relax, such as cousin Daisy Suckley and his former mistress, Lucy Mercer Rutherford. Roosevelt's choleric wife could exacerbate his high blood pressure.[28] In November 1944, Eleanor had called FDR on the phone to complain about new State Department appointees and "raised the devil with him," according to their daughter, Anna. The president "hung up" on the First Lady.[29] As relief for her father, Anna herself facilitated his meetings with Lucy. One contemporary noted: "Eleanor Roosevelt has many virtues but she is not a restful woman." Unlike Eleanor, daughter Anna took on a protective role with FDR. Whereas Eleanor brought problems and pressure to her husband, Anna attempted to push them away. She observed: "It was immaterial to me whether my job was helping to plan the 1944 campaign, pouring tea for General de Gaulle or filling Father's empty cigarette case. All that mattered was relieving a greatly overburdened man of a few details of work and trying to make his life as pleasant as possible when a few moments opened up for relaxation." Anna's son, John R. Boettiger, wrote: "Anna was conscious that she helped fill for her father an important emotional need, yet she also knew, and did not wish to exacerbate, her mother's distress at Franklin's easier companionship with less serious and demanding women."[30]

Harry Hopkins tried to carry on, but was regularly hospitalized.[31] After the announcement of Hopkins's engagement in 1942, General Marshall wrote Hopkins's fiancée: "To be very frank, I am intensely interested in Harry's health and happiness, and therefore, in your approaching marriage. . . . He is of great importance to our national interests at the present time, and he is one of the most imprudent people regarding his health that I have ever known."[32] After the 1943 summit at Quebec, Hopkins violated doctors' orders to rest: "All those boys at the front are fighting & getting hurt & dying. I have a job to do here, & I'm going to do it."[33] Daisy Suckley observed that Hopkins "has only half a stomach & should never touch liquor, but he hasn't the sense to resist it. Besides that, he was kept alive by having regular blood transfusions for the past months—perhaps a year or two."[34]

FDR suffered the flu during the month before the Teheran conference. Hopkins was as debilitated as the president, but Roosevelt remarked that "it will break his heart if I don't take him with me" on the grueling trip.[35] When Hopkins returned from Teheran, he was again hospitalized for several weeks. "I've seen him [Hopkins] trying to feed up on regular food & drinking cocktails, etc. when he should be on gruel & baby foods," wrote Suckley disapprovingly of Hopkins.[36] By September 1944, Suckley had grown increasingly concerned about Roosevelt: "He gets so awfully tired and has no chance to rest. This campaign [for a fourth term] will wear him still further."[37] Former Senator Byrnes recalled that because Hopkins was usually resting in his room, "Members of our delegation frequently held meetings there because Dr. McIntyre insisted he [Hopkins] remain in bed."[38]

Hopkins had played perhaps the central role as liaison among the Anglo-American leaders. Pamela Churchill, later Pamela Harriman, observed that Hopkins had "a marvelous capacity to explain president to prime minister as well as the reverse," adding that "he had a sensitive and clever understanding of the two."[39] Historian Walter Reid wrote of an incident in January 1940, when Churchill asked for a million rifles. Hopkins called Roosevelt and returned to tell Churchill that a million rifles would be shipped on the following day. Churchill was visibly moved to tears, as he often was. Reid wrote that "Hopkins understood the magic of moments such as this, and what they meant to Churchill—and to an extent to Roosevelt. Such alchemy could impart a romantic and emotional dimension from time to time into a relationship that was otherwise cold, calculating and often unappealing."[40] When Churchill overwhelmed a parliamentary revolt in July 1942, Hopkins wrote him: "We are delighted by today's action in the House of Commons. The military defeats you suffer are ours also and we will share together the certain victories to come, so I know you will be of good heart. . . . Your own courage and tenacity and strength and everlasting confidence will bring your country through and you know that the President does not quit."[41] When Hopkins, who enjoyed unprecedented access to both Roosevelt and Churchill, was not available to manage the relationship in 1943–1944, discord ensued. Possessive of their intimate friendship, Churchill and Roosevelt often preferred direct communication. In June 1944, Churchill telegraphed Roosevelt: "Your telegrams to me in the recent crisis worked wonders. . . . Why can you and I not keep this in our own hands, considering how we see eye to eye about so much of it?"[42]

Differences between Great Britain and America arose in negotiations with Joseph Stalin. Roosevelt decided to set up his own direct relationship with the Russian dictator, whom he first met at the Teheran conference, in November 1943. FDR flattered himself that he could handle Stalin. As he began to accommodate Stalin, the deferential Hopkins leaned more frequently against Churchill's harder attitude toward Stalin. President Roosevelt had angled to meet Stalin alone at the Teheran summit before seeing Churchill. When Churchill's physician questioned Hopkins about the propriety of such a move, Hopkins became defensive: "What possible objection could there be to the President meeting Stalin by himself for a heart-to-heart talk?"[43] Churchill wrote in his memoirs that on the second day of the Teheran conference, "I suggested that the President and I might lunch together before the second plenary meeting that afternoon. Roosevelt declined the invitation, sending Harriman to me to explain that he did not want Stalin to know that he and I were meeting privately. I was surprised at this, for I thought we all three should treat each other with equal confidence."[44] FDR desired to persuade Stalin that Soviet Russia and democratic America had much in common, compared to imperial Britain, despite the well-known fact that the United Kingdom was a full-fledged democracy, and the Soviet empire a brutal tyranny. That the president refused to meet with Churchill, in deference to Stalin, surely complicated the Anglo-American positions at the Teheran summit.

Both the timing of the cross-channel invasion, Operation OVERLORD, and the future of colonial territories divided Churchill from Roosevelt. Dr. Wilson wrote in his diary at Teheran: "The President, Hopkins said, made it clear that he was anxious to relieve the pressure on the Russian front by invading France. Stalin expressed his gratification, and when the President went on to say [in Churchill's absence] that he hoped Malaya, Burma and other British colonies would be 'educated in the arts of self-government' the talk became quite intimate. The President felt encouraged by Stalin's grasp of the democratic issue at stake, but he warned him not to discuss India with the Prime Minister."[45] Churchill believed there was much sanctimony in American anti-imperialism, even hypocrisy in American rhetoric about the British colonies. At the White House back in September, Roosevelt had observed Churchill's interaction with Helen Reid, the influential wife of the *New York Tribune* publisher. Challenged by Mrs. Reid about India, Churchill had responded: "Before we proceed let me get one thing clear. Are we talking about the brown Indians in India, who have multiplied alarmingly under the benevolent British rule? Or are we speaking of the red Indians in America, who, I understand, are almost extinct?"[46] FDR was listening, and Churchill's implied meaning was inescapable: India under the British Empire had prospered, while Native Americans had been displaced by American democracy.

The president would stoop low to ingratiate himself with Stalin—actually ridiculing Churchill in Stalin's presence, even encouraging Stalin to do so as well. FDR's translator, Russian expert and experienced diplomat Charles Bohlen, disapproved of FDR's response to Stalin's hectoring of Churchill: "Roosevelt should have come to the defense of a close friend and ally, who was really being put upon by Stalin. Of course it was true that Roosevelt was arguing on the same side that Stalin was, so in effect this anti-Churchill attitude was justified. Roosevelt never explained his attitude in my presence, but his apparent belief that ganging up on the Russians was to be avoided at all cost was, in my mind, a basic error, stemming from Roosevelt's lack of understanding of the Bolsheviks."[47] FDR, however, knew the story of the Bolshevik Revolution. It was his vanity, his desire to be liked, his belief in his charm, and, tactically, his desire to get Stalin into the war against Japan that moved him to belittle his loyal ally, Churchill.[48]

During late 1943 and early 1944, Hopkins fell from Roosevelt's favor—even as Hopkins became less sympathetic to the prime minister's hesitations about the invasion of western France, his preoccupation with Mediterranean operations, and his resistance to discussing postwar political changes. As early as March 1943, Hopkins told a Foreign Office aide that he worried about "the P.M., his age, his unteachability. He was not the man to make the peace."[49] Just before the Teheran summit in November 1943, Dr. Wilson "[r]an into Harry Hopkins, and found him full of sneers and jibes. He had just come from a meeting of the Combined Chiefs of Staff, who were framing a plan to put before Stalin at Teheran. According to Harry, Winston hardly stopped talking, and most of it was about 'his bloody Italian war.'" Hopkins stated in his dry aggressive way: "Winston said he was a hundred percent for OVERLORD. But it was very important to capture Rome, and then we ought to take Rhodes."[50]

At Teheran, Hopkins took responsibility for personally informing Churchill that Operation OVERLORD must go forward without any further delays.[51] General Marshall repeatedly poured cold water on the prime minister's peripheral schemes, such as the capture of Greek islands off Turkey. But Churchill argued that substantial military resources were then undeployed. Thus, the prime minister, a warrior to the core, objected to a situation in which military personnel or equipment were not actively engaged in the war effort. Churchill wrote in his memoirs that he pressed at Teheran for an operation to take Rhodes: "If Rhodes were taken the whole Ægean could be dominated by our Air Force and direct sea contact established with Turkey. If, on the other hand, Turkey could be persuaded to enter the war, or to strain her neutrality by lending us the airfields we had built for her, we could equally dominate the Ægean and the capture of Rhodes would not be necessary. Either way it would work."[52] Stalin undercut Churchill's arguments, pressing for a second front in the west—denying the importance of "Turkey, Rhodes, Yugoslavia and even the capture of Rome."[53] Despite Churchill's tactical arguments, Roosevelt and Stalin at this stage wanted nothing to delay the cross-channel invasion of France in the spring of 1944. Churchill and Brooke had correctly opposed the cross-channel operation in 1942 and 1943 as premature. After Teheran, effective opposition came to an end. By the spring of 1944, General Eisenhower and his team had completed the colossal preparations for D-Day.

It was in 1943 that the Churchill-Roosevelt relationship had begun to fray, as America gradually became the senior partner in the Anglo-American alliance. Moreover, in 1944, Hopkins fell into political and medical eclipse for nearly nine months. He was not invited to the September 1944 Anglo-American summit in Quebec, but he was invited to Hyde Park immediately afterward, to help with the FDR-Churchill follow-up meeting. At that Quebec summit, the president and the prime minister (wishing to accommodate FDR) embarrassed themselves by initialing a memo, summarizing a highly controversial plan drawn up by Treasury Secretary Morgenthau. The plan, if implemented, would have deindustrialized and pastoralized postwar Germany. By virtue of the plan, Germany would become primarily an agricultural nation, thus leaving all Europe, unto the English Channel, totally vulnerable to the enormous occupying Russian army so close to the French border. Churchill's first and serious reaction to Morgenthau's plan, at a dinner on September 13, had been an uncharacteristically angry outburst at FDR: "Is *this* what you asked me to come all the way here to discuss?" He added: "I'm all for disarming Germany. But we ought not prevent her living decently." He added: "Kill the criminals, but don't carry on the business for years." Under the influence of his very anti-German advisor "Prof" Lindemann, but more in deference to FDR, Churchill temporarily did an about-face.[54] The next morning, Morgenthau, Lindemann, and Anglo-American advisors met, giving momentum to the Morgenthau Plan. Churchill later dictated a short memo on the plan that he and Roosevelt initialed with neither careful analysis nor consultation. Morgenthau wrote in his diary: "Naturally, I am terrifically happy over it as we got just what we started out to get."[55] Morgenthau's senior Treasury deputy, Harry Dexter White, had inspired the idea and the plan.

When he arrived in Quebec, Eden told Churchill: "You can't do this. After all, you and I publicly have said quite the opposite. Furthermore, we have a lot of things in the works in London which are quite different."[56] They then had a rare disagreement in front of American leaders. Eden, who was much less sensitive than Churchill on Jewish questions, wrote in his diary that he was "irritated by this German Jew's [Morgenthau's] bitter hatred of his own land." (An astonishing comment in view of the well-known Holocaust.) Ultimately, Morgenthau would be trumped by British and American policy makers taking a longer-range, strategic view of the reconstruction of Germany—linked primarily to Soviet deterrence. Moreover, in the summer of 1944, there was a growing "skepticism in London about the willingness of the United States to play any useful role in defending postwar Europe," according to Fraser Harbutt. In fact, FDR had given notice that the United States would not remain tied down in Europe. As a consequence, British strategists increasingly thought "that the vital western industrial part of Germany must be drawn into the postwar British defensive orbit as a necessary counter to any potential Soviet aggression."[57] British strategy would ultimately prevail in 1951 when West Germany joined the European Coal and Steel Community, then in 1957 the fledgling Common Market of Western Europe.

White House aide Robert Sherwood, a playwright who served as an FDR speechwriter and director of the Office of War Information Overseas Branch, wrote:

> It is not improbable that one of the factors in restoring Hopkins to his former position with Roosevelt was the Morgenthau Plan episode. Roosevelt admitted that he had yielded to the importunities of an old and loyal friend [Morgenthau] when he affixed his initials to this document, and this was precisely the kind of thing against which Hopkins—who was no respecter of old friendships—was practiced in protecting him. Hopkins had agreed with Stimson and Hull on the general outline for treatment of Germany and would have been quick to detect the dangerous implications in the Morgenthau Plan and Roosevelt realized this and was sorry that he had not taken Hopkins with him to Quebec.[58]

When the initial endorsement of the Morgenthau Plan was revealed to the Roosevelt cabinet, it caused a major division. Secretary of War Stimson and Secretary of State Hull would strongly oppose the president's action.[59]

FDR, ever opportunistic in his use of subordinates, resurrected Hopkins for the post-Quebec meeting with Churchill at Hyde Park. "Harry Hopkins was . . . obviously invited to please me," wrote Churchill in his memoirs of the September 1944 meeting. "He explained to me his altered position. He had declined in the favour of the President. There was a curious incident at luncheon, when he arrived a few minutes late, and the president did not even greet him. It was remarkable how definitely my contacts with the president improved and our affairs moved quicker as Hopkins appeared to regain his influence. In two days it seemed to be like old times."[60] Clementine Churchill, however, believed the afterthought of Hopkins's inclusion was "sad and rather embarrassing."[61] Hopkins, however, proved he was still the grease that lubricated the Churchill-Roosevelt relationship. After the Hyde

Park meeting, Beaverbrook wrote Hopkins: "I have seen Churchill and have had his account of his conversation with you. All the old warmth and affection is bubbling over. He is full of praise for God's work in restoring you to health."[62] Historian Warren Kimball noted that "Churchill mistakenly believed [Hopkins] to be Britain's best friend at the White House." This was probably true in 1940–1941. But by early 1944, Hopkins was sick and out of the loop, only returning to FDR's favor in the autumn. When Churchill insisted on visiting Moscow before the 1944 presidential election, FDR wrote him on October 4, 1944: "I can well understand the reasons why you feel that an immediate meeting between yourself and Uncle Joe is necessary before the three of us can get together. The questions which you will discuss there are ones which are, of course, of real interest to the United States, as I know you will agree. I have therefore instructed Harriman to stand by and to participate as my observer, if agreeable to you and Uncle Joe, and I have so informed Stalin."[63] FDR had become increasingly peremptory with Churchill—Hopkins less willing and less able to patch up disagreements.

Hopkins's role as a lightning rod for presidential critics occasionally limited his usefulness to FDR. Historian H. W. Brands wrote that even Eleanor Roosevelt regretted the actions she took in 1938, to bring Hopkins closer to FDR's inner circle: "His actions as czar of relief stole headlines she thought should have been Franklin's. And when he attracted criticism she resented the bad light he brought on the administration. Conservatives repeated endlessly a statement attributed to Hopkins that he forever denied having made, but that seemed to summarize the Hopkins attitude towards relief [welfare] and politics: 'We shall tax and tax, and spend and spend, and elect and elect.' At every opportunity the conservatives slapped him down."[64] In 1938, FDR had invited Hopkins to the White House to promote Hopkins as a possible presidential successor in 1940. World war and bad health interfered with those aspirations.[65] Charles Bohlen, who served as State Department liaison to the White House in 1944–1945, wrote that Hopkins's "influence with Roosevelt was entirely personal and therefore went up and down, depending on Roosevelt's mood. Sometimes he enjoyed Roosevelt's total confidence and at other times, for no apparent reason, he was cast aside and for weeks never even saw the President. Hopkins became a master at recognizing the President's moods and knew intuitively when to offer a suggestion and when to keep silent. There is no doubt that throughout the war Roosevelt relied more on Hopkins than on any other adviser."[66] FDR biographer Joseph P. Lash, himself a close associate of Eleanor Roosevelt, observed that Hopkins "provided Roosevelt with the disinterested companionship that the president so desperately needed."[67]

In 1944, British and American military authorities had been debating a crucial issue for two years—the timing of a cross-channel invasion. At one point, American planners in Washington speculated that the British felt that "continued Mediterranean operations coupled with [Operation] POINTBLANK [the Anglo-American air campaign to destroy Germany's infrastructure] and the crushing Russian offensive, will be sufficient to cause the internal collapse of Germany and thus bring about her military defeat without undergoing what they consider an almost certain 'bloodbath.' The conclusion that the forces being built up in the United Kingdom will never be used for a military offensive against Europe, but are intended [by the British] as a gigantic deception plan and an occupying force, is inescapable."[68] General Leslie Hollis recalled that memories of gruesome World War I casualties influenced British strategy: "The British Empire lost one million men dead—the pick of a generation—in that war, most of them in France. Churchill was determined that this fearful slaughter should not be approached in the Second World War." Churchill told Eisenhower in 1944: "When I think of the beaches of Normandy choked with the flowers of American and British youth and when in my mind's eye I see the tides running red with their blood I have my doubts—I have my doubts Ike, I have my doubts."[69] British military authorities also believed the Americans were naive about the weather, tides, equipment, and supply problems of the Normandy invasion.[70] These were serious problems, but the Americans had determined to solve them.

The British finally agreed at the 1943 Quebec summit to a spring 1944 invasion, but they continued to focus on the difficulties. After the conclave, Hopkins told Dr. Wilson: "Winston is no longer against Marshall's plan for landing on the coast of France. At least, so he says."[71] The Americans, especially General Marshall, had thought the British duplicitous in 1942—first voicing support, and then finding arguments for military campaigns in what Churchill called the "soft underbelly" of Europe. Military historian Max Hastings wrote: "Churchill's uncertainty concerned not whether to invade Europe and the Mediterranean, but when to do so. Looking back over the strategic debate that took place between 1941 and 1944, it is impossible to acquit America's leadership of naivety, just as it is difficult to deny the inability of Britain's service chiefs to match the American genius for overcoming difficulties."[72] Early in the war, Churchill lacked confidence in the British Army and the fighting esprit of the British soldier. This, too, would change.

British planners well understood the immense obstacles to a successful invasion. They respected the stubborn bravery of the battle-tested German soldiers and officers. General Brooke predicted before D-Day: "At the best, it will come very far short of the expectations of the bulk of the people, namely all those who know nothing about its difficulties. At its worst, it may well be the most ghastly disaster of the whole war."[73] The enormous difficulties faced by Allied forces in the first two months after D-Day gave credibility to the concerns of the prime minister and General Brooke. Max Hastings, a distinguished historian of D-Day, wrote that "the inescapable reality of the battle for Normandy was that when Allied troops met Germans on anything like equal terms, the German almost always prevailed." Churchill was mortified by this fact. Moreover, the Allies had not fully prepared themselves to deal with the tactical difficulties of the Normandy terrain. Many commanders showed insufficient resourcefulness overcoming the obstacles they met. Hastings argued that "nowhere did the Allies achieve decisive penetrations against high-quality German formations until these had been worn down by attrition and ruined by air attack." Total dominance of the air was crucial, but the Allied advance was tortuously slow. The British had underestimated the fact that the Allies completely commanded the air over the Channel and Normandy. Still, German ground troops were tenacious. Hastings added: "The Allies in Normandy faced the finest fighting army of the war, one of the greatest that the world has ever seen."[74] Churchill, speaking to Allied military leaders in April 1944, said that "the time was now *ripe.* We had experienced commanders, a great allied army, a great air force. Our equipment had improved. All the preparations, strategical and tactical, had been made with the greatest skill and care. We were now going to write a glorious page in the history, not of one country or of two, but of the world."[75] The Allies still did not reckon fully on the skilled German defenses General Rommel had put in place in northwest France. This the Germans accomplished despite the gigantic war of survival that German armies were waging in Russia on the vast eastern front.[76] The scale of the eastern front dwarfed the western front, even at full strength long after D-Day. As a measure of the scale of fighting on the two fronts, four out of five German soldiers who died in battle were killed on the eastern front, reenforcing Stalin's claim to the centrality of the Soviet Union's victories on the eastern front—victories achieved at a far higher cost of human lives. Stalin and Soviet generals were heedless of the cost in soldiers' lives.

General Eisenhower would mount more than a heroic invasion of northwestern France. He would plan the huge Operation ANVIL, designed to invade southern France from the Mediterranean, the better to supply Allied troops on the way to Germany. The prime minister opposed Operation ANVIL, causing increasing friction in 1944 between Churchill and the American leadership. He objected that ANVIL would jeopardize the slowly moving Allied campaign in Italy. But American military and civilian leaders decided to focus Allied armies on ANVIL and OVERLORD. Churchill wrote in his memoirs: "Eisenhower himself firmly believed in the vital importance of 'Anvil', and thought it would be a mistake to impoverish it for the sake of strengthening 'Overlord'."[77] Churchill criticized the planning and the conduct of the invasion of southern France, believing it a diversion from Allied operations underway not only in Italy, but also in northwest France. The prime minister wrote that "it was no use landing in the south of France unless we did so at the right time. The mere threat of an assault would suffice to keep German troops in the region; a real invasion might induce the enemy to reinforce them; but once we joined battle in Normandy, 'Anvil's' value was much reduced, because Hitler was not likely to detach troops from the main struggle in the north for the sake of keeping his hold on Provence."[78] In July 1944, Churchill complained to General Omar Bradley, "Why, why break down the back door when the front door has already been opened by your magnificent American army?"[79] In early August, Churchill tried to enlist Harry Hopkins to back his strategic argument. Hopkins, no longer so close to FDR, replied: "While there has been no reply as yet from the president to your message relative to the same matter [ANVIL], I am sure his answer will be in the negative."[80] On August 15, Churchill would personally observe the ANVIL invasion. Later, he wrote in his memoirs: "The army which we had landed on the Riviera at such painful cost to our operations in Italy arrived too late to help Eisenhower's first main struggle in the north, while Alexander's offensive [in Italy] failed by the barest of margins, to achieve the success it deserved and we so badly needed."[81] Never did Churchill's faith waiver about the relative importance of the Italian campaign, not least because it immobilized an immense, high-quality, well-led German army in Italy. There mountainous topography proved much harder for the Allies than the "soft underbelly" that Churchill had once described to Stalin.

In different circumstances, the president and the prime minister were both tactical opportunists, shifting like the fox this way, then that way. U.S. Army Chief of Staff Marshall and General Eisenhower, like the hedgehog, set their assault in one direction. They had decided to attack the German army head-on in France. General Marshall, early on, opposed all diversions from this main strategic thrust. President Roosevelt, the American commander in chief, had been consistently opportunistic in domestic policy and early war strategy. Joseph Persico wrote that during the run up to war in 1939–1941, FDR's "tacking from belligerence to prudence revealed something that isolationists did not believe and that interventionists did not want to accept. He would keep the United States out of the war if, at the same time, he could sufficiently strengthen Britain to hold out against Germany."[82] Cordell Hull described American policy more systematically: "From Pearl Harbor until my resignation, our policy toward Britain embraced three objectives. First, to arrive at the maximum cooperation in the prosecution of the war. Second, to work closely with the United Kingdom, the Soviet Union, China, and other countries toward creating institutions to deal with the problems arising from the war and problems that would face us after the war. Third, to solve specific Anglo-American post-war problems by direct negotiation before the end of hostilities."[83] Although the U.S. Department of State had a streak of Anglophobia, Hull acknowledged the heroic character of Churchill: "When the supreme crisis arrived during the Dunkirk period, involving life or death to Britain, Churchill's was the one single voice that could be heard above the din at home and abroad, instilling into every man, woman, and child in Britain a determination to resist German invasion to the last breath."[84]

Admiration for Churchill in the United States was not sufficient to sustain the Roosevelt-Churchill relationship. Surely one important cause was that Roosevelt rapidly declined physically (and, to some extent, mentally) in 1944–1945.The weakened prime minister, despite his ailments, fortified by remarkable recovery powers, carried on tenaciously. For tactical and strategic reasons, as well as postwar planning purposes, the exhausted president tended to avoid Churchill toward the end of the war. Churchill's physician noted the growing split: "Winston was moved only by a growing concern about the conduct of the war; there was nothing personal in his differences with the President. He always maintained that Franklin Roosevelt was a very great man, and became angry when he heard criticism." By the end of the war, the colossal American war production machine—supplying both the eastern front, the western front, and the home front—rendered a tiring Churchill the junior partner in the Anglo-American coalition. Dr. Wilson noted that during the final year of the war, "Hopkins, in a temper, blurted out that it did not seem just to the President that Winston should take all the credit as leader of the Free World. Roosevelt had become jealous of Winston. Lord Halifax confirmed this when I put a direct question to him."[85] The Churchill-Roosevelt honeymoon had deteriorated (along with health problems), by reason of sincere policy differences, confirming that nations have no permanent friends, only interests. Furthermore, Anglo-American disputes were increasingly marked by different, emerging political strategies for the postwar world—especially how to contain an expansive, victorious Soviet Union, its armies occupying most of Eastern Europe.

President Roosevelt and Prime Minister Churchill showing the strains of the Casablanca Conference, January 1943.
FRANKLIN D. ROOSEVELT PRESIDENTIAL LIBRARY

XVIB

The Wages of War: Health Problems in the Alliance

Franklin D. Roosevelt suffered a minor heart attack in February 1940, during a dinner with Ambassador William Bullitt and secretary Missy LeHand.[1] Nearly four years later, during the opening dinner at the Teheran conference, in November 1943, FDR was beset by another attack. He was temporarily speechless and flushed with sweat, but recovered by the next morning. Like Roosevelt, Winston Churchill endured a series of health defects—including a mild heart attack while visiting Roosevelt at the White House in December 1941. During the war, the pressures of work aggravated the health problems of military and civilian officials on both sides of the Atlantic, most of whom smoked too much and got too little exercise; some even drank too much.

These health issues hovered over Anglo-American relations. The stress of war took its toll on Churchill, Roosevelt, and company. Secretary of the Treasury Henry Morgenthau's son suggested that one reason FDR did not want Hopkins around, in the summer of 1944, was that he reminded the president of his own mortality: "Harry was not only a very ill man, but his brown, tobacco-stained lips, teeth, and fingers, his pallor, and his rumpled, cadaverous appearance were an uncomfortable reminder of the physical limits of fellow mortals under stress."[2] On a rough sea voyage across the Atlantic in August 1941, Churchill himself treated senior aide John Martin's seasickness. "The PM dosed me most tenderly with Mothersill, which he finds an unfailing remedy; but self-respect was restored on the last day of the homeward voyage, when it was again stormy and it was *he* who had to take the Mothersill."[3]

Bronchial attacks persisted among Anglo-American leaders. Max Beaverbrook and Leslie Hollis suffered from serious asthma and commiserated over the failure of medical science to find a remedy.[4] Admiral William Leahy came down with bronchitis on the way to the Casablanca summit; he remained at Trinidad to recuperate, and never even reached Africa. When General Hastings Ismay fell ill from exhaustion after the 1943 Teheran conference, Churchill questioned Ismay's aide, Colonel Hollis, about his health. "Sir, I am perfectly fit," replied Hollis. "*You'd better be!*" responded Churchill.[5] Hollis might have to step in for Ismay. Soon thereafter, Churchill came down with pneumonia, General Ismay then came down with bronchitis, and Hollis was called on to perform Ismay's role for nearly two months in North Africa.

Respiratory problems were an occupational hazard; Harriman suffered from sinus problems on the way back from Moscow in October 1941. As ambassador in Moscow, his sinus infections continued. "Even after he recovered, there were many winter days when he never left the house, never received an official visitor, and stayed abed until late morning, reading and writing cables."[6] Roosevelt himself received medical treatment from Admiral McIntire for his sinus difficulties while being briefed on military affairs. Air travel aggravated sinus infections.[7] The sinus problems of the crucial Deputy CIGS John N. Kennedy became so bad in 1944 that he spent the rest of the war on sick leave in Scotland.

Roosevelt aides Harry Hopkins and Averell Harriman suffered recurring stomach troubles; Harriman's ulcer required hospitalization in April 1940. Harriman's Moscow aide, George Kennan, also suffered from ulcers while serving in London. Former Ambassador Joseph Davies repeatedly refused reassignment to Moscow, because of his own intestinal difficulties.[8] Foreign Secretary Anthony Eden's health was often problematic. Eden aide Oliver Harvey wrote in his diary, in May 1943, that Eden "was genuinely fussed, as he always is over his health, at his tiredness and general exhaustion."[9] Fellow cabinet member Hugh Dalton met with Eden in August 1941: "Eden drinks some milk and admits that he has a tendency to duodenal ulcers. He says that he had a good deal of pain from this about a year ago. I am told that this complaint comes from excessive worry, and no doubt Eden is, more than most men, a nervy fusser."[10] When Eden took several weeks off from his duties in April 1944, Churchill told him: "You are my right arm; we must take care of you."[11] Eden's duodenal ulcer became so troublesome in June 1945 that the foreign secretary could not attend his mother's funeral, and the 70-year-old prime minister took over one more burden, the Foreign Office. Secretary of State Cordell Hull suffered from a chronic autoimmune disorder, sarcoidosis, as well as diabetes and claustrophobia, which eventually led to his resignation.[12] Newly developed medication that Hull subsequently received helped him live another decade. Secretary of War Henry Stimson and Secretary of the Treasury Henry Morgenthau suffered from migraines, occasionally disabling them.[13]

Under Secretary of State Sumner Welles frequently suffered from symptoms that resembled heart attacks, but soldiered on—his health furthered impaired by alcoholism. Welles feared that if Hull knew of his medical problems, the secretary would replace him.[14] John Maynard Keynes suffered from subacute bacterial endocarditis. His breathing problems frequently required bed rest, especially after a heart attack experienced at the Bretton Woods conference in 1944.[15] This heart attack left the road open to Harry Dexter White. Chancellor of the Exchequer Kingsley Wood, who had brought Keynes into the government, died of a heart attack in September

1943. Army Air Corps Chief Harold "Hap" Arnold suffered four heart attacks during the war; the last one prevented him from attending the Yalta summit.[16]

After several of his own heart attacks, Secretary of the Navy Frank Knox died in April 1944. In the same year, British Admiral Dudley Pound died of a brain tumor, and British General John Dill died of aplastic anaemia. Suffering from high blood pressure, a devoted FDR aide, Edwin "Pa" Watson, had a heart attack at Yalta in February 1945, and died after a stroke on the way back from the Yalta summit.[17] The unusually stoic President Roosevelt appeared deeply affected by Watson's death. FDR's secretary, Missy LeHand, had suffered a stroke and a mental breakdown in 1941 and never returned to work—leaving a void in FDR's inner circle.

Stalin also suffered health problems. He had contracted smallpox as a boy. Heavy smoking contributed to arteriosclerosis. During World War II, health was one of Stalin's excuses for not flying to overseas summits—particularly after he suffered attacks of the flu in the fall of 1943 and the summer of 1944.[18] Churchill ignored worse problems.

General Bernard Montgomery once told Churchill: "I don't drink or smoke and I'm one hundred percent fit."[19] Still, generals were not immune to the ravages of war. Churchill, sitting in meetings with Eisenhower's chief of staff in the summer of 1942, had noticed that General Walter Bedell Smith was seriously sick. "If you want Bedell in this battle you should send him to hospital this very night, no matter what he says," Churchill advised Eisenhower. Smith required two blood transfusions.[20] In the midst of Operation TORCH, General Eisenhower came down with walking pneumonia.[21] Over the next three years, smoking and stress, even drinking too much, aggravated Eisenhower's repeated bronchial attacks. By early 1945, the chain-smoking general was irritable and agitated. "Look at you," General Smith told him. "You've got bags under your eyes. Your blood pressure's higher than it's ever been, and you can hardly walk across the room."[22] By the autumn of 1945, Eisenhower was hospitalized with full-blown pneumonia.

U.S. Assistant Treasury Secretary Harry Dexter White (left) and John Maynard Keynes, honorary advisor to the British Treasury, meet at the inaugural meeting of the International Monetary Fund's Board of Governors in Savannah, Georgia, March 1946.
INTERNATIONAL MONETARY FUND COLLECTIONS

XVIIA

Harry Dexter White and John Maynard Keynes

[T]he Harry White [postwar monetary] scheme is not a firm offer. The real risk is that there will be no plan at all and that Congress will run away from their own proposal. No harm, therefore, at least it seems to me, if the Americans work up a certain amount of patriotic fervour for their own version. Much can be done in detail hereafter to improve it. The great thing at this stage is that they should get thoroughly committed to there being some plan; or, what is perhaps another way of putting the same thing, that their public should get thoroughly used to the idea that such a plan is inevitable.[1]

***John Maynard Keynes** (1883–1946), letter to Frederick Phillips, April 1944. Keynes was a distinguished British intellectual and economist who authored several major economic works. He served as the primary British negotiator at Bretton Woods in July 1944. On most financial and monetary issues, Keynes was the principal British representative to the American government. He would underestimate Harry Dexter White, the senior U.S. Treasury official at Bretton Woods. His health, too, would hinder Keynes.*

One thing is certain. No matter how long the war lasts nor how it is won, we shall be faced with three inescapable problems: to prevent the disruption of foreign exchanges and the collapse of monetary and credit systems; to assure the restoration of foreign trade; and to supply the huge volume of capital that will be needed virtually throughout the world for reconstruction, for relief and for economic recovery.[2]

***Harry Dexter White** (1892–1948), from his 1942 version of the "White Plan." White was a relatively obscure academic and Treasury Department official during most of the first and second terms of the Roosevelt administration. By FDR's third term, Treasury Secretary Henry Morgenthau Jr. had come to rely on his trusted deputy, White, for advice and plans on international finance and diplomacy. White acted as an assistant secretary of the Treasury at Morgenthau's request. White took charge of all Treasury planning for postwar international monetary policy, financial policy, and the Bretton Woods conference* *of July 1944. Because Morgenthau lacked financial sophistication, White, an unmasked Soviet spy, became the most important Treasury official during the war.*[3]

Absorbed with wartime military strategy and postwar political strategy, neither President Roosevelt nor Prime Minister Churchill focused much on the critical issue of postwar monetary and economic policy. President Roosevelt ignored it, never understanding its importance. The prime minister had gained experience with the issues as chancellor of the exchequer from 1924 to 1929, but he had little time left over for economic issues during the war.[4] Instead, the two national leaders turned such planning over to Secretary of the Treasury Henry Morgenthau Jr. and Chancellor of the Exchequer John Anderson, the successor to Kingsley Wood after Wood's death in 1943. With almost no experience or knowledge of economic or monetary affairs, Morgenthau relied on subordinates, more than Anderson did, to make plans and negotiate all-important deals for the peacetime global economy. For most of his life, Anderson had been a very capable civil servant, entering the House of Commons only in 1938, before serving in a series of cabinet jobs focused on domestic policy. Morgenthau, an apple farmer before serving FDR, had inherited sufficient wealth to make him independent.

Morgenthau's appointment as secretary of the Treasury had come entirely from his close personal relationship to FDR. Anderson earned his position by distinction in the civil service and election as a member of Parliament, but he was never close to Churchill, although the prime minister admired him.[5] Unlike Morgenthau, Anderson was a brilliant student who had entered the civil service in 1905, after earning degrees in mathematics, philosophy, and economics. Churchill's physician observed that there was "nothing quite like him [Anderson] in the Civil Service. His astonishing efficiency depends on an unusual combination of qualities. In the first place, he has an appetite for facts, which he has indulged freely for many years, so that it is almost impossible to catch him out in anything. The grip of detail is reinforced by what Maynard Keynes termed 'the gift of instinctive judgment.'" Churchill would praise "Sir John's firm spirit."[6] Anderson's "company and his appearance were pontifical. [Fellow cabinet member] Brendan Bracken, who had a *penchant* for creating nicknames, called him God's Butler, but he was on a par with Lord Hankey as one of Britain's greatest twentieth-century administrators," wrote Churchill aide John Colville. "The smoothness with which the country's civil administration was conducted, and its economic resources maintained, was in large part due to his calm and steady administrative skill."[7]

Henry Morgenthau, like Harry Hopkins, was neither a politician nor a financial man, but instead a true FDR loyalist—one of the few on whom Roosevelt could depend and in whom he confided. Historian David Rees wrote that "while of different temperament, Roosevelt and Morgenthau shared similar backgrounds. Neither were radicals, neither were intellectuals, and both possessed a patrician feeling for the land and for public service."[8] Like FDR, an heir to his family's fortune, Morgenthau had endeared himself to Roosevelt in the early 1920s, by regularly visiting him when he was largely confined by polio to Hyde Park.[9] Dean Acheson later wrote of Morgenthau that he was "naturally timid, nervous, and apprehensive of Congress and of what he called 'going out on a limb.'"[10] Morgenthau himself wrote: "Mr. Roosevelt often asked me to do things for the Government which had nothing to do with regular Treasury work. He would usually ask these things of me after some Cabinet member had failed with the result that I made many enemies."[11]

Reporting to Anderson and Morgenthau as chief deputies were the two key Anglo-American planners and negotiators of the international postwar economy. Keynes and White were both clever, arrogant, and willful men. They aggravated and insulted each other, as well as their colleagues. Each was jealous and defensive of his point of view. The president and the prime minister, their political leaders, ceded to Morgenthau and Anderson the immense and decisive peacetime responsibility of devising a stable postwar monetary and financial order. The early execution of the plans also fell to White and Keynes.

Harry Dexter White, Morgenthau's deputy, has been described by economic historian Benn Steil as "the brash, dogged technocrat raised in working-class Boston by Lithuanian Jewish immigrants," a marked contrast to Steil's description of John Maynard Keynes as the "servant-reared scion of Cambridge academics."[12] Even White's mentor, Secretary Morgenthau, belatedly recalled that White was "quick-tempered, overly ambitious, and power went to his head."[13] Some coworkers were severe in their criticism of White.[14] Morgenthau's son and biographer wrote that "White, by nature short-tempered and arrogant, was meticulously civil to anyone in a position to afford him access to the powerful"—in short, a sycophant and a bully.[15] Unlike the famous, self-confident Keynes, White was a relatively colorless and anonymous bureaucrat, without extensive cultural and political contacts. But within the Roosevelt administration, White had been well positioned by Morgenthau. Curiously, Secretary of State Hull called White "a very high class fellow," attesting to White's deferential way with important superiors.[16] Keynes and White, each in his own way, were inside political operators who cared little for electoral politics. Unlike White, the respected Keynes was a prominent writer and a skilled manipulator of the press.

The supercilious Keynes showed little deference to the powerful, beginning a 1928 letter to then Chancellor of the Exchequer Churchill, whom he knew and had advised: "What an imbecile Currency Bill you have introduced!" Churchill tactfully responded: "I will read your article enclosed and reflect carefully, as I always do, on all you say."[17] Keynes reveled in the sound of his own sarcasm. White, equally opinionated, abused colleagues and subordinates, but deferred to superiors. Mustachioed, bespectacled, and balding, both economists suffered frequent bouts of bad health, made worse by the public tensions of complicated wartime negotiations, which probably shortened their lives. (Keynes would die in 1946, and White in 1948.) Economist Milton Friedman, who worked at the Treasury Department from 1941 to 1943, recalled a meeting in Morgenthau's office during the war "with perhaps a dozen or so persons present, at which there was a difference of opinion about something or other and the discussion became very heated, with White somehow differing with the secretary. Suddenly, White stood up, face livid, and said something like, 'I'd better leave before I say something I shouldn't,' and stomped out of the room. The atmosphere was like that of a schoolboy squabble." Friedman wrote: "Morgenthau's limited intellectual capacity meant that he was inordinately dependent on consultants and subordinates. . . . He surrounded himself with an extraordinarily able group of subordinates."[18]

White and Keynes were an oddly matched pair, each with very different social and intellectual biographies and economic objectives. At six feet six inches, Keynes was as conspicuous as White was inconspicuous at five feet six inches. In 1918, White had married a Ukrainian-born woman, who became a writer of children's books after his death. In 1925, Keynes married a Russian-born ballerina and actress, who accompanied him on all his travels during his life. He had become a self-important collector and patron of the arts; he chaired a government Council for the Encouragement of Music and the Arts during World War II. His ambition included "making London the artistic capital of Europe," wrote biographer Robert Skidelsky.[19] Born to the English intellectual elite, Keynes became independently wealthy as a result of his investments. He could afford to volunteer his services to government. Far more circumscribed financially, White depended on his government salary and entirely on Secretary of the Treasury Morgenthau for his position. Keynes operated independently, sometimes against the policies of his own government. His fame was actually a negotiating handicap, because it raised American suspicions that he might trap the United States in a deal good for Britain but bad for America. (Similar fears about the persuasive Churchill preoccupied American civilian and military officials.) Keynes traveled to the United States six times during World War II. On his first trip in the spring of 1941, he complained that decision-making in Washington was "almost incredibly inefficient. One wonders how decisions are ever reached at all. There is no clear hierarchy of authority. The different departments of the Government criticise one another in public and produce rival programmes."[20] In this observation, the British economist corroborated the testimony of others about the disorganized and chaotic administration of the American president. Keynes's remarks came after three successful elections for FDR, and two less successful terms in office.

White was as powerful as the untutored Morgenthau made him, and that was very powerful indeed, because of the crucial international policies that he generated for Morgenthau and Roosevelt to study and adopt. With the benefit of hindsight, historians now understand why these ideas often turned out to be good for Stalin's Russia, rarely good for Britain. Whittaker Chambers, who was White's Communist Party contact in the 1930s, wrote that White "talked endlessly about the 'Secretary' . . . whose moods were a fair barometer of White's. If White's spirits were up, I knew that the Secretary was smiling. If he was depressed, I knew that the Secretary had had a bad day."[21] As early as 1938, Morgenthau named White director of monetary research, a title that understated his growing policy influence with Morgenthau, who relied on White's comprehensive memos on a growing variety of topics related to international finance and diplomacy. In April 1938, White became part of the 9:30 A.M. morning meeting of the secretary's closest advisors. Biographer David Rees wrote that "as White's career progressed in the Treasury, and he became Morgenthau's principal adviser, he was the beneficiary of some of the authority that fell by the osmosis of power from Roosevelt to Morgenthau. As the problems of the Depression gave way to those of the war and the postwar world, that authority remained as intangible as the governing principle, but also as certain as the friendship between the Hudson Valley Squires."[22]

In the late 1930s, White had emerged as Treasury's expert on international loans and credit, especially with the Chinese government, which the Roosevelt administration was attempting to prop up. White's analytical disposition acted as a counterbalance to Morgenthau's inexperienced intuition. White had a crisper, more analytic mind than Morgenthau. He was able to summarize and synthesize Morgenthau's own thoughts better than Morgenthau.[23] The first day after Pearl Harbor, Morgenthau named White an *ad hoc* assistant secretary of the Treasury, and one of his top three advisors. "To make life easier for me . . . I want to give Harry White the status of Assistant Secretary. I can't make him an Assistant Secretary," said Morgenthau, acknowledging only Congress could confer that title. "He will be in charge of foreign affairs for me." Concerning foreign issues, Morgenthau added: "I want it all in one brain, and I want it in Harry White's brain."[24] It was not until more than three years later that White officially got the title to go with the responsibilities he had been carrying. He stayed on into the Truman administration, after Morgenthau quit. White's influence, however, steadily fell in late 1945 and early 1946, as his Soviet ties could not be hidden, even as President Truman and the Senate approved his nomination to the Board of the International Monetary Fund.[25]

In 1939, as conflict broke out in Europe, the Treasury Department had increasingly taken on important international responsibilities. As a discreet Soviet agent, White was unsurprisingly a strong proponent of aid to Russia, long before Germany invaded the Soviet Union.[26] When it came to providing aid to Britain and France, FDR used Treasury to get around isolationists, the Neutrality Acts, and congressional restrictions.[27] The president's failure to set clear lines of authority and policy caused friction among the State Department, the Treasury Department, and eventually the War Department.

In April 1935, Secretary of State Hull "had circulated a memorandum to American embassies in Europe stating that the United States should cooperate with the British on the basis of conservative monetary policies, including the restoration of the pre-1933 dollar-sterling exchange rates," wrote historian David Rees. "An enraged Morgenthau protested to Roosevelt, who was also apparently angry, and the offending memorandum was withdrawn, with a recognition by the State Department of the Treasury's jurisdiction over [currency] stabilization negotiations."[28] In May 1941, White himself was highly critical of the "half measures, miscalculation, timidity, machinations or incompetence of the State Departments of the United States, England and France."[29] During 1941, White and the Treasury Department became deeply involved in the negotiations with Japan, seeking to reach an agreement that would avoid war—what White called an "all-out" effort. Although White came up with a comprehensive peace proposal, by November 1941, he had become a hard-liner on Japan.[30] In his memoirs, Hull wrote of his growing conflict with Morgenthau:

> The Secretary of the Treasury, Henry Morgenthau, Jr., who ranked next to me in the Cabinet, often acted as if he were clothed with authority to project himself into the field of foreign affairs and inaugurate efforts to shape the course of foreign policy in given

> instances. He had an excellent organization in the Treasury Department, ably headed by Harry White, but he did not stop with work at the Treasury. Despite the fact that he was not at all fully or accurately informed on a number of questions of foreign policy with which he undertook to interfere, we found from his earliest days in the Government that he seldom lost an opportunity to take long steps across the line of State Department jurisdiction. Emotionally upset by Hitler's rise and his persecution of the Jews, he often sought to induce the President to anticipate the State Department or act contrary to our better judgment. We sometimes found him conducting negotiations with foreign governments which were the function of the State Department.[31]

Keynes was not only older and much taller than White; he was also socially more confident and experienced than White. Keynes had excelled at Cambridge University and begun work as a promising civil servant in 1906. He served two years in the India Office before he returned to teach at Cambridge University, where he had concentrated on philosophy and mathematics as an undergraduate. By contrast, much of White's twenties had been spent in the family hardware business in Massachusetts, then service in World War I as an army lieutenant. White came late to academics, but he became a serious student who excelled at Stanford. He did not earn his Ph.D. from Harvard until 1930, when he was 38, the year that the already-famous Keynes published *A Treatise on Money.*[32] Unlike the polymath Keynes, White had been professionally trained in economics. After several years of college teaching, White accepted a job with the Treasury Department as a monetary analyst in 1934. His job was classified as "emergency work." Thus, he was never hired under normal civil service rules, avoiding thereby some background checks that might have revealed his communist associations.[33] White's appointment came one year after Keynes published *The Means to Prosperity* (1933), and just two years before Keynes published his famous treatise with the grandiose title, *The General Theory of Employment, Interest and Money* (1936). His criticism of the Versailles treaty, *The Economic Consequences of the Peace* (1919), as well as *The Economic Consequences of Mr. Churchill* (1925), had made him a famous polemicist.

A fervent critic of the Soviet Union, Keynes wrote that Russia "exhibits the worst example which the world, perhaps, has ever seen of administrative incompetence and of the sacrifice of almost everything that makes life worth living."[34] On the other hand, White was an admirer of what the Soviet Union had supposedly accomplished, writing in an undated memo that "in Russia, hundreds of thousands of small farms are leased and operated by individuals; carpenters, cobblers, and all means of services are sold to consumers in the same manner as in cap[italist] countries; people receive royalties on publications, and own govt. bonds and receive interest there on; wage rates though determined by govt. are influenced by the principle of supply and demand almost just as much as in capitalist countries."[35] One of White's sympathetic colleagues noted that White was "quite willing to deal with Communist officials to achieve his objectives. The Soviet Union shared his political objectives regarding postwar Germany, and he believed that Soviet officials would support the [International Monetary] Fund and the [World] Bank proposals. He did not share the pervasive fear that the Communist ideology would spread to the rest of the world, or that the Soviet Union might dominate the world by military conquest. He believed that a Communist state could operate under a system of nondiscriminatory trade rules, abiding by the trade and exchange obligations of his plan."[36] In fact, White actively promoted Soviet interests, as documented evidence would subsequently reveal.

Morgenthau biographer John Morton Blum wrote that White "often tried to circumvent [opposition] by going outside ordinary bureaucratic channels—a habit that could be identified with furtiveness or even confused with subversion. He appointed some assistants who were almost certainly members of the Communist Party, though Morgenthau did not know they were, and those assistants, in White's view, were as free to pass along information about Treasury policy to the Russians as was Averell Harriman, for example, free to talk to the British. But White did not himself hew to the line of the Communist Party."[37] This was academic rationalization by sympathetic Professor Blum; White's full espionage role was discovered years later.

White was a strong supporter of the increasing use of the dollar as an international reserve currency, aiming to displace the British pound sterling, also a Soviet policy intended to disrupt the financial system of the British Empire. Keynes understood the deteriorating position of the British pound, so he favored the creation of a new international currency, called the "bancor," to be issued by a future International Monetary Fund, to settle balance of payments deficits and surpluses, thus helping to finance Britain's perennial deficits. White saw a continued role for gold; Keynes did not. Benn Steil wrote that Keynes's mission was "conserving what he could of bankrupt Britain's historic imperial prerogatives. . . . His unlikely emergence as Britain's last-ditch financial ambassador—its chief voice in the Bretton Woods, Lend-Lease, and British loan negotiations—was grounded in the repeated failure of his country's politicians and mandarin class to make headway in what amounted to increasingly desperate begging operations in Washington."[38] Indeed, the United Kingdom was technically insolvent as early as December 1940. White's aim to end the reserve currency role of the pound sterling spelled doom for the British imperial financial and trade preference system—an objective shared by Stalin and FDR.

Of the two architects of the Bretton Woods agreements in 1944, Keynes was much better known. White's rise in the U.S. Treasury had been spectacular in the 1930s, but out of the public eye, with the relative anonymity necessary for a Soviet agent. Keynes had been in the public eye for decades, serving as Britain's chief economic advisor at the Paris Peace Conference in 1919. Neither man operated at the highest levels of war leadership, though the influence of Keynes was fortified by his position as a world-famous writer and economist. Neither had regular contact with Churchill or Roosevelt, but Keynes knew the prime minister well. They had differed on monetary policy when Churchill was chancellor of the exchequer. In 1925, Keynes had published a fierce critique of Churchill's monetary policies, in particular the parity at which Churchill reluctantly established the gold-exchange standard under pressure from the Bank of England and other advisors. Nevertheless, in 1927, Keynes was invited to join the exclusive "Other Club," which Churchill had cofounded. Historian H. W. Arndt observed that although Keynes and Churchill often disagreed, "throughout their public lives, they expressed mutual regard."[39] Keynes met FDR several times and wrote him several letters, to which there are no known replies—not atypical for the president. The ambitious White proved the more influential in World War II policy, having the ear of Treasury Secretary Morgenthau, who in turn had the ear of his Hudson River neighbor, FDR.[40]

Benn Steil described Keynes before Bretton Woods: "Fifty-six years old, in poor health, and too uncontrollable a force to be woven into Whitehall, he was not among the economists initially drafted into service. That did not stop him from forcefully stating his views, on paper and in person, on every subject . . . with anyone in government who was in a position to push through policy."[41] Steil wrote: "Keynes had a preternatural ability to see relationships between complex phenomena entirely differently than generations of experts before him."[42] Moreover, Keynes was a very public figure and a prominent commentator on contemporary economic issues.[43] White was an obscure bureaucrat making his case in long memos, operating effectively inside the corridors of power. He was comfortable at his desk, not in drawing rooms. Keynes thought White a boor. A member of established British society, Keynes was a graduate of Eton and Cambridge. A member too of the fashionable Bloomsbury Group, Keynes was more adept than White in social situations and more persuasive in political negotiations.[44] The clever but treasonous White—sponsored by the untutored Morgenthau, who was empowered by the busy FDR—represented America's decisive economic and political power in negotiations to establish the postwar international financial system.

Neither Keynes nor White understood intimately the intricate economic and political institutions of the other's country. The influence of White, supposedly confined to the Treasury Department in which he advised the secretary, penetrated deep into the State and War Departments through numerous "fellow travelers" working in the Roosevelt administration and the White House. The free-floating Keynes knew no constraint, freely sending memos outside of normal channels. Harry Hopkins complained to Morgenthau about a "long-winded letter" he had received from Keynes. "I don't like his style and approach. My own opinion is that except from the point of view of the British Treasury, he'd just be well off at home."[45] Keynes met with the American president on three occasions during the war. After their first meeting on May 28, 1941, Keynes had concluded that FDR "does not really care for [economic policy] any more than our own Prime Minister does."[46] At their second meeting, in July 1941, Keynes thought the president "weak and tired." Lord Halifax noted of this meeting that Roosevelt, who did not work hard to understand monetary policy and other complex economic issues, "was not greatly interested in the detail of Keynes's subject."[47] Keynes recognized no protocol, thus becoming a pervasive thorn in Anglo-American relations. Economic historian Ed Conway wrote: "Within a few weeks of his arrival in the country [in the spring of 1941], Keynes managed to irritate almost everyone. The British embassy was put out when he insisted on going in to see the Treasury secretary alone, without [British Treasury representative Frederick] Phillips; the State Department was horrified about his attitude toward Lend-Lease; and Morgenthau was simply infuriated by everything he did."[48]

White, a neophyte at the Treasury, had first met Keynes in 1935, when White had toured Europe. For sheer orneriness, White would prove a match for Keynes. One government economist noted that "normally, Harry is the unpleasantest man in Washington."[49] Conway wrote: "White was studiously civil to anyone in a position to help him advance—and brutally rude to those who could not."[50] Keynes himself complained of White: "Any reserves we may have about him are a pale reflection of what his colleagues feel. He is over-bearing, a bad colleague, always trying to bounce you, with harsh rasping voice, aesthetically oppressive in mind and manner; he has not the faintest conception how to behave or observe the rules of civilised intercourse. At the same time, I have a very great respect and even liking for him. In many respects he is the best man here. . . . The best way to reach him is to respect his purpose, arouse his intellectual interests . . . and to tell him off frankly and firmly without any finesse when he has gone off the rails of relevant argument or appropriate behaviour."[51]

Considering Anglo-American economic arrangements early in the war is useful for understanding what happened toward the end of World War II. When Roosevelt and Churchill met at Placentia Bay in 1941, they produced (but never signed) a document that asserted the basis for economic cooperation, but also gave rise to subsequent conflict among Anglo-American economic agents. The Atlantic Charter of August 1941 had stated that the United States and the United Kingdom "will endeavor, with due respect for their existing obligations, to further the enjoyment by all States, great or small, victor or vanquished, of access, on equal terms, to the trade and to the raw materials of the world which are needed for their economic prosperity." The key phrase, which the British had insisted on including, in order to insulate imperial preference from American free-trade ideology, was "respect for existing obligations." Churchill thus did not worry about the agreement. At Chequers in late August 1941, noted an aide, Churchill discussed with Halifax "the fourth point of the Atlantic Charter, which declares for freedom of trade and access to raw materials. The PM thought this would in fact be achieved and foresaw a great increase in wealth as a result. Halifax said the Tories would not object, except perhaps [Leo] Amery."[52] Churchill knew more about economic policy than is credited to him. As a Liberal Party leader in pre–World War I cabinets, as well as in parliamentary debate, Churchill had been a devoted free trader. As a Tory chancellor of the exchequer from 1924 to 1929, he accepted with reservations the restoration, in 1925, of the pre–World War I sterling-gold parity and the Tories' imperial protectionist system. In Parliament, he presented and argued orally the annual British government budget, holding his own in sophisticated debate.

In World War II, power and contracts trumped abstract economic ideologies. The crucial basis for Anglo-American planning during World War II was spelled out in Article VII of the Lend-Lease agreement between the United States and Britain of February 23, 1942:

> In the final determination of the benefits to be provided to the United States of America by the Government of the United Kingdom in return for aid furnished under the Act of Congress of March 11, 1941, the terms and conditions thereof shall be such as not to burden

> commerce between the two countries, but to promote mutually advantageous economic relations between them and the betterment of world-wide economic relations. To that end, they shall include provision for agreed action by the United States of America and the United Kingdom, open to participation by all other countries of like mind, directed to the expansion, by appropriate international and domestic measures, of production, employment, and the exchange and consumption of goods, which are the material foundations of the liberty and welfare of all peoples; to the elimination of all forms of discriminatory treatment in international commerce, and to the reduction of tariffs and other trade barriers; and, in general, to the attainment of all the economic objectives set forth in the Joint Declaration made on August 14, 1941, by the President of the United States of America and the Prime Minister of the United Kingdom.[53]

Article VII dictated quick action: "At an early convenient date, conversations shall be begun between the two Governments with a view to determining, in the light of governing economic conditions, the best means of attaining the above stated objectives by their own agreed action and of seeking the agreed action of other like-minded Governments."[54] These clauses were legalese for the gospel of free trade, preached by Secretary of State Hull. Neither FDR nor Churchill, preoccupied with military operations, expected prompt follow-through.

Keynes visited Washington in May 1941, to work on implementing Lend-Lease. American officials intended to use Lend-Lease to limit Britain's postwar economic options by stripping her of both monetary reserves and imperial preferences in trade.[55] Democratic Party policy opposed the British Empire trade policy on principle, and correctly calculated Britain to be a bad credit risk. The failure of the United Kingdom to repay its debts to America, after World War I, aggravated opposition to the British Empire. American policy makers concluded that Britain should be held to very tough standards. British officials, who had stood alone against the Nazis in 1940, thought American credit policy demeaning, counterproductive, and destabilizing. Reacting to Anglophobia in the Treasury Department, Keynes said that Morgenthau treated the British "worse than we have ever ourselves thought it proper to treat the humblest and least responsible Balkan country."[56]

In the late 1930s, White, already a power in Morgenthau's Treasury Department, had begun work on plans for a new international economic order. The collapse of the international gold standard in World War I, and the ensuing currency disorder of the 1920s and 1930s, dominated international economic policy making during the interwar period. As the issue of monetary stabilization during the late 1930s came to preoccupy Morgenthau, so rose White's influence.[57] When White's plan was presented to FDR in May 1942, Roosevelt balked at the required international conference to formalize the plan. Instead, FDR showed the plan to interested officials at the State Department. Keynes had meanwhile been working on his own plan, an "International Clearing Union" to help finance balance-of-payments deficits and surpluses, using a new international currency Keynes labeled the "bancor," which would be issued by a postwar monetary authority. In the summer of 1942, the two plans were exchanged.[58] Robert Skidelsky wrote: "The desultory nature of the long-distance contacts between Washington and London was briefly interrupted by the visit of Morgenthau and White to London in October 1942, to inspect armament factories and to discuss the currency arrangements to be implemented in North Africa following the impending, and, they presumed, successful, Allied invasion [Operation TORCH]. Winant, with Morgenthau's agreement, arranged a private meeting between Keynes and White. They met at the ambassador's residence on 23 October, with both American and British officials in attendance."[59] With Winant deftly chairing the group, some progress was made. In an effort to drum up support, the competing plans were distributed to other countries, and ultimately to the press. Progress was slow "because despite Secretary Hull's November 1942 statement that the Americans were ready for consultation on Article VII, this was far from the case," wrote Keynes biographer Donald Moggridge. "The White Plan was redrafted seven times between November 1942 and January 1943 before it was officially transmitted to the British at the beginning of February" of that year.[60]

In April 1943, the plans were officially released. Keynes, elevated to the peerage in June 1942, defended his plan in a speech to the House of Lords in May 1943. Redrafting by both nations continued over the next year. In the early autumn of 1943, a joint commission met in Washington to work out differences. A senior Foreign Office diplomat, Richard Law, led the British, but much of the work filtered through four subgroups. Keynes and White went head-to-head as the key negotiators on monetary policy, although the stress of the meetings sometimes made White too sick to attend.[61] At one point, according to a member of the British delegation, Keynes erupted at the presentation of an American document: "This is intolerable. It is yet another Talmud. We had better simply break off negotiations." White sarcastically responded: "We will try to produce something which Your Highness *can* understand."[62]

The British returned to London with a document to present to the War Cabinet in the winter of 1943–1944.[63] Churchill would not—or could not, given the press of war responsibilities—devote the time necessary to master the complex arrangements.[64] Lord Beaverbrook, always suspicious of American free-trade designs, and protective of imperial trade preferences, opposed the White-Keynes plans, claiming they would revive the gold standard, promote free trade, and doom imperial preference. At cabinet and subcabinet meetings in February 1944, Beaverbrook ranted against the plan. "The Beaver has put in a ludicrous paper, making a direct frontal attack, on the ground (a) that this is the Gold Standard all over again, and (b) that we are abolishing Imperial Preference," wrote fellow minister Hugh Dalton. Professor Frederick Lindemann, by now Lord Cherwell, meanwhile supported the proposed agreement. "The P.M., a little torn between Cherwell and the Beaver, says he knows nothing about these things and has not had time to pass this paper through his mind, but that it is clear that the majority of the Cabinet are in favour of going forward with the negotiations on the lines suggested, and that a small committee of ministers should look at it and report again to the Cabinet," wrote Dalton.[65] Churchill knew much more than a little "about these things." His comments may have been a cover for his deference to FDR, as well as his own unwillingness to devote the required time to studying them.[66]

Beaverbrook wrote Keynes on March 10, 1944: "I would not be prepared to support a proposition that destroyed imperial preference and sacrificed agriculture on account of compensations which appear to be both dubious and inadequate."[67] Beaverbrook was not alone in his doubts. Economist Richard Gardner wrote that "there was profound skepticism throughout the [British] establishment that a system based on open, multilateral trade would be in the country's interests. The Federation of British Industries and the London Chamber of Commerce were hostile. Many felt that [because of wartime precedents] the wave of the future was barter trade, managed markets, discriminatory arrangements, and currency controls."[68] Beaverbrook meanwhile complained directly to Keynes about the plan: "I find myself in disagreement with each portion of it. I am at variance with the underlying doctrine because it is essentially international and free trade."[69] Keynes, well known for his denunciation of the gold standard as a "barbarous relic," denied that any revival of the gold standard was contemplated. Skidelsky argued that Keynes "fought virtually single-handed to protect the Joint Statement agreed in Washington from Treasury scepticism, Bank of England opposition and widespread political hostility."[70] Economic historian Gregory A. Fossedal noted: "Keynes reported chiefly to Sir John Anderson, chancellor of the Exchequer, though Churchill himself was an active force in the negotiations, penciling in a suggestion here, a change of phrase there."[71] (By contrast, FDR, impatient with monetary policy, showed little interest in the economic details of sterling-dollar diplomacy, even less in the monetary talks. As a result, American responsibility for these problems fell primarily into the hands of the Treasury and Harry Dexter White.)

Keynes had conceived of an international lending agency, leading to a supranational central bank empowered to help finance balance-of-payment deficits among nations. Keynes knew Britain was insolvent, desperately in need of a mechanism to finance essential imports. Keynes got neither his supranational central bank nor bancor, his proposed new currency to be issued by the supranational agency. Keynes's bancor was designed to settle residual balance-of-payments deficits between countries, especially the perennial sterling payments deficits. The United States, wary of the impact of such a system on U.S. finances, rejected the Keynes plan. What puzzled British diplomats and economists throughout this period was the tendency of many in the U.S. State Department and Treasury Department to treat Britain as the economic enemy and Russia as a desirable economic model. Skidelsky wrote that "the main aim of his [White's] personal policymaking was to secure a political and economic alliance with the Soviet Union through the instrument of large American loans."[72] (It was at this crucial moment that White's spy contacts with the Soviet Union shifted directly to his Russian NKVD handler.) Indeed, the American attitude toward British finances was very different from the U.S. Treasury's indulgent attitude toward Soviet finances. At one point in 1944, Keynes complained to Under Secretary of State Stettinius that "the US Administration was very careful to take every possible precaution to see that the British were as near as possible bankrupt before any assistance was given."[73]

Morgenthau testified before Congress on April 21, 1944, about the Anglo-American agreement and his intention to call an international conference to negotiate its approval. The conference could not be called too quickly, because tight security in

Britain was restricting overseas travel as a military precaution leading up to D-Day, only weeks away. The Roosevelt administration aimed to get bipartisan support in Congress before presidential electioneering intensified, and then to get credit for the economic agreement before voting occurred in November. Morgenthau pledged to Congress that some of their members would be among the delegates to the international conference.[74] The British hesitated to commit to the conference; so, too, did the Russians. Morgenthau told White that "England and Russia have to make up their minds" whether to go it alone or commit to cooperation and the conference. "Unless we get a clean cut answer from Russia and England, I will not ask the President to call this conference." Morgenthau added: "In all of these years that I have worked with Mr. Roosevelt, I have always been prepared to let him have what is good, and I have always been prepared to take what is bad. I can afford to take it. After all, if it gets too bad, I can always go back and raise apples."[75] The Anglo-American negotiated plan, "Joint Statement by Experts on the Establishment of an International Monetary Fund," was published in April 1944. The Treasury Department made plans for the full conference in May, with Dean Acheson representing the State Department. They were approved by FDR on May 25, with the patronizing comment: "Here's where you get a medal, Henry."[76]

Under White's direction, technical aspects of the agreement were reviewed at a conference in Atlantic City in June 1944, although Morgenthau determined that political questions should be reserved for him and the full conference. The Treasury secretary knew that powerful business and banking interests opposed the White Plan, but much of White's technical plan remained obscure. Economic historian Ed Conway wrote that White made "sure none of the other big fish [in the Roosevelt administration] would actually be present at Atlantic City, so that the real work of the final detailed drafting for Bretton Woods could be done [by White] unimpeded." Even Morgenthau complained about the secrecy: "Harry, you're leaving me completely high and dry, and all the rest of the American delegates, and then you expect us to come up there and sign on the dotted line, and it won't work."[77] As Assistant Secretary of State Dean Acheson left for the international conference, he observed: "Neither I nor the other delegates know what the hell we are doing and we can't get the Treasury to take time off to work it out with us. But somehow I think we can get along."[78]

On July 1, 1944, the Anglo-Americans gathered representatives of 45 nations from around the world at Bretton Woods, New Hampshire, to plan the postwar framework for the international monetary system. They met at a sprawling mountain resort, recently renovated and reopened prematurely to accommodate the conference. The location was chosen for a variety of reasons, among them that Keynes detested the oppressive heat and humidity of Washington in the summer.[79] Moreover, the Roosevelt administration needed a Republican ally in the Senate to assure approval of the agreement. New Hampshire Senator Charles Tobey, who faced a potentially difficult reelection campaign, was placed on the delegation and duly supported the Bretton Woods agreement.

The Mount Washington resort had been closed for two years, but was scheduled to reopen in the summer of 1944. Delegates started to arrive on July 1. There were so many representatives that some had to be housed in nearby hotels. Timing was critical for the Roosevelt administration, which wanted an agreement to promote in the presidential election of November 1944. For that purpose, the conference had to be an Anglo-American show from start to finish. It was. With his customary disdain, Keynes described the proceedings as "the most monstrous monkey-house assembled for years," populated by nations that had little or nothing to contribute to the proceedings.[80] Moreover, participants were denied time to review carefully the proposed complex agreements. Information was in short supply, but alcohol was not.

Secretary of the Treasury Morgenthau was elected president of the conference, which lasted longer than expected, inconveniencing private guests who had summer reservations at the hotel. Morgenthau declared inanely that the conference's purpose was "to drive the usurious money lenders from the temple of international finance."[81] The actual work of Bretton Woods was divided into three commissions. The first was headed by White and charged with the development of the International Monetary Fund.[82] The second was headed by Keynes and charged with the development of the Bank for Reconstruction and Development, later called the World Bank. Commission III, "Other Means of International Financial Cooperation," was headed by Eduardo Suárez, secretary of finance for the government of Mexico. White had arrogated to himself control of the key commission, which would rule on international monetary policy.[83] The Americans exacted British agreement to White's plan for the International Monetary Fund. Keynes was not in control.[84]

"Delegates were issued over 500 documents filling some 1,200 printed pages; the need to make translations caused proceedings to bog down yet further," noted economist Judy Shelton.[85] The White Plan confused nontechnicians. Nomenclature further confused its broad outlines, calling the development fund a "bank" (the World Bank), and the lending and clearing bank a "fund" (the International Monetary Fund). White maintained that one crucial purpose of the IMF was to set "the rate of the various exchanges of the countries of the world on a multilateral basis and . . . provide a mechanism for keeping orderly exchanges."[86] In the end, the IMF would substantially adopt *de facto* exchange rates. Nations haggled over their quotas for the World Bank and drawing rights at the IMF, in negotiations with Morgenthau and Fred Vinson, who would succeed Morgenthau in 1945, but who was at the time director of the Office of Economic Stabilization.[87] White himself focused on the design of the International Monetary Fund.

The work was exhausting, particularly for Keynes, who spent a good deal of time in bed. "A controlled Bedlam was what White wanted," wrote Skidelsky. "It would make easier the imposition of the *fait accompli*."[88] Keynes too ramrodded material through his commission, aware that only he was sufficiently familiar with the documents to identify particular sections. Keynes, generally considered the more intellectually sophisticated economist and adroit negotiator, was effectively outmaneuvered and deceived by White. The ailing British economist did preside over his own commission. The American delegation, headed by Morgenthau but masterminded by White, conducted the key bilateral negotiations, made the necessary concessions, and changed the document's final wording in places, without review by Keynes. One amendment to the agreement made the dollar the only international currency convertible to gold—in effect establishing the dollar as the world's sole, official, reserve currency. "White's personal obsession was making the dollar as good as gold," wrote Steil. "To the extent that could be done by decree, he intended to use the IMF as his vehicle. Keynes, however, had fiercely resisted White's earlier attempts to give the dollar any form of special status. So it would have to be done out of his sight."[89] The dominant world reserve currency role of the dollar, born under Bretton Woods fixed exchange rates, has enabled the United States to finance its perennial balance of payments deficits, up to the present day—a monetary world of floating, manipulated exchange rates since 1971.

The agenda of the conference, originally shoehorned into 19 days, required three extra days in order to force through the necessary agreements. Serious examination of the documents and issues by the conference delegates as a whole did not take place. What White intended was more a charade than a conference; he would give the appearance of deliberations, without the reality. White's goal was to minimize, eliminate, or evade any opposition to the agreement—either inside or outside the American government. The American delegation altered quota allocations in the IMF to get the requisite support from other nations. Keynes erupted over the proposed future of the Bank for International Settlements (BIS)—a point on which he really did not disagree with the Americans, but nevertheless exploded out of sheer frustration and exhaustion.[90] Nevertheless, Morgenthau observed on July 19: "I don't know what the experience of the rest of you has been with Keynes, but mine is, I feel that he has been absolutely sincere and wants this meeting to be a success. . . . B. M. Baruch has fed me full of this stuff that you can't believe Keynes, and Keynes double crossed him at Versailles, so forth and so on, and I have been looking for it, but I have seen no evidence of it."[91] That very night, Keynes took to his bed with a heart attack.[92]

Bretton Woods focused on many necessary incidental issues—such as siting of the headquarters for the new international organizations. Keynes wanted the location to be determined in the future, but the American delegation stubbornly insisted that the headquarters should be in the United States.[93] Steil wrote: "The American delegation was steadfast behind him [White]—few of them were tutored in the technicalities of monetary architecture, but they knew Congress would insist on the physical edifice being within walking distance" in Washington.[94] As the U.S. dollar displaced the British pound sterling as the chief world reserve currency, so New York would displace London as the world's financial center.

The Americans knew they held the economic trump cards. They were determined to play them. As the most powerful country with the most powerful currency, and a near monopoly on world gold reserves (about three-quarters of the world's official reserves), the United States dominated the proceedings. White proved far more sympathetic to the role of gold in international trade than Keynes. National currencies were to be defined in gold. The American dollar alone was to be convertible to gold, so in effect all currencies were pegged to the dollar. Steil wrote: "White wanted to make the U.S. dollar, and only the U.S. dollar, synonymous with gold, which would give the U.S.

government a virtual free hand to set interest rates and other monetary conditions at will—not just for the United States, but for the world. Keynes wanted to wean the world off gold, and dollars, by creating a new supranational currency [bancor], issuance of which would follow economic principles consistent with an 'expansionist' policy."[95] Historian R. Bruce Craig portrayed the hero of Bretton Woods as White, who "assumed the dominant role in the creation" of both the International Monetary Fund and the World Bank. "He, more than any other single individual, most properly deserves credit as the 'father' of the Bretton Woods System. Not only did he shepherd the conference through the force of his personality, but unlike Keynes, who rarely bothered to attend the plenary sessions and constantly irritated members who served under him while performing his committee charge, White was far more diligent in his behind-the-scenes efforts to see that the delegates reached a consensus."[96]

White was also in better health. Keynes was very sick during the conference. Thus, he was much more accommodating than usual when he participated. "I should like to pay a particular tribute to our lawyers. All the more so because I have to confess that, generally speaking, I do not like lawyers," remarked the supercilious Keynes to the delegates at the close of the conference. "When I first visited Mr. Morgenthau in Washington some three years ago accompanied only by my secretary, the boys in your Treasury enquired of him—where is your lawyer? When it was explained that I had none—'who then does your thinking for you?' was the rejoinder." Keynes acknowledged, however, "certain final technical matters we haven't considered at all, what the lawyers call the final act, which embodies the results of this Conference." Speaking of the cooperation among the delegations, Keynes optimistically declared that "if we can so continue . . . [t]he brotherhood of man will have become more than a phrase." Keynes understood that the agreement had been rushed: "We all of us had to sign of course, before we had a chance of reading through a clean and consecutive copy of the document. All we had seen of it was the dotted line. Our only excuse is the knowledge that our hosts had made final arrangements to throw us out of the hotel, unhoused, disappointed, unannealed, within a few hours."[97]

Keynes admitted he had "never seen the final text of the clauses now under discussion at the time I signed the paper."[98] But, as Keynes biographer Donald Moggridge observed, the final document had been set in stone because the U.S. government did not want any changes as it pushed for congressional approval.[99] The White-Keynes plans did become points of pride for the two economists; the prestige of becoming architects of the postwar monetary world would substitute for careful analysis about whether the architecture would actually work in the long run.

White believed, not least because of his Soviet sympathies, that postwar collaboration with Russia was not only possible, but to some extent would come on Russian terms. In 1948, well after President Truman turned hostile to an aggressive Stalin, the compromised White would argue implausibly: "No influential person, as far as I can remember, expressed the expectation or the fear that international relations would worsen."[100] (Certainly, Churchill did.) White subsequently played a key role in promoting ratification of the Bretton Woods agreement. A distinguished opponent and future presidential hopeful, Senator Robert Taft of Ohio, pressed White for answers at a congressional committee hearing. The patronizing White arrogantly responded: "There is no use my trying to explain it to you, Senator, you wouldn't understand anyway."[101]

Designed in secrecy and ratified in haste, the Bretton Woods agreement would be revealed in time as a flawed international monetary system for the United States, for Britain, and for the world.[102] Concessions were repeatedly granted to the Soviet Union in order to assure its support, but concessions sought by Britain were denied.[103] Both Stalin and FDR aimed to disassemble the British Empire, producing the irony that America's loyal British ally after Pearl Harbor became the target of American anti-imperialism, even as the Soviet Empire was commandeering Eastern Europe. Steil contended: "There are three foundations on which Bretton Woods was built. First is that the British empire could be peaceably and profitably dismantled. Second is that Germany could and would be deindustrialized after the war. Third is that the Soviet Union could be permanently co-opted into a global alliance with the United States."[104] Thus, the U.S. delegation had devoted a disproportionate effort to pleasing the Soviet delegation, so that Russia would sign the agreement, not unlike FDR's deference to Stalin at Teheran and Yalta. However, the Soviet Union never ratified Bretton Woods. A White advisor later wrote that "the Soviet Union shared his [White's] political objectives regarding postwar Germany [deindustrialization and pastoralization], and he believed that Soviet officials would support the Fund and the Bank proposals."[105] As a Soviet spy, White had reason to believe this, even if the Russians did not cooperate.

At the time, it was not clearly understood at the top leadership level that White was a Soviet agent. Historians and American officials, guided by witnesses and evidence, came to know that White passed on critical information to Russian agents.[106] Keynes's most respected biographer, Robert Skidelsky, wrote: "White was associated, politically and socially, with the American communist underground and was passing confidential information to it which was being transmitted to Soviet intelligence; and that some of the Treasury people—including White's appointees—were also underground communists or agents or both. White did not believe that Soviet interests conflicted with American interests."[107] Perhaps, but it is equally plausible that White well understood the conflict of interests, but as a Soviet spy he was indifferent to them.

The White House was warned of White's Soviet connections in November 1945, the State Department as early as 1939. But despite the informed opposition of FBI head J. Edgar Hoover and Secretary of State James Byrnes, White was appointed and confirmed, with President Truman's approval, as the first U.S. director of the International Monetary Fund, an appointment falsely rationalized later as an effort to get White out of his more sensitive Treasury position without alerting the Russians to American suspicions.[108] White was no fool, acknowledged Benn Steil: "White's role as the chief architect of Bretton Woods, where he outmaneuvered his far more brilliant but willfully ingenuous British counterpart, marks him as an unrelenting nationalist, seeking to extract every advantage out of the tectonic shift in American and British geopolitical circumstances put in motion by the Second World War."[109] The evidence suggests that White intended the United States to share world economic and political hegemony with the Soviet Union.

Harry Dexter White, April 25, 1945
HARRIS AND EWING PHOTO, COURTESY HARRY S. TRUMAN PRESIDENTIAL LIBRARY & MUSEUM

XVIIB

The Soviet Connection of Harry Dexter White

A widespread network of Soviet agents and traitors in the United States and Britain undermined Churchill, Roosevelt, and company. Harry Dexter White, assistant secretary of the Treasury and the most powerful man at Treasury except for Secretary Morgenthau, was a spy for Russia. Academic controversy persists over the semantics of what constitutes a spy or a Communist. The same controversy involves historians' assumptions concerning White's intentions. That he provided secret Allied information to the Soviets during wartime is beyond dispute. Moreover, some historians and economists doubt the wisdom of the monetary and economic policies White pursued, and whether Russia was the intended major beneficiary of his policies.[1] White's behavior during World War II revealed that he knew he was acting contrary to law and American interests, as both the transcripts of the U.S. Army Signal Intelligence Service's "Venona" archival files, and the archival information, later gleaned from the Russian KGB, confirm.[2] White was extremely well placed within the Treasury Department to advance Soviet intelligence. He was Secretary of the Treasury Henry Morgenthau's right-hand man on all international affairs. He wrote important policy-making proposals and had ready access to other crucial documents and plans from the highest levels of American government. He passed on sensitive documents from the Treasury, State, and War Departments to Soviet agents or Communists, as he saw fit.[3] Moreover, Morgenthau's secretary, Henrietta Klotz, was a close social friend of White, his wife, Anne, and White's espionage conspirators.[4]

Perhaps the best analysis of White's espionage activities appears in a section of John Earl Haynes and Harvey Klehr's *Venona: Decoding Soviet Espionage in America*, where they wrote: "Eighty-five deciphered KGB cables, dating from 1942 to 1945, mention one or more of the persons [Soviet courier Elizabeth] Bentley named as members of the [Nathan Gregory] Silvermaster [spy] group. Eleven of the fourteen persons she named feature in Venona messages: both Silvermasters, Ullmann, Silverman, Coe, both Golds, Bursler, Currie, Adler, and White."[5] The facts regarding White's collaboration with Communist and Russian agents are not debatable; the compelling evidence has accumulated in the decades since his death, despite the fact that Soviet spies in the Roosevelt administration were careful to limit a paper trail that might incriminate them.[6]

It was Lauchlin Currie, a high-level aide to FDR in the White House and a Soviet agent, who apparently learned that the Army Signal Intelligence Service had begun efforts to decode Russian transmissions that might expose the espionage network of which he was a part.[7] In 1943, Currie notified Soviet spymasters about the American efforts. Currie, known in Russian decrypts as "Page," defended his betrayal to a colleague with the fatuous cover story that he wanted to avoid "sowing of seeds of distrust between the allies."[8] From 1938 on, professional Soviet agents steadily took over the American spy network from the U.S. Communist Party, and assumed direct control over their spies within the Roosevelt administration.[9] In early 1945, Russian operatives circumvented Roosevelt administration middlemen, in an effort to speak directly to Currie in the White House. (Currie had become a friend of White during their days as doctoral students at Harvard.) Currie then met several times with Anatoly Gromov, a senior Soviet diplomat who was also the lead KGB spy in Washington.[10]

The top-level secrets that White himself passed on to his Russian contacts show him to be one of the most important traitors of World War II. Haynes and Klehr wrote: "There are fifteen deciphered KGB messages during 1944 and 1945 in which White was discussed or which reported information he was providing to Soviet intelligence officers. The KGB mentioned that White offered advice concerning how far the Soviets could push the United States on abandoning the [London-based] Polish government-in-exile (which was hostile to Stalin) and assured the Soviets that U.S. policy-makers, despite their public opposition, would acquiesce to the USSR's annexation of Latvia, Estonia, and Lithuania."[11] Before the United Nations conference in San Francisco in April 1945, the Russian spy chiefs ordered Iskhak Akhmerov, then the top illegal resident spy in the United States, to arrange for a Russian espionage agent to meet with White and Silvermaster during the event.[12] White's reports to the Soviets were self-evidently treasonous. "Truman and Stettinius want to achieve the success of the conference at any price," White told the Russian agents. According to Haynes and Klehr, the documents showed that White "advised that if Soviet diplomats held firm to their demand that the Soviet Union get a veto of UN actions, that the United States 'will agree.' He [White] offered other tactical advice on how the Soviets might defeat or water down positions being advanced by his own [U.S.] government and that of Great Britain. The KGB officer meeting with White even carried with him a questionnaire on a variety of issues about which Soviet diplomats wanted to know the American strategy; White answered in detail."[13] It is impossible to know how many personal tragedies White's betrayal may have caused by his collaboration on Soviet policies.

For three years in the mid-1990s, when the Soviet archives were opened, Russian writer Alexander Vassiliev, himself a former Soviet security officer, reviewed KGB records and conducted an analysis of White's actions. Vassiliev's reports of KGB records show that White gave information to the KGB verbally.[14] Vassiliev worked with American historian Allen Weinstein in writing *The Haunted Wood: Soviet Espionage in America—The Stalin Era*, after he had filled eight notebooks with transcripts from the KGB archives. The notebooks were subsequently deposited in the U.S. Library of Congress. Historian R. Bruce Craig wrote of the Vassiliev reports: "Taken individually, one could argue that some of the documents indicate that White may have not always been aware that his information was being passed on to Moscow, but taken collectively Vassiliev's documentation leaves little wiggle room for White's defenders to continue to assert that he was not involved in an activity that, at least by present day legal standards, constitutes espionage."[15] Even by conventional standards, White was nothing less than a traitor.

Out of government in 1948, White appeared before the House Un-American Activities Committee (HUAC) in August. White effectively stonewalled the committee on his connections with the Soviet spy network. He was never subjected to tough or penetrating questioning about his associations and activities. At the time, HUAC did not have access to the accumulating hidden evidence of White's work as a crucial conduit for confidential information sent to Soviet Russia. In 1936, writer Whittaker Chambers, then a Soviet spy working for the federal government, had become White's primary Soviet contact. About two years later, Chambers broke with the party and then broke with White. As early as September 2, 1939, Assistant Secretary of State Adolf Berle met with Chambers and Isaac Don Levine, an anti-Communist journalist.[16] Levine was an émigré from Russia who was writing an exposé on Russian espionage, eventually published as *Stalin's Secret Service* in 1939.

Marvin McIntyre, FDR's appointments secretary, whom Levine had first approached with his information, suggested the Berle meeting.[17] Chambers had wanted a meeting with the president, which McIntyre rejected. McIntyre told Levine that Berle was in charge of intelligence questions for FDR. Levine went to the State Department to see Berle, who agreed to meet the informant to be known as "Carl."[18] Over drinks in Berle's backyard, Chambers laid out the network of Communist Party members and agents within the government—including a top State Department official, Alger Hiss—but neglected to mention White. Chambers claimed in his memoirs: "Two names I deliberately omitted from my conversation with Berle. They were those of George Silverman and Harry Dexter White. I still hoped that I had broken them away from the Communist Party."[19] Chambers recalled: "Around midnight, we went into the house. What we said there is not in question because Berle took it in the form of penciled notes. Just inside the front door, he sat at a little desk or table with a telephone on it and while I talked he wrote, abbreviating swiftly as he went along. These notes did not cover the entire conversation on the lawn. They were what we recapitulated quickly at a late hour after a good many drinks. I assumed that they were an exploratory skeleton on which further conversations and investigation would be based." As Chambers and Levine left his home, Berle made a phone call. "I supposed that he was calling the White House," Chambers recalled.[20]

Berle apparently did report back to McIntyre, but he never communicated with the FBI. Berle wrote in his diary: "Through a long evening, I slowly manipulated Mr X [Chambers] to a point where he told some of the ramifications hereabout; and it becomes necessary to take a few simple measures. I expect more of this kind of thing, later. A good deal of the Russian espionage was carried on by Jews; we know now that they [the Russians] are exchanging information with Berlin [during the Nazi-Soviet pact in 1939–1941]; and the Jewish units are furious to find that they are, in substance, working for the Gestapo."[21] In 1952, after Chambers's remarkable memoir, *Witness*, was released, Berle recalled: "I never did know what McIntyre had reported to the President." Berle added: "I have vague recollections of having mentioned the matter to the President when shortly thereafter we were working on the Foreign Agents Registration Act, which was the real, tangible outcome of this, though there were plenty of other lines leading to it. I was struck with the fact that no law was violated by having foreign-controlled sympathizers around, and that in this respect the Nazi pattern of having propaganda agents was almost exactly the same as the Communist pattern, but there was no law against it." Berle added that "the story as Chambers told it to me would not hold up against the reputation of any honest man."[22] Civil rights lawyer Berle was opposed to the State Department's role in investigating espionage. Democratic academic Berle shared the mind set of Republican Henry L. Stimson, who had closed down an espionage division, naively declaring: "Gentlemen do not read each other's mail."[23] Bolshevik agents were not gentlemen. Furthermore, Communist and Russian sympathies were at that time pervasive in America and Britain, especially in the academic world, and during the war as respect and sympathy increased for Russian armies.[24]

Berle's notes were collected in a sketchy memo titled "Underground Espionage Agent" and did not include White's name. R. Bruce Craig argued that Berle "knew White fairly well and, consequently, had Chambers named White, in all likelihood it would have clearly stuck in Berle's mind and would have been reflected in his notes."[25] Although Berle's notes did not mention White, those made of the meeting by journalist Levine did include White.[26] Levine wrote that when Chambers mentioned White, Berle had replied: "But I know Harry Dexter White very well, and I cannot believe it!"[27] Berle's failure to follow up on the meeting is mysterious. His failure to include White may have been because he desired to protect him. Berle biographer Jordan A. Schwarz wrote: "Berle did nothing with Chambers' information until he turned it over to the FBI in 1941 for an investigation of Chambers' charges. While Chambers' list surfaced in the State Department in 1943 again, nothing was done until Chambers showed up once more in 1948, to repeat his charges to the House Committee on Un-American Activities."[28] Berle apparently had shared Chambers's revelations with FDR, but Chambers wrote that the president "simply laughed." When Berle tried to press the issue, Roosevelt responded in a colorful phrase that Chambers felt he should paraphrase: "[G]o jump in a lake."[29] Testifying before HUAC in August 1948, White evaded perjury by saying he could not recall having met Chambers.[30]

In his memoir, *Witness*, Chambers wrote: "Harry Dexter White, then the chief monetary expert of the Treasury Department, had been in touch with the Communist Party for a long time, not only through his close friend, George Silverman, but through other party members whom he had banked around him in the Treasury Department. He was perfectly willing to meet me secretly; I sometimes had the impression that he enjoyed the secrecy for its own sake. But his sense of inconvenience was greater than his sense of precaution, and he usually insisted on meeting me near his Connecticut Avenue apartment."[31] In 1941, two FBI agents visited Chambers. In his memoirs, Chambers wrote: "I no longer recall most of the details of that first conversation with the F.B.I., except that I told Special Agent Smith that in talking to Berle, I had omitted the names of Harry Dexter White and George Silverman." The FBI apparently made no follow-up to that conversation.[32] Thus, White was allowed to continue to operate under the radar of official suspicion from 1939 until the end of the war, suggesting indifference by the Roosevelt administration from the top down.

One of the key pieces of Chambers's evidence against White was the distribution by Chambers of four expensive rugs purchased in December 1936, on orders from Chambers's Soviet handler, an officer in the GRU (Russian military intelligence organization), for delivery to four key contacts in the Roosevelt administration, including White and Alger Hiss in the State Department.[33] Another rug went to George Silverman, a White friend from Harvard who, during World War II, acted as a conduit for material passed on from White to Soviet sources.[34] Nathan Gregory Silvermaster subsequently noticed the rug in White's residence and guessed its provenance and White's own espionage connections.[35] In November 1948, Chambers recovered four pages of notes written by White that had been hidden in the Brooklyn apartment of Chambers's nephew.[36] Chambers further suggested that another document he submitted to Congress might have come from White in 1938.[37]

In 1941, a top NKVD agent, Vitali Pavlov, met with White at the Old Ebbitt Grill in Washington, regarding American policy toward Japan. According to Pavlov, he cleverly avoided suggesting to White "anything that would be outside the bounds of legality or would be detrimental to the USA."[38] Introducing himself as a friend of another Russian agent, Bill Greinke (aka Iskhak Akhmerov), Pavlov said he tried to bring coherence and collaboration to Russian and American policies regarding Japan. R. Bruce Craig argued that "the account offers concrete evidence from one of the highest-ranking NKVD Soviet officials involved with intelligence gathering in America that there were several active Soviet agents operating in the Treasury Department prior to World II and, more important, prior to the formation of the Silvermaster Group."[39] Pavlov notified his superiors in Russia that "everything is all right, as planned."[40] Pavlov, a savvy spy, would use a cover by saying, of the 1939–1940 period: "I can testify to the fact that Harry Dexter White never was one of our agents," and leaving open the possibility that he may have played a different role.[41] Pavlov's revelations were contained in *Operation Snow: Half a Century at KGB Foreign Intelligence*. Economic historian Benn Steil observed: "The significance of Operation Snow lay not in White acting as he did because he was so prodded, and certainly not in acting against what he believed to be American interests; rather, it is that the Soviets believed that White was influential and impressionable enough, and that conflict between the United States and Japan was important enough, that they chose to use him in pursuit of their aims."[42] Indeed, Pavlov's conversation with White was based on the fact that White had a prior relationship with Iskhak Akhmerov, a key Russian spy in the United States in the late 1930s, who would return to the United States as a top Soviet spy chief in the last three years of World War II. Since Akhermov had no diplomatic cover, he based himself in Baltimore, where he used a clothing and fur business as a front for his spying during the war.[43]

There is a gap in surviving evidence about White's Russian contacts from 1938 until 1941. Then, Nathan Gregory Silvermaster, a War Production Board economist, became a Russian agent and White's chief Soviet contact. The gap may be explained because Stalinist purges in the late 1930s had reduced the number of Russian agents available to handle and transfer documents to Moscow. Isaac Don Levine wrote: "Most of the secret agents outside the Soviet Union were recalled for 'consultations' at headquarters, never to emerge alive."[44] In June 1941 came Operation Barbarossa, the colossal Nazi invasion of Russia that shocked Stalin, despite warnings from multiple sources. The Nazi invasion prompted orders from Moscow for more intelligence assets in Washington.[45]

Silvermaster had become a key spymaster in the Communist espionage apparatus of Washington, where he arrived from California in 1935. Harry Dexter White had become a critical asset for Silvermaster's operations. Silvermaster was the subject of four federal investigations into his Communist links in 1942, by HUAC, the FBI, the Civil Service Commission, and the Office of Naval Intelligence. Remarkably, most of the investigations led to no action, but the navy forced Silvermaster out of the Treasury Department in June 1942. So porous was the Roosevelt administration that after a short break and relocation to the Farm Security Administration, Silvermaster resumed his spying with the Board of Economic Warfare.[46] When the FBI and other security agencies raised questions about Silvermaster in 1943, Roosevelt aide Lauchlin Currie vouched there was no basis for them.[47] The top U.S. spy for Russia reported that Silvermaster informed his handlers that Currie "made every effort to liquidate his [Silvermaster's] case."[48] Haynes and Klehr noted: "The [Silvermaster] transfer, however, triggered objections from the Office of Naval Intelligence and the War Department counterintelligence. Neither agency had evidence that [the Russian-born] Silvermaster was engaged in espionage, but both believed that he was a hidden Communist and regarded him as a security risk at an agency with access to U.S. intelligence information." They wrote that White contacted Under Secretary of War Robert Patterson "and told him that the suspicions about Silvermaster were baseless." Lauchlin Currie called Patterson to vouch for Silvermaster. "Patterson chose to trust and accommodate these highly placed persons and overruled military counterintelligence."[49] Haynes and Klehr concluded: "Thanks to the influence of Assistant Secretary Harry D. White, the Treasury Department was a congenial home for Soviet agents. Six of the eight known Soviet sources in the department were connected with the Division of Monetary Research, headed first by White and then by a second Soviet source, Frank Coe, after White moved farther up in the Treasury hierarchy."[50] In effect, FDR's disorganized wartime administration not only rendered decision-making difficult, but it created a permeable wartime security system, easily penetrated by Soviet spies at the highest levels of the presidential administration.

Silvermaster and his wife, Helen, were both spies, as was William Ullmann, their live-in friend and photography specialist, who worked at Treasury first for Coe and later for White. In his 1948 congressional testimony, White admitted to playing Ping-Pong at the Silvermaster residence in the basement, where Ullmann's spy darkroom was located. Asked about Silvermaster, White called him "a very charming chap and a very fine chap."[51] Silvermaster informed the Russians in late 1944 that he had spoken to White's wife, who informed him that White was considering leaving government so that he could earn money to pay for his daughter's college costs. The Russians responded that they wanted White to remain in government and were willing to cover the daughter's expenses "as a mark of our gratitude."[52] Still, Silvermaster was turf conscious. John Earl Haynes and Harvey Klehr wrote: "The Venona messages show that Silvermaster had protested the KGB's bypassing him and meeting directly with White, an objection that was overridden. White did not meet just with Americans who were part of Soviet intelligence, but also directly with Soviet intelligence officers. An August 1944 deciphered cable reported on a July meeting between Kolstov, the cover name of an unidentified KGB [NKVD] officer, and Jurist, White's cover name at the time."[53] White "knows where his info goes," Silvermaster told Akhmerov, "which is precisely why he transmits it in the first place."[54] White, like so many Soviet spies of this era, did not become a traitor for money, but instead was a volunteer, a Communist loyal to the Soviet Union and Stalin because of ideological conviction.

The text of one Venona decrypt (of a meeting held on July 31 with a Russian agent), from August 1944, confirmed White's state of mind and comprehension that he had become a security risk, and that White's wife was aware of his spy activities: "As regards the technique of further work with us Jurist [White] said that his wife was ready for any self-sacrifice; he himself did not think about his personal security, but a compromise would lead to a political scandal and the discredit of all supporters of the new course [Communism], therefore he would have to be very cautious. . . . Jurist has no suitable apartment for a permanent meeting place; all his friends are family people. Meetings could be held at their houses in such a way that one meeting devolved on each every 4–5 months. He proposes infrequent conversations lasting up to a half a hour while driving in his automobile."[55] According to Haynes and Klehr, the term "family people" was NKVD language for Communists and fellow travelers.[56] "After discussing Germany and monetary policy [after Bretton Woods], White revealed to [the Russian agent] that a trip he and Morgenthau planned to make to Moscow had been delayed indefinitely," wrote Herbert Romerstein and Eric Breindel. "In general, the Soviets believed that White was in a position to advise them on the thinking of high-level U.S. government officials." Because of his pro-Soviet bias, White "sometimes misled them" into too optimistic a view about official American receptivity to Russian policies.[57] Still, FDR's increasing embrace of Stalin in 1943–1945, and the president's coolness toward Churchill, must have encouraged the Soviet spymasters in Washington. FDR's indifference to Soviet spying compounded the problem. Indeed, it enabled Soviet spies to operate with impunity, protected as they were by high-level Americans in the Roosevelt administration who were either Soviet agents or sympathetic Communists.

After Secretary Morgenthau was forced from office in July 1945, there was a direct meeting between a KGB agent and White, an effort to keep him from resigning his Treasury post. "It was pointed out to Reed [White] how important it was to us for him to keep his post and so forth. Reed replied, however, that we wouldn't lose anything from his departure, since Peak [Frank Coe] would replace him perfectly well," the Soviet agent reported of the October meeting. Only a month later, White's utility to the Russians evaporated, when they shut down their Washington spy network after Soviet spy Elizabeth Bentley defected.[58] Bentley could identify the American spies working for the Soviet Union.

Russian spymasters had not been satisfied with the timeliness or the readability of the documents that the Silvermaster group was supplying through Ullmann's darkroom photos. In mid-1944, the Russians complained about the late delivery of a "three-page draft memorandum composed by White for Morgenthau about amendments to the Soviet-American agreement on lend-lease and about granting an immense loan to the Soviet Union for reconstructing the national economy."[59] White might have done even more damage to American security had not his relationship with Silvermaster deteriorated as a result of Silvermaster's abrasiveness. They apparently quarreled when White refused to support Silvermaster's pursuit of a promotion; White believed necessary security investigations would expose the Treasury Department ring to investigation.[60]

Spying must create anxiety and tension—in egotistical spies, even more.[61] Elizabeth Bentley, an admitted Communist who revealed information about Soviet spying to the FBI, alleged that in the Silvermaster home, William "Lud" Ullmann, a Treasury Department staffer, regularly photographed documents for transfer to Russia.[62] Ullmann, a close friend of White, was "perhaps the most important collector of information in the entire group," wrote Craig.[63] Like George Silverman, Ullmann worked for several years at the Air Material and Services Division, a dream job for anyone interested in photographing military secrets. Ullmann's affair with Silvermaster's wife, Helen, contributed to domestic strife and led one top

Russian spy to complain: "Surely these unhealthy relations between them cannot help but influence their behavior."[64] The affair could have affected Silvermaster's personality, described by one Soviet agent as "exceptionally self-willed, stubborn, confident of his superiority over all others and behaving . . . as a dictator or 'fuhrer.'"[65] Silvermaster, like other Soviet operatives, was both nervous about discovery of his treason and jealous of his espionage turf.[66]

In November 1942, Soviet intelligence officials in Moscow had wired their top New York spy that "at one time [White] was a probationer [agent] of the neighbors [Silvermasters]." White was identified as worthy of "singling out a special 'illegal' to work with him."[67] White was not easy for the Russians to manage, because of his oversized ego and his underlying insecurity. Allen Weinstein and Alexander Vassiliev wrote that White "was a reluctant recruit: agitated constantly over the possibility of exposure, concerned with career advancement within Treasury, and generally (in [top KGB agent Vasily] Zurbin's words) 'a very nervous and cowardly person.'"[68] In late 1943, responsibility for the Silvermaster group passed to senior Soviet operative Iskhak Akhmerov, who reported home that Silvermaster was "sincerely devoted to the party and the Soviet Union." Akhmerov called Silvermaster "politically literate, knows Marxism, a deeply Russian man."[69] This judgment applied to many Americans who committed treason as Soviet spies, most academically well trained.

In 1944, when Silvermaster's position at the War Department ended, White vouched for him to Under Secretary of Agriculture Paul Appleby, who wrote: "The other day when Harry White, of the Treasury Department, was in to see me on other business, he lingered to ask whether or not I could do anything about placing Gregory Silvermaster, who has been in Farm Security Administration for some years. . . . Silvermaster has been under some attack by the [Martin] Dies committee [HUAC], I believe, principally or exclusively because he happens to have been born in Russia and has been engaged most of his life as an economist and more particularly a labor economist. He is a highly intelligent person and is very close both to Harry White and Lauch Currie. There is no reason to question his loyalty and good citizenship."[70] The irony of Appleby's comments suggests that in the Roosevelt administration, spies like Currie and White vouched for spies, and thus blew away the clouds of suspicion of treason that might otherwise have settled on them. As a result, the process of investigations, indictments, and convictions could be scuttled early on.

"White had a vast network of personal and professional contacts to draw on when he recruited staff," whom Craig dubbed the "Econ-umists."[71] Some of them were "Communists or fellow-travelers," including brothers Robert and Frank Coe, who worked at the Treasury.[72] Frank Coe moved among federal agencies; at one point, he worked for the Board of Economic Warfare, and later served as technical secretary of the Bretton Woods Conference.[73] Coe's was one of the names of Russian contacts that Whittaker Chambers had provided Berle in 1938. Before the end of World War II, Coe took over White's old post as director of monetary research at Treasury. Allen

Weinstein and Alexander Vassiliev wrote of the twisted irony that Coe "complained frequently to handlers that his agent work was hindering his 'official' career."[74]

White moved in social and official circles of Soviet spies and fellow travelers who shared sympathy and information with Russia. Another key contact for White was economist Abraham George Silverman, whom White had met at Stanford; their relationship continued at Harvard, where Silverman received his doctorate. Chambers wrote that Silverman was viewed as "a whiner" by his Communist Party contact, J. Peters (a pseudonym for the Hungarian-born Communist Sándor Goldberger). Anxious to get Silverman off his hands in 1936, Peters had suggested that Chambers use Silverman as a contact for White. "I got along with Silverman easily and pleasantly by the simple method of recognizing that he was a highly intelligent child, and by letting him, in so far as possible, do whatever he wanted in his own way," recalled White. "I also listened patiently and sympathetically to his personal and financial woes." Those problems included bad stock market advice he received from FDR aide Currie; it was a curious complaint from an anticapitalist member of the Communist Party. Silverman "soon introduced me [Chambers] to White, delaying, as he explained to me, only until he was satisfied that I could handle that odd character."[75]

After Chambers had become frightened by Russian brutality and disillusioned by the cynical Hitler-Stalin agreement of August 1939, he decided to end his spying. He met with Silverman and explained "that I would surely denounce him if he continued the apparatus which, I assured him, I meant to wreck. He confessed that he sometimes had his own doubts about the Communist Party. We parted gently."[76] Chambers had already met with White and tried to scare the Treasury official out of any Russian contacts: "The fact is that I have broken with the Communist Party and I am here to break you away from the apparatus," Chambers told White. "If you do not break, I will denounce you."[77] Chambers wrote that White "and Silverman were almost fraternally close. Of the two, White was the more successful bureaucrat, and, in his special field, perhaps had the better mind. But in all other fields, Silverman was much more intelligent, and knew it. Their relationship seemed to have hinged for years on Silverman's willingness to let himself be patronized by White, to whom his sympathy was indispensable whenever, for example, the Secretary [Morgenthau] was snappish and White had one of his crises of office nerves."[78] Chambers's memoir, *Witness*, shows that his own defection from the Soviet spy network was a total ideological conversion, a repudiation of the Stalinist system.

Silverman's first regular government job had been at the Railroad Retirement Board, but he shifted to the Treasury Department, and then to the Air Staff Material and Services command from 1942 to 1943, whereupon he returned to the Treasury Department. Silverman had been a Communist Party member since the 1930s.[79] "A heavy, broad-shouldered man with thick glasses and untidy hair, he seemed brilliant but odd to his co-workers," wrote historian Kathryn S. Olmsted. "Some of his fellow Communists thought he was offensive, indiscreet, and insufferably dogmatic." Still, like many of his colleagues, Silverman was terrified of getting caught.[80] The Venona transcripts show that Silverman provided the Russians with detailed reports from the Treasury Department.[81] Coe and White frequently joined Silverman for a Saturday lunch. Chambers wrote that Silverman's "chief business, and a very exacting and unthankful one too, was to keep Harry Dexter White in a buoyant and co-operative frame of mind."[82]

In 1944, the ex-wife of Victor Perlo wrote to the White House alleging Perlo's complicity in Russian espionage, with more than two dozen others in Washington. Perlo, an economist and a key Soviet agent who worked in several government agencies during the 1930s and 1940s, had taken over the Communist cell in Washington, once headed by Harold Ware until his death in 1935. Math whiz Perlo had worked for a number of federal agencies, including the National Recovery Administration and the Federal Home Loan Bank Board, before going to work for the Commerce Department in 1940, then headed by Harry Hopkins. Perlo later moved to the War Production Board in 1943, and in 1945 was hired at the Treasury Department on White's recommendation.[83] The Perlos had engaged in a bitter divorce in 1943. Although Katherine Wills Perlo wrote the White House under a pseudonym, her identity was quickly uncovered. Herself a onetime Communist, Katherine Perlo complained that a chief Russian operative was George Abraham Silverman, who "works through close friends who are indebted to him including Lauchlin Currie – Harry White etc." Perlo made no specific allegations against White, and some of her allegations were undermined by mental illness.[84]

As usual, federal officials failed to follow up on the Perlo leads. This systematic indifference of the Roosevelt administration toward Soviet spying has no easy explanation. In March 1945, the top State Department security official, Ray Murphy, interviewed Whittaker Chambers and wrote a memorandum about the conversation on March 20: "Harry White of the Treasury was described as a member at large [of the Communist Party] but rather timid. He put on assistants in the Treasury, [Harry] Glasser, a member of the underground group, and an [Solomon] Adler or Odler, another party member. The two Coe brothers, also Party members were also put on by White."[85] Chambers did not then mention the espionage activities by White, even in a subsequent meeting with Murphy in August 1946: "Harry White was reported to be a member of one of the cells, not a leader, and his brother-in-law, a dentist in New York, is said to be a fanatical Communist."[86] Beginning in 1937, Nathan Glasser worked under White as assistant director of the Division of Monetary Research. By late 1938, Glasser had been assigned by his Soviet handler as a "control" for White, who Russian agents thought was not delivering sufficient information. Glasser and his wife, members of the Perlo group of spies, dutifully reported that his mentor White "was turning over everything of importance that came into his hands."[87]

"Although Glasser was an able economist, his rise in the Treasury Department was assisted by the network of fellow underground Communists inside Treasury," wrote Haynes and Klehr. After the Molotov-Ribbentrop agreement of 1939, White moved Glasser and Frank Coe away from Treasury, according to Morgenthau's son.[88] In 1940, Glasser began a two-year stint in Ecuador, as an economic advisor.

Glasser later informed the KGB that "the FBI's secret police were conducting an investigation. I was unable to get any information about the nature of this investigation, except for a suspicion that it was my membership in the Comparty [Communist Party] that was under investigation." Apparently as a result, Berle initially refused to grant White a diplomatic passport for Glasser, but "[u]nder pressure and attack from Harry White, Berle gave up" and approved Glasser's passport.[89] Glasser's relations with White protected him again in 1941. Haynes and Klehr wrote that Glasser's "promotions and job ratings were also reviewed and backed by Harry Dexter White. . . . This hidden network also helped Glasser when security officers first ran across evidence of his Communist background. In December 1941 the Secret Service . . . forwarded a report indicating that it had evidence of Glasser's involvement in Communist activities. Had the report been acted on, Glasser's subsequent work for Stalin's intelligence agencies might never have taken place. The report, however, went to Harry White, and nothing happened."[90]

In December 1944, a Russian spymaster in Washington wrote that Russian Ambassador Andrei Gromyko "charged me with meeting 'Richard' [White] for the purpose of receiving additional explanations from Morgenthau's department about German postage-stamps prepared by him. On the same day, [White] phoned me and asked me to come and get the information Gromyko was interested in. On December 11, I went to Morgenthau's department. [White] was not in the office, but one of his secretaries showed me to his assistant, on whose office door was written: Assistant to the Director of the Division of Monetary Research. [White's] assistant turned out to be [Harold Glasser]. We have tried to organize [Glasser's] work through [Elizabeth Bentley, Victor Perlo,] and others."[91] In 1945, Glasser's production of documents earned him a recommendation for the Soviet "Order of the Red Star."[92] Among the 74 documents shipped to Russia via Glasser, in the first five months of 1945, were several sensitive memos or drafts by Secretary of the Treasury Morgenthau.[93] During that period, White met with Russian agents in San Francisco during United Nations talks.

In August of 1945, federal authorities received compelling information they could not ignore, but they nevertheless failed to act. Elizabeth Bentley came to the FBI with allegations about her role as a courier and handler for the Soviet agents, including Silverman, Silvermaster, and Perlo. After Chambers had withdrawn from the Soviet-Communist spy network, Jacob Golos, a Ukrainian-born Communist, took his place as a contact. Bentley worked with Golos and became his mistress. When Golos died in November 1943, she pushed to take over his responsibilities, but Bentley's Russian boss, Iskhak Akhmerov, complained to Moscow: "Sometimes, by her remarks, I can feel that at heart, she doesn't like us."[94] Distrust grew as control of the Silvermaster group moved directly to Akhmerov in September 1944. At one point, Akhmerov considered trying to interest Bentley in a romance with another Russian agent, in order to ease her depression, but she became increasingly alienated from her Soviet handlers. In December 1944, Anatoly Gorsky (aka Gromov), who was first secretary of the Russian embassy, transferred Bentley's remaining contacts. Gorsky found Bentley sloppy and unreliable. The Russians cut her off and she drifted toward the FBI during 1945.[95] It was not until Bentley returned to the FBI a second time in October that government agents took her seriously and launched an investigation into her statements.[96] In November, a very high-ranking British spy, the infamous traitor Kim Philby, alerted Russian spymasters to this development, and they closed their Washington espionage operation abruptly. Akhmerov quickly left for Russia.[97] In early 1963, Philby himself would flee from the Middle East to Moscow.

Although Bentley worked with both the Perlo and Silvermaster spy rings, and those connected professionally with White, she did not have access to White himself, and she subsequently misstated and exaggerated her activities.[98] As Steil wrote: "Unlike Chambers, Bentley never claimed to have met White, and had no physical evidence supporting her allegations against him."[99] FBI agents followed White and bugged his conversations, but they failed to come up with any evidence to use against him at trial.[100] Part of the FBI's problem was that illegal, unauthorized wiretaps were not admissible in court.

According to Kathryn S. Olmsted, author of *Red Spy Queen: A Biography of Elizabeth Bentley*, FBI Director J. Edgar Hoover shared the initial information about Bentley's revelations on November 9, with British spy chief William Stephenson. From London, Soviet spy Kim Philby, head of British counterintelligence, passed the news on to the KGB, on November 20, about ten days before Bentley signed her long report. Olmsted wrote: "In a November 23 cable, the Soviets instructed all station chiefs in the United States to 'cease immediately their connection with all persons known to Bentley in our work [and] to warn the agents about Bentley's betrayal.'"[101] As Philby often did during his career as a Soviet spy, he saved other Soviet spies from detection in his role as the head of British counterintelligence. In the Bentley case, Philby saved White and his colleagues in the Treasury Department. By December, 72 FBI agents were tailing and investigating the spies whom Elizabeth Bentley had named, but it was too late. By then, the forewarned spies were avoiding espionage activities.[102]

FBI Director Hoover became frustrated by the lack of incriminating evidence, and his top aide, Clyde Tolson, worried that it was a "great mistake" to use the phrase "Soviet espionage agent" to describe White and others, based only on Bentley's statements.[103] The mistake was not as important as the Soviet warning to cease espionage activity. FBI agents interviewed White in August 1947, and were solicitous of his health, which had been weakened by a recent heart attack. Bentley testified before HUAC in July 1948, and painted an image of a duplicitous White who placed "people in strategic places."[104] When Bentley testified before HUAC in the summer of 1948, she said White "gave information to Mr. Silvermaster which was relayed to me."[105]

Several specific incidents generated more suspicion about White. Craig wrote that White "stands accused of everything from placing Communists in high government positions to selling out American interests in China and thus precipitating the 'loss' of China to the communists. Indeed, subversion of American policy is the heart of the accusation against White."[106] Craig further argued that there was little evidence of White plotting the "fall of China" by stopping shipments of gold (with which to pay for material to fight the Japanese) to the corrupt regime of Chiang Kai-shek. In truth, there was in Washington a great deal of opposition to the gold transfers. Many officials thought the shipments would do little to stabilize the shaky Nationalist regime.[107] Regarding the Chinese gold transfer, John Earl Haynes and Harvey Klehr suggested that more than simple diligence by White was involved: "White, Coe and [Solomon] Adler were right about the corruption of the Nationalist regime, but their position that China needed to institute a monetary reform in the midst of World War II, with the Japanese occupying China's most productive regions, was an excuse rather than a reason. They effectively delayed the transfer of gold while only going through the motions of offering alternatives. By mid-1945 Morgenthau, who had supported delaying the transfer, realized that he had been misled on key points."[108] Beginning in May, White and Coe alternated in urging that Morgenthau resist pressure to expedite gold transfers to China from businessman T. V. Soong, Chiang's personal representative to the U.S. government. Coe wrote a memo declaring that previous gold transfers had been wasted, and that the only advantage from future sales would be to cronies of Soong.

President Truman delegated Morgenthau to handle the problem of gold transfers. Although there were doubts about the program, there was agreement from both the War and State Departments that the Chiang Kai-Shek government should be strengthened. After a meeting on May 8, with Soong and a wide array of federal officials, Morgenthau grew embarrassed by Coe's recommendations, and complained the next day that Coe's staff had put him "in an absolutely dishonorable position, and I think it's inexcusable." Annoyed at being boxed in, Morgenthau complained: "After all, you were so worried about saving face, what about my face."[109] Haynes and Klehr concluded that the Treasury secretary "thought his aides had merely mishandled the gold transfer but were well motivated, and he never suspected that they had an entirely separate agenda from his."[110] It was a rare case in which Coe and White failed to get their way at Treasury.

Historian R. Bruce Craig argued that contrary to Elizabeth Bentley's testimony, White's role in the 1944 preparation and delivery to Russia of sensitive American printing plates for German occupation currency had been overrated. Bentley's claims about her participation in the affair have been widely discounted, but doubts remain about White's role. Craig differed with White biographer David Rees, who argued that White performed "an important and perhaps central role."[111] Craig agreed with historian John Morton Blum and Secretary Morgenthau that Morgenthau, not White, was the key decision maker.[112] American policy makers were anxious to appease the Russians, who had been adamant in demanding that the Soviet Union be given equal status in printing new German currency.[113] The major opponent was Alvin W. Hall, the longtime director of the Bureau of Engraving and Printing.[114] Craig wrote that "neither White nor anyone else in the Treasury Department could possibly have anticipated the enormous temporary drain on the U.S. Treasury caused by the failure of the War Department to establish a sound currency redemption policy."[115] Craig did indicate, however, that on April 14, 1944, White misrepresented a lack of objections from the economically unsophisticated Combined Chiefs of Staff as "approval" of the Russian request for transfer of the currency plates.[116] Bentley's contention in her memoir that "I was able through Harry Dexter White to arrange that the United States Treasury Department turn the actual printing plates over to the Russians!" was not true, according to Steil.[117] But the fact remains that the U.S. Treasury authorized the inflationary decision to transfer printing plates for German currency to the Soviets. The Soviets abused the power to print currency, prompting inflation and delaying stabilization of the German economy until implementation of the reforms created by German economist Ludwig Erhard in 1948–1949.[118]

Morgenthau was anxious to expedite the transfer of plates, as was the State Department.[119] Two decades after the event, Morgenthau claimed: "My decision was correct both politically and militarily. The Russians had been holding up the Germans while the United States and England prepared for the invasion. There was every reason to trust them."[120] Morgenthau biographer Blum argued: "The decision about the duplicate plates subordinated technical to military and political judgments. It was not primarily White's decision but the joint decision of the Treasury, State, and War Departments, the Combined Chiefs of Staff and the British Government with General John Hilldring [who was the army's chief of civilian policy], Assistant Secretary of State James Dunn, and Morgenthau as the major contributors to the final policy. No one of those men was in any sense a Communist or Communist sympathizer."[121] This was not true of White, who participated in the decision and had a major influence on Morgenthau. The result was a currency and inflation disaster, as Russia printed about eight times as many German marks (convertible to dollars, then to gold) as the United States did, costing the U.S. government an immense loss of reserves.[122] U.S. reserves were held mainly in gold.

After World War II ended, White became the target for Republicans and others who mistrusted Soviet influence on the new post–Bretton Woods international economic organizations he had helped to create. Compelling evidence of White's secret espionage activities was slow to emerge. Some evidence was not revealed until after White's death. Much is still sealed in Russian KGB archives, access to which has been largely closed since the early 1990s.[123] The most damning evidence against White comes from the Venona transcripts, in which the NKVD identified White as "JURIST," "LAWYER," and "Richard." The NKVD archives stated that by 1945, White "doesn't pass information or documents."[124] Biographer Rees acknowledged "a number of inconsistencies and inaccuracies in the Bentley-Chambers testimony," but concluded, "it is tentatively assumed here that, on the whole, the story of the witnesses regarding White was correct."[125] Steil concluded: "White was an enormously valuable resource [to the Soviet Union] because he had access to virtually all the Treasury Department's confidential material, as well as secret information the Treasury received from other departments. White was also willing and able to pull strings to help other [Soviet] agents in difficulty."[126]

White cleverly stonewalled the House Un-American Activities Committee when he testified on August 13, 1948. He prudently sidestepped perjury and used the customary defense by Soviet spies, namely his belief in American civil liberties. HUAC members ineffectively followed up on White's diversions and evasions. He specifically denied any recollection of having met Whittaker Chambers.[127] The word "recollection" obviated perjury by the legally cagey White. A few days later, Chambers heard of White's death in New Hampshire, from an apparent heart attack. Chambers was in the middle of his own interviews with the House Un-American Activities Committee. He reflected: "White is luckier than the rest of us. He at least is well out of it."[128]

A curious and still mystifying series of errors of omission and commission characterized the Roosevelt administration when judging reliable reports on Soviet security threats. The State Department's Adolf Berle never followed up on Whittaker Chambers's conversation. The FBI never followed up on later conversations with Chambers or Katherine Perlo. The FBI never told military intelligence that Silvermaster was an NKVD spy. Communist spies and Russian sympathizers, working throughout the Roosevelt administration, vouched for each other when suspicions were raised. Few inside the government knew of the work on the incriminating Venona transcripts, and that work took decades to bear fruit. Too late it was that the FBI followed up on Bentley's information on Russian spies. The Soviet conspirators inside government had already closed down their spy network.

When in November 1945 the FBI's J. Edgar Hoover sent Truman aide Harry Vaughan a memo on Bentley's allegations, no action was taken. (Copies also went to other top Truman administration officials, including Secretary of State Byrnes.)[129] Despite compelling information and testimony that White was a Soviet spy, President Truman went ahead and nominated White for the IMF post in January 1946, prompting Hoover to send a second, more detailed memo on White to Vaughan. Truman later claimed implausibly, perhaps falsely, that he let the White nomination go forward in order to protect the FBI investigation.[130] Byrnes, however, had urged Truman to rescind the appointment.[131] Haynes and Klehr noted that the Venona decrypts remain only a fraction of the incriminating evidence of Soviet penetration of the Roosevelt administration: "The bulk of the reports from sources and copies of stolen documents were sent by courier and resides in still-closed Russian archives. Only occasional items of exceptional interest or time-sensitive information were cabled. The Venona messages, the testimony of defectors, and the confessions of apprehended spies provide general descriptions of the type of information that was being transmitted but few details and, of course, little about what the Soviets did with the information."[132] The evidence from Allied summits shows that Stalin was very well briefed about relevant intelligence, and that he used his knowledge shrewdly to outmaneuver and deceive FDR completely, and Churchill to a lesser extent.

Acceptance of White's collusion with the Russians was slow to develop. In 1948, FDR's erstwhile pro-Russian Vice President Henry Wallace confirmed that had Wallace been elevated to the presidency, Harry Dexter White would have been his choice for secretary of the Treasury.[133] In early 1952, after White's protector, FDR's Treasury Secretary Henry Morgenthau Jr., reviewed White's FBI files, Morgenthau concluded that there was "no question but that White was working for the Russians."[134]

Treasury Secretary Henry Morgenthau Jr. (left) and President Roosevelt, February 1934.
FRANKLIN D. ROOSEVELT PRESIDENTIAL LIBRARY

XVIII

The Morgenthau Plan

> [T]he Ruhr . . . lies [at] the heart of German industrial power, the caldron of wars. This area should not only be stripped of all presently existing industries but so weakened and controlled that it can not in the foreseeable future become an industrial area.[1]
>
> ***Henry Morgenthau Jr.*** *to President Roosevelt, "Suggested Post-Surrender Program for Germany," September 5, 1944, a program designed largely by Harry Dexter White.*

> In substance, my point is that these resources [the Ruhr and surrounding industrial areas] constitute a natural and necessary asset for the productivity of Europe. In a period when the world is suffering from destruction and from want of production, the concept of the total obliteration of these values is to my mind wholly wrong. My insistence is that these assets be conserved and made available for the benefit of the whole of Europe, including particularly Great Britain.[2]
>
> ***Henry L. Stimson,*** *memorandum to President Roosevelt, September 9, 1944.*

In the summer of 1944, after Bretton Woods, Harry Dexter White accompanied Treasury Secretary Morgenthau to Europe. At the time, Morgenthau's son later wrote, the Treasury secretary "and Harry White were experiencing a high that stimulated their hunger for a new challenge." On the long flight across the Atlantic, they discussed postwar Germany, based on their review of CCS 551, a document from the War Department that foresaw Germany's economic revival.[3] According to a Treasury staffer who overhead their conversation, White declared: "What we ought to be doing is making Germany basically a deindustrialized nation, not rebuilding them and making them a strong industrial nation." This too was Soviet policy. During the trip, the Treasury secretary and White hatched the Morgenthau Plan, calling for the deindustrialization of a newly pastoral Germany. Morgenthau was persuaded that the State Department and War Department strategy for reparations and Germany's future economic revival were wrong, and White's idea regarding German deindustrialization was right.[4]

On August 10, Morgenthau proposed to British Chancellor of the Exchequer John Anderson that "we could divide Germany up into a number of small provinces, stop all industrial production and convert them into small agricultural landholders."[5] On August 12, Morgenthau convened a meeting with White, Winant, and other American officials, at a British country home. White followed up Morgenthau's rambling ideas for postwar Germany with a more coherent explanation: "Our objective was to see that Germany was never again in a position to wage war. Everything else was incidental to that objective. If, to obtain that objective, it was necessary to reduce Germany to the status of a fifth-rate power, that should be done." One diplomat present observed: "Whatever might be thought of the opinions of Mr. Morgenthau, it was impossible to deny the resourcefulness of Dr. White in mastering the main points of the interdepartmental committee's report just before the meeting and in transferring the secretary's sketchy and spasmodic exposition of his views into a clear, amplified and well organized restatement composed in fifteen minutes after Mr. Morgenthau had finished speaking and, coming as nearly as possible to clothing a bad thesis with an appearance of intellectual respectability."[6] It was White who provided the structure and substance of the Morgenthau Plan, a toned-down version of which was initialed by Roosevelt.[7] Morgenthau's son wrote: "Although the so-called Morgenthau Plan seems to have been conceived in the mind of Harry Dexter White, Morgenthau's response to White's proposals went far beyond anything that White himself had hoped for. In no time Morgenthau was proceeding with a driving fury, confounding even his most ardent and loyal supporters."[8] At this meeting, Ambassador Winant doubted that Morgenthau's agrarian plan for Germany would be a bulwark against militarism: "Farmers make good fighters." White retorted: "Not farmers without modern industrial equipment." Morgenthau's deputy insisted that the Allies should not restore Germany to "a position where she will again endeavor to become master of the world."[9]

Work on the Morgenthau Plan continued under White's supervision through August 1944, but without any real guidance from President Roosevelt, with whom Morgenthau met on August 19. "Nobody has been studying how to treat Germany roughly along the lines you wanted," said Morgenthau. FDR declared his intention to crack down on "the German people—not just the Nazis. You either have to castrate the German people or you have got to treat them in such a manner so that they can't just go reproducing people who want to continue the way they have in the past."[10] Morgenthau, motivated in part by his revulsion at the Holocaust, resolved to put structure behind the president's tough words. Morgenthau convinced himself he could devise a plan to "be tough to the Germans" and that FDR would endorse it. The British would be forced to accept it. Meeting with FDR on August 25, Morgenthau told the president: "Look, Mr. President you can't be expected to give these directives on how to treat Germany unless somebody does the work for you. Everything that has been done so far is worthless."[11] Morgenthau's views were significantly tougher than White's. Many American officials thought the White-Morgenthau Plans too harsh.[12] The president impetuously contributed to the drive of the Morgenthau Plan by commenting at an August 25 cabinet meeting that Germans should be restricted to "a subsistence level of food." After FDR had tentatively approved the Morgenthau Plan, he then confused matters by endorsing the suggestion of Secretary of War Stimson (opposed to the plan) for a four-man cabinet committee (with Harry Hopkins, Stimson, Hull, and Morgenthau) to consider American plans for Germany after the war.[13]

Work continued on his plan while Morgenthau went back to New York for a brief vacation. White sent his version of the plan to Morgenthau on September 1. The Treasury secretary shared the plan with the president on September 2, without any substantive response from FDR. The same day, White met in Hopkins's office to discuss the plan with representatives from the State and War Departments. State Department officials presented their own plan. The War Department represented a strong competing influence. White persisted in pushing his plan that would depopulate and deindustrialize the Ruhr. On September 4, Morgenthau presented his plan to Stimson over dinner at Stimson's home. On September 5, Morgenthau, Stimson, and Hull met with Hopkins to discuss competing plans. Hull and Hopkins appeared to side with Morgenthau, over Stimson's objections.[14] Stimson noted in his diary that night: "Hull has been rather crotchety about the whole thing and showed it in this meeting. I fear that he regards it as a reflection upon the prerogatives of the State Department." The secretary of war was outnumbered by Hull and Morgenthau—and by Harry Hopkins, who had decided for Morgenthau. "We will have to meet with Roosevelt quick before somebody else changes his mind," Hopkins told Morgenthau.[15]

On September 6, the full cabinet met and, as he often did, FDR conveyed contradictory signals. On one hand, he indicated that the Germans could be comfortable with outhouses and soup kitchens, but he delayed any decisions on the future of the Ruhr and seemed to favor a measure of German reconstruction.[16] Morgenthau called it "a very unsatisfactory meeting," but added that FDR now thought it possible to return Germany "back to 1810, where they would be perfectly comfortable but wouldn't have any luxuries."[17] Roosevelt typically avoided decisions by "telling a long, rambling story and then terminating the discussion abruptly," reported Morgenthau. That night, FDR's son-in-law, John Boettiger, called on Morgenthau and asked for his approval of changes in the original War Department "handbook" for Germany, which had sparked the intracabinet fight.[18] The most important underlying issue was not yet paramount in the cabinet arguments over Germany. With Russian arms dominating Eastern Europe, what would stop an aggressive Soviet Union from an advance to the English Channel if France remained prostrate and Germany had been reduced to soup kitchens and outhouses?

In a conversation with Hull on September 8, Morgenthau complained; "The trouble is, Cordell, the President has never given a directive on how he feels Germany should be treated. The first thing we know, we will be in Germany and we will have no policy." Hull responded: "Well, you heard the President say he wants to put the Germans on a soup kitchen diet and Stimson wants to give them luxuries."[19] The cabinet secretaries again met with Roosevelt on September 9; Hull, Morgenthau, and Stimson all presented their plans. Stimson presented his objections to the Morgenthau Plan, arguing: "I cannot treat as realistic the suggestion that such an area [the Ruhr and the Saar] in the present economic [depressed] condition of the world can be turned into a nonproductive ghost territory."[20] Roosevelt avoided taking sides, but historian David Rees argued that FDR indicated he was "closer to Morgenthau on Germany than to his other advisers when the Cabinet Committee ended."[21] The president seemed impressed by an implausible statement in Morgenthau's plan: "It is a fallacy that Europe needs a strong industrial Germany." Roosevelt commented: "This is the first I have seen this stated," and impulsively agreed "with this idea," adding, "I believe in an agricultural Germany."[22] Over the next two days, Hull seemed to drift toward opposition to the Morgenthau Plan, annoyed "that the President didn't consult him."[23] While Hull vacillated, Stimson saw danger. As historian Warren Kimball observed: "[t]he Morgenthau Plan was a design for a radical reconstruction of Germany. Imbued with the belief of many New Dealers in the efficacy of grand plans as the solution to problems, it called for a total change in the occupations and life-styles of most Germans." And there would be consequences. Kimball wrote: "Echoing the arguments of John Maynard Keynes two decades earlier regarding the so-called Carthaginian Peace following World War I, Stimson predicted that such harsh measures would generate resentment and war rather than peaceful acceptance."[24] In his diary, Stimson wrote that he was "troubled" that Roosevelt "is going up there [to Quebec] without any real preparation for the solution of the underlying and fundamental problem of how to treat Germany."[25]

Roosevelt's handling of the Morgenthau Plan reflected his instinct for impulsive, unprepared decision-making, both during the run-up to the Quebec summit and at the summit itself in mid-September 1944.[26] The Treasury secretary did not at first accompany the president to meet Churchill at Quebec; Hull declined an invitation to attend. Roosevelt had promised Hull he would be summoned if political questions were raised. The chronically sick Hull had complained that he was too tired to attend.[27] Soon, both Morgenthau and White were summoned to Quebec, where they arrived on September 13.[28] White thought, incorrectly, that he had Keynes's support for the Morgenthau Plan, and Morgenthau thought incorrectly he had the support of Anthony Eden.[29] When a meeting convened at Quebec on September 15, Eden would express his dislike for the plan, adding in his memoirs: "nor was I convinced that it was to our national advantage." He wrote that Churchill "resented my criticism of something which he and the president had approved, not, I am sure on his account, but on the President's."[30] Churchill, now the junior partner, accommodated FDR more often than he agreed with the president.

The Morgenthau Plan demonstrated how far Churchill was willing to go for guarantees of indispensable American assistance to Britain. The president appeared to toy with Churchill at Quebec, holding up approval of Stage II Lend-Lease aid until agreement was reached on the Morgenthau Plan.[31] Because Roosevelt delayed signing a new Lend-Lease agreement, Churchill caustically complained: "What do you want me to do? Get on my hind legs and beg like [FDR's dog] Fala?"[32] Churchill did not like to beg, but he could not afford to offend Roosevelt. Britain was insolvent and desperately needed American aid. At first, Churchill reacted very negatively at the September 14 dinner at which Morgenthau presented his plan. Morgenthau wrote: "After I had finished my piece he [Churchill] turned on me the full flood of his rhetoric, sarcasm and violence. He looked on the Treasury plan, he said, as he would on chaining himself to a dead German. He was slumped in his chair, his language biting, his flow incessant, his manner merciless. I have never had such a verbal lashing in my life."[33]

The prime minister later explained himself. "At first I was violently opposed to the [Morgenthau Plan]," admitted Churchill. "But the President and Mr. Morgenthau—

from whom we had much to ask—were so insistent that in the end we agreed to consider it."[34] In a word, the prime minister abandoned his objection to the Morgenthau Plan, hoping FDR would approve the indispensable Stage II Lend-Lease aid to an insolvent Britain. After Lindemann met with Morgenthau and White the next morning, Churchill dictated a memo that reflected the plan's intent:

> At the conference between the President and the Prime Minister upon the best measures to prevent renewed rearmament by Germany, it was felt that an essential feature was the future disposition of the Ruhr and the Saar.
>
> The ease with which the metallurgical, chemical and electrical industries in Germany can be converted from peace to war has already been impressed upon us by bitter experience. It must also be remembered that the Germans have devastated a large portion of the industries of Russia and of other neighboring Allies, and it is only in accordance with justice that these injured countries should be entitled to remove the machinery they require in order to repair the losses they have suffered. The industries referred to in the Ruhr and in the Saar would therefore be necessarily put out of action and closed down. It was felt that the two districts should be put under some body under the world organization which would supervise the dismantling of these industries and make sure that they were not started up again by some subterfuge.
>
> This programme for eliminating the war-making industries in the Ruhr and in the Saar is looking forward to converting Germany into a country primarily agriculture and pastoral in its characters.[35]

This Churchill summary of the Morgenthau Plan proved a short-lived triumph for White and the Treasury secretary. The combined weight of the British and American government, after rethinking the negative consequences of deindustrialization, reaffirmed Churchill's original opposition, and quickly crushed the Morgenthau-White Plan—at the same time exposing the internal rifts within the Roosevelt administration. While FDR had gone to Quebec, Stimson had traveled to his Long Island estate. Reading the Morgenthau Plan that weekend, Stimson angrily wrote on it: "Childish folly!" Stimson concluded a September 15 memo to the president: "I plead for no 'soft' treatment of Germany. I urge only that we take steps which in the light of history are reasonably adapted to our purpose, namely, the prevention of future wars. The Carthaginian aspect of the proposed plan would, in my judgment, provide a reaction on the part of the people in this country and in the rest of the world which would operate not only against the measures advocated but in its violence would sweep away the proper and reasonable restrictive measures that we could justifiably impose."[36]

During this period, Britain had embraced at least three major goals: (1) assuring continued U.S. assistance; (2) assuring continuation of the British Empire and imperial preference; and (3) using Germany and France as a bulwark between the Russian armies in Eastern Europe and the English Channel. As the war came to an end, much economic goodwill had been dissipated on both sides of the Atlantic. Morgenthau was depressed by the vituperation that accompanied post-Quebec publicity about his plan. He explained the path of events to Under Secretary of State Stettinius: "On September 6, a week before he went to Quebec (he was there from the thirteenth to the fifteenth) he sent copies of his so-called 'Control Germany' plan to the president, to Hull, and to Stimson. At no time did Mr. Hull express dissatisfaction. In one letter, Morgenthau spoke of his being gratified that Mr. Hull thought the plan was good. Morgenthau stated that at a White House meeting, Mr. Hull nudged him and said, 'Henry, go on and present your plan.'"[37] Morgenthau met with Hull and Stimson on September 20, to report on the Quebec agreement, which Stimson called "the narration of a pretty heavy defeat for everything that we had fought for."[38] Hull thought FDR had acted with "irresponsibility and deviousness."[39]

Shortly after the Quebec conference, Secretary of War Stimson forcefully dissented from the Morgenthau Plan: "It is not within the realm of possibility that the whole nation of seventy million people, who have been outstanding for many years in the arts and the sciences and who through their efficiency and energy have attained one of the highest industrial levels in Europe, can by force be required to abandon all their previous methods of life, be reduced to a level with virtually complete control of industry and science left to other peoples. . . . Enforced poverty is even worse, for it destroys the spirit not only of the victim but debases the victor. It would be just such a crime as the Germans themselves hoped to perpetrate upon their victims—it would be a crime against civilization itself."[40] Morgenthau biographer Blum wrote: "Neither Stimson nor Morgenthau understood the motives of the other, perhaps largely because both were so confident of their own integrity and so zealous in their quest for the allegiance of the President."[41] Morgenthau thought he had been scapegoated, and that, as Stettinius wrote in his diary: "somewhere between the War Department and State Department there is a coordinated attack on him that he feels unfair and anti-Semitic."[42]

Morgenthau and Stimson had both been victims of Roosevelt's devious tendency to allow contenders on both sides of a critical issue to believe they had his support. Hypocritically, FDR himself later complained: "Henry pulled a boner."[43] The president, however, refused to act to counter the bad press the controversy had stirred, or to ask for a new plan to replace Morgenthau's.[44] Of the document to which he had affixed his initials, FDR in early October pleaded disingenuously to Stimson: "Henry, I have not the faintest recollection of this at all!" Roosevelt said: "About this pastoral, agricultural Germany, that is just nonsense. I have not approved of anything like that. I am sure I have not."[45] Stimson did not let the president off easy, telling him he "must not poison" the moral principles on which FDR had waged the war.[46] White House aide Robert Sherwood wrote: "Roosevelt subsequently made no secret of his regret that he had ever agreed to initial the proposal."[47] Secretary of State Hull was equally angry. On September 26, Hull's deputy, Breckinridge Long, wrote that Hull's treatment "is a repudiation. . . . He feels that a rift between him and the President has become real and that his position under these circumstances may not long be tenable."[48] Within a month, Hull would make the decision to resign.

Soon after Quebec, a press war broke out among the cabinet secretaries.[49] Morgenthau grew very testy about the resulting publicity, especially as reported by Drew Pearson, and complained to Stettinius on the night of October 24, calling to say that "if he had been rude he was sorry—the attacks on him are terrific from all sides and he is getting burned out and says things he doesn't mean."[50] By then, the plan had become an issue on both sides of the Atlantic.[51] Germany had not yet surrendered, so the Nazis were using the proposal to terrify the German people, to stimulate them to fight fiercely, and to prevent any accommodation toward the Allies. In the United States, Republican presidential candidate Thomas Dewey used it as a campaign issue.[52] After Roosevelt's reelection, the debate continued.[53]

Different visions of what would prevent another world war motivated Stimson and Morgenthau. Both clearly perceived different threats to a postwar world. Morgenthau insisted: "Any program which has as its purpose the building up of Germany as a bulwark against Russia and communism will inevitably lead to a third World War." Stimson argued that "the course proposed by the Treasury would in the long run certainly defeat what we hope to attain by a complete military victory—this, the peace of the world, and the assurance of social, economic, and political stability of the world." Similarly, Ambassador Winant told a Treasury Department official that "there is going to be all sorts of misery and disorder in Germany and it will be such that it is going to create just the thing we are fighting against—another Hitler." The British Foreign Office predicted the Morgenthau Plan would create two million unemployed who "would be very difficult" to absorb "if at the same time 3 to 5 million workers from the ceded territories of the East had also to be absorbed."[54] Allied military officers had a better understanding of the reconstruction requirements of Germany than the faraway civilians in the Treasury Department. At a dinner with American Air Chief Henry Arnold in early 1945, British Air Marshal Arthur Tedder declared: "Stalin fully realizes he controls the German bread basket through his hold on Roumania, the Ukraine, Poland, and Hungary. Without these sources of food, Germany starves unless we, the United States and Great Britain, keep them alive, for Germany has not the [food] production to support itself. That may well be a source of trouble in the future."[55]

In the end, the Morgenthau Plan withered away under Roosevelt's tendency to postpone decisions, and the compelling pressure of Stalin's push westward. Russia's territorial expansion created the obvious strategic necessity of a Franco-German bulwark between the Soviet Empire and the English Channel, supported by America. Stung by the consequences of his disingenuous handling of the Morgenthau Plan, FDR postponed serious postwar planning. In a September 29 memo from Secretary Hull to FDR, the State Department defined the economic objectives for postwar Germany: "The primary and continuing objectives of our economic policy are: (1) to render Germany incapable of waging war, and (2) to eliminate permanently German economic domination of Europe. A shorter term objective is to require the performance by Germany of acts of restitution and reparation for injuries done to the United Nations."[56] On October 20, FDR responded to Hull: "In view of the fact that we have not occupied Germany, I cannot agree at this moment as to what kind of a Germany we want in every detail."[57] After a meeting with Roosevelt in November 1944, John Maynard Keynes told Secretary of State Stettinius that "the president emphasized the fact that he did not feel there was any great hurry in reaching a final decision regarding economic treatment of Germany, that we wanted to see what damage our bombs had done and what the general conditions were."[58] The struggle for a postwar German policy would continue.

Churchill, Stalin, Roosevelt, and aides at the conference table at Yalta, February 1945.
FRANKLIN D. ROOSEVELT PRESIDENTIAL LIBRARY

XIX

Yalta and Victory

I would minimize the general Soviet problem as much as possible because these problems, in one form or another, seem to arise every day, and most of them straighten out. . . . We must be firm, however, and our course thus far is correct.[1]

Franklin D. Roosevelt *to Winston S. Churchill, April 11, 1945.*

There is not much comfort in looking into a future where you and the countries you dominate, plus the communist parties in many other States, are all drawn up on one side, and those who rally to the English-speaking nations and their associates or Dominions are on the other. It is quite obvious that their quarrel would tear the world to pieces and that all of us leading men on either side who had anything to do with that would be shamed before history. Even embarking on a long period of suspicions, of abuse and counter-abuse, and of opposing policies would be a disaster hampering the great developments of world prosperity for the masses which are attainable only by our trinity.[2]

Winston Churchill*, letter to Joseph Stalin, April 29, 1945.*

Winston Churchill undertook his relationship with Franklin D. Roosevelt as an anxious suitor. FDR, however, was a fickle mistress who became wary, even jealous, of the heroic and famous biography that the prime minister brought into the alliance. By 1943, the president well understood that the United States was by far the dominant Anglo-American partner—and he acted that way. After 1943, for many reasons, Roosevelt deferred to Russian power and Stalin's primacy in Europe. The president had decided it was necessary to bring Stalin into the war against Japan. After the war, as FDR said, the United States would avoid deep American involvement in Europe—thus increasing Stalin's leverage on Britain and the European continent. Moreover, as the war entered its fourth year, the Churchill-Roosevelt relationship had become more a marriage of convenience, in which each national leader respected the good qualities in his alliance partner. Neither was blind to the perceived defects of the other. It was in late 1943 that Roosevelt became not only solicitous of Stalin, but at the same time disparaging of Churchill—a transparent attempt by the president to ingratiate himself with the Soviet leader.

Meeting with Churchill at a stopover in Cairo, just before the Teheran summit in November 1943, Roosevelt had arranged that Chinese leader Chiang Kai-shek and his problems would absorb all the time that otherwise might have been available to discuss Anglo-American strategy with Churchill. The prime minister had planned to talk about other crucial matters with the president. And he was prepared. Similarly, at a stopover in Malta just before the Yalta summit in February 1945, Roosevelt avoided any substantive discussions with the prime minister.[3] FDR was unprepared, as his secretary of state discovered. Foreign Secretary Eden complained: "The President was so unpredictable that the Prime Minister and I became uneasy at this void."[4] (This reaction to the president's conduct was typical of his own cabinet members.) Matters did not improve once the Yalta conclave began. "Dinner with the Americans; a terrible party I thought," wrote Eden of the first night. "President vague and loose and ineffective. W. understanding that business was flagging made desperate efforts and too long speeches to get things going again. Stalin's attitude to small countries struck me as grim, not to say sinister."[5] Ever the improviser, the "vague and loose" Roosevelt, in deference to Stalin, continued to avoid bilateral discussions at Yalta with Churchill and Eden. FDR was also sick and frail.

Historians have differed on the intimacy of the relationship between the prime minister and the president. Historian Warren Kimball wrote: "By the time of Roosevelt's death, the Churchill-Roosevelt relationship had become routine—more than a facade, but less than the personal, near friendship that it had been."[6] In private, according to FDR's son Elliott, Roosevelt would ungenerously ridicule Churchill. At the Casablanca summit, Roosevelt said: "Winnie is a great man for the status quo. He even *looks* like the status quo, doesn't he?"[7] Historian Keith Sainsbury wrote: "The wartime friendship between Franklin Roosevelt and Winston Churchill was not precisely all it seemed to be; nor was it totally a myth. It was one of those half-truths which played a valuable part in the conduct of the Second World War." He called the two men "uneasy partners."[8] Churchill did not argue with FDR's tendency unrealistically to treat the alliance as a global United Nations. At the Cairo conference in 1943, after listening to Harry Hopkins's complaints about the prime minister, Churchill's physician exclaimed: "What I find so shocking is that to the Americans, the P.M. is the villain of the piece; they are far more sceptical of him than they are of Stalin."[9] Hopkins, of course, reflected FDR's attitude toward Stalin.

Still, the prime minister would persist in the romance. In January 1943, Churchill had written his wife from North Africa, after meeting "Don Quixote" (Roosevelt) and "Sancho Panza" (Harry Hopkins): "I am lunching with the Don, Harry Hopkins and Averell alone. We have touched on several things, plunging right into the matter straight away. I think he was delighted to see me, and I have a very strong sense of the friendship which prevails between us."[10] Shortly before FDR died in

1945, Churchill wrote the president about his dispute with Eisenhower—that the general should try to outrun the Russians to Berlin: "I regard the matter as closed and to prove my sincerity I will use one of my very few Latin quotations, 'Amantium irae amoris integratio est.'" (Lovers' quarrels are a part of love.)[11] Churchill clearly grasped America's new economic and military preeminence among the nations, and the shrinking relative importance of the United Kingdom. After the 1944 presidential election, Churchill had wired FDR on November 28 about the prime minister's views of the postwar world. The United States "will have the greatest Navy in the world. You will have, I hope, the greatest air force. You will have the greatest trade. You have all the gold. But these things do not oppress my mind with fear because I am sure the American people under your re-acclaimed leadership will not give themselves over to vain-glorious ambitions, and that justice and fair-play will be the lights that guide them."[12] As General Eisenhower's son John observed: "One of Winston Churchill's claims to greatness—not recognized generally—was his ability to rise above disappointments, even humiliations. He never let these considerations becloud the goal of victory."[13]

The Yalta Conference, in February 1945, proved the last great conclave of the original Allied leaders. Roosevelt had carefully avoided serious meetings alone with Churchill before Yalta.[14] The conference did not begin happily, nor did it end well. Even before the summit, Churchill told Hopkins: "We could not have found a worse place for a meeting if we had spent ten years on research."[15] Stalin chose the Crimean resort for his convenience—with the excuse that his doctors forbade more distant travel. Churchill led the British delegation that included Foreign Secretary Eden, Under-Secretary Cadogan, Ambassador to Russia Clark Kerr, Cabinet Secretary Edward Bridges, Field Marshal Brooke, Air Marshal Portal, Field Marshall Alexander, Admiral Cunningham, and General Ismay. FDR's delegation included Secretary of State Stettinius, Hopkins, Chief of Staff Leahy, former Supreme Court Justice James Byrnes, General Marshall, Admiral King, and Ambassador to Russia Harriman. Stalin's delegation consisted of Foreign Minister Molotov, Deputy Foreign Minister Maisky, Admiral Nikolay Gerasimovich Kuznetsov, General Aleksei Antonov, Air Marshal Sergei Khudyakov, Stalin operative Andrey Vyshinski, Ambassador to Great Britain Feodor T. Gousev, and Ambassador to the United States Andrei Gromyko. It was a fateful conclave. When the Potsdam Conference convened almost six months later in July, FDR would be dead and the war in Europe over. Relations with Russia would turn ice cold.[16]

During the last year and a half of the war, FDR had become ever more evasive, slippery, even devious in his dealings with Churchill, as he became ever more solicitous of the Russian dictator.[17] He became indifferent, even harsh toward the feelings of the British prime minister. At the beginning of the Yalta summit, Hopkins tried to reverse Roosevelt's desire to sideline Churchill. On February 3, the bedridden Hopkins complained to FDR's daughter, Anna Boettinger, arguing "that FDR must see Churchill in the morning . . . that it was imperative that FDR and Churchill have some prearrangements before the Big Conference started." She "asked him if he didn't think this course might stir up some distrust among our Russian brethren, and Harry passed me off very lightly." Anna in turn dismissed Hopkins: "Certainly it didn't seem to me that his mind was clicking or his judgment good, or maybe it's just that I had never quite realized how pro-British Harry is."[18] Hopkins believed correctly that the prime minister was the loyal, dependable ally. Hopkins could be forgiven for his loyalty to his "pro-British" view, as he knew how crucial Churchill had been in 1940–1941, and he respected the prime minister's experience. Churchill's physician had a better-informed opinion of Hopkins's judgment than FDR's daughter: "He knows the President's moods like a wife watching the domestic climate. He will sit patiently for hours, blinking like a cat, waiting for the right moment to put his point; and if it never comes, he is content to leave it to another time."[19]

For months in 1944, in deference to Stalin, Roosevelt had failed to take up the serious issues regarding Poland's future, despite the fact that the American Polish constituency was loyal to FDR's Democratic Party. Even Ambassador Harriman observed that FDR "consistently shows very little interest in Eastern European matters except as they affect [political] sentiment in America."[20] But the president had given public notice that after the war, the United States would not be tied down in Europe. Thus, America and Britain had little leverage in negotiations with Stalin about Eastern Europe. Churchill got it right in January 1945. "The only hope for the world," observed the prime minister to Foreign Secretary Eden, "is the agreement of the three Great Powers. If they quarrel, our children are undone."[21] As it turned out, the postwar world would be dominated by the Cold War between the Soviet Union and the United States. A free Western Europe would be restored because Presidents Truman and Eisenhower kept American troops on the continent, creating NATO and the Marshall Plan for European redevelopment.

At Yalta, in February 1945, FDR had aimed to get agreement on certain issues and then depart. Churchill had other ideas, telling Roosevelt: "I do not feel that we should hurry away from the Crimea leaving these vital problems unresolved or reach hasty decisions. These are among the most important days that any of us shall live. Of course you could all go away and leave me in this delightful spot but I do urge that we stay a little bit longer to conclude our discussions satisfactorily."[22] As Yalta historian S. M. Plokhy observed: "The final draft of the Allied declaration on Poland . . . was in all but form an act of surrender to the Soviets."[23] In hindsight, this was no surprise. Conviction in Washington about the need to cooperate with Russia went much deeper than FDR alone—especially among those who had no experience dealing with Stalin. Increasingly, military planners viewed Russia as "decisive" in Europe. To them, Russia was the great bear in the room.[24] Appeasing the Russian bear had become a continuing military and diplomatic priority. But Stalin was not easily satisfied, given his leverage; six million Soviet soldiers in arms dwarfed the Anglo-American presence in Europe.

At Yalta, Roosevelt again vainly believed he could charm and flatter Stalin—in part by publicly diminishing Churchill. At one meeting, Churchill arrived to discover that FDR was closeted with Stalin. When Secretary Stettinius suggested that

Admiral Leahy inform the president of the prime minister's arrival, the message from Leahy was "Let him wait"—callously delivered in front of British diplomats. Stettinius apologized to Eden, who responded that he "thoroughly understood the whims of their masters and not to be upset about it." Historian Andrew Roberts politely observed: "Perhaps Eden ought to have taken this act of casual rudeness on the part of the President as yet another sign of his willingness to appear somewhere between grandly nonchalant and simply offhand towards Churchill."[25] The prime minister told his doctor: "The President is behaving very badly. He won't take any interest in what we are trying to do."[26] FDR not only behaved badly. He was also very sick and very weak.

Previously, when Roosevelt wanted to block State Department participation in international conferences, he would say that only military matters would be discussed. Yalta represented the first summit to which the top foreign policy officials were invited. In this case, Stettinius, Eden, and Molotov played key roles, working through issues at their midday meetings, before they were discussed by the Big Three later in the afternoon. Nevertheless, key issues, such as Russian demands regarding China and Japan, were kept out of their hands. Stalin and Roosevelt worked them out together on February 8—without Churchill. As victory neared, British and American policies diverged, though in 1944, Churchill had told Roosevelt: "I simply can't go on without you" when FDR's fourth term seemed in doubt.[27] FDR saw his advantage and increasingly took unilateral action without consulting the prime minister. Yalta scholar S. M. Plokhy wrote: "Churchill was struggling, caught between true admiration for a close friend and ally and the disappointment that he felt increasingly after Teheran, when Roosevelt began to shift toward Stalin at the expense of the prime minister." Plokhy summed up: "The days of easy intimacy between Churchill and Roosevelt were gone."[28]

Communication had broken down. Hopkins himself wrote:

> The last night before the Yalta conference broke up, the President flabbergasted Churchill by telling him for the first time that he was going to fly to Egypt and had arranged for the King of Egypt [Farouk], [Saudi Arabia's King] Ibn Saud and [Ethiopia's Emperor] Hailie Selassie to hold conferences with him aboard the cruiser in Great Bitter Lake on three successive days. There were a number of people present when the President told Churchill about what these visits were all about. Later that night he, Churchill, sought me out, greatly disturbed and wanted to know what were the President's intentions in relation to these three sovereigns. Fortunately I could tell him I did not know because I had asked the President the same thing. I had already made up my mind that it was, in the main, a lot of horseplay and that the President was going to thoroughly enjoy the colorful panoply of the sovereigns of this part of the world who thought that President Roosevelt of the United States could probably cure all their troubles. I did know he intended to talk to Ibn Saud about the Palestine situation. Nothing I said, however, was comforting to Churchill because he thought we had some deep laid plot to undermine the British Empire in these areas.[29]

Interviewed aboard ship by American correspondents on his way back from Yalta, Roosevelt cavalierly said of Prime Minister Churchill's constitutional responsibility for the British Empire that he was "mid-Victorian. . . . Dear old Winston will never learn on that point." Biographer Jon Meacham wrote that Roosevelt "was falling back on an old, unattractive trait: self-importance, the unfortunate flip side of his wonderful confidence."[30]

FDR tired easily at Yalta. Unlike the prime minister, the president did not want to resist the Russians, or to fight it out on the crucial issues that would determine the future of European and world politics. Leahy complained that the Poland agreement was "so elastic that the Russians can stretch it all the way from Yalta to Washington without even technically breaking it." FDR replied: "[I]t's the best I can do for Poland at this time."[31] Confronted by Adolf Berle at the White House about Yalta's treatment of Eastern Europe, Roosevelt reiterated: "Adolf, I didn't say the result was good. I said it was the best I could do."[32] Perhaps so, as these countries were occupied by Soviet troops, but was that sufficient ground for humoring Stalin while abandoning Eastern Europe without tenacious argument?

In the fall and winter of 1944–1945, Hopkins had returned to his role as a bridge between Roosevelt and Churchill. Hopkins biographer Sherwood noted that prior to the Yalta Conference, on "January 21, Hopkins took off for London in 'The Sacred Cow.' It had been decided that he should spend two or three days with Churchill in an attempt to promote a more amiable mood prior to the gathering at Yalta, for the tensions created during December [over Greece] had evidently not been entirely relaxed."[33] Hopkins stopped in Paris on the way to Yalta, dining with Colonel Elliott Roosevelt: "Harry did what he was *so* good at: he was a charming and interesting companion, flashing with ideas and with wit, and we had a very good time."[34] The trip took its toll on Hopkins. Churchill's physician described him at Yalta as "ghastly—his skin was a yellow-white membrane stretched tight over the bones."[35]

Once at the Crimean site, the exhausted Hopkins spent much of his time in bed, his role with FDR largely performed by Admiral Leahy. Roosevelt's top priorities focused on Russian agreement on the United Nations and Soviet entry into the war against Japan.[36] On other issues, the president saw himself as a referee between Stalin and Churchill.[37] Leahy attended the political and military meetings "in order," said Roosevelt, "that we have someone in whom I have full confidence who will remember everything that we have done."[38] Hopkins was seldom available to manage the Anglo-American divide. "Hopkins is of course a valuable ally," wrote Churchill's physician, "particularly now, when the President's opinions flutter in the wind."[39] Hopkins was sick much of the time and, when fit, concentrated mainly on smoothing the way toward postwar collaboration with Russia. Secretary Stettinius wrote that on February 8: "Hopkins and I had a discussion in which he suggested that we should start to work immediately on the preparation of a communique about the coming world security conference. If we did not, he warned, the Prime Minister would sit up in bed some morning and dash it off himself. From past experience, Hopkins added, he knew it would be difficult to change it once it was on paper."[40]

Hopkins was so weak after Yalta that he flew back to Washington rather than accompany the president by ship. "Why did Harry have to get sick on me?" complained Roosevelt.[41] In September 1943, FDR had acknowledged "that when a group of men are arguing and haggling over the details of some problem, and perhaps talking at cross purposes, Harry will be sitting quietly saying nothing, taking it all in, and then, in one sentence, he will put his finger on the point of the argument, and clarify the whole thing."[42] Leahy noted in his memoirs: "Churchill's jesting title [for Hopkins], 'Lord Root of the Matter,' was an accurate description. Hopkins had an excellent mind. His manner of approach was direct and nobody could fool him, not even Churchill. He was never influenced by a person's rank." Leahy added: "Roosevelt trusted him implicitly and Hopkins never betrayed that trust."[43] In an alliance in which the rules of the game determined how cooperation played out, Hopkins was one of the few who understood and could set a few of the rules. Exhausted after Yalta, FDR and Hopkins parted in North Africa. They would not meet again.

As the surrender of Germany drew near in early May 1945, Anthony Eden, Vyacheslav Molotov, and Edward Stettinius wired Hopkins from San Francisco: "At a dinner last night we three drank a special toast to you in sincere recognition of the outstanding part you personally have played in bringing our three countries together in the common cause."[44] Days later, Churchill wired Hopkins: "Among all those in the grand alliance, warriors or statesmen who struck deadly blows at the enemy and brought peace nearer, you will ever hold an honored place."[45] Soon thereafter, Hopkins retired from government. He briefly reentered the diplomatic scene on May 23, to travel to Moscow. President Truman took the unusual step of sending Anglophile Hopkins to Moscow and Russophile Joseph Davies to London.[46] Davies had been one of the few Americans who, early in the war, had thought that Russia would survive the Nazi onslaught. As ambassador to Moscow, he had become a sympathetic friend of Stalin. Hopkins proved more successful in his mission than the pro-Soviet Davies, who quickly alienated Churchill. Hopkins, like FDR, was sympathetic to Stalin. Russian specialist Charles E. Bohlen observed that Hopkins "was always more optimistic about Soviet policy than I. He clung to one central idea, that good relations between the United States, the Soviet Union, and Great Britain were the most important factor in the world, and everything should be done to promote them. . . . Harry was inclined to dismiss ideology, feeling that patient, careful dealings with Moscow were the proper answer to the problem."[47] Bohlen knew from experience that to ignore ideology was to ignore the history of the Bolshevik Revolution, and to ignore Stalin's communist worldview.

When Hopkins died in January 1946, Churchill wrote: "I have a great regard for that man, who always went to the root of the matter and scanned our great affairs with pierceing [sic] eye."[48] One of Hopkins's last letters was to Churchill, regretting that his health had not allowed him to greet Churchill on a visit to Florida.[49] Churchill, however, was no longer prime minister. It was Hopkins who had shrewdly understood that Churchill was indispensable in wartime, but not in peace. At a Washington dinner party in December 1942, Hopkins had declared: "Churchill would be Premier only for the war period, and after that undoubtedly the British people would select somebody else." After the dinner, a less perceptive Treasury Secretary Morgenthau had thought Hopkins a "funny fellow' and "wondered why Harry had emphasized so strongly that Churchill would be through when the peace came."[50]

Throughout the war, Roosevelt and Churchill had for strategic reasons courted Stalin. John Colville noted that in October 1944, the prime minister "flew to Moscow . . . largely, so he said, to convince Stalin that the Quebec Conference did not mean the Anglo-Saxons were 'ganged up' to the exclusion of Russia."[51] He knew only too well that it was primarily the Russian army that had destroyed the German army, and that Russia was powerful enough at that moment to be the master of Europe. This was no delusion.[52] Eden recalled a conversation he had had with Stalin in December 1941. The Russian dictator had declared: "Hitler has shown he has one fatal defect. He does not know where to stop." At that, Eden had broken into a slight smile, causing Stalin some consternation for a few moments before the Soviet dictator responded: "I realize now why you are smiling, Mr. Eden. You are wondering if I myself will know where to stop. But I can assure you that I will always know where to stop."[53] After Yalta, it was Presidents Truman and Eisenhower who would say: "Stop!"

Roosevelt was surely more gullible about the Soviet leader than Churchill. "You know, I really think the Russians will go along with me about having no spheres of influence and about agreements for free ports all over the world," the president told Secretary of Labor Perkins, after meeting Stalin at Teheran. She noted that FDR "felt himself on very good personal terms with Marshall Stalin. He [FDR] liked him and found him extremely interesting."[54] Historian James MacGregor Burns wrote that Roosevelt, unlike Stalin and Churchill, "was handicapped, when it came to considerations of peace, by the belief that better days must lie ahead."[55] The tragedy of Yalta was that a sick and weakened Roosevelt, too solicitous of Stalin, did not mediate equitably between Churchill and Stalin; nor did he press hard to negotiate a postwar world in which Eastern Europe might escape Soviet totalitarianism. Indeed, only the creation of American-led NATO in 1949–1950 would assure protection of Western Europe and the Atlantic, reversing as it did FDR's intention to withdraw from Europe at war's end.

During Hopkins's first meeting with Stalin in the summer of 1941, the Russian dictator had argued without realizing the irony of his remarks: "Hitler's greatest weakness was found in the vast numbers of oppressed people who hated Hitler and the immoral ways of his Government. He believed these people and countless other millions in nations still unconquered could receive the kind of encouragement and moral strength they needed to resist Hitler from only one source, and that was the United States."[56] Duplicitous as he was, Stalin had a clear view of geopolitical realities, a strong sense of military strategy, and at the end of the war a much stronger military position. He was well informed and better prepared than FDR, often more prepared than Churchill. Hard-nosed General Brooke wrote in his diary of Stalin that he was "impressed by his astuteness and his crafty cleverness. He is a realist with little flattery about him, and not looking for much flattery either."[57] After World War II, Stalin himself used the third person to relate a story about what happened at Yalta: "Churchill, Roosevelt and Stalin went hunting. They finally killed their bear." As Stalin told the story, Churchill said, "I'll take the bearskin. Let Roosevelt and Stalin divide the meat." Roosevelt said, "No, I'll take the skin. Let Churchill and Stalin divide the meat." When Stalin stayed, Churchill and Roosevelt inquired, "Mister Stalin, what do you say?" Stalin responded, "The bear belongs to me—after all, I killed it."[58] Churchill would grow increasingly alarmed by aggressive Russian behavior. He wrote Eden that he did not wish "to go back on our desire to establish friendly relationships with Russia, but our and especially *my* courteous and even effusive personal approaches have had a bad effect."[59]

The Allied leaders had their vices. "Roosevelt was vain; Churchill was conceited," noted Colville.[60] But Churchill and Roosevelt were so very different from Stalin: an ideological Bolshevik, a ruthless bully in Eastern Europe, and a murderer at home. Churchill understood the asymmetric nature of Anglo-American power relations. He grasped—with difficulty—that not all Americans loved him or his countrymen. When Judge Samuel I. Rosenman, counsel to the president, visited the prime minister shortly before the German surrender in May 1945, Churchill worried about the postwar election in Britain. "Do you remember when I came over to your country in the summer of 1944 when your election campaigning was beginning? Do you remember that when I arrived, I said something favorable to the election of the President, and immediately the associates of the President sent word to me in no uncertain terms to 'lay off' discussing the American election. Do you remember I was told that if I wanted to help the President get re-elected, the best thing I could do was to keep my mouth shut; that the American people would resent any interference or suggestion by a foreigner about how they should vote?" Rosenman well remembered the incident because he had so advised Roosevelt. The prime minister continued with intentional irony: "Now what I want you to tell the President is this. When he comes over here in May [when FDR had been invited] I shall be in the midst of a political campaign myself; we shall be holding our own elections about that time. I want you to tell him that I impose no such inhibitions upon him as he imposed upon me."[61]

A few days later, FDR was dead. "I am much weakened in every way by his loss," lamented Churchill.[62] But Churchill did not go to Washington for the funeral. At the end of the war, he was needed every day in London to make decisions. The president and the prime minister, both outsized personalities, had made their personal chemistry a vital necessity to Anglo-American cooperation before and after the United States entered the war. British historian John Charmley, a revisionist, had argued that Churchill excessively accommodated American interests.[63] Surely Charmley underestimated Britain's desperate insolvency in 1940–1941, and thus its total dependence on the United States for the means to defend itself in a long war. Indeed, many U.S. officials thought Churchill failed sufficiently to accommodate American strategic priorities like Project ANVIL, the invasion of southern France in August 1944.[64] British Admiral Andrew Cunningham diplomatically recalled: "Maybe we erred in criticizing the American desire to land in southern France in the summer of 1944, and Eisenhower's strategical conduct of the campaign in the north. On the other hand, we were beset by Admiral [Ernest] King's deeply rooted aversion to the employment of the British Fleet in the Pacific, while I remember the vexation we were caused by the President's sudden offer to the Russians of one-third of the Italian fleet, which was made without previous consultation with us."[65] The evidence suggests that early in the war, Churchill's brilliant and subtle diplomacy bridged these profound differences between the British and the Americans, and to some extent, the Russians. Roosevelt changed after 1943, but Churchill never gave up his faith in the Anglo-American special relationship.

The prime minister and the president deployed personal charm as a weapon of persuasion, but not all human targets were charmed. Churchill's daughter Mary Soames wrote: "One could hardly fail to be dazzled by the magnetic quality of [FDR's] charm, but Clementine never really fell under 'FDR's' powerful spell, spotting very quickly that his personal vanity was inordinate. However, they got on very well, although she complained to me after an early encounter, that she thought it 'great cheek of him calling me Clemmie!' It was surely meant as a compliment; but my mother always regarded the use of her own, or other people's, Christian names as a privilege marking close friendship or long association."[66] The self-confident Clementine, like General Marshall, resisted FDR's false intimacy. Eleanor Roosevelt made a positive impression on Clementine when the First Lady visited Britain in October 1942: "Each time she said something significant, fresh and true, and she gave all who heard her a sense of being in the presence of a remarkable and benevolent personality."[67] Mrs. Roosevelt, for her part, admired but did not trust Winston Churchill's worldview. In 1942, she wrote: "I like Mr. Churchill, he's loveable & emotional & very human, but I don't want him to write the peace or carry it out."[68] Eleanor Roosevelt, an anticolonial liberal, correctly believed Mr. Churchill a Tory determined to defend the British Empire. The prime minister was proud to admit this devotion.

Alan Brooke could be sharply critical of both Allied leaders, whom the patronizing Brooke thought wanting in steady and wise military judgment and strategy. "He knows no details, has only got half the picture in his mind, talks absurdities and makes my blood boil to listen to his nonsense," complained Brooke of Churchill, while on the transatlantic voyage to the Quebec summit of September 1944. "And the wonderful thing is that ¾ of the population of the world imagine that Winston Churchill is one of the Strategists of History, a second Marlborough, and the other ¼ have no conception of what a public menace he is and has been throughout this war!"[69] Writing in his diary on November 29, 1943, at the Teheran summit conference, Brooke evaluated the second "long 3 hour conference! Bad from beginning to end. Winston was not good and Roosevelt even worse." Brooke concluded: "After listening to the arguments put forward during the last 2 days I feel more like entering a lunatic asylum or a nursing home than continuing with my present job."[70]

Brooke and his key deputy, however, acknowledged that the warden of the asylum was a unique and dynamic leader. "Winston certainly inspires confidence," General John Kennedy wrote in his diary in July 1942. "I do admire the unhurried way in which he gets through such a colossal amount of work, and yet never seems otherwise than at leisure. He was particularly genial and good-humoured today. I can well understand how those around him become devoted to him—and dominated by him. I remember [Admiral of the Fleet] Dudley Pound once saying, 'You cannot help loving that man,' and I can quite see the truth of this sentiment. There is one thing that Winston's enemies and critics must admit—he has only one interest in life at this moment and that is to win the war."[71] Brooke's diaries ring with similar sentiments, even as his entries sometimes demeaned Churchill's mastery of strategy and condemned his work habits.

"There's only one thing worse than undertaking a war with allies," Churchill told General Eisenhower prior to D-Day. "Waging a war without allies."[72] British General Leslie Hollis thought Anglo-American differences over strategy were primarily "psychological." He argued: "America, a large country, adopted—like a large man—frontal tactics. They wanted quick and terrible hammer blows that would speedily finish the fight; in this case, a very early landing in Europe, and then on down through France into Germany, and so over with the war." The United Kingdom's perspective differed. "Britain, a small country with a long history of frequently successful engagements against opponents that could have overwhelmed her with their numbers, adopted—like a small man faced by a large enemy—more subtle tactics. Over the centuries we had established an Empire by a policy of small operations which could be consolidated. Frequently we had gone 'in at the back door.' . . . In Churchill's view (and mine) we could have destroyed Germany in the First War had the back door in Gallipoli been less ineptly opened."[73] Here, General Hollis would mitigate Churchill's greatest humiliation at war—the disastrous campaign in World War I at the Dardanelles, the gateway to Turkey and the Black Sea—arguing, as a minority of others have, that Churchill's strategy was correct, but the military execution a failure.

In the last months of FDR's life, Churchill struggled to hold together Anglo-American cooperation. As the war had made progress, Churchill believed that only a strengthened relationship between the United States and the United Kingdom, given the expansion of the Soviet Empire, could uphold and enlarge the free world. Roosevelt demurred. Distracted by appearances, he minimized the early success of the intimate Churchill-Roosevelt relationship. Of course, FDR feared giving offense to some segments of the American electorate, and he was ever more careful not to offend Stalin and Soviet official opinion. Thus, after late 1943, FDR tried to avoid Anglo-American collaboration, as he focused on charming Uncle Joe and trying to coopt Russia on behalf of his postwar vision. Churchill critic John Charmley wrote: "Roosevelt had made it clear ever since Tehran that he was not going to enter some exclusive special relationship with the British. He had always avoided going to London and doing anything which might allow Churchill to claim that he had an entrée to the President. Indeed, even at Yalta he had opposed British attempts to build up France as a Great Power because he did not want to see the British developing a sphere of influence in Western Europe."[74] The Anglo-American alliance, designed to defeat Hitler and imperial Japan, was indispensable, but the Wilsonian in FDR focused on the abstract idea of the United Nations to replace the global role of the British Empire. At the same time, the president would include the Soviet Empire as an equal in the United Nations.

One night at Malta, in early 1945, Dr. Charles Wilson and Ambassador Gil Winant discussed courage and failure, as viewed differently by the Americans and the British. A publisher had just rejected Wilson's book, *The Anatomy of Courage.* Winant observed that the British had a special reverence for strength in adversity: "It's not failure you like, but the fact that some men grow in adversity. I think it is because you people are so interested in character and put it before anything else that you find failure not unattractive." Ambassador Winant and Dr. Wilson agreed that Americans put much more stock in success—more so than did the British. Wilson observed: "Winston seems to me a hundred percent American in his feelings about failure." In his diary that night, Wilson wrote: "Unless a man has done something in life, something really worth doing, he does not interest Winston. . . . It is what a man does, not what he is, that counts."[75]

Even before World War II, Winston Churchill decided he must prepare to *do* what counted—destroy the Nazi monster. As Admiral Leahy wrote in his memoirs: "There were two men at the top who really fought and finally agreed on the major moves that led to victory. They were Franklin Roosevelt and Winston Churchill. They really ran the war [in Western Europe and the Pacific, but not in Eastern Europe]. Of course, they had to have some people like us to help them, but we were just artisans building definite patterns of strategy from the rough blueprints handed to us by our respective Commanders-in-Chief."[76] General Brooke notwithstanding, Churchill himself devised the original blueprint and strategy against Hitler—the United Kingdom carrying on alone in 1940. On February 8, 1945, at the Yalta summit, Stalin toasted Churchill "as the bravest governmental figure in the world. He said that due in large measure to Mr. Churchill's courage and staunchness, England, when she stood alone, had divided the might of Hitlerite Germany at a time when the rest of Europe was falling flat on its face before Hitler. He said that Great Britain under Mr. Churchill's leadership, had carried on the fight alone irrespective of existing or potential allies." Then Stalin concluded that "he knew of few examples in history where the courage of one man had been so important to the future history of the world. He drank a toast to Mr Churchill, his fighting friend and a brave man."[77]

Churchill never gave up, despite the grave defeats of 1940–1942. The prime minister became the indispensable bulwark against Nazi triumphalism. The bridge he created to FDR, across the Atlantic, was his handiwork and it made ultimate victory possible. As one fierce American critic of British military strategy observed: "The diversions into the Mediterranean area would never have been possible had it not been for the so-called charisma of the prime minister."[78] The inescapable British response to this American conceit had to be that the so-called British diversions in the Mediterranean forced Hitler to reduce manpower and equipment on the Russian front at the critical moment. Without this reduction of German armed forces, diverted by Hitler to the Mediterranean, the Nazis would probably have taken Moscow, Leningrad, and Stalingrad, destroyed the Russian army, and then turned their full fury on Great Britain and the Atlantic. In his memoirs, Churchill wrote:

> In the military as in the commercial or production spheres the American mind runs naturally to broad, sweeping, logical conclusions on the largest scale. It is on these that they build their practical thought and action. They feel that once the foundation has been planned on true and comprehensive lines all other stages will follow naturally and almost inevitably. The British mind does not work quite in this way. We do not think that logic and clear-cut principles are necessarily the sole keys to what ought to be done in swiftly changing and indefinable situations. In war particularly we assign a larger importance to opportunism and improvisation, seeking rather to live and conquer in accordance with unfolding events than to aspire to dominate it often by fundamental decisions.[79]

The British fox contrasted with the American hedgehog.

When it counted and where it mattered, the Americans and Churchill built an intimate, effective Anglo-American alliance. It was Churchill who pressed for the Soviet alliance, despite his hatred for Bolshevism. That the Anglo-American alliance came together with the massive Russian army is itself a partial explanation of the total defeat of Hitler. At a dinner at the Foreign Office during World War II, Lady Halifax reported Churchill in a grumpy mood. "As his wrath died down and the champagne began to have its usual mellowing effect he started talking about himself—I got slightly confused as to his meaning when he said with some emotion: 'That old man up there intended me to be where I am at this time,' until I [Lady Halifax] realized that he was talking about the Almighty and His Divine Providence and Purpose."[80] After the British Navy had sunk the German battleship *Bismarck* in May 1941, Churchill had referred Roosevelt to 2 Corinthians 6:1–2: "For he saith, I have heard thee in a time accepted, and in the day of salvation I have succoured thee; behold, *now* is the accepted time; behold *now* is the day of salvation."[81]

The Casablanca Conference. At the table: Admiral Ernest King, Prime Minister Churchill, President Roosevelt. Standing: unknown, Major General Hastings Ismay, Lord Louis Mountbatten, unknown, and Field Marshall John Dill.
NATIONAL ARCHIVES

Epilogue: Themes and Conclusions

> It is not given to us to peer into the mysteries of the future. Still I avow my hope and faith, sure and inviolate, that in the days to come the British and American people will for their own safety and for the good of all walk together in majesty, in justice and in peace.
>
> ***Winston S. Churchill****, December 27, 1941, speech to U.S. Congress, Washington, 20 days after Pearl Harbor.*

> No petty differences in the world of trade, traditions, or national pride should ever blind us to our identities in priceless values. If we keep our eyes on this guidepost, then no difficulties along our path of mutual co-operation can ever be insurmountable. Moreover, when this truth has permeated to the remotest hamlet and heart of all peoples, then indeed may we beat our swords into plowshares and all nations can enjoy the fruitfulness of the earth.[1]
>
> ***Dwight D. Eisenhower****, June 12, 1945, speech at the Guildhall, London, a month after Germany's surrender and two months before Japan's surrender.*

It was President Roosevelt who decided on December 31, 1941, that the Allies should be called "United Nations" rather than "Associated Powers." Prime Minister Winston Churchill, anxious to please his American host, quickly agreed. To name the alliance was easy. To sustain the alliance, through years of defeats until victory, required leadership and statecraft rarely exercised in the history of wartime alliances. The prime minister admitted in 1942: "My whole system is founded on friendship with Roosevelt."[2] Two years later, just before D-Day, Churchill told Charles de Gaulle: "Each time I must choose between you and Roosevelt, I shall always choose Roosevelt."[3] The prime minister did not neglect Stalin, signing some communications with the Soviet dictator: "Your friend and war-time comrade." But true comradeship with a cynical and aggressive Stalin at times proved impossible. FDR maintained his faith that the personal relationships among Churchill, Stalin, and himself could make the alliance work. In October 1944, the president wrote Stalin: "I am firmly convinced that the three of us, and *only* the three of us, can find the solution to the still unresolved questions."[4]

After World War II, Averell Harriman wrote that FDR had decided to establish "a close personal relationship with Stalin in wartime, to build confidence among the Kremlin leaders [so] that Russia, now an acknowledged major power, could trust the West." Roosevelt's envoy wrote: "Churchill had a more pragmatic attitude. He too would have liked to build on wartime intimacy to achieve postwar understandings. But his mind concentrated on the settlement of specific political problems and spheres of influence. He despised Communism and all its works. He turned pessimistic about the future earlier than Roosevelt. And he foresaw much greater difficulties at the end of war."[5] In these judgments, Churchill was the more prescient.

Stalin's victories in the east gave him great confidence. Of the Allies, it was primarily Russian arms that destroyed the German army. The Anglo-American armies played an important but supporting role on the western front. At sea, the U.S. Navy played the commanding role after 1942, the British navy the lesser role. The combined forces of the U.S. Navy, Marines, Army, and Air Force led to victory over Japan. No matter these historic triumphs, the wartime alliance of America, the Soviet Union, and the United Kingdom could not keep the peace, the goal envisioned for the postwar United Nations. Stalin himself declared, in 1945 at Yalta: "It is not so difficult to keep unity in time of war since there is a joint aim to defeat the common enemy, which is clear to everyone. The difficult task will come after the war when diverse interests tend to divide the Allies. It is our duty to see that our relations in peacetime are as strong as they have been in war."[6]

Diplomacy requires patience and hard work, especially when cooperation turns to competition. None took the initiative and worked harder at those relationships than Winston Churchill and Harry Hopkins. "I came here as a representative of the President of the United States," said Hopkins at the end of his second visit to Britain in July 1941. "His hatred for the things that Hitler stands for is the hatred of our people against tyranny."[7] At the beginning of 1941, during the ABC talks among American, British, and Canadian military officials in Washington, it had been established that Europe and the Atlantic would be the primary military theater of the war. Churchill continued to argue successfully for this priority. In June 1941, Hitler invaded the Soviet Union. Russia would join the Anglo-American alliance. Even the Japanese attack at Pearl Harbor did not alter the strategic decision—Europe first. With the attack on December 7, 1941, the Anglo-American alliance mobilized in the Pacific to defeat Japan. Four days after Pearl Harbor, Hitler declared war on the United States. The truly global war would now engage the Allies against the Axis powers in the greatest armed conflict of history.

Harry Hopkins proved himself indispensable in dealing with the Big Three leaders because, as FDR's son observed, "Harry could disarm you. He could make you his friend in the first five minutes of a conversation and that must have been pretty rough with Stalin who was a tough old bird. . . . Harry had the ability to win him over."[8] Russian Marshal Georgy Zhukov recalled meeting Hopkins in Berlin, on his way back from Moscow in June 1945: "I had never met Hopkins, but according to Stalin, he was an outstanding personality. Hopkins had done a great deal to strengthen business contacts between the United States and the Soviet Union." He recalled Hopkins saying: "It's a pity President Roosevelt didn't live to see these days, it was easier with him." Roosevelt's longtime aide maintained: "I respect Churchill, but he is a difficult person to get along with. The only man who found no difficulty in talking with him was Franklin Roosevelt."[9]

Hopkins proved a skilled observer and analyst of important people. He had a gift for saying the right thing at the right time. Hopkins's friend Robert Sherwood wrote: "The Prime Minister and the President, as Hopkins saw them, were widely different characters, but they both possessed to a superlative degree the ability to provoke loyalty, enthusiasm, devotion, even a kind of adoration—and also the ability merely to provoke."[10] In January 1941, Churchill sketched his vision of postwar Europe before asking Hopkins for his reaction. Hopkins then said "there were two kinds of men: those who talked and those who acted. The President, like the Prime Minister, was one of the latter." John Colville reported in his diary: "Although Hopkins had heard him [FDR] sketch out an idea very similar to the P.M.'s, Roosevelt refused to listen to those who talked so much of war aims and was intent only upon one end: the destruction of Hitler."[11] In fact, Churchill was even more single-minded. Victory at all costs was his early, overarching priority.

The alliance would sustain unstinting diplomacy, negotiations, and compromise. There was little collaboration among the Axis powers. In early December 1941, Russian, British, and American interests fused, as German troops were repelled from the outskirts of Moscow, just days before the Japanese attacked Pearl Harbor. In a press conference at the White House in late December, Churchill declared: "I can't describe the feelings of relief with which I find Russia victorious, the United States and Great Britain standing side by side. It is incredible to anyone who has lived through the lonely months of 1940. It is incredible. Thank God."[12] At the lighting of the White House Christmas tree a few days earlier, Churchill had observed: "I cannot feel myself a stranger here in the center and at the summit of the United States. I feel a sense of unity and fraternal association which, added to the kindliness of your welcome, convinces me that I have a right to sit at your fireside and share your Christmas joys."[13] When Churchill spoke before the U.S. Congress a few days later, he opened by saying: "the fact that my American forebears have for so many generations played their part in the life of the United States and that here I am, an Englishman, welcomed in your midst makes this experience one of the most moving and thrilling of my life."[14]

Two and a half years later, serious disagreement would develop over the planned invasion of southern France, Project ANVIL, which FDR refused to cancel despite Churchill's complaints. The prime minister wrote Roosevelt: "I am sure that if we could have met, as I so frequently proposed, we should have reached a happy agreement. I send you every personal good wish. However we may differ on the conduct of the war, my personal gratitude to you for your kindness to me and all you have done for the cause of freedom will never be diminished."[15] Correspondence sustained the Roosevelt-Churchill relationship. Historian Robert Nisbet observed: "Any reader's first reaction to the two thousand communications, covering nearly six years of war, is one of astonishment that two war leaders could have maintained the high level of civility, of warmth, and of mutual courtesy that are to be found in their voluminous correspondence with each other." Nisbet added: "Courtesy and warmth notwithstanding, there were genuine strains and tensions between the two men."[16]

Cooperation within FDR's administration was as problematic as Allied relations abroad. Inadvertently, Hopkins contributed to Roosevelt's threadbare relationship with the State Department. As long as Hopkins lived in the White House, he remained FDR's primary foreign policy advisor. Other than Harriman, Hopkins was the only American who had an ongoing relationship with both Churchill and Stalin. "Roosevelt handled foreign policy out of his own pocket," observed historians Walter Isaacson and Evan Thomas, and he whimsically changed pockets impulsively. There was, in Roosevelt's intuitive decision-making, an impetuous arrogance. "He could indulge or ignore a Kennan, or a Bohlen, or even an Acheson. Be it at Teheran or Yalta or in the White House Map Room, Roosevelt relied on no State Department briefing books or even a Secretary of State."[17] Hence he was never as well prepared as Churchill and Stalin. Moreover, the president often seemed more interested in appearances than harsh political reality. He concentrated on building a new world organization without mastering what he viewed to be past balance-of-power failures that he believed to be the cause of war. As the Foreign Office's Cadogan observed: "The Americans have an astonishing phobia about 'spheres of influence.'"[18] But American policy indulged the Soviet Union as it established a sphere of influence in Eastern Europe. Indeed, Churchill tended to view "spheres of influence" as stabilizing elements in the anarchy of international politics.

The three Allied foreign ministries played a subordinate role in diplomacy, directed as they were by powerful heads of government—and not by the heads of foreign ministries. The Soviet foreign ministry could not initiate proposals without the explicit approval of Stalin. Deputy Foreign Minister Andrey Vyshinsky told Harriman, in September 1941, that he should not worry about inflexibility of Russian officials; none could decide anything without conferring with Stalin.[19] The indifference of the White House, and the disorder of the State Department and its isolation from FDR, severely limited what American diplomats could do. Foreign Secretary Eden caustically wrote in January 1943: "The Americans don't help themselves but are always ready to criticize the efforts of others."[20] Roosevelt deceived himself that he could co-opt Stalin. However, noted historian Keith Sainsbury, "It is difficult to believe that the Soviet leader ever thought possible the kind of partnership and genuine co-operation between capitalist America and communist Russia which Roosevelt desired."[21] In this observation can be found the secret of Stalin's success. His ideological convictions, his cynical realism, his tenacious focus, and his careful preparation before summits made a mockery of FDR's unprepared, intuitive, airy idealism. As a result, Stalin prevailed in negotiations. Herbert Feis wrote that Stalin "was always measuring Roosevelt and Churchill. He never became so absorbed in his relations with them as to be distracted from essential Soviet purposes." Feis described the murderous Soviet dictator as "opportunist, sly, malevolent, persistent, most skilled in the graduation of pressures, ablest of all dissemblers."[22] Above all, he had committed his life to the revolutionary ideology of global communism.

Cooperation among Allies does require trust, but trust was not part of Joseph Stalin's character. In fact, Russia's murderous Bolshevik regime produced few leaders who trusted one another. "Stalin's whole life and character—and beliefs—would have predisposed him to suspicion of someone who purported to be as frank and unreserved as Roosevelt," wrote historian Keith Sainsbury.[23] In truth, Stalin was shrewd enough to recognize the pretense and purpose in FDR's frankness, charm, and flattery. Stalin saw through the crafty president. The cunning Stalin was more devious than FDR, but he was more disciplined and better informed.[24] For the Russians, the consumption of vodka was also a high priority.[25] Russian social events often turned into drinking contests, in which Anglo-American representatives gave way. After one epic drinking session in November 1943, Ambassador Archibald Clark Kerr reported to London: "They tell me that I left under my own steam, which I find hard to believe, and that Molotov had to be propelled by a large group of his followers." The next day, Molotov told Clark Kerr "that it was a pity we could not have parties like that more often."[26]

The Churchill administration was well organized and better managed than that of FDR. British officials were kept well informed by the prime minister, and he was well informed by them. Such was rarely the case with FDR's official family. During Treasury Secretary Morgenthau's August 1944 trip to Britain, Anthony Eden revealed that he had notes from the Teheran summit—notes to which FDR had denied American cabinet members access. Eden reluctantly acceded to Morgenthau's request to hear some excerpts. When Morgenthau returned to the United States, he met with Roosevelt on August 19 and announced what he had heard, but added that Cordell "Hull told me that he had never been told what was in the minutes of the Teheran meeting." Roosevelt was not pleased, neither by Eden's revelation, nor by Morgenthau's interference in non-Treasury matters. Morgenthau stirred cabinet discontent with FDR's failure to keep them informed. The Treasury secretary wrote that FDR "looked very embarrassed, and I repeated it so that he would be sure to get it."[27] The incident was symptomatic of the paradox that Robert Nisbet described as FDR's "strict avoidance of all experts."[28] Such a habit may have given the president the illusion of self-sufficiency and control, but it created dissension and, worse yet, inadequate preparation for crucial decisions.

At the October 1943 summit of foreign ministers in Moscow, it was Foreign Secretary Eden who often led the discussions. Eden aide Oliver Harvey wrote in his diary on October 22: "Hull takes little part in the discussion, but when he does, he is helpful and even to the point—quite a new Hull. A.E. does practically all. We are carrying the American delegation."[29] The secretary of state went home with a very different recollection of the Moscow meeting: "Eden made a poor impression and Hull reports that Stalin sort of waived [sic] him aside—paid little attention to his proposals or recommendations."[30] Although the foreign ministers made progress on some issues, the tough questions were left for the Teheran summit a few weeks later.

To gain respect and deference among the Anglo-American leaders required political will and political vision executed under stress. Churchill's character epitomized such will and vision. "One must have a bull's eye," Churchill told Violet Bonham Carter in January 1943. "We are fighting this war against Hitler." She responded: "No—against *evil.*"[31] The prime minister had made this point repeatedly. On December 30, 1941, speaking to the Canadian Parliament, Churchill had declared: "There shall be no halting, or half measures, there shall be no compromise, or parley. These gangs of bandits have sought to darken the light of the world. . . . They shall themselves be cast into the pit of death and shame, and only when the earth has been cleansed and purged of their crimes and their villainy shall we turn from the task which they have forced upon us; a task we were reluctant to undertake, but which we shall now most faithfully and punctiliously discharge."[32] Even Churchill critic John Connell wrote: "Churchill's strategic ideas may have been amateurish, his judgment on people and events often mercurial, and his attitude towards senior commanders ambivalent; but his courage and his zest in a dark time were matchless."[33]

Churchill's labors required stamina, bravery, and creativity—each a testimony to his gritty character. There were fifteen Allied summits during World War II—all for the prime minister, just three for Stalin. Historian John Keegan wrote of Churchill: "The necessity for him was to meet the others of the Big Three face-to-face, as often as possible, so that Britain's importance as a combatant, diminishing as it was, might be sustained by treaty or diplomacy. Altogether he met Roosevelt eleven times during the war, always, except at Casablanca, Cairo, Teheran, and Yalta—in North America."[34] Roosevelt and Stalin preferred to stay home, but the older Churchill would undertake the punishing and dangerous missions to reinforce collaboration of the Supreme Command of the alliance. Suggesting that the British leader be awarded the coveted Victoria Cross, the highest military medal of the British Empire, General Douglas MacArthur wrote that "foreign and hostile lands may be the duty of young pilots, but for a Statesman burdened by the world's cares, it is an act of inspiring gallantry and valor." Of the Victoria Cross, MacArthur said: "No one of those who wear it deserves to wear it more than he [Churchill]."[35]

For complete success in war and peace, the presence of profound goodwill and common interests among the Allies would have been necessary, but it was not to be. National interests and personal chemistry often divided the Allies. So did differences of ideology, principle, and strategy. There was much distrust among the Big Three civilian leaders, often more among their military chiefs. Somehow, deep distrust had to be overcome in order to prevail over fierce and determined enemies, Nazi Germany and imperial Japan. One major Allied issue was whether to use precious resources to help countries beleaguered by Germany, such as France, Greece, Russia, and even

Britain, when they seemed to be on the cusp of defeat. Was such help in the national or Allied interest? Would it hurt or help the cause in the long run? "How can we help the French in the battle without hurting ourselves mortally, and in a way that will encourage the French to feel that we are doing all in our power?" inquired Churchill in early June 1940, with French defeat inevitable as the Germans closed in on Paris. The prime minister wanted to help France, but because France had all but given up, Churchill decided he might be "sacrificing its [Britain's] future ability to defend itself."[36] In mid-December 1940, he drafted a telegram for FDR which he never sent: "If you were to 'wash your hands of us' i.e. give us nothing we cannot pay for with suitable [cash] advances, we should certainly not give in, and I believe we could save ourselves and our own National interests for the time being. But we should certainly not be able to beat the Nazi tyranny and gain you the time you require for your re-armament."[37] In May 1941, FDR's election won, Churchill entreated FDR to enter the war: "Mr President, I am sure that you will not misunderstand me if I speak to you exactly what is in my mind. The one decisive counterweight I can see to balance the growing pessimism in Turkey, the Near East, and in Spain would be if United States were immediately to range herself with us as a belligerent power. If this were possible I have little doubt that we could hold the situation in the Mediterranean until the weight of your munitions gained the day."[38]

Churchill found it hard to beg, especially because Britain had to reveal its insolvency—its desperate need for supplies, food, and armaments—while at the very same time convince the United States of its will and ability to carry on. After Pearl Harbor, utter reliance on the United States led to conflicts within the prime minister's government. "For Churchill the important thing remained to do nothing to endanger the Anglo-American alliance," wrote historian David Dutton. "Britain should therefore support the United States to the limit of her ability in the Pacific war. . . . Eden, by contrast, was as sceptical about America's conduct in the Far East as he was about its policy towards [Vichy] France."[39] The prime minister worked day and night to minimize friction, even late in the war, managing the contentious rivalries among American and British generals. Churchill wrote FDR on January 7, 1945: "CIGS [Brooke] and I have passed the last two days with Eisenhower and Montgomery and they both feel the battle very heavy but are confident of success. I hope you understand that, in case any troubles should arise in the press, His Majesty's Government have complete confidence in General Eisenhower and feel acutely any attacks made on him. . . . He and Montgomery are very closely knit and also Bradley and Patton, and it would be disaster which broke up this combination which has, in nineteen forty-four, yielded us results beyond the dreams of military avarice."[40]

Despite the decisive Allied victory, the Anglo-American alliance deteriorated after the war—as it had toward the end of the war. Roosevelt had already undermined Anglo-American negotiating strength in Europe and the Pacific, by emphasizing the return stateside of American soldiers from Europe. FDR wrote Churchill twice in February 1944: "I am absolutely unwilling to police France and possibly Italy and the Balkans as well. After all, France is your baby and will take a lot of nursing in order to bring it to the point of walking alone. It would be very difficult for me to keep in France my military force or management for any length of time."[41] A second time, FDR warned: "Do please don't ask me to keep any American forces in France. I just cannot do it! I would have to bring them all back home. As I suggested before, I denounce and protest the paternity of Belgium, France and Italy. You really ought to bring up and discipline your own children. In view of the fact that they may be your bulwark in future days you should at least pay for their schooling now."[42] Churchill knew too well that FDR wanted to withdraw from Europe. In November 1944, the president told the prime minister: "You know, of course, that after Germany's collapse I must bring American troops home as rapidly as transportation problems will permit."[43] Stalin knew FDR's intentions; they emboldened him.

Roosevelt's policy of withdrawal influenced Foreign Secretary Eden to focus on the future security of Europe. Thus, in August 1944, Eden wrote that "the foundations of our postwar European policy must be the Anglo-Soviet alliance." He saw "no reason why within this framework we should not work to consolidate our position in three groups of European countries with which our relations have been traditionally close and intimate. . . . France, the Low Countries and the Iberian peninsula, especially Portugal; the Scandinavian countries; and the Mediterranean Group, comprising Turkey, Greece, and eventually, Italy." Eden saw clearly the overpowering force of Russian arms in Eastern Europe.[44] American diplomat George Kennan observed: "When it came to Europe, we were sternly insistent that there must be no discussion, while the war was on, of the postwar political and territorial changes. But by virtue of that curious inconsistency which causes Americans to reverse so many principles when the gaze goes westward rather than eastward, all this seems not to have applied to the Far East."[45] Thus at Yalta, FDR was willing to give away pieces of China and Japan to Russia.

As early as 1936, Kennan had concluded there was "little future for Russian-American relations other than a long series of misunderstandings, disappointments and recriminations on both sides."[46] By 1945, the balance of power within the tripartite relationship had passed to Stalin, supported by his armies as far west as Berlin. As usual, the Soviet leader was well informed of British and American thinking. From the vast Soviet espionage network, as well as from the spy reports of physicist Klaus Fuchs, Stalin knew of the development of the atom bomb. In fact, the alliance was unbalanced by a mismatch in intelligence. The Russians had key espionage operatives reporting from high levels within the Washington and London governments on matters that the Americans and British had decided to withhold from the Russians. When Anglo-Americans visited Moscow, their rooms were always bugged, as were their embassies. At the summits of Teheran and Yalta, Stalin was regularly briefed on American and British intentions and plans, the content of the briefings derived from the bugging devices.[47]

Moreover, the Anglo-American diplomats in Russia were prevented from close association with top Russian officials. There was, of course, a serious downside for the Allied cause from this spying, noted historian Donald Gillies: "All the Communist spies of the era produced exactly [the] same result: far from averting schism and maintaining the alliance, their actions gave evidence to Stalin that [Allied] collaboration was limited, and destroyed whatever spirit of goodwill there could have been."[48] Russian spies intensified mistrust by reporting to Moscow what its English-speaking allies were doing and saying. Germany defeated, the question arose within the Moscow government about who would be the next big enemy of the Soviet Union and how strategic advantages might be obtained.[49]

Russian strategy appeared to be better defined than that of either Britain or the United States. Charles Bohlen summarized FDR's position on Europe in a December 1943 memo: "Germany is to be broken up and kept broken up. The states of eastern, southeastern and central Europe will not be permitted to group themselves into any federations or associations. France is to be stripped of her colonies and strategic bases beyond her borders and will not be permitted to maintain any appreciable military establishment. Poland and Italy will remain approximately their present territorial size, but it is doubtful if either will be permitted to maintain any appreciable armed force. The result would be that the Soviet Union would be the only important military and political force on the continent of Europe. The rest of Europe would be reduced to military and political impotence."[50] The shrewd and experienced Bohlen understood the European consequences of FDR's policies. Nothing substantial would stand between the armies of the Soviet Union and the English Channel. Why FDR did not grasp that reality is a mystery. In September 1944, Bohlen's friend Kennan reported to Washington from Moscow about the difficulty of Americans understanding the Russian mind-set: "The apprehension of what is valid in the Russian world is unsettling and displeasing to the American mind."[51]

Russia self-consciously and correctly claimed the majority of credit for containing and destroying German ground forces, invariably demanding more U.S. assistance and support. But Russia would not acknowledge the massive, indispensable Anglo-American aid. When Ambassador Standley in Moscow pushed for more Soviet public recognition in 1943, Lend-Lease legislation then before Congress became problematic. Molotov denied there was a problem. He told Standley: "the Russian people are aware of the receipt of Lend-Lease aid. The man in the street knows by heart the number of tanks and planes we have received from America." Standley rightly denied any such knowledge by ordinary Russians. "You see, Mr. Molotov, the way we look at things in America, good will is a two-way street; only one side of it is being used because the Russian people have been kept from knowing of the sympathy and help which the American people are trying to extend to the Russian people."[52] Abetted by Sumner Welles and the State Department, American journalists portrayed the disagreement as "a great diplomatic blunder." Others like Averell Harriman were "secretly pleased at the way Standley spoke out in Moscow even if this was an indiscretion. The feeling is growing here that we will build trouble for the future if we allow ourselves to be kicked around by the Russians."[53] Thanks to the boldness of Ambassador Standley, the Russians finally gave American aid the public recognition previously denied. British Ambassador Clark Kerr admired Standley, whom he called "the best colleague I have ever had."[54] Distrust of Russia, sublimated during the early war years, grew gradually among American officials as the war neared conclusion.

Roosevelt and Churchill tried to put the best interpretation on the unsatisfactory results of the Yalta summit. Speaking to the House of Commons after he returned from Yalta in February 1945, Churchill said: "I decline absolutely to embark here on a discussion about Russian good faith. It is quite evident that these matters touch the whole future of the world. Sombre indeed would be the fortunes of mankind if some awful schism arose between the Western democracies and the Russian Soviet Union."[55] Churchill wrote, but did not deliver, the following lines: "No one can guarantee the future of the world. There are some who fear it will tear itself to pieces and that an awful lapse in human history may occur. I do not believe it. There must be hope. The alternative is despair, which is madness. The British race has never yielded to counsels of despair."[56] The prime minister would never give up his unflagging effort to prepare the postwar world for a defensible political arrangement, an effort he would continue into his second administration (1951–1955).

At war's end, the threads of trust linking London, Washington, and Moscow were unraveling. "A Soviet foreign policy divorced from the restraining influence of enlightened public opinion and hypersensitive in all matters affecting national prestige is likely to offer serious impediments to the development of postwar inter-allied relations in an atmosphere free from recurring tension," reported Clark Kerr in August 1944.[57] U.S. Ambassador Harriman had become more critical of Stalin's government and more insistent on a firm stand. Talking to State Department colleagues in April 1945, Harriman declared: "We have always dealt directly and fair and with full candor" with the Soviet government. "This the Russians, accustomed to an atmosphere of suspicion and intrigue, do not understand. Furthermore, they have undoubtedly viewed our attitude as a sign of weakness."[58]

In the complex diplomacy among Roosevelt, Stalin, and Churchill, it was the prime minister who worked diligently to mitigate strained relations. "Churchill himself remarked that he had wooed Stalin as a young man might woo a maid, and that no lover had ever studied every whim of his mistress as he had those of Roosevelt," wrote historian Robin Edmonds. "The style of the attitude that he adopted towards Stalin was indeed as nothing by comparison with the degree of deference that he practiced in almost all his exchanges with Roosevelt."[59] Fraser J. Harbutt wrote that the prime minister "was, in many ways, an impressively self-conscious practitioner of the diplomatic arts seemingly called for in a British prime minister trying to maintain himself and his country's fundamental interests in a difficult coalition with two more powerful partners." Deferring important decisions to FDR often led to delay and confusion in the poorly organized Roosevelt administration. The weakened and sick FDR compounded Anglo-American vulnerability to Russian initiatives. For example, key Americans questioned continued aid to both Britain and Russia in 1944–1945. George Kennan, posted to Portugal, Britain, and Russia during the war, later doubted "the decision to continue Lend-Lease aid from the United States to Russia in 1944–1945." Kennan acknowledged "both the overriding compulsion of military necessity under which our statesmen were working and also the depth of their conviction that one had no choice but to gamble on the possibility that Soviet suspicions might be broken down and Soviet collaboration won for the postwar period, if there were to be any hope of permanent peace."[60] So long as FDR presumed Russian aid necessary to defeat Japan, American aid to the Soviet Union would continue.

It was difficult to maintain trust when the Russians bugged Anglo-American offices and residences in Moscow, while maintaining extensive espionage operations in Britain and the United States. Moreover, the Russians practiced a peculiar brand of "good-cop bad-cop" diplomacy, to which Anglo-Americans were not accustomed. In August 1942, British Air Marshal Arthur Tedder accompanied Churchill to Moscow. Tedder grew anxious when Churchill spoke about his contentious talks with Stalin, in the villa to which they had been assigned by the Russian government, which was undoubtedly bugged. Tedder recalled: "Unfortunately in his account of it all to us he rather let himself go, speaking of Stalin as just a peasant whom he, Winston, knew exactly how to handle. Being fairly certain that the whole villa was a network of microphones, I scribbled *mefiez vous* [beware], and passed it to him. He gave me a glare which I shall never forget, but I am afraid it was too late. The damage was done."[61] It was Churchill's first summit with the Soviet dictator. At their second Kremlin session, Stalin predictably had grown more belligerent, as he often did at second meetings with Anglo-American diplomats. Churchill was offended and depressed. British Ambassador Clark Kerr attempted to smooth things over during a walk in the forest away from Soviet ears and bugs in the villa. As Churchill rushed through the woods, the ambassador urged the prime minister to take a different approach. As Clark Kerr recalled: "After the first day when I had watched him use his charm with admirable effect, he had put them all away. His approach to the Russians had become all wrong. What was wrong was that he was an aristocrat and a man of the world and he expected these people to be like him. They weren't. They were straight from the plough or the lathe. They were rough and inexperienced."[62] Some were also ruthless gangsters.

Unlike Roosevelt, who seldom confronted Stalin over difficult issues, Churchill alternated charm and argument in dealing with the Russian leader. But, at the end of the war, the prime minister no longer had any leverage with Stalin. In 1940–1941, he had provided the moral force of the alliance, but in 1945, Churchill led from relative weakness.[63] Allied success had always depended on coordinated reaction, and those actions depended on necessity and trust. But mutual confidence was often in short supply. More importantly, Churchill did not want to believe that by mid-1943, he had played his best cards and his was no longer a strong hand. His ill-advised adventures on obscure islands in the Mediterranean had dissipated some of his credibility with the Americans.[64] American military planners objected to almost any Churchillian idea that deviated from U.S. priorities. Moreover, the military planners led by Marshall were determined to work with FDR, rather than against him as they had in 1942 during the debates over Operation TORCH. The president listened increasingly to his military advisors, less to Churchill. In some ways, Churchill's success with Operation TORCH in 1942, and at the Casablanca summit in 1943, had weakened his influence, because American military authorities resolved not to let the prime minister divert them again from a cross-channel invasion. Latent American and FDR distrust of British imperialism contributed to anti-British feelings.[65]

Churchill's preoccupation with military operations in Italy and his advocacy of island campaigns in the eastern Mediterranean could not be sustained by his relative weakness among the Allied leaders. Americans believed his ideas to be diversions from the main goal—invading northern France and defeating Germany on the ground. Even though the prime minister advocated action that he argued would achieve real results, especially when there were idle war resources, he did not prevail. His strong support for bombing Germany early in the war did prevail when no other means of hitting the Nazis directly was available. However, under changed circumstances, his proposals for diversionary maneuvers in Italy, the Balkans, the Dodecanese islands, and elsewhere in the Mediterranean—when the cross-channel invasion became all-important—undermined his relationships with American decision makers. Even his loyal friend Harry Hopkins became annoyed. Churchill's persistent caution about Operation OVERLORD had diplomatic consequences; FDR "in effect refused to meet Prime Minister alone for any considerable period in advance" of Teheran, wrote historian David Carlton. At Cairo, before the Teheran summit, Admiral William Leahy complained in his diary: "The Prime Minister used every artifice of his charm to induce the President to assist in obtaining from the Chiefs of Staff approval of the British proposal that the Burma Campaign be reduced in order that naval, air and ground forces may be made available for the seizure of Rhodes and other islands in the Aegean Sea. Mr Eden did little to assist him and the President persisted in his stand that promises made to Chiang Kai-shek be fully carried out."[66]

At Cairo in 1943, Churchill had summarized his military program: "Rome in January and Rhodes in February; to renew supplies to the Yugoslavs, settle the Command arrangements, and to open the Ægean, subject to the outcome of an approach to Turkey; all preparations for 'Overlord' to go ahead full steam within the framework of the foregoing policy for the Mediterranean."[67] Of Churchill's Mediterranean strategy, the goal of Rome would be attained five months later than Churchill forecast because of able German generalship and the bravery of crack German troops. At Teheran, Stalin confronted the prime minister directly about Britain's support for OVERLORD. Historian Warren Kimball noted that Stalin saw in Italy what Churchill could not: Hitler would immobilize "as many allied Divisions as possible in Italy where no decision could be reached."[68] The prime minister had told British envoy Harold Macmillan as they flew to Teheran in late 1943: "Germany is finished, though it may take some time to clean up the mess. The real problem is Russia. I *can't* get the Americans to see it."[69] Churchill's tactical military adventures could distract him, but he was already envisioning the Russian problem of postwar Europe. His American partner unwilling to discuss the harsh realities of postwar Europe, Churchill turned to Stalin in 1944 to negotiate some sensitive Eastern European issues.

Suspicions, recriminations, and misunderstandings now characterized the Allied relationships on all sides. Churchill, Roosevelt, and Stalin each had his own hobbyhorses for the postwar world. FDR talked about international organization, a system of trusteeships for colonies, and other areas deemed not ready for self-government. Churchill would support both representative government and monarchies, depending upon the circumstances. He defended the British Empire and its imperial preference system for goods traded within the empire. Roosevelt promised repeatedly to keep Britain apprised of atomic energy research, and then breached the agreement. Neither man had always kept the other informed of every important development. Roosevelt tried to set up a bilateral meeting with Stalin in 1943, without informing Churchill. When Churchill met with Stalin at Moscow in October 1944, he cut his own deals, excluding Harriman, who represented FDR.

The focus of Anglo-American diplomacy meant that certain issues received scant attention. China was not part of Britain's agenda. France was not an FDR priority. Churchill, alienated by de Gaulle, failed to act aggressively enough to build a European alternative to Big Three consensus politics. (Out of office in 1946, he would correct this mistake.) By early 1944, the Russians had taken the military offensive on the eastern front. Thus, they had become less quarrelsome about Anglo-American delays in launching a second front in France, especially as the Soviets saw all of Eastern Europe as a target for occupation and safe buffer zones.

The Soviet Union developed a confident postwar policy based on Stalin's "correlation of forces." As the armed victor who occupied and governed the conquered territory, Russia could easily justify such action on the basis of its immense wartime sacrifices.[70] The cost of victory for the Soviet Union was unique in the history of warfare. Russian historian Roy Medvedev argued that "the Soviet victory cost 20 million lives (or more probably between 25 and 30 million). No less than 10 million came back from the war as invalids."[71] Although the British Empire had sustained the conflict with Germany alone in 1940, the United States after March 1941 supplied the global military effort with food and military equipment. In addition, the United States bankrolled the alliance. But Russia absorbed the most severe impact of the brutal Nazi aggression. As Eden aide Oliver Harvey observed in February 1943: "The Russians are very tiresome allies, importunate, graceless, ungrateful, secretive, suspicious, ever asking for more," but he acknowledged that the Russians were winning the war for Britain.[72]

The strong and resilient egos of the Allied supreme leaders proved a blessing and a curse, but mostly a blessing, in a seven-year international conflict. As historian Richard Hough observed, Churchill's "confidence in his own genius was limitless, his power of application and dedication unsurpassed, his attention to the smallest detail exceeded only by his talent for encompassing, like the sweep of a radar aerial, a complete strategic concept. His sheer physical endurance, remarkable for a man of sixty-five, was quite as great as when he had been at the Admiralty [during World War I] twenty-six years earlier."[73] Because his forecasts were right about some key events, he presumed too often that he would be right about others.

Churchill made himself indispensable, but he needed strong colleagues, not sycophants. "Britain was fortunate during the Second World War in having admirals such as Pound and Cunningham in office, and generals such as Brooke," wrote historian Christopher M. Bell. "These men applied the necessary brakes on numerous occasions, and more than once deflected Churchill from ideas that would have needlessly increased the navy's losses."[74] The Americans generally considered British Chief of the Air Staff Charles Portal the smartest of the British chiefs, and also the easiest to get along with.[75] Historian Vincent Orange wrote: "In his better moments, Portal was one of a handful of officers emerging to meet desperate crises in all three services who had the professional knowledge and personal character to challenge Churchill."[76] The prime minister was also well served by the civilians he sent abroad, such as Mideast representative Harold Macmillan, a future British prime minister, who developed a strong working relationship with Eisenhower, as well as with Robert Murphy, Macmillan's counterpart from the State Department.[77] The outgoing, self-confident Murphy and the reserved, more anxious Macmillan were instrumental in bringing about a "marriage" of Generals Giraud and de Gaulle at the Casablanca summit, and later counseling the French and Italians through rough patches.[78]

As victory came closer, the war aims of the Allies diverged. Roosevelt had agreed with Churchill that the first priority must be to defeat Nazi Germany, but neither man had developed a coherent, accepted plan for postwar Europe. William Manchester and Paul Reid wrote: "Where Roosevelt weighed issues regarding Europe in terms of American politics, Churchill weighed them in terms of Europe, its future, and Britain's role in postwar Europe."[79] From the outset, the prime minister subordinated all priorities—even his long hatred for Bolshevik revolution—to the defeat of Hitler. He stated in June 1941, after Hitler's invasion of Russia: "This is no class war, but a war in which the whole British Empire and Commonwealth of Nations is engaged without distinction of race, creed, or party. It is not for me to speak of the action of the United States, but this I will say: if Hitler imagines that his attack on Soviet Russia will cause the slightest division of aims or slackening of effort in the great Democracies who are resolved upon his doom, he is woefully mistaken."[80] It was in part Churchillian diplomacy and single-mindedness that enabled the alliance with Russia.

The Roosevelt-Churchill marriage had begun as courtship. Then on December 7, 1941, it became a shotgun wedding. FDR must be given credit for initiating the relationship by correspondence. Historian John Keegan noted: "It was Roosevelt who had proposed the creation of a personal relationship, as early as September 11, 1939, and their exchange of letters (two thousand, eventually) and telephone calls had sustained him throughout the hardest years."[81] But it was FDR who caused a growing separation between them, as the American president would woo Russia's dictator from late 1943 to the war's conclusion. Churchill's character was different from that of FDR. Historian Norman Davies noted that Churchill "had practised democratic politics for nearly forty years. He had the constitution of a horse, a head for hard liquor, and a fearless disregard for the quirks of fortune. Psychologically, he was a fighter, a man who could not be bullied, who freely chose his ever more dominant partner. Roosevelt was far more devious, an adept at political marketing, a smooth-talking operator who, by the time of his third term, was confident of his historic mission to bring the USA from Depression to world dominance."[82]

One issue in particular strained U.S.-British relations. As prime minister, Churchill embraced the duty and determination to maintain the integrity of the British Empire and Commonwealth. Roosevelt aimed to disassemble the British Empire. So did the Soviets. John Colville wrote:

> In the last eighteen months of Roosevelt's life, I thought the [previous] open heartedness diminished. By the beginning of 1944, the United States had become the senior partner, even though the British Commonwealth and Empire still had twice as many men in combat with the enemy. Britain had given all she had in five years of war. Her resources were exhausted and it was clear that after the final British effort of sending one million men across the Normandy beaches, almost the entire future supply of material and manpower would have to come from America. The brotherly tone of the President's messages seemed to change: there were times when I thought others might have drafted them, and this became a certainty after the Second Quebec Conference as Roosevelt grew increasingly frail.[83]

The alliance grew weaker as FDR weakened; Churchill much less so. "From the Quebec conference onward," historian John Keegan wrote, "Churchill was increasingly to find himself the odd man out among the Big Three. The change of status was demeaning, however successfully he disguised it in public and from himself."[84]

Churchill worked at building the Anglo-American relationship more intensely than did Roosevelt. Speaking to a group of American officials at a British embassy lunch in May 1943, Churchill observed: "I could see small hope for the world unless the United States and the British Commonwealth worked together in fraternal association." However, the numbers told their own story. Colville wrote: "At the end of the war the RAF and the US Army Air Force had each dropped approximately 680,000 tons of bombs on Germany, and over Europe as a whole the RAF had lost 10,800 aircraft against America's 8300. The British and the Americans both had approximately one million men on French soil during the summer of 1944 and, in the Far East, the British Imperial Forces guarding India and fighting Japan in Burma were as numerous as the Americans deployed in the whole Pacific theatre of war."[85] Britain was small and insolvent, America large and rich. Colville's point was relative British sacrifices exceeded those of the United States.[86]

Among the Allies, there continued to be moments of rhetorical optimism, such as Churchill's comment to Parliament on February 27, 1945, regarding Russia, despite his private doubts of Soviet Russia: "The impression I brought back from the Crimea [Yalta], and from all my other contacts, is that Marshall Stalin and the Soviet leaders wish to live in honourable friendship and equality with the Western democracies. I feel also that their word is also their bond. I know of no government which stands to its obligations . . . more solidly than the Russian Soviet government."[87] This misleading bromide came shortly after Churchill had been heartened by his successful peacemaking in Greece, which Stalin had accepted in accordance with their October 1944 agreement. But in London and Washington, reality soon set in again as the Russians broke all their pledges in Poland. When news of FDR's death on April 12 reached the prime minister, Churchill bodyguard Walter H. Thompson listened to a tearful prime minister ruminate about his friend: "No one realized what that man meant to the country. No Englishman can ever quite know it altogether. They can only half sense it. Perhaps, in time. In later years."[88] No other Englishman could know it fully, because no Englishman but Churchill brought FDR into an intimate Anglo-American alliance.

At the formal surrender of Germany in Berlin, early on the morning of May 9, 1945, Allied differences nearly derailed the ceremony. British Air Marshal Arthur Tedder was Eisenhower's trusted representative. He insisted that American Carl Spaatz and Frenchman Jean de Lattre de Tassigny also sign the surrender. Deputy Russian Foreign Minister Andrey Vyshinsky objected. "We have to have an American name because 140,000,000 people are involved and we have to have France because 40,000,000 are involved," declared Tedder. "We have three flags to consider, you have one." Vyshinsky finally agreed that the American and French signatures could be affixed just below that of Tedder and Russian Marshal Georgy Zhukov. The division of East and West could be foreseen in this dispute. The next day, General Eisenhower responded to a congratulatory note from First Sea Lord Cunningham:

> [J]ust the other day someone asked me what particular period I would probably remember longest in this war. The subject was intriguing enough to demand an hour's conversation and out of it I came to the conclusion that the hours that you and I spent together in the dripping tunnels of Gibraltar will probably remain as long in my memory as will any other. It was there I first understood the indescribable and inescapable strain that comes over one when his part is done—when the issue rests with fate and the fighting men he has committed to action.[89]

Along the road to Allied victory, there were plenty of grievous misjudgments. For example, in the 1930s, Churchill, then a supporter of the early expansion of the British air force, had declared that "an aeroplane cannot sink a battleship . . . because the armour is too thick."[90] In early 1938, Churchill said: "The air menace against properly-armed and protected ships of war will not be of a decisive character."[91] World War II naval warfare proved Churchill wrong. Stalin refused to believe authentic warnings from numerous sources, in the spring of 1941, that a German invasion was imminent. Stalin's myopia caused disaster and death to strike the Russian people. Churchill's scientific advisor thought the German V1 and V2 weapons were fantasies. They were only too real for the residents of southern England. "The [atom] bomb will never go off," said U.S. Admiral William Leahy, "and I speak as an expert on explosives."[92] Air Marshal Arthur Harris convinced himself that unrestrained bombing could defeat Germany. Admiral Andrew Cunningham noted at a meeting in May 1944, just weeks before D-Day: "Bomber Harris complained what a nuisance this Overlord operation was and how it interfered with the right way to defeat Germany, i.e., by bombing."[93]

Churchill did forecast the ultimate victory of the Anglo-American-Russian alliance. Despite mistrust, spying, and divergent national interests, the ground-sea-air alliance held together. "No one could, alone, have brought about this result," General Eisenhower told an elite London audience on June 12, 1945. "Had I possessed the military skill of a Marlborough, the wisdom of Solomon, the understanding of Lincoln, I still would have been helpless without the loyalty, the vision, the generosity of thousands upon thousands of British and Americans. Some of them were my companions in the high command, many were enlisted men and junior officers carrying the fierce brunt of the battle, and many others were back in the U.S. and here in Great Britain, in London. Moreover, back of us were always our great national war leaders and their civil and military staffs that supported and encouraged us through every trial, every test. The whole was one great team."[94] General Brooke, never an Eisenhower fan, commented in his diary: "Ike made a *wonderful* speech and impressed all hearers in the Guildhall including the Cabinet. . . . I had never realized that Ike was as big a man until his performance today."[95] As Eisenhower himself would write a friend several months later: "War is a matter of teamwork!"[96]

Acknowledgments

I acknowledge with gratitude my outstanding readers—Larry Arnn, James Basker, Richard Carwardine, Thomas Lehrman, Andrew Roberts, Nicole Seary, and Frank Trotta. The reach of their scholarship, the clarity of their advice and recommendations have proved invaluable. There are others to whom I am grateful, men who were not readers of this volume: Professor Robin Winks with whom, long ago, I studied as a Carnegie Teaching Fellow at Yale. He was a scholar of British Imperial and Commonwealth history at Yale; Correlli Barnett, an outstanding British imperial and military historian, received me at Churchill College, Cambridge with great generosity. He is the former keeper of the Churchill Archives at Churchill College, Cambridge University. When I was a Woodrow Wilson Fellow at Harvard, Professor Frank Freidel shared his incomparable research on FDR; Professor Merle Fainsod his mastery of Soviet history in the twentieth century.

Larry Arnn carries on the monumental work of Randolph Churchill and Martin Gilbert, for whom he was director of research. He is now completing the vast, official, multi-volume biography of Winston Spencer Churchill with 19 volumes of supporting original documents. It was through Larry Arnn that I came to know Martin Gilbert, a biographer and historian with few peers. Professor James Basker, president of the Gilder Lehrman Institute, a master of the English language, has combed this book with his well-tutored eye. Professor Richard Carwardine is the emeritus Rhodes Professor of American History at Oxford University. He is a prize-winning biographer of Abraham Lincoln, and he is also engaged in twentieth-century Anglo-American history. Thomas Lehrman, my son, has the eye and the touch of a fact-based historian; he specializes in the history of science and technology, intellectual history, and the history of economic thought; he is a careful reader, with no fear of his father's reaction to shrewd criticisms. Professor Andrew Roberts of King's College London, in the opinion of fellow scholars, on both sides of the Atlantic, is one of the great masters of modern and military history; he is a rigorous reader, with a matchless command of the period upon which this book concentrates. Nicole Seary of the Gilder Lehrman Institute is surely one of the best copyeditors. Her painstaking preliminary copyedit was deeply appreciated. At Stackpole Books, Judith Schnell, David Reisch, and Stephanie Otto, publisher and editors, have been indispensable. They are masters of the craft of publishing; Dave Reisch, himself, is an expert in the historical period of this book. As they surely know, I am grateful for their every effort and support. My copyeditor at Stackpole, Amy Rafferty, was outstanding, calling my attention to errors of all types.

In one of my previous books, *Lincoln at Peoria* (the history of Mr. Lincoln's anti-slavery campaign from 1854 until 1865), I did acknowledge many men and women to whom I am still very grateful. Their influence carries on indirectly into *Churchill, Roosevelt & Company: Studies in Character and Statecraft.* It goes without saying that those named in the bibliography of *Churchill, Roosevelt & Company* and in its end-notes are scholars and writers to whom I am also indebted.

Richard Behn, my research associate, was a crucial ally in the plumbing of the vast research material available in primary and secondary sources. Our problem consisted in selection and limitation. I am only too aware how much more there is to study. I am ever grateful to the staff in my business office who carry on when I must disappear to study, to write, and to edit: Deja Hickcox, Mary MacKenzie, Steve Szymanski, Susan Tang, and Frank Trotta (a very careful reader, too). Deja Hickcox and Susan Tang coordinated my work with the readers and publishers, making my labors on this book the more efficient.

Many thanks also to David Dilks, accomplished author of *Churchill and Company*, whose title gave me the idea to call this book *Churchill, Roosevelt & Company: Studies in Character and Statecraft.*

The unstinting efforts of my readers and editors, my friends and colleagues, have helped me to avoid errors of commission and omission.

All remaining errors are mine alone.

Lewis E. Lehrman

Appendix A

At the Beginning

Fireside Chat by Franklin D. Roosevelt on the Cusp of War: "Arsenal of Democracy" (December 29, 1940)

My friends:

This is not a fireside chat on war. It is a talk on national security, because the nub of the whole purpose of your President is to keep you now, and your children later, and your grandchildren much later, out of a last-ditch war for the preservation of American independence and all of the things that American independence means to you and to me and to ours.

Tonight, in the presence of a world crisis, my mind goes back eight years to a night in the midst of a domestic crisis. It was a time when the wheels of American industry were grinding to a full stop, when the whole banking system of our country had ceased to function.

I well remember that while I sat in my study in the White House, preparing to talk with the people of the United States, I had before my eyes the picture of all those Americans with whom I was talking. I saw the workmen in the mills, the mines, the factories; the girl behind the counter; the small shopkeeper; the farmer doing his spring plowing; the widows and the old men wondering about their life's savings.

I tried to convey to the great mass of American people what the banking crisis meant to them in their daily lives.

Tonight, I want to do the same thing, with the same people, in this new crisis which faces America.

We met the issue of 1933 with courage and realism.

We face this new crisis—this new threat to the security of our nation—with the same courage and realism.

Never before since Jamestown and Plymouth Rock has our American civilization been in such danger as now.

For, on September 27th, 1940, this year, by an agreement signed in Berlin, three powerful nations, two in Europe and one in Asia, joined themselves together in the threat that if the United States of America interfered with or blocked the expansion program of these three nations—a program aimed at world control—they would unite in ultimate action against the United States.

The Nazi masters of Germany have made it clear that they intend not only to dominate all life and thought in their own country, but also to enslave the whole of Europe, and then to use the resources of Europe to dominate the rest of the world.

It was only three weeks ago their leader stated this: "There are two worlds that stand opposed to each other." And then in defiant reply to his opponents, he said this: "Others are correct when they say: With this world we cannot ever reconcile ourselves. . . . I can beat any other power in the world." So said the leader of the Nazis.

In other words, the Axis not merely admits but the Axis proclaims that there can be no ultimate peace between their philosophy of government and our philosophy of government.

In view of the nature of this undeniable threat, it can be asserted, properly and categorically, that the United States has no right or reason to encourage talk of peace, until the day shall come when there is a clear intention on the part of the aggressor nations to abandon all thought of dominating or conquering the world.

At this moment, the forces of the states that are leagued against all peoples who live in freedom are being held away from our shores. The Germans and the Italians are being blocked on the other side of the Atlantic by the British, and by the Greeks, and by thousands of soldiers and sailors who were able to escape from subjugated countries. In Asia the Japanese are being engaged by the Chinese nation in another great defense.

In the Pacific Ocean is our fleet.

Some of our people like to believe that wars in Europe and in Asia are of no concern to us. But it is a matter of most vital concern to us that European and Asiatic war-makers should not gain control of the oceans which lead to this hemisphere.

One hundred and seventeen years ago the Monroe Doctrine was conceived by our Government as a measure of defense in the face of a threat against this hemisphere by an alliance in Continental Europe. Thereafter, we stood (on) guard in the Atlantic, with the British as neighbors. There was no treaty. There was no "unwritten agreement."

And yet, there was the feeling, proven correct by history, that we as neighbors could settle any disputes in peaceful fashion. And the fact is that during the whole of this time the Western Hemisphere has remained free from aggression from Europe or from Asia.

Does anyone seriously believe that we need to fear attack anywhere in the Americas while a free Britain remains our most powerful naval neighbor in the Atlantic? And does anyone seriously believe, on the other hand, that we could rest easy if the Axis powers were our neighbors there?

If Great Britain goes down, the Axis powers will control the continents of Europe, Asia, Africa, Australia, and the high seas—and they will be in a position to bring enormous military and naval resources against this hemisphere. It is no exaggeration to say that all of us, in all the Americas, would be living at the point of a gun—a gun loaded with explosive bullets, economic as well as military.

We should enter upon a new and terrible era in which the whole world, our hemisphere included, would be run by threats of brute force. And to survive in such a world, we would have to convert ourselves permanently into a militaristic power on the basis of war economy. Some of us like to believe that even if (Great) Britain falls, we are still safe, because of the broad expanse of the Atlantic and of the Pacific.

But the width of those oceans is not what it was in the days of clipper ships. At one point between Africa and Brazil the distance is less from Washington than it is from Washington to Denver, Colorado—five hours for the latest type of bomber. And at the North end of the Pacific Ocean America and Asia almost touch each other.

Why, even today we have planes which could fly from the British Isles to New England and back again without refueling. And remember that the range of the modern bomber is ever being increased.

During the past week many people in all parts of the nation have told me what they wanted me to say tonight. Almost all of them expressed a courageous desire to hear the plain truth about the gravity of the situation. One telegram, however, expressed the attitude of the small minority who want to see no evil and hear no evil, even though they know in their hearts that evil exists. That telegram begged me not to tell again of the ease with which our American cities could be bombed by any hostile power which had gained bases in this Western Hemisphere. The gist of that telegram was: "Please, Mr. President, don't frighten us by telling us the facts."

Frankly and definitely there is danger ahead—danger against which we must prepare. But we well know that we cannot escape danger, or the fear of danger, by crawling into bed and pulling the covers over our heads.

Some nations of Europe were bound by solemn non-intervention pacts with Germany. Other nations were assured by Germany that they need never fear invasion. Non-intervention pact or not, the fact remains that they were attacked, overrun, thrown into the modern form of slavery at an hour's notice, or even without any notice at all. As an exiled leader of one of these nations said to me the other day, "The notice was a minus quantity. It was given to my Government two hours after German troops had poured into my country in a hundred places."

The fate of these nations tells us what it means to live at the point of a Nazi gun.

The Nazis have justified such actions by various pious frauds. One of these frauds is the claim that they are occupying a nation for the purpose of "restoring order." Another is that they are occupying or controlling a nation on the excuse that they are "protecting it" against the aggression of somebody else.

For example, Germany has said that she was occupying Belgium to save the Belgians from the British. Would she then hesitate to say to any South American country, "We are occupying you to protect you from aggression by the United States?"

Belgium today is being used as an invasion base against Britain, now fighting for its life. And any South American country, in Nazi hands, would always constitute a jumping-off place for German attack on any one of the other republics of this hemisphere.

Analyze for yourselves the future of two other places even nearer to Germany if the Nazis won. Could Ireland hold out? Would Irish freedom be permitted as an amazing pet exception in an unfree world? Or the Islands of the Azores which still fly the flag of Portugal after five centuries? You and I think of Hawaii as an outpost of defense in the Pacific. And yet, the Azores are closer to our shores in the Atlantic than Hawaii is on the other side.

There are those who say that the Axis powers would never have any desire to attack the Western Hemisphere. That is the same dangerous form of wishful thinking which has destroyed the powers of resistance of so many conquered peoples. The plain facts are that the Nazis have proclaimed, time and again, that all other races are their inferiors and therefore subject to their orders. And most important of all, the vast resources and wealth of this American Hemisphere constitute the most tempting loot in all of the round world.

Let us no longer blind ourselves to the undeniable fact that the evil forces which have crushed and undermined and corrupted so many others are already within our own gates. Your Government knows much about them and every day is ferreting them out.

Their secret emissaries are active in our own and in neighboring countries. They seek to stir up suspicion and dissension to cause internal strife. They try to turn capital against labor, and vice versa. They try to reawaken long slumbering racist and religious enmities which should have no place in this country. They are active in every group that promotes intolerance. They exploit for their own ends our own natural abhorrence of war. These trouble-breeders have but one purpose. It is to divide our people, to divide them into hostile groups and to destroy our unity and shatter our will to defend ourselves.

There are also American citizens, many of them in high places, who, unwittingly in most cases, are aiding and abetting the work of these agents. I do not charge these American citizens with being foreign agents. But I do charge them with doing exactly the kind of work that the dictators want done in the United States.

These people not only believe that we can save our own skins by shutting our eyes to the fate of other nations. Some of them go much further than that. They say that we can and should become the friends and even the partners of the Axis powers. Some of them even suggest that we should imitate the methods of the dictatorships. But Americans never can and never will do that.

The experience of the past two years has proven beyond doubt that no nation can appease the Nazis. No man can tame a tiger into a kitten by stroking it. There can be no appeasement with ruthlessness. There can be no reasoning with an incendiary bomb. We know now that a nation can have peace with the Nazis only at the price of total surrender.

Even the people of Italy have been forced to become accomplices of the Nazis, but at this moment they do not know how soon they will be embraced to death by their allies.

The American appeasers ignore the warning to be found in the fate of Austria, Czechoslovakia, Poland, Norway, Belgium, the Netherlands, Denmark and France.

They tell you that the Axis powers are going to win anyway; that all of this bloodshed in the world could be saved, that the United States might just as well throw its influence into the scale of a dictated peace, and get the best out of it that we can.

They call it a "negotiated peace." Nonsense! Is it a negotiated peace if a gang of outlaws surrounds your community and on threat of extermination makes you pay tribute to save your own skins?

Such a dictated peace would be no peace at all. It would be only another armistice, leading to the most gigantic armament race and the most devastating trade wars in all history. And in these contests the Americas would offer the only real resistance to the Axis powers.

With all their vaunted efficiency, with all their parade of pious purpose in this war, there are still in their background the concentration camp and the servants of God in chains.

The history of recent years proves that the shootings and the chains and the concentration camps are not simply the transient tools but the very altars of modern dictatorships. They may talk of a "new order" in the world, but what they have in mind is only a revival of the oldest and the worst tyranny. In that there is no liberty, no religion, no hope.

The proposed "new order" is the very opposite of a United States of Europe or a United States of Asia. It is not a government based upon the consent of the governed. It is not a union of ordinary, self-respecting men and women to protect themselves and their freedom and their dignity from oppression. It is an unholy alliance of power and pelf to dominate and to enslave the human race.

The British people and their allies today are conducting an active war against this unholy alliance. Our own future security is greatly dependent on the outcome of that fight. Our ability to "keep out of war" is going to be affected by that outcome.

Thinking in terms of today and tomorrow, I make the direct statement to the American people that there is far less chance of the United States getting into war if we do all we can now to support the nations defending themselves against attack by the Axis than if we acquiesce in their defeat, submit tamely to an Axis victory, and wait our turn to be the object of attack in another war later on.

If we are to be completely honest with ourselves, we must admit that there is risk in any course we may take. But I deeply believe that the great majority of our people agree that the course that I advocate involves the least risk now and the greatest hope for world peace in the future.

The people of Europe who are defending themselves do not ask us to do their fighting. They ask us for the implements of war, the planes, the tanks, the guns, the freighters which will enable them to fight for their liberty and for our security. Emphatically we must get these weapons to them, get them to them in sufficient volume and quickly enough, so that we and our children will be saved the agony and suffering of war which others have had to endure.

Let not the defeatists tell us that it is too late. It will never be earlier. Tomorrow will be later than today.

Certain facts are self-evident.

In a military sense Great Britain and the British Empire are today the spearhead of resistance to world conquest. And they are putting up a fight which will live forever in the story of human gallantry.

There is no demand for sending an American Expeditionary Force outside our own borders. There is no intention by any member of your Government to send such a force. You can, therefore, nail, nail any talk about sending armies to Europe as deliberate untruth.

Our national policy is not directed toward war. Its sole purpose is to keep war away from our country and away from our people.

Democracy's fight against world conquest is being greatly aided, and must be more greatly aided, by the rearmament of the United States and by sending every ounce and every ton of munitions and supplies that we can possibly spare to help the defenders who are in the front lines. And it is no more unneutral for us to do that than it is for Sweden, Russia and other nations near Germany to send steel and ore and oil and other war materials into Germany every day in the week.

We are planning our own defense with the utmost urgency, and in its vast scale we must integrate the war needs of Britain and the other free nations which are resisting aggression.

This is not a matter of sentiment or of controversial personal opinion. It is a matter of realistic, practical military policy, based on the advice of our military experts who are in close touch with existing warfare. These military and naval experts and the members of the Congress and the Administration have a single-minded purpose—the defense of the United States.

This nation is making a great effort to produce everything that is necessary in this emergency—and with all possible speed. And this great effort requires great sacrifice.

I would ask no one to defend a democracy which in turn would not defend everyone in the nation against want and privation. The strength of this nation shall not be diluted by the failure of the Government to protect the economic well-being of its citizens.

If our capacity to produce is limited by machines, it must ever be remembered that these machines are operated by the skill and the stamina of the workers. As the Government is determined to protect the rights of the workers, so the nation has a right to expect that the men who man the machines will discharge their full responsibilities to the urgent needs of defense.

The worker possesses the same human dignity and is entitled to the same security of position as the engineer or the manager or the owner. For the workers provide the human power that turns out the destroyers, and the planes and the tanks. The nation expects our defense industries to continue operation without interruption by strikes or lockouts. It expects and insists that management and workers will reconcile their differences by voluntary or legal means, to continue to produce the supplies that are so sorely needed. And on the economic side of our great defense program, we are, as you know, bending every effort to maintain stability of prices and with that the stability of the cost of living.

Nine days ago I announced the setting up of a more effective organization to direct our gigantic efforts to increase the production of munitions. The appropriation of vast sums of money and a well coordinated executive direction of our defense efforts are not in themselves enough. Guns, planes, ships and many other things have to be built in the factories and the arsenals of America. They have to be produced by workers and managers and engineers with the aid of machines which in turn have to be built by hundreds of thousands of workers throughout the land.

In this great work there has been splendid cooperation between the Government and industry and labor, and I am very thankful.

American industrial genius, unmatched throughout all the world in the solution of production problems, has been called upon to bring its resources and its talents into action. Manufacturers of watches, of farm implements, of linotypes, and cash registers, and automobiles, and sewing machines, and lawn mowers and locomotives are now making fuses, bomb packing crates, telescope mounts, shells, and pistols and tanks.

But all of our present efforts are not enough. We must have more ships, more guns, more planes—more of everything. And this can only be accomplished if we discard the notion of "business as usual." This job cannot be done merely by superimposing on the existing productive facilities the added requirements of the nation for defense.

Our defense efforts must not be blocked by those who fear the future consequences of surplus plant capacity. The possible consequences of failure of our defense efforts now are much more to be feared.

And after the present needs of our defense are past, a proper handling of the country's peacetime needs will require all of the new productive capacity—if not still more.

No pessimistic policy about the future of America shall delay the immediate expansion of those industries essential to defense. We need them.

I want to make it clear that it is the purpose of the nation to build now with all possible speed every machine, every arsenal, every factory that we need to manufacture our defense material. We have the men—the skill—the wealth—and above all, the will.

I am confident that if and when production of consumer or luxury goods in certain industries requires the use of machines and raw materials that are essential for defense purposes, then such production must yield, and will gladly yield, to our primary and compelling purpose.

So I appeal to the owners of plants—to the managers—to the workers—to our own Government employees—to put every ounce of effort into producing these munitions swiftly and without stint. With this appeal I give you the pledge that all of us who are officers of your Government will devote ourselves to the same whole-hearted extent to the great task that lies ahead.

As planes and ships and guns and shells are produced, your Government, with its defense experts, can then determine how best to use them to defend this hemisphere.

The decision as to how much shall be sent abroad and how much shall remain at home must be made on the basis of our overall military necessities.

We must be the great arsenal of democracy. For us this is an emergency as serious as war itself. We must apply ourselves to our task with the same resolution, the same sense of urgency, the same spirit of patriotism and sacrifice as we would show were we at war.

We have furnished the British great material support and we will furnish far more in the future. There will be no "bottlenecks" in our determination to aid Great Britain. No dictator, no combination of dictators, will weaken that determination by threats of how they will construe that determination.

The British have received invaluable military support from the heroic Greek army and from the forces of all the governments in exile. Their strength is growing. It is the strength of men and women who value their freedom more highly than they value their lives.

I believe that the Axis powers are not going to win this war. I base that belief on the latest and best of information.

We have no excuse for defeatism. We have every good reason for hope—hope for peace, yes, and hope for the defense of our civilization and for the building of a better civilization in the future.

I have the profound conviction that the American people are now determined to put forth a mightier effort than they have ever yet made to increase our production of all the implements of defense, to meet the threat to our democratic faith.

As President of the United States I call for that national effort. I call for it in the name of this nation which we love and honor and which we are privileged and proud to serve. I call upon our people with absolute confidence that our common cause will greatly succeed.

Appendix B

At the End

BBC Broadcast by Winston S. Churchill: "Five Years of War" (May 13, 1945)

It was five years ago on Thursday last that His Majesty the King commissioned me to form a National Government of all parties to carry on our affairs. Five years is a long time in human life, especially when there is no remission for good conduct. However, aided by loyal and capable colleagues and sustained by the entire British nation at home and all our fighting men abroad, and with the unswerving cooperation of the Dominions far across the oceans and of our Empire in every quarter of the globe, it became clear last week that things had worked out pretty well and that the British Commonwealth and Empire stands more united and more effectively powerful than at any time in its long romantic history. Certainly we were in a far better state to cope with the problems and perils of the future than we were five years ago.

For a while our prime enemy, our mighty enemy, Germany, overran almost all Europe. France, who bore such a frightful strain in the last great war was beaten to the ground and took some time to recover. The Low Countries, fighting to the best of their strength, were subjugated. Norway was overrun. Mussolini's Italy stabbed us in the back when we were, as he thought, at our last gasp. But for ourselves, our lot, I mean the British Commonwealth and Empire, we were absolutely alone.

In July, August, and September, 1940, forty or fifty squadrons of British fighter aircraft broke the teeth of the German air fleet at odds of seven or eight to one in the Battle of Britain. Never before in the history of human conflict was so much owed by so many to so few. The name of Air Chief Marshal Lord Dowding will ever be linked with this splendid event. But conjoined with the Royal Air Force lay the Royal Navy, ever ready to tear to pieces the barges, gathered from the canals of Holland and Belgium, in which an invading army could alone have been transported. I was never one to believe that the invasion of Britain would be an easy task. With the autumn storms, the immediate danger of invasion in 1940 had passed.

Then began the blitz, when Hitler said he would rub out our cities. This was borne without a word of complaint or the slightest signs of flinching, while a very large number of people—honor to them all—proved that London could take it and so could the other ravaged centers.

But the dawn of 1941 revealed us still in jeopardy. The hostile aircraft could fly across the approaches to our island, where 46,000,000 people had to import half their daily bread and all the materials they need for peace or war, from Brest to Norway in a single flight or back again, observing all the movements of our shipping in and out of the Clyde and Mersey and directing upon our convoys the large and increasing numbers of U-boats with which the enemy bespattered the Atlantic—the survivors or successors of which are now being collected in British harbors.

The sense of envelopment, which might at any moment turn to strangulation, lay heavy upon us. We had only the northwestern approach between Ulster and Scotland through which to bring in the means of life and to send out the forces of war. Owing to the action of Mr. de [Eamon] Valera, so much at variance with the temper and instinct of thousands of southern Irishmen, who hastened to the battlefront to prove their ancient valor, the approaches which the southern Irish ports and airfields could so easily have guarded were closed by the hostile aircraft and U-boats.

This was indeed a deadly moment in our life, and if it had not been for the loyalty and friendship of Northern Ireland we should have been forced to come to close quarters with Mr. de Valera or perish forever from the earth. However, with a restraint and poise to which, I say, history will find few parallels, we never laid a violent hand upon them, which at times would have been quite easy and quite natural, and left the de Valera Government to frolic with the German and later with the Japanese representatives to their heart's content.

When I think of these days I think also of other episodes and personalities. I do not forget Lieutenant-Commander Esmonde, V.C., D.S.O., Lance-Corporal Keneally, V.C., Captain Fegen, V.C., and other Irish heroes that—I could easily recite, and all bitterness by Britain for the Irish race dies in my heart. I can only pray that in years which I shall not see the shame will be forgotten and the glories will endure, and that the peoples of the British Isles and of the British Commonwealth of Nations will walk together in mutual comprehension and forgiveness.

My friends, we will not forget the devotion of our merchant seamen, the vast, inventive, adaptive, all-embracing and, in the end, all-controlling power of the Royal Navy, with its ever more potent new ally, the air, which have kept the life-line open. We were able to breathe; we were able to live; we were able to strike. Dire deeds we had to do. The destruction or capture of the French fleet which, had it ever passed into German hands would, together with the Italian fleet, have perhaps enabled the German Navy to face us on the high seas. The dispatch to Wavell all round the Cape at our darkest hour, of tanks—practically all we had in the island—enabled us as far back as November, 1940, to defend Egypt against invasion and hurl back with the loss of a quarter of a million captives the Italian armies at whose tail Mussolini had planned a ride into Cairo or Alexandria.

Great anxiety was felt by President Roosevelt, and indeed by thinking men throughout the United States, about what would happen to us in the early part of 1941. This great President felt to the depth of his being that the destruction of Britain would not only be a fearful event in itself, but that it would expose to mortal danger the vast and as yet largely unarmed potentialities and future destiny of the United States.

He feared greatly that we should be invaded in that spring of 1941, and no doubt he had behind him military advice as good as any in the world, and he sent his recent Presidential opponent, Mr. Wendell Willkie, to me with a letter in which he had written in his own hand the famous lines of Longfellow, which I quoted in the House of Commons the other day:

> Sail on, O Ship of State!
> Sail on, O Union strong and great!
> Humanity with all its fears,
> With all the hopes of future years,
> Is hanging breathless on thy fate!

We were in a fairly tough condition by the early months of 1941 and felt very much better about ourselves than in the months immediately after the collapse of France. Our Dunkirk army and field force troops in Britain, almost a million strong, were nearly all equipped or reequipped. We had ferried over the Atlantic a million rifles and a thousand cannon from the United States, with all their ammunition, since the previous June.

In our munition works, which were becoming very powerful, men and women had worked at their machines till they dropped senseless with fatigue. Nearly one million of men, growing to two millions at the peak, working all day had been formed into the Home Guard, armed at least with rifles and armed also with the spirit "Conquer or Die."

Later in 1941, when we were still all alone, we sacrificed, to some extent unwillingly, our conquests of the winter in Cyrenaica and Libya in order to stand by Greece, and Greece will never forget how much we gave, albeit unavailingly, of the little we had. We did this for honor. We repressed the German-instigated rising in Iraq. We defended Palestine. With the assistance of General de Gaulle's indomitable Free French we cleared Syria and the Lebanon of Vichyites and of German intrigue. And then in June, 1941, another tremendous world event occurred.

You have no doubt noticed in your reading of British history that we have sometimes had to hold out all alone, or to be the mainspring of coalitions, against a Continental tyrant or dictator for quite a long time—against the Spanish Armada, against the might of Louis XIV, when we led Europe for nearly twenty-five years under William III and Marlborough and 130 years ago, when Pitt, Wellington, and Nelson broke Napoleon, not without the assistance of the heroic Russians of 1812. In all these world wars our island kept the lead of Europe or else held out alone.

And if you hold out alone long enough there always comes a time when the tyrant makes some ghastly mistake which alters the whole balance of the struggle. On

June 22, 1941, Hitler, master as he thought himself of all Europe, nay indeed soon to be, he thought, master of the world, treacherously, without warning, without the slightest provocation, hurled himself on Russia and came face to face with Marshal Stalin and the numberless millions of the Russian people. And then at the end of the year Japan struck her felon blow at the United States at Pearl Harbor, and at the same time attacked us in Malaya and at Singapore. Thereupon Hitler and Mussolini declared war on the republic of the United States.

Years have passed since then. Indeed every year seems to me almost a decade. But never since the United States entered the war have I had the slightest doubt but that we should be saved and that we had only to do our duty in order to win. We have played our part in all this process by which the evildoers have been overthrown. I hope I do not speak vain or boastful words. But from Alamein in October, 1942, through the Anglo-American invasion of North Africa, of Sicily and of Italy, with the capture of Rome, we marched many miles and never knew defeat.

And then last year, after two years' patient preparation and marvelous devices of amphibious warfare—in my view our scientists are not surpassed by any nation, specially when their thought is applied to naval matters—last year on June 6 we seized a carefully selected little toe of German-occupied France and poured millions in from this island and from across the Atlantic until the Seine, the Somme, and the Rhine all fell behind the advancing Anglo-American spearheads. France was liberated. She produced a fine Army of gallant men to aid her own liberation. Germany lay open.

And now from the other side, from the East, the mighty military achievements of the Russian people, always holding many more German troops on their front than we could do, rolled forward to meet us in the heart and center of Germany. At the same time in Italy Field-Marshal Alexander's Army of so many nations, the largest part of which was British or British Empire, struck their final blow and compelled more than 1,000,000 enemy troops to surrender. This Fifteenth Army Group, as we call it, are now deep in Austria joining their right hand with the Russians and their left with the United States Armies under General Eisenhower's command.

It happened that in three days we received the news of the unlamented departures of Mussolini and Hitler, and in three days also surrenders were made to Field-Marshal Alexander and Field-Marshal Montgomery of over 2,500,000 soldiers of this terrible warlike German Army.

I shall make it clear at this moment that we have never failed to recognize the immense superiority of the power used by the United States in the rescue of France and the defeat of Germany.

For our part we have had in action about one-third as many men as the Americans, but we have taken our full share of the fighting, as the scale of our losses shows. Our Navy has borne incomparably the heavier burden in the Atlantic Ocean, in the narrow seas and Arctic convoys to Russia, while the United States Navy has used its massive strength mainly against Japan. It is right and natural that we should extol the virtues and glorious services of our own most famous commanders, Alexander and Montgomery, neither of whom was ever defeated since they began together at

Alamein, both of whom had conducted in Africa, in Italy, in Normandy and in Germany battles of the first magnitude and of decisive consequences. At the same time we know how great is our debt to the combining and unifying of the command and high strategic direction of General Eisenhower.

Here is the moment when I must pay my personal tribute to the British Chiefs of the Staff with whom I have worked in the closest intimacy throughout these hard years. There have been very few changes in this powerful and capable body of men who, sinking all Service differences and judging the problems of the war as a whole, have worked together in the closest harmony with each other. In Field-Marshal Brooke, Admiral Pound, Admiral Andrew Cunningham, and Marshal of the R.A.F. Portal a power was formed who deserved the highest honor in the direction of the whole British war strategy and its agreement with that of our Allies.

It may well be said that never have the forces of two nations fought side by side and intermingled into line of battle with so much unity, comradeship, and brotherhood as in the great Anglo-American army. Some people say, "Well, what would you expect, if both nations speak the same language and have the same outlook upon life with all its hope and glory." Others may say, "It would be an ill day for all the world and for the pair of them if they did not go on working together and marching together and sailing together and flying together wherever something has to be done for the sake of freedom and fair play all over the world."

There was one final danger from which the collapse of Germany has saved us. In London and the southeastern counties we have suffered for a year from various forms of flying bombs and rockets and our Air Force and our Ack-Ack Batteries have done wonders against them. In particular the Air Force, turned on in good time on what then seemed very slight and doubtful evidence, vastly hampered and vastly delayed all German preparations.

But it was only when our Armies cleaned up the coast and overran all the points of discharge, and when the Americans captured vast stores of rockets of all kinds near Leipzig, and when the preparations being made on the coasts of France and Holland could be examined in detail, that we knew how grave was the peril, not only from rockets and flying bombs but from multiple longrange artillery.

Only just in time did the Allied Armies blast the viper in his nest. Otherwise the autumn of 1944, to say nothing of 1945, might well have seen London as shattered as Berlin. For the same period the Germans had prepared a new U-boat fleet and novel tactics which, though we should have eventually destroyed them, might well have carried anti-U-boat warfare back to the high peak days of 1942. Therefore we must rejoice and give thanks not only for our preservation when we were all alone but for our timely deliverance from new suffering, new perils not easily to be measured.

I wish I could tell you tonight that all our toils and troubles were over. Then indeed I could end my five years' service happily, and if you thought you had had enough of me and that I ought to be put out to grass, I assure you I would take it with the best of grace. But, on the contrary, I must warn you, as I did when I began this five years' task—and no one knew then that it would last so long—that there is still a lot to do and that you must be prepared for further efforts of mind and body and further sacrifices to great causes if you are not to fall back into the rut of inertia, the confusion of aim, and the craven fear of being great. You must not weaken in any way in your alert and vigilant frame of mind, and though holiday rejoicing is necessary to the human spirit, yet it must add to the strength and resilience with which every man and woman turns again to the work they have to do, and also to the outlook and watch they have to keep on public affairs.

On the continent of Europe we have yet to make sure that the simple and honorable purposes for which we entered the war are not brushed aside or overlooked in the months following our success, and that the words freedom, democracy, and liberation are not distorted from their true meaning as we have understood them. There would be little use in punishing the Hitlerites for their crimes if law and justice did not rule, and if totalitarian or police governments were to take the place of the German invaders.

We seek nothing for ourselves. But we must make sure that those causes which we fought for find recognition at the peace table in facts as well as words, and above all we must labor that the world organization which the United Nations are creating at San Francisco, does not become an idle name; does not become a shield for the strong and a mockery for the weak. It is the victors who must search their hearts in their glowing hours and be worthy by their nobility of the immense forces that they wield.

We must never forget that beyond all lurks Japan, harassed and failing but still a people of a hundred millions, for whose warriors death has few terrors. I cannot tell you tonight how much time or what exertions will be required to compel them to make amends for their odious treachery and cruelty. We have received—like China so long undaunted—we have received horrible injuries from them ourselves, and we are bound by the ties of honor and fraternal loyalty to the United States to fight this great war at the other end of the world at their side without flagging or failing.

We must remember that Australia, New Zealand, and Canada were and are all directly menaced by this evil Power. They came to our aid in our dark times, and we must not leave unfinished any task which concerns their safety and their future. I told you hard things at the beginning of these last five years; you did not shrink, and I should be unworthy of your confidence and generosity if I did not still cry, "Forward, unflinching, unswerving, indomitable, till the whole task is done and the whole world is safe and clean."

Endnotes

The bibliography incorporates, by reference, all books, articles, and essays in these endnotes.

THE HISTORICAL RECORD

1. Richard Langworth, ed, *Churchill by Himself*, p. 275 (May 7, 1941).
2. *Public Papers of the Presidents of the United States: F. D. Roosevelt, 1943*, Volume 12, p. 81.
3. Mark A. Stoler, *George C. Marshall, Soldier-Statesman of the American Century*, p. 129 (Marshall to Churchill, April 3, 1945).
4. Winston S. Churchill, *Their Finest Hour: The Second World War*, Volume II, p. 5.
5. Martin S. Gilbert, *Winston S. Churchill: Finest Hour, 1939–1941*, p. 413.
6. Mark A. Stoler, *George C. Marshall, Soldier-Statesman of the American Century*, p. 103.
7. Carlo D'Este, *Eisenhower: A Soldier's Life*, p. 424.
8. After participation in the British cabinet during World War I, Lord Beaverbrook wrote *Politicians and the Press* and *Politicians and the War.* After World War II, Beaverbrook wrote *Men and Power 1917–1918* and *The Decline and Fall of Lloyd George.*
9. FDR's speeches were the joint work product of himself, Samuel I. Rosenman, Robert E. Sherwood, Harry Hopkins, and other aides. Samuel I. Rosenman, *Working with Roosevelt*, p. 317. Robert E. Sherwood, *Roosevelt and Hopkins: An Intimate History*, pp. 183–184.
10. Donald E. Moggridge, *Maynard Keynes: An Economist's Biography*, p. xv.
11. "I calculate his total of words in print, including published speeches, to be between 8 and 10 million." Paul Johnson, p. 11. A study by Churchill scholar Richard Langworth found about 15 million published words. http://www.winstonchurchill.org/resources/quotations/quotes-falsely-attributed.
12. David Dilks observed that Churchill's "letters and minutes, and the records of meetings, are far fuller and more revealing than a diary." David Dilks, *Churchill and Company*, p. 43.
13. Martin S. Gilbert, *Winston S. Churchill: Finest Hour, 1939–1941*, p. 15.

14. Martin S. Gilbert, *Winston S. Churchill: Finest Hour, 1939–1941*, p. 274.

15. John Colville, *The Fringes of Power: The Incredible Inside Story of Winston Churchill*, p. 309 (December 12, 1940).

16. Isaiah Berlin, *Personal Impressions*, p. 22.

17. Urged to keep a journal in 1942, Marshall rejected the advice: "Such a practice tends to cultivate a state of mind unduly concerned with possible investigations rather than a complete concentration on the business of victory." Andrew Roberts, *Masters and Commanders*, p. 23.

18. David Dilks, ed, *The Diaries of Sir Alexander Cadogan, O.M., 1938–1945*, p. 407 (September 29, 1941).

19. David Dilks, ed, *The Diaries of Sir Alexander Cadogan, O.M., 1938–1945*, p. 16.

20. David Dilks, ed, *The Diaries of Sir Alexander Cadogan, O.M., 1938–1945*, p. 720 (February 22, 1945).

21. James Leutze, ed, *The London Observer: The Journal of General Raymond E. Lee*, p. 356 (September 17, 1940).

22. James Leutze, ed, *The London Observer: The Journal of General Raymond E. Lee*, p. 340 (July 15, 1941).

23. John Oliver, ed, *The War Diaries of Oliver Harvey, 1941–1945*, p. 176 (November 3, 1943).

24. Donald Gillies, *Radical Diplomat: The Life of Archibald Clark Kerr, Lord Inverchapel, 1882–1951*, p. 130.

25. Will Brownell and Richard N. Billings, *So Close to Greatness: A Biography of William C. Bullitt*, pp. 270–280.

26. Diaries of Henry Morgenthau Jr., April 27, 1933–July 27, 1945: Franklin D. Roosevelt Presidential Library & Museum, http://www.fdrlibrary.marist.edu/archives/collections/franklin/index.php?p=collections/findingaid&id=535.

27. Breckinridge Long wrote in his diary on February 7, 1941: Hull "is much worried about the British—thinks they are in a *very* bad way and are *very* stupid." In January 1942, after Hull experienced rebuffs from Roosevelt over the Free French takeover of the St. Pierre and Miquelon islands off Canada, and from Churchill over Hull's attempt to insert free-trade language in the Lend-Lease agreement, Hull went into a deep funk, during which he prepared to leave office. He told Assistant Secretary Long that Churchill was "selfish, vindictive, vicious." Fred L. Israel, ed, *The War Diary of Breckinridge Long: Selections from the Years, 1939–1944*, pp. 175, 242.

28. Fraser J. Harbutt, *Yalta 1945: Europe and America at the Crossroads*, p. 240.

29. Winston S. Churchill, *The Hinge of Fate: The Second World War*, Volume IV, p. 616. John Colville wrote that Churchill told him in late 1952, after Eisenhower had been elected president: "he must omit part of what he intended to include in Volume VI of his war history. He could no longer tell in full the story of how the United States, to please the Russians, gave away vast tracts of territory they had occupied and how suspicious they were of his pleas for caution." John Colville, *Winston Churchill and His Inner Circle*, p. 135.

30. Winston S. Churchill, *Their Finest Hour: The Second World War*, Volume II, p. 143.

31. Albert Resis, ed, *Molotov Remembers: Inside Kremlin Politics*, p. 59.

32. Albert Resis, ed, *Molotov Remembers*, pp. 21, 23.

33. "TOP GENERAL: ZHUKOV," *TIME*, February 21, 1955, http://content.time.com/time/subscriber/article/0,33009,892966-1,00.html. Zhukov had no contact with Anglo-American officials until the very end of the war, when he participated in surrender ceremonies and got to know Allied commander Dwight D. Eisenhower.

34. Roy Medvedev, *Let History Judge: The Origins and Consequences of Stalinism*, pp. 768–769. (from A. M. Vasilevsky, *Delo vsei zhizni*, pp. 126–127).

35. Richard Evans, *The Third Reich in History and Memory*; and Andrew Roberts, *The Storm of War*, *passim*.

36. Stalin biographer Robert Service wrote that Stalin would not "witness conditions at the front; indeed he scarcely left Moscow apart from completely unavoidable trips to the Allied conferences at Tehran and Yalta. While urging audacity upon his commanders, he took no risks with his personal security." When he did go near the front in 1942, Stalin remained thirty miles away from military action and "never saw a shot fired." Robert Service, *Stalin: A Biography*, pp. 456–457.

37. Medvedev quoted a top Russian military official, Nikolay N. Voronov: "I rarely saw Stalin in the first days of the war. He was depressed, nervous, and off balance. When he gave assignments, he demanded that they be completed in an unbelievably short time, without considering real possibilities. In the first weeks of the war, in my opinion, he misconceived the scale of the war, and the forces and equipment that could actually stop the advancing enemy on a front stretching from sea to sea." Roy Medvedev, *Let History Judge: The Origins and Consequences of Stalinism*, pp. 770, 757.

38. Ivan Maisky, *Memoirs of a Soviet Ambassador: The War, 1939–1943*, p. 231. Maisky's detailed London diaries, *The Maisky Diaries: Red Ambassador to the Court of St James's, 1932–1943*, were edited by Gabriel Gorodetsky in 2015.

39. Albert Resis, ed, *Molotov Remembers*, p. 69.

40. Roy Medvedev, *Let History Judge: The Origins and Consequences of Stalinism*, p. 769.

41. Albert Resis, ed, *Molotov Remembers*, p. 69.

42. Historian David Reynolds wrote out in the sixth book of Churchill's series on *The Second World War*: "Churchill's main object in *Triumph and Tragedy* was to prove that he had been a far-sighted prophet of the Soviet threat" and to paint the Americans as naive. "This was not easy, for two reasons. First, he had been in charge of British foreign policy in 1944–1945, carving up the Balkans with Stalin in Moscow in October and reaching a Polish settlement with him at Yalta the following February. . . . Second, he wanted to shift responsibility for Western mistakes onto the Americans." David Reynolds, *In Command of History*, p. 436.

43. John Lewis Gaddis, *The Cold War*, pp. 16–25.

44. Fraser J. Harbutt, *Yalta 1945: Europe and America at the Crossroads*, p. 46.

45. Fraser J. Harbutt, *Yalta 1945: Europe and America at the Crossroads*, p. 50.

46. Warren Kimball, *Forged in War: Roosevelt, Churchill, and the Second World War*, p. 14.

47. Baron Charles McMoran Wilson Moran, *Churchill: Taken from the Diaries of Lord Moran: The Struggle for Survival, 1940–1965*, p. 193.

48. Charles Bohlen, *Witness to History*, p. 137. Although he did not like others to have records of their meetings with him, Roosevelt had a recording system installed in his office so that the president could have a record of exactly what was said. Joseph Persico, *Roosevelt's Secret War: FDR and World War II Espionage*, p. 40.

49. Winston S. Churchill, *Their Finest Hour: The Second World War*, Volume II, p. 17 (Churchill to Hastings Ismay, July 19, 1940).

50. Martin S. Gilbert, *Winston S. Churchill: Road to Victory 1941–1945*, p. 139.

51. Isaiah Berlin, *Personal Impressions*, p. 6.

52. Martin S. Gilbert, ed, *Winston Churchill: The Power of Words*, p. 273 (Speech to House of Commons, November 12, 1940).

53. Walter Reid, *Churchill: 1940–1945, Under Friendly Fire*, p. 145.

54. Richard M. Langworth, *The Definitive Wit of Winston Churchill*, pp. 82–83.
55. Winston S. Churchill, *The Grand Alliance: The Second World War*, Volume II, p. 20.
56. John Martin, *Downing Street: The War Years*, p. 39.
57. Robert H. Ferrell, *The Dying President: Franklin D. Roosevelt, 1944–1945*, p. 143.
58. David Reynolds, *In Command of History: Churchill Fighting and Writing the Second World War*, p. 520.
59. Richard Langworth, ed, *Churchill by Himself*, p. 288 (May 13, 1945).

FORMER NAVAL PERSONS: WINSTON AND FRANKLIN

1. Winston S. Churchill, *Their Finest Hour*, Volume II, p. 198.
2. *The Public Papers and Addresses of Franklin D. Roosevelt, 1940: War and Aid to Democracies*, p. 261 (Address at the University of Virginia, June 10, 1940).
3. David Dilks, ed, *The Diaries of Sir Alexander Cadogan, O.M., 1938–1945*, p. 663 (September 10, 1944).
4. Ben Pimlott, ed, *The Second World War Diary of Hugh Dalton, 1940–45*, p. 693 (January 1–2, 1944).
5. Jonathan Rose, *The Literary Churchill: Author, Reader, Actor*, p. 297.
6. Churchill biographer Martin Gilbert wrote that in July 1940, "Churchill's confidence was reflected in his private conversation. Commenting at Chequers . . . on the much anticipated invasion, he said that he thought it 'highly unlikely', and added: 'Hitler must invade or fail. If he fails he is bound to go east and fail he will.'" Martin S. Gilbert, *Winston S. Churchill: Finest Hour, 1939–1941*, p. 663. Hitler issued his invasion orders on July 16: "Since England, in spite of her hopeless military situation, shows no signs of being ready to come to an understanding, I have decided to prepare a landing operation against England, and, if necessary, to carry it out." Martin S. Gilbert, *Winston S. Churchill: Finest Hour, 1939–1941*, p. 668. The Battle of Britain commenced in earnest in August. Churchill wrote FDR in early October 1940: "I cannot feel that the invasion danger is passed. The gent has taken off his clothes and put on his bathing suit, but the water is getting colder and there is an autumn nip in the air." Warren Kimball, ed, *Churchill & Roosevelt: The Complete Correspondence*, Volume I, p. 74 (Churchill to Roosevelt, October 4, 1940).
7. John Kennedy, *The Business of War: The War Narrative of Major-General Sir John Kennedy*, p. 156.
8. Louis Adamic, *Dinner at the White House*, p. 66. Eleanor Roosevelt, who invited Adamic, was chagrined by his book, which she called "anti-British and anti-Churchill." Eleanor Roosevelt, *This I Remember*, p. 246.
9. John Colville, *The Fringes of Power: The Incredible Inside Story of Winston Churchill*, p. 122 (May 10, 1940).
10. David Dilks, *Churchill and Company*, p. 54.
11. Gabriel Gorodetsky, ed, *Maisky Diaries: Red Ambassador to the Court of St. James's 1932–1943*, p. 318 (November 4, 1940, based on a conversation on July 3, 1940).
12. Martin S. Gilbert, *Winston S. Churchill, Finest Hour, 1939–1941*, p. 358.
13. Shortly after Pearl Harbor, recalled General Alan Brooke, "someone [at a British COS meeting] was still adopting the careful attitude that had been necessary before the entry of the USA to ensure that we did not let ourselves into a war with Japan without the USA being in it. Winston turned to him, and with a wicked leer in his eye, said: 'Oh! That is the way

we talked to her while we were wooing her; now that she is in the harem we talk to her quite differently!'" Alex Danchev and Daniel Todman, eds, *War Diaries, 1939–1945: Field Marshal Lord Alanbrooke*, p. 209.

14. John Lukacs, *The Duel: 10 May–31 July 1940: The Eighty-Day Struggle Between Churchill and Hitler*, p. 220.

15. Henry L. Stimson and McGeorge Bundy, *On Active Service in Peace and War*, p. 429. *Foreign Relations of the United States: Conferences at Washington and Quebec, 1943*, p. 444.

16. Paul Addison, *Churchill: The Unexpected Hero*, p. 180.

17. David Lawrence, *Diary of a Washington Correspondent*, p. 311 (December 31, 1942).

18. Roosevelt ingratiated himself with Churchill by commenting in his letter: "I am glad you did the Marlboro [Marlborough] volumes before this thing started—and I much enjoyed reading them." Warren Kimball, *Forged in War: Roosevelt, Churchill, and the Second World War*, p. 31 (Roosevelt to Churchill, September 11, 1939).

19. Jon Meacham, *Franklin and Winston: An Intimate Portrait of an Epic Friendship*, p. 37.

20. Roosevelt's trip to California, Hawaii, and Alaska in the summer of 1944 exemplified his mastery of the dramatic. Jonathan W. Jordan wrote that it was Roosevelt's "way of dramatizing his role as commander-in-chief—and making sure the voters knew who was calling the shots." Jonathan W. Jordan, *American Warlords: How Roosevelt's High Command Led America to Victory in World War II*, p. 379.

21. Meeting FDR for the first time in August 1941, British Foreign Under-Secretary Alexander Cadogan, normally a tough observer of humanity, thought FDR "has great, and natural, charm." David Dilks, ed, *The Diaries of Sir Alexander Cadogan, O.M., 1938–1945*, p. 397.

22. Richard Snow, *A Measureless Peril: America in the Fight for the Atlantic, the Longest Battle of World War II*, p. 108. In November 1942, Secretary Stimson described one unproductive meeting at the White House, which "had all the typical difficulties of a discussion in the Roosevelt Cabinet. The President was constantly interrupting me with discursive stories which popped into his mind while we were talking, and it was very hard to keep a steady thread." Nigel Hamilton, *The Mantle of Command: FDR at War, 1941–1942*, p. 414 (November 6, 1942).

23. Samuel I. Rosenman, *Working with Roosevelt*, p. 355.

24. Winston S. Churchill, *The Hinge of Fate: The Second World War*, Volume IV, p. 713.

25. In 1944, after his dismissal as commerce secretary, Jesse Jones observed that Roosevelt was a "hypocrite . . . lacking in character, but you just can't help liking that fellow." Conrad Black, *Franklin Delano Roosevelt: Champion of Freedom*, p. 1042. Dean Acheson, who served as a high-ranking official at both the State and Treasury Departments under Roosevelt, observed after his death that FDR's "responses seemed too quick, his reasons too facile for considered judgement; one could not tell what lay beneath them. He remained a formidable man, a leader who won admiration and respect. In others, he inspired far more, affection and devotion." Dean Acheson, *Morning and Noon*, p. 165. Acheson's relationship with Roosevelt was complicated. "I respected his ability to rule, but I did not like him." Walter Isaacson and Evan Thomas, *The Wise Men: Six Friends and the World They Made*, pp. 136. State Department official Charles Bohlen concluded: "Among those who worked with him in the White House for long periods of time, there was real affection for him, but not the kind of human feeling that springs from personal love." Charles Bohlen, *Witness to History: 1929–1969*, p. 210.

26. Winston S. Churchill, *The Hinge of Fate: The Second World War*, Volume IV, p. 62.

27. Susan Ware, *Partner and I: Molly Dewson, Feminism, and New Deal Politics*, p. 237.

28. Conrad Black, *Franklin Delano Roosevelt: Champion of Freedom*, p. 1118.

29. Warren Kimball, ed, *Churchill & Roosevelt: The Complete Correspondence*, Volume I, p. 123 (Churchill to Roosevelt, December 31, 1940).

30. Frances Perkins, *The Roosevelt I Knew*, p. 33. Chief of Naval Operations Harold Stark similarly reported that FDR "could sit and plot all the towns that would be passed on a flight down Brazil and over to India." Joseph Persico, *Roosevelt's Secret War*, p. 84. General Dwight D. Eisenhower observed that Roosevelt "amazed me with his intimate knowledge of world geography." Dwight D. Eisenhower, *Crusade in Europe*, p. 218. Anthony Eden took a much more skeptical view of FDR's geographical knowledge. "Roosevelt was familiar with the history and geography of Europe. Perhaps his hobby of stamp-collecting had helped him to this knowledge, but the academic yet sweeping opinions which he built upon it were alarming in their cheerful fecklessness. He seemed to see himself disposing of the fate of many lands, allied no less than enemy." Anthony Eden, *The Reckoning: The Memoirs of Anthony Eden, Earl of Avon*, p. 433.

Roosevelt's geographic knowledge could be problematic, even a mark of vanity. In October 1943, FDR told Secretary of State Cordell Hull that as a result of his childhood trips through Germany, he was more familiar with the country than Hull. On the way to the Teheran summit in November, FDR carved up Germany on a map from *National Geographic*. Michael Beschloss, *The Conquerors*, pp. 20, 22. When it came to finding a site for the second tripartite Allied summit, Stettinius wrote that FDR "studied maps to find a possible location for the next conference at a warm-weather port in Russian territory." Edward R. Stettinius Jr., *Roosevelt and the Russians: The Yalta Conference*, p. 23.

31. Nigel Hamilton, *The Mantle of Command*, pp. 150–152.

32. Some of Roosevelt's knowledge of Germany came from bicycle trips he took while his parents summered at Bad Nauheim in an attempt to restore the health of FDR's father. Geoffrey C. Ward, *Before the Trumpet: Young Franklin Roosevelt*, p. 176.

33. Robert Dallek, *Franklin Roosevelt and American Foreign Policy, 1932–1945*, pp. 5–7.

34. Winston S. Churchill, *Their Finest Hour: The Second World War*, Volume II, p. 489.

35. David Kaiser, *No End Save Victory: How FDR Led the Nation into War*, pp. 237, 203.

36. James Leasor, *War at the Top: The Experiences of General Sir Leslie Hollis, KCB KBE*, p. 63.

37. Ronald Lewin, *Churchill as Warlord*, p. 11.

38. Warren Kimball, *The Juggler: Franklin Roosevelt as Wartime Statesman*, p. 7 (Henry Morgenthau, May 15, 1942). After Roosevelt's death, Douglas MacArthur quipped that FDR was "a man who would never tell the truth when a lie would serve him just as well." Mark Perry, *The Most Dangerous Man in America*, p. 328.

39. Robert Dallek, *Franklin Roosevelt and American Foreign Policy, 1932–1945*, p. 355.

40. Harold LeClair Ickes, *The Secret Diary of Harold L. Ickes*, Volume II, p. 659. Aide Samuel I. Rosenman wrote that FDR's "unwillingness to be unpleasantly frank was notorious among those who knew him well. But it was a characteristic that visitors who came to see him with new ideas or suggestions sometimes had to learn the hard way. They often left his office thinking they had convinced him of the soundness of their views, when what had happened was that he had refrained from telling them frankly that he disagreed with them. By smiling and nodding, and saying, 'I see,' or 'That's very interesting,' or 'Thanks for taking the trouble to come in and give me your slant on this' . . . he would have given them the impression that he had been completely convinced." Samuel I. Rosenman, *Working with Roosevelt*, p. 440.

41. Anthony Eden, *The Reckoning: The Memoirs of Anthony Eden, Earl of Avon*, p. 433.

42. Lord Halifax argued that "Winston's virtues were, in a sense, a handicap when we came to present our case in Washington in the war years. The Americans had never met anyone like him. He seemed to them a museum piece, a rare relic." Baron Charles McMoran Wilson Moran, *Churchill: Taken from the Diaries of Lord Moran: The Struggle for Survival, 1940–1965*, p. 791 (July 3, 1958).

43. James MacGregor Burns, *Roosevelt: The Soldier of Freedom*, p. 9.

44. Isaiah Berlin, *Personal Impressions*, p. 17.

45. During the abdication crisis of 1936, Clementine Churchill had quipped that her husband was "the last believer in the Divine Right of Kings." John Pearson, *The Private Lives of Winston Churchill*, p. 283.

46. Churchill complained to Bernard Baruch in June 1940: "We shall be all right here but your people are not doing much. . . . If things go wrong with us it will be bad for them." Martin S. Gilbert, *Winston S. Churchill: Finest Hour, 1939–1941*, p. 607 (June 28, 1940).

47. Joseph Persico, *Roosevelt's Centurions: FDR and the Commanders He Led to Victory in World War II*, p. 176.

48. One contemporary wrote of Churchill's recruitment of Lindemann for the Admiralty in 1939: "It was not enough, amid the heavy pressure of his duties at the Admiralty, to have a cursory knowledge of matters outside his province; he wanted to have a deeply critical knowledge, and what better person to aid him towards getting than the Prof?" Martin S. Gilbert, *Winston S. Churchill: Finest Hour, 1939–1941*, p. 49. In early September 1940, Churchill told Lindemann: "This was a war of science, a war which could be won with new weapons." John Colville, *The Fringes of Power: The Incredible Inside Story of Winston Churchill*, p. 238 (September 1, 1940).

49. At the beginning of the war, Churchill was reluctant to rush to share British military innovations with U.S. authorities. Martin Gilbert wrote that after Lindemann proposed giving the Americans British secrets "to get *immediate delivery* of a thousand or more" Noreen bomb-sights, Churchill refused, saying: "I am waiting for a further development of the American attitude." Martin S. Gilbert, *Winston S. Churchill: Finest Hour, 1939–1941*, p. 474.

50. Warren Kimball, *Forged in War: Roosevelt, Churchill, and the Second World War*, p. 19.

51. Elliott Roosevelt, *As He Saw It*, p. 19.

52. H. W. Brands, *Traitor to His Class: The Privileged Life and Radical Presidency of Franklin Delano Roosevelt*, p. 630.

53. Merriman Smith, *Thank You, Mr. President: A White House Notebook*, p. 54.

54. Merriman Smith, *Thank You, Mr. President*, p. 68.

55. Robert E. Sherwood, *Roosevelt and Hopkins: An Intimate History*, p. 157.

56. Historian James MacGregor Burns wrote that FDR "seemed unduly sensitive to both congressional and public opinion; he used public opinion polls much more systematically than was realized at the time, even to the point one time of polling people on the question of who should succeed Knox as Secretary of the Navy." James MacGregor Burns, *Roosevelt: The Soldier of Freedom*, p. 607.

57. Winston S. Churchill, *Closing the Ring: The Second World War*, Volume V, p. 123.

58. W. Averell Harriman and Elie Abel, *Special Envoy to Churchill and Stalin, 1941–1946*, p. 216.

59. John Q. Barrett, ed, *That Man: An Insider's Portrait of Franklin D. Roosevelt*, p. 15.

60. James MacGregor Burns, *Roosevelt: the Lion and the Fox*, p. 84.

61. Theodore H. White, ed, *The Stilwell Papers*, pp. 13–16 (December 27, 1941). Two years later, the curmudgeonly Stilwell emerged from a meeting with FDR in Cairo, equally

disillusioned because the president had reneged on a promise to initiate a plan to open up a route to China through Burma. "The man is a flighty fool. Christ, but he's terrible." Jonathan W. Jordan, *American Warlords: How Roosevelt's High Command Led America to Victory in World War II*, p. 313.

62. Robert Dallek, *Franklin D. Roosevelt and American Foreign Policy, 1932–1945*, p. 322.

63. Gustavus Ohlinger, "Winston Spencer Churchill: A Midnight Interview," *Michigan Quarterly Review*, Volume 5, No. 2, p. 76.

64. Randolph acknowledged his difficulty "living under the shadow of the great oak tree—the small sapling, so close to the parent tree." Randolph Spencer Churchill, *Twenty-One Years*, p. 136.

65. R. Crosby Kemper II, ed, *Winston Churchill: Resolution, Defiance, Magnanimity, Good Will*, p. 120 (John R. Colville, "The Personality of Winston Churchill").

66. Isaiah Berlin, *Personal Impressions*, p. 21.

67. Robert E. Sherwood, *Roosevelt and Hopkins: An Intimate History*, p. 9.

68. Keith Eubank, *Summit at Teheran*, p. 351. At the Yalta summit, for example, when Churchill started to talk about Poland, FDR wrote a note to Secretary of State Stettinius: "Now we are in for ½ hour of it." Edward R. Stettinius Jr., *Roosevelt and the Russians: The Yalta Conference*, p. 185.

69. Alex Danchev and Daniel Todman, eds, *War Diaries, 1939–1945: Field Marshal Lord Alanbrooke*, p. 544.

70. John Lukacs, *The Duel: 10 May–31 July 1940: The Eighty-Day Struggle Between Churchill and Hitler*, p. 22.

71. Richard Holmes, *Churchill's Bunker*, p. 109.

72. Warren Kimball, *Forged in War: Roosevelt, Churchill, and the Second World War*, pp. 18–19.

73. Robert E. Sherwood, *Roosevelt and Hopkins: An Intimate History*, p. 209.

74. Arthur M. Schlesinger Jr., *The Coming of the New Deal: 1933–1935, The Age of Roosevelt*, Volume II, p. 528. Isaiah Berlin noted: "Roosevelt believed in flexibility, improvisation, the fruitfulness of using persons and resources in an infinite variety of new and unexpected ways; his bureaucracy was somewhat chaotic, perhaps deliberately so. His own office was not tidily organized, he practiced a highly personal form of government. He maddened the advocates of institutional authority, but it is doubtful whether he could have achieved his ends in any other way." Surely Berlin, an academic intellectual, was wrong in this assertion that there was not "any other way." Isaiah Berlin, *Personal Impressions*, p. 21.

75. Arthur Krock, *Memoirs: Sixty Years on the Firing Line*, p. 202.

76. Robert Skidelsky, *John Maynard Keynes: Fighting for Freedom, 1937–1946*, pp. 115–116.

77. John Harvey, ed, *War Diaries of Oliver Harvey*, p. 32 (August 15, 1941).

78. General Leslie Hollis recalled: "In the middle [between the Americans and Churchill] stood Brooke, backing Churchill against the often naïve ideas of the Americans, and backing himself against Churchill's own ambitious projects." James Leasor, *War at the Top: The Experiences of General Sir Leslie Hollis, KCB KBE*, pp. 11, 168, 225.

79. Winston S. Churchill, *The Hinge of Fate: The Second World War*, Volume IV, p. 339.

80. Doris Kearns Goodwin, *No Ordinary Time*, p. 411.

81. James MacGregor Burns, *Roosevelt: The Lion and the Fox*, pp. 382–383.

82. Frances Perkins, *The Roosevelt I Knew*, p. 362.

83. Constitutional historian Ivor Jennings wrote: "Mr. Churchill was not a dictator. He had not even the personal power of the President of the United States. Anything that

was physically possible was politically practicable to him, but only because he had a united War Cabinet, a united Parliament, and a united people behind him. He had therefore to observe the constitutional forms: he needed the consent of his colleagues in Cabinet, and the Cabinet was dependent upon the unswerving support of the House of Commons." Ivor Jennings, *Cabinet Government*, pp. 197–198. Harry Hopkins observed the difference between the British and American leadership styles at the Placentia Bay conference, where "Roosevelt was completely on his own" and "Churchill was constantly reporting to and consulting the War Cabinet in London." Robert E. Sherwood, *Roosevelt and Hopkins: An Intimate History*, p. 361.

84. Simon Berthon, *Allies at War: The Bitter Rivalry among Churchill, Roosevelt and de Gaulle*, p. 284 (Churchill to Harold Macmillan, June 1943).

85. Jean Edward Smith, *FDR*, p. 578. "Since Churchill knew of Roosevelt's habits of going to bed early, he made a pretense of retiring himself at a fairly reasonable hour," wrote Robert E. Sherwood of Churchill's first visit to the White House, "but Roosevelt knew that his tireless guest and Hopkins would go on talking and he did not want to miss any of it so he stayed up much later than usual." Robert E. Sherwood, *Roosevelt and Hopkins: An Intimate History*, p. 442.

86. Baron Charles McMoran Wilson Moran, *Churchill: Taken from the Diaries of Lord Moran: The Struggle for Survival, 1940–1965*, p. 791 (July 3, 1958).

87. John Q. Barrett, ed, *That Man: An Insider's Portrait of Franklin D. Roosevelt*, p. 15.

88. U.S. envoy W. Averell Harriman was one of Churchill's favorite partners for bezique. "Over the course of the war, he and Churchill played hundreds of hours in good times and bad—in the garden of Chequers, at Churchill's hideaway at Chartwell, in heavy seas crossing the Atlantic, on the Prime Minister's train, and aboard thundering America bombers," wrote Harriman biographer Rudy Abramson. "While Harriman dealt the cards, the PM would try out proposals he was thinking of putting to Roosevelt, ruminate over problems with Beaverbrook, or formulate climactic lines for speeches." Harriman usually beat Churchill and collected on their small wagers. Rudy Abramson, *Spanning the Century: The Life of W. Averell Harriman, 1891–1986*, pp. 298–299.

89. On Saturday night, September 2, 1939, FDR concluded a White House poker game by declaring: "Gentlemen, by noon tomorrow, war [in Europe] will have been declared." John Q. Barrett, ed, *That Man: An Insider's Portrait of Franklin D. Roosevelt*, p. 77.

90. Sympathetic FDR biographer Conrad Black wrote: "Despite his moodiness and indifferent manners at times, he [Churchill] was probably more companionable than Roosevelt once matters progressed much beyond the superficialities of the card table or the fishing party." Conrad Black, *Franklin Delano Roosevelt: Champion of Freedom*, p. 1132.

91. Frances Perkins, *The Roosevelt I Knew*, p. 31.

92. Winston S. Churchill, *Their Finest Hour: The Second World War*, Volume II, p. 22.

93. David Dilks, *Churchill and Company*, p. 161.

94. William D. Hassett, *Off the Record with FDR 1942–1945*, p. 335 (April 12, 1945).

95. Robert E. Sherwood, *Roosevelt and Hopkins: An Intimate History*, p. 227.

96. No President," wrote Alexander DeConde in *The American Secretary of State: An Interpretation*, "so frequently undercut the authority of his Secretary of State as did Franklin D. Roosevelt. . . . None of the President's advisers, however, angered Hull quite as much as did Sumner Welles, the Assistant Secretary of State in charge of Latin American Affairs. . . . Welles continually slighted Hull and acted as if he were the President's personal assistant, not amenable to the authority of the Secretary of State." At cabinet meetings,

foreign policy was seldom discussed. "When I accepted this office, I knew that I would be misrepresented, lied about, let down, and that there would be humiliations that no man in private life could accept and keep his self-respect," said Hull in 1944. "But I made up my mind in advance that I would accept all these things and just do my job. I have suffered all these things but have just kept right on." Alexander DeConde, *The American Secretary of State: An Interpretation*, pp. 24–25, 108–109.

97. Michael C. Fullilove, *Rendezvous with Destiny: How Franklin D. Roosevelt and Five Extraordinary Men Took America into the War and into the World*, p. 26. An Associated Press reporter wrote: "Mr. Welles is six feet, three inches tall and every inch of him is impressive. So impressive, in fact, that you are sometimes not quite certain whether or not there's a human being beneath all that polish and austerity. . . . All his life he has been mistaken for an Englishman." Lucrece Hudgins, "How to Thaw Out Sumner Welles; Get Him to Talk about his Dog," *St. Petersburg Times*, October 21, 1941, p. 10. Historian Theodore A. Wilson wrote Welles "always dressed impeccably in Savile Row suits, and had a resonant, precise voice that recalled the deep tones of actor Basil Rathbone." Wilson added that Welles's "brilliance served not a class but rather the nation and, insofar as calculation allowed, the cause of international peace and cooperation." Theodore A. Wilson, *The First Summit: Roosevelt & Churchill at Placentia Bay, 1941*, p. 31. Like Roosevelt, Welles was a graduate of the Groton School, as were several other high-ranking Roosevelt administration officials including Attorney General Francis Biddle and State Department officials Joseph Grew, Dean Acheson, and Averell Harriman.

98. Dean Acheson, *Present at the Creation: My Years in the State Department*, pp. 9, 11. Acheson had been under secretary of the Treasury at the beginning of the Roosevelt administration, but quickly left in a conflict over the Roosevelt administration's manipulation of money. David Rees, *Harry Dexter White: A Study in Paradox*, p. 46. Nevertheless, FDR viewed Acheson's resignation letter as a model of "how a gentleman resigns." Walter Isaacson and Evan Thomas, *The Wise Men: Six Friends and the World They Made*, p. 135. Hull admitted he didn't "see the President very often." Benjamin Welles, *Sumner Welles: FDR's Global Strategist*, p. 276. Hull's resentment of Welles's access boiled over when FDR selected Welles to accompany him to the August 1941 conference with Churchill at Placentia Bay. Hull told Assistant Secretary Breckinridge Long that "he resented not being asked for suggestions and being kept in the dark about it all—and he was mad that the incident should have come close to wrecking his work for settlement" of issues with Japan. Fred L. Israel, ed, *The War Diary of Breckinridge Long*, p. 215 (August 31, 1941).

99. Robert Dallek, *Franklin Roosevelt and American Foreign Policy, 1932–1945*, p. 421.

100. In his memoirs, Hull wrote critically of Welles: "I had looked to him to supervise the administration of the State Department in the most efficient manner possible. This was the normal function of an Under Secretary, permitting the Secretary of State to devote more time to the formulation of policy. He seemed, however, to become engrossed with other matters, with the result that most of us in the Department in position to judge were keenly disappointed by the result of his administrative services. After Stettinius became Under Secretary I encharged him with a complete administrative reorganization of the Department." Cordell Hull, *The Memoirs of Cordell Hull*, Volume II, p. 1230.

101. Irving Gellman, *Secret Affairs: Franklin Roosevelt, Cordell Hull, and Sumner Welles*, p. 188. After the two-hour meeting, Welles nevertheless described Churchill as "one of the most fascinating personalities he had ever met." Churchill told Welles that Nazi "objectives . . . endangered the security of the United States as much as they imperilled the safety of the British Em-

pire." Michael Fullilove, *Rendezvous with Destiny: How Franklin D. Roosevelt and Five Extraordinary Men Took America into the War and into the World*, p. 53–54. Under-Secretary Alexander Cadogan decided not to inform Churchill how impressed Welles had been with their meeting, but took "comfort from the fact that Mr. Churchill will already have that conviction, so nothing is lost." David Dilks, ed, *The Diaries of Sir Alexander Cadogan, O.M., 1938–1945*, p. 261.

102. Sumner Welles, *Seven Major Decisions*, p. 46.

103. Winston S. Churchill, *Their Finest Hour: The Second World War*, Volume II, p. 87.

104. Winston S. Churchill, *Their Finest Hour: The Second World War*, Volume II, p. 104.

105. Winston S. Churchill, *Their Finest Hour: The Second World War*, Volume II, p. 129.

106. Robert E. Sherwood, *Roosevelt and Hopkins: An Intimate History*, pp. 363–364.

107. W. Averell Harriman and Elie Abel, *Special Envoy to Churchill and Stalin 1941–1946*, p. 191.

108. Talking in 1945 of Churchill's willingness to travel, Stalin told Harriman that the prime minister was "the healthiest old man . . . a desperate fellow." Herbert Feis, *Churchill-Roosevelt-Stalin: The War They Waged and the Peace They Sought*, p. 497.

109. Winston S. Churchill, *The Hinge of Fate: The Second World War*, Volume IV, p. 621.

110. Martin S. Gilbert, *Winston S. Churchill, Road to Victory: 1941–1945*, p. 304. Max Hastings says the telegram was to Attlee.

111. Winston S. Churchill, *The Hinge of Fate: The Second World War*, Volume IV, p. 622

112. Baron Charles McMoran Wilson Moran, *Churchill: Taken from the Diaries of Lord Moran: The Struggle for Survival, 1940–1965*, p. 86 (January 19, 1943).

113. Baron Charles McMoran Wilson Moran, *Churchill: Taken from the Diaries of Lord Moran: The Struggle for Survival, 1940–1965*, pp. 86–87 (January 19, 1943).

CHAPTER I. THE JOSEPH KENNEDY CONUNDRUM

1. Amanda Smith, ed, *Hostage to Fortune: The Letters of Joseph P. Kennedy*, p. 393 (Diary, October 5, 1939).

2. Fred L. Israel, ed, *The War Diary of Breckinridge Long*, p. 148 (November 7, 1940).

3. In the 1938–1940 period, FDR encouraged a wide variety of officials to think of themselves as potential successors to the presidency. General Raymond E. Lee, the top American military official in London, wrote in September 1940 that "Kennedy has the speculator's smartness but also his *sharpshooting* and *facile* insensitivity to the great forces which are now playing like heat lightning over the map of the world." James Leutze, ed, *The London Observer: The Journal of General Raymond E. Lee*, p. 62.

4. David E. Koskoff, *Joseph P. Kennedy*, pp. 116–117.

5. John Lukacs, *The Duel: 10 May–31 July 1940: The Eighty-Day Struggle Between Churchill and Hitler*, p. 73.

6. Kennedy did not conform himself to Roosevelt administration policies during his term as ambassador, nor did he keep the administration fully informed of his activities. "During Kennedy's early ambassadorial period, Roosevelt and Hull wanted America—and at least its ambassadors—to remain aloof from developments, while Kennedy wanted America to use its weight to preserve peace," wrote biographer David E. Koskoff. Peace meant appeasement of Hitler. "Later, the President and Secretary became convinced of the wisdom of massive aid for the allies while Kennedy became more and more isolationistic. Positions reversed, but throughout, Kennedy pursued his own policies." David E. Koskoff, *Joseph P. Kennedy: A*

Life and Times, pp. 292–293. By October 1939, Kennedy was upset by FDR's outreach to Churchill, which he described in his diary: "Another instance of Roosevelt's conniving mind, which never indicates he knows how to handle any organization. It's a rotten way to treat his Ambassador and I think shows him up to the other people. I am disgusted." Amanda Smith, ed, *Hostage to Fortune: The Letters of Joseph P. Kennedy*, p. 392 (Diary, October 5, 1939).

7. Martin S. Gilbert, *Churchill and America*, p. 172.

8. Thomas Maier, *When Lions Roar: The Churchills and the Kennedys*, pp. 78–81.

9. Kennedy biographer Thomas Maier contended: "For years, the president accommodated Kennedy because of his close friendship with Roosevelt's oldest son, James." Kennedy had promoted James Roosevelt's insurance business in Massachusetts in the early 1930s, and James in turn went with Kennedy to Britain in 1933 to promote Kennedy's desire to obtain liquor franchises for postprohibition America. Later, James Roosevelt promoted Kennedy's political ambitions to his father. As ambassador, Kennedy promoted the interests of his Haig and Haig whiskey franchise. Thomas Maier, *When Lions Roar: The Churchills and the Kennedys*, pp. 154–157, 179–184. When FDR appeared to back away from the ambassadorial appointment, Kennedy declared: "FDR promised me London, and I told Jimmy to tell his father that's the job, and the only one, I'll accept." Arthur Krock, *Memoirs: Sixty Years on the Firing Line*, p. 333. The alternative job for Kennedy of commerce secretary eventually went to Harry Hopkins. Kennedy also befriended future FDR son-in-law, Clarence John Boettiger, and got him a job with the Motion Picture Producers and Distributors of America. John R. Boettiger, *A Love in the Shadow*, p. 191. Roosevelt and Kennedy shared some disappointments. Both had been humiliated when they had been blackballed from Harvard's elite Porcellian Club. During World War I, Roosevelt had called his rejection "the biggest disappointment of my life." Unlike the Episcopalian Roosevelt, Kennedy had the excuse for rejection that he was Irish-Catholic, whereas Roosevelt had the requisite social standing. Some contemporaries have suggested that his rejection at Porcellian caused FDR to become bitter toward his own elite social class. See Maier, p. 72, and Geoffrey C. Ward, *Before the Trumpet: Young Franklin Roosevelt*, pp. 235–238.

10. Amanda Smith, ed, *Hostage to Fortune: The Letters of Joseph P. Kennedy*, pp. 425–426 (May 15, 1940). Kennedy repeatedly made false or exaggerated comments about Churchill's drinking such as: "Churchill is a remarkable man, or as remarkable as any man can be who's loaded with brandy by ten o'clock in the morning." David E. Koskoff, *Joseph P. Kennedy: A Life and Times*, p. 249.

11. Amanda Smith, *Hostage to Fortune: The Letters of Joseph P. Kennedy*, p. 425 (Kennedy to Roosevelt and Hull, May 15, 1940).

12. Warren Kimball, ed, *Churchill & Roosevelt: The Complete Correspondence*, Volume I, p. 37 (Churchill to Roosevelt, May 15, 1940).

13. John Lukacs, *The Duel: 10 May–31 July 1940: The Eighty-Day Struggle Between Churchill and Hitler*, p. 71.

14. In October 1940, General Raymond E. Lee wrote that Herschel Johnson, the widely respected American embassy counselor, "says that Bullitt is a treacherous and mischievous individual who completely deceived the French about American feeling and intentions, while at the same time informing our President about the French." James Leutze, ed, *The London Observer: The Journal of General Raymond E. Lee*, p. 84 (October 8, 1940).

15. Orville H. Bullitt, ed, *For the President: Personal and Secret: Correspondence Between Franklin D. Roosevelt and William C. Bullitt*, p. 419 (Bullitt to Hull and Roosevelt, May 15, 1940).

16. Orville H. Bullitt, ed, *For the President: Personal and Secret: Correspondence Between Franklin D. Roosevelt and William C. Bullitt*, pp. 427–428 (Bullitt to Roosevelt, May 16, 1940).

17. Cordell Hull, *The Memoirs of Cordell Hull*, Volume I, p. 774.

18. Air Chief Marshall Hugh Dowding insisted that British fighters be preserved to defend Britain, writing Churchill: "I believe that, if an adequate fighter force is kept in this country, if the fleet remains in being, and if Home Forces are suitably organised to resist invasion, we should be able to carry on the war single-handed for some time, if not indefinitely. But, if the Home Defence Force is drained away in desperate attempts to remedy the situation in France, defeat in France will involve the final complete and irremediable defeat of this country." John Ellis, *Brute Force: Allied Strategy in the Second World War*, p. 20.

19. Joseph P. Lash, *Roosevelt and Churchill, 1939–1941*, pp. 113, 134.

20. David Nasaw, *The Patriarch: The Remarkable Life and Turbulent Times of Joseph P. Kennedy*, p. 449.

21. Amanda Smith, ed, *Hostage to Fortune: The Letters of Joseph P. Kennedy*, pp. 474 (Diary, September 24, 1940).

22. Joseph Lash, *Roosevelt and Churchill, 1939–1941*, p. 146.

23. Warren Kimball, ed, *Churchill & Roosevelt: The Complete Correspondence*, Volume I, p. 40 (Churchill to Roosevelt, May 20, 1940).

24. John Q. Barrett, ed, *That Man: An Insider's Portrait of Franklin D. Roosevelt*, p. 84.

25. John Lukacs, *The Duel: 10 May–31 July 1940: The Eighty-Day Struggle Between Churchill and Hitler*, p. 138.

26. Winston S. Churchill, *Their Finest Hour*, p. 201 (Winston S. Churchill to Lord Lothian, June 28, 1940).

27. *Foreign Relations of the United States*, 1939, Volume I, p. 500.

28. The clerk, Tyler Kent, had once been suspected of engaging in spying for Russia when he was posted in Russia. In London, he passed his information along to Anna Wolkoff, a White Russian who passed the cables Kent collected along to the Nazis. Ronald Kessler, *The Sins of the Father: Joseph P. Kennedy and the Dynasty He Founded*, p. 203. David Nasaw, *The Patriarch*, pp. 444–447.

29. Amanda Smith, ed, *Hostages to Fortune: The Letters of Joseph P. Kennedy*, pp. 452–453 (Diary, August 1, 1940).

30. Richard J. Whalen, *The Founding Father: The Story of Joseph P, Kennedy*, p. 278.

31. David Nasaw, *The Patriarch: The Remarkable Life and Turbulent Times of Joseph P. Kennedy*, p. 505.

32. Cordell Hull, *The Memoirs of Cordell Hull*, Volume I, p. 766. Kennedy wrote Hull on May 15, after meeting with Churchill: "He said it was his intention to ask for the loan of 30 or 40 of our old destroyers and also whatever airplanes we could spare right now." *Foreign Relations of the United States,* 1940, Volume III, p. 30 (Kennedy to Hull, May 15, 1940). At the end of September, Kennedy wrote Hull: "I was delighted to see that the president said he was not going to enter the war, because to enter this war, imagining for a minute that the English have anything to offer in the line of leadership or productive capacity in industry that could be of the slightest value to us, would be a complete misapprehension. . . . If by any chance we should ever come to the point of getting into this war we can make up our minds that it will be the United States against Germany, Italy, and Japan, aided by a badly shot to pieces country which in the last analysis can give little." David E. Koskoff, *Joseph P. Kennedy: A Life and Times*, p. 263 (Joseph P. Kennedy to Cordell Hull, September 27, 1940).

33. On July 26, 1940, Churchill forwarded to Lord Lothian a shopping list compiled by the Admiralty: "Need of American destroyers is more urgent than ever in view of losses and the need of coping with invasion threat as well as keeping Atlantic approaches open and dealing with Italy. All was clearly set out in my telegram of June 15. There is nothing that America can do at this moment that would be of greater help than to send fifty destroyers, except sending a hundred. The flying-boats also are of the greatest importance now in the next two months. As I have repeatedly explained, the difficulty is to bridge the gap until our new war-time production arrives in a flood." Martin S. Gilbert, *Winston S. Churchill: Finest Hour, 1939–1941*, p. 681.

34. Amanda Smith, ed, *Hostages to Fortune: The Letters of Joseph P. Kennedy*, pp. 462–463 (Diplomatic dispatch from Joseph P. Kennedy to Franklin Roosevelt, August 27, 1940). It was Lord Lothian who had first broached the bases deal on May 27. Martin S. Gilbert, *Winston S. Churchill: Finest Hour, 1939–1941*, p. 410.

35. Richard J. Whalen, *The Founding Father: The Story of Joseph P. Kennedy*, p. 307.

36. *Foreign Relations of the United States*, 1940, Volume III, p 33. (Joseph P. Kennedy to Hull, June 6, 1940).

CHAPTER II. WILLIAM J. DONOVAN AND WILLIAM STEPHENSON: MASTER SECRET AGENTS

1. Richard Dunlop, *Donovan: America's Master Spy*, p. 275.

2. Richard Dunlop, *Donovan: America's Master Spy*, p. vii.

3. David Stafford, *Roosevelt and Churchill: Men of Secrets*, p. 8. Carter visited the State Department's Adolf Berle shortly after he began his intelligence activities in early 1941. "He wanted an advance of some kind against the compensation which he would eventually receive for his work," reported Berle. "I am not, of course, familiar with what the President has asked him to do, nor do I wish to be." Joseph Persico, *Roosevelt's Secret War*, p. 58. Carter's role was not unique. Historian Jeffery M. Dorwart observed that one of Roosevelt's "favorite methods for gathering data was employment of confidential agents who reported to him personally and privately." Jeffery M. Dorwart, "The Roosevelt-Astor Espionage Ring," *New York History*, Volume 62, July 1981, p. 312. When William Donovan tried to recruit one Middle East expert for his spy operations, he was embarrassed to discover that the proposed operative already was working in the Carter spy group. Joseph Persico, *Roosevelt's Secret War*, p. 118.

4. Jeffery M. Dorwart, "The Roosevelt-Astor Espionage Ring, *New York History*, Volume 62, July 1981, pp. 319–322. After a June 1940 meeting with Astor, FDR wrote Chief of Naval Operations Harold Stark: "I have requested him [Astor] to coordinate work in the New York area, and, of course, want him given every assistance. Among other things, I would like to have great weight given his recommendation on the selection of candidates because of his wide knowledge of men and affairs." Joseph Persico, *Roosevelt's Secret War*, pp. 50–56.

5. Roosevelt asked Carter to check on Astor as part of his responsibilities. Joseph Persico, *Roosevelt's Secret War*, p. 58.

6. Thomas F. Troy, *Wild Bill and Intrepid: Donovan, Stephenson, and the Origin of the CIA*, pp. 4–5. The medal was for services during World War II and is no longer awarded.

7. See David Stafford, "'Intrepid': Myth and Reality," *Journal of Contemporary History*, Volume 22 (1978), pp. 303–317. Bill MacDonald tried to untangle the Stephenson myth and the inaccuracies of previous biographies in *The True 'Intrepid': Sir William Stephenson and the Un-*

known Agents. Former CIA historian Thomas F. Troy tried to untangle the Stephenson-Donovan relationship in *Wild Bill and Intrepid: Donovan, Stephenson, and the Origin of the CIA.*

8. Roald Dahl, a British agent who became a famous writer, recalled that Stephenson was "an enigma. And how much wool did he pull over people's eyes, and how much truly good work did he do? But there's no question he did some truly good work." Bill MacDonald, *The True 'Intrepid': Sir William Stephenson and the Unknown Agents*, p. 263.

9. Trevor-Roper acknowledged in his review of *A Man Called Intrepid* that Stephenson and Churchill were friends and that Stephenson was the intermediary for ULTRA reports sent to Roosevelt. In a later article, Trevor-Roper cast doubts on the Churchill-Stephenson relationship and accused the British-American spy network of propagating fiction: "To the old OSS hands and their CIA successors, Stephenson was the mythical figure who in the heroic past had stood behind their semi-mythical founder Donovan." Bill MacDonald, *The True 'Intrepid': Sir William Stephenson and the Unknown Agents*, pp. 153–154.

10. See Bill MacDonald, *The True 'Intrepid': Sir William Stephenson and the Unknown Agents, passim.*

11. Thomas F. Troy, *Wild Bill and Intrepid: Donovan, Stephenson, and the Origin of the CIA*, pp. 14, 160–161, 195–196.

12. Keith Jeffery, *The Secret History of MI6*, p. 451.

13. Keith Jeffery, *The Secret History of MI6*, p. 450.

14. Anthony Cave Brown, *"C": The Secret Life of Sir Stewart Menzies, Spymaster to Winston Churchill*, p. 264.

15. Douglas Waller, *Wild Bill Donovan*, p. 63.

16. Thomas F. Troy, *Wild Bill and Intrepid: Donovan, Stephenson, and the Origin of the CIA*, p. 156.

17. Thomas F. Troy, *Wild Bill and Intrepid: Donovan, Stephenson, and the Origin of the CIA*, pp. 186–191.

18. Keith Jeffery, *The Secret History of MI6*, pp. 439–440.

19. Anthony Cave Brown, *"C": The Secret Life of Sir Stewart Menzies, Spymaster to Winston Churchill*, p. 263.

20. Frank Knox had been the 1936 Republican candidate for vice president.

21. Richard Dunlop, *Donovan: America's Master Spy*, p. 206 (July 12, 1940).

22. Richard Dunlop, *Donovan: America's Master Spy*, pp. 211–212.

23. Richard Dunlop, *Donovan: America's Master Spy*, p. 209.

24. Richard Dunlop, *Donovan: America's Master Spy*, p. 217.

25. Douglas Waller, *Wild Bill Donovan, The Spymaster Who Created the OSS and Modern American Espionage*, pp. 59–60.

26. Martin S. Gilbert, *Winston S. Churchill: Finest Hour, 1939–1941*, p. 672.

27. David Stafford, *Roosevelt and Churchill: Men of Secrets*, p. xxiii.

28. Kennedy was also upset by the arrival in August of a military mission under Rear Admiral Robert L. Ghormley and General George V. Strong. Kennedy complained that "it has been a bit embarrassing to have the entire British Cabinet know that an Admiral was coming here for staff talks when nobody in the Embassy knew anything about it." David E. Koskoff, *Joseph P. Kennedy: A Life and Times*, p. 245.

29. Elliott Roosevelt, ed, *F.D.R.: His Personal Letters: 1928–1945*, Volume IV, p. 1061. (Roosevelt to Joseph Kennedy, August 28, 1941). Kennedy had complained to Hull about Donovan's mission and a follow-up military mission about which he had not been informed

in advance: "I do not like it and I either want to run this job or get out. At this time, this job is a delicate one and to do the job well, requires that I know what is going on. Not to know what is going on causes embarrassment and confusion. I want to know, in other words, what is going to happen before the British are notified. Not to tell me, is very poor treatment of me, and is bad organization." Amanda Smith, ed, *Hostage to Fortune: The Letters of Joseph P. Kennedy*, p. 459 (Joseph P. Kennedy to Cordell Hull, August 7, 1940).

30. Kennedy wrote Hull on August 7 "that over here, the newspapermen were familiar before I was with their [Donovan's and Mower's] appointment. I casually mentioned that an Admiral had been appointed as my Naval Attache. This was known to the British Departments and Cabinet while I knew nothing about it." Amanda Smith, ed, *Hostage to Fortune: The Letters of Joseph P. Kennedy*, pp. 458–459 (Joseph P. Kennedy to Cordell Hull, August 7, 1940). After Kennedy presented his complaints to the State Department, Hull attempted to mollify him by writing that Secretary "Knox appreciates fully the excellent reporting of the Embassy and the Military and Naval Attaches, and does not desire that this step will interfere in any way with the functions of the Embassy or the Attachés." Michael Fullilove, *Rendezvous with Destiny*, p. 79.

31. Joan Bright, a key employee of the Defence Ministry, wrote: "The contact with Mr Stephenson and this visit convinced him [Donovan] that when the United States entered the war it would be profitable to draw into one body the many intelligence agencies which worked independently of each other in the department of War, Navy, and State and to include in the body the study and implementation of unorthodox methods of war such as were now being pursued in England." Joan Bright Astley, *The Inner Circle: A View of War at the Top*, pp. 49–50.

32. Martin S. Gilbert, *Winston S. Churchill: Finest Hour, 1939–1941*, p. 738. At the urging of Secretary of War Frank Knox, Donovan and *Daily News* reporter Edgar Ansel Mowrer wrote a set of articles about the dangers of a German fifth column in America. Richard Dunlop, *Donovan: America's Master Spy*, p. 223. Mowrer subsequently went to work for Robert Sherwood at the Office of War Information.

33. Douglas Waller, *Wild Bill Donovan: The Spymaster Who Created the OSS and Modern American Espionage*, p. 77.

34. David Stafford, *Roosevelt and Churchill: Men of Secrets*, p. 61.

35. Winston S. Churchill, *Their Finest Hour: The Second World War*, Volume II, pp. 358–359 (Memo from Winston S. Churchill to Lord Halifax, August 7, 1940).

36. Winston S. Churchill, *Their Finest Hour: The Second World War*, Volume II, pp. 359 (Winston S. Churchill to Lord Lothian, August 7, 1940).

37. The situation that Churchill communicated to America needed to be grave and critical, but not impossible. Churchill wrote Roosevelt in October 1940: "You will see, therefore, Mr. President, how very great are our problems and dangers. We feel, however, confident of our ability, if we are given the necessary supplies, to carry the war to a successful conclusion, and anyhow we are going to try our best." He added: "You will, however, allow me to impress upon you the extreme urgency of accelerating the delivery of the programme of aircraft and other munitions which has already been laid before you." Martin S. Gilbert, *Winston S. Churchill: Finest Hour, 1939–1941*, p. 875 (October 27, 1940). Lend-Lease legislation was still five months in the future.

38. *Foreign Relations of the United States*, 1940, Volume III, pp. 48–49 (Joseph P. Kennedy to Hull, September 27, 1940).

39. Richard J. Whalen, *The Founding Father: The Story of Joseph P, Kennedy*, pp. 324–325.

40. Gill Bennett, *Churchill's Man of Mystery: Desmond Morton and the World of Intelligence*, p. 258. Dick Ellis claimed: "Stephenson was able through his contacts in Washington, to obtain results on a number of matters that would have been quite impossible at that time done through the embassy." Bill MacDonald, *The True 'Intrepid': Sir William Stephenson and the Unknown Agents*, p. 76.

41. Lynne Olson, *Those Angry Days*, p. 339.

42. Douglas Waller, *Wild Bill Donovan*, p. 62.

43. Joseph Persico, *Roosevelt's Secret War*, p. 91.

44. Richard Dunlop, *Donovan: America's Master Spy*, p. 297. In London, General Raymond Lee worried about duplication and overlap of intelligence work. "We are now managing to make the most simple, straightforward things so complicated and tangled that they all get bogged down in Washington." James Leutze, ed, *The London Observer: The Journal of General Raymond E. Lee*, p. 393 (September 10, 1941).

45. Lynne Olson, *Those Angry Days*, p. 340.

46. Arthur Meier Schlesinger, *A Life in the Twentieth Century: Innocent Beginnings, 1917–1950*, p. 305. Historian Joseph Persico wrote: "Donovan, perhaps a managerial calamity, was, more importantly, a natural leader, a master of theater, a man who floated above the mundane, much like the President he served." Joseph Persico, *Roosevelt's Secret War*, p. 112. Donovan upset his bureaucratic counterparts. Assistant Secretary of State Breckinridge Long wrote in his diary on December 20, 1941: "One most important thing to be controlled is Donovan. His organization is composed largely of inexperienced people—inexperienced in so far as dealing with high powered confidential information is concerned. They get all our information and use it ad lib. Sometimes there is a definite flare-back because of lack of judgment in its use." Fred L. Israel, ed, *The War Diary of Breckinridge Long*, p. 234 (December 20, 1941).

47. Douglas Waller, *Wild Bill Donovan*, p. 104.

48. David Stafford, *Roosevelt and Churchill: Men of Secrets*, p. 63.

49. David Stafford, *Roosevelt and Churchill: Men of Secrets*, p. 165.

50. David Stafford, *Roosevelt and Churchill: Men of Secrets*, pp. 179–188.

51. David Stafford, *Roosevelt and Churchill: Men of Secrets*, p. 189.

52. In February 1942, Berle reported in his diary that an FBI agent had reported to him that a British agent was trying to dig up dirt on Berle. "This would be amusing if it did not illustrate the precise danger which is run from having these foreigners operate." Beatrice Bishop Berle, ed, *Navigating the Rapids, 1918–1971: From the Papers of Adolf A. Berle*, p. 402 (February 13, 1942).

53. David Stafford, *Roosevelt and Churchill: Men of Secrets*, p. 160. Thomas E. Mahl wrote: "British intelligence formed one part, the most secret part, of a three-sided relationship—the Roosevelt White House and the Eastern foreign policy elite formed the other sides. President Roosevelt allowed British intelligence broad latitude in its American operations before and during World War II." Among the many efforts in which they engaged was publication of fake public opinion polls. Thomas E. Mahl, *Desperate Deception: British Covert Operations in the United States, 1939–44*, pp. 178–179. Berle's anti-British sentiments apparently led British intelligence to assign an agent to uncover dirt on Berle; when the investigation was discovered, the British agent was expelled from the United States. Bill MacDonald, *The True 'Intrepid': Sir William Stephenson and the Unknown Agents*, p. 205. Berle nevertheless subsequently admitted: "It was impossible not to like Bill Stephenson." Thomas F. Troy, *Wild Bill and Intrepid: Donovan, Stephenson, and the Origin of the CIA*, p. 31.

54. Lynne Olson, *Those Angry Days*, p. 298. In March 1940, Berle wrote: "Britain is a small country of 45 million population and may not be able to hold the far-flung empire together. Should it go under, it is a very fair question whether the United States might not have to take them all over, in some fashion or other." David Reynolds, *The Creation of the Anglo-American Alliance 1937–41: A Study in Competitive Co-Operation*, p. 121.

55. Dean Acheson, *Present at the Creation: My Years in the State Department*, p. 13.

56. Fred L. Israel, ed, *The War Diary of Breckinridge Long: Selections from the Years 1939–1944*, p. 67 (March 15, 1940).

57. In 1949, Berle would charge in testimony before the House Un-American Activities Committee that then Assistant Secretary Dean Acheson was too influenced by the "pro-Russian" Alger Hiss, supposedly Acheson's assistant, in a confrontation over policy toward Russia in the fall of 1944. Whittaker Chambers had personally warned Berle about Hiss and other Russian agents in September 1939, but Berle had curiously failed to follow up on that information. Beatrice Bishop Berle, ed, *Navigating the Rapids, 1918–1971: From the Papers of Adolf A. Berle*, pp. 249–250, 582–584, 598–599.

58. Anthony Cave Brown, *"C": The Secret Life of Sir Stewart Menzies*, p. 368.

59. Anthony Cave Brown, *"C": The Secret Life of Sir Stewart Menzies*, p. 484.

60. Anthony Cave Brown, *"C": The Secret Life of Sir Stewart Menzies*, p. 391. Berle concluded: "Why should anyone have a spy system in the United States? And what will it look like a little later when someone finds out about it?" Bill MacDonald, *The True 'Intrepid': Sir William Stephenson and the Unknown Agents*, p. 102.

CHAPTER III. ROOSEVELT: HIS OWN SECRETARY OF STATE

1. Alexander DeConde, *The American Secretary of State: An Interpretation*, p. 109.

2. General Raymond E. Lee, the top American military official in London, wrote that in July 1941, Harry Hopkins reported: "Bill Donovan is encountering tremendous opposition in trying to put over his Intelligence idea; that he is in a frightful row with Stimson and Knox and Marshall and Stark." Lee wrote: "Hopkins's recital of how the thing was bungled with everyone set at loggerheads is an illuminating commentary on how affairs are conducted in Washington." James Leutze, ed, *The London Observer: The Journal of General Raymond E. Lee*, pp. 344–345 (July 21, 1941).

3. William Stevenson, *A Man Called Intrepid*, p. 213. In his second Roosevelt-sponsored trip to Europe, Donovan travelled from Britain to the Mediterranean, North Africa, the Middle East, and throughout the Balkans. He was accompanied by a directive from the Churchill government: "The Prime Minister directs that every facility should be afforded to Colonel Donovan who has been taken fully into our confidence." Among Donovan's efforts was a meeting with Bulgaria's King Boris in an attempt to prevent his submission to Hitler. Richard Dunlop, *Donovan: America's Master Spy*, pp. 239, 249–251. Donovan reported briefly on his trip to Roosevelt, Knox, and Hopkins on March 19, 1941, but his major influence may have been to suggest to the British that they should support the Greek government in the face of a German invasion. After Donovan visited the Balkans, the minutes of a February 24 cabinet meeting "recalled that Colonel Donovan had stressed in a telegram to the President the importance of a Balkan front. If we now forsook Greece, it would have a bad effect in the United States." Martin S. Gilbert, ed, *The Churchill War Papers: The Ever-Widening War, 1941*, p. 258.

4. James MacGregor Burns, *Roosevelt: The Lion and the Fox*, pp. 371–373.

5. Winston S. Churchill, *The Hinge of Fate: The Second World War*, Volume IV, p. 78.

6. Arthur Krock, *Memoirs: Sixty Years on the Firing Line*, p. 207.

7. Dean Acheson, *Present at the Creation: My Years in the State Department*, p. 88.

8. Charles Bohlen, *Witness to History*, p. 129. Secretary of State Edward Stettinius wrote in his memoirs of the Yalta summit that he believed the "lack of proper co-ordination between the White House and the State Department in the determination and execution of foreign policy was a serious weakness. One of the first steps that I took as Secretary of State was to establish a closer liaison between the White House and the Department by appointing Charles E. Bohlen as liaison officer." Edward R. Stettinius Jr., *Roosevelt and the Russians: The Yalta Conference*, p. 12. Bohlen also served as FDR's translator at the Teheran and Yalta summits.

9. Charles Bohlen, *Witness to History*, p. 121. FDR emasculated the State Department, establishing a trend that continues to this very day.

10. Raoul Aglion, *Roosevelt & de Gaulle: Allies in Conflict, a Personal Memoir*, p. 112.

11. W. Averell Harriman and Elie Abel, *Special Envoy to Churchill and Stalin, 1941–1946*, p. 15.

12. Frances Perkins, *The Roosevelt I Knew*, p. 327.

13. Charles Bohlen, *Witness to History*, p. 129. Hull was also too "vague" and "pig-headed" for the taste of British Under-Secretary of Foreign Affairs Alexander Cadogan, who referred to Hull as the "old lady" in his diary. David Dilks, *The Diaries of Sir Alexander Cadogan, O.M., 1938–1945*, p. 553 (August 20, 1943) and p. 560 (September 12, 1943).

14. Benjamin Welles, *Sumner Welles: FDR's Global Strategist*, p. 263.

15. Charles Bohlen, *Witness to History*, p. 129.

16. Dean Acheson, *Present at the Creation: My Years in the State Department*, p. 12.

17. Anthony Eden, *The Reckoning*, p. 436. Eden wrote: "There was at this time a strange dichotomy in the conduct of American foreign affairs, the President preferring to work through Sumner Welles, yet having regard for his Secretary of State's authority, especially with the Senate. I liked Mr. Cordell Hull, and right up to the time of his death I would never visit Washington without calling upon him in his retirement. But these were the days of authority. Looking like an old eagle, and gently waving his pince-nez, he had almost old fashioned good manners. . . . Yet it was impossible to forget the beak and claws. . . . I felt that he . . . could pursue a vendetta to the end." Anthony Eden, *The Reckoning*, p. 440.

18. Joseph P. Lash, *Roosevelt and Churchill, 1939–1941*, pp. 181–182. "Hull was a very silent member of the cabinet," observed Attorney General Jackson. Unlike the quiet Hull, Welles spoke up when he attended cabinet meetings. "If Welles were representing the State Department, as frequently he was, he usually gave a quick and very intelligent resume of the week's developments and trends." Benjamin Welles, *Sumner Welles: FDR's Global Strategist*, pp. 264–265.

19. Writing about the drafting of a message to Winston Churchill in June 1940 regarding American assistance, Assistant Secretary Adolf Berle wrote: "The Secretary was not happy about Welles having over-ruled him in the White House on the message. He likes to mull things over, where Welles likes to act fast. But I think in this particular case there is a difference of principle. Welles and the President are emotionally much more engaged than the Secretary." Beatrice Bishop Berle, ed, *Navigating the Rapids, 1918–1971: From the Papers of Adolf A. Berle*, pp. 323–324 (June 13, 1940).

20. Sumner Welles, *Seven Major Decisions*, pp. 118–121. Hull became furious with Welles's work at the 1942 Rio conference, getting Latin American support for breaking diplomatic relations with Germany. Welles pointed out: "I had received specific authoriza-

tion from President Roosevelt to take precisely [the] action that I had taken" in getting a compromise on language. In the subsequent confrontation, FDR specifically backed Welles, undoubtedly fueling Hull's animosity to his subordinate. Benjamin Welles, *Sumner Welles: FDR's Global Strategist*, p. 320.

21. Cordell Hull, *The Memoirs of Cordell Hull*, Volume II, p. 1227.

22. Cordell Hull, *The Memoirs of Cordell Hull*, Volume II, p. 1229. Hull wrote: "I felt that, notwithstanding his education and training in foreign affairs, he was narrower and less sound than my other associates on quite a number of major questions and policies. Before the war in Europe came we differed on armed intervention in Cuba and on our evaluation of the results of the Munich Conference. After war came, we differed on the Western Hemisphere Neutrality Zone and on the proposed ultimatum to Japan to which Roosevelt and Churchill agreed at the Atlantic Conference, and in the formulation of which he had been an adviser. I felt this would have brought on war with the Japanese at a time when we were less prepared than at the time of Pearl Harbor. After Pearl Harbor we differed on the handling of Argentina at the Rio conference, on the nature of his speeches, and on the structure of the postwar international security organization. . . . These divergences were due at times to a difference of philosophy and at others to differences over the more practical and effective means of handling crucial questions and issues, to say nothing of Welles's frequent unwillingness to do teamwork with me." Cordell Hull, *The Memoirs of Cordell Hull*, Volume II, p. 1129.

23. Sumner Welles, *Seven Major Decisions*, p. 29. The second volume was written after Cordell Hull's own memoirs, and thus settled more scores with Hull than the first volume had.

24. Cordell Hull, *The Memoirs of Cordell Hull*, Volume II, p. 1474.

25. Arthur Krock, *Memoirs: Sixty Years on the Firing Line*, p. 208.

26. Jordan A. Schwarz, *Liberal: Adolf A. Berle and the Vision of an American Era*, p. 134.

27. Irving Gellman, *Secret Affairs: Franklin Roosevelt, Cordell Hull, and Sumner Welles*, p. 302.

28. In March of 1940, Bullitt stayed in Florida rather than meet with Welles on the under secretary's tour of Europe. Michael Fullilove wrote that Hull "was black with rage at the news of Welles's appointment because he regarded himself as FDR's principal adviser on European affairs." Michael Fullilove, *Rendezvous with Destiny: How Franklin D. Roosevelt and Five Extraordinary Men Took America into the War and into the World*, p. 31. In June 1940, Bullitt refused to move from Paris with the retreating French government. He then ignored orders from the Roosevelt administration, lied about receiving them, and booked a flight home from Portugal. Bullitt thought himself a possibility for the cabinet, but instead found himself *persona non grata*. By early 1941, Bullitt was devoting himself to exacting revenge on Welles, whom he blamed for his diplomatic exile. Benjamin Welles, *Sumner Welles: FDR's Global Strategist*, pp. 260, 272–273.

29. Dean Acheson wrote in his memoirs that the "malign" Bullitt possessed a "singularly ironic middle name," Christian. Dean Acheson, *Present at the Creation: My Years in the State Department*, p. 46. Bullitt, however, was prescient on one subject—the danger posed by Stalin, whom Bullitt called "a Caucasian bandit whose only thought when he got something for nothing was that the other fellow was an ass." As the first post-revolution American Ambassador to Moscow from 1933 to 1936, Bullitt knew Stalin firsthand. Bullitt wrote FDR repeatedly about the Soviet threat. Mark A. Stoler, *Allies and Adversaries: The Joint Chiefs of Staff, the Grand Alliance, and U.S. Strategy in World War II*, p. 134. When in August 1943, Ambassador Bullitt warned Roosevelt about Russian domination of Europe, FDR responded: "I just have a hunch that Stalin is not that kind of man. Harry [Hopkins] says he's not and that he doesn't want anything but security for his country, and I think that if I give him everything I possibly can and

ask nothing from him in return, noblesse oblige, he won't try to annex anything and will work with me for a world of democracy and peace." Wilson D. Miscamble, *From Roosevelt to Truman: Potsdam, Hiroshima, and the Cold War*, p. 52. More than any policy, FDR's personal vanity and desire to please Stalin enabled Stalin to use the Yalta accords to dominate Eastern Europe.

At the very beginning of his biography of his father, journalist Benjamin Welles confirmed the details of the homosexual incident which occurred on September 16, 1940, when Sumner Welles drank for hours on the trip back from the funeral. About 4 A.M., Welles had propositioned the porters and been rejected. Benjamin Welles, *Sumner Welles: FDR's Global Strategist*, p. 2.

30. Benjamin Welles wrote: "As [J. Edgar] Hoover's report implies, the President himself was loath to raise an embarrassing issue with his Under Secretary; and the two officials whom Welles consulted—Berle and [Attorney General Robert] Jackson were friends anxious to shield the administration from scandal. In short, no one, went to the mat with Welles." Benjamin Welles, *Sumner Welles: FDR's Global Strategist*, p. 275.

31. Welles had a very serious problem with alcohol that led his wife to write him, probably in the summer of 1941, that "when you leave me at night I know you will be drinking." She declared her desire to leave him, but she did not. Benjamin Welles, *Sumner Welles: FDR's Global Strategist*, pp. 274–275, 277–278.

32. Kenneth S. Davis, *FDR: The War President, 1940–1945*, pp. 331–332.

33. H. W. Brands, *Traitor to His Class: The Privileged Life and Radical Presidency of Franklin Delano Roosevelt*, p. 750. More than two decades later, Adolf Berle recalled the story in his diary and wrote that Bullitt and FDR never met again after the confrontation. "Bullitt was a flashing, effective, ego-filled knight-errant." Beatrice Bishop Berle and Travis Beal Jacobs, eds, *Navigating the Rapids, 1918–1971: From the Papers of Adolf A. Berle*, p. 829 (February 16, 1967).

34. Geoffrey C. Ward, ed, *Closest Companion: The Unknown Story of the Intimate Friendship between Franklin Roosevelt and Margaret Suckley*, p. 226.

35. According to Hull, "The President himself had begun to appreciate the extent of Under Secretary Welles's disloyalty to me. . . . In early summer, 1943, the President himself realized that the situation in the State Department could not continue. He decided on his own that in the light of all existing circumstances the efficiency of the Department would be improved by Welles's retirement. We agreed that Welles's resignation should be rendered easier for him by the President's offer to send him to South America as roving Ambassador or to Russia on a special mission." Cordell Hull, *The Memoirs of Cordell Hull*, Volume II, p. 1230. At the end of August, as Welles cleaned out his office, Welles told Berle that he was leaving. "Almost at once the left-wing press in the United States began to make Sumner a hero," wrote Berle in his diary. "They spoke of him as the only friend of Russia in the Department: the sole bulwark against a Fascist State Department; they opened a general attack all along the line on everyone else notably Breckinridge Long, Jimmy Dunn and myself, and, to some extent, Secretary Hull, whom they had not hitherto attacked." Beatrice Bishop Berle and Travis Beal Jacobs, eds, *Navigating the Rapids, 1918–1971: From the Papers of Adolf A. Berle*, p. 444 (September 1, 1943). It is a mistake to underestimate the extent of press sympathy for Soviet Russia in both the United Kingdom and the United States.

36. Geoffrey C. Ward, ed, *Closest Companion: The Unknown Story of the Intimate Friendship between Franklin Roosevelt and Margaret Suckley*, p. 234 (September 2, 1943).

37. H. W. Brands, *Traitor to His Class: The Privileged Life and Radical Presidency of Franklin Delano Roosevelt*, p. 751.

38. Jordan A. Schwarz, *Liberal: Adolf A. Berle and the Vision of an American Era*, p. 192.

39. Dean Acheson, *Present at the Creation: My Years in the State Department*, p. 14.

40. Beatrice Bishop Berle and Travis Beal Jacobs, eds, *Navigating the Rapids, 1918–1971: From the Papers of Adolf A. Berle*, p. 377 (October 24, 1941).

41. Winchell had a regular table at the Stork Club in Manhattan, where he gathered gossip. Gilles Playfair, who worked with BSC, recalled: "He would be given stories and inside information on what was happening in Britain and so on and so forth." Benjamin deForest Bayly, an electrical engineer and inventor who worked with Stephenson, recalled: "Winchell was a man who actually got a reputation for being a very straightforward person, and he did a lot of propaganda work for Bill Stephenson. If Bill could sell him on why the US should do this, and if it did that then Winchell would be your man." Bill MacDonald, *The True 'Intrepid': Sir William Stephenson and the Unknown Agents*, pp. 278, 351.

42. Mahl wrote that Lippmann's brother-in-law, "John F. C. 'Ivar' Bryce . . . worked for both the SOE and OSS." Mahl quotes a letter that Bryce wrote Lippmann in March 1943: "If you felt at all inclined to write anything about the danger to S. America, I could give you any number of facts which have never been published, but which my friends here would like to see judiciously made public, at this point." Thomas E. Mahl, *Desperate Deception: British Covert Operations in the United States, 1939–44*, pp. 56, 179.

43. Thomas E. Mahl, *Desperate Deception: British Covert Operations in the United States, 1939–44*, p. 53.

44. In his memoirs, the *New York Times'* Arthur Krock recalled the case against Welles in December 1943. Hull argued that beginning in 1941, Welles "joined with Vice-President Wallace" in an effort to supplant Hull. Welles "set out to cultivate certain publishers, columnists, and radio broadcasters, some of whom were led to believe that the choice of them to serve on secret Department committees, made by the Secretary himself, were made by Welles, and that he was the man to approach for 'favors.'" Hull contended that he might have helped Welles get through the railroad porter scandal if Welles had come to him for help. Arthur Krock, *Memoirs: Sixty Years on the Firing Line*, pp. 205–207.

45. Pearson promoted Welles's work in a way that grated on Hull. In a 1939 column that credited Welles with the success of a recent Pan-American conference, Pearson wrote: "For seven years he [Welles] has been doing the spade work for Pan-American conferences. He plowed the field where his chief Cordell Hull reaped." Pearson had gone on to write: "Welles is a tall and austere gentleman who looks like the proverbial British diplomat but is not nearly as forbidding as he looks. Caught off guard, he will laugh at a good story, even tell one himself." He concluded by noting that Roosevelt and Welles were the "team today which really directs the foreign affairs of the United States." Drew Pearson and Robert S. Allen, "Sumner Welles Mainly Responsible for Success of Good Neighbor Policy," *St. Petersburg Times*, October 14, 1939, p. 4.

46. James MacGregor Burns, *Roosevelt: The Soldier of Freedom*, p. 398.

47. Irwin F. Gellman, *Secret Affairs: Franklin Roosevelt, Cordell Hull, and Sumner Welles*, pp. 316, 322–323. In his diary, Adolf Berle wrote: "The Hiss boys (Alger and Donald) were of the appeasement faction of the State Department. Anything that went through their office leaked, usually to Drew Pearson." Beatrice Bishop Berle and Travis Beal Jacobs, eds, *Navigating the Rapids, 1918–1971: From the Papers of Adolf A. Berle*, p. 583 (August 9, 1948).

48. W. Averell Harriman and Elie Abel, *Special Envoy to Churchill and Stalin, 1941–1946*, p. 230. Eden aide Oliver Harvey wrote in his diary on August 30, 1943, after the Quebec summit: "A.E. came up after lunch. He has had frightful tussles with the P.M. and F.D.R. over Stalin whose rude messages have infuriated them. The P.M., he thinks, is now getting dangerously anti-Russian. A.E. had no idea of the strength of the anti-French recognition opposition.

He had battle after battle with Hull whom he found quite hopeless. The old man went off in a very sour mood at the end. He was certainly responsible for driving out Sumner Welles and when the President had tentatively suggested using S.W. for visiting Moscow, he looked even sourer than usual." John Harvey, ed, *War Diaries of Oliver Harvey*, p. 288.

49. In these memoirs, Welles mentioned Secretary Hull just once: "The greatest positive achievement of the first Roosevelt Administration in the realm of international co-operation lay in the trade agreements policy for which Secretary of State Hull is wholly responsible, and which he has furthered with a single-minded and indefatigable devotion." Fellow State Department officials were virtually ignored. Sumner Welles, *Time for Decision*, p. 55.

50. Robert H. Jackson, who served as solicitor general and attorney general before he was elevated to the Supreme Court in 1941, recalled: "Roosevelt had a happy disregard of channels, ranks and priorities and often would confer with or give instructions to lower-string men about subjects he should have taken up with their superiors. He once asked me, as Attorney General, to get Secretary Hull and Secretary Morgenthau together and settle their disagreement about a foreign financial policy. After the Cabinet meeting, I pointed out to him that it would be impossible for me to arbitrate between two men, both my senior in years, both my senior in Cabinet rank, both my senior in service there, and who, moreover, both had sources of information on the subject matter that I could not possibly have. Only one man could possibly settle that difficulty, and that was the President himself, but he shrank from doing so." In FDR's character, there was an aversion to dealing directly with thorny problems. Roosevelt's tolerance of differing views contributed to policy confusion. After acknowledging that he seldom cleared his speeches with the White House, Jackson wrote of FDR, "I sometimes thought he was too tolerant, for the good of the Administration, of individuality in matters that required team play. The President to a large extent relied on the good faith and good sense of people about him not to precipitate needless controversies within the Administration." John Q. Barrett, ed, *That Man: An Insider's Portrait of Franklin D. Roosevelt*, pp. 112, 115. With Roosevelt, proximity tended to enhance power and feed his impulsive temperament. Aides and subordinates were therefore anxious to accompany him on fishing trips and other excursions. Treasury secretary Henry Morgenthau's influence was enhanced by the proximity of his Hudson River home to FDR's Hyde Park estate. Morgenthau's influence did not depend on his financial acumen. "I don't know how [FDR] could appoint my son Secretary of the Treasury. He's not up to it," proclaimed Morgenthau's domineering father. "*I* could do the job." Michael Beschloss, *The Conquerors*, p. 49. John Maynard Keynes argued, "Morgenthau has easier access to his [FDR's] presence than to his mind." Donald E. Moggridge, *Maynard Keynes: An Economist's Biography*, p. 779.

51. Charles Bohlen, *Witness to History: 1929–1969*, p. 210.

52. Historian Robert Nisbet wrote that Stalin made a "near career" based "upon the exploitation of those who came bearing gifts and seeking friendship. From the mid-1930s such seasoned experts as Loy Henderson, Kennan, and Bullitt, among others, were aware of this pathological but real and unalterable bent of Stalin's. At least two Roosevelt-dispatched ambassadors to the Kremlin, [William H.] Standley and [W. Averell] Harriman, early became aware of Stalin's nature and tried to warn the President, who would not, however, be warned." Robert Nisbet, *Roosevelt and Stalin: The Failed Courtship*, p. 27.

53. Robert E. Sherwood, *Roosevelt and Hopkins: An Intimate History*, p. 757.

54. John Morton Blum, *From the Morgenthau Diaries: Years of War, 1941–1945*, pp. 241–242 (July 9, 1943).

55. H. W. Brands, *Traitor to His Class: The Privileged Life and Radical Presidency of Franklin Delano Roosevelt*, p. 748.

CHAPTER IV. ROOSEVELT AS COMMANDER IN CHIEF

1. Doris Kearns Goodwin, *No Ordinary Time: Franklin & Eleanor Roosevelt: The Home Front in World War II*, p. 345 (Stimson diary, June 20, 1942).

2. William D. Leahy, *I Was There*, p. 322.

3. Joseph P. Lash, *Roosevelt and Churchill, 1939–1941*, p. 269.

4. British officials were often better informed than their American counterparts. When U.S. General John R. Deane was reassigned to Russia, he learned of his posting from his British counterpart on the Combined Chiefs of Staff. John R. Deane, *The Strange Alliance: The Story of Our Efforts at Wartime Cooperation with Russia*, p. 9.

5. Andrew Roberts, *Masters and Commanders*, p. 582. Among the military skeptics and Anglophobes was Lt. General Stanley D. Embick, who came out of retirement to serve as the influential chief of the Joint Strategic Survey Committee (JSSC) and chairman of the Inter-American Defense Board, who before the war was skeptical of any U.S. military action outside the continental United States. Embick's son-in-law, future General Albert C. Wedemeyer, who worked in the War Plans Division (WPD) and headed the Strategy and Planning Group from 1942 to 1943, was even more anti-British and anti-Churchill, although he did author the Germany-first Victory Program of 1941. Historian Mark A. Stoler noted that when Embick joined Marshall's staff, Embick "refused to equate" Britain's "survival with the continuation of the entire British Empire or the government of Churchill, an individual whose strategic and political judgments he had distrusted since World War I. Indeed, he [Embick] informed a surprised Marshall on April 16 [1941] that neither the loss of the Middle East nor Churchill's fall would weaken England, and he concluded that the United States should not be 'duped' again, as it had been in 1917, into entering the conflict voluntarily at this time." Marshall was the balance wheel between the pro-war faction of the War Department, led by Stimson, and the anti-war, anti-British group led by Embick and officers in the Intelligence Division. Wedemeyer's Strategy and Policy Group argued that Britain placed an overreliance on naval operations while Russia did the hard groundwork against Germany. In essence, skeptics and Anglophobes believed that Britain was fighting not to win the war, but to preserve the empire and to win the postwar negotiations. In one memo, Wedemeyer wrote that "the British may be expected to insist upon operations which will create most favorable circumstances at the peace table while weakening the positions of all other participating nations, particularly Germany and Russia." Mark A. Stoler, *Allies and Adversaries: The Joint Chiefs of Staff, the Grand Alliance, and U.S. Strategy in World War II*, pp. 10–14, 42–43, 46–67, 108, 113, 115. One officer within Wedemeyer's group argued the contrary in January 1943: "We are fighting for a secure and orderly world where we can exploit our American genius. The British empire is the most satisfactory order-producing agency that is, or will be, available in the Middle East either now or at war's end. So, in simple self interest, we are—or should be—fighting to preserve at least large slices of the British Empire." Walter L. Hixson, ed, *The American Experience in World War II: The United States in the European Theater*, p. 22. In his 1958 memoirs, Wedemeyer argued that a cross-channel invasion of France could have succeeded in 1943. Albert C. Wedemeyer, *Wedemeyer Reports!*, pp. 132–145. Wedemeyer was particularly scathing in October 1944, in referring to Churchill's "eternal and infernal Balkan enterprises." Stoler, p. 223. Although Wedemeyer was posted to Southeast Asia in 1943, Embick continued to be a force for cooperation with Russia until the end of war. Stoler, p. 251. In the summer of 1943, Wedemeyer was Averell Harriman's choice as the new military representative for the U.S. embassy in Moscow, but Harry Hopkins vetoed the selection. Rudy Abramson, *Spanning the Century: The Life of W. Averell Harriman, 1891–1986*, pp. 350–351.

6. Alex Danchev and Daniel Todman, eds, *War Diaries, 1939–1945: Field Marshal Lord Alanbrooke*, p. 594.

7. Max Hastings, *Winston's War: Churchill, 1940–1945*, p. 197.

8. Alex Danchev and Daniel Todman, eds, *War Diaries, 1939–1945: Field Marshal Lord Alanbrooke*, p. 210. British General John Kennedy described Dill as "a completely dedicated man. Soldiering to him was more than a profession; it was a vocation. The Army came before everything else." Bernard Fergusson, ed, *The Business of War: The War Narrative of Major-General Sir John Kennedy*, p. 1.

9. Ed Cray, *General of the Army: George C. Marshall*, p. 271 (Dill to Brooke, December 28, 1941).

10. In 1942, Dill had an operation for a hernia, followed by an infection.

11. Winston S. Churchill, *The Grand Alliance: The Second World War*, Volume III, p. 610.

12. When Dill died, Marshall wrote Churchill: "I doubt if you or your Cabinet associates fully realize the loss you have suffered." Alex Danchev, *Very Special Relationship: Field-Marshall Sir John Dill and the Anglo-American Alliance, 1941–44*, p. 32.

13. John Q. Barrett, ed, *That Man: An Insider's Portrait of Franklin D. Roosevelt*, p. 81.

14. Kenneth S. Davis, *FDR: The War President, 1940–1945*, pp. 52–53.

15. Benjamin Welles, *Sumner Welles: FDR's Global Strategist*, p. 271.

16. Sumner Welles, *Seven Major Decisions*, p. 54.

17. Sumner Welles, *Seven Major Decisions*, pp. 54–56.

18. Joseph P. Lash, *Roosevelt and Churchill, 1939–1941*, p. 269.

19. Winston S. Churchill, *Their Finest Hour: The Second World War*, Volume II, p. 450.

20. FDR said on September 11, in a campaign speech to the Teamsters Union convention: "I hate war, now more than ever. I have one supreme determination—to do all that I can to keep war away from these shores for all time. I stand, with my party, and outside of my party as President of all the people, on the platform . . . that was adopted in Chicago less than two months ago. It said: 'We will not participate in foreign war, and we will not send our army, naval, or air forces to fight in foreign lands outside of the Americas, except in case of attack.'" William L. Langer and S. Everett Gleason, *The Undeclared War, 1940–1941*, p. 202.

21. Sumner Welles, *Seven Major Decisions*, p. 71.

22. Sumner Welles, *Seven Major Decisions*, p. 59.

23. Walter R. Borneman, *The Admirals: Nimitz, Halsey, Leahy, and King—The Five-Star Admirals Who Won the War at Sea*, p. 266.

24. Andrew Roberts, *Masters and Commanders*, p. 71.

25. Forest Pogue, *George C. Marshall: Ordeal and Hope, 1939–1942*, p. 299.

26. Leahy's longevity contrasted with the swift departure of many Roosevelt loyalists after FDR died. By the end of the summer of 1945, Truman had replaced Secretary of State Edward Stettinius (June 22 with James F. Byrnes), Henry Morgenthau Jr. (July 22 with Fred Vinson), and Henry L. Stimson (September 21 with Robert Patterson). Attorney General Biddle left on June 26. Secretary of Agriculture Claude R. Wickard lasted until June 29. Secretary of Labor Frances Perkins left on June 30. Interior Secretary Harold Ickes lasted until February 1946. Secretary of the Navy James Forrestal lasted until September 1947, when he became the nation's first defense secretary. Former Vice President Henry A. Wallace had only been in office as secretary of commerce for a month when FDR died; he lasted until September 1946, when Truman asked for his resignation. In 1948, Wallace challenged Truman for the presidency.

27. Mark A. Stoler, *Allies and Adversaries: The Joint Chiefs of Staff, the Grand Alliance, and U.S. Strategy in World War II*, p. 91. Stoler wrote: "The chiefs' power was . . . increased by

the exceptionally close and direct relationship they developed with Roosevelt. Throughout the war the JCS existed solely at his discretion, with FDR rejecting their request for a formal charter as 'superfluous' as well as possibly restrictive and using them as his personal military advisers and planners." After the JCS setback over FDR's support for Churchill and approval of Operation TORCH in July 1942, JCS members improved their political skills in dealing with the president. In addition to Leahy, Marshall maintained a back channel to FDR through Hopkins. Stoler, pp. 65, 104.

28. William D. Leahy, *I Was There*, pp. 98–99.

29. William D. Leahy, *I Was There*, p. 101.

30. Mark A. Stoler, *Allies and Adversaries: The Joint Chiefs of Staff, the Grand Alliance, and U.S. Strategy in World War II*, p. 108.

31. Harry Hopkins, who dutifully wrote memos after important events, was a conspicuous exception.

32. Mark A. Stoler, *Allies and Adversaries: The Joint Chiefs of Staff, the Grand Alliance, and U.S. Strategy in World War II*, p. 65.

33. S. M. Plokhy, *Yalta: The Price of Peace*, p. 9.

34. Thomas Parrish, *Roosevelt and Marshall: Partners in Politics and War, The Personal Story*, pp. 250–251.

35. William D. Leahy, *I Was There*, p. 102.

36. Thomas Parrish, *Roosevelt and Marshall: Partners in Politics and War, the Personal Story*, p. 515.

37. Thomas B. Buell, *Master of Seapower: A Biography of Fleet Admiral Ernest J. King*, p. 332.

38. William D. Leahy, *I Was There*, p. 97.

39. Walter R. Borneman, *The Admirals: Nimitz, Halsey, Leahy, and King—The Five-Star Admirals Who Won the War at Sea*, p. 271.

40. Henry L. Stimson and McGeorge Bundy, *On Active Service in Peace and War*, p. 414.

41. William D. Leahy, *I Was There*, pp. 150–151, 138.

42. Mark Stoler wrote: "Throughout the war the JCS thus continued to rely on the service secretaries, the British, and one another to remain apprised of presidential decisions." Mark A. Stoler, *Allies and Adversaries: The Joint Chiefs of Staff, the Grand Alliance, and U.S. Strategy in World War II*, p. 108.

43. Stimson recalled lecturing Roosevelt "on the necessity of his taking the lead and that without a lead on his part it was useless to expect the people would voluntarily take the initiative in letting him know whether or not they would follow him if he did take the lead." Henry L. Stimson and McGeorge Bundy, *On Active Service in Peace and War*, p. 369 (from diary, April 22, 1941).

44. Attorney General Jackson later wrote: "Secretary Stimson, Secretary Knox, Secretary Morgenthau, and Secretary Ickes were much more convinced that war was inevitable and they were much more ready to meet it on the basis that it was inevitable than some of the rest of us, and more, I think, than the President himself. He thought it was avoidable much longer than did some of the others. Roosevelt had a great confidence that something would happen to bring things out right. He felt that by some stroke of diplomacy, or some other stroke, it will come out all right." John Q. Barrett, ed, *That Man: An Insider's Portrait of Franklin D. Roosevelt*, p. 106.

45. David Kaiser, *No End Save Victory: How FDR Led the Nation into War*, p. 302.

46. FDR contended even to his cabinet that aid to Britain was not a prelude to war. Stimson did not buy Roosevelt's reasoning. "To me it seems a clearly hostile act [helping Britain] to the Germans, and I am prepared to take the responsibility of it. He seems to be trying to hide it into the character of a purely reconnaissance action which really it is not. However, as he fully realizes that he will probably get into a clash with the Germans by what he does, it doesn't make much difference what he calls it." Jonathan W. Jordan, *American Warlords: How Roosevelt's High Command Led America to Victory in World War II*, p. 75.

47. Robert Dallek, *Franklin Roosevelt and American Foreign Policy, 1932–1945*, p. 264. Admiral Ernest King contended that Roosevelt's "basic idea was to inch into war little by little." Jonathan W. Jordan, *American Warlords: How Roosevelt's High Command Led America to Victory in World War II*, p. 76.

48. Harold LeClair Ickes, *The Secret Diary of Harold L. Ickes: The Lowering Clouds, 1939–1941*, p. 511 (May 10, 1941).

49. On the eve of the presidential election, October 30, 1940, FDR said in Boston: "Your boys are not going to be sent into any foreign wars. They are going into training to form a force so strong that, by its very existence, it will keep the threat of war far away from our shores." David Kaiser, *No End Save Victory: How FDR Led the Nation into War*, p. 134.

50. Robert Dallek, *Franklin D. Roosevelt and American Foreign Policy, 1932–1945*, p. 256.

51. Nigel Hamilton, *The Mantle of Command: FDR at War, 1941–1942*, p. 292. *Foreign Relations of the United States. The Conferences at Washington, 1941–1942, and Casablanca, 1943* (1941–1943), p. 421.

52. Nigel Hamilton, *The Mantle of Command: FDR at War, 1941–1942*, pp. 297–298 (Stimson diary, June 20, 1942).

53. Henry L. Stimson and McGeorge Bundy, *On Active Service in Peace and War*, p. 426.

54. American emphasis on the Pacific theater where it had been first attacked possessed logic, but not military foresight. Andrew Roberts wrote: "The collapse of Japan within four months of Hitler's death was a powerful vindication of the Germany First policy adopted by the Allies after Pearl Harbor. Had the Allies pursued a Pacific First policy—as advocated by the US Navy in the wake of Pearl Harbor—it would have allowed Hitler considerably more time and resources with which to defeat the Soviet Union, and establish himself as master of the Greater European land mass." Andrew Roberts, *The Storm of War*, p. 564.

55. Mark A. Stoler, *Allies and Adversaries: The Joint Chiefs of Staff, the Grand Alliance, and U.S. Strategy in World War II*, p. 79.

56. James Leasor, *War at the Top: The Experiences of General Sir Leslie Hollis, KCB KBE*, p. 209.

57. Mark A. Stoler wrote: "Despite his firm rejection of their proposal and clear directive regarding future operations, neither Marshall nor King had abandoned the proposed Pacific offensives. During the ensuing weeks they would continue to fight for a major revision of Allied strategy and would achieve limited success." Mark A. Stoler, *Allies and Adversaries: The Joint Chiefs of Staff, the Grand Alliance, and U.S. Strategy in World War II*, p. 87.

58. Forrest C. Pogue, *George C. Marshall: Ordeal and Hope, 1939–1942*, p. 400.

59. When FDR saw the King-Marshal plan for shifting U.S. priorities to the Pacific, he responded: "My first impression is that it is exactly what Germany hoped the United States would do following Pearl Harbor." Leonard Moseley, *Marshall, Hero for Our Times*, p. 206.

60. As Mark A. Stoler wrote: "Convinced he [FDR] was pursuing a militarily and politically disastrous approach as a result of Churchill's baneful influence, they continued to resist the North African invasion and created a de facto Pacific-first strategy in the face of direct

presidential orders to the contrary." Mark A. Stoler, *Allies and Adversaries: The Joint Chiefs of Staff, the Grand Alliance, and U.S. Strategy in World War II*, p. 101.

61. Maurice Matloff and Edwin M. Snell, *Strategic Planning for Coalition Warfare, 1941–1942*, p. 295.

62. Mark A. Stoler, *Allies and Adversaries: The Joint Chiefs of Staff, the Grand Alliance, and U.S. Strategy in World War II*, pp. 91–92.

63. Nigel Hamilton, *The Mantle of Command: FDR at War, 1941–1942*, p. 298.

64. Many important lessons were learned from TORCH about the readiness for the cross-channel invasion. "TORCH hardly began as a flaming success," wrote Eisenhower in his World War II memoirs. "[T]hrough a crazy mixture of mistakes and oversights in the United States, the first materiel for the North African invasion arrived without one crate or box properly labeled." In addition, "for the drive on Algiers, all signal equipment for the *entire* task force had been put on one ship. When that vessel was shot up by an enemy ship, the task force was badly embarrassed." Dwight D. Eisenhower, *At Ease: Stories I Tell to Friends*, p. 253. Harry Hopkins, himself a strong advocate of Marshall's cross-channel invasion, later ruminated: "In trying to figure out whether we could have got across the Channel successfully in 1942 or 1943, you've got to answer the unanswerable question to whether Eisenhower, Bradley, Spaatz, Patton, Beedle Smith, and also Montgomery and Tedder and a lot of others, could have handled the big show as they did if they hadn't had the experience fighting Germans in North Africa and Sicily." Robert E. Sherwood, *Roosevelt and Hopkins: An Intimate History*, p. 807.

65. Walter Reid, *Churchill: 1940–1945, Under Friendly Fire*, p. 143.

CHAPTER V. HARRY HOPKINS

1. Robert E. Sherwood, *Roosevelt and Hopkins: An Intimate History*, p. 817.

2. Joseph Persico, *Roosevelt's Centurions: FDR and the Commanders He Led to Victory in World War II*, p. 92.

3. John Colville, *Footprints in Time*, p. 146. "I have seen the Fairy Queen," young Diana had told her father. Michael Fullilove, *Rendezvous with Destiny*, p. 143.

4. Doris Kearns Goodwin, *No Ordinary Time: Franklin & Eleanor Roosevelt: The Home Front in World War II*, p. 89.

5. Hopkins drank, smoked, and was a fan of the *Daily Racing Form*. "Harry seemed to get so much genuine pleasure out of contact with gay but more or less artificial society," groused Eleanor. Eleanor Roosevelt, *This I Remember*, p. 173. Historian George McJimsey wrote: "Hopkins's relations with Eleanor Roosevelt also revealed his connection with wartime liberalism. As he moved into the president's inner circle and devoted his energies to managing the war, he drew away from Eleanor, not because of any difference on their part but because Eleanor and Franklin had long since taken up separate lives. Anyone who entered the White House faced two strong personalities who demanded undivided loyalty." George McJimsey, *Harry Hopkins: Ally of the Poor and Defender of Democracy*, p. 330.

6. Robert E. Sherwood, *Roosevelt and Hopkins: An Intimate History*, p. 212.

7. Fraser J. Harbutt, "Churchill, Hopkins, and the 'Other' Americans: An Alternative Perspective on Anglo-American Relations, 1941–1945," *The International History Review*, Volume 8, No. 2, May 1986, p. 237.

8. John Harvey, ed, *War Diaries of Oliver Harvey*, p. 233 (March 17, 1943).

9. Robert E. Sherwood, *Roosevelt and Hopkins: An Intimate History*, p. 231.

10. Thomas Parrish, *To Keep the British Isles Afloat: FDR's Men in Churchill's London, 1941*, p. 123.
11. Jean Monnet, *Memoirs*, p. 166.
12. Thomas Parrish, *To Keep the British Isles Afloat: FDR's Men in Churchill's London, 1941*, p. 125.
13. W. Averell Harriman and Elie Abel, *Special Envoy to Churchill and Stalin, 1941–1946*, p. 10.
14. Robert E. Sherwood, *Roosevelt and Hopkins: An Intimate History*, p. 734.
15. Winston S. Churchill, *The Grand Alliance: The Second World War*, Volume III, pp. 20–21.
16. Robert E. Sherwood, *Roosevelt and Hopkins: An Intimate History*, p. 243.
17. H. W. Brands, *Traitor to His Class: The Privileged Life and Radical Presidency of Franklin Delano Roosevelt*, p. 584.
18. Sir John Martin, *Downing Street: The War Years*, p. 39.
19. Lord General Hastings Ismay, *The Memoirs of General Lord Ismay*, pp. 214–215.
20. Winston S. Churchill, *The Grand Alliance: The Second World War*, Volume III, p. 21.
21. Lord General Hastings Ismay, *The Memoirs of General Lord Ismay*, p. 217.
22. Thomas Parrish, *To Keep the British Isles Afloat: FDR's Men in Churchill's London, 1941*, p. 87.
23. David Roll, *The Hopkins Touch*, p. 97 (Hopkins to Churchill, February 9, 1941).
24. Harold L. Ickes, *The Secret Diary of Harold L. Ickes: The Lowering Clouds, 1939–1941*, p. 429 (February 8, 1941).
25. Robert E. Sherwood, *Roosevelt and Hopkins: An Intimate History*, p. 247.
26. Winston S. Churchill, *The Grand Alliance: The Second World War*, Volume III, p. 111 (Churchill to Hopkins, February 28, 1941).
27. Winston S. Churchill, *The Hinge of Fate: Second World War*, Volume IV, p. 366 (Hopkins to Churchill, July 2, 1942).
28. John Kennedy, *The Business of War: The War Narrative of Major-General Sir John Kennedy*, p. 156.
29. Thomas Parrish, *To Keep the British Isles Afloat: FDR's Men in Churchill's London, 1941*, p. 49. According to Roosevelt's physician, Hopkins's "symptoms were markedly similar to those of sprue, a food-deficiency disease fairly common in tropical countries." He "called in Rear Admiral Stitt, formerly surgeon general of the Navy, along with other specialists. Study developed that Harry's trouble came from an imbalance of proteins in the blood stream, and the use of blood substitutes soon helped him to a better assimilation of his food. Keeping him to a routine, however, proved an impossibility." Ross T. McIntire, *White House Physician*, p. 94. In 1937, Joseph P. Kennedy Sr. had arranged for Hopkins to recuperate from his surgery at his Palm Beach home. Thomas Maier, *When Lions Roar: The Churchills and the Kennedys*, p. 267.
30. Charles Bohlen, *Witness to History*, p. 122. Hopkins's language was often direct and earthy. While working late one night in February 1942, with Robert Sherwood and Samuel I. Rosenman on a Roosevelt speech, Hopkins declared: "One thing the President does not want to do is to kid the American people into believing that this is anything but a tough son-of-a-bitch of a war against the toughest and cruelest bastards on earth. He wants them to realize right at the start what they are up against." Samuel I. Rosenman, *Working with Roosevelt*, p. 5.
31. Winston S. Churchill, *The Grand Alliance: The Second World War*, Volume III, p. 21.

32. W. Averell Harriman and Elie Abel, *Special Envoy to Churchill and Stalin 1941–1946*, p. 12.

33. John Gilbert Winant, *Letter from Governor Square*, pp. 29–30.

34. Lord General Hastings Ismay, *The Memoirs of General Lord Ismay*, p. 217. Tom Johnston was the regional commissioner for Scotland.

35. Stalin was oblivious to the signs of the impending invasion of three million German soldiers and deaf to repeated Anglo-American warnings, among others, that a Nazi attack was pending. Russian historian Roy Medvedev observed: "The blindness of Stalin and his advisors in those days of June is unparalleled. While the German embassy in Moscow was systematically reducing the number of German citizens in the USSR, almost every day new Soviet officials were arriving in Germany with their families." Medvedev noted: "The Commissariat of Defense warned Stalin once again about the possibility of a German attack a few days before it happened. 'You are creating panic over nothing,' he replied." Roy Medvedev, *Let History Judge: The Origins and Consequences of Stalinism*, p. 744. When he was first informed of the German assault, Stalin believed that it was a renegade action not authorized by Hitler. Stalin biographer Simon Sebag Montefiore wrote: "Stalin did not collapse. [Anastas] Mikoyan thought he was 'subdued.' Zhukov noticed he was 'pale' and 'bewildered' sitting at the green baize table, 'a pipe in his hand.' Voronov thought him 'depressed and nervy,' but he was in command of his office at least. Outside the fronts were in anarchy. But here, Chadaev, the Sovnarkom assistant, remembered that Stalin 'spoke slowly, choosing his words carefully, occasionally his voice broke down. When he had finished, everybody was silent for some time and so was he.'" Simon Sebag Montefiore, *Stalin: The Court of the Red Czar*, p. 365.

36. Winston S. Churchill, *The Grand Alliance: The Second World War*, Volume III, p. 378.

37. Henry H. Adams, *Harry Hopkins: A Biography*, p. 232.

38. John Gilbert Winant, *Letter from Grosvenor Square*, p. 207.

39. Robert E. Sherwood, *Roosevelt and Hopkins: An Intimate History*, p. 318 (Harry Hopkins to Franklin D. Roosevelt, July 23, 1941).

40. Joseph P. Lash, *Roosevelt and Churchill, 1939–1941*, p. 387. Churchill wrote Stalin: "I must tell you that there is a flame in this man for democracy and to beat Hitler. He is the nearest personal representative of the President. A little while ago when I asked him for a quarter of a million rifles they came at once. The President has now sent him full instructions and he leaves my house tonight to go to you. You will be advised of his arrival through the proper channels. You can trust him absolutely. He is your friend and our friend. He will help you to plan for the future victory and for the long-term supply of Russia." Martin S. Gilbert, *Winston S. Churchill: Finest Hour, 1939–1941*, p. 1143.

41. Henry H. Adams, *Harry Hopkins: A Biography*, p. 235.

42. David Kaiser, *No End Save Victory: How FDR Led the Nation into War*, p. 261.

43. Robert E. Sherwood, *Roosevelt and Hopkins: An Intimate History*, p. 343.

44. David Roll, *The Hopkins Touch*, p. 135.

45. Henry H. Adams, *Harry Hopkins: A Biography*, p. 239. It was Bohlen who, after Roosevelt's death in April 1945, suggested to Harriman that Stalin might be comforted by a visit from Hopkins.

46. Charles Bohlen, *Witness to History, 1929–1969*, p. 244.

47. Robert E. Sherwood, *Roosevelt and Hopkins: An Intimate History*, p. 781.

48. Robert E. Sherwood, *Roosevelt and Hopkins: An Intimate History*, p. 343.

49. Lord General Hastings Ismay, *The Memoirs of General Lord Ismay*, p. 228.

50. Elliott Roosevelt, *As He Saw It*, p. 22.

51. Walter H. Thompson, *Assignment: Churchill*, p. 226.

52. Warren Kimball, ed, *Churchill and Roosevelt, The Complete Correspondence*, Volume I, p. 226 (Churchill to Roosevelt, August 5, 1941).

53. Robert E. Sherwood, *Roosevelt and Hopkins: An Intimate History*, p. 351.

54. Sir John Martin, *Downing Street: The War Years*, p. 57.

55. Robert E. Sherwood, *Roosevelt and Hopkins: An Intimate History*, p. 350.

56. David Dilks, ed, *The Diaries of Sir Alexander Cadogan, O.M., 1938–1945*, pp. 554–555 (August 23, 1943).

57. Winston S. Churchill, *Closing the Ring: The Second World War*, Volume V, p. 340.

58. W. Averell Harriman and Elie Abel, *Special Envoy to Churchill and Stalin, 1941–1946*, p. 75.

59. Geoffrey C. Ward, ed, *Closest Companion: The Unknown Story of the Intimate Friendship between Franklin Roosevelt and Margaret Suckley*, p. 141 (Roosevelt to Suckley, beginning on August 5, 1941).

60. Elliott Roosevelt, *As He Saw It*, p. 35.

61. Martin S. Gilbert, *Churchill and America*, p. 234.

62. Elliott Roosevelt, *As He Saw It*, pp. 35–36.

63. Paul Addison, *Churchill: The Unexpected Hero*, p. 199.

64. Lord Halifax had told Alexander Cadogan to use the meeting to develop a working relationship with Sumner Welles. "I have hobnobbed with him a lot and have tried to get through his reserve," wrote Cadogan. "I believe him to be sound at heart and Edward [Halifax] assures me this is so." Cadogan wrote in his diary that Welles "improves on acquaintance, but it is a pity that he swallowed a ramrod in his youth." David Dilks, ed, *The Diaries of Sir Alexander Cadogan, O.M., 1938–1945*, p. 399.

65. The Atlantic Charter was first drafted by Sumner Welles and then revised by Churchill and Roosevelt. Tragically, Britain's chief Lend-Lease administrator in Washington, Arthur Purvis, was killed in a plane crash on the way to the conference. Martin Gilbert wrote: "The man who, more than any other, had worked to secure this new and essential trans-Atlantic lifeline was the British-born explosives expert, and Canadian industrialist, described by Churchill in his memoirs as 'our agent, the highly competent and devoted Mr Purvis.'" Martin S. Gilbert, *Winston S. Churchill: Finest Hour, 1939–1941*, p. 513.

66. John Charmley, *Churchill's Grand Alliance The Anglo-American Special Relationship, 1940–1957*, p. 37.

67. Winston S. Churchill, *The Grand Alliance: The Second World War*, Volume III, p. 398.

68. Walter H. Thompson, *Sixty Minutes with Winston Churchill*, p. 60.

69. John Gilbert Winant, *Letter from Grosvenor Square*, p. 118.

70. Michael Beschloss, *The Conquerors*, p. 94.

71. Ickes wrote: "It seemed to me that Harry showed evidence of feeling his importance and the great power that he undoubtedly has." Harold L. Ickes, *The Secret Diary of Harold L. Ickes: The Lowering Clouds, 1939–1941*, p. 471 (April 12, 1940). After Hopkins's first trip to Britain, Ickes had responded to Roosevelt's glowing praise of the Hopkins mission by writing in his diary: "I suspect that if, as his personal representative, the President should send to London a man with the bubonic plague, Churchill would, nevertheless, see a good deal of him." Harold L. Ickes, *The Secret Diary of Harold L. Ickes: The Lowering Clouds, 1939–1941*, p. 429 (February 7, 1941).

72. John Q. Barrett, ed, *That Man: An Insider's Portrait of Franklin D. Roosevelt*, p. 116.

73. James MacGregor Burns, *Soldier of Freedom: Roosevelt*, p. 60.

74. Alex Danchev and Daniel Todman, eds, *War Diaries of Field Marshal Lord Alanbrooke*, p. 269. When after the fall of Tobruk, FDR wanted 300 new Sherman tanks shipped to the Middle East for Britain, Marshall responded: "Mr. President, the tanks have just been issued to the 1st Armored Division. It is a terrible thing to take weapons out of a soldier's hand, but if the British need is so great, they must have them." Leonard Moseley, *Marshall, Hero for Our Times*, p. 253.

75. Stettinius noted that Churchill "had complete confidence in Hopkins, as well as great affection for him." Edward R. Stettinius Jr. *Roosevelt and the Russians: The Yalta Conference*, pp. 48, 55.

76. William D. Hassett, *Off the Record with FDR 1942–1945*, p. 161 (March 9, 1943). Beaverbrook had given Hopkins's bride, Louise Macy, a diamond brooch as a wedding present; some press accounts vastly overstated its £1260 cost. George McJimsey, *Harry Hopkins: Ally of the Poor and Defender of Democracy*, p. 320.

77. David Stafford, *Roosevelt & Churchill: Men of Secrets*, p. 227.

78. Winston S. Churchill, *The Grand Alliance: Second World* War, Volume III, p. 21.

79. Charles Bohlen, *Witness to History, 1929–1969*, p. 244.

80. Kenneth S. Davis, *FDR: The War President, 1940–1945*, p. 543.

81. Robert E. Sherwood, *Roosevelt and Hopkins: An Intimate History*, pp. 804–805, 809.

82. Warren Kimball, *The Juggler: Franklin Roosevelt as Wartime Statesman*, p. 9.

CHAPTER VI. JOHN GILBERT WINANT

1. Lynne Olson, *Citizens of London*, pp. 183–184.

2. Winston S. Churchill, *Their Finest Hour: The Second World War*, Volume II, p. 330.

3. John Gilbert Winant, *Letter from Grosvenor Square*, pp. 64–65.

4. Omar N. Bradley and Clay Blair, *A General's Life: An Autobiography by General of the Army Omar N. Bradley*, p. 230.

5. Baron Charles McMoran Wilson Moran, *Churchill: Taken from the Diaries of Lord Moran: The Struggle for Survival, 1940–1965*, p. 134 (November 16, 1943).

6. John Colville, *Winston and His Inner Circle*, p. 121.

7. John Colville, *Fringes of Power*, p. 372 (April 8, 1941). Assistant Secretary of State Breckinridge Long wrote in his diary: "Winant is an odd person. He is thoroughly intense. He has a fervor that is constant, and I should think it would wear him out mentally and nervously. He has a sort of dischevelled [sic] personal appearance as to hair and clothes. His features are good and his eyes are brilliant. They burn with a sort of intensity which controls his whole being even in the most casual conversation and on ordinary trivial subjects." *The War Diary of Breckinridge Long*, p. 204 (June 6, 1941).

8. Martin S. Gilbert, ed, *The Churchill War Papers: The Ever-Widening War, 1941*, p. 365 (March 18, 1941).

9. Lynne Olson, *Citizens of London*, p. 26.

10. Richard Langworth, ed, *Churchill by Himself*, p. 378 (March 27, 1941).

11. John Gilbert Winant, *Letter from Grosvenor Square*, pp. 162–163.

12. R. A. Butler: *The Art of the Possible: The Memoirs of Lord Butler*, p. 87.

13. Baron Charles McMoran Wilson Moran, *Churchill: Taken from the Diaries of Lord Moran: The Struggle for Survival, 1940–1965*, pp. 134–135 (November 16, 1943).

14. John Colville, *Footprints in Time: Memories*, p. 155.

15. John Colville, *Winston and His Inner Circle*, p. 121.

16. Baron Charles McMoran Wilson Moran, *Churchill: Taken from the Diaries of Lord Moran: The Struggle for Survival, 1940–1965*, p. 135 (November 16, 1943). Eden aide Oliver Harvey, often tart in his criticisms, wrote in his diary: "Winant is a curious man. He never seems to invite anyone to his house. In some ways he is rather a great man. He is certainly an unorthodox man. No one knows how much, if any influence he wields with the President, though the State Dept. dislike him. He is untidy in his mind and his ways. His Embassy is unbelievably inefficient. He (or his staff) loses papers, doesn't acknowledge letters, doesn't answer invitations or requests. He has a shyness which is superficially attractive and a Lincoln caste [sic] of countenance but we still ask ourselves what it conceals." John Harvey, ed, *War Diaries of Oliver Harvey*, p. 278 (July 21, 1943).

17. John Colville, *Footprints in Time*, p. 153.

18. Lynne Olson, *Citizens of London*, pp. 91–92.

19. John Colville, *The Fringes of Power: The Incredible Inside Story of Winston Churchill*, p. 374 (April 13, 1941).

20. Rudy Abramson, *Spanning the Century: The Life of W. Averell Harriman*, p. 303.

21. James Leutze, ed, *The London Observer: The Journal of General Raymond E. Lee*, p. 353 (July 15, 1941). General Lee wrote at the end of July 1940, as Harriman returned to the United States: "I like him and have nothing against him as an individual, but I hope he will stay at home for a good long visit. This will give the Ambassador a chance to really take hold of things here. Never did any Ambassador undertake such a new appointment with such a handicap as another man, bearing a wide-open letter from the President which describes him as his personal representative and authorizes him to interfere in anything and everything. Winant had been entirely too patient." James Leutze, ed, *The London Observer: The Journal of General Raymond E. Lee*, pp. 358–359 (July 30, 1941). About a month later, while Harriman was still in the United States, Winant asked Lee whether he thought Harriman would come back to London. "I said that I did not. It is easy to see that he would prefer that Harriman not do so." James Leutze, ed, *The London Observer: The Journal of General Raymond E. Lee*, p. 382 (August 29, 1941).

22. Eleanor Roosevelt, *This I Remember*, p. 266. In her memoirs, she wrote that Winant "was a shy person, but he had great intellectual integrity, a vivid imagination which enabled him to understand situations that he had never experienced, and a sensitiveness to other people that enabled him to accomplish things many of his friends thought beyond his powers. . . . I know Mr. Churchill had a real respect and affection for him."

23. Kenneth S. Davis, *FDR: The War President, 1940–1943*, pp. 643–644.

24. John Colville, *Footprints in Time*, p. 155.

25. James Leasor, *War at the Top: The Experiences of General Sir Leslie Hollis, KCB KBE*, p. 156.

26. Robert E. Sherwood, *Roosevelt and Hopkins: An Intimate History*, pp. 754–755.

CHAPTER VII. LORD BEAVERBROOK

1. Kenneth Young, *Churchill and Beaverbrook: A Study in Friendship and Politics*, p. 249.

2. Winston S. Churchill, *The Hinge of Fate: Second World War*, Volume IV, p. 66.

3. Anne Chisholm and Michael Davie, *Lord Beaverbrook: A Life*, p. 376. White House aide Robert Sherwood wrote that Churchill and Beaverbrook "both were supreme patriots on an

imperial scale, both were tireless and tenacious, both extremely worldly, with great zest and capacity for good living, both were superb showmen with an alert ability for spotting and appreciating the main chance; and each of the main disagreements between them seemed utterly irreconcilable until a common contempt for the purely transient issue brought them together again." Robert E. Sherwood, *Roosevelt and Hopkins: An Intimate History*, p. 248.

4. Winston S. Churchill, *Their Finest Hour: The Second World War*, Volume II, p. 12.

5. Kenneth Young, *Churchill and Beaverbrook: A Study in Friendship and Politics*, pp. 150–151. The impact of Beaverbrook and his team on aircraft production was impressive. Andrew Roberts noted that "as minister of aircraft production, [he] managed to treble the rate of aircraft production during 1940, when the Germans only doubled theirs." Andrew Roberts, *The Storm of War*, p. 92.

6. In August 1940, Beaverbrook opposed use of Canadian training schools for RAF navigators. Churchill remonstrated: "I attach the greatest importance to your opinion, but you must either face the facts and answer them effectively and with a positive plan or allow the opinion of those who are responsible to prevail." Martin S. Gilbert, *Winston S. Churchill: Finest Hour, 1939–1941*, p. 759 (August 27, 1940). Churchill could not have won the Battle of Britain without the aircraft commissioned under Chamberlain. From "The Finest Hour" journal, http://www.winstonchurchill.org/publications/finest-hour/257-finest-hour-160/3188-around-about.

7. Anne Chisholm and Michael Davie, *Lord Beaverbrook: A Life*, p. 375. (King George VI to Winston Churchill, May 10, 1940).

8. Oliver Viscount Chandos Lyttelton, *The Memoirs of Lord Chandos*, p. 164.

9. Robert Rhodes James, *Churchill: A Study in Failure, 1900–1939*, pp. 379–380.

10. Anne Chisholm and Michael Davie, *Lord Beaverbrook: A Life*, p. 349.

11. Kenneth Young, *Churchill and Beaverbrook*, p. 128.

12. Anne Chisholm and Michael Davie, *Lord Beaverbrook: A Life*, p. 401.

13. Kenneth Young, *Churchill and Beaverbrook: A Study in Friendship and Politics*, p. 144.

14. John Colville *The Fringes of Power: The Incredible Inside Story of Winston Churchill*, p. 395 (June 5, 1941).

15. Kenneth Young, *Churchill and Beaverbrook: A Study in Friendship and Politics*, p. 145 (Max Beaverbrook to Samuel Hoare, June 11, 1940).

16. Edward Spears, *Assignment to Catastrophe: Fall of France, June 1940*, Volume II, p. 215.

17. Cordell Hull, *The Memoirs of Cordell Hull*, Volume I, p. 775.

18. Thomas Maier, *When Lions Roar: The Churchills and the Kennedys*, pp. 211–212.

19. William Stevenson, *A Man Called Intrepid: The Secret War*, p. 154.

20. Michael R. Beschloss, *Kennedy and Roosevelt: The Uneasy Alliance*, p. 213.

21. Amanda Smith, ed, *Hostage to Fortune: The Letters of Joseph P. Kennedy*, p. 475 (Roosevelt to Joseph P. Kennedy, October 17, 1940).

22. Michael R. Beschloss, *Kennedy and Roosevelt: The Uneasy Alliance*, p. 214.

23. David E. Koskoff, *Joseph P. Kennedy: A Life and Times*, p. 297.

24. Amanda Smith, ed, *Hostage to Fortune: The Letters of Joseph P. Kennedy*, pp. 478–480. Having been burned by statements by Ambassador William Bullitt, FDR wired Kennedy: "A great deal of unnecessary confusion and undesirable complications have been caused in the last few months by statements which have been made to the press by some of our chiefs of mission who have been coming back to this country. I am, consequently, asking you, specifically, not to make any statements to the press on your way over, nor when you arrive in New York, until you and I have a chance to agree upon what should be said. Please come straight through to Washington on your arrival since I will want to talk with you as soon as you get

here." Benjamin Welles, *Sumner Welles: FDR's Global Strategist*, pp. 262–263 (Roosevelt to Kennedy, October 17, 1940).

25. As FDR invited Kennedy by phone "to come to the White House tonight for a little family dinner," the president made a hand gesture of slitting his throat, recalled then Congressman Lyndon B. Johnson. Michael R. Beschloss, *Kennedy and Roosevelt: The Uneasy Alliance*, p. 215.

26. Amanda Smith, ed, *Hostage to Fortune: The Letters of Joseph P. Kennedy*, pp. 481–482. Arthur Krock, *Memoirs: Sixty Years on the Firing Line*, p. 336. During the meeting, FDR purportedly pledged a "real house-cleaning" at the State Department after the election. Michael R. Beschloss, *Kennedy and Roosevelt: The Uneasy Alliance*, p. 218.

27. Back in London, General Raymond E. Lee, the head of the American military mission in London, expressed surprise, writing that "Kennedy certainly left London all primed for a vindictive and vigorous assault on Roosevelt." James Leutze, ed, *The London Observer: The Journal of General Raymond E. Lee*, p. 115 (October 30, 1940).

28. Michael R. Beschloss, *Kennedy and Roosevelt: The Uneasy Alliance*, pp. 219–221.

29. William D. Pederson, *The FDR Years*, p. 392 (October 30, 1940).

30. W. Averell Harriman and Elie Abel, *Special Envoy to Churchill and Stalin, 1941–1946*, p. 61.

31. Anne Chisholm and Michael Davie, *Lord Beaverbrook: A Life*, p. 406.

32. Alex Danchev and Daniel Todman, eds, *War Diaries, 1939–1945: Field Marshal Lord Alanbrooke*, p. 100.

33. Andrew Roberts, *Masters and Commanders*, pp. 12–13.

34. Randolph Churchill had warned Pamela about Beaverbrook. "You must not get under the Beaverbrook spell because nothing amuses Beaverbrook more than to have complete control of people's lives, smash them or put them together as he sees fit. And one thing I ask you is not to come under his spell." Thomas Maier, *When Lions Roar: The Churchills and the Kennedys*, p. 293.

35. Sally Bedell Smith, *Reflected Glory: The Life of Pamela Churchill Harriman*, p. 91.

36. Sally Bedell Smith, *Reflected Glory: The Life of Pamela Churchill Harriman*, p. 92.

37. Sally Bedell Smith, *Reflected Glory: The Life of Pamela Churchill Harriman*, p. 100.

38. James Leasor, *War at the Top: The Experiences of General Sir Leslie Hollis, KCB KBE*, pp. 10–11.

39. James Leasor, *War at the Top: The Experiences of General Sir Leslie Hollis, KCB KBE*, pp. 101–102.

40. James Leasor, *War at the Top: The Experiences of General Sir Leslie Hollis, KCB KBE*, p. 100.

41. Henry H. Arnold, *Global Mission*, pp. 217–218.

42. Kenneth Young, ed, *The Diaries of Sir Robert Bruce Lockhart*, Volume II, p. 483.

43. W. Averell Harriman and Elie Abel, *Special Envoy to Churchill and Stalin, 1941–1946*, p. 202.

44. W. Averell Harriman and Elie Abel, *Special Envoy to Churchill and Stalin, 1941–1946*, p. 206.

45. Smith became Earl Birkenhead in 1922.

46. Woodrow Wyatt, *Distinguished for Talent: Some Men of Influence and Enterprise*, pp. 42–43.

47. Martin S. Gilbert, *Winston S. Churchill: Finest Hour, 1939–1941*, p. 619 (Churchill to Beaverbrook, July 4, 1940).

48. Kenneth Young, *Churchill and Beaverbrook: A Study in Friendship and Politics*, pp. 168–169.

49. Elliott Roosevelt, *As He Saw It*, p. 45.

50. Robert E. Sherwood, *Roosevelt and Hopkins: An Intimate History*, p. 810.

51. Robert E. Sherwood, *Roosevelt and Hopkins: An Intimate History*, p. 811.

52. Robert E. Sherwood, *Roosevelt and Hopkins: An Intimate History*, p. 836. (Beaverbrook to Hopkins, October 23, 1944).

53. British economist John Maynard Keynes called Britain's depletion of its gold reserves in 1940 the "story of financial imprudence that has no parallel in history. Nevertheless, that imprudence may have been a face of that single-minded devotion, without which the war would have been lost. So we beg leave to think that it was worthwhile—for us, and also for you." Randall Bennett Woods, *A Changing of the Guard: Anglo-American Relations, 1941–1946*, p. 185. See Correlli Barnett, *The Collapse of British Power*, pp. 12–15, 588–593.

54. Thomas Parrish, *To Keep the British Isles Afloat: FDR's Men in Churchill's London, 1941*, p. 30.

55. Winston S. Churchill, *The Grand Alliance: The Second World War*, Volume V, p. 402.

56. Robert E. Sherwood, *Roosevelt and Hopkins: An Intimate History*, p. 393

57. Robert E. Sherwood, *Roosevelt and Hopkins: An Intimate History*, p. 393.

58. Admiral William H. Standley, who was part of the Beaverbrook-Harriman mission, wrote of his return to Washington: "We had started the flow of supplies, which would become a flood of Lend-Lease aid to Russia, the extent and effects of which would be more surprising, and, in the end, would extend into fields and would continue in time far beyond the expectation of those original negotiators. We had been ordered to 'give and give' and we had carried out those orders with efficiency and despatch, but little did we know, in those Fall days of 1941, that a few years later we would also be 'taken' by the Russians without even a 'Thank you' by way of return." William H. Standley and Arthur A. Ageton, *Admiral Ambassador to Russia*, pp. 76–77.

59. W. Averell Harriman and Elie Abel, *Special Envoy to Churchill and Stalin, 1941–1946*, p. 105.

60. Robert E. Sherwood, *Roosevelt and Hopkins: An Intimate History*, p. 470.

61. Baron Charles McMoran Wilson Moran, *Churchill: Taken from the Diaries of Lord Moran: The Struggle for Survival, 1940–1965*, p. 22 (January 1, 1942).

62. Robert E. Sherwood, *Roosevelt and Hopkins: An Intimate History*, p. 474.

63. Kenneth Young, *Churchill and Beaverbrook: A Study in Friendship and Politics*, p. 151.

64. Winston S. Churchill, *The Hinge of Fate: The Second World War*, Volume IV, p. 67.

65. Winston S. Churchill, *The Hinge of Fate: The Second World War*, Volume IV, p. 73 (Max Beaverbrook to Winston S. Churchill, February 17, 1942).

66. Winston S. Churchill, *The Hinge of Fate: The Second World War*, Volume IV, p. 74.

67. W. Averell Harriman and Elie Abel, *Special Envoy to Churchill and Stalin, 1941–1946*, pp. 206–207.

68. W. Averell Harriman and Elie Abel, *Special Envoy to Churchill and Stalin, 1941–1946*, p. 208.

69. W. Averell Harriman and Elie Abel, *Special Envoy to Churchill and Stalin, 1941–1946*, pp. 209–210.

70. Kenneth Young, *Churchill and Beaverbrook: A Study in Friendship and Politics*, p. 240–241. The Foreign Office's Oliver Harvey wrote in his diary on March 21, 1942: "At last too the Beaver has been got off. Fifteen film-stars couldn't have been more temperamental,

changing his mind and saying he didn't want to go (which he did) and saying he wouldn't go unless the P.M. *asked* him to go. . . . He will advocate our Russian policy at any rate. Russia has become his obsession and for that we must be thankful." John Harvey, ed, *War Diaries of Oliver Harvey*, pp. 111–112 (March 21, 1942).

71. Robert E. Sherwood, *Roosevelt and Hopkins: An Intimate History*, p. 553.

72. Kenneth Young, *Churchill and Beaverbrook: A Study in Friendship and Politics*, pp. 251 (Max Beaverbrook to Samuel Hoare, February 2, 1943).

73. Robert E. Sherwood, *Roosevelt and Hopkins: An Intimate History*, pp. 728–729.

74. Beaverbrook was not averse to criticizing his own government, writing Hopkins in early 1942: "Britain has no foreign policy toward Russia." Lloyd C. Gardner, *Spheres of Influence: The Great Powers Partition Europe, from Munich to Yalta*, p. 122.

CHAPTER VIII. LORD LOTHIAN AND LORD HALIFAX

1. Nicholas Tarling, *Britain, Southeast Asia and the Onset of the Pacific War*, p. 128. See Thomas Martin Sobottke, *The Management of the American Relationship: British Foreign Policy and the United States: 1940*, p. 77.

2. David Reynolds, *The Creation of the Anglo-American Alliance*, p. 101.

3. David Reynolds, "Lord Lothian and Anglo-American Relations, 1939–1940," *Transactions of the American Philosophical Society*, Volume 73, Part 2 (1983), p. 2.

4. General Raymond E. Lee wrote that Lothian "knew quite a lot about the Empire and also quite a lot about politics. But what really fixed him in the United States was the fact that he had written for the newspapers and could therefore parade himself as a journalist. This immediately put him on a first-rate basis with the newspaper fraternity in Washington, and he exploited it to the utmost." James Leutze, ed, *The London Observer: The Journal of General Raymond E. Lee*, p. 174 (December 12, 1940).

5. Joseph Persico, *Roosevelt's Secret War*, p. 59.

6. Earl of Halifax, *Fullness of Days*, p. 239.

7. David Reynolds, "Lord Lothian and Anglo-American Relations, 1939–1940," *Transactions of the American Philosophical Society*, Volume 73, Part 2 (1983), pp. 2, 5.

8. David Reynolds, "Lord Lothian and Anglo-American Relations, 1939–1940," *Transactions of the American Philosophical Society*, Volume 73, Part 2 (1983), p. 11.

9. David Reynolds, "Lord Lothian and Anglo-American Relations, 1939–1940," *Transactions of the American Philosophical Society*, Volume 73, Part 2 (1983), pp. 40–42.

10. David Reynolds, "Lord Lothian and Anglo-American Relations, 1939–1940," *Transactions of the American Philosophical Society*, Volume 73, Part 2 (1983), p. 25.

11. David Reynolds, "Lord Lothian and Anglo-American Relations, 1939–1940," *Transactions of the American Philosophical Society*, Volume 73, Part 2 (1983), p. 29.

12. Thomas Parrish, *To Keep the British Isles Afloat: FDR's Men in Churchill's London, 1941*, p. 101.

13. Winston S. Churchill, *Their Finest Hour: The Second World War*, Volume II, p. 490.

14. Speaking to the War Cabinet on August 25, 1941, Churchill said he "sometimes wondered whether the President realised the risk which the United States were running by keeping out of the war. If Germany beat Russia to a standstill and the United States had made no further advance towards entry into the war, there was a great danger that the war might take a turn against us. While no doubt we could hope to keep going, this was a very

different matter from imposing our will on Nazi Germany." Martin S. Gilbert, *Churchill: Finest Hour, 1939–1941*, p. 1173. A few days later, Churchill wrote his son: "The President, for all his warm heart and good intentions, is thought by many of his admirers to move with public opinion rather than to lead and form it. I thank God however that he is where he is." Martin S. Gilbert, *Winston S. Churchill: Finest Hour, 1939–1941*, p. 1177 (Winston S. Churchill to Randolph Churchill, August 29, 1941).

15. David Reynolds, "Lord Lothian and Anglo-American Relations, 1939–1940," *Transactions of the American Philosophical Society*, Volume 73, Part 2 (1983), p. 20 (Winston S. Churchill to Mackenzie King, June 5, 1940). There was a desperate quality to Churchill's messages during the desperate days of June, as he struggled to keep France in the war and, at the very least, prevent the Germans from obtaining use of the French fleet. Churchill wrote in his memoirs that he took French Admiral François Darlan aside on June 12: "Darlan, you must never let them get the French Fleet." According to Churchill, Darlan "promised solemnly that he would never do so." Winston S. Churchill, *Their Finest Hour: The Second World War*, Volume II, p. 141.

16. Winston S. Churchill, *Their Finest Hour: The Second World War*, Volume II, p. 355 (Telegram from Winston S. Churchill to Lord Lothian, June 9, 1940).

17. Winston S. Churchill, *Their Finest Hour: The Second World War*, Volume II, p. 357.

18. Winston S. Churchill, *Their Finest Hour: The Second World War*, Volume II, p. 358.

19. Winston S. Churchill, *Their Finest Hour: The Second World War*, Volume II, pp. 358–359 (Winston S. Churchill to Lord Halifax, August 7, 1940).

20. Winston S. Churchill, *Their Finest Hour: The Second World War*, Volume II, p. 367 (Telegram from Winston S. Churchill to Franklin D. Roosevelt, August 31, 1940).

21. Winston S. Churchill, *Their Finest Hour: The Second World War*, Volume II, pp. 354, 503.

22. John Wheeler-Bennett, *Special Relationships: America in Peace and War*, p. 112. William L. Langer and S. Everett Gleason wrote: "Lord Lothian's blunt statement to the reporters upon his return was regarded in Washington as a most undiplomatic *faux pas*. Both the President and Mr. Morgenthau feared that it would arouse the suspicions of Congress and jeopardize such prospects as there were for approval of increased assistance to Britain. Mr. Hull was not only annoyed, but also skeptical as to whether the British financial picture was as black as Lothian painted it." William L. Langer and S. Everett Gleason, *The Undeclared War, 1940–1941*, p. 224.

23. David Reynolds, "Lord Lothian and Anglo-American Relations, 1939–1940," *Transactions of the American Philosophical Society*, Volume 73, Part 2 (1983), p. 48.

24. David Reynolds, "Lord Lothian and Anglo-American Relations, 1939–1940," *Transactions of the American Philosophical Society*, Volume 73, Part 2 (1983), p. 50 (Memo from Churchill to Lord Lothian, November 30, 1940).

25. David Reynolds, "Lord Lothian and Anglo-American Relations, 1939–1940," *Transactions of the American Philosophical Society*, Volume 73, Part 2 (1983), p. 51 (Telegram from Lord Lothian to Lord Halifax, November 28, 1940). Churchill wrote Lord Lothian at the end of June: "I don't think words count for much now. Too much attention should not be paid to eddies of United States opinion. Only force of events can govern them." Winston S. Churchill, *Their Finest Hour: The Second World War*, Volume II, p. 201 (June 28, 1940).

26. Robert E. Sherwood, *Roosevelt and Hopkins: An Intimate History*, pp. 221–222.

27. Winston S. Churchill, *Their Finest Hour: The Second World War*, Volume II, p. 501. Lothian became a consistent advocate of full disclosure in dealing with the Americans. Martin

Gilbert wrote: "Lothian believed that it was 'imperative' for Churchill to inform Roosevelt 'as soon as possible' of the numbers, types and tonnages of destroyers lost, of the numbers damaged, of the time taken to repair these, 'and any other information necessary to convince him of our case.' The American Press, Lothian added ominously, had been carrying a statement 'that we have already made good all destroyers.'" Martin S. Gilbert, *Winston S. Churchill: Finest Hour, 1939–1941*, p. 493.

28. Winston S. Churchill, *Their Finest Hour: The Second World War*, Volume II, p. 502. Roosevelt's language mimicked a memo sent him in August 1940, by Secretary of the Interior Harold L. Ickes. "It seems to me, we Americans are like the householder who refuses to lend or sell his fire extinguishers to help put out the fire in the house that is right next door although that house is all ablaze and the wind is blowing from that direction." Martin S. Gilbert, *Winston S. Churchill: Finest Hour, 1939–1941*, p. 694.

29. Robert E. Sherwood, *Roosevelt and Hopkins: An Intimate History*, p. 224.

30. Historian Richard Toye wrote that Lloyd George twice had meetings in December with Churchill about the position, convincing the prime minister of what others already knew—that the 77-year-old Lloyd George had lost both physical stamina and mental acuity. Churchill remarked that "he babbled of pigs." Lloyd George took himself out of consideration and would become increasingly critical of Churchill's conduct of the war. Richard Toye, *Lloyd George & Churchill*, pp. 376–377, 384–385.

31. John Lukacs, *The Duel: 10 May–31 July 1940: The Eighty-Day Struggle Between Churchill and Hitler*, p. 90. John Colville wrote of these critical discussions: "The Cabinet are feverishly considering our ability to carry on the war alone in such circumstances and there are signs that Halifax is being defeatist. He says our aim can no longer be to crush Germany, but rather to preserve our own integrity and independence." John Colville, *The Fringes of Power*, pp. 140–141 (May 27, 1940). Because Halifax did not want to be prime minister on May 10, 1940, did not mean that Halifax did not intend to be prime minister in the future. Historian Walter Reid wrote that Halifax "almost certainly hoped that he would have the opportunity of taking over in more congenial circumstances before long." Walter Reid, *Churchill: 1940–1945, Under Friendly Fire*, p. 27.

32. British Labour leader Herbert Morrison recalled: "Halifax was a man of deep sincerity and pleasing personality. In the Churchill coalition he gave the impression of being a competent statesman though not, perhaps, one destined for immortal fame. Churchill seemed to get on well enough with him, but there was a certain coolness which suggested that he had not entirely forgotten Halifax's connexion with a cabinet which had pursued, in his judgment, wrong policies before and after war broke out. He was one of the men of Munich." Herbert Morrison, *An Autobiography*, p. 200.

33. Winston S. Churchill, *Their Finest Hour: The Second World War*, Volume II, p. 504.

34. Richard Langworth, ed, *Churchill by Himself*, p. 344 (January 9, 1941).

35. Nigel Hamilton, *The Mantle of Command: FDR at War 1941–1942*, p. 78.

36. R. A. Butler: *The Art of the Possible: The Memoirs of Lord Butler*, p. 85.

37. Warren Kimball, ed, *Churchill and Roosevelt, The Complete Correspondence*, Volume I, p. 116 (Churchill to Roosevelt, December 21, 1940).

38. Thomas Parrish, *To Keep the British Isles Afloat: FDR's Men in Churchill's London, 1941*, p. 167. General Raymond E. Lee accompanied Halifax on this voyage across the Atlantic. As they approached the United States, it was announced "that the President will meet us at Annapolis and board us if possible. Thus Lord Halifax is to be passed from Churchill to Roosevelt, almost like a bit of cut glass or a jewel." James Leutze, ed, *The London Observer: The*

Journal of General Raymond E. Lee, p. 231 (January 23, 1941). From Britain, Hopkins wrote FDR that his shipboard greeting of Halifax was "received warmly here" in the press. Michael Fullilove, *Rendezvous with Destiny*, p. 141.

39. Sir John Wheeler-Bennett, *Special Relationships*, p. 118. Interior secretary Harold Ickes, often critical of others in his diary, had relatively kind words for Halifax. "Either Lord Halifax has a good memory or he was well posted because he recalled, in flattering detail, our former meeting in his office and even what I had said on that occasion. I thought that he looked more tired than when I saw him in London almost three years ago. He is certainly grave and courteous, and I am convinced, a perfectly sincere man." Harold LeClair Ickes, *The Secret Diary of Harold L. Ickes: The Lowering Clouds, 1939–1941*, p. 428 (February 8, 1941).

40. John Colville, *Winston Churchill and His Inner Circle*, p. 123. The new ambassador was taken aback when he was invited to dinner with a group of forty Republican congressmen. The custom was for each to ask the ambassador a question. One prefaced his remarks by stating, "I would like you to know that every one of us in this room thinks President Roosevelt is as dangerous a dictator as Hitler or Mussolini, and that he is taking this country to hell just as fast as he can." Ambassador Halifax could also be tough on American critics of appeasement: "In this business the American critics were like people who had collected to watch a great fight and expressed disappointment that the entertainment was called off. But never had they intended to be more than spectators of the fight." Earl of Halifax, *Fullness of Days*, pp. 241–242.

41. Warren Kimball, *The Juggler: Franklin Roosevelt as Wartime Statesman*, p. 21 (Lord Halifax to John Simon, March 21, 1941).

42. Gordon Martel, ed, *American Foreign Relations Reconsidered: 1890–1993*, p. 20 (J. Garry Clifford: "'They don't come out where you expect': institutions of American diplomacy and the policy of process.")

43. Joseph P. Lash, *Roosevelt and Churchill, 1939–1941*, p. 302.

44. Baron Charles McMoran Wilson Moran, *Churchill: Taken from the Diaries of Lord Moran: The Struggle for Survival, 1940–1965*, p. 791 (July 3, 1958). In his memoirs, Halifax did speak generously of FDR's hospitality and congeniality. "One of the greatest of his gifts was the power that he had of putting any visitor immediately and completely at ease," wrote Halifax. "Conversation ranged widely, and ran on without the least inhibition of ceremonious restraint. He would deal with any subject that came up, and once satisfied that his confidence would be respected would discuss freely." Earl of Halifax, *Fullness of Days*, p. 249.

45. Sir John Wheeler-Bennett, *Special Relationships*, p. 119.

46. Robert Dallek, *Franklin Roosevelt and American Foreign Policy, 1932–1945*, p. 289.

47. Andrew Roberts, *Masters and Commanders*, pp. 83–84.

48. David Lawrence, *Diary of a Washington Correspondent*, pp. 280–281 (December 31, 1942).

49. Nigel Hamilton, *The Mantle of Command: FDR at War, 1941–1942*, p. 293.

50. Earl of Birkenhead, *Halifax: The Life of Lord Halifax*, p. 538.

51. Earl of Birkenhead, *Halifax: The Life of Lord Halifax*, pp. 534–535.

52. Earl of Birkenhead, *Halifax: The Life of Lord Halifax*, p. 538. Eden aide Oliver Harvey wrote of the ambassador in his diary on March 15, 1943: "Poor H. is most helpful and yet he kills everything that comes near him. He devitalises his staff. . . . Yet H. has a very good mind and has very attractive sides. He has a devastating simplicity but I remind myself that it conceals a harsh and ruthless nature." John Harvey, ed, *War Diaries of Oliver Harvey*, p. 231 (March 15, 1943).

53. Earl of Birkenhead, *Halifax: The Life of Lord Halifax*, p. 537.

54. Kenneth Young, *Churchill and Beaverbrook: A Study in Friendship and Politics*, p. 171.

55. Kenneth Young, *Churchill and Beaverbrook: A Study in Friendship and Politics*, p. 255 (Memo from Max Beaverbrook to Winston S. Churchill, July 19, 1943).

CHAPTER IX. PEARL HARBOR

1. Franklin D. Roosevelt, *The War Messages of Franklin D. Roosevelt*, December 8, 1941, to April 13, 1945, p. 11.

2. Fraser J. Harbutt, *Yalta 1945: Europe and America at the Crossroads*, p. 34.

3. John Gilbert Winant, *Letter from Grosvenor Square*, pp. 273–275.

4. Brian Lavery, *Churchill Goes to War*, p. 67.

5. Baron Charles McMoran Wilson Moran, *Churchill: Taken from the Diaries of Lord Moran: The Struggle for Survival, 1940–1965*, p. 10.

6. John Gilbert Winant, *Letter from Grosvenor Square*, p. 278.

7. John Gilbert Winant, *Letter from Grosvenor Square*, p. 278.

8. David Reynolds, *In Command of History*, p. 264.

9. Winston S. Churchill, *The Grand Alliance: The Second World War*, Volume III, p. 538. In a letter Kathleen Harriman wrote but never mailed, she observed that after the news, "P.M. pacing in dragon wrapper, danced a jig. Ave standing by the fireplace." Marie Brenner, "To War in Silk Stockings," *Vanity Fair*, November 2011.

10. Robert E. Sherwood, *Roosevelt and Hopkins: An Intimate History*, pp. 426, 430–431, 432. On December 6, 1941, Harriman wired Hopkins: "The President should be informed of Churchill's belief that in the event of aggression by the Japanese it would be the policy of the British to postpone taking any action—even though this delay might involve some military sacrifice—until the President has taken such action as, under the circumstances, he considers best. Then Churchill will act 'not within the hour but within the minute.'" W. Averell Harriman and Elie Abel, *Special Envoy to Churchill and Stalin, 1941–1946*, p. 111.

11. William L. Langer and S. Everett Gleason, *The Undeclared War, 1940–1941*, p. 938.

12. Ross T. McIntire, *White House Physician*, p. 137.

13. John Q. Barrett, ed, *That Man: An Insider's Portrait of Franklin D. Roosevelt*, p. 104.

14. William L. Langer and S. Everett Gleason, *The Undeclared War, 1940–1941*, p. 936.

15. Michael Fullilove, *Rendezvous with Destiny*, pp. 341–345.

16. Arthur Krock, *Memoirs: Sixty Years on the Firing Line*, p. 203.

17. It was lucky for the Allies that three U.S. aircraft carriers had been ordered to sea and were not in Pearl Harbor when Japan attacked. The U.S. Navy was thereby forced to rely on carriers rather than battleships in its war against Japan. This proved providential at the Battle of Midway. Andrew Roberts, *The Storm of War*, p. 189.

18. Dean Acheson, *Present at the Creation: My Years in the State Department*, p. 38.

19. Robert Dallek, *Franklin Roosevelt and American Foreign Policy, 1932–1945*, p. 305.

20. Robert Dallek, *Franklin Roosevelt and American Foreign Policy, 1932–1945*, pp. 309–311.

21. Robert E. Sherwood, *Roosevelt and Hopkins: An Intimate History*, p. 427. See Elting Morison, *Turmoil and Tradition*, p. 525.

22. Robert Dallek, *Franklin Roosevelt and American Foreign Policy, 1932–1945*, p. 309.

23. Michael Fullilove, *Rendezvous with Destiny*, p. 340.

24. Ross T. McIntire, *White House Physician*, p. 77.

25. David Stafford, *Roosevelt and Churchill: Men of Secrets*, p. 123.
26. Lynne Olson, *Citizens of London*, p. 33.
27. Joseph Persico, *Roosevelt's Centurions: FDR and the Commanders He Led to Victory in World War II*, p. 97.
28. Joseph E. Persico, *Roosevelt's Secret War: FDR and World War II Espionage*, p. 136.
29. Murrow conferred with Hopkins in his bedroom before Hopkins finally went to bed. After describing the Japanese attack as a "Godsend" for uniting the country behind the war effort, Hopkins lamented: "Oh, God—if I only had the strength." Christopher D. O'Sullivan, *Harry Hopkins: FDR's Envoy to Churchill and Stalin*, p. 76.
30. Robert H. Pilpel, *Churchill in America, 1895–1961*, p. 140.
31. Winston S. Churchill, *The Grand Alliance: The Second World War*, Volume III, p. 588.
32. Kenneth S. Davis, *FDR: The War President, 1940–1945*, pp. 381–382.
33. Robert E. Sherwood, *Roosevelt and Hopkins: An Intimate History*, p. 478.

CHAPTER X. ANTHONY EDEN

1. Anthony Eden, *The Reckoning*, p. 512.
2. Anthony Eden, *The Reckoning*, p. 594.
3. Jonathan Schneer, *Ministers at War: Winston Churchill and His War Cabinet*, pp. 47–48.
4. Winston S. Churchill, *Their Finest Hour: The Second World War*, Volume II, p. 21.
5. Historian Keith Sainsbury wrote: "To the wider British public he [Eden] was better known than any other of Churchill's colleagues and already commanded great public prestige. Alone of the wartime ministers he had regularly accompanied Churchill to wartime conferences, besides leading missions himself on occasions, thus getting to know most of the Allied leaders. . . . No one questioned his grasp of foreign affairs or his skill and patience in negotiations." Sainsbury acknowledged that Eden's "vanity led him sometimes to overestimate the worth of agreements which he had been able to reach, and judge their real value too uncritically. He was sometimes indecisive. He was also apt to immerse himself too much in details, at the expense of the wider picture. He lacked the broad creative vision of Churchill: in a word, he lacked inspiration." Keith Sainsbury, *The Turning Point: Roosevelt, Stalin, Churchill, and Chiang-Kai-Shek, 1943*, p. 44. Historian R. W. Thompson was even more critical, writing that Eden was "a poor and dangerous counselor, for he lived in a rarified political air of his own, incapable of relating political ends to military means, a condition that would bring him to ruin" in the Suez Canal crisis of 1956. R. W. Thompson, *Winston Churchill: The Yankee Marlborough*, p. 291.
6. Winston S. Churchill, *The Grand Alliance: The Second World War*, Volume III, p. 60 (February 12, 1941).
7. John Harvey, ed, *War Diaries of Oliver Harvey*, p. 50 (October 9, 1941).
8. John Harvey, ed, *War Diaries of Oliver Harvey*, p. 143 (July 24, 1942).
9. Anthony Eden, *The Reckoning*, p. 445 (April 21, 1943).
10. Winston S. Churchill, *Their Finest Hour: The Second World War*, Volume II, p. 448.
11. Winston S. Churchill, *Their Finest Hour: The Second World War*, Volume II, p. 480.
12. S. M. Plokhy, *Yalta: The Price of Peace*, p. 64.
13. John Gilbert Winant, *Letter from Grosvenor Square*, pp. 95–96.
14. John Harvey, ed, *War Diaries of Oliver Harvey*, p. 26 (August 4, 1941).

15. John Harvey, ed, *War Diaries of Oliver Harvey*, p. 68 (December 2, 1941). Eden did not enjoy unproductive confrontations such as those in which Beaverbrook and Bracken often engaged with Churchill. In May 1945, as Churchill tried to put together a Conservative government before parliamentary elections, both Bracken and Beaverbrook bickered with Churchill. "I loathe these scenes," wrote Eden in his diary. "They are a hideous waste of time & after my father's rages, these storms only bore me." Robert Rhodes James, *Anthony Eden: A Biography*, p. 295. A key Churchill administration official told Churchill's physician: "Of course Anthony always gave way to Winston. We were often furious with him at the F.O. He would return and say Winston had been very nice to him and they had agreed. But this was because he cannot bear scenes or any sort of unpleasantness. However, when his mind is made up on a policy, no one sticks to it with the same tenacity as Anthony." Lord Moran, *Churchill: The Struggle for Survival 1945–60*, p. 720 (July 10, 1955).

16. Robert Rhodes James, *Anthony Eden: A Biography*, p. 237 (Anthony Eden to Winston S. Churchill, November 30, 1940).

17. David Dilks, *Churchill and Company*, p. 160.

18. Anthony Eden, *The Reckoning: The Memoirs of Anthony Eden, Earl of Avon*, p. 426.

19. John Harvey, ed, *War Diaries of Oliver Harvey*, p. 274 (July 14, 1943).

20. Historian David Dilks observed that as foreign secretary, Eden "traveled once to Ankara, twice to Washington and Quebec, thrice to Athens and Moscow and four times to Cairo, in addition to attending the conferences at Tehran, Yalta, San Francisco and Potsdam." David Dilks, ed, *The Diaries of Sir Alexander Cadogan, O.M., 1938–1945*, p. 345.

21. Warren Kimball, ed, *Churchill & Roosevelt: The Complete Correspondence*, Volume II, p. 54 (Roosevelt to Churchill, December 3, 1942).

22. Warren Kimball, ed, *Churchill & Roosevelt: The Complete Correspondence*, Volume II, p. 74 (Roosevelt to Churchill, December 14, 1942).

23. W. Averell Harriman and Elie Abel, *Special Envoy to Churchill and Stalin, 1941–1946*, p. 177.

24. Fraser J. Harbutt, *Yalta 1945: Europe and America at the Crossroads*, p. 59 (Anthony Eden, "Policy towards Russia," January 28, 1942).

25. Albert Resis, ed, *Molotov Remembers*, p. 50.

26. Anthony Eden, *The Reckoning*, p. 376.

27. Elisabeth Barker wrote: "Differences between Churchill and Eden over Stalin were tactical, or the product of momentary moods or circumstances, rather than matters of fundamental strategy. Eden liked it to be known in the Foreign Office that he sometimes thought differently from Churchill." Elisabeth Barker, *Churchill and Eden at War*, p. 230.

28. Winston S. Churchill, *The Hinge of Fate: The Second World War*, Volume IV, p. 650 (Roosevelt to Churchill, February 12, 1943).

29. Geoffrey C. Ward, ed, *Closest Companion: The Unknown Story of the Intimate Friendship between Franklin Roosevelt and Margaret Suckley*, p. 232 (August 28, 1943).

30. Winston S. Churchill, *The Hinge of Fate: The Second World War*, Volume IV, p. 662 (Roosevelt to Churchill, March 17, 1943).

31. Geoffrey C. Ward, ed, *Closest Companion: The Unknown Story of the Intimate Friendship between Franklin Roosevelt and Margaret Suckley*, p. 207 (April 2, 1943).

32. John Harvey, ed, *War Diaries of Oliver Harvey*, p. 228 (March 11, 1943).

33. Geoffrey C. Ward, ed, *Closest Companion: The Unknown Story of the Intimate Friendship between Franklin Roosevelt and Margaret Suckley*, p. 207 (August 28, 1943).

34. Eden's great-great-grandfather, Robert Eden, had been Maryland's last colonial governor and a friend of George Washington. Anthony Eden, *The Reckoning*, p. 435.

35. Anthony Eden, *The Reckoning*, p. 395 (August 20, 1943).

36. Anthony Eden, *The Reckoning*, p. 470 (September 10, 1943).

37. Anthony Eden, *The Reckoning*, p. 593.

38. Fraser J. Harbutt, *Yalta 1945: Europe and America at the Crossroads*, p. 95.

39. Benjamin Welles, *Sumner Welles: FDR's Global Strategist*, pp. 296–297.

40. Elisabeth Barker, *Churchill and Eden at War*, p. 75. By early 1944, Roosevelt tried to change his tone. After Eisenhower asked for instructions for dealing with de Gaulle in the preparations for D-Day, FDR wrote Marshall denying that he was "anti-de Gaulle. . . . I am perfectly willing to have de Gaulle made President, or Emperor, or King or anything else so long as the action comes in an untrammeled and unforced way from the French people themselves." Ed Cray, *General of the Army: George C. Marshall, Soldier and Statesman*, p. 462. Robert Dallek wrote that "other FDR comments on de Gaulle belie these words. 'The only thing I am interested in,' he told Stettinius in May [1944], 'is not having de Gaulle and the National Committee named as the government of France.' He expected no cooperation from de Gaulle, he advised Churchill in June. 'It seems clear that prima donnas do not change their spots.' He 'would not now permit that "jackenape" to seize the government,' he told Stimson ten days after the Allies had landed in France." Robert Dallek, *Franklin Roosevelt and American Foreign Policy, 1932–1945*, p. 459.

41. Cordell Hull, *The Memoirs of Cordell Hull*, Volume II, pp. 1232–1233.

42. Anthony Eden, *The Reckoning*, p. 466 (August 20, 1943).

43. Ed Cray, *General of the Army: George C. Marshall*, p. 463.

44. Walter Reid, *Churchill: 1940–1945, Under Friendly Fire*, p. 225.

45. Lord General Hastings Ismay, *The Memoirs of General Lord Ismay*, p. 327.

46. William D. Hassett, *Off the Record with FDR, 1942–1945*, p. 218 (November 1, 1943).

47. Winston S. Churchill, *Closing the Ring: The Second World War*, Volume V, pp. 265–266.

48. Anthony Eden, *The Reckoning*, p. 595. Alone among the major Anglo-American diplomats during World War II, Eden had conferred with Stalin before the war in 1935.

49. Richard Langworth, ed, *Churchill by Himself*, p. 340 (February 27, 1945).

CHAPTER XI. GEORGE C. MARSHALL AND DWIGHT D. EISENHOWER

1. Dwight D. Eisenhower, *At Ease: Stories I Tell to Friends*, pp. 389–390.

2. Andrew Roberts, *Masters and Commanders*, p. 28.

3. Ed Cray, *General of the Army: George C. Marshall, Soldier and Statesman*, p. 132.

4. Doris Kearns Goodwin, *No Ordinary Time*, p. 24. Jonathan W. Jordan wrote: "When Roosevelt did ask Marshall for his opinions, he gave them straight and to the point. He counseled subordinates to put written recommendations to the president in plain English, without flourish, preferably condensed to one page. 'He is quickly bored by papers, lengthy discussions, and by anything short of a few pungent sentences of description,' Marshall told them. 'You have to intrigue his interest.'" Jonathan W. Jordan, *American Warlords: How Roosevelt's High Command Led America to Victory in World War II*, p. 28.

5. Lord General Hastings Ismay, *The Memoirs of General Lord Ismay*, p. 253. Dr. Wilson recalled Churchill calling Marshall the "noblest Roman of them all" at Potsdam. Baron Charles McMoran Wilson Moran, *Churchill: Taken from the Diaries of Lord Moran: The Struggle for Survival, 1940–1965*, p. 292 (July 17, 1945). As Churchill flew on to North Africa, he wrote Clementine from Gibraltar in May 1943: "I got the President to let General Marshall come with me in order that the work I am now about to do at Algiers should run evenly, and that there should be no suggestion I had exerted a one-sided influence. I think very highly of Marshall. He wrote a paper the day before yesterday in the airplane on general strategy. It was one of the most masterly I have seen, and with which I am in the fullest accord. There is no doubt he has a massive brain and a very high and honourable character." Mary Soames, ed, *Winston and Clementine: The Personal Letters of the Churchills*, p. 473 (Winston Churchill to Clementine Churchill, May 28, 1943).

6. Winston S. Churchill, *The Hinge of Fate: Second World War*, Volume IV, pp. 726–727.

7. Joan Bright Astley, *The Inner Circle: A View of War at the Top*, p. 197.

8. Baron Charles McMoran Wilson Moran, *Churchill: Taken from the Diaries of Lord Moran: The Struggle for Survival, 1940–1965*, p. 22 (January 1, 1942).

9. Randolph S. Churchill, ed, *The Sinews of Peace, Post-War Speeches by Winston S. Churchill*, pp. 108–109 (Speech to General Assembly of Virginia, March 8, 1946).

10. Winston S. Churchill, *The Hinge of Fate: The Second World War*, Volume IV, p. 472.

11. Elisabeth Barker, *Churchill and Eden at War*, p. 134.

12. Walter Reid, *Churchill: 1940–1945, Under Friendly Fire*, p. 276.

13. Forrest C. Pogue, *George C. Marshall: Ordeal and Hope, 1939–1942*, pp. 305–306.

14. Forrest C. Pogue, *George C. Marshall: Ordeal and Hope, 1939–1942*, p. 313.

15. A decade after the war ended, Marshall admitted that General Montgomery's carping got to him at a meeting in early 1945. "I was under terrific urge to whittle him down. And then I thought, now this is Eisenhower's business and not mine, and I had better not meddle, though it was very hard for me to restrain myself." Larry I. Bland, ed, *George C. Marshall: Interviews and Reminiscences for Forest C. Pogue*, p. 345 (November 15, 1956).

16. Arthur Bryant, *Triumph in the West*, p. 162 (John Dill to Alan Brooke, July 7, 1944).

17. Lord General Hastings Ismay, *The Memoirs of General Lord Ismay*, p. 251.

18. Omar N. Bradley, *A Soldier's Story*, p. 204.

19. Andrew Roberts noted that the American difficulty in subduing the remnants of Rommel's Afrika Corps, cornered in Tunisia in early 1943, "perfectly illustrates the formidable and apparently ubiquitous German capacity for counter-attack, and illustrates why Marshall's plan for an early attack on north-west France was probably impracticable." Andrew Roberts, *The Storm of War*, p. 310.

20. Alex Danchev and Daniel Todman, eds, *War Diaries, 1939–1945: Field Marshal Lord Alanbrooke*, p. 246 (April 9, 1942).

21. Alex Danchev and Daniel Todman, eds, *War Diaries, 1939–1945: Field Marshal Lord Alanbrooke*, p. 249.

22. Robert E. Sherwood, *Roosevelt and Hopkins: An Intimate History*, p. 787. Badgered by Stalin to name an OVERLORD chief at Teheran, FDR told Admiral Leahy: "That old Bolshevik is trying to force me to give him the name of our Supreme Commander. I just can't tell him because I have not yet made up my mind." William D. Leahy, *I Was There*, p. 208.

23. Robert E. Sherwood, *Roosevelt and Hopkins: An Intimate History*, p. 759. Determined to keep Marshall in Washington, the crafty Admiral King launched a covert press campaign

to suggest that any OVERLORD appointment for Marshall would be bad for the war effort. Thomas B. Buell, *Master of Sea Power: A Biography of Fleet Admiral Ernest J. King*, pp. 410–411.

24. Henry Hitch Adams, *Witness to Power: The Life of Fleet Admiral William D. Leahy*, p. 225.

25. Henry L. Stimson and McGeorge Bundy, *On Active Service in Peace and War*, p. 437 (Memo from Henry Stimson to Franklin D. Roosevelt, August 10, 1943).

26. First Sea Lord Andrew B. Cunningham, who briefly served in Washington in 1942, recalled: "We at home have our inter-service rivalries and jealousies; but the dislike existing between the American Army and Navy was an eye-opener to me and was carried to extraordinary lengths. I sometimes wondered if it was drilled into the embryo officers at West Point and Annapolis. General Marshall, Admiral Stark and a few other senior officers were above this constant and acrimonious bickering; but I do not think the same could be said of many others." Viscount Andrew Browne Cunningham, *A Sailor's Odyssey: The Autobiography of Admiral of the Fleet, Viscount Cunningham of Hyndhope*, pp. 466–467.

27. Mark A. Stoler, *George C. Marshall, Soldier-Statesman of the American Century*, p. 89.

28. Viscount Andrew Browne Cunningham, *A Sailor's Odyssey: The Autobiography of Admiral of the Fleet, Viscount Cunningham of Hyndhope*, p. 466. John S. D. Eisenhower indicated his father reciprocated the admiration. "A meeting with Cunningham was always enough to lift one's spirits, for his courage, cheerfulness, and optimism were contagious." John S. D. Eisenhower, *Allies: Pearl Harbor to D-Day*, p. 174. Admiral William Leahy was also a Cunningham fan "because, in the first place, he was a splendid sailor. He was a daring, experienced, and successful British sea commander, worthy of the tradition of Britain's Nelson." William D. Leahy, *I Was There*, p. 106.

29. John Colville, *Winston and His Inner Circle*, p. 122.

30. Carlo D'Este, *Eisenhower: A Soldier's Life*, p. 293.

31. Henry L. Stimson and McGeorge Bundy, *On Active Service in Peace and War*, p. 438 (Henry L. Stimson to Franklin D. Roosevelt, August 10, 1943). After visiting Eisenhower in North Africa in late July 1943, Stimson wrote Roosevelt about Operation OVERLORD: "I believe therefore that the time has come for you to decide that your government must assume the responsibility of leadership in this great final movement of the European war which is now confronting us. We cannot afford to begin the most dangerous operation of the war under halfhearted results. Nearly two years ago the British offered us this command. I think now it should be accepted—if necessary, insisted on." As he consistently did, Stimson pushed for the appointment of Marshall. John S. D. Eisenhower, *Allies: Pearl Harbor to D-Day*, p. 360. Hopkins also pushed for Marshall's appointment.

32. Henry L. Stimson and McGeorge Bundy, *On Active Service in Peace and War*, p. 422 (Diary, December 18, 1943).

33. William D. Leahy, *I Was There*, p. 192.

34. John S. D. Eisenhower, *Allies: Pearl Harbor to D-Day*, pp. 389–390.

35. Robert E. Sherwood, *Roosevelt and Hopkins: An Intimate History*, p. 803.

36. When informed by Averell Harriman that Eisenhower had been chosen to command OVERLORD, Stalin responded: "I am satisfied. He is an officer of great experience in amphibious warfare and a man of determination." Herbert Feis, *Churchill-Roosevelt-Stalin: The War They Waged and the Peace They Sought*, p. 309. General Brooke also commended the choice of Eisenhower: "The selection of Eisenhower rather than Marshall was a good one. Eisenhower had now had a certain amount of experience as a commander and was beginning

to find his feet." Brooke added: "Marshall had never commanded anything in war except, I believe, a company in the First World War." Alex Danchev and Daniel Todman, eds, *War Diaries, 1939–1945: Field Marshal Lord Alanbrooke*, p. 491.

37. Leonard Mosley, *Marshall: Hero for Our Times*, p. 309.

38. John Wheeler-Bennett, *Special Relationships: America in Peace and War*, pp. 178–179.

39. Alex Danchev and Daniel Todman, eds, *War Diaries, 1939–1945: Field Marshal Lord Alanbrooke*, p. 575 (July 27, 1944).

40. Andrew Roberts, *Masters and Commanders*, pp. 216–217.

41. Kay Summersby, *Eisenhower Was My Boss*, p. 20.

42. Harry C. Butcher, *Three Years with Eisenhower: The Personal Diary of Captain Harry C. Butcher, USNR, Naval Aide to General Eisenhower, 1942–1945*, p. 804 (April 18, 1945).

43. Harry C. Butcher, *Three Years with Eisenhower: The Personal Diary of Captain Harry C. Butcher, USNR, Naval Aide to General Eisenhower, 1942–1945*, pp. 257 (February 7, 1943).

44. James C. Humes, *Eisenhower and Churchill: The Partnership that Saved the World*, p. 124.

45. Robert H. Ferrell, ed, *The Eisenhower Diaries*, p. 70 (July 5, 1942).

46. Kay Summersby, *Past Forgetting: My Love Affair with Dwight D. Eisenhower*, pp. 166–167. Ike was not alone in his complaint of Churchill's habits. In the fall of 1943, there was a small party of British officials and Averell Harriman. General Leslie "Jo" Hollis, a key Churchill military aide, arrived in a bad mood. Just before Hollis prepared for the social event, "I was summoned to the PM's suite. He was in his bath and there was steam everywhere." Added to the steam was "the biggest dressing down I've ever had in my life." His wife consoled him: "Well, my darling Jo. . . . Surely you're the only man who has been given a dressing down by the PM in the nude." Joanna Moody, *From Churchill's War Rooms: Letters of a Secretary 1943–45*, p. 62.

47. Carlo D'Este, *Eisenhower: A Soldier's Life*, p. 315. Admiral Andrew B. Cunningham, the naval commander for Operation TORCH, reported back to the British government "that in this most difficult of all types of operation with a number of services involved and despite the difficulties inherent in welding together the systems of command organization, there reigned a spirit of comradeship and understanding which provided that vital force which brought success to our undertakings. The embodiment of that spirit was exemplified in our Commander-in-Chief, General Dwight D. Eisenhower: we count it a privilege to follow in his train." Viscount Andrew Browne Cunningham, *A Sailor's Odyssey: The Autobiography of Admiral of the Fleet, Viscount Cunningham of Hyndhope*, p. 493.

48. James C. Humes, *Eisenhower and Churchill: The Partnership that Saved the World*, p. 185.

49. Stephen E. Ambrose, *The Supreme Commander: The War Years of General Dwight D. Eisenhower*, p. 582.

50. Omar N. Bradley and Clay Blair, *A General's Life: An Autobiography by General of the Army Omar N. Bradley*, pp. 380, 399.

51. British diplomat Harold Macmillan wrote in his diary of Eisenhower in October 1943: "Although completely ignorant of Europe and wholly uneducated (in any normal sense of the word), he has two great qualities which make him much easier to deal with than many superficially better endowed American or British generals. First, he will always listen to and try to grasp the point of an argument. Second, he is absolutely fair-minded and, if he has prejudices, never allows them to sway his final judgment. Compared with the wooden heads and desiccated hearts of many British soldiers I see here, he is a jewel of broad-mindedness and wisdom." Carlo D'Este, *Eisenhower: A Soldier's Life*, p. 457 (October 18, 1943).

52. David Reynolds, *In Command of History: Churchill Fighting and Writing the Second World War*, p. 437 (Winston S. Churchill to Dwight D. Eisenhower, April 9, 1953).

53. Winston S. Churchill, *Triumph and Tragedy: The Second World War*, Volume VI, p. 476 (Winston S. Churchill to Harry Truman, May 9, 1945).

54. James Leasor, *War at the Top: The Experiences of General Sir Leslie Hollis, KCB KBE*, p. 267.

55. Alex Danchev and Daniel Todman, eds, *War Diaries, 1939–1945: Field Marshal Lord Alanbrooke*, p. 365.

56. To rectify that discrepancy, Marshall, MacArthur, Eisenhower, and Arnold were consecutively promoted to the five-star rank "General of the Army" in December 1944.

57. Omar N. Bradley and Clay Blair, *A General's Life: An Autobiography by General of the Army Omar N. Bradley*, pp. 231–232.

58. U.S. Admiral Ernest King caustically said that the Mediterranean had the "soft underbelly of a turtle." Jonathan W. Jordan, *American Warlords: How Roosevelt's High Command Led America to Victory in World War II*, p. 221.

59. Omar N. Bradley and Clay Blair, *A General's Life: An Autobiography by General of the Army Omar N. Bradley*, p. 117.

60. Kay Summersby, *Past Forgetting: My Love Affair with Dwight D. Eisenhower*, pp. 24–25.

61. Arthur Bryant, *The Turn of the Tide: A History of the War Years Based on the Diaries of Field-Marshal Lord Alanbrooke, Chief of the Imperial General Staff*, p. 19 (Montgomery to Brooke, January 1, 1946).

62. Nigel Hamilton, *Montgomery: D-Day Commander*, pp. 6–12.

63. Vincent Orange, *Tedder: Quietly in Command*, p. 218.

64. Montgomery produced his own, unrealistic plan for the invasion of Sicily. Admiral Cunningham wrote back to London on April 28, 1943: "I am afraid Montgomery is a bit of a nuisance; he seems to think that all he has to do is to say what is to be done and everyone will dance to the tune of his piping. Alexander appears quite unable to keep him in order. Tedder is also absolutely opposed to this new plan." Lord Tedder, *With Prejudice: The War Memoirs of Marshal of the Royal Air Force*, p. 430.

65. Richard Langworth, ed, *Churchill by Himself: The Definitive Collection of Quotations*, p. 362 (Winston S. Churchill to Clementine Churchill, August 9, 1942).

66. Max Hastings, *Overlord: D-Day and the Battle for Normandy*, p. 32.

67. Carlo D'Este, *Eisenhower: A Soldier's Life*, p. 511.

68. Alex Danchev and Daniel Todman, eds, *War Diaries, 1939–1945: Field Marshal Lord Alanbrooke*, p. 566 (July 6, 1944).

69. Stephen E. Ambrose, *Eisenhower: Soldier and President*, p. 163.

70. Viscount Montgomery of Alamein, *The Memoirs of Field-Marshal Montgomery*, p. 484.

71. Winston S. Churchill, *The Hinge of Fate: The Second World War*, Volume IV, pp. 419–420.

72. Andrew Roberts, *Masters and Commanders*, p. xxxix. The pugnacious Charles de Gaulle was even more diplomatic in his memoirs, waxing lyrical in his description of Churchill's eloquence and leadership. "Whatever his audience—crowd, assembly, council, even a single interlocutor—whether he was before a microphone, on the floor of the House, at table, or behind a desk, the original, poetic, stirring flow of his ideas, arguments, and feelings brought him an almost infallible ascendancy in the tragic atmosphere in which the poor world was gasping. Well tried in politics, he played upon that angelic and diabolical gift to rouse the

heavy dough of the English as well as to impress the minds of foreigners." Charles de Gaulle, *War Memoirs: The Call to Honour, 1940–1942*, p. 57.

73. King's famous advice to a subordinate was: "Your big weakness, McCrea, is that you are not a son of a bitch. And a good naval officer has to be a son of a bitch." Walter R. Borneman, *The Admirals: Nimitz, Halsey, Leahy, and King—The Five-Star Admirals Who Won the War at Sea*, p. 330. King's daughter declared that the admiral was "the most even-tempered man in the Navy. He is always in a rage." Mark A. Stoler, *Allies and Adversaries: The Joint Chiefs of Staff, the Grand Alliance, and U.S. Strategy in World War II*, p. 69. Marshall worked hard to keep a working relationship with the navy chief. In May 1942, King stormed off after being kept waiting to see Marshall. The army chief went directly to King's office and told him that "if you and I begin fighting at the very start of the war, what in the world will the public have to say about us? They won't accept it for a minute." After composing himself, King responded: "Well, you've been very magnanimous in coming over here the way you have. We will see if we can get along, and I think we can." Thomas Parrish, *Roosevelt and Marshall: Partners in Politics and War, The Personal Story*, p. 249.

74. Oliver Warner, *Admiral of the Fleet: Cunningham of Hyndhope: The Battle for the Mediterranean; a Memoir*, p. 179.

75. Carlo D'Este, *Eisenhower: A Soldier's Life*, p. 297.

76. Lord General Hastings Ismay, *The Memoirs of General Lord Ismay*, p. 253.

77. Stilwell himself was known for his anti-Chinese and anti-British comments. Theodore H. White, ed, *The Stilwell Papers*, p. 245.

78. Alex Danchev and Daniel Todman, eds, *War Diaries, 1939–1945: Field Marshal Lord Alanbrooke*, p. 364 (January 20, 1943).

79. Viscount Andrew Browne Cunningham, *A Sailor's Odyssey: The Autobiography of Admiral of the Fleet, Viscount Cunningham of Hyndhope*, p. 612.

80. When King's career appeared to dead end in 1940, Stark had him named to head the Atlantic naval command, a position from which King developed a strong relationship with FDR. In December 1941, Roosevelt appointed King as commander in chief, U.S. Fleet. It was Stark who, in February 1942, suggested to FDR that King also be named chief of naval operations. B. Mitchell Simpson III, *Admiral Harold R. Stark: Architect of Victory, 1939–1945*, pp. 117–118, 126.

81. B. Mitchell Simpson III, *Admiral Harold R. Stark: Architect of Victory, 1939–1945*, p. 137. Stark's usefulness was clearly understood by First Sea Lord Dudley Pound. Pound biographer Robin Brodhurst wrote that Lord Dudley Pound decided "that Stark should know everything that he knew. He, and indeed the whole Board of Admiralty, knew how much they already owed to Stark and as a result Pound wanted something more than just the normal liaison." Robin Brodhurst, *Churchill's Anchor: The Biography of Admiral of the Fleet Sir Dudley Pound, OM, GCB, GCVO*, p. 217. When shortly before D-Day, Stark ran into British recalcitrance on an engineering problem relating to the floating harbors, the American admiral went to the British king, whom Stark had met and befriended in World War I aboard the HMS *Iron Duke*. As one Stark subordinate recalled: "Stark had cut the Gordian knot, bypassed all chains of command, American and British, civil and military, and regardless of all repercussions and their probable effects on him, had gone directly to his old shipmate, his last remaining hope in avoiding catastrophe, with his problem. [King] George, once a seagoing naval officer himself, saw it as his friend Stark saw it, as vitally important. There was but one man in Britain who could make Churchill do anything, and that man was [King] George." Edward Ellsberg, *The Far Shore: An American at D-Day*, pp. 113–114.

82. B. Mitchell Simpson III, *Admiral Harold R. Stark: Architect of Victory, 1939–1945*, pp. 155–182. Stark dealt with the prickly de Gaulle with frankness and firmness, but without rancor. He had to keep de Gaulle informed of repeated postponements of his invitation to visit Washington in late 1942.

83. Mark A. Stoler, *Allies and Adversaries: The Joint Chiefs of Staff, the Grand Alliance, and U.S. Strategy in World War II*, pp. 268–269.

84. Maurice Matloff, *US Army in WW2: War Department, Strategic Planning for Coalition Warfare*, pp. 344–345.

85. A. H. Birse, *Memoirs of an Interpreter*, p. 176.

CHAPTER XII. UNSUNG STALWARTS OF THE ALLIANCE

1. Mary Soames, ed, *Winston and Clementine: The Personal Letters of the Churchills*, p. 523 (Winston Churchill to Clementine Churchill, April 6, 1945).

2. Keith Eubank, *Summit at Teheran: The Untold Story*, p. 254.

3. John Colville, *Footprints in Time: Memories*, p. 144.

4. James Leutze, ed, *The London Observer: The Journal of General Raymond E. Lee*, p. 37.

5. James Leutze, ed, *The London Observer: The Journal of General Raymond E. Lee*, p. 178.

6. In January 1942, General Chaney became the first commander of U.S. forces in Britain. He was replaced in June 1942 by Gen, Dwight Eisenhower.

7. James Leutze, ed, *The London Observer: The Journal of General Raymond E. Lee*, p. 357 (July 27, 1941). Seven billion dollars in 1940 is equivalent to $70–100 billion today. For monetary equivalents in 2015, multiply World War II figures by at least 10.

8. Martin S. Gilbert, *Winston S. Churchill: Road to Victory 1941–1945*, p. 843.

9. James Leutze, ed, *The London Observer: The Journal of General Raymond E. Lee*, p. 429. Mark A. Stoler, *Allies and Adversaries: The Joint Chiefs of Staff, the Grand Alliance, and U.S. Strategy in World War II*, p. 35.

10. David Rees, *Harry Dexter White: A Study in Paradox*, pp. 96–97.

11. In June 1941, for example, British Air Marshal Charles Portal stubbornly argued against shifting bombers to the U-boat fight. "I am convinced that great value to the war effort as a whole would be obtained from these two squadrons if they remain in Bomber Command than if they are lent to Coastal Command. I am so strongly convinced of this that I regard the loss of these two squadrons to Bomber Command as unacceptable." What historian Correlli Barnett called the "Battle of the Air" continued through the fall of 1941, as the Admiralty and RAF fought over the use of needed bombers. "Churchill still allowed the 'Battle of the Air' to drag on without a final decision, even permitting the circulation to the War Cabinet of fundamentalist tracts by [Arthur] Harris and old [Hugh] Trenchard, the still living Messiah of strategic bombing." Correlli Barnett, *Engage the Enemy More Closely*, pp. 467–471.

12. James Leutze, ed, *The London Observer: The Journal of General Raymond E. Lee*, p. 295 (May 27, 1940).

13. James Leutze, ed. *The London Observer: The Journal of General Raymond E. Lee*, p. 300 (June 1, 1941).

14. George McJimsey, *Harry Hopkins: Ally of the Poor and Defender of Democracy*, pp. 228, 237. The conservative Douglas had been FDR's first director of the budget, serving until 1934, when he resigned in a conflict over New Deal spending.

15. Oliver Viscount Chandos Lyttelton, *The Memoirs of Lord Chandos*, p. 311.

16. Robert E. Sherwood, *Roosevelt and Hopkins: An Intimate History*, p. 581 (Hopkins to Churchill, June 7, 1942).

17. Dwight D. Eisenhower, *Crusade in Europe*, pp. 369.

18. Eric Larrabee, *Commander-in-Chief: Franklin Delano Roosevelt, His Lieutenants and Their War*, pp. 500–501. Lord General Hastings Ismay, *The Memoirs of General Lord Ismay*, p. 258.

19. Correlli Barnett, *Engage the Enemy More Closely*, p. 843.

20. Winston S. Churchill, *Triumph and Tragedy*, p. 476 (Churchill to Harry S. Truman, May 9, 1945).

21. Donald Gillies, *Radical Diplomat: The Life of Archibald Clark Kerr, Lord Inverchapel, 1882–1951*, p. 143. Ambassador Standley wrote his wife: "Davies arrived yesterday, clowning as usual, but he is a friendly clown, and if I have to put up with clowns and publicity hounds, I'd rather it be a friendly one . . . he [Davies] is here in the interests of Davies." Davies insisted on delivering his letter to Stalin outside of Standley's presence. Standley reported to the State Department: "Mr. Davies held a press conference yesterday afternoon in which he took such violent exception to criticism of Soviet officials' failure to give U.S. needed military information about Germans that discussion became heated and correspondents left conference extremely annoyed with attitude of Mr. Davies. Wisdom of sending to Moscow a man with such violent views pro or contra is questionable." William H. Standley and Arthur A. Ageton, *Admiral Ambassador to Russia*, pp. 366, 372. Davies's mission and Roosevelt's persistent efforts to arrange a meeting with Stalin are detailed by Keith Eubank in *Summit at Teheran: The Untold Story*, pp. 65–89.

22. In early 1941, Secretary of the Treasury Morgenthau insisted that the British compile a detailed balance sheet on their resources in order to push Lend-Lease legislation through Congress. William L. Langer and S. Everett Gleason wrote: "Secretary Morgenthau and his Treasury associates remained convinced that H.R. 1776 would fail of enactment unless the entire dismal picture of Britain's financial position were revealed to the Congressional committees and, thus, to the world. . . . Though the responsibility for making these revelations weighed heavily upon the Secretary of the Treasury, he consoled himself with the argument that to disguise the facts would be dangerous. Hitler probably knew the worst anyway. The British eventually resigned themselves to the disclosure and placed themselves in the Secretary's hands. Sir Frederick Phillips warned him [Morgenthau], however, that if the legislation were defeated after such vital information had been broadcast, the British would be 'through.'" William L. Langer and S. Everett Gleason, *The Undeclared War, 1940–1941*, p. 260.

23. Robert E. Sherwood, *Roosevelt and Hopkins: An Intimate History*, p. 860.

24. John S. D. Eisenhower, *Allies: Pearl Harbor to D-Day*, p. 18.

25. Lord General Hastings Ismay, *The Memoirs of General Lord Ismay*, p. 259.

26. Andrew Roberts, *Masters and Commanders*, pp. 336–337.

27. The combined chiefs had many arguments at their Cairo meeting in November 1943, with particular tension between British Admiral Cunningham and America's Admiral King. King biographer Thomas Buell noted that after the argument, the chiefs went for dinner together. "Passions by then had subsided, and the amazing ability of the chiefs to leave their differences on the doorstep was again apparent. King's colleagues observed King's birthday, and the evening passed pleasantly in good food, good conversation, and good fellowship." Thomas B. Buell, *Master of Sea Power: A Biography of Fleet Admiral Ernest J. King*, pp. 427–428. Their fights were over military strategy, not global politics. Historian Herbert Feis wrote: "The top American military men—Marshall, King, Eisenhower—paid strict homage

to the idea that, in making military plans, their assignment, their only assignment, was to win the war as soon and with as little loss of life as possible. They wanted to do whatever would serve this end, and they did not want to do anything that might interfere with it." Herbert Feis, *Churchill-Roosevelt-Stalin: The War They Waged and the Peace They Sought*, p. 349. For Brooke, politicians could be maddening. At the Teheran conference, he wrote in his diary: "I am *absolutely* disgusted with the politicians' method of waging a war!! Why will they imagine they are experts at a job they know nothing about! It is lamentable to listen to them!" Alex Danchev and Daniel Todman, eds, *War Diaries, 1939–1945: Field Marshal Lord Alanbrooke*, p. 485 (November 29, 1943).

28. Henry Adams, *Harry Hopkins: A Biography*, p. 266.

29. Elisabeth Barker wrote: "Over oil and civil aviation Beaverbrook took the lead in championing British interests; Eden sympathised but sometimes thought Beaverbrook made tactical mistakes by over-dramatising things, and would have liked to use more diplomatic methods, working through friendly members of the State Department." Elisabeth Barker, *Churchill and Eden at War*, p. 202.

30. The Earl of Birkenhead, *Halifax: The Life of Lord Halifax*, p. 500.

31. B. Mitchell Simpson III, *Admiral Harold R. Stark: Architect of Victory, 1939–1945*, p. 129.

32. Leonard Moseley, *Marshall: Hero for Our Times*, p. 274.

33. Halifax wrote in his memoirs that Marshall and Dill "were entirely devoid of any thought of self-seeking and were heart and soul devoted to the achievement of Allied victory. With complete confidence in each other's motive, they could examine every case without risk of the conclusion being affected by any consideration smaller than the merits of it." Lord Halifax, *Fullness of Days*, pp. 259–260.

34. James Leutze, ed, *The London Observer: The Journal of General Raymond E. Lee*, pp. 351–352.

35. Christopher M. Bell, *Churchill and Sea Power*, p. 237 (February 17, 1941).

36. Christopher M. Bell, *Churchill and Sea Power*, p. 196 (September 3, 1940).

37. Winston Churchill, *Their Finest Hour: The Second World War*, Volume II, p. 567 (Churchill to Beaverbrook, July 8, 1940).

38. Eisenhower's son wrote that Tedder was the "key man in the air question" regarding D-Day. "With no set doctrine to fetter him, Tedder has seriously studied the question of the air role in support of the invasion." American air chief Carl Spaatz and British counterpart Arthur Harris both opposed the Transportation Plan to bomb French rail hubs as in conflict with their preferred strategies—oil facilities for Spaatz and cities for Harris. John S. D. Eisenhower, *Allies: Pearl Harbor to D-Day*, p. 444. Admiral Cunningham supported the plan and complained in his diary: "Considerable sob stuff about children with legs blown off & blinded old ladies but nothing about the saving of risk to our young soldiers landing on a hostile shore." Andrew Roberts, *Masters and Commanders: The Military Geniuses Who Led the West to Victory in World War II*, p. 476.

39. Ed Cray, *General of the Army: George C. Marshall, Soldier and Statesman*, p. 518.

40. Anthony Eden, *The Reckoning*, p. 544.

41. Tedder's position was undermined by Churchill and General Bedell Smith, Eisenhower's chief of staff, both of whom sought to exclude Tedder from key meetings. Carlo D'Este, *Eisenhower: A Soldier's Life*, pp. 485–486.

42. Stephen E. Ambrose, *Eisenhower: Soldier and President*, p. 126.

43. John Keegan, *The Second World War*, p. 415.

44. Andrew Roberts, *The Storm of War*, p. 451.

45. Henry Probert, *Bomber Harris: His Life and Times: The Biography of Marshal of the Royal Air Force Sir Arthur Harris*, pp. 293–294, 302–303.

46. Historian Samuel Eliot Morison, who described Stark as a "born diplomat," wrote: "Gentle in manner and unobtrusive in personality, he had one of the best brains in the Navy; and what was equally important, he possessed in a high degree the Washingtonian capacity for selecting from a welter of conflicting opinions the right course to follow. Although unmethodical in habits of work, and slow to make up his mind, he expressed himself with perfect clarity when it was made up, and acted with energy and decision." Samuel Eliot Morrison, *History of United States Naval Operations in World War II: The Battle of the Atlantic, September 1939–May 1943*, p. 41.

47. Winston S. Churchill, *Finest Hour*, pp. 614–615 (November 20, 1940).

48. Stark was a gentleman, while King was rough-cut. History has not been kind to Stark, who generally drops out of history books after his replacement as chief of naval operations. Early in the war, even Eisenhower once described Stark as a "nice old lady." Carlo D'Este, *Eisenhower: A Soldier's Life*, p. 297.

49. Ernest J. King and Walter Muir Whitehill, *Fleet Admiral King: A Naval Record*, p. 633.

50. B. Mitchell Simpson III, *Admiral Harold R. Stark: Architect of Victory, 1939–1945*, p. 279.

51. Correlli Barnett wrote: "Ramsay's orders laid down in the minutest detail (complete with diagrams and timetables) the interlocking movements of this mass of vessels of every shape, size, and speed so that they would arrive off the Normandy shore in correct sequence on D-Day." Correlli Barnett, *The Lords of War: From Lincoln to Churchill*, p. 211.

52. Correlli Barnett, *Engage the Enemy More Closely*, p. 796, 142. Barnett wrote that Ramsay considered Kirk "a pompous and whingeing fusspot." Correlli Barnett, *The Lords of War: From Lincoln to Churchill*, p. 208.

53. Robert H. Ferrell, ed, *The Eisenhower Diaries*, p. 91 (June 11, 1943). Ramsay was tragically killed on January 2, 1945, when his plane crashed on takeoff.

54. Carlo D'Este, *Eisenhower: A Soldier's Life*, p. 498.

55. Lord Tedder, *With Prejudice: The War Memoirs of Marshal of the Royal Air Force*, p. 646–647.

56. Ed Cray, *General of the Army: George C. Marshall, Soldier and Statesman*, p. 425.

CHAPTER XIII. W. AVERELL HARRIMAN

1. W. Averell Harriman and Elie Abel, *Special Envoy to Churchill and Stalin, 1941–1946*, p. 218.

2. Milovan Djilas, *Conversations with Stalin*, p. 114.

3. W. Averell Harriman and Elie Abel, *Special Envoy to Churchill and Stalin, 1941–1946*, p. 19.

4. W. Averell Harriman and Elie Abel, *Special Envoy to Churchill and Stalin, 1941–1946*, p. 17.

5. W. Averell Harriman and Elie Abel, *Special Envoy to Churchill and Stalin, 1941–1946*, p. 22.

6. John Colville, *Winston Churchill and His Inner Circle*, p. 120.

7. Churchill visited Ditchley Park on those weekends when a full moon dangerously exposed Chequers to enemy attack.

8. W. Averell Harriman and Elie Abel, *Special Envoy to Churchill and Stalin, 1941–1946*, p. 14.

9. Lynne Olson, *Citizens of London*, p. 117.

10. John Colville, *Fringes of Power*, p. 374 (April 13, 1941).

11. John Colville, *Fringes of Power*, p. 382 (May 2, 1941).

12. Lynne Olson, *Citizens of London*, pp. 100–104, 109–110, 174–175, 239–245.

13. Fraser J. Harbutt, "Churchill, Hopkins, and the 'Other' Americans: An Alternative Perspective on Anglo-American Relations, 1941–1945," *The International History Review*, Volume 8, No. 2 (May 1986), p. 239.

14. Winston S. Churchill, *The Grand Alliance: The Second World War*, Volume III, p. 709 (Churchill to Archibald Wavell, June 4, 1941).

15. Historian James MacGregor Burns noted: "Along with his democratic manner and instincts he had that curious interest in royal and noble personages and doings. He told a friend, rather improbably, that he had been hurt in England after the first war when he had not been invited to Buckingham Palace." James MacGregor Burns, *Roosevelt: The Soldier of Freedom*, p. 603. FDR had an aristocratic manner and, like some insecure, well-born Americans, he aspired to the society of foreign nobility.

16. Walter Isaacson and Evan Thomas, *The Wise Men: Six Friends and the World They Made*, p. 211.

17. Winston S. Churchill, *The Grand Alliance: The Second World War*, Volume III, p. 402.

18. Winston S. Churchill, *The Grand Alliance: The Second World War*, Volume III, p. 411 (Joseph Stalin to Winston S. Churchill, September 15, 1941).

19. Winston S. Churchill, *The Grand Alliance: The Second World War*, Volume III, p. 402.

20. Winston S. Churchill, *The Grand Alliance: The Second World War*, Volume III, p. 403 (Churchill to Beaverbrook, August 30, 1941).

21. Lord General Hastings Ismay, *The Memoirs of General Lord Ismay*, p. 231.

22. Walter Isaacson and Evan Thomas, *The Wise Men: Six Friends and the World They Made*, p. 212.

23. A. J. P. Taylor, *Beaverbrook*, p. 487. After the Moscow meetings, Harriman wrote: "Stalin made no effort to conceal his enthusiasm. It was my impression that he was completely satisfied that Britain and America meant business." W. Averell Harriman and Elie Abel, *Special Envoy to Churchill and Stalin 1941–1946*, p. 92.

24. Max Hastings, *Inferno: The World at War, 1939–1945*, p. 646.

25. Lord General Hastings Ismay, *The Memoirs of General Lord Ismay*, p. 379.

26. Walter Isaacson and Evan Thomas, *The Wise Men: Six Friends and the World They Made*, p. 210.

27. Alex Danchev and Daniel Todman, eds, *War Diaries, 1939–1945: Field Marshal Lord Alanbrooke*, p. 660 (February 8, 1945).

28. Walter Isaacson and Evan Thomas, *The Wise Men: Six Friends and the World They Made*, p. 228.

29. Charles Bohlen, *Witness to History*, p. 127.

30. Walter Isaacson and Evan Thomas, *The Wise Men: Six Friends and the World They Made*, p. 216.

31. William Averell Harriman, *America and Russia in a Changing World: A Half Century of Personal Observation*, p. 24.

32. Harriman recalled, "Churchill, who loved to gamble for modest stakes, used to say that while it might seem undignified for His Majesty's First Minister to play cards with subordinates,

it was entirely appropriate for him to play with 'the President's personal envoy.'" W. Averell Harriman and Elie Abel, *Special Envoy to Churchill and Stalin, 1941–1946*, p. 202.

33. Hopkins noted that Churchill could "play backgammon and discuss British and American politics, the war, Vichy France, Pierre Laval (and you should hear him on Laval), the movies, books, personalities, and speculate on what the winter will bring to Russia—all this and not miss a move in backgammon." Theodore A. Wilson, *The First Summit: Roosevelt & Churchill at Placentia Bay, 1941*, p. 71.

34. W. Averell Harriman and Elie Abel, *Special Envoy to Churchill and Stalin, 1941–1946*, pp. 202–203.

35. W. Averell Harriman and Elie Abel, *Special Envoy to Churchill and Stalin, 1941–1946*, p. 205.

36. Fraser J. Harbutt, "Churchill, Hopkins, and the 'Other' Americans: An Alternative Perspective on Anglo-American Relations, 1941–1945," *The International History Review*, Volume 8, No. 2 (May 1986), p. 239.

37. W. Averell Harriman and Elie Abel, *Special Envoy to Churchill and Stalin, 1941–1946*, pp. 216–217.

38. Harriman biographer Rudy Abramson wrote that Davies and his wife, heiress Marjorie Merriweather Post, had "made a spectacle of themselves with their excesses. . . . Davies amused himself collecting Russian antiques and yachting on the Baltic. He fawned over Stalin and the Soviet government, and Harriman considered him to have been utterly inept." Rudy Abramson, *Spanning the Century: The Life of W. Averell Harriman, 1891–1986*, p. 347. Donald Gillies noted that Davies was "unpopular with both the US Embassy and the press corps because of his self-publicity and unrealistic pro-Soviet stance." Donald Gillies, *Radical Diplomat: The Life of Archibald Clark Kerr, Lord Inverchapel, 1882–1951*, p. 143.

39. Charles Bohlen and George Kennan, who had both served under Ambassador Davies, scorned the book as "Submission to Moscow." Walter Isaacson and Evan Thomas, *The Wise Men: Six Friends and the World They Made*, p. 279.

40. Russian diplomat Ivan Maisky noted that Davies "arrived in Moscow, bringing Stalin a letter from Roosevelt dated 5 May 1943. In his letter the President expressed the wish to meet personally with Stalin on 'an informal and completely simple visit,' somewhere in the area of the Bering Straits, accompanied by the most restricted number of people. Roosevelt proposed to bring with him only Hopkins, an interpreter and a stenographer. It was clear from the letter [that] the meeting should take place without Churchill. 'You and I would talk very informally and get what we call a meeting of minds." Ivan Maisky, *Memoirs of a Soviet Ambassador: The War, 1939–1943*, p. 363.

41. Steinhardt, a Roosevelt political supporter, had poor relations with Stalin. When Beaverbrook and Harriman met with Stalin in September 1941, noted Walter Isaacson and Evan Thomas, "Harriman had pointedly excluded from the negotiations the U.S. ambassador, Laurence Steinhardt, who had become quite embittered during his tenure in Moscow. Such disillusionment was an occupational hazard for American envoys." Walter Isaacson and Evan Thomas, *The Wise Men: Six Friends and the World They Made*, p. 213. Steinhardt went on serve as U.S. Ambassador in Turkey and Czechoslovakia.

42. Standley's job was made more difficult by the independence of General Philip R. Faymonville, the Lend-Lease mission chief in Moscow. Rudy Abramson, *Spanning the Century: The Life of W. Averell Harriman, 1891–1986*, p. 346. "Stop acting like a Santa Claus, Chief," Standley told Roosevelt in October 1942. "And let's get something from Stalin in return. [Lt. Col. Philip R.] Faymonville agrees to give them everything in the world they ask for, from a

darning needle to a tire factory, which they won't have operating ten years after the war. My advice is to treat Stalin like an adult, keep any promises we make to him, but insist that he keep his promises too." William H. Standley and Arthur A. Ageton, *Admiral Ambassador to Russia*, pp. 305–310.

43. William H. Standley and Arthur A. Ageton, *Admiral Ambassador to Russia*, p. 195.

44. Rudy Abramson, *Spanning the Century: The Life of W. Averell Harriman, 1891–1986*, p. 345.

45. Lynne Olson, *Citizens of London*, p. 243.

46. Walter Isaacson and Evan Thomas, *The Wise Men: Six Friends and the World They Made*, p. 213.

47. Walter Isaacson and Evan Thomas, *The Wise Men: Six Friends and the World They Made*, p. 219.

48. Walter Isaacson and Evan Thomas, *The Wise Men: Six Friends and the World They Made*, p. 233.

49. By 1944, Kennedy's patience with FDR had worn out. On August 12, Joe's namesake had been killed in an airplane explosion. "Harry, what the hell are you doing campaigning for that crippled son of a bitch that killed my son Joe?" he complained to Senator Harry Truman. Kennedy wrote Max Beaverbrook: "For a fellow who didn't want this war to touch your country or mine, I have had a rather a bad dose—Joe dead . . . my son Jack in the Naval Hospital." Arthur M. Schlesinger, *Robert Kennedy and His Times*, p. 56.

50. Walter Isaacson and Evan Thomas, *The Wise Men: Six Friends and the World They Made*, p. 244. Neither President Truman nor his new Secretary of State James Byrnes treated Harriman with as much deference as Roosevelt. Harriman's request to attend the Potsdam Conference, in July 1945, was initially rebuffed by Stettinius, but later approved by Byrnes. Rudy Abramson, *Spanning the Century: The Life of W. Averell Harriman, 1891–1986*, p. 400. Walter Isaacson and Evan Thomas, *The Wise Men: Six Friends and the World They Made*, p. 298.

51. Rudy Abramson, *Spanning the Century: The Life of W. Averell Harriman, 1891–1986*, p. 271. The aide, Robert Meiklejohn, wrote of Harriman's behavior as ambassador: "He asks endless questions, rarely with any view to gaining information but rather to bring out his own detailed knowledge of the matter in question or to put the other party on the defensive. I suppose these are techniques that are useful in diplomatic conversation or business deals but they certainly make him a person to be avoided so far as recreational conversation is concerned." Abramson, p. 354. Russian Foreign Minister Molotov once observed of Harriman: "How can a man with $100 million look so sad?" Walter Isaacson and Evan Thomas, *The Wise Men: Six Friends and the World They Made*, p. 243.

52. Rudy Abramson wrote: "Most of the time, the circumstances called for nothing more than a messenger and an analyst with infinite patience, and Averell was not a patient man." Rudy Abramson, *Spanning the Century: The Life of W. Averell Harriman, 1891–1986*, p. 367.

53. W. Averell Harriman and Elie Abel, *Special Envoy to Churchill and Stalin, 1941–1946*, p. 220.

54. Rudy Abramson, *Spanning the Century: The Life of W. Averell Harriman, 1891–1986*, p. 360.

55. Kennan wrote that Harriman was a demanding boss, demanding of himself as well as his subordinates. "The normal leisurely pace of an embassy chancery, and the coordination of its work with the other normal demands, social and personal, of a diplomatic existence, was

not for him. An order once given, in no matter how trivial an affair, he expected . . . it to be executed forthwith. . . . Small wonder that he was often peremptory. He didn't shout you down, for he never shouted, but he had a way of riding roughshod over unsolicited suggestions. A hundred times I came away from our common labors asking myself, without finding an answer: 'Why do I still like this man?'" George F. Kennan, *Memoirs, 1925–1950*, pp. 232–233. Kennan would later change his views during the Cold War. British diplomat-academic Isaiah Berlin recalled that Kennan "was not at all like the people in the State Department I knew in Washington during my service there. He was more thoughtful, more austere, and more melancholy than they were. He was terribly absorbed—personally involved, somehow—in the terrible nature of the [Stalin] regime, and in the convolutions of its policy." Kennan developed a close working relationship with his British counterpart in Moscow, Frank Roberts. John Lewis Gaddis, *George F. Kennan: An American Life*, p. 209–212.

56. George Kennan wrote Charles Bohlen just before the Yalta summit of February 1945: "I recognize that Russia's war effort has been masterful and effective and must, to a certain extent, find its reward at the expense of other peoples in eastern and central Europe. But with all of this, I fail to see why we must associate ourselves with this political program [of the Soviet Union], so hostile to the interests of the Atlantic Community as a whole, so dangerous to everything which we need to see preserved in Europe. Why could we not make a decent and definitive compromise with it—divide Europe frankly into spheres of influence—keep ourselves out of the Russian sphere and keep the Russians out of ours?" S. M. Plokhy, *Yalta: The Price of Peace*, pp. 150–151.

57. Walter L. Hixson, ed, *The American Experience in World War II: The United States in the European Theater*, p. 318. After the war, John R. Deane detailed his experiences in *The Strange Alliance: The Story of Our Efforts at Wartime Cooperation with Russia.* On April 16, 1945, Deane wrote: "Not only have we a Russia that is victorious over the Germans, but one that is so sure of her strength as to assume an attitude of dominance with respect to her Allies. I have felt this situation developing since my arrival in Russia. It has reached a climax since the Crimea Conference." Mark A. Stoler, *Allies and Adversaries: The Joint Chiefs of Staff, the Grand Alliance, and U.S. Strategy in World War II*, p. 235.

58. S. M. Plokhy, *Yalta: The Price of Peace*, p. 209. Sooner rather than later, Roosevelt appointees generally came to appreciate Stalin's danger and duplicity, even if FDR did not.

59. Mark A. Stoler, *Allies and Adversaries: The Joint Chiefs of Staff, the Grand Alliance, and U.S. Strategy in World War II*, p. 213.

60. Mark A. Stoler noted six key factors "for the Joint Chiefs' refusal to propose or sanction any change in their Soviet policy: the need for continued Russian military action and cooperation in the war against Germany; the desire for Soviet participation in the war against Japan; anger at Britain and belief that it was to blame for many of the problems that had arisen; the fact that cooperation remained White House policy; recognition that Axis strategy was to split the Allies; and the belief that everything must be done to avoid an unwinnable World War III with the USSR." Mark A. Stoler, *Allies and Adversaries: The Joint Chiefs of Staff, the Grand Alliance, and U.S. Strategy in World War II*, pp. 215–216, 220.

61. S. M. Plokhy, *Yalta: The Price of Peace*, p. 17.

62. W. Averell Harriman and Elie Abel, *Special Envoy to Churchill and Stalin, 1941–1946*, p. 438.

63. Walter Isaacson and Evan Thomas, *The Wise Men: Six Friends and the World They Made*, pp. 225–226. Historian Norman Davies wrote: "Soviet propaganda had worked won-

ders in concealing the true horrors of Soviet history and of current Soviet conditions. Wide sections of British and American opinion had been convinced that Soviet Communism was a force for good. Whilst Fascist sympathizers were locked up, Communist Party members operated freely in the civil service, and even in the armed forces. Fellow-travellers abounded in academe and in the press. And a large number of professional Soviet spies had penetrated all levels of the political, economic and scientific establishments." Norman Davies, *No Simple Victory*, p. 174.

64. Norman Davies, *Rising '44: The Battle for Warsaw, passim.*

65. Thomas B. Buell, *Master of Seapower: A Biography of Fleet Admiral Ernest J. King*, p. 431.

66. Alex Danchev and Daniel Todman, eds, *War Diaries, 1939–1945: Field Marshal Lord Alanbrooke*, p. 484.

67. James MacGregor Burns, *Roosevelt: The Lion and the Fox*, p. 464.

68. David Dilks, ed, *The Diaries of Sir Alexander Cadogan, O.M., 1938–1945*, p. 706 (February 8, 1945).

69. Winston S. Churchill, *Closing the Ring: The Second World War*, Volume V, pp. 341–342.

70. Winston S. Churchill, *Triumph and Tragedy: The Second World War*, Volume VI, p. 190.

71. Martin S. Gilbert, *Road to Victory: Winston S. Churchill, 1941–1945*, p. 983.

72. Winston S. Churchill, *Triumph and Tragedy: The Second World War*, Volume VI, pp. 211–212 (Churchill to Stalin, October 20, 1944).

73. Anthony Eden, *The Reckoning*, p. 595.

74. Lord General Hastings Ismay, *The Memoirs of Lord General Ismay*, p. 377.

75. Edward R. Stettinius Jr., *Roosevelt and the Russians: The Yalta Conference*, p. 95. Harriman's style occasionally grated on Secretary of State Stettinius, who complained about his visit to Truman in April 1945. "I am burned up with the way in which Harriman has been acting. He went to see the President without any of us knowing about it and has not reported to anyone yet what took place." Walter Isaacson and Evan Thomas, *The Wise Men: Six Friends and the World They Made*, p. 263.

76. Edward R. Stettinius Jr., *Roosevelt and the Russians: The Yalta Conference*, p. 95.

77. Edward R. Stettinius Jr., *Roosevelt and the Russians: The Yalta Conference*, p. 92.

78. On February 11, 1942, Churchill spoke about Cripps to Violet Bonham Carter. "What has he ever done? What post has he ever held? He wasn't a success in Russia. Stalin didn't care about him. Stalin never even said goodby to him. He behaved most discourteously to Cripps." Mark Pottle, ed, *Champion Redoubtable: The Diaries and Letters of Violet Bonham Carter, 1914–1945*, p. 236 (February 11, 1942). Eden aide Oliver Harvey wrote in his diary on August 19, 1941: "Cripps is so clumsy and impetuous in his work. He is quarrelsome with the Russians in matters where quarrels aren't wanted, and it is certainly time he was changed. He himself wants to come home, but he must be put at once into the Government or he'll be an infernal nuisance. But it will need careful handling, or else the F.O. will be accused by the press of having jockeyed out Cripps which won't be true." John Oliver, ed, *The War Diaries of Oliver Harvey, 1941–1945*, p. 34.

79. Winston S. Churchill, *The Hinge of Fate: The Second World War*, Volume IV, p. 56.

80. Donald Gillies, *Radical Diplomat: The Life of Archibald Clark Kerr, Lord Inverchapel, 1882–1951*, p. 141.

81. Churchill was taken aback when the pipe-smoking Clark Kerr remonstrated with Stalin at the Teheran summit when the Soviet leader began to smoke a cigarette. "It's cissy to

smoke cigarettes." Stalin switched to his pipe. Donald Gillies, *Radical Diplomat: The Life of Archibald Clark Kerr, Lord Inverchapel, 1882–1951*, p. 156.

82. Donald Gillies, *Radical Diplomat: The Life of Archibald Clark Kerr, Lord Inverchapel, 1882–1951*, p. 154. Frustrated with Clark's Kerr attempt to conciliate with Stalin, Churchill once told Eden that Clark Kerr "would give up anything to appease Stalin." Fraser J. Harbutt, *Yalta 1945: Europe and America at the Crossroads*, p. 151.

83. Charles Bohlen, *Witness to History*, p. 355.

84. Baron Charles McMoran Wilson Moran, *Churchill: Taken from the Diaries of Lord Moran: The Struggle for Survival, 1940–1965*, p. 244 (February 9, 1945).

85. Donald Gillies, *Radical Diplomat: The Life of Archibald Clark Kerr, Lord Inverchapel, 1882–1951*, p. 167.

86. Rudy Abramson, *Spanning the Century: The Life of W. Averell Harriman, 1891–1986*, p. 340. Clark Kerr was less likely to flatter Churchill than were many Americans. The two clashed during an August 1942 summit in Moscow. "I fancy that he saw the battle in my eye and this made him peevish. It wasn't much fun and the sycophancy of the US Ambassador at luncheon and the sustained bumsucking of Harriman made me feel and probably look like an angry ram." At a subsequent lunch, "the PM was at his bloody worst. He seemed to concentrate his ill-humour upon me. It was difficult to sit through the meal with any semblance of patience and good manners. I fear I didn't make a success of that, for I felt like giving him a good root up the arse." Clark Kerr's colorful commentary was not appreciated by the Foreign Office, to which he reported, after one contentious meeting, that Churchill had "got up and had a walk, pulling from his heated buttocks the seat of his trousers which had clearly stuck to them. It was indeed a warm night. There was something about this dumpy figure, plucking at his backside, which suggested immense strength but little distinction." Donald Gillies, *Radical Diplomat: The Life of Archibald Clark Kerr, Lord Inverchapel, 1882–1951*, pp. 131–133.

87. Rudy Abramson, *Spanning the Century: The Life of W. Averell Harriman, 1891–1986*, p. 339.

88. Lynne Olson, *Citizens of London: The Americans Who Stood with Britain in Its Darkest, Finest Hour*, p. 169.

89. Andrew Roberts, *Masters and Commanders*, p. 444. At the Teheran summit in 1943, Air Chief Henry Arnold recalled: "Stalin surprised me with his knowledge of our planes. He knew details of their performance, their characteristics, their armament, and their armor much better than many of the senior officers in our own Air Force." Henry H. Arnold, *Global Mission*, p. 466.

90. William Manchester and Paul Reid, *The Last Lion: Winston Spencer Churchill: Defender of the Realm, 1940–1965*, p. 729.

91. Warren Kimball, ed, *Churchill & Roosevelt: The Complete Correspondence*, Volume I, p. 421 (Roosevelt to Churchill, March 18, 1942).

92. Frank Costigliola, *Roosevelt's Lost Alliances: How Personal Politics Helped Start the Cold War*, p. 313.

93. W. Averell Harriman and Elie Abel, *Special Envoy to Churchill and Stalin, 1941–1946*, p. 448. Walter Isaacson and Evan Thomas concluded: "Harriman, the shrewd and practical businessman, deeply believed in the desirability of achieving a workable arrangement. He urged a tough policy not because he felt it inevitable that Soviet-American cooperation would fail, but because he thought such a strategy had the best chance of succeeding." Walter Isaacson and Evan Thomas, *The Wise Men: Six Friends and the World They Made*, p. 249.

94. Geoffrey C. Ward, ed, *Closest Companion: The Unknown Story of the Intimate Friendship between Franklin Roosevelt and Margaret Suckley*, p. 162 (June 19, 1942, diary). Admiral William Standley concluded, during his service as U.S. ambassador in Moscow: "With Molotov and to a lesser degree with Stalin, I always felt that they understood a lot more of what we said in English than I ever did of their Russian." William H. Standley and Arthur A. Ageton, *Admiral Ambassador to Russia*, p. 114.

95. Winston S. Churchill, *The Hinge of Fate: The Second World War*, Volume IV, p. 447.

96. Ben Pimlott, ed, *The Second World War Diary of Hugh Dalton 1940–45*, p. 489 (September 7, 1942).

97. Anthony Eden, *The Reckoning*, p. 595. Molotov recalled: "Roosevelt knew how to conceal his attitude toward us." He was "[s]ociable . . . a nice person." He compared Truman unfavorably to Roosevelt: "He was far from having Roosevelt's intellect." Molotov recalled of Churchill, "He was a man of great character and perseverance. But character is not enough; one must have understanding." Albert Resis, ed, *Molotov Remembers*, p. 51, 55, 414. Historian Keith Sainsbury wrote: "As a diplomat and negotiator Molotov was stubborn, unyielding, patient, and humourless." Sainsbury wrote that Molotov "was an 'old Bolshevik', a veteran survivor of the Revolution. In Stalin's Russia of the 1930s, 'survival' had been the appropriate word. Molotov had achieved that feat, where others had gone to the wall, but he had known many anxious moments. Like every other Soviet minister he feared Stalin and knew that not merely his job but possibly his life depended on retaining the dictator's favour. Deep-rooted suspicion of his fellow men was almost inevitable after such a career, and was intensified with foreigners. Travelling to overseas countries, even allied ones, he slept with a revolver by his bedside." Keith Sainsbury, *The Turning Point: Roosevelt, Stalin, Churchill, and Chiang-Kai-Shek, 1943*, pp. 46–47.

98. W. Averell Harriman and Elie Abel, *Special Envoy to Churchill and Stalin, 1941–1946*, p. 441. Molotov would get his education when he met with President Truman on April 23. Truman took a tough line on fulfilling the Yalta agreements, then abruptly said: "That will be all, Mr. Molotov. I would appreciate it if you would transmit my views to Marshall Stalin." When Molotov complained, "I've never been talked to like that in my life," Truman replied: "Carry out your agreements and you won't get talked to like that." Harry S. Truman, *Memoir: Year of Decisions*, p. 82.

CHAPTER XIV. EDWARD STETTINIUS JR.

1. S. M. Plokhy, *Yalta: The Price of Peace*, p. 315.

2. James F. Byrnes Jr., *Speaking Frankly*, p. 23.

3. Historian George McJimsey noted that Hopkins had recommended Byrnes for appointment as head of Office of War Mobilization, but that after Byrnes took office, he told Hopkins: "There's just one suggestion I want to make to you Harry, and that is to keep the hell out of my business." George McJimsey, *Harry Hopkins: Ally of the Poor and Defender of Democracy*, pp. 324–325. Hopkins did not quickly forget.

4. Robert E. Sherwood, *Roosevelt and Hopkins: An Intimate History*, p. 833.

5. Thomas M. Campbell and George C. Herring, *The Diaries of Edward R. Stettinius, Jr., 1943–1946*, p. xvii.

6. Dean Acheson, *Present at the Creation: My Years in the State Department*, p. 88.

7. Dean Acheson, *Present at the Creation: My Years in the State Department*, p. 90. Stettinius would have many critics, inside and outside the State Department. Senator Arthur Vandenberg wrote that Stettinius was "only a presidential messenger. He does *not* have the background and experience for such a job at such a critical time—altho[ugh] he is a *grand person* with every good intention and high honesty of purpose." Wilson D. Miscamble, *From Roosevelt to Truman: Potsdam, Hiroshima, and the Cold War*, p. 96. When British Under-Secretary of Foreign Affairs Alexander Cadogan met Stettinius in London in April 1945, Cadogan patronizingly wrote the first day: "Looks like a dignified and more monumental Charlie Chaplin." When Stettinius departed about two weeks later, Cadogan wrote that Stettinius was "very easy and friendly and understanding, though I don't know what he's like really." David Dilks, ed, *The Diaries of Sir Alexander Cadogan, O.M., 1938–1945*, pp. 617–618, 624. (April 12, 1944, and April 25, 1944).

8. Thomas M. Campbell and George C. Herring, *The Diaries of Edward R. Stettinius, Jr., 1943–1946*, pp. 4–5.

9. Having been led to believe that he was FDR's choice for vice president to replace Henry Wallace in 1944, Byrnes probably believed he deserved a consolation prize. FDR instead took Byrnes along to the Yalta summit, where his lack of access to meetings infuriated Byrnes. S. M. Plokhy, *Yalta: The Price of Peace*, pp. 9, 81. Byrnes had a difficult relationship with other members of the Roosevelt administration because, in the words of Secretary of the Treasury Morgenthau, Byrnes believed "what he reads in the papers, namely that he is Acting-President." In an acrimonious Oval Office confrontation in September 1943, animosity between Byrnes and Morgenthau boiled over. "I wouldn't agree with you on anything," Byrnes told Morgenthau. Peter Moreira, *The Jew Who Defeated Hitler: Henry Morgenthau Jr., FDR, and How We Won the War*, pp. 208, 212.

10. Fred L. Israel, ed, *The War Diary of Breckinridge Long*, pp. 387–388.

11. Arthur Krock, *Memoirs: Sixty Years on the Firing Line*, p. 209. Morgenthau himself was incensed by Krock's stories about the Morgenthau Plan's abandonment. "This isn't the first time that I have been the whipping boy for the President," said Morgenthau to his aides, but FDR refused to see him when Morgenthau went to the White House to complain. Peter Moreira, *The Jew Who Defeated Hitler: Henry Morgenthau Jr., FDR, and How We Won the War*, p. 266.

12. Berle contended that the English believed that the British and Americans were the lone civilized groups in the world, but "I am not sure that they let us in, except when they are talking to us." The alternative administration view was "that the entire Continent of Europe ought to be written off as a total loss. The Treasury takes this view." Beatrice Bishop Berle and Travis Beal Jacobs, eds, *Navigating the Rapids, 1918–1971: From the Papers of Adolf A. Berle*, p. 365 (March 17, 1941).

13. Jordan A. Schwarz, *Liberal: Adolf A. Berle and the Vision of an American Era*, p. 178.

14. Jordan A. Schwarz, *Liberal: Adolf A. Berle and the Vision of an American Era*, pp. 180–181.

15. Robert Sherwood wrote that Stettinius "made a determined effort to reorganize the State Department and bring it up to date. He drew up an enormous and impressive chart with myriad boxes in orderly array. But he found out that this rearrangement could produce no real change in the character of the State Department as long as the occupants of the boxes, particularly on the upper middle level of divisional chiefs, remained the same; and they did the same." Robert E. Sherwood, *Roosevelt and Hopkins: An Intimate History*, p. 757. Perhaps it was not only the occupants of the boxes that impeded change. The State Department was a bureaucratic agency with manifold rules.

16. David S. McLellan and David C. Acheson, *Among Friends: Personal Letters of Dean Acheson*, p. 48. Acheson himself took on different duties at the State Department.

17. H. W. Brands, *Traitor to His Class: The Privileged Life and Radical Presidency of Franklin Delano Roosevelt*, p. 787. Robert E. Sherwood noted that Hopkins was "given a large share of responsibility for the new appointments and suddenly found himself in the unaccustomed position of being criticized as a convert to Toryism." Robert E. Sherwood, *Roosevelt and Hopkins: An Intimate History*, p. 837.

18. Thomas M. Campbell and George C. Herring, *The Diaries of Edward R. Stettinius, Jr., 1943–1946*, pp. 37–38.

19. Thomas M. Campbell and George C. Herring, *The Diaries of Edward R. Stettinius, Jr., 1943–1946*, p. 58.

20. Thomas M. Campbell and George C. Herring, *The Diaries of Edward R. Stettinius, Jr., 1943–1946*, p. 60.

21. Thomas M. Campbell and George C. Herring, *The Diaries of Edward R. Stettinius, Jr., 1943–1946*, p. 63.

22. Thomas M. Campbell and George C. Herring, *The Diaries of Edward R. Stettinius, Jr., 1943–1946*, p. 65.

23. Thomas M. Campbell and George C. Herring, *The Diaries of Edward R. Stettinius, Jr., 1943–1946*, pp. 73–74.

24. "Old Stone Face" Gromyko was an improvement over Russia's first wartime ambassador, the ever-boorish Konstantin Oumansky, whom Dean Acheson said possessed "no redeeming qualities." Acheson wrote that "Gromyko's gaucheness was relieved by a grim, sardonic humor." The ambassador between Oumansky and Gromyko was Maxim Litvinov, a Russian Jew who had married an English Jew while living outside Russia for a decade before the Russia Revolution. Litvinov's English proficiency was an advantage for his job, but his relations with Stalin himself were strained. Acheson described Litvinov was "an old bolshevik but an old-school Russian as well" who "understood the forms and uses of courtesy, as some of the new types in the Soviet establishment did not. Roly-poly, short, and voluble, he presented an amusing antithesis to Lord Halifax, never bothering to cloak stubbornness, but makes his points clearly and courteously." Dean Acheson, *Present at the Creation: My Years in the State Department*, pp. 34, 68.

25. Thomas M. Campbell and George C. Herring, *The Diaries of Edward R. Stettinius, Jr., 1943–1946*, p. 184 (November 27, 1944).

26. John Charmley, *Churchill's Grand Alliance The Anglo-American Special Relationship, 1940–1957*, p. 148.

27. Thomas M. Campbell and George C. Herring, *The Diaries of Edward R. Stettinius, Jr., 1943–1946*, pp. 184–185.

28. The pragmatic Roosevelt continued to use Byrnes—taking him along to the Yalta summit and using him to help project its accomplishments.

29. Mark A. Stoler, *Allies and Adversaries: The Joint Chiefs of Staff, the Grand Alliance, and U.S. Strategy in World War II*, p. 196.

30. Winston S. Churchill, *Triumph and Tragedy: The Second World War*, Volume VI, p. 67 (Telegram from Winston S. Churchill to Franklin D. Roosevelt, June 11, 1944).

31. Warren Kimball, *Forged in War*, p. 283.

32. Thomas M. Campbell and George C. Herring, *The Diaries of Edward R. Stettinius, Jr., 1943—1946*, p. 192.

33. Warren Kimball, *The Juggler: Franklin Roosevelt as Wartime Statesman*, p. 165 (Winston S. Churchill to Harry Hopkins, December 11, 1944).

34. Winston S. Churchill, *Triumph and Tragedy: The Second World War*, Volume VI, p. 255.

35. Winston S. Churchill, *Triumph and Tragedy: The Second World War*, Volume VI, p. 256 (December 8, 1944).

36. Winston S. Churchill, *Triumph and Tragedy: The Second World War*, Volume VI, p. 259 (Winston S. Churchill to Harry Hopkins, December 9, 1944).

37. Warren Kimball, ed, *Churchill & Roosevelt: The Complete Correspondence*, Volume III, p. 456 (Roosevelt to Churchill, December 13, 1944).

38. Winston S. Churchill, *Triumph and Tragedy: The Second World War*, Volume VI, pp. 262–263 (Churchill to Roosevelt, December 14, 1944).

39. Winston S. Churchill, *Triumph and Tragedy: The Second World War*, Volume VI, p. 264 (Hopkins to Churchill, December 16, 1944).

40. Winston S. Churchill, *Triumph and Tragedy: The Second World War*, Volume VI, p. 264 (Churchill to Hopkins, December 17, 1944).

41. Lloyd Gardner, *Spheres of Influence: The Great Powers Partition Europe, from Munich to Yalta*, p. 207 (December 20, 1944).

42. Winston S. Churchill, *Triumph and Tragedy: The Second World War*, Volume VI, p. 273 (Telegraph from Winston S. Churchill to Franklin D. Roosevelt, December 26, 1944).

43. Robert E. Sherwood, *Roosevelt and Churchill: An Intimate History*, p. 843.

44. Thomas M. Campbell and George C. Herring, *The Diaries of Edward R. Stettinius, Jr., 1943–1946*, p. 231 (February 1, 1945).

45. Roosevelt was "under immense pressure . . . by our military leaders," according to Stettinius, "to bring Russia into the Far Eastern war." Conrad Black, *Franklin Delano Roosevelt: Champion of Freedom*, p. 1059.

46. Conrad Black, *Franklin Delano Roosevelt: Champion of Freedom*, p. 1055.

CHAPTER XV. CHURCHILL AND ROOSEVELT: INCREASINGLY SUSPICIOUS

1. Warren Kimball, ed, *Churchill & Roosevelt: The Complete Correspondence*, Volume III, p. 207 (Roosevelt to Churchill, June 26, 1944).

2. Geoffrey C. Ward, ed, *Closest Companion: The Unknown Story of the Intimate Friendship between Franklin Roosevelt and Margaret Suckley*, p. 230 (August 15, 1943).

3. Geoffrey C. Ward, ed, *Closest Companion: The Unknown Story of the Intimate Friendship between Franklin Roosevelt and Margaret Suckley*, p. 420 (April 12, 1945).

4. Geoffrey C. Ward, ed, *Closest Companion: The Unknown Story of the Intimate Friendship between Franklin Roosevelt and Margaret Suckley*, p. 236 (September 6, 1943).

5. Samuel I. Rosenman, *Working with Roosevelt*, p. 544.

6. William D. Hassett, *Off the Record with FDR, 1942–1945*, p. 171 (May 29, 1943).

7. Elisabeth Barker, *Churchill and Eden at War*, p. 299. Albert E. Kersten wrote that "the attention he gave to Princess Juliana and Prince Bernhard exceeded this formal relationship. From Roosevelt's utterances to intimates of his entourage, it is evident that he greatly appreciated Queen Wilhelmina's courage and dedication. According to his son James, Queen Wilhelmina was 'one of the few living persons of whom he was slightly in awe.' Roosevelt's private

secretary, William Hassett, revealed that Roosevelt used to call the Queen 'Minie' and made her like it." Cornelis A. Van Minnen and John F. Sears, eds, *FDR and His Contemporaries*, p. 89 (Albert E. Kersten, "Wilhelmina and Franklin D. Roosevelt: A Wartime Relationship").

8. Winston S. Churchill, *The Grand Alliance: The Second World War*, Volume III, p. 393.

9. Nigel Hamilton, *The Mantle of Command: FDR at War, 1941–1942*, p. 244.

10. Estimates of the number who died during the partition of India and Pakistan in 1947–1948 range from one to two million. Another 15 million were forced to move. William Dalrymple, "The Great Divide," *The New Yorker*, June 29, 2015, p. 65.

11. Thomas M. Campbell and George C. Herring, *The Diaries of Edward R. Stettinius, Jr., 1943–1946*, pp. 304–305.

12. Thomas M. Campbell and George C. Herring, *The Diaries of Edward R. Stettinius, Jr., 1943–1946*, p. 39 (March 17, 1944).

13. Anthony Eden, *The Reckoning*, p. 593. The simplicity of FDR's approach to the British Empire was reflected in a conversation he had with Ambassador Halifax: "One day, raising a subject that was to come into more serious prominence in a later connexion, he [Roosevelt] said to me, 'Is Hong Kong a Crown Colony?' and when I [Halifax] said it was, he went on to ask whether that meant it was a personal possession of the King. I told him that it was not perhaps quite as simple as that, but that it was generally the case that Crown Colonies were not self-governing and were very much more under the control of Whitehall. After a little more such constitutional exchange, the President said he had had an idea about Hong Kong, on which he would like my opinion. At the present time it was likely to become more and more of a political headache for us; China was bound to get more restive about it; American opinion thought it was just a survival of the bad old imperialism; and it would be a good thing all round if we could find some means of taking the sting out of it." Halifax wrote that Roosevelt's idea was "let the King send a telegram to Chiang Kai-shek, saying how impressed he had been with the Chinese resistance to the Japanese aggressors over many years, and that to mark his admiration of Chinese resistance, he wished to present his Crown Colony of Hong Kong to China as a free gift in perpetuity." Lord Halifax, *Fullness of Days*, pp. 249–250. FDR's maternal grandfather, Warren Delano, had grown rich in the 19th century as a result of his trade in opium. FDR grew up with family lore about China. Geoffrey Ward, *A First Class Temperament: The Emergence of Franklin Roosevelt*, pp. 71–72.

14. Robert E. Sherwood, *Roosevelt and Hopkins: An Intimate History*, p. 512.

15. Richard Langworth, ed, *Churchill by Himself: The Definitive Collection of Quotations*, p. 93 (November 9, 1942).

16. Warren Kimball, *The Juggler: Franklin Roosevelt as Wartime Statesman*, p. 149. (Winston S. Churchill to Anthony Eden, December 31, 1944).

17. Cordell Hull, *The Memoirs of Cordell Hull*, Volume II, pp. 1477–1478.

18. Cordell Hull, *The Memoirs of Cordell Hull*, Volume II, p. 1475.

19. Cordell Hull, *The Memoirs of Cordell Hull*, Volume II, p. 1478.

20. Elliott Roosevelt, *As He Saw It*, pp. 41–42.

21. Elliott Roosevelt, *As He Saw It*, p. 25. One small but telling reason to doubt Elliott Roosevelt is that Churchill had beautiful hands, not stubby but long fingers, of which the prime minister was proud. "His hands and fingers, which were a shiny ivory white like the skin on the rest of body, were much smaller and better shaped than one might have expected on such a rotund figure and they were always kept in perfect condition no matter what they were called up on to do." Walter Graebner, who worked with Churchill, added: "The beauty of his hands in fact meant much to Churchill, and it irked him enormously one day to read in

Robert E. Sherwood's book, 'Roosevelt and Hopkins,' that Harry Hopkins had once referred to his hands as 'flabby.'" Walter Graebner, *Spokane Daily Chronicle*, January 30, 1965.

22. Fraser J. Harbutt, "Churchill, Hopkins, and the 'Other' Americans: An Alternative Perspective on Anglo-American Relations, 1941–1945," *The International History Review*, Volume 8, No. 2 (May 1986), p. 255.

23. John Charmley, "Churchill and the American Alliance," *Transactions of the Royal Historical Society*, Volume 11 (2001), p. 368.

24. Winston Churchill. *The Gathering Storm: The Second World War*, Volume I, p. 10.

25. Warren Kimball, *Swords or Ploughshares? The Morgenthau Plan for Defeated Nazi Germany, 1943–1946*, pp. 95–96 (from Morgenthau memorandum of conversation with Roosevelt, August 19, 1944).

26. Lord Beaverbrook protested the American demand for South African gold: "It should be made amply clear that we are not prepared to relinquish any more gold here or in South Africa and that we must retain any interest we possess in gold in the Dominions. These are the last resources of the British people and should be held intact to provide us with essential means in the case of a compelling necessity to obtain foodstuffs for our people." Martin S. Gilbert, *Winston S. Churchill: Finest Hour, 1939–1941*, p. 971 (December 26, 1940).

27. Walter Reid, *Churchill: 1940–1945, Under Friendly Fire*, p. 153.

28. Thomas M. Campbell and George C. Herring, *The Diaries of Edward R. Stettinius, Jr., 1943–1946*, p. 61.

29. The policy of imperial preference for products traded within the British Empire and its dominions was codified at a conference in Ottawa in 1932. At the Placentia Bay summit in 1941, according to Sumner Welles, "Churchill stated quite frankly that, while he himself throughout his political career had vigorously opposed Imperial preferences, and had consistently favored the liberal trade principles of the latter part of the nineteenth century, he was not empowered constitutionally to enter into any commitments of this character without the consent of the other members of the British Commonwealth of Nations." Sumner Welles, *The Time for Decision*, p. 176.

30. John Maynard Keynes advised in July 1941: "The President ought to be left free to concentrate on issues of strategy, diplomacy and politics without having to consider the pressing and difficult details of economic policy, which he does not really care for any more than our own Prime Minister." H. W. Arndt, "The Wizard and the Pragmatist/Keynes and Churchill," *Finest Hour* 153 (Winter 2011–12).

31. Dean Acheson, *Present at the Creation: My Years in the State Department*, p. 55.

32. Warren Kimball, *The Juggler: Franklin Roosevelt as Wartime Statesman*, pp. 44–47.

33. Warren Kimball, *The Juggler: Franklin Roosevelt as Wartime Statesman*, p. 59.

34. Warren Kimball, ed, *Churchill and Roosevelt: The Complete Correspondence*, Volume III, p. 35 (Churchill to Roosevelt, March 9, 1944).

35. Fraser J. Harbutt, "Churchill, Hopkins, and the 'Other' Americans: An Alternative Perspective on Anglo-American Relations, 1941–1945," *The International History Review*, Volume 8, No. 2 (May 1986), pp. 254–255.

36. Walter Reid, *Churchill: 1940–1945, Under Friendly Fire*, p. 126.

37. Kenneth Young, *Churchill and Beaverbrook: A Study in Friendship and Politics*, pp. 176–177 (Beaverbrook to Churchill, December 26, 1940).

38. Acheson wrote: "When, as always happens, the original Cabinet committee descended to what arrogant subordinates called the 'working level'—Harry White (Treasury), John J. McCloy (War), and myself (State)—the battle continued over the level of British gold and

dollar reserves which might be accumulated under lend-lease." Dean Acheson, *Present at the Creation: My Years in the State Department*, p. 28.

39. Kenneth Young, *Churchill and Beaverbrook: A Study in Friendship and Politics*, p. 261.

40. Warren Kimball, *The Juggler: Franklin Roosevelt as Wartime Statesman*, p. 55.

41. George McJimsey, *Harry Hopkins: Ally of the Poor and Defender of Democracy*, p. 159.

42. Anthony Eden, *The Reckoning*, p. 494.

43. Sarah Churchill, *A Thread in the Tapestry*, pp. 62–63.

44. Baron Charles McMoran Wilson Moran, *Churchill: Taken from the Diaries of Lord Moran: The Struggle for Survival, 1940–1965*, p. 243 (February 7, 1945). As Roosevelt departed from Casablanca, Churchill told an American diplomat; "If anything should happen to that man, I couldn't stand it. He is the truest friend; he has the farthest vision; he is the greatest man I've ever known." Doris Kearns Goodwin, *No Ordinary Time*, p. 408.

45. James MacGregor Burns, *Roosevelt: The Soldier of Freedom*, p. 607.

46. Baron Charles McMoran Wilson Moran, *Churchill: Taken from the Diaries of Lord Moran: The Struggle for Survival, 1940–1965*, p. 793 (July 24, 1958).

47. Martin S. Gilbert, ed, *The Churchill War Papers: The Ever-Widening War, 1941*, pp. 1283–1284.

48. Martin S. Gilbert, ed, *The Churchill War Papers: The Ever-Widening War, 1941*, p. 895 (Churchill to J.A. Spender, July 3,1941).

49. R. Crosby Kemper II, ed, *Winston Churchill: Resolution, Defiance, Magnanimity, Good Will*, p. 113 (John R. Colville, "The Personality of Winston Churchill").

50. Robert E. Sherwood, *Roosevelt and Hopkins: An Intimate History*, p. 405. At the Yalta summit, Churchill called China the "Great American Illusion." Edward R. Stettinius Jr., *Roosevelt and the Russians: The Yalta Conference*, p. 71.

51. William McNeill argued that Hull's intransigence about the takeover, combined with his poor chemistry with Churchill, led to Hull's political eclipse from the White House. William McNeill, *America, Britain and Russia: Their Co-operation and Conflict, 1941–1946*, p. 118.

52. Robert E. Sherwood, *Roosevelt and Hopkins: An Intimate History*, pp. 481–489. Sherwood noted: "As an elder statesman and a figure of great dignity, Hull had established for himself a position that was almost sacrosanct. It was bewildering as well as infuriating for him to find himself the target of the kind of insults and gibes to which many of his colleagues in the Administration had long since become accustomed." p. 483.

53. Cordell Hull, *The Memoirs of Cordell Hull*, Volume II, p. 1137.

54. Benjamin Welles, *Sumner Welles: FDR's Global Strategist*, p. 287.

55. Thomas M. Campbell and George C. Herring, *The Diaries of Edward R. Stettinius, Jr., 1943–1946*, pp. 90–91. Charles E. Bohlen recalled visiting the White House in March 1945. He "checked in at the Map Room to look at telegrams, and dropped in to see Admiral Leahy. My conversations with Leahy followed a definite pattern. In his snapping-turtle manner, he usually had some crack to make about General de Gaulle, and I would go to a map on the wall and point out the crucial geographical location of France, which he knew better than I did. A military man who made no pretense to political acumen, Leahy would then grudgingly admit that we had to take care of our relations with France." Charles Bohlen, *Witness to History*, p. 206.

56. Harold Macmillan, *War Diaries: The Mediterranean 1943–1945*, p. 455 (June 5, 1944).

57. Walter Reid, *Churchill: 1940–1945, Under Friendly Fire*, p. 249.

58. Warren Kimball, ed, *Churchill & Roosevelt: The Complete Correspondence*, Volume II, p. 255 (Roosevelt to Churchill, June 17, 1943).

59. Walter Reid, *Churchill: 1940–1945, Under Friendly Fire*, p. 298.

60. Eden aide Oliver Harvey wrote in his diary on July 27, 1943, that Ambassador Winant got himself in trouble for advocating recognition of the Free French: "We learn that Roosevelt *had* seen the P.M.'s telegram urging recognition in terms of our formula when he sent his last foolish message about 'acceptance'. Winant is at a loss what to do and says 'he is in the dog-kennel', which apparently means he is in disgrace for having advocated recognition. He believes Hull drafted the President's message and says even Harry Hopkins, who agrees with us, can do nothing." John Harvey, ed, *War Diaries of Oliver Harvey*, p. 280 (July 27, 1943). Prime Minister Churchill and General Eisenhower understood what FDR did not. De Gaulle had increasingly won the hearts of the Free French movement.

61. David Reynolds, *In Command of History: Churchill Fighting and Writing the Second World War*, pp. 414–415.

CHAPTER XVIA. CHURCHILL AND ROOSEVELT: INCREASINGLY EXHAUSTED

1. Mark Pottle, ed, *Champion Redoubtable: The Diaries and Letters of Violet Bonham Carter, 1914–1945*, pp. 312–313 (August 1, 1944).

2. Winston S. Churchill, *Triumph and Tragedy*, p. 242 (Churchill to Roosevelt, January 6, 1945).

3. Warren Kimball, ed, *Churchill & Roosevelt: The Complete Correspondence*, Volume III, p. 499 (Churchill to Roosevelt, January 7, 1945).

4. Eleanor Roosevelt wrote of Churchill: "It was astonishing to me that anyone could smoke so much and drink so much and keep perfectly well." Robert H. Pilpel, *Churchill in America, 1895–1961: An Affectionate Portrait*, p. 156.

5. Brian Lavery, *Churchill Goes to War*, p. 119. Churchill uses the same phrase in *The Hinge of Fate*, p. 350. In North Africa, Churchill confided to his bodyguard: "Thompson, I am tired out in body, soul and spirit." A few minutes later, he added: "All is planned and ready, in what better place could I die than here—in the ruins of Carthage?" W. H. Thompson, *Sixty Minutes with Winston Churchill*, p. 77.

6. Warren Kimball, ed, *Churchill & Roosevelt: The Complete Correspondence*, Volume I, p. 156 (Roosevelt to Churchill, March 17, 1943).

7. Warren Kimball, *The Juggler: Franklin Roosevelt as Wartime Statesman*, p. 15.

8. S. M. Plokhy, *Yalta: The Price of Peace*, pp. 11, 34.

9. Warren Kimball, *Forged in War: Roosevelt, Churchill, and the Second World War*, p. 340.

10. Ross T. McIntire, *White House Physician*, p. 132.

11. Defensively, McIntire contended that a loss of weight and heart trouble were his major concerns. He denied that Roosevelt's condition suggested a possible cerebral hemorrhage." Ross T. McIntire, *White House Physician*, pp. 234, 236, 239. In the weeks after Yalta, Roosevelt "spoke frequently and with great sadness about Pa Watson," reported secretary Grace Tully, "the first instance in which he had ever displayed any morbid afterthoughts following the death of a friend or associate." Grace Tully, *FDR: My Boss*, p. 355.

12. James MacGregor Burns, *Roosevelt: The Soldier of Freedom, 1940–1945*, p. 507.

13. Warren Kimball, ed, *Churchill & Roosevelt: The Complete Correspondence*, Volume II, p. 157 (Roosevelt to Churchill, March 17, 1943).

14. Warren Kimball, ed, *Churchill & Roosevelt: The Complete Correspondence*, Volume II, p. 621 (Roosevelt to Churchill, December 17, 1943).

15. Baron Charles McMoran Wilson Moran, *Churchill: Taken from the Diaries of Lord Moran: The Struggle for Survival, 1940–1965*, p. 233 (January 30, 1945).

16. Martin S. Gilbert wrote: "In 1932 he had suffered an attack of paratyphoid, and in the years that followed had been a victim of painful dyspepsia." Winston S. Churchill, *Finest Hour, 1939–1941*, p. 390.

17. Robert H. Ferrell, *The Dying President: Franklin D. Roosevelt, 1944–1945*, pp. 24–25.

18. Ferrell argued that Admiral McIntire's various diagnoses allowed FDR to be mystified about his health problems until March 1944, when a "heart man" was specifically assigned to oversee FDR. Robert H. Ferrell, *The Dying President: Franklin D. Roosevelt, 1944–1945*, pp. 36–37, 139.

19. Robert H. Ferrell, *The Dying President: Franklin D. Roosevelt, 1944–1945*, p. 41.

20. Robert H. Ferrell, *The Dying President: Franklin D. Roosevelt, 1944–1945*, p. 24.

21. Grace Tully, *FDR: My Boss*, p. 274.

22. Frank Freidel, *Franklin D. Roosevelt: A Rendezvous with Destiny*, p. 507.

23. Robert H. Ferrell details in *The Dying President: Franklin D. Roosevelt, 1944–1945* the incompetence of Admiral McIntire's oversight of the president's health. The president notoriously did not like to be told bad news about his health. When Dr. Frank H. Lahey told FDR that "you may not care for what I have to say" about the state of FDR's health, the president responded: "That will be all, Dr. Lahey." Neither FDR nor Churchill placed much faith in doctors. Robert H. Ferrell, *The Dying President: Franklin D. Roosevelt, 1944–1945*, pp. 19, 140–141. At one point, secrecy about the president's health literally became an FBI case when J. Edgar Hoover was called in to investigate leaks about his health. FDR stood for election to a fourth term in November 1944. If the electorate had known his true health condition, his victory might have been in doubt.

24. Baron Charles McMoran Wilson Moran, *Churchill: Taken from the Diaries of Lord Moran: The Struggle for Survival, 1940–1965*, p. 242 (February 7, 1945).

25. Robert H. Ferrell, *The Dying President: Franklin D. Roosevelt, 1944–1945*, p. 108.

26. Charles Bohlen, *Witness to History*, p. 206.

27. Herbert Levy, *Henry Morgenthau, Jr: The Remarkable Life of FDR's Secretary of the Treasury*, pp. 396–398.

28. One family friend observed FDR with Princess Martha and commented that the Norwegian princess "says nothing, just giggles and looks adoringly at him. But he seems to like it tremendously—and there is a growing flirtacious [sic] intimacy which is of course not at all serious." Frank Freidel, *Roosevelt: A Rendezvous with Destiny*, p. 510.

29. Robert H. Ferrell, *The Dying President: Franklin D. Roosevelt, 1944–1945*, p. 114.

30. John R. Boettiger, *A Love in Shadow: The Story of Anna Roosevelt and John Boettiger*, p. 254.

31. Geoffrey C. Ward, ed, *Closest Companion: The Unknown Story of the Intimate Friendship between Franklin Roosevelt and Margaret Suckley*, p. 229 (August 14, 1943). "You must not wear yourself out, you are too important to the situation," wrote Harriman to Hopkins in the spring of 1941. "Everyone here constantly speaks of you and all look upon you as their truest friend." Michael Fullilove, *Rendezvous with Destiny*, p. 221.

32. Christopher D. O'Sullivan, *Harry Hopkins: FDR's Envoy to Churchill and Stalin*, p. 81.

33. Geoffrey C. Ward, ed, *Closest Companion: The Unknown Story of the Intimate Friendship between Franklin Roosevelt and Margaret Suckley*, p. 233 (August 31, 1943).

34. Geoffrey C. Ward, ed, *Closest Companion: The Unknown Story of the Intimate Friendship between Franklin Roosevelt and Margaret Suckley*, p. 239 (September 14, 1943). Roosevelt remained concerned about Hopkins, although the president thought heavy responsibilities were good for his aide. "Dr. Roosevelt knows what's good for Harry," proclaimed FDR about prescribing hard work for his aide in the summer of 1941. The Anglo-American intermediaries worried about each other's health. "You must not wear yourself out, you are too important to the situation," wrote Harriman to Hopkins in the spring of 1941. "Everyone here constantly speaks of you and all look upon you as their truest friend." Michael Fullilove, *Rendezvous with Destiny*, pp. 255, 221. Ahead of Hopkins's trip to Britain in April 1942, FDR wrote Churchill to "[m]ake Harry go to bed early & let him obey Dr. Fulton, U.S.N., whom I am sending with him as super-nurse with full authority." Warren Kimball, ed, *Churchill & Roosevelt: The Complete Correspondence*, Volume I, p. 441 (Roosevelt to Churchill, April 3, 1942). At one point in the summer of 1942, Roosevelt gave Harry Hopkins a *Book of Psalms*. The president had indicated verses he "wanted me to study . . . with a view to future speeches—and one that he marked was the last verse of the thirty-ninth psalm: 'O spare me, that I may recover strength, before I go hence, and shall be no more.'" Robert E. Sherwood, *Roosevelt and Hopkins: An Intimate History*, p. 626. By the time he returned to America from Yalta, Hopkins was suffering from pneumonia.

35. Geoffrey C. Ward, ed, *Closest Companion: The Unknown Story of the Intimate Friendship between Franklin Roosevelt and Margaret Suckley*, p. 250 (October 30, 1943).

36. Geoffrey C. Ward, ed, *Closest Companion: The Unknown Story of the Intimate Friendship between Franklin Roosevelt and Margaret Suckley*, p. 273 (no date).

37. Geoffrey C. Ward, ed, *Closest Companion: The Unknown Story of the Intimate Friendship between Franklin Roosevelt and Margaret Suckley*, p. 327 (September 11, 1944).

38. James F. Byrnes, *Speaking Frankly*, p. 23.

39. Sally Bedell Smith, *Reflected Glory: The Life of Pamela Churchill Harriman*, p. 102.

40. Walter Reid, *Churchill: 1940–1945, Under Friendly Fire*, p. 150. "How I wish I could be with you to see our war machine in operation," Roosevelt wired Churchill on June 1944. Warren Kimball, ed, *Churchill & Roosevelt: The Complete Correspondence*, Volume III, p. 167 (Roosevelt to Churchill, June 6, 1944).

41. Robert E. Sherwood, *Roosevelt and Hopkins: An Intimate History*, p. 602.

42. Warren Kimball, ed, *Churchill & Roosevelt: The Complete Correspondence*, Volume III, p. 180 (Churchill to Roosevelt, June 11, 1944).

43. Baron Charles McMoran Wilson Moran, *Churchill: Taken from the Diaries of Lord Moran: The Struggle for Survival, 1940–1965*, p. 144 (November 28, 1943).

44. Winston S. Churchill, *Closing the Ring: The Second World War*, Volume V, p. 320.

45. Baron Charles McMoran Wilson Moran, *Churchill: Taken from the Diaries of Lord Moran: The Struggle for Survival, 1940–1965*, pp. 144–145 (November 28, 1943).

46. Richard Langworth, ed, *Churchill by Himself: The Definitive Collection of Quotations*, p. 553 (September 5, 1943).

47. Charles Bohlen, *Witness to History, 1929–1969*, p. 146.

48. Roosevelt told Frances Perkins why he decided to make fun of Churchill: "I thought it over all night and made up my mind I had to do something desperate. I couldn't stay in Teheran forever. I had to cut through this icy surface so that later I could talk by telephone or letter in a personal way [with Stalin]. I had scarcely seen Churchill alone during the conference.

I had a feeling that the Russians did not feel right about seeing us conferring together in a language which we understood and they didn't." Frances Perkins, *The Roosevelt I Knew*, p. 81.

49. John Harvey, ed, *War Diaries of Oliver Harvey*, p. 239 (March 28, 1942).

50. Baron Charles McMoran Wilson Moran, *Churchill: Taken from the Diaries of Lord Moran: The Struggle for Survival, 1940–1965*, p. 140 (November 25, 1943).

51. Charles Bohlen, *Witness to History, 1929–1969*, p. 148.

52. Winston S. Churchill, *Closing the Ring: The Second World War*, Volume V, p. 305.

53. Robert E. Sherwood, *Roosevelt and Hopkins: An Intimate History*, p. 788.

54. Churchill's physician was "bewildered by a sharp right-about-turn. . . . It was plain that the Prof. had got hold of him." Lindemann later told Moran his reasoning: "I explained to Winston that the plan would save Britain from bankruptcy by eliminating a dangerous competitor. Somebody must suffer for the war, and it was surely right that Germany and not Britain should foot the bill. Winston had not thought of it in that way, and he said no more about a cruel threat to the German people." Baron Charles McMoran Wilson Moran, *Churchill: Taken from the Diaries of Lord Moran: The Struggle for Survival, 1940–1965*, pp. 190–191 (September 13, 1944). Lindemann would later argue: "The question now is not whether German factories should be destroyed or not. They *have* been destroyed. The question is whether they should be rebuilt in Germany and employ German labour or whether the goods they could produce for export should be made here." He added: "It is far more important to this country to re-establish British exports than to obtain German manufactured goods as reparations. For this reason alone, we should discourage the restoration of German industry. But quite apart from this, such a policy would give far greater military security than any other scheme likely to be devised. . . . Britain must expand her exports or starve. Germany can live without." Adrian Fort, *Prof: The Life of Frederick Lindemann*, p. 314. In the absence of John Maynard Keynes, Lindemann was in effect Britain's chief economic negotiator at Quebec. After the summit, Lindemann stayed in the United States to assess progress on building an atomic bomb.

55. John Morton Blum, ed, *From the Morgenthau Diaries: Years of War 1941–1945*, pp. 369–371. Henry Morgenthau III, *Mostly Morgenthaus: A Family History*, pp. 379–386.

56. John Morton Blum, ed, *From the Morgenthau Diaries: Years of War 1941–1945*, p. 371. In his memoirs, Churchill wrote of the Morgenthau Plan: "Even if it had been practicable, I do not think it would have been right to depress Germany's standard of life in such a way; but at that time, when German militarism based on German industry had done such appalling damage to Europe, it did not seem unfair to agree that her manufacturing capacity need not be revived beyond what was needed to give her the same standards of life as her neighbours." Winston S. Churchill, *Triumph and Tragedy, The Second World War*, Volume VI, pp. 138–139. Eden recalled in his memoirs that at the morning meeting, he expressed his dislike for the plan, adding "nor was I convinced that it was to our national advantage." Eden wrote that Churchill "resented my criticism of something which he and the president had approved, not I am sure on his account, but on the President's." Anthony Eden, *The Reckoning*, p. 552.

57. Fraser J. Harbutt, *Yalta 1945: Europe and America at the Crossroads*, p. 169.

58. Robert E. Sherwood, *Roosevelt and Hopkins: An Intimate History*, p. 832. According to Cordell Hull, FDR "forgot, despite Churchill's initialing of the agreement, that the British Government was the last to desire the conversion of Germany into a pastoral country, because Britain's livelihood would be impaired if Europe's economy collapsed because of a wrecked Germany." Cordell Hull, *The Memoirs of Cordell Hull*, Volume II, p. 1621.

59. John Morton Blum, ed, *From the Morgenthau Diaries: Years of War 1941–1945*, p. 375–383. The British government must have learned early of the Morgenthau Plan because

it issued a memo: "A policy which condenses or favours chaos is not hard; it is simply inefficient, we do not favour a soft policy towards Germany; but the suffering which she must undergo should be the price of useful results for the United Nations, ordered and controlled by ourselves." Warren Kimball, *Swords or Ploughshares? The Morgenthau Plan for Defeated Nazi Germany, 1943–1946*, p. 121.

60. Winston S. Churchill, *Triumph and Tragedy: The Second World War*, Volume VI, p. 142.

61. Brian Lavery, *Churchill Goes to War*, p. 280.

62. Fraser J. Harbutt, "Churchill, Hopkins, and the 'Other' Americans: An Alternative Perspective on Anglo-American Relations, 1941–1945," *The International History Review*, Volume 8, No. 2 (May 1986), p. 257 (Beaverbrook to Hopkins, September 27, 1944).

63. Winston S. Churchill, *Triumph and Tragedy: The Second World War*, Volume VI, p. 190.

64. H. W. Brands, *Traitor to His Class: The Privileged Life and Radical Presidency of Franklin Delano Roosevelt*, p. 502.

65. H. W. Brands, *Traitor to His Class: The Privileged Life and Radical Presidency of Franklin Delano Roosevelt*, pp. 502–503.

66. Charles Bohlen, *Witness to History*, p. 244.

67. Joseph P. Lash, *Roosevelt and Churchill, 1939–1941*, p. 115.

68. Max Hastings, *Overlord: D-Day and the Battle for Normandy*, p. 22.

69. James C. Humes, *Eisenhower and Churchill: The Partnership That Saved the World*, p. 181.

70. James Leasor, *War at the Top: The Experiences of General Sir Leslie Hollis, KCB KBE*, p. 173.

71. Hopkins added that Churchill "might change his mind again, as he did last year. I don't believe he is really converted." Baron Charles McMoran Wilson Moran, *Churchill: Taken from the Diaries of Lord Moran: The Struggle for Survival, 1940–1965*, p. 117 (August 18, 1943).

72. Max Hastings, *Overlord: D-Day and the Battle for Normandy*, p. 23.

73. Alex Danchev and Daniel Todman, eds, *War Diaries, 1939–1945: Field Marshal Lord Alanbrooke*, p. 554 (June 5, 1944).

74. Max Hastings, *Overlord: D-Day and the Battle for Normandy*, p. 315.

75. John N. Kennedy, *The Business of War*, p. 327.

76. Andrew Roberts, *Storm of War*, pp. 520–563.

77. Winston S. Churchill, *Closing the Ring: The Second World War*, Volume V, p. 451. Operation ANVIL was originally scheduled to occur concurrent with Operation OVERLORD. When it occurred two months later, the British thought its impact had been muted. John N. Kennedy, *The Business of War*, pp. 334–336.

78. Winston S. Churchill, *Triumph and Tragedy: The Second World War*, Volume VI, p. 51.

79. Omar N. Bradley, *A Soldier's Story*, p. 369.

80. Winston S. Churchill, *Triumph and Tragedy: The Second World War*, Volume VI, p. 61 (Harry Hopkins to Winston Churchill, August 7, 2014).

81. Winston S. Churchill, *Triumph and Tragedy: The Second World War*, Volume VI, p. 111.

82. Joseph Persico, *Roosevelt's Centurions: FDR and the Commanders He Led to Victory in World War II*, p. 54.

83. Cordell Hull, *The Memoirs of Cordell Hull*, Volume II, p. 1472.

84. Cordell Hull, *The Memoirs of Cordell Hull*, Volume II, p. 1473.

85. Baron Charles McMoran Wilson Moran, *Churchill: Taken from the Diaries of Lord Moran: The Struggle for Survival, 1940–1965*, p. 837.

CHAPTER XVIB. THE WAGES OF WAR: HEALTH PROBLEMS IN THE ALLIANCE

1. Will Brownell and Richard N. Billings, *So Close to Greatness: A Biography of William C. Bullitt*, p. 247.
2. Henry Morgenthau III, *Mostly Morgenthaus: A Family History*, p. 381.
3. John Martin, *Downing Street: The War Years*, p. 57.
4. Leslie Hollis, *A Mariner's Tale*, pp. 125–126.
5. James Leasor, *War at the Top: The Experiences of General Sir Leslie Hollis, KCB KBE*, p. 264. Leslie Hollis, *A Mariner's Tale*, pp. 111–112.
6. Rudy Abramson, *Spanning the Century: The Life of W. Averell Harriman, 1891–1986*, p. 352.
7. Edward R. Stettinius Jr., *Roosevelt and the Russians: The Yalta Conference*, p. 75.
8. Michael Dobbs, *Six Months in 1945: FDR, Stalin, Churchill, and Truman—from World War to Cold War*, p. 216.
9. John Harvey, ed, *War Diaries of Oliver Harvey*, p. 258 (May 19, 1943).
10. Ben Pimlott, ed, *The Second World War Diary of Hugh Dalton 1940–45*, p. 265 (August 8, 1941).
11. David Dilks, ed, *The Diaries of Sir Alexander Cadogan, O.M., 1938–1945*, p. 617.
12. Robert H. Ferrell, ed, *FDR's Quiet Confidant: The Autobiography of Frank C. Walker*, p. 127.
13. Michael Beschloss, *The Conquerors*, pp. 18, 52. Peter Moreira, *The Jew Who Defeated Hitler: Henry Morgenthau Jr., FDR, and How We Won the War*, p. 274.
14. Benjamin Welles, *Sumner Welles: FDR's Global Strategist*, p. 317.
15. Ed Conway, *The Summit: Bretton Woods, 1944*, pp. 6, 91.
16. Bill Yenne, *Hap Arnold: Inventing the Air Force*, pp. 215–216.
17. Thomas Parrish, *Roosevelt and Marshall: Partners in Politics and War, the Personal Story*, p. 497.
18. Charles Bohlen, *Witness to History*, p. 131.
19. Richard Langworth, ed, *Churchill by Himself: The Definitive Collection of Quotations*, p. 522.
20. Winston S. Churchill, *The Hinge of Fate: The Second World War*, Volume IV, p. 473.
21. John S. D. Eisenhower, *Allies: Pearl Harbor to D-Day*, p. 205.
22. Carlo D'Este, *Eisenhower: A Soldier's Life*, p. 680.

CHAPTER XVIIA. HARRY DEXTER WHITE AND JOHN MAYNARD KEYNES

1. Donald E. Moggridge, *Maynard Keynes: An Economist's Biography*, p. 692.
2. David Rees, *Harry Dexter White: A Study in Paradox*, p. 137.
3. That White acted as a Soviet spy remains a contested issue. See Chapter XVIIB for an analysis of this issue.
4. After a meeting with top business and government officials in April 1945, Keynes wrote: "Winston was quite magnificent throughout, in his best form, taking a profound interest in our Treasury problems for once, thoroughly understanding the points at issue."

H. W. Arndt, "The Wizard and the Pragmatist/Keynes and Churchill," *Finest Hour* 153 (Winter 2011–12), p. 20.

5. Chris Wrigley, *Winston Churchill: A Biographical Companion*, pp. 18–19. Anderson had his critics among fellow Conservatives like Beaverbrook and Bracken who called him "Pomposo" behind his back. Historian Jonathan Schneer wrote: "The urbane Eden never indulged in such behavior, but confided to his diary about Anderson: 'A good committee man, but zero in Cabinet.' The prime minister may have judged that such a figure was unlikely to initiate comprehensive measures" of domestic reform. Jonathan Schneer, *Ministers at War: Winston Churchill and His War Cabinet*, p. 180.

6. Baron Charles McMoran Wilson Moran, *Churchill: Taken from the Diaries of Lord Moran: The Struggle for Survival, 1940–1965*, p. 129 (September 22, 1943).

7. John Colville, *Fringes of Power*, p. 771.

8. David Rees, *Harry Dexter White: A Study in Paradox*, p. 50.

9. Just as Henry Jr. bonded with FDR, Henry Sr. had bonded with Woodrow Wilson and had been rewarded with appointment as ambassador to the Ottoman Empire.

10. Dean Acheson, *Present at the Creation: My Years in the State Department*, p. 28.

11. David Rees, *Harry Dexter White: A Study in Paradox*, p. 52.

12. Benn Steil, *The Battle of Bretton Woods*, p. 3.

13. John Morton Blum, *From the Morgenthau Diaries: Years of War, 1941–1945*, p. 90.

14. R. Bruce Craig, *Treasonable Doubt: The Harry Dexter White Spy Case*, p. 292, footnote 9. Edward Bernstein, a Harvard monetary economist hired by White, thought his boss "temperamental." Bernstein said White "really wasn't a top-notch technician, but if you could think of somebody having a mind for economic policy, he had it." Henry Morgenthau III, *Mostly Morgenthaus: A Family History*, p. 313. Like several other colleagues, Bernstein noted; "I had the impression that he did not like me nor did I especially like him." Henry Morgenthau III, *Mostly Morgenthaus: A Family History*, p. 314. Historian Michael Beschloss wrote: "Blunt, sardonic, hardworking, rapaciously ambitious, White strode with blue eyes darting from side to side down the Treasury halls." Michael Beschloss, *The Conquerors*, p. 151.

15. The son of the Treasury secretary wrote that "as he came to fathom the complexities of a wartime economy and of the peace to follow, he began to depend increasingly on the advice of Harry White, placing great faith in his intelligence and judgment." The younger Morgenthau added: "I can remember observing White on occasions when my father invited me to sit in on one of the 9:30 staff meetings in his large office. Harry would walk into the room with the quick, coordinated step of the good tennis and Ping-Pong player that he was. A man of medium stature and compact frame, he wore dark, conservative suits and ties. . . . When he spoke his rapid-fire comments sounded disdainfully critical, though he always tried to show respect when addressing my father directly." It was "White's anti-German passion that made him particularly attractive to my father, blinding him to the more complex, sometimes contradictory facets of White's persona." Henry Morgenthau III, *Mostly Morgenthaus: A Family History*, pp. 311, 313, 310.

16. John Morton Blum, *From the Morgenthau Diaries: Years of War, 1941–1945*, p. 89.

17. H. W. Arndt, "The Wizard and the Pragmatist/Keynes and Churchill," *Finest Hour* 153 (Winter 2011–12), p. 20. Eugene V. Rostow, who served in the Roosevelt administration during World War II, wrote: "Keynes was a formidable, overbearing man, with a flair for the dramatic. His literary style was an elegant combination of sardonic wit and prophetic majesty. He spoke ex cathedra and in his day, it required unusual courage to point out that like most people he sometimes talked nonsense." Eugene V. Rostow, *Toward Managed Peace: The National Security Interests of the United States, 1759 to the Present*, p. 224.

18. Milton Friedman and Rose D. Friedman, *Two Lucky People: Memoirs*, pp. 116–118.

19. Robert Skidelsky, *John Maynard Keynes, 1883–1946: Economist, Philosopher, Statesman*, p. 729.

20. Ed Conway, *The Summit: Bretton Woods, 1944*, p. 113. Robert Skidelsky, *John Maynard Keynes: Fighting for Freedom, 1937–1946*, p. 115.

21. Whittaker Chambers, *Witness*, p. 384. White was not so different from Morgenthau. "When Roosevelt smiled at him, Morgenthau was exuberant. When he ignored him, he was despondent," wrote historian Michael R. Beschloss. When Morgenthau told FDR's wife about FDR's "bullying" treatment, she responded that the president treated badly "people close to him." Michael R. Beschloss, *The Conquerors*, p. 51. White colleague Edward Bernstein recalled that Morgenthau asked White to leave the room after he had used a profanity. When Bernstein saw White outside the room, White was crying. "White had a short temper," recalled Bernstein, "and he was easily upset by the Secretary of the Treasury because he depended for his influence on his close relationship with the Secretary." Ed Conway, *The Summit: Bretton Woods, 1944*, pp. 79–80.

22. David Rees, *Harry Dexter White: A Study in Paradox*, pp. 131, 53.

23. R. Bruce Craig, *Treasonable Doubt: The Harry Dexter White Spy Case*, p. 163.

24. John Morton Blum, *From the Morgenthau Diaries: Years of War, 1941–1945*, p. 89.

25. FBI Director J. Edgar Hoover worked hard to "undermine White's nomination" according to R. Bruce Craig, but he did not have sufficient evidence to prove him a spy, or prove his disloyalty in court. Contrary to the 1953 allegations by Attorney General Herbert Brownell, Hoover had not advised the White House that White was a spy, and when Brownell made the allegation in a November speech, Hoover contradicted him privately. By 1946, White was under investigation for alleged espionage—as Hoover informed Secretary of the Treasury Fred Vinson in February 1946. As Craig noted, Hoover "recognized the importance of precision in language." Craig noted that contrary to Truman's misstatements, "the FBI had not requested that White be placed in the IMF position nor had the FBI suggested that White be retained at the IMF so that the Bureau could catch a whole spy ring." Truman's duplicity about the government's handling of White was as misleading as Brownell's. R. Bruce Craig, *Treasonable Doubt: The Harry Dexter White Spy Case*, pp. 198–199, 233–235. Hoover was called to testify before Congress along with Brownell, and said that he advised the Truman administration that White was "unfit" for appointment to the IMF, although he did not then have sufficient evidence that might convict White of a crime. David Rees, *Harry Dexter White: A Study in Paradox*, p. 422.

26. David Rees, *Harry Dexter White: A Study in Paradox*, p. 162.

27. David Rees, *Harry Dexter White: A Study in Paradox*, p. 99.

28. David Rees, *Harry Dexter White: A Study in Paradox*, p. 57.

29. Benn Steil, *The Battle of Bretton Woods*, p. 51.

30. David Rees, *Harry Dexter White: A Study in Paradox*, pp. 114–127.

31. Cordell Hull, *Memoirs of Cordell Hull*, Volume I, pp. 207–208.

32. Like Whittaker Chambers, White had studied at Columbia, but they apparently never met. At Harvard, however, White met fellow economist Lauchlin Currie, who, as a Roosevelt administration official, was a member of the Soviet espionage network and a collaborator of White. R. Bruce Craig, *Treasonable Doubt: The Harry Dexter White Spy Case*, pp. 25, 29. Roger James Sandilands, *The Life and Political Economy of Lauchlin Currie: New Dealer, Presidential Adviser, and Development Economist*, p. 23. In 1943, Morgenthau alienated Secretary of War

Stimson by pushing for the appointment of Currie to the Combined Civil Affairs Committee to oversee the occupation administration of Germany.

33. David Rees, *Harry Dexter White: A Study in Paradox*, p. 43.

34. Robert Skidelsky, *John Maynard Keynes, 1883–1946: Economist, Philosopher, Statesman*, p. 488.

35. Benn Steil, *The Battle of Bretton Woods*, p. 41. Historian R. Bruce Craig has attempted to refute the importance that Benn Steil placed on the document: "White's exuberance for the Soviet-styled planned economy was well known to his contemporaries, including Edward Bernstein, Raymond Mikesell, and scores of others who worked on White's Treasury staff. White's views were equally well known to his contemporaries in the State and War departments and even to several in the White House." http://www.rbrucecraig.com/black-chamber-review-blog/white-lies-about-bretton.html.

36. Raymond F. Mikesell, *Foreign Adventures of an Economist*, p. 56.

37. John Morton Blum, *From the Morgenthau Diaries: Years of War, 1941–1945*, p. 90. John Morton Blum, an academic historian at Yale, was intent on defending Morgenthau, and rationalized White's role as a Soviet spy.

38. Benn Steil, *The Battle of Bretton Woods*, p. 3.

39. H. W. Arndt, "The Wizard and the Pragmatist: Keynes and Churchill," *Finest Hour* 153 (Winter 2011–12), p. 20. Outside of Benn Steil's *The Battle of Bretton Woods*, World War II monetary policy deliberations have generally not received the analysis they deserved. Bretton Woods was never even mentioned in Churchill's six-volume *The Second World War*. Bretton Woods has been generally ignored or skipped over by Roosevelt's biographers. It was as if international monetary policy, despite its centrality in the global economy, was too difficult for FDR and his biographers to understand. In *Franklin D. Roosevelt and American Foreign Policy, 1932–1945*, Robert Dallek never mentioned Bretton Woods. In *Roosevelt 1940–1945*, James MacGregor Burns devoted three paragraphs to the meeting and the problems associated with it. James MacGregor Burns, *Roosevelt: Soldier of Freedom*, p. 514. Lord Keynes, whose writings fill 30 volumes, has received more attention, but seldom outside the work of Robert Skidelsky has there been detailed examination of his work leading up to Bretton Woods. White, in comparison, has received much more attention for the controversy surrounding his transfer of government documents to Russian agents. Even as astute a historian as A. J. P. Taylor got it completely wrong in his biography of Max Beaverbrook, asserting that by 1944, Keynes "had now been converted to the gold standard and free trade." A. J. P. Taylor, *Beaverbrook*, p. 556. Like Secretary of State Cordell Hull, White was a strong free trader. R. Bruce Craig, *Treasonable Doubt: The Harry Dexter White Spy Case*, p. 39.

For an in-depth examination of Anglo-American economic relations, see Randall Bennett Woods, *A Change of the Guard: Anglo-American Relations, 1941–1946*. See also Lloyd Gardner, *Economic Aspects of New Deal Diplomacy*, and Richard N. Gardner, *Sterling Dollar Diplomacy: Anglo-American Collaboration in the Reconstruction of Multilateral Trade*.

40. White was an activist idea generator and persuasive debater. R. Bruce Craig, *Treasonable Doubt: The Harry Dexter White Spy Case*, p. 37.

41. Benn Steil, *The Battle of Bretton Woods*, p. 95.

42. Benn Steil, *The Battle of Bretton Woods*, p. 89.

43. In 1931, Keynes urged: "Therefore, O patriotic housewives, sally out tomorrow early into the streets and go to the wonderful sales." Benn Steil, *The Battle of Bretton Woods*, p. 84.

44. Keynes social habits, however, could be more coarse than White's, and even offended members of his Bloomsbury Group colleagues. Ed Conway, *The Summit: Bretton Woods, 1944*, p. 31.

45. Robert Skidelsky, *John Maynard Keynes: Fighting for Britain, 1937–1946*, p. 122.

46. Ed Conway, *The Summit: Bretton Woods, 1944*, p. 117.

47. Robert Skidelsky, *John Maynard Keynes, 1883–1946: Economist, Philosopher, Statesman*, p. 629. Benn Steil, *The Battle of Bretton Woods*, p. 114. Keynes met with FDR once more on November 26, 1944, and discussed the Morgenthau Plan, but Keynes found the president "obviously extremely fluid over the whole question" and intending to delay decisions indefinitely, as was FDR's habit. Donald E. Moggridge, *Maynard Keynes: An Economist's Biography*, p. 777.

48. Ed Conway, *The Summit: Bretton Woods, 1944*, pp. 113–114.

49. Donald E. Moggridge, *Maynard Keynes: An Economist's Biography*, p. 684. White's discourtesy was indiscriminate. In his memoirs, Dean Acheson, the State Department representative at the Bretton Woods conference, wrote: "I have often been so outraged by Harry White's capacity for rudeness in discussion that the charges made against him would have seemed mild compared to expressions I have used, but he could be equally pleasant and amusing, as I well remember from an evening when we joined the Keyneses for dinner at the Whites'." Dean Acheson, *Present at the Creation: My Years at the State Department*, pp. 81–82. In a 1969 interview, Acheson described White as "profoundly jealous" of his British counterpart Keynes. David Rees, *Harry Dexter White: A Study in Paradox*, p. 230. American Treasury colleague Ray Mikesell wrote: "I do not recall White's embarrassing any staff member by dressing him down, but he showed another side when he was involved in negotiations outside the Treasury Department. He was often brusque, even crude, in his meetings with Keynes and the British delegation. When annoyed, he sometimes cynically addressed Keynes as 'Your Royal Highness' or 'Your Lordship.'" Ray Mikesell, *Foreign Adventures of an Economist*, pp. 54–55. British economist Lionel Robbins, who served on the British delegation, described White as "brash, truculent, and, I suspect, somewhat unscrupulous where his own interests were concerned." Lord Robbins, *Autobiography of an Economist*, p. 198.

50. Ed Conway, *The Summit: Bretton Woods, 1944*, p. 79.

51. Donald Moggridge, *Maynard Keynes: An Economist's Biography*, p. 684.

52. John Colville, *The Fringes of Power*, p. 433 (August 30, 1941).

53. Franklin D. Roosevelt, Public Papers of the Presidents, F.D. Roosevelt, Volume XII, p. 512 (A Report to Congress on Reverse Lend-Lease, November 11, 1943).

54. Preliminary Agreement Between the United States and the United Kingdom, February 23, 1942, http://avalon.law.yale.edu/20th_century/decade04.asp.

55. Keynes noted that he made "three vows . . . before a visit to America, namely, one that I will drink no cocktails, two that I will obey my wife, and three that I will never allow myself to be betrayed into speaking the truth." Randall Bennett Woods, *A Changing of the Guard: Anglo-American Relations, 1941–1946*, p. 181.

56. Paul Addison, *Churchill: The Unexpected Hero*, p. 179.

57. David Rees, *Harry Dexter White: A Study in Paradox*, p. 62.

58. After reviewing White's draft in July 1942, Keynes wrote: "The general attitude of mind seems to me most helpful and also enlightening. But the actual technical solution strikes me as quite hopeless. He has not seen how to get around the gold standard difficulties and has forgotten all about the useful concept of bank money. But is there any reason why, when once the advantages of bank money have been pointed out to him, he should not collect and

rearrange his other basic ideas around this technique?" Donald Moggridge, *Maynard Keynes: An Economist's Biography*, p. 687.

59. Robert Skidelsky, *John Maynard Keynes, 1883–1946: Economist, Philosopher, Statesman*, p. 701.

60. Donald Moggridge, *Maynard Keynes: An Economist's Biography*, p. 689.

61. British economist Lionel Robbins wrote of one meeting that White "shouted all day like a man directing the movements of a ship without a rudder in a hurricane." Lord Robbins, *Autobiography of an Economist*, p. 198.

62. Robert Skidelsky, *John Maynard Keynes, 1883–1946: Economist, Philosopher, Statesman*, p. 743. British economist James Meade wrote in his diary: "What absolute Bedlam these discussions are! Keynes and White sit next [to] each other, each flanked by a long row of his own supporters. Without any agenda or any prepared idea of what is going to be discussed they go for each in a strident duet of discord which after a crescendo of abuse on either side leads up to a chaotic adjournment." Donald Moggridge, *Maynard Keynes: An Economist's Biography*, p. 727. At another point, Meade wrote that "it augurs ill for the future unless these negotiations can somehow or another be got out of the hands of two such prima donnas as White and Keynes." Susan Howson and Donald Edward Moggridge, eds, *The Wartime Diaries of Lionel Robbins and James Meade, 1943–45*, p. 133.

63. John Maynard Keynes wrote: "I always regard a visit [to Washington] as in the nature of a serious illness to be followed by a convalescence." Ed Conway, *The Summit: Bretton Woods, 1944*, p. 119.

64. Robert Skidelsky, *John Maynard Keynes, 1883–1946: Economist, Philosopher, Statesman*, p. 750.

65. Ben Pimlott, ed, *The Second World War Diary of Hugh Dalton, 1940–1945*, pp. 704–706 (February 11, 1944).

66. See Churchill's speeches on free trade in Parliament before World War I and his two-budget speeches as chancellor of the exchequer.

67. A. J. P. Taylor, *Beaverbrook*, p. 556 (Max Beaverbrook to John Maynard Keynes, March 10, 1944).

68. James M. Boughton and K. Sarwar Lateef, eds, *Fifty Years after Bretton Woods: The Future of the IMF and the World Bank*, p. 64 (Richard Gardner, "Establishing a Vision for Promoting Economic Development").

69. Robert Skidelsky, *John Maynard Keynes: Fighting for Freedom, 1937–1946*, p. 333 (Max Beaverbrook to John Maynard Keynes, March 11, 1944).

70. Robert Skidelsky, *John Maynard Keynes, 1883–1946: Economist, Philosopher, Statesman*, p. 755.

71. Gregory A. Fossedal, *Our Finest Hour: Will Clayton, the Marshall Plan, and the Triumph of Democracy*, p. 114.

72. Robert Skidelsky, *John Maynard Keynes, 1883–1946: Economist, Philosopher, Statesman*, p. 697. The Venona Project of the U.S. Army Signal Intelligence Agency, established to intercept and decode communication between Russia and espionage agents, produced evidence of White's spying for the Soviet Union. See "Report of the Commission on Protecting and Reducing Government Secrecy," United States Government Printing Office, 1997.

73. Robert Skidelsky, *John Maynard Keynes, 1883–1946: Economist, Philosopher, Statesman*, p. 756.

74. At Bretton Woods, Morgenthau told Keynes that he had included congressmen in the American delegation "solely for the purpose of getting this legislation through, because they

are sensitive to their constituency." The Treasury secretary blamed Woodrow Wilson's failure to get ratification of the League of Nations on Wilson's neglecting to include Senator Henry Cabot Lodge in his discussions. John Morton Blum, *From the Morgenthau Diaries: Years of War, 1941–1945*, p. 270.

75. John Morton Blum, *From the Morgenthau Diaries: Years of War, 1941–1945*, p. 250.

76. John Morton Blum, *From the Morgenthau Diaries: Years of War, 1941–1945*, p. 251.

77. Morgenthau told White: "If I don't read it, it's my own fault, but if I don't have anything from you, then it's your fault." Ed Conway, *The Summit: Bretton Woods, 1944*, pp. 184, 187, 188.

78. James Chace, *Acheson: The Secretary of State Who Created the American World*, p. 97.

79. Keynes had implored that White "not take us to Washington in July, which should surely be a most unfriendly act. We were hoping, you will remember, that the new round [of talks] would be here [in England]. If that is impossible, then at least you must arrange for some pleasant resort in the Rocky Mountains, if you are going to keep your flock in a reasonably good temper." Ed Conway, *The Summit: Bretton Woods, 1944*, p. 6.

80. Benn Steil, *The Battle of Bretton Woods: John Maynard Keynes, Harry Dexter White, and the Making of a New World Order*, p. 190.

81. Eric Helleiner, *Forgotten Foundations of Bretton Woods: International Development and the Making of the Postwar Order*, p. 121.

82. When in March 1943, White asked Morgenthau if FDR backed the proposed International Monetary Fund, the Treasury secretary replied that the ailing Roosevelt "very seldom, Harry, shows any enthusiasm these days. It is very rare. So don't be disappointed." Peter Moreira, *The Jew Who Defeated Hitler: Henry Morgenthau Jr., FDR, and How We Won the War*, p. 209.

83. Benn Steil, *The Battle of Bretton Woods: John Maynard Keynes, Harry Dexter White, and the Making of a New World Order*, pp. 201–249.

84. Economic historian Ed Conway wrote: "Consigned as they were to their own committees, Keynes and White by this stage had little face-to-face contact. Only occasionally did they bump into each other in the corridors and lobbies of the hotel, and when they did there was barely time for more than small talk, which usually entailed complaints about the volume of work." Ed Conway, *The Summit: Bretton Woods, 1944*, p. 240.

85. Judy Shelton, *Money Meltdown*, p. 43.

86. John Morton Blum, *From the Morgenthau Diaries: Years of War, 1941–1945*, p. 255.

87. Fred Vinson's designated assistant from the Treasury Department, economist Raymond F. Mikesell, wrote: "The lack of candor regarding quotas at Bretton Woods was unfortunate because it created considerable controversy and mistrust. White used an arbitrarily determined procedure to produce the recommended quotas and then tried to keep the formula from most of the delegates." Raymond F. Mikesell, *Foreign Adventures of an Economist*, p. 51.

88. Robert Skidelsky, *John Maynard Keynes, 1883–1946: Economist, Philosopher, Statesman*, p. 764.

89. Benn Steil, *The Battle of Bretton Woods*, p. 214. Ironically, the crucial amendment "according to which the criteria of payment of official gold subscription should be expressed as official holdings of gold and United States dollars" was made by one of the British delegates, well-known economist Dennis Robertson. Keynes would belatedly discover the change. Ed Conway, *The Summit: Bretton Woods, 1944*, pp. 244–247.

90. Benn Steil, *The Battle of Bretton Woods*, pp. 226–228. Keynes's emotional response probably precipitated a heart attack that night. American officials had been incensed by the

role of the Bank for International Settlements in 1939, in shifting Czech gold reserves to Germany's account, and thereafter targeted the BIS for termination. Ed Conway, *The Summit: Bretton Woods, 1944*, pp. 270–272.

91. John Morton Blum, *From the Morgenthau Diaries: Years of War, 1941–1945*, p. 268.

92. Keynes's heart condition was so severe that his wife refused to let him go to conference receptions and insisted they eat alone in their suite. Keynes himself admitted: "The flow of alcohol is appalling." Liaquat Ahamed, *Lords of Finance: The Bankers Who Broke the World*, p. 494.

93. British bankers were worried that the financial center of the world would shift from London to the United States, but Secretary Morgenthau opposed the attempts by the State Department's Dean Acheson to seek a compromise. Morgenthau insisted that "the financial center of the world is going to be New York and we don't want to postpone this thing until another day where we may not be in as advantageous a position and maybe have then to get in a horse-trading position and maybe end up by having it in London." Ed Conway, *The Summit: Bretton Woods, 1944*, p. 269.

94. Benn Steil, *The Battle of Bretton Woods*, p. 222.

95. Benn Steil, *The Battle of Bretton Woods*, p. 148.

96. R. Bruce Craig, *Treasonable Doubt: The Harry Dexter White Spy Case*, pp. 144–145.

97. Donald Moggridge, *Maynard Keynes: An Economist's Biography*, pp. 746–747. Robert Skidelsky, *John Maynard Keynes: Fighting for Freedom, 1937–1946*, p. 355. One Treasury economist recalled: "Keynes frequently complained that Americans were too dependent on attorneys, and once suggested that 'when the Mayflower sailed from Plymouth, it must have been entirely filled with lawyers.'" Raymond F. Mikesell, *Foreign Adventures of an Economist*, p. 57.

98. Benn Steil, *The Battle of Bretton Woods*, p. 251. Randall Bennett Woods wrote: "The true British architect of the monetary system constructed at Bretton Woods was not Keynes but Frederick Lindemann. . . . Lindemann, who peppered Churchill with memos on foreign economic policy throughout this period, also saw the fund and bank, and multilateralism in general, as important aids in the battle to save capitalism" in Britain. Randall Bennett Woods, *A Changing of the Guard; Anglo-American Relations, 1941–1946*, p. 147.

99. Donald Moggridge, *Maynard Keynes: An Economist's Biography*, pp. 747–748.

100. R. Bruce Craig, *Treasonable Doubt: The Harry Dexter White Spy Case*, p. 147.

101. Henry Morgenthau III, *Mostly Morgenthaus: A Family History*, p. 400.

102. Historian William Hardy McNeill wrote that "the deliberations at Bretton Woods were hardly adequate to the occasion." McNeill argued that the Bretton Woods architects "had little idea of the vastness and the persistence of the 'dollar shortage' which was to plague the post-war world; nor did the scheme take into account the devices for economic exploitation of neighbouring countries which the Soviet Government were to develop in the immediate post-war period." William Hardy McNeill, *America, Britain and Russia: Their Co-operation and Conflict, 1941–1946*, p. 450. Similarly, historian Randall B. Woods wrote: "Liquidity was the key to making any multilateral system work, and the Bretton Woods agreements did not provide that liquidity." David B. Woolner, Warren Kimball, David Reynolds, eds, *FDR's World*, p. 184 ("Roosevelt's New Economic Order"). On the contrary, the Bretton Woods system led to excessive liquidity, criticized as 'irrigation in a flood" by one of its chief critics. Jacques Rueff, *Balance of Payments*, *passim*.

103. Benn Steil, *The Battle of Bretton Woods*, pp. 243–244.

104. Neil Irwin, "How a Soviet Spy Outmaneuvered John Maynard Keynes to Ensure U.S. Financial Dominance," *Washington Post*, March 14, 2013.

105. Raymond F. Miesell, "The Bretton Woods Debates: A Memoir," *Essays in International Finance*, No 192, March 1994, p. 42.

106. See Chapter XVIIB for a discussion of the evidence of the espionage conducted by White and his colleagues.

107. Robert Skidelsky, *John Maynard Keynes, 1883–1946: Economist, Philosopher, Statesman*, p. 696.

108. R. Bruce Craig, *Treasonable Doubt: The Harry Dexter White Spy Case*, p. 199.

109. Benn Steil, *The Battle of Bretton Woods*, p. 5.

CHAPTER XVIIB. THE SOVIET CONNECTION OF HARRY DEXTER WHITE

1. In 2000, the IMF's James M. Broughton published *The Case Against Harry Dexter White: Still Not Proven*. Broughton argued that White did indeed pass information to the Soviets, but that it was of little value and did not undermine U.S. interests. John Earl Haynes and Harvey Klehr decisively refute Broughton's claims in their book *In Denial: Historians, Communism, and Espionage* (2005), wherein they showed that Broughton "manipulated the truth in an attempt to rescue Harry Dexter White" (p. 182). Economic historian Ed Conway argued: "Whether you believe White was a spy depends largely on your definition of the word. What White did might be classified as a form of espionage. But as spies go, he was a pretty lousy one. He was reluctant to provide much in the way of detailed information." Ed Conway, *The Summit: Bretton Woods, 1944*, p. 159. Conway's view is disputed by Benn Steil, John Earl Haynes, and Harvey Klehr.

2. Russia's main security service was the NKVD during World War II. It operated both at home and abroad. Under Nikita Khruschev, it became the KGB in 1954. The military security service during World War II was the GRU. Benn Steil wrote that "the 18 cables referencing White which I found among 13,000 pages of FBI documentation on him, dated from March 1944 to January 1946 (considerably longer than the range indicated by Boughton), reveal far more than this. They show White passing confidential strategic information to Soviet intelligence through American moles, as well as directly to Soviet operatives, and expressing grave concern over whether and how his activities can continue to be kept secret." Benn Steil, "The Lonely Crusade of an IMF Historian to Whitewash the Spy Career of the Fund's Founder," Forbes.com, August 15, 2013, http://www.forbes.com/sites/realspin/2013/08/15/the-lonely-crusade-of-an-imf-historian-to-whitewash-the-spy-career-of-the-funds-founder/.

3. White had a strong aversion to State Department officials. Treasury staffer Raymond F. Mikesell, who proclaimed his own belief in White's patriotism, recalled: "White sought to conduct his own foreign policy independently of the State Department. He dealt directly with foreign officials in Washington, and members of the Monetary Research staff in American embassies in Allied countries, including myself, secretly reported directly to White without going through their embassies. White sometimes used the press to promote his policies that were in opposition to those of the State Department. On one occasion, while I was alone with him in his office, he dictated over the phone a long, top-secret State Department statement to a reporter." Raymond F. Mikesell, *Foreign Adventures of an Economist*, pp. 55–56.

4. According to Morgenthau's son, "Mrs. Klotz said she assumed at the time a lot of Harry's friends were Communists. But thrown into a situation that confused her, she 'didn't know

what a Communist was to begin with.'" Henry Morgenthau III, *Mostly Morgenthaus: A Family History*, p. 312. Klotz's explanation, too, was a typically disingenuous explanation of an accomplice caught in the act. Morgenthau III wanted to exonerate his father.

5. John Earl Haynes and Harvey Klehr, *Venona: Decoding Soviet Espionage in America*, p. 130.

6. Former secretary Morgenthau wrote to White's widow: "Harry was a top flight public servant who served his country well. If I get around to writing the real story of my life, Harry will occupy an important place in the book. He served his country well." Henry Morgenthau III, *Mostly Morgenthaus: A Family History*, p. 424.

7. Federal Reserve Chairman Marriner Eccles recalled that FDR called him on the phone in 1939 and announced, "I am going to steal Lauch Currie from you. I need him here as one of my assistants." The president added: "I am sure you will realize that it is not such a bad thing after all as far as the Board and you are concerned. You, of course, see the advantages at once of having a friend in court who can represent and speak for your point of view." Biographer Roger James Sandilands noted that while at the Federal Reserve, Currie had acted as a liaison to the Treasury and friend Harry Dexter White. Currie himself recalled that once at the White House, he recruited economists for positions throughout the Roosevelt administration. "Our position in the Treasury was getting stronger as Harry White gained influence." Currie noted: "We did not sleep much, but when we did the General Theory kept working." Roger James Sandilands, *The Life and Political Economy of Lauchlin Currie*, pp. 96–98.

8. John Earl Haynes and Harvey Klehr, *In Denial*, pp. 170–172. Currie was designated in 1941 by Harry Hopkins as the point person for Lend-Lease aid to China. George McJimsey, *Harry Hopkins: Ally of the Poor and Defender of Democracy*, p. 290.

9. Christopher Andrew and Vasili Mitrokhin, *The Sword and the Shield: The Mitrokhin Archive and the Secret History of the KGB*, p. 105.

10. John Earl Haynes and Harvey Klehr, *In Denial*, p. 175. According to Haynes and Klehr, "More than two dozen KGB documents in Vassiliev's notebooks, the earliest from 1941 and the latest from 1948 . . . show that Currie actively assisted Soviet intelligence via Silvermaster and Silverman from 1941 until 1945." John Earl Haynes, Harvey Klehr, and Alexander Vassiliev, *Spies: The Rise and Fall of the KGB in America*, p. 265.

11. John Earl Haynes and Harvey Klehr, *Venona: Decoding Soviet Espionage in America*, p. 140–141.

12. Herbert Romerstein and Eric Breindel, *The Venona Secrets*, p. 49. John Earl Haynes and Harvey Klehr, *Venona: Decoding Soviet Espionage in America*, p. 154–155.

13. John Earl Haynes and Harvey Klehr, *Venona: Decoding Soviet Espionage in America*, p. 141.

14. See Alexander Vassiliev,"How I Came to Write My Notebooks, Discover Alger Hiss, and Lose to His Lawyer," in John Earl Haynes, Harvey Klehr, and Alexander Vassiliev, *Spies: The Rise and Fall of the KGB in America*, pp. xxvii–liii.

15. R. Bruce Craig, "Setting the Record Straight: Harry Dexter White and Soviet Espionage," History News Network, April 30, 2012, http://historynewsnetwork.org/article/145913.

16. A civil libertarian, Berle was philosophically averse to the espionage role that FDR had assigned him and complained about preventing "crimes; at the same time to prevent this machinery from being used hysterically, in violation of civil liberties." Joseph Persico, *Roosevelt's Secret War*, p. 42.

17. Meeting with Levine in New York, Chambers was not anxious to reveal his knowledge without "immunity from prosecution." Chambers insisted: "I wouldn't trust anybody's word

but that of President Roosevelt himself." As a result, Levine promised to try to arrange a private meeting with FDR." Isaac Don Levine, *Eyewitness to History*, p. 192.

18. Isaac Don Levine, *Eyewitness to History*, p. 193. Sam Tanenhaus, *Whittaker Chambers: A Biography*, pp. 160–161. Jordan A. Schwarz, *Liberal: Adolf A. Berle and the Vision of an American Era*, p. 299. Schwarz wrote that when Berle testified before HUAC in August 1949, "Berle's testimony was vague and confused. He insisted that the men Chambers named as spies were no more than a group of Communist sympathizers intent upon organizing a Marxist study group in the State Department. Although Chambers had named names, Berle did not attach any great significance to them; some were already out of government." Schwarz, p. 299. Berle and Dean Acheson detested each other. When Acheson was up for confirmation as secretary of state in 1949, Berle and Acheson had a very public disagreement, during which Acheson argued: "Mr. Berle's memory has gone badly astray" about a 1944 conversation about either Alger Hiss (Berle) or Donald Hiss (Acheson). Schwarz, p. 301. The dysfunctionality within the State Department may have contributed to Berle's failure to follow up on Chambers's revelations, but there may have been other reasons as well. Stettinius wrote in his memoirs: "Shortly after I became Under Secretary of State—October 1943—with the approval of the President and Mr. Hull I called in the FBI to conduct a security examination of the State Department. Assistant Secretary of State G. Howland Shaw served as liaison with the FBI during this examination. I never heard of any questioning of Mr. Hiss's loyalty from anyone inside or outside of the State Department or from the FBI during my time of service in the Department." Edward R. Stettinius Jr., *Roosevelt and the Russians: The Yalta Conference*, p. 31. With the benefit of hindsight, Berle's competence and judgment must be questioned.

19. Whittaker Chambers, *Witness*, p. 470.

20. Whittaker Chambers, *Witness*, p. 465.

21. Beatrice Bishop Berle and Travis Beal Jacobs, eds, *Navigating the Rapids, 1918–1971: From the Papers of Adolf A. Berle*, p. 250 (September 4, 1939). Berle complained about Chambers's memoirs: "Read carefully, the book (as far as I have got it) is not in detail inaccurate, but the whole impression is wrong. At no time does he record what he said to me, and thus gives the impression that he told me everything he told many years later in the Hiss case." Berle and Jacobs, p. 598 (March 18, 1952). Christopher Andrew and Vasili Mitrokhin, *The Sword and the Shield: The Mitrokhin Archive and the Secret History of the KGB*, p. 107.

22. Sam Tanenhaus, *Whittaker Chambers: A Biography*, pp. 161–162. Beatrice Bishop Berle and Travis Beal Jacobs, eds, *Navigating the Rapids, 1918–1971: From the Papers of Adolf A. Berle*, pp. 598–599 (March 18, 1952). In his diary, writing more than 12 years after his meeting, Berle wrote that Chambers "did not state anything he told me as personal knowledge—but as something he had heard about while in the Communist Party in New York. He did not even remotely indicate that he personally had been engaged in the operation. He did not charge individuals with espionage—they were merely 'sympathizers' who would be hauled out later when the great day came. He would not take his story to the FBI. I would not even stand to it himself. He would not himself verify or stick to the story. He really wanted to see the President." Berle and Jacobs, p. 598. Chambers wanted immunity from prosecution.

23. Henry L. Stimson, *On Active Service in Peace and War*, p. 188. Berle wrote in his diary on July 11, 1941: "I have asked the Federal Bureau of Investigation to continue their surveillance over Communist activities here. A party line which could change from one of hostility to one of collaboration overnight could change back with equal speed. Anyhow, freedom from subversive activities (in plain English, from plotting, sabotage, political strikes, and in some

cases, murder) ought not to rest on the grace of a foreign government. It ought to rest on our own strength." Beatrice Bishop Berle and Travis Beal Jacobs, eds, *Navigating the Rapids, 1918–1971: From the Papers of Adolf A. Berle*, p. 373 (July 11, 1941).

24. Norman Davies, *No Simple Victory*, p. 174.

25. R. Bruce Craig, *Treasonable Doubt: The Harry Dexter White Spy Case*, p. 297, footnote 57.

26. Levine first revealed that mention in a magazine he edited, *Plain Talk*, October 1948. David Rees, *Harry Dexter White: A Study in Paradox*, p. 86. In his memoirs, Levine wrote: "Upon my return after midnight to the Hay-Adams House, where I took leave of Whittaker Chambers, I jotted down on a sheet of hotel stationery most of the names that had been revealed during the evening." Levine said he remained quiet about Chambers and the Berle meeting "in order not to compromise Whitaker Chambers's position on *Time* magazine." Isaac Don Levine, *Eyewitness to History: Memoirs and Reflections of a Foreign Correspondent for Half a Century*, pp. 195, 182.

27. Isaac Don Levine, *Eyewitness to History: Memoirs and Reflections of a Foreign Correspondent for Half a Century*, p. 195.

28. Jordan A. Schwarz, *Liberal: Adolf A. Berle and the Vision of an American Era*, p. 299.

29. Whittaker Chambers, *Witness*, p. 470.

30. David Rees, *Harry Dexter White: A Study in Paradox*, p. 85.

31. Whittaker Chambers, *Witness*, p. 383.

32. Whittaker Chambers, *Witness*, p. 492.

33. Sam Tanenhaus, *Whittaker Chambers: A Biography*, p. 110. John Earl Haynes and Harvey Klehr, *In Denial*, pp. 186–187. White was the target of many gifts, many of which were misdirected to a carpenter named Harvey D. White who also lived in Washington. When, in 1944, the other White, Harvey, received a gift of liquor and cigarettes from "[t]he Government Purchasing Commission of the Soviet Union in the USA, he called the Treasury Department and was told by Harry Dexter White to send half the gift on to him and keep the rest for himself." Ed Conway, *The Summit: Bretton Woods, 1944*, pp. 151–152.

34. R. Bruce Craig, *Treasonable Doubt: The Harry Dexter White Spy Case*, pp. 46–47.

35. Benn Steil, *The Battle of Bretton Woods*, p. 295.

36. Sam Tanenhaus, *Whittaker Chambers: A Biography*, p. 291. Isaac Don Levine, *Eyewitness to History: Memoirs and Reflections of a Foreign Correspondent for Half a Century*, p. 206.

37. R. Bruce Craig, *Treasonable Doubt: The Harry Dexter White Spy Case*, p. 51.

38. R. Bruce Craig, *Treasonable Doubt: The Harry Dexter White Spy Case*, p. 249. Vitalii Pavlov, *Operation Snow: Half a Century at KGB Foreign Intelligence*. Pavlov's book is not available in English. The Pavlov-White encounter is related in John Koster, *Operation Snow*, pp. 2–8.

39. R. Bruce Craig, *Treasonable Doubt: The Harry Dexter White Spy Case*, p. 251.

40. Herbert Romerstein and Eric Breindel, *The Venona Secrets*, p. 44.

41. R. Bruce Craig, *Treasonable Doubt: The Harry Dexter White Spy Case*, p. 251. See Vitalii Pavlov, *Operation Snow: Half a Century at KGB Foreign Intelligence*.

42. Benn Steil, *The Battle of Bretton Woods*, p. 58. Herbert Romerstein and Eric Breindel noted: "White wrote a memorandum shortly after this meeting and sent it to Secretary Henry Morgenthau. In substance, it was an exact repetition of the points Pavlov had given him." They wrote that, later, "White rewrote his hard-line memorandum for Morgenthau, who signed it and sent it to President Roosevelt and Secretary of State Cordell Hull." They contended that White's response to Pavlov was reassuring to Russia because it "made . . . clear that Akhmerov's American network was more pro-Soviet than it was anti-Nazi." Herbert Romerstein and Eric Breindel, *The Venona Secrets*, pp. 41–44.

43. Christopher Andrew and Vasili Mitrokhin, *The Sword and the Shield: The Mitrokhin Archive and the Secret History of the KGB*, p. 109.

44. Isaac Don Levine, *Eyewitness to History*, p. 183.

45. Benn Steil, *The Battle of Bretton Woods*, p. 295. Russians thought that Anglo-American warnings about an impending German invasion were meant to provoke a confrontation. Marshal Georgy Zhukov wrote in his memoirs: "The spring of 1941 was marked by a new wave of false rumors in the Western countries about large-scale Soviet war preparations against Germany. The German press raised a great outcry over three rumors and complained that such information clouded German-Soviet relations." Zhukov said Stalin responded: "You see, they are trying to frighten us with the Germans and the Germans with us, setting us one against the other." Marshal Georgy Zhukov, *The Memoirs of Marshal Zhukov*, p. 224.

46. John Earl Haynes and Harvey Klehr, *Venona: Decoding Soviet Espionage in America*, pp. 131–133. Allen Weinstein and Alexander Vassiliev, *The Haunted Wood: Soviet Espionage in America—The Stalin Era*, pp. 158–161.

47. Allen Weinstein and Alexander Vassiliev speculated that Currie was the Soviet source of Harry Hopkins's report on his July 1941 visit to Moscow, a report sent back to Moscow. Allen Weinstein and Alexander Vassiliev, *The Haunted Wood: Soviet Espionage in America—The Stalin Era*, p. 159.

48. Allen Weinstein and Alexander Vassiliev, *The Haunted Wood: Soviet Espionage in America—The Stalin Era*, p. 161.

49. John Earl Haynes and Harvey Klehr, *Venona: Decoding Soviet Espionage in America*, p. 132. Jacob Golos reported on Patterson's conversation with Currie: "A large number of people was dismayed by [Silvermaster's] dismissal. The head of the Farm Security Administration . . . was very angry. Currie called Assistant Secretary of War Patterson to protest. He told Patterson that 'P' [Silvermaster] did not follow the 'Party line,' that 'P.' had supported general military efforts long before the attack on the Sov. Union and that his position had not abruptly changed after 22 June 1941. Patterson replied that this changed things to a considerable degree and asked him to produce documentary evidence." John Earl Haynes, Harvey Klehr, and Alexander Vassiliev, *Spies: The Rise and Fall of the KGB in America*, p. 266.

50. John Earl Haynes and Harvey Klehr, *Venona: Decoding Soviet Espionage in America*, p. 331.

51. David Rees, *Harry Dexter White: A Study in Paradox*, p. 412.

52. John Earl Haynes and Harvey Klehr, *Venona: Decoding Soviet Espionage in America*, p. 141. Herbert Romerstein and Eric Breindel, *The Venona Secrets*, p. 50. Ed Conway maintained that Venona transcripts indicate the Russians did send $2,000 to help with college costs, but that the money made it only as far as Silvermaster's pockets. Ed Conway, *The Summit: Bretton Woods, 1944*, p. 157.

53. John Earl Haynes and Harvey Klehr, *Venona: Decoding Soviet Espionage in America*, p. 141.

54. John Earl Haynes, Harvey Klehr, and Alexander Vassiliev, *Spies: The Rise and Fall of the KGB in America*, p. 260.

55. John Earl Haynes and Harvey Klehr, *Venona: Decoding Soviet Espionage in America*, p. 142.

56. John Earl Haynes and Harvey Klehr, *In Denial*, p. 191. Beschloss wrote: "White arranged for another meeting after his return with Morgenthau from Europe in mid-August." Michael Beschloss, *The Conquerors*, p. 152.

57. Herbert Romerstein and Eric Breindel, *The Venona Secrets*, p. 46.

58. John Earl Haynes, Harvey Klehr, and Alexander Vassiliev, *Spies: The Rise and Fall of the KGB in America*, p. 261.

59. Allen Weinstein and Alexander Vassiliev, *The Haunted Wood: Soviet Espionage in America—The Stalin Era*, pp. 163–164. Benn Steil noted that in January 1945, White pushed Morgenthau for better loan terms for Russia, according to the Venona decrypts. Ben Steil, "The Lonely Crusade of an IMF Historian to Whitewash the Spy Career of the Fund's Founder," Forbes.com, August 15, 2013, http://www.forbes.com/sites/realspin/2013/08/15/the-lonely-crusade-of-an-imf-historian-to-whitewash-the-spy-career-of-the-funds-founder/. Robert Skidelsky described White's efforts to "enabl[e] better calibration between the timing of Soviet demands and policy proposals being discussed within the US government" and that the "most striking instance of this is the co-ordination of Soviet requests for an American loan in 1944–5 with White's attempts to get approval for such a loan in Washington. White was keeping Moscow informed of the program of his own loan initiative in Washington, of those members of the administration who favoured it and of the reasons for the delay." Robert Skidelsky, *John Maynard Keynes: Fighting for Freedom, 1937–1946*, p. 259.

60. Allen Weinstein and Alexander Vassiliev, *The Haunted Wood: Soviet Espionage in America—The Stalin Era*, p. 167. Michael Beschloss, *The Conquerors*, p. 156.

61. White's ego was an irritation to his Russian contacts. "Jurist is rough around the edges and a lot of work has to be done on him before he will make a valuable informant," complained Vasily Zurbin in 1944. "To date he has reported only what he deemed necessary himself." But Zurbin thought White was worth the effort, writing "we consider it advisable to assign a special illegal to work with him." John Earl Haynes, Harvey Klehr, and Alexander Vassiliev, *Spies: The Rise and Fall of the KGB in America*, p. 259.

62. David Rees, *Harry Dexter White: A Study in Paradox*, p. 199.

63. R. Bruce Craig, *Treasonable Doubt: The Harry Dexter White Spy Case*, p. 105.

64. Allen Weinstein and Alexander Vassiliev, *The Haunted Wood: Soviet Espionage in America—The Stalin Era*, p. 164.

65. Allen Weinstein and Alexander Vassiliev, *The Haunted Wood: Soviet Espionage in America—The Stalin Era*, pp. 165–166.

66. Silvermaster was jealous of his authority over his spy network and complained to Akmerov that White "had started putting on airs and acting independently" of the Silvermaster group, because he had a direct KGB contact. John Earl Haynes, Harvey Klehr, and Alexander Vassiliev, *Spies: The Rise and Fall of the KGB in America*, p. 509. Jealousy pervaded the Russian spy network in Washington. There was jealousy between Silvermaster and the Perlo espionage group, to which Harold Glasser reported. John Earl Haynes, Harvey Klehr, and Alexander Vassiliev, *Spies: The Rise and Fall of the KGB in America*, p. 511.

67. Allen Weinstein and Alexander Vassiliev, *The Haunted Wood: Soviet Espionage in America—The Stalin Era*, p. 158.

68. Allen Weinstein and Alexander Vassiliev, *The Haunted Wood: Soviet Espionage in America—The Stalin Era*, p. 158.

69. Allen Weinstein and Alexander Vassiliev, *The Haunted Wood: Soviet Espionage in America—The Stalin Era*, p. 162. R. Bruce Craig, *Treasonable Doubt: The Harry Dexter White Spy Case*, p. 109.

70. John Earl Haynes and Harvey Klehr, *Venona: Decoding Soviet Espionage in America*, p. 133.

71. R. Bruce Craig, *Treasonable Doubt: The Harry Dexter White Spy Case*, pp. 83–112.

72. R. Bruce Craig, *Treasonable Doubt: The Harry Dexter White Spy Case*, p. 84, 89–90.

73. Many of White's fellow Russian spies were part of the American delegation at Bretton Woods. Also in attendance was Nikolai F. Chechulin, an NKVD agent who also served as deputy director of the Russian state bank, who conferred with White at Bretton Woods. Ed Conway wrote: "White provided at least some information that may have undermined the efforts of his fellow negotiators." Ed Conway, *The Summit: Bretton Woods, 1944*, pp. 152, 163, 198, 249–250.

74. Allen Weinstein and Alexander Vassiliev, *The Haunted Wood: Soviet Espionage in America—The Stalin Era*, p. 158.

75. Whittaker Chambers, *Witness*, p. 383.

76. Whittaker Chambers, *Witness*, p. 69.

77. Whittaker Chambers, *Witness*, p. 67.

78. Whittaker Chambers, *Witness*, p. 384.

79. David Rees, *Harry Dexter White: A Study in Paradox*, pp. 198–200. R. Bruce Craig, *Treasonable Doubt: The Harry Dexter White Spy Case*, pp. 94–96.

80. Kathryn S. Olmsted, *Red Spy Queen: A Biography of Elizabeth Bentley*, p. 48.

81. R. Bruce Craig, *Treasonable Doubt: The Harry Dexter White Spy Case*, p. 96.

82. Whittaker Chambers, *Witness*, p. 29.

83. R. Bruce Craig, *Treasonable Doubt: The Harry Dexter White Spy Case*, p. 100. John Earl Haynes, Harvey Klehr, and Alexander Vassiliev, *Spies: The Rise and Fall of the KGB in America*, pp. 271–272.

84. R. Bruce Craig, *Treasonable Doubt: The Harry Dexter White Spy Case*, p. 61.

85. David Rees, *Harry Dexter White: A Study in Paradox*, p. 408.

86. Murphy did not give his notes to the FBI, but two years later, a Catholic priest did. Herbert Romerstein and Eric Breindel, *The Venona Secrets*, p. 126.

87. Whittaker Chambers, *Witness*, p. 430. John Earl Haynes, Harvey Klehr, and Alexander Vassiliev, *Spies: The Rise and Fall of the KGB in America*, p. 15.

88. John Earl Haynes and Harvey Klehr, *Venona: Decoding Soviet Espionage in America*, p. 128. Henry Morgenthau III, *Mostly Morgenthaus: A Family History*, p. 314.

89. John Earl Haynes, Harvey Klehr, and Alexander Vassiliev, *Spies: The Rise and Fall of the KGB in America*, p. 273.

90. John Earl Haynes and Harvey Klehr, *Venona: Decoding Soviet Espionage in America*, p. 128.

91. Allen Weinstein and Alexander Vassiliev, *The Haunted Wood: Soviet Espionage in America—The Stalin Era*, pp. 265–266.

92. Allen Weinstein and Alexander Vassiliev, *The Haunted Wood: Soviet Espionage in America—The Stalin Era*, p. 268.

93. Allen Weinstein and Alexander Vassiliev, *The Haunted Wood: Soviet Espionage in America—The Stalin Era*, pp. 270–272. After White's official promotion to assistant secretary in early 1945, Silvermaster promoted Glasser to replace White as Morgenthau's assistant. If the promotion were successful, Silvermaster advocated Glasser to be moved to Silvermaster's espionage group. Romerstein and Eric Breindel, *The Venona Secrets*, p. 47. According to Haynes and Klehr, by "1945 the KGB Washington station, with very good reason, regarded Glasser as its most valuable source." John Earl Haynes, Harvey Klehr, and Alexander Vassiliev, *Spies: The Rise and Fall of the KGB in America*, p. 273.

94. Kathryn S. Olmsted, *Red Spy Queen: A Biography of Elizabeth Bentley*, p. 67.

95. Kathryn S. Olmsted, *Red Spy Queen: A Biography of Elizabeth Bentley*, pp. 69–79. Christopher Andrew and Vasili Mitrokhin, *The Sword and the Shield: The Mitrokhin Archive and the Secret History of the KGB*, pp. 129–130. Top Russian spies were upset with the sloppiness of the Washington spy ring and the knowledge that American contacts had about each other's involvement; the Russians criticized "the lack of understanding by our operational workers of the most elementary rules in our work." Andrew and Mitrokhin, p. 142.

96. Benn Steil, *The Battle of Bretton Woods*, p. 294.

97. Allen Weinstein and Alexander Vassiliev, *The Haunted Wood: Soviet Espionage in America—The Stalin Era*, p. 170. Philby and his British fellow members of the "Cambridge Five" were key sources of Russian intelligence. S. M. Plokhy wrote: "Owing to the activities of the Cambridge Five in Britain and the United States, the Soviet intelligence services were able to supply their masters with copies of most secret American and British documents related to the Yalta Conference." S. M. Plokhy, *Yalta: The Price of Peace*, p. xxv.

98. R. Bruce Craig, *Treasonable Doubt: The Harry Dexter White Spy Case*, pp. 68–71.

99. Benn Steil, *The Battle of Bretton Woods*, p. 296.

100. R. Bruce Craig, *Treasonable Doubt: The Harry Dexter White Spy Case*, pp. 71–72.

101. Kathryn S. Olmsted, *Red Spy Queen: A Biography of Elizabeth Bentley*, pp. 105–106.

102. Kathryn Olmsted wrote that Bentley initially "said that she had never met Harry Dexter White. She did mention that she regarded him as a 'valuable adjunct' to the spy network because of his friendship with the treasury secretary. But she did not hint at the vast conspiracies she would later attribute to him once the newsreel cameras were turned on." Kathryn S. Olmsted, *Red Spy Queen: A Biography of Elizabeth Bentley*, pp. 101–103.

103. R. Bruce Craig, *Treasonable Doubt: The Harry Dexter White Spy Case*, pp. 73.

104. R. Bruce Craig, *Treasonable Doubt: The Harry Dexter White Spy Case*, pp. 76–79.

105. Benn Steil, *The Battle of Bretton Woods*, p. 318.

106. R. Bruce Craig, *Treasonable Doubt: The Harry Dexter White Spy Case*, p. 14.

107. R. Bruce Craig, *Treasonable Doubt: The Harry Dexter White Spy Case*, pp. 178–196.

108. John Earl Haynes and Harvey Klehr, *Venona: Decoding Soviet Espionage in America*, p. 143.

109. John Morton Blum, ed, *From the Morgenthau Diaries: Years of War 1941–1945*, p. 440. Morgenthau was greatly annoyed that his staff was undermining what he thought was a U.S. commitment, while his staff was annoyed that Morgenthau faulted them for the problem. "[M]y word and the promise of Franklin Roosevelt" had assured the Chinese that the gold shipment would be made, maintained the Treasury secretary. Peter Moreira, *The Jew Who Defeated Hitler: Henry Morgenthau Jr., FDR, and How We Won the War*, p. 283.

110. John Earl Haynes and Harvey Klehr, *Venona: Decoding Soviet Espionage in America*, p. 143.

111. David Rees, *Harry Dexter White: A Study in Paradox*, p. 174.

112. R. Bruce Craig, *Treasonable Doubt: The Harry Dexter White Spy Case*, p. 134.

113. John Morton Blum, ed, *From the Morgenthau Diaries: Years of War 1941–1945*, pp. 185–188.

114. John Morton Blum, ed, *From the Morgenthau Diaries: Years of War 1941–1945*, pp. 179–181.

115. R. Bruce Craig, *Treasonable Doubt: The Harry Dexter White Spy Case*, p. 127.

116. R. Bruce Craig, *Treasonable Doubt: The Harry Dexter White Spy Case*, p. 124.

117. Benn Steil, *The Battle of Bretton Woods*, p. 296.

118. Alfred C. Mierzejewski, *Ludwig Erhard: A Biography*, pp. 62–85.

119. R. Bruce Craig, *Treasonable Doubt: The Harry Dexter White Spy Case*, pp. 124–125.

120. John Morton Blum, ed, *From the Morgenthau Diaries: Years of War 1941–1945*, p. 188.

121. John Morton Blum, ed, *From the Morgenthau Diaries: Years of War 1941–1945*, p. 192.

122. David Rees, *Harry Dexter White: A Study in Paradox*, p. 190.

123. Many records compiled by former KGB officer Vasili Mitrokhin are now housed at Churchill College of Cambridge University. Copies of Alexander Vassiliev's eight notebooks transcribing KGB records are held at the Library of Congress, and are available in Russian and English through the Wilson Center's digital archives, http://digitalarchive.wilsoncenter.org/document/113862.

124. Allen Weinstein and Alexander Vassiliev, *The Haunted Wood: Soviet Espionage in America—The Stalin Era*, p. 169.

125. David Rees, *Harry Dexter White: A Study in Paradox*, p. 425.

126. Benn Steil, *The Battle of Bretton Woods*, p. 295. "There was . . . a breathtaking gulf between the intelligence supplied to Stalin on the United States and that available to Roosevelt on the Soviet Union." Russia had agents everywhere in the British and American governments, including the spy agencies, but the United States had no agents in Russia. Christopher Andrew and Vasili Mitrokhin, *The Sword and the Shield: The Mitrokhin Archive and the Secret History of the KGB*, p. 111.

127. David Rees, *Harry Dexter White: A Study in Paradox*, pp. 411–415.

128. Whittaker Chambers, *Witness*, p. 601. Chambers was not an enthusiastic HUAC witness. He had stumbled rather unwittingly into the hornet's nest by testifying earlier in August, about White and Alger Hiss, then president of the Carnegie Endowment for International Peace. Isaac Don Levine, *Eyewitness to History*, pp. 201–202. Chambers, pp. 535–537. In November 1948, Chambers recovered several espionage documents from their hiding place in Brooklyn—including an incriminating four-page memorandum written in White's handwriting. David Rees, *Harry Dexter White: A Study in Paradox*, p. 418.

129. According to Hoover, White was "a valuable adjunct to an underground Soviet espionage organization operation in Washington D.C. Material which came into his possession as a result of his official capacity allegedly was made available . . . to the Soviet Union." Herbert Romerstein and Eric Breindel, *The Venona Secrets*, p. 51.

130. Benn Steil, *The Battle of Bretton Woods*, pp. 297–299.

131. Herbert Romerstein and Eric Breindel, *The Venona Secrets*, pp. 51–52. Byrnes, who had been dismissed as secretary of state by Truman, testified before a congressional committee that the FBI's report had said White "was known to be engaged in espionage activity." Sam Tanenhaus, *Whittaker Chambers*, p. 480.

132. John Earl Haynes and Harvey Klehr, *Venona: Decoding Soviet Espionage in America*, p. 332.

133. John Earl Haynes and Harvey Klehr, *Venona: Decoding Soviet Espionage in America*, p. 139.

134. Michael Beschloss, *The Conquerors*, p. 153.

CHAPTER XVIII. THE MORGENTHAU PLAN

1. Warren Kimball, *Swords or Ploughshares? The Morgenthau Plan for Defeated Nazi Germany, 1943–1946*, p. 102.

2. Warren Kimball, *Swords or Ploughshares? The Morgenthau Plan for Defeated Nazi Germany, 1943–1946*, p. 112.

3. Henry Morgenthau III, *Mostly Morgenthaus: A Family History*, pp. 352–353. Donald Moggridge, *Maynard Keynes: An Economist's Biography*, p. 771.

4. Henry Morgenthau III, *Mostly Morgenthaus: A Family History*, pp. 353–354. Morgenthau biographer John Morton Blum implausibly wrote that this notion did not necessarily seem punitive to Morgenthau, who "was a Jeffersonian, a devotee of agricultural society as the nearest equivalent of Eden on earth." John Morton Blum, *From the Morgenthau Diaries: Years of War 1941–1945*, p. 377.

5. At a meeting later in the day, Churchill complained: "Morgenthau, you have been reported to me in the last year as having turned against us and becoming rather hard in your attitude toward us." Morgenthau promised to be of more help. Michael Beschloss, *The Conquerors*, pp. 75–76. Churchill's wife was not impressed by Morgenthau, writing her husband that she could not "imagine him managing" a sidewalk vendor's stall, "but perhaps the Treasury is easier." Michael Beschloss, *The Conquerors*, p. 79. Morgenthau was an unsuccessful apple farmer. Clementine was an acerbic and astute observer of character.

6. David *Rees, Harry Dexter White: A Study in Paradox*, p. 248.

7. Inadvertently, a meeting during the trip, between Morgenthau and General Eisenhower, may have provided fuel for Morgenthau's thinking. As Eisenhower later recalled the meeting: "[M]y personal opinion is that, following upon the conclusion of hostilities, there must be no room for doubt as to who won the war. Germany must be occupied. More than this, the German people must not be allowed to escape a sense of guilt, of complicity in the tragedy that has engulfed the world." Dwight D. Eisenhower, *Crusade in Europe*, p. 287. Morgenthau's son wrote: "Morgenthau took Eisenhower's words in the tent at Portsmouth as a clear signal that he could advocate a tough policy for Germany with the general's complete approval." Henry Morgenthau III, *Mostly Morgenthaus: A Family History*, p. 356.

8. Henry Morgenthau III, *Mostly Morgenthaus: A Family History*, p. 364. Michael Beschloss wrote: "In his instigation and support of the key elements of the Morgenthau Plan, we may never know whether White was chiefly moved by his own economic-political philosophy, Soviet bribes or other forms of pressure, a higher allegiance to the Soviet Union or an arrogant certainty that he knew best how to handle America's trusted ally." Michael Beschloss, *The Conquerors*, p. 156.

9. Michael Beschloss, *The Conquerors*, p. 77. Morgenthau tended to act from limited knowledge and even more limited foresight. When he and White visited North Africa in the spring of 1943, he insisted to Eisenhower advisor Robert Murphy that French financial administrator Maurice Couve de Murville must be removed from his position of *de facto* French minister of finance. Murphy noted: "It proved impossible to get this decision reversed in Washington, so we were compelled to inform French headquarters that the man who probably was their most effective civilian administrator in Algiers was sidetracked. This excursion by Morgenthau into the field of foreign policy was based upon the assumption, very common among Americans in 1943, that any Frenchman who had remained in France and served the Vichy Government was thereby suspect." De Gaulle, no fan of Vichy supporters, quickly

picked up Couve de Murville and eventually used him as a diplomat. As Murphy later wrote: "Morgenthau seriously disturbed the French civil administration." In the 1960s, President de Gaulle would name Couve de Murville as foreign minister for a decade, and later premier. Robert Murphy, *Diplomat Among Warriors*, pp. 148–149.

10. Henry Morgenthau III, *Mostly Morgenthaus: A Family History*, p. 365. Morgenthau countered: "Well, Mr. President, nobody is considering the question along those lines in Europe. In England they want to build up Germany so that she can pay reparations." Morgenthau said that FDR "left no doubt in my mind that he and I are looking at this thing in the same way, but the people down the line aren[']t. Warren Kimball, *Swords or Ploughshare? The Morgenthau Plan for Defeated Nazi Germany, 1943–1946*, p. 96 (memorandum, August 19, 1944).

11. Michael Beschloss, *The Conquerors*, pp. 86–93.

12. R. Bruce Craig, *Treasonable Doubt: The Harry Dexter White Spy Case*, pp. 160, 165.

13. David Rees, *Harry Dexter White: A Study in Paradox*, p. 253. There emerged a fundamental split in the Roosevelt administration. "In considering how to treat a defeated Germany," wrote historians Walter Isaacson and Evan Thomas, "those with internationalist economic outlook—most notably Stimson, [John J.] McCloy, [Robert A.] Lovett, Harriman, and Acheson—felt that destroying that nation's industry would remove the 'spark plug' . . . of the European economy. With its capacity to export manufactured goods and import raw materials, Germany could play a critical role in a system of world trade." They wrote that "behind the Treasury Secretary's back, McCloy embarked on a merciless campaign to discredit what had become known as the 'Morgenthau Plan.' Each afternoon he and Lovett would get together and think up absurd methods for pastoralizing Germany and gleefully spread their satiric barbs through the Washington bureaucracy." Walter Isaacson and Evan Thomas, *The Wise Men: Six Friends and the World They Made*, pp. 235–236.

14. George McJimsey, *Harry Hopkins: Ally of the Poor and Defender of Democracy*, p. 344.

15. Michael Beschloss, *The Conquerors*, pp. 105, 107. Historian Herbert Feis, who served under Hull at the time, wrote: "In these White House talks, Hull—judging from the accounts later written by Stimson and Morgenthau—seems to have given each of them the sense that he had come around to his side." Herbert Feis, *Churchill-Roosevelt-Stalin: The War They Waged and the Peace They Sought*, p. 369.

16. Michael Beschloss, *The Conquerors*, p. 108.

17. John Morton Blum, ed, *From the Morgenthau Diaries: Years of War 1941–1945*, p. 363.

18. John Morton Blum, ed, *From the Morgenthau Diaries: Years of War 1941–1945*, pp. 363–364.

19. John Morton Blum, ed, *From the Morgenthau Diaries: Years of War 1941–1945*, p. 366.

20. Herbert Levy, *Henry Morgenthau, Jr.: The Remarkable Life of FDR's Secretary of the Treasury*, p. 390.

21. David Rees, *Harry Dexter White: A Study in Paradox*, p. 264.

22. John Morton Blum, ed, *From the Morgenthau Diaries: Years of War 1941–1945*, p. 367.

23. Henry Morgenthau III, *Mostly Morgenthaus: A Family History*, p. 375.

24. Warren Kimball, *Swords or Ploughshares? The Morgenthau Plan for Defeated Nazi Germany, 1943–1946*, pp. 31–32.

25. Herbert Feis, *Churchill-Roosevelt-Stalin: The War They Waged and the Peace They Sought*, p. 369 (September 11, 1944, diary entry).

26. Analyzing the history of the Morgenthau Plan, historian Warren F. Kimball wrote: "Franklin Roosevelt's administrative style made for uncertainty and competition within the

American government, and the jealousy which characterized relations between the War and State departments finds no better illustration than in planning for Germany." Warren Kimball, *Swords or Ploughshares? The Morgenthau Plan for Defeated Nazi Germany, 1943–1946*, p. 21.

27. Britain's Alexander Cadogan was in Washington when he was summoned to Quebec by Churchill. When he informed Stettinius, the under secretary reported back that Hull believed it a "tragic mistake" for Cadogan to "go to Quebec. . . . His arguments were that Q. was 'ostensibly' a military meeting: it would be known I was there, and that would seem to inject into it diplomatic and political questions." Stettinius told Cadogan that he had complained to President Roosevelt that "the constant attendance of Harriman and Hopkins at international conferences had caused deep resentment in the State Department." FDR agreed, telling Stettinius: "Quebec is to be entirely military; if any other subjects come up I shall call Cordell right away." David Dilks, *The Diaries of Sir Alexander Cadogan, O.M., 1938–1945*, pp. 664–666.

28. Hearing of Morgenthau's sudden invitation to Quebec, Stimson wrote in his diary that Roosevelt took "the man who really represents the minority and is so biased by his Semitic grievances that he really is a very dangerous adviser to the President at this time." To counter Morgenthau, Stimson tried to convene the cabinet working group on Germany, but Hull declined to participate. Michael Beschloss, *The Conquerors*, p. 127.

29. After a meeting in Washington on August 20, White wrote that he and Keynes "briefly discussed the reparations problem and he said that he was heartily in agreement with our view of the desirability of dismembering Germany and as to the relative unimportance of reparations. . . . In short, Keynes seems to be in our corner." Donald Moggridge, *Maynard Keynes: An Economist's Biography*, pp. 771–772. Henry Morgenthau III, *Mostly Morgenthaus: A Family History*, p. 365. Michael Beschloss, *The Conquerors*, p. 78. When Keynes arrived in Washington in October 1944, for talks with Morgenthau and White, they shared the Morgenthau Plan, which Keynes in turn was only to share with his boss, John Anderson. Keynes wrote the chancellor of the exchequer that Morgenthau "by no means considers himself defeated on this issue, and is still on the warpath. . . . When Harry White broached the same subject I took the line that all plans relating to Germany which I had seen so far struck me as equally bad, and the only matter I was concerned with was that it should not be the British Treasury which had to pay reparations or support Germany. I gathered that the plan is not quite as crude as it appeared in the reports from Quebec. All the same it seems pretty mad, and I asked White how the inhabitants of the Ruhr were to be kept from starvation; he said that there would have to be bread lines but on a very low level of subsistence." Donald Moggridge, *Maynard Keynes: An Economist's Biography*, p. 776.

30. Anthony Eden, *The Reckoning*, p. 552. British officials had been prepared to oppose the Morgenthau Plan. When Harry Hopkins met with Lord Halifax on September 7, he suggested that economic sanctions against Germany include "physical destruction of the Ruhr heavy industry." Warren Kimball, *Swords or Ploughshares? The Morgenthau Plan for Defeated Nazi Germany, 1943–1946*, p. 115. A week later on September 14, the Foreign Office prepared a memo for Eden that stated: "A policy which condones or favours chaos is not hard; it is simply inefficient, we do not favour a soft policy towards Germany; but the suffering which she must [undergo] should be the price of useful results for the United Nations, ordered and controlled by ourselves." Warren Kimball, *Swords or Ploughshares? The Morgenthau Plan for Defeated Nazi Germany, 1943–1946*, p. 121.

31. Benn Steil, *The Battle of Bretton Woods*, pp. 268–271.

32. Michael Beschloss, *The Conquerors*, p. 130.

33. John Morton Blum, ed, *From the Morgenthau Diaries: Years of War 1941–1945*, p. 369.

34. Winston S. Churchill, *Triumph and Tragedy: The Second World War*, Volume 6, p. 138. Dr. Wilson, who attended the Quebec Conference, wrote of Churchill's recollection: "It would be possible I suppose to dismiss the somewhat ambiguous sentences as no more than a good example of the political art of presenting a bad case in its least damaging form." Baron Charles McMoran Wilson Moran, *Churchill: Taken from the Diaries of Lord Moran: The Struggle for Survival, 1940–1965*, p. 196.

35. Herbert Feis, *Churchill-Roosevelt-Stalin: The War They Waged and the Peace They Sought*, pp. 369–370. Warren Kimball wrote: "As Morgenthau later pointed out, the word 'pastoral' came from Churchill, not the Treasury Department." Warren Kimball, *Swords or Ploughshares? The Morgenthau Plan for Defeated Nazi Germany, 1943–1946*, p. 40.

36. Warren Kimball, *Swords or Ploughshares? The Morgenthau Plan for Defeated Nazi Germany, 1943–1946*, p. 124.

37. Thomas M. Campbell and George C. Herring, eds, *The Diaries of Edward R. Stettinius, Jr., 1943–1946*, pp. 160–161 (October 26, 1944).

38. John Morton Blum, ed, *From the Morgenthau Diaries: Years of War 1941–1945*, p. 376.

39. Arthur Krock, *Memoirs: Sixty Years on the Firing Line*, p. 209.

40. Anthony Kubek, "The Morgenthau Plan and the Problem of Policy Perversion," *Journal of Historical Review*, August 2007, vho.org/GB/Journals/JHR/9/3/Kubek287-304.html.

41. John Morton Blum, ed, *From the Morgenthau Diaries: Years of War 1941–1945*, p. 377.

42. Thomas M. Campbell and George C. Herring, *The Diaries of Edward R. Stettinius, Jr., 1943–1946*, p. 161.

43. Wilson D. Miscamble, *From Roosevelt to Truman: Potsdam, Hiroshima, and the Cold War*, p. 71.

44. When Cordell Hull suggested that FDR convene a meeting to work through differences, Morgenthau responded that, unfortunately, Roosevelt wouldn't "do it. That isn't the way he works." Michael Beschloss, *The Conquerors*, p. 142.

45. Michael Beschloss, *The Conquerors*, p. 149. In his diary, Stimson wrote that FDR "was frankly staggered by this and said he had no idea he could have initialed this; that he had evidently done it without much thought." Herbert Feis, *Churchill-Roosevelt-Stalin: The War They Waged and the Peace They Sought*, p. 372.

46. Godfrey Hodgson, *The Colonel: The Life and Wars of Henry Stimson, 1867–1950*, p. 265.

47. Robert E. Sherwood, *Roosevelt and Hopkins: An Intimate History*, p. 818.

48. Fred L. Israel, ed, *The War Diary of Breckinridge Long*, p. 383 (September 26, 1944).

49. Warren Kimball, *Swords or Ploughshares? The Morgenthau Plan for Defeated Nazi Germany, 1943–1946*, pp. 41–43.

50. Thomas M. Campbell and George C. Herring, eds, *The Diaries of Edward R. Stettinius, Jr., 1943–1946*, p. 158.

51. Late in 1944, Keynes wrote: "What frightens me most in the whole problem is that these issues are extremely likely to be settled by those (as I know by first-hand conversations), who have not given continuous or concentrated thought to it." He added that "there is *no* good solution. *All* the solutions which are now being talked about are, not only bad, but very bad." Donald E. Moggridge, *Maynard Keynes: An Economist's Biography*, p. 777.

52. The conflicts over German occupation reconstruction between the Departments of State, Treasury, and War were renewed in March 1945. This time, it was a State Department document that caused a round of internecine warfare. A weakened Roosevelt again failed to play a leadership role as he shifted between his fantasy of a rural Germany expounded by Morgenthau, and the practicalities of Germany's reconstruction pushed by the War and State Departments. Morgenthau's position was repeatedly undermined by FDR's daughter Anna, who neither liked nor trusted her father's friend. At a meeting on March 22, Roosevelt backpedaled further from his Morgenthau Plan approval at Quebec, where he said he had been sold "a bill of goods." Incredibly, he blamed the reluctant Churchill for their initialed memo and denied he wanted to "eliminate" German factories. Michael Beschloss, *The Conquerors*, pp. 185–202. Publication of the Morgenthau Plan was equivalent to "ten fresh German divisions," argued Republican presidential candidate Thomas E. Dewey in the 1944 campaign. John Morton Blum, ed, *From the Morgenthau Diaries: Years of War 1941–1945*, pp. 382, 400–414. Roger Norton, *Thomas E. Dewey and His Times*, p. 432.

53. Michael Beschloss, *The Conquerors*, pp. 160–177. John Dietrich, *The Morgenthau Plan: Soviet Influence on American Postwar Policy*, pp. 79–81. In December 1944, Roosevelt's son-in-law, Major John Boettiger, was dispatched by Assistant Secretary of War John J. McCloy to explain to Morgenthau what Boettiger had seen of northwestern Germany. "You can tell McCloy I will be delighted to see him, but as of today my position hasn't changed one iota. I don't want to destroy Germany," responded the Treasury secretary. "I want them to take care of themselves." Peter Moreira, *The Jew Who Defeated Hitler: Henry Morgenthau Jr., FDR, and How We Won the War*, p. 273.

54. Warren Kimball, *Swords or Ploughshares? The Morgenthau Plan for Defeated Nazi Germany, 1943–1946*, pp. 145, 122, 147, 141.

55. Henry H. Arnold, *Global Mission*, p. 550.

56. Warren Kimball, *Swords or Ploughshares? The Morgenthau Plan for Defeated Nazi Germany, 1943–1946*, p. 127.

57. Warren Kimball, *Swords or Ploughshares? The Morgenthau Plan for Defeated Nazi Germany, 1943–1946*, p. 128.

58. *Foreign Relations of the United States: Diplomatic Papers*, 1944, Volume III, p. 79.

CHAPTER XIX. YALTA AND VICTORY

1. Warren Kimball, ed, *Churchill & Roosevelt: The Complete Correspondence*, Volume III, p. 630 (Roosevelt to Churchill, April 11, 1945).

2. Winston S. Churchill, *Triumph and Tragedy: The Second World War*, p. 433 (Churchill to Stalin, April 29, 1945).

3. S. M. Plokhy, *Yalta: The Price of Peace*, p. 29.

4. Anthony Eden, *The Reckoning*, p. 592.

5. Anthony Eden, *The Reckoning*, p. 593.

6. Warren Kimball, *Forged in War*, p. 331.

7. Elliott Roosevelt, *As He Saw It*, p. 71.

8. Keith Sainsbury, *Churchill and Roosevelt at War*, p. 1.

9. Baron Charles McMoran Wilson Moran, *Churchill: Taken from the Diaries of Lord Moran: The Struggle for Survival, 1940–1965*, p. 142 (November 25, 1943).

10. Mary Soames, ed, *Winston and Clementine: The Personal Letters of the Churchills*, p. 473 (Winston Churchill to Clementine Churchill, January 15, 1943).

11. Warren Kimball, ed, *Churchill & Roosevelt: The Complete Correspondence*, Volume III, p. 612 (Churchill to Roosevelt, April 5, 1945).

12. Warren Kimball, ed, *Churchill & Roosevelt: The Complete Correspondence*, Volume III, p. 421 (Churchill to Roosevelt, November 28, 1944).

13. John S. D. Eisenhower, *Allies: Pearl Harbor to D-Day*, p. 38.

14. S. M. Plokhy, *Yalta: The Price of Peace*, p. 34.

15. Robert E. Sherwood, *Roosevelt and Hopkins: An Intimate History*, p. 847. Hopkins had first raised the possibility of a meeting at Crimea. After Stalin had eliminated the ten other suggestions FDR made, Crimea became the only possibility. S. M. Plokhy, *Yalta: The Price of Peace*, pp. 26–27.

16. Of Potsdam, Marshal Zhukov wrote: "Stalin was extremely particular with regard to the slightest attempt by the US and British delegations to take decisions to the detriment of Poland, Czechoslovakia, Hungary and the German people. He had particularly sharp disputes with Churchill both at the Conference itself and during reciprocal visits." Marshal Georgy Zhukov, *The Memoirs of Marshal Zhukov*, p. 675. Zhukov meant by "detriment" any dispute over total, existing Soviet domination.

17. The conceit that Anglo-American leaders could deal successfully with Stalin would continue. After his first meeting with Stalin at Potsdam, President Harry Truman wrote in his diary on July 17, 1945: "I can deal with Stalin. He is honest, but smart as hell." More than a decade later, Truman acknowledged that he had been taken in by the "little son-of-a-bitch" at Potsdam. Robert H. Ferrell, ed, *Off the Record: The Private Papers of Harry S. Truman*, pp. 53, 348–349. At Potsdam, however, ill-advised by former Ambassador Davies, Truman attempted to placate Russia. Two years later, while campaigning for president, Truman declared: "I like old Joe." Wilson D. Miscamble, *From Roosevelt to Truman: Potsdam, Hiroshima, and the Cold War*, p. 193. Molotov recalled: "Our diplomacy was not bad. But it was Stalin, not some diplomat, who played the decisive role in it." Molotov said that Stalin was "close to a genius in tactics; in theory and strategy he was weaker." Molotov recalled that "Stalin had an astounding capacity for work. . . . He had a thorough knowledge of what he needed and stuck to the point. And he considered a question in all its aspects." Albert Resis, ed, *Molotov Remembers*, pp. 70, 166, 179. Stalin's "genius" had conspicuously failed him in the first half of 1941, as Anglo-American leaders tried to warn him of Germany's impending invasion. "Over a hundred warnings of the pending invasion are estimated to have reached the Kremlin. Operation Barbarossa had become the worst-kept secret of the war." Joseph Persico, *Roosevelt's Secret War*, p. 101. Stalin ignored all of the warnings; millions of Russians paid the price for Stalin's belief in Hitler's good intentions and the Hitler-Stalin pact of 1939.

18. Christopher D. O'Sullivan, *Harry Hopkins: FDR's Envoy to Churchill and Stalin*, pp. 120–121.

19. Baron Charles McMoran Wilson Moran, *Churchill: Taken from the Diaries of Lord Moran: The Struggle for Survival, 1940–1965*, p. 241 (February 5, 1945). Hopkins was particularly influential in pushing FDR to accept France and de Gaulle in the postwar agreements on Germany. S. M. Plokhy, *Yalta: The Price of Peace*, p. 254.

20. W. Averell Harriman and Elie Abel, *Special Envoy to Churchill and Stalin, 1941–1946*, p. 366. Handling of Poland was a troublesome issue on both sides of the Atlantic. On March 1, Max Beaverbrook wrote Hopkins about discontent in Britain regarding how Yalta treated Poland. He said "the opposition is . . . led by a powerful Tory group who are the erstwhile

champions of Munich. These followers of Chamberlain make the undercover case that Churchill beat them up in 1938 for selling the Czechs down the river, and now has done to the Poles at Yalta exactly what Chamberlain did to the Czechs at Munich." Warren Kimball, *Forged in War*, p. 320 (Max Beaverbrook to Harry Hopkins, March 1, 1945).

21. John Charmley, *Churchill's Grand Alliance The Anglo-American Special Relationship, 1940–1957*, p. 133 (Memo from Winston S. Churchill to Anthony Eden, January 25, 1945).

22. S. M. Plokhy, *Yalta: The Price of Peace*, p. 245.

23. S. M. Plokhy, *Yalta: The Price of Peace*, p. 249.

24. Mark A. Stoler, *Allies and Adversaries: The Joint Chiefs of Staff, the Grand Alliance, and U.S. Strategy in World War II*, pp. 123–130.

25. Andrew Roberts, *Masters and Commanders*, p. 554.

26. Baron Charles McMoran Wilson Moran, *Churchill: Taken from the Diaries of Lord Moran: The Struggle for Survival, 1940–1965*, p. 247 (February 11, 1945).

27. Geoffrey C. Ward, ed, *Closest Companion: The Unknown Story of the Intimate Friendship between Franklin Roosevelt and Margaret Suckley*, p. 421 (April 14, 1945).

28. S. M. Plokhy, *Yalta: The Price of Peace*, pp. 190–191.

29. Robert E. Sherwood, *Roosevelt and Hopkins: An Intimate History*, p. 871.

30. Jon Meacham, *Franklin and Winston: An Intimate Portrait of an Epic Friendship*, p. 328.

31. Doris Kearns Goodwin, *No Ordinary Time*, p. 582.

32. Beatrice Bishop Berle and Travis Beal Jacobs, eds, *Navigating the Rapids, 1918–1971: From the Papers of Adolf A. Berle*, p. 477 (Speech at Kalamazoo College, May 26, 1965).

33. Robert E. Sherwood, *Roosevelt and Hopkins: An Intimate History*, pp. 846–847.

34. Elliott Roosevelt, *As I See It*, p. 231.

35. Baron Charles McMoran Wilson Moran, *Churchill: Taken from the Diaries of Lord Moran: The Struggle for Survival, 1940–1965*, p. 243 (February 8, 1945).

36. "The State Department was not a factor in the Far Eastern agreement," wrote Stettinius of Yalta. "Although Ambassador Harriman had conducted conversations with Stalin on the question, he had a unique assignment at Moscow. There was nothing, during the war, quite like it. His task was totally different from that of a mere ambassador. He was the over-all co-ordinator of both civilian and military matters in Moscow." Edward R. Stettinius Jr., *Roosevelt and the Russians: The Yalta Conference*, p. 95.

37. Historian S. M. Plokhy observed: "The Soviet refusal during the first days of the conference to discuss joint operations against Japan convinced Roosevelt that there would be no effective cooperation with the Red Army, and perhaps even no Soviet participation in the war in the Far East, unless Stalin's conditions [regarding new Russian territorial accessions in Manchuria and Japan] were met. Many would later wonder whether the cost to China and, eventually, to the United States had been too high." S. M. Plokhy, *Yalta: The Price of Peace*, pp. 228, 261.

38. Thomas Parrish, *Roosevelt and Marshall: Partners in Politics and War*, p. 481.

39. Baron Charles McMoran Wilson Moran, *Churchill: Taken from the Diaries of Lord Moran: The Struggle for Survival, 1940–1965*, p. 241 (February 5, 1945).

40. Edward R. Stettinius Jr., *Roosevelt and the Russians: The Yalta Conference*, pp. 189–190.

41. David Stafford, *Roosevelt & Churchill: Men of Secrets*, p. 285.

42. Geoffrey C. Ward, ed, *Closest Companion: The Unknown Story of the Intimate Friendship between Franklin Roosevelt and Margaret Suckley*, p. 239 (September 14, 1944).

43. William D. Leahy, *I Was There*, p. 138.

44. Robert E. Sherwood, *Roosevelt and Hopkins: An Intimate History*, p. 885 (Telegram from Anthony Eden, Molotov, and Stettenius to Harry Hopkins, May 4, 1945).

45. Robert E. Sherwood, *Roosevelt and Hopkins: An Intimate History*, p. 885 (Telegram from Winston S. Churchill to Harry Hopkins, May 8, 1945).

46. Ambassador Harriman pushed Truman to send Hopkins, because Stalin would understand Hopkins was "speaking for Roosevelt as well as you." Rudy Abramson, *Spanning the Century: The Life of W. Averell Harriman, 1891–1986*, p. 397.

47. Charles Bohlen, *Witness to History*, p. 243.

48. Chris Wrigley, *Winston Churchill: A Biographical Companion*, p. 223 (Churchill to Truman, January 29, 1946).

49. Robert E. Sherwood, *Roosevelt and Hopkins: An Intimate History*, p. 930.

50. John Morton Blum, ed, *The Price of Vision: The Diary of Henry A. Wallace 1942–1946*, pp. 148–149.

51. John Colville, *Winston and His Inner Circle*, p. 128.

52. Andrew Roberts, *The Storm of War*, pp. 561–562.

53. Sumner Welles, *Seven Major Decisions*, p. 192.

54. Frances Perkins, *The Roosevelt I Knew*, p. 367. Historian John Lewis Gaddis wrote: "A division of Europe into spheres of influence—as implied by the Churchill-Stalin agreement [of October 1944]—would leave little room for the Europeans to determine their future: that is why Roosevelt worried about it. However much as he might have justified the war to himself in balance of power terms, he had explained it to the American people as Wilson might have done—as a fight for self-determination. Churchill had gone along with this in 1941 by accepting the Atlantic Charter, F.D.R.'s restatement of Wilsonian principles. A major Anglo-American objective, therefore, was to reconcile these ideals with Stalin's territorial demands, as well as his insistence on a sphere of influence that would ensure the presence of 'friendly' nations, along the Soviet Union's postwar borders. Roosevelt and Churchill repeatedly pressed Stalin to allow free elections in the Baltic States, Poland and elsewhere in Eastern Europe. At the Yalta Conference he agreed to do so, but without the slightest intention of honoring his commitment. 'Do not worry,' he reassured his foreign minister Vyacheslav Molotov. 'We can implement it in our own way later. The heart of the matter is the correlation of forces.'" John Lewis Gaddis, *The Cold War*, pp. 20–21. Stalin deceived FDR and worried Churchill.

55. James MacGregor Burns, *Roosevelt: The Lion and the Fox*, p. 470.

56. Robert E. Sherwood, *Roosevelt and Hopkins: An Intimate History*, p. 342.

57. Alex Danchev and Daniel Todman, eds, *War Diaries, 1939–1945: Field Marshal Lord Alanbrooke*, p. 299 (August 13, 1942).

58. Simon Sebag Montefiore, *Stalin: The Court of the Red Czar*, p. 484.

59. Elisabeth Barker, *Churchill and Eden at War*, pp. 288–289 (April 1, 1944).

60. John Colville, *Winston and His Inner Circle*, p. 132.

61. Samuel I. Rosenman, *Working with Roosevelt*, pp. 546–547.

62. Martin S. Gilbert, *Churchill and America*, p. 342.

63. John Charmley, "Churchill and the American Alliance," *Transactions of the Royal Historical Society*, Volume 11 (2001), pp. 353–371.

64. Eric Larrabee wrote that Marshall "and Eisenhower both believed that the port of Marseilles was essential to Overlord for at least three reasons: for supplying the armies that would otherwise be dependent on the Normandy beaches, for bringing fresh American forma-

tions more rapidly and directly from the United States, and (this was much in Eisenhower's thought) for enabling the French divisions we had at some expense been equipping in North Africa to participate in the liberation of their homeland." Eric Larrabee, *Commander-in-Chief: Franklin Delano Roosevelt, His Lieutenants and Their War*, p. 451.

65. Viscount Andrew Browne Cunningham, *A Sailor's Odyssey: The Autobiography of Admiral of the Fleet, Viscount Cunningham of Hyndhope*, pp. 641–642.

66. Mary Soames, *Clementine Churchill: The Biography of a Marriage*, p. 448.

67. Mary Soames, *Clementine Churchill: The Biography of a Marriage*, p. 420.

68. Doris Kearns Goodwin, *No Ordinary Time*, p. 312.

69. Alex Danchev and Daniel Todman, eds, *War Diaries, 1939–1945: Field Marshal Lord Alanbrooke*, p. 590 (September 10, 1944).

70. Alex Danchev and Daniel Todman, eds, *War Diaries, 1939–1945: Field Marshal Lord Alanbrooke*, p. 485 (November 29, 1943).

71. John Kennedy, *The Business of War: The War Narrative of Major-General Sir John Kennedy*, pp. 255–256.

72. James C. Humes, *Eisenhower and Churchill: The Partnership That Saved the World*, pp. 189–190.

73. James Leasor, *War at the Top: The Experiences of General Sir Leslie Hollis, KCB KBE*, p. 239.

74. John Charmley, *Churchill's Grand Alliance The Anglo-American Special Relationship, 1940–1957*, p. 145.

75. Baron Charles McMoran Wilson Moran, *Churchill: Taken from the Diaries of Lord Moran: The Struggle for Survival, 1940–1965*, p. 138 (November 17, 1943).

76. William D. Leahy, *I Was There*, p. 106.

77. Robert E. Sherwood, *Roosevelt and Hopkins: An Intimate History*, p. 868. General John Deane complained bitterly in December 1944, about the superficiality of Russian hospitality. Writing to Marshall from Moscow, Deane declared: "I have sat at innumerable Russian banquets and become gradually nauseated by Russian food, vodka and protestations of friendship. Each person high in public life proposes a toast a little sweeter than the preceding one on Soviet-British-American friendship. It is amazing how these toasts go down past the tongues in the cheeks. . . . After the banquets, we send the Russians another thousand airplanes, and they approve a visa that has been hanging for months. We then scratch our heads to see what other gifts we can send, and they scratch theirs to see what else they can ask for." Keith Eubank, *Summit at Teheran*, pp. 430–431.

78. Andrew Roberts, *Masters and Commanders*, p. 582.

79. Winston S. Churchill, *The Grand Alliance: The Second World War*, Volume III, pp. 596–597.

80. Andrew Roberts, *"The Holy Fox": The Life of Lord Halifax*, p. 289.

81. Martin S. Gilbert, *Churchill and America*, p. 225.

EPILOGUE: THEMES AND CONCLUSIONS

1. Winston S. Churchill, *The Grand Alliance: The Second World War*, Volume III, p. 596.

2. Max Hastings, *Winston's War*, p. 196 (Churchill to Eden, November 5, 1942).

3. Stephen E. Ambrose, *The Supreme Commander: The War Years of General Dwight D. Eisenhower*, p. 385.

4. Jon Meacham, *Franklin and Winston: An Intimate Portrait of an Epic Friendship*, p. 305. Department of State: *The Conferences at Malta and Yalta*, p. 6 (Roosevelt to Stalin, October 4, 1944).

5. W. Averell Harriman and Elie Abel, *Special Envoy to Churchill and Stalin, 1941–1946*, p. 170.

6. James F. Byrnes, *Speaking Frankly*, p. 44.

7. Michael Fullilove, *Rendezvous with Destiny*, pp. 275–276.

8. Michael Fullilove, *Rendezvous with Destiny*, p. 333.

9. Marshal Georgy Zhukov, *The Memoirs of Marshal Zhukov*, pp. 666–667.

10. Robert E. Sherwood, *Roosevelt and Hopkins: An Intimate History*, p. 248.

11. John Colville, *The Fringes of Power: The Incredible Inside Story of Winston Churchill during World War II*, pp. 333–334 (January 11, 1941).

12. Robert H. Pilpel, *Churchill in America, 1895–1861*, p. 147.

13. Winston S. Churchill, *The Grand Alliance: The Second World War*, Volume III, p. 594 (December 24, 1941).

14. Martin S. Gilbert, ed, *Churchill: The Power of Words: His Remarkable Life Recounted Through His Writings and Speeches*, p. 291 (December 24, 1941).

15. Warren Kimball, ed, *Churchill & Roosevelt: The Complete Correspondence*, Volume III, p. 229 (Churchill to Roosevelt, July 1, 1944).

16. Robert Nisbet, *Roosevelt and Stalin: The Failed Courtship*, p. 8.

17. Walter Isaacson and Evan Thomas, *The Wise Men: Six Friends and the World They Made*, pp. 256–257.

18. Lloyd C. Gardner, *Spheres of Influence: The Great Powers Partition Europe, from Munich to Yalta*, p. 188.

19. W. Averell Harriman and Elie Abel, *Special Envoy*, p. 96.

20. Fraser J. Harbutt, *Yalta 1945: Europe and America at the Crossroads*, p. 141.

21. Keith Sainsbury, *The Turning Point: Roosevelt, Stalin, Churchill, and Chiang-Kai-Shek, 1943*, p. 227.

22. Herbert Feis, *Churchill-Roosevelt-Stalin: The War They Waged and the Peace They Sought*, p. 669.

23. Keith Sainsbury, *The Turning Point: Roosevelt, Stalin, Churchill, and Chiang-Kai-Shek, 1943*, p. 300.

24. Michael Dobbs wrote: "After the collapse of communism, his [Stalin's] personal files were found to contain a copy of an internal State Department memorandum prepared in December 1944, opposing the transfer of the Kurile Islands to the Soviet Union. Roosevelt could not be bothered to read the review of his own experts on such matters, but Stalin devoured every nuance." Michael Dobbs, *Six Months in 1945: FDR, Stalin, Churchill, and Truman—from World War to Cold War*, p. 69.

25. Any dinner hosted by the Russians involved copious amounts of vodka. When Wendell Willkie visited Russia, he said that on September 25, he had consumed 53 vodka shots accompanying toasts at Soviet banquets. Donald Gillies, *Radical Diplomat: The Life of Archibald Clark Kerr, Lord Inverchapel, 1882–1951*, p. 137.

26. Donald Gillies, *Radical Diplomat: The Life of Archibald Clark Kerr, Lord Inverchapel, 1882–1951*, pp. 151–152.

27. Michael Beschloss, *The Conquerors*, p. 85.

28. Robert Nisbet, *Roosevelt and Stalin: The Failed Courtship*, p. 4.

29. John Harvey, ed, *War Diaries of Oliver Harvey*, p. 311 (October 22, 1943).

30. Fred L. Israel, ed, *The War Diary of Breckinridge Long: Selections from the Years, 1939–1944*, p. 333 (November 18, 1943).

31. Mark Pottle, ed, *Champion Redoubtable, The Diaries and Letters of Violet Bonham Carter, 1914–1945*, pp. 252–253 (January 6, 1943).

32. Martin S. Gilbert, *Churchill: The Power of Words: His Remarkable Life Recounted Through His Writings and Speeches*, p. 296 (December 30, 1941).

33. John Connell, *Wavell, Scholar and Soldier*, p. 454.

34. John Keegan, *Winston Churchill*, p. 153.

35. William Manchester and Paul Reid, *The Last Lion: Winston Spencer Churchill: Defender of the Realm, 1940–1965*, p. 596.

36. Martin S. Gilbert, *Winston S. Churchill: Finest Hour, 1939–1941*, p. 470.

37. Martin S. Gilbert, *Winston S. Churchill: Finest Hour, 1939–1941*, p. 969.

38. Warren Kimball, ed, *Churchill & Roosevelt: The Complete Correspondence*, Volume I, p. 182 (Churchill to Roosevelt, May 4, 1941).

39. David Dutton, *Anthony Eden: A Life and Reputation*, p. 156.

40. Warren Kimball, ed, *Churchill & Roosevelt: The Complete Correspondence*, Volume III, p. 498 (Churchill to Roosevelt, January 6, 1945).

41. Warren Kimball, ed, *Churchill & Roosevelt: The Complete Correspondence*, Volume II, pp. 710–711 (Roosevelt to Churchill, February 7, 1944).

42. Warren Kimball, ed, *Churchill & Roosevelt, The Complete Correspondence*, Volume II, p. 767. (Roosevelt to Churchill, February 29, 1944).

43. Fraser J. Harbutt, *Yalta 1945: Europe and America at the Crossroads*, p. 164 (Roosevelt to Churchill, November 18, 1944).

44. Fraser J. Harbutt, *Yalta 1945: Europe and America at the Crossroads*, p. 169 (Anthony Eden, "Soviet Policy in Europe," August 9, 1944).

45. George Kennan, *Russia and the West Under Lenin and Stalin*, p. 373.

46. Walter Isaacson and Evan Thomas, *The Wise Men: Six Friends and the World They Made*, p. 167.

47. At Teheran, Stalin told NKVD chief Lavrenti Beria's son Sergo: "I must know everything in detail, be aware of all the shades of meaning. I am asking you for all that because it is now that the question of the second front will be settled. I know that Churchill is against it. It is important that the Americans support us in this matter." Young Beria noted that Stalin was well prepared, even while briefed by him, "having at hand files on every question that interested him." Beria recalled: "I was able to establish from my eavesdropping that Roosevelt felt great respect and sympathy for Stalin. Admiral Leahy tried several times to persuade him to be firmer with the Soviet leader. Every time he received the reply: 'That doesn't matter. Do you think you can see further than I can? I am pursuing this policy because I think it is more advantageous. We are not going to pull the chestnuts out of the fire for the British.'" Sergo Beria, *My Father: Inside Stalin's Kremlin*, pp. 93–94. In addition to the bugs, all the staff waiting on the American diplomats were probably NKVD agents. Keith Eubank, *Summit at Teheran: The Untold Story*, p. 196.

48. Donald Gillies, *Radical Diplomat: The Life of Archibald Clark Kerr, Lord Inverchapel, 1882–1951*, p. 145.

49. George Kennan wrote fellow Sovietologist Charles Bohlen before Yalta: "A basic conflict is thus arising over Europe between the interests of Atlantic seapower, which demand the preservation of vigorous and independent political life on the European peninsula, and the interests of the jealous Eurasian land power, which must always seek to extend itself to the west

and will never find a place, short of the Atlantic Ocean, where it can from its own standpoint safely stop." John Lewis Gaddis, *George F. Kennan: An American Life*, pp. 188–189.

50. Fraser J. Harbutt, *Yalta 1945: Europe and America at the Crossroads*, p. 131.

51. Donald Gillies, *The Life of Archibald Clark Kerr, Lord Inverchapel, 1882–1951*, p. 160.

52. *Foreign Relations of the United States: Diplomatic Papers*, Volume III, p. 636.

53. Robert E. Sherwood, *Roosevelt and Hopkins, An Intimate History*, p. 706.

54. Donald Gillies, *Radical Diplomat: The Life of Archibald Clark Kerr, Lord Inverchapel, 1882–1951*, p. 143.

55. Martin S. Gilbert, *Winston S. Churchill: Road to Victory 1941–1945*, p. 1234.

56. Martin S. Gilbert, *Winston S. Churchill: Road to Victory 1941–1945*, p. 1235 (February 27, 1945).

57. Donald Gillies, *Radical Diplomat: The Life of Archibald Clark Kerr, Lord Inverchapel, 1882–1951*, p. 160.

58. Walter Isaacson and Evan Thomas, *The Wise Men: Six Friends and the World They Made*, p. 262. *Foreign Relations of the United States: Diplomatic Papers, 1945*, Volume 5, p. 839.

59. Robin Edmonds, *The Big Three: Churchill, Roosevelt & Stalin in Peace and War*, p. 454.

60. George Kennan, *American Diplomacy*, pp. 74–76.

61. Vincent Orange, *Churchill and His Airmen*, p. 185.

62. Donald Gillies, *Radical Diplomat: The Life of Archibald Clark Kerr, Lord Inverchapel, 1882–1951*, p. 134.

63. Orme Sargent, of the British Foreign Office, wrote in May 1945 that "in the minds of our two big partners, especially in that of the United States . . . Great Britain is now a secondary Power and can be treated as such, and that in the long run all will be well if they—the United States and the Soviet Union—as the two supreme World Powers of the future, understand one another. It is this misconception which it must be our policy to combat." David Dutton, *Anthony Eden: A Life and Reputation*, pp. 174–175.

64. Churchill did like to keep military units occupied, but he did not like military exercises without a real objective. For example, in January 1941, he rejected a plan to destroy a Norwegian power station, writing that he "did not wish to disturb the Norwegian coast for a trifle like this." Christopher M. Bell, *Churchill and Sea Power*, p. 211. In July 1941, Churchill told Stalin that "petty raids" on the French coast "would only lead to fiascos doing far more harm than good to both of us." Winston S. Churchill, *The Grand Alliance: The Second World War*, Volume III, p. 344. Bell noted that even Churchill's highly criticized decision to send Admiral Tom Phillips to the Far East with the HMS *Prince of Wales* and *Repulse* was designed to avert war with Japan, not to engage Japan. The prime minister argued, albeit incorrectly: "The Japanese Navy is not likely to venture far from its home bases so long as the superior battle-fleet is maintained at Singapore or Honolulu. The Japanese would never attempt a siege of Singapore with a hostile, superior American Fleet in the Pacific." Churchill was not alone in incorrectly assessing Japanese intent; the Americans did too. Christopher M. Bell, *Churchill and Sea Power*, pp. 230–237.

65. Mark A. Stoler, *Allies and Adversaries: The Joint Chiefs of Staff, the Grand Alliance, and U.S. Strategy in World War II*, p. 120.

66. David Carlton, *Anthony Eden*, p. 230.

67. Winston S. Churchill, *Closing the Ring: The Second World War*, Volume V, p. 295.

68. Warren Kimball, *Forged in War*, p. 259.

69. John W. Wheeler-Bennett and Anthony Nicholls, *The Semblance of Peace*, p. 290.

70. Stalin responded to Molotov's complaints about agreeing to the Declaration on Liberated Europe: "We can deal with it our own way later. The point is the correlation of forces." Michael Dobbs, *Six Months in 1945: FDR, Stalin, Churchill, and Truman—from World War to the Cold War*, p. 87.

71. Roy Medvedev, *Let History Judge: The Origins and Consequences of Stalinism*, p. 770.

72. John Oliver, ed, *The War Diaries of Oliver Harvey, 1941–1945*, p. 219 (February 10, 1943).

73. Richard Hough, *Winston and Clementine*, p. 411.

74. Christopher M. Bell, *Master of Sea Power*, p. 339.

75. John S. D. Eisenhower wrote: "Air Chief Marshal Sir Charles R. ('Peter') Portal was making a real contribution to harmony between the British and Americans. While conscious of the position of the air forces—and of British interests versus American—Peter Portal was a favorite of the Americans, as he possessed the breadth of vision to understand their point of view." He added: "Among the three [British chiefs], Portal was definitely the British chief with whom George Marshall preferred to deal." John S. D. Eisenhower, *Allies: Pearl Harbor to D-Day*, p. 219. Air Marshal Tedder thought Portal "the real brains" of the COS. "Brooke would often fume, rattling off in his staccato fashion objections and complaints about Churchill's impossible demands. When he had finished, Portal would quietly point out how by a concession here and an alteration there an agreed policy could quickly be reached without the sacrifice of essentials." Lord Tedder, *With Prejudice: The War Memoirs of Marshal of the Royal Air Force*, p. 534.

76. Vincent Orange, *Churchill and His Airmen: Relationships, Intrigue and Policy Making 1914–1945*, p. 214.

77. Though Murphy was a State Department official, he was ordered by the president to report directly to him in working with Vichy French leaders in North Africa: "Don't worry; I'll take care of Cordell." John S. D. Eisenhower, *Allies: Pearl Harbor to D-Day*, pp. 238, 132. From his first meeting with Ike, Harold Macmillan sensed "an inherent goodness and firmness of character. If sometimes impetuous, he was always fair." Harold Macmillan, *The Blast of War*, p. 222. In his diary, Macmillan sometimes complained about Murphy, writing early in their relationship: "My American colleague is very difficult to handle. He seems to be without any fixed purpose or plan and is affected by every changing mood of local opinion or Washington rumour. He is very pleasant, but without character or decision, and I am very much afraid I shall not be able to keep him up to the mark." Harold Macmillan, *War Diaries: Politics and War in the Mediterranean: January 1943–May 1945*, p. 66 (April 23, 1943). Almost a year later, Macmillan wrote that Murphy "is a pleasant enough creature and amenable to kind and firm treatment. But he has neither principles nor judgment." p. 393 (March 23, 1944). By the time that Murphy was shifted from North Africa to Italy in August 1944, Macmillan wrote: "By and large he has been an excellent colleague and a cheerful and genial friend. His Irish characteristics have made him sometimes a little difficult to deal with, but he has been to me personally I think loyal and helpful." p. 505 (August 20, 1944).

78. George McJimsey, *Harry Hopkins: Ally of the Poor and Defender of Democracy*, pp. 274–275. Murphy's work was not always appreciated in London or Washington, but Macmillan had determined from the outset, in January 1943, "that we should work closely together, and that I should gain his confidence." He noted: "I knew that Generals Eisenhower and Bedell Smith, and indeed all the American officers, were suspicious of my appointment and would resent any premature attempt to influence their decisions." In the early days, Macmillan

"had many talks with Murphy, who generously shared with me his knowledge of all the background. Although he naturally defended his own policies, I thought him singularly objective and fair-minded. Even at this rather difficult time, before we had learned to understand each other, he was helpful and forthcoming." Harold Macmillan, *The Blast of War*, pp. 224–227. Together, Macmillan and Murphy tried to present a united front, especially in dealing with the French in North Africa.

79. William Manchester and Paul Reid, *The Last Lion: Winston Spencer Churchill, Defender of the Realm, 1940–1965*, p. 805.

80. Martin S. Gilbert, *Churchill: The Power of Words: His Remarkable Life Recounted Through His Writings and Speeches*, p. 286.

81. John Keegan, *Winston Churchill*, p. 161.

82. Norman Davies, *No Simple Victory: World War II in Europe, 1939–1945*, p. 56.

83. John Colville, *Footprints in Time: Memories*, pp. 141–142.

84. John Keegan, *Winston Churchill*, p. 161.

85. John Colville, *Footprints in Time: Memories*, pp. 163–164.

86. When civilian and military deaths are combined, there were more deaths among British citizens than among Americans.

87. Winston S. Churchill, *Triumph and Tragedy*, p. 351.

88. Walter H. Thompson, *Assignment: Churchill*, p. 303.

89. Viscount Andrew Browne Cunningham, *A Sailor's Odyssey: The Autobiography of Admiral of the Fleet, Viscount Cunningham of Hyndhope*, p. 493.

90. Adrian Fort, *Prof: The Life of Frederick Lindemann*, p. 241.

91. Paul Addison, *Churchill: The Unexpected Hero*, p. 142.

92. Walter Isaacson and Evan Thomas, *The Wise Men: Six Friends and the World They Made*, p. 274.

93. Andrew Roberts, *The Storm of War*, p. 451.

94. Dwight D. Eisenhower, *At Ease: Stories I Tell My Friends*, p. 390.

95. Alex Danchev and Daniel Todman, eds, *War Diaries, 1939–1945: Field Marshal Lord Alanbrooke*, p. 697 (June 11, 1945).

96. Michael Korda, *Ike: An American Hero*, p. 603.

Selected Bibliography

All titles in the Endnotes are, by reference, included in this Selected Bibliography. This bibliography is but a fraction of the important works, even a smaller fraction of the primary sources, on this period of history.

Abramson, Rudy. *Spanning the Century: The Life of W. Averell Harriman.* New York: William Morrow & Co., 1992.

Acheson, Dean. *Present at the Creation: My Years in the State Department.* New York: W. W. Norton & Company, 1969.

Adams, Henry H. *Harry Hopkins: A Biography.* New York: Putnam, 1977.

———. *Witness to Power: The Life of Fleet Admiral William D. Leahy.* Annapolis, Maryland: Naval Institute Press, 1985.

Addison, Paul. *Churchill: The Unexpected Hero.* New York: Oxford University Press, 2005.

———. *Churchill on the Home Front, 1900–1955.* London: Jonathan Cape, 1992.

———. *The Road to 1945: British Politics and the Second World War.* London: Pimlico, 1994.

———. *Winston Churchill.* New York: Oxford University Press, 2007.

Aglion, Raoul. *Roosevelt & de Gaulle: Allies in Conflict, a Personal Conflict.* New York: The Free Press, 1988.

Ambrose, Stephen E. *Eisenhower: Soldier and President.* New York: Simon & Schuster, 1991.

———. *The Supreme Commander: The War Years of Dwight D. Eisenhower.* New York: Doubleday, 1970.

Andrew, Christopher, and Vasili Mitrokhin. *The Sword and the Shield: The Mitrokhin Archive and the Secret History of the KGB.* New York: Basic Books, 1999.

Arndt, H. W. "The Wizard and the Pragmatist/Keynes and Churchill," *Finest Hour* 153, Winter 2011–12.

Arnn, Larry. ed. *The Churchill Documents Volume 18: One Continent Redeemed, January–August, 1943.* Hillsdale, Michigan: Hillsdale College Press, 2015.

———, *Churchill's Trial: Winston Churchill and the Salvation of Free Government.* Nashville, Tennessee: Thomas Nelson, 2015.

Arnold, Henry H. *Global Mission*. New York: Harper, 1949.

Astley, Joan Bright. *The Inner Circle: A View of War at the Top*. Boston: Little, Brown & Co., 1971.

Barker, Elisabeth. *Churchill and Eden at War*. New York: St. Martin's Press, 1978.

Barnard, Ellsworth. *Wendell Willkie: Fighter for Freedom*. Marquette, Michigan: Northern Michigan University Press, 1966.

Barnett, Correlli. *The Desert Generals*. London: Castle Books, 2004.

———. *Engage the Enemy More Closely*. New York: Norton, 1991.

———. *The Lords of War: From Lincoln to Churchill: Supreme Leadership from Lincoln to Churchill*. London: Pen and Sword, 2013.

Barrett, John Q., ed. *That Man: An Insider's Portrait of Franklin D. Roosevelt*. New York: Oxford University Press, 2004.

Bedell Smith, Sally. *Reflected Glory: The Life of Pamela Churchill Harriman*. New York: Touchstone, 1996.

Bell, Christopher M. *Churchill and Sea Power*. New York: Oxford University Press, 2013.

Bellush, Bernard. *He Walked Alone: A Biography of John Gilbert Winant*. The Hague: Mouton, 1968.

Ben-Moshe, Tuvia. *Churchill: Strategy and History*. Boulder, Colorado: Lynne Rienner Publishers, 1991.

Bercuson, David, and Holger Herwig. *One Christmas in Washington: The Secret Meeting Between Roosevelt and Churchill that Changed the World*. Woodstock, New York: Overlook Press, 2005,

Beria, Sergo. *My Father: Inside Stalin's Kremlin*. London: Duckworth, 2001.

Berle, Beatrice Bishop, and Travis Beal Jacobs, eds. *Navigating the Rapids, 1918–1971: From the Papers of Adolf A. Berle*. New York: Harcourt Brace Jovanovich, 1973.

Berlin, Isaiah. *Personal Impressions*. New York: Viking Press, 1981.

Berthon, Simon. *Allies at War: The Bitter Rivalry Among Churchill, Roosevelt, and de Gaulle*. New York: Carrol & Graf, 2001.

———. *Warlords*. Cambridge, Massachusetts: De Capo Press, 2006.

Beschloss, Michael. *The Conquerors: Roosevelt, Truman, and the Destruction of Hitler's Germany, 1941–1945*. New York: Simon & Schuster, 2002.

———. *Kennedy and Roosevelt: The Uneasy Alliance*. New York: W. W. Norton & Co., 1981.

Best, Geoffrey. *Churchill: A Study in Greatness*. Oxford: Oxford University Press, 2003.

Birkenhead, Earl Frederick Winston Furneau Smith. *Halifax: The Life of Lord Halifax*. Boston: Houghton Mifflin Company, 1966.

Birse, Arthur. *Memoirs of an Interpreter*. New York: Coward-McCann, 1967.

Black, Conrad. *Franklin Delano Roosevelt: Champion of Freedom*. New York: Public Affairs, 2003.

Black, Stanley W., and Edward M. Bernstein. *A Levite Among the Priests: Edward M. Bernstein and the Origins of the Bretton Woods System*. Boulder, Colorado: Westview Press, 1991.

Blake, Robert, and William Roger Louis. *Churchill*. New York: W. W. Norton, 1993.

Bland, Larry I., ed. *George C. Marshall: Interviews and Reminiscences for Forrest C. Pogue*. Lanham, Maryland: Lexington, 1996.

Blum, John Morton, ed. *From the Morgenthau Diaries, Years of War 1941–1945*. Boston: Houghton Mifflin, 1967.

———. *The Price of Vision: The Diary of Henry A. Wallace 1942–1946*. Boston: Houghton Mifflin, 1973.

Boettiger, John R. *A Love in Shadow: The Story of Anna Roosevelt and John Boettiger.* New York: Norton, 1978.

Bohlen, Charles. *Witness to History, 1929–1969.* New York: W. W. Norton & Company, Inc., 1973.

Borneman, Walter, R. *The Admirals: Nimitz, Halsey, Leahy, and King—The Five-Star Admirals Who Won the War at Sea.* Boston: Little, Brown, 2012.

Bradley, Omar N. *A Soldier's Story.* New York: Holt, 1994.

Bradley, Omar N., and Clay Blair. *A General's Life: An Autobiography by General of the Army Omar N. Bradley.* New York: Simon & Schuster, 1983.

Brands, H. W. *Traitor to His Class: The Privileged Life and Radical Presidency of Franklin Delano Roosevelt.* New York: Anchor, 2009.

Brodhurst, Robin. *Churchill's Anchor: Admiral of the Fleet Sir Dudley Pound.* Barnsley: Leo Cooper, 2000.

Browder, Robert Paul, and Thomas G. Smith. *Independent: A Biography of Lewis W. Douglas.* New York: Alfred A. Knopf, 1986.

Brown, Anthony Cave. *"C": The Secret Life of Sir Steward Menzies, Spymaster to Winston Churchill.* New York: Macmillan Publishing Company, 1987.

Buell, Thomas B. *Master of Sea Power: A Biography of Fleet Admiral Ernest J. King.* Boston: Little, Brown, 1980.

Buhite, Russell D. *Patrick J. Hurley and American Foreign Policy.* Ithaca, New York: Cornell University Press, 1973.

Bullitt, Orville H., ed. *For the President: Personal and Secret: Correspondence Between Franklin D. Roosevelt and William C. Bullitt.* Boston: Houghton Mifflin, 1972.

Burgess, Simon. *Stafford Cripps: A Political Life.* London: Victor Gollanez, 1999.

Burns, James MacGregor. *Roosevelt: The Lion and the Fox.* New York: Harcourt, Brace & World, 1956.

———. *Roosevelt: Soldier of Freedom.* New York: Harcourt Brace Jovanovich, 1970.

Butcher, Harry C. *Three Years with Eisenhower: The Personal Diary of Captain Harry C. Butcher, USNR, Naval Aide to General Eisenhower, 1942–1945.* New York: Simon & Schuster, 1946.

Butler, J. R. M. *Lord Lothian, Philip Kerr, 1882–1940.* London, Macmillan; New York: St. Martin's Press, 1960.

Butler, R. A. *The Art of the Possible: The Memoirs of Lord Butler.* Boston: Gambit Inc., 1972.

Byrnes, James F. *All in One Lifetime.* New York: Harper, 1958.

———. *Speaking Frankly.* New York: Harper, 1947.

Calder, Angus. *The People's War: Britain, 1939–45.* London: Pimlico, 1992.

Callahan, Raymond. *Churchill and His Generals.* Lawrence, Kansas: University Press of Kansas, 2007.

Campbell, Thomas M., and George C. Herring. *The Diaries of Edward R. Stettinius, Jr., 1943–1946.* New York: New Viewpoints, 1975.

Carlton, David. *Anthony Eden.* London: Allen & Unwin, 1981.

———. *Churchill and the Soviet Union.* Manchester: Manchester University Press, 1999.

Chace, James. *Acheson: The Secretary of State Who Created the American World.* New York: Simon & Schuster, 1998.

Chambers, Whittaker. *Witness.* New York: Random House, 1952.

Charmley, John. "Churchill and the American Alliance." *Transactions of the Royal Historical Society,* Volume 11, 2001.

———. *Churchill's Grand Alliance: The Anglo-American Special Relationship 1940–1957.* London: Hodder & Stoughton, 1995.

Chisholm, Anne, and Michael Davie. *Lord Beaverbrook: A Life.* New York: Knopf, 1992.

Churchill, Sarah. *A Thread in the Tapestry.* New York: Dodd, Mead & Company, 1967.

Churchill, Winston S. *Their Finest Hour: The Second World War,* Volume II. Boston: Houghton Mifflin, 1985.

———. *The Grand Alliance: The Second World War,* Volume III. Boston: Houghton Mifflin, 1985.

———. *The Hinge of Fate: The Second World War,* Volume IV. Boston: Houghton Mifflin, 1985.

———. *Closing the Ring: The Second World War,* Volume V. Boston: Houghton Mifflin, 1985.

———. *Triumph and Tragedy: The Second World War,* Volume VI. Boston: Houghton Mifflin, 1985.

Colville, John. *Footprints in Time: Memories.* Norwich: Michael Russell, 1984.

———. *The Fringes of Power: The Incredible Inside Story of Winston Churchill During World War II.* Guilford, Connecticut: The Lyons Press, 1985.

———. *Winston and His Inner Circle.* New York: Wyndham Books, 1981.

Conant, Jennet. *The Irregulars: Roald Dahl and the British Spy Ring in Wartime Washington.* New York: Simon & Schuster, 2009.

Connell, John. *Auchinleck: A Biography of Field-Marshal Sir Claude Auchinleck.* London: Cassell, 1959.

———. *Wavell, Scholar and Soldier.* New York: Harcourt Brace & World, 1964.

Conquest, Robert. *Stalin: Breaker of Nations.* New York: Penguin Books, 1992.

Conway, Ed. *The Summit: Bretton Woods, 1944: J. M. Keynes and the Reshaping of the Global Economy.* New York: Pegasus Books, 2015.

Cooper, Alfred Duff. *Old Men Forget.* London: Readers Union/Rupert Hart-Davis, 1955.

Costigliola, Frank. *Roosevelt's Lost Alliances: How Personal Politics Helped Start the Cold War.* Princeton, New Jersey: Princeton University Press, 2012.

Craig, R. Bruce. *Treasonable Doubt: The Harry Dexter White Spy Case.* Lawrence, Kansas: University Press of Kansas, 2004.

Cray, Ed. *General of the Army: George C. Marshall.* New York: W. W. Norton & Co., Inc., 1990.

Cunningham, Viscount Andrew Browne. *A Sailor's Odyssey: The Autobiography of Admiral of the Fleet, Viscount Cunningham of Hyndhope.* London: Hutchinson, 1956.

Dallek, Robert. *Franklin Roosevelt and American Foreign Policy, 1932–1945.* New York: Oxford University Press, 1995.

Danchev, Alex. "'Dilly-Dally,' or Having the Last Word: Field Marshall Sir John Dill and Prime Minister Churchill," *Journal of Contemporary History,* Volume 22, 1987.

———. *Very Special Relationship: Field-Marshall Sir John Dill and the Anglo-American Alliance, 1941–44.* London: Brassey's (UK) Ltd., 1986.

Danchev, Alex, and Daniel Todman, eds. *War Diaries, 1939–1945: Field Marshall Lord Allanbrooke.* London: Phoenix, 2002.

Davenport-Hines, Richard. *Universal Man: The Lives of John Maynard Keynes.* New York: Basic Books, 2015.

Davies, Norman. *No Simple Victory: World War II in Europe, 1939–1945.* New York: Viking, 2007.

———. *Rising '44: The Battle for Warsaw.* New York: Viking Penguin, 2004.

Davis, Kenneth S. *FDR: The War President, 1940–1945.* New York: Random House, 2000.

Dawson, Raymond H. *The Decision to Aid Russia, 1941*. Chapel Hill, North Carolina: University of North Carolina Press, 1959.

Deane, John R. *The Strange Alliance: The Story of Our Efforts at Wartime Cooperation with Russia*. Bloomington, Indiana: Indiana University Press, 1973.

DeConde, Alexander. *The American Secretary of State: An Interpretation*. Westport, Connecticut: Greenwood Press, 1975.

De Gaulle, Charles. *War Memoirs: The Call to Honour, 1940–1942*. New York: Viking Press, 1955.

———. *War Memoirs: Unity, 1942–1944*. New York: Simon and Schuster, 1959.

D'Este, Carlo. *Eisenhower: A Soldier's Life*. New York: Henry Holt, 2002.

———. *Warlord: A Life of Winston Churchill at War, 1874–1945*. New York: HarperCollins, 2008.

Dilks, David. *Churchill and Company*. New York: I. B. Taurus, 2012.

———, ed. *The Diaries of Sir Alexander Cadogan, O.M., 1938–1945*. New York: G. P. Putnam's 1972.

Dobbs, Michael. *Six Months in 1945: FDR, Stalin, Churchill, and Truman—from World War to Cold War*. New York: Knopf, 2012.

Dobson, Alan P. *US Wartime Aid to Britain*. London: Croom Helm, 1986.

Donoughue, Bernard, and G. W. Jones, *Herbert Morrison: Portrait of a Politician*. London: Widenfeld and Nicolson, 1973.

Dunlop, Richard. *Donovan, America's Master Spy*. Chicago: Rand McNally & Company, 1982.

Dunn, Dennis J. *Caught Between Roosevelt and Stalin: America's Ambassadors to Moscow*. Lexington, Kentucky: University Press of Kentucky, 1998.

Dutton, David. *Anthony Eden: Life and Reputation*. New York: St. Martin's Press, 1997.

Eade, Charles, ed. *Churchill by His Contemporaries*. London: Morrison and Gibb, Limited, 1955.

Eden, Anthony. *The Reckoning: The Eden Memoirs, Earl of Avon*. Boston: Houghton Mifflin Co., 1965.

Edmonds, Robin. *The Big Three: Churchill, Roosevelt and Stalin in Peace and War*. London: Penguin, 1991.

Eisenhower, Dwight D. *At Ease: Stories I Tell to Friends*. Eastern Acorn Press, June 1981.

———. *Crusade in Europe*. New York: Doubleday & Co., 1948.

———. *The Eisenhower Diaries*. New York: Norton, 1981.

Eisenhower, John S. D. *Allies: Pearl Harbor to D-day*. Garden City, New York: Doubleday & Co., 1982.

———. *General Ike: A Personal Reminiscence*. New York: The Free Press, 2003.

Ellsberg, Edward. *The Far Shore*. New York: Dodd, Mead, 1960.

Eubank, Keith. *Summit at Teheran*. New York: William Morrow & Co., 1985.

Evans, Richard. *The Third Reich at War*. New York: Penguin Press, 2009.

Feis, Herbert. *Churchill-Roosevelt-Stalin: The War They Waged and the Peace They Sought*. Princeton, New Jersey: Princeton University Press, 1974.

Fenby, Jonathan. *Alliance: The Inside Story of How Roosevelt, Stalin and Churchill Won One War and Began Another*. San Francisco, California: MacAdam Cage, 2006.

Fergusson, Bernard, ed. *The Business of War: The War Narrative of Major-General Sir John Kennedy*. London: Hutchinson of London, 1957.

Ferrell, Robert H. *The Dying President: Franklin D. Roosevelt, 1944–1945*. Columbia, Missouri: University of Missouri Press, 1998.

———, ed. *FDR's Quiet Confidant: The Autobiography of Frank C. Walker*. Boulder, Colorado: University Press of Colorado, 1997.

Folly, Martin. *Churchill, Whitehall and the Soviet Union, 1940–45*. Basingstoke, United Kingdom: Palgrave Macmillan, 2000.

Fort, Adrian. *Prof: The Life of Frederick Lindemann*. London: Jonathan Cape, 2003.

Fraser, David. *Alanbrooke*. London: Hamlyn Paperback, 1983

Freidel, Frank. *Franklin D. Roosevelt: A Rendezvous with Destiny*. Boston: Little Brown, 1990.

Fromkin, David. "Churchill's Way: The Great Convergence of Britain and the United States." *World Policy Journal*, Volume 15, No. 1 (Spring 1998).

Fullilove, Michael. *Rendezvous with Destiny: How Five Extraordinary Men Took America into the War and into the World*. New York: Penguin Press, 2013.

Gaddis, John Lewis. *The Cold War: A New History*. New York: Penguin Press, 2005.

———. *George F. Kennan: An American Life*. New York: Penguin Books, 2012.

Gardner, Lloyd. *Architects of Illusion: Men and Ideas in American Foreign Policy, 1941–1949*. Chicago: Quadrangle Books, 1970.

———. *Economic Aspects of New Deal Diplomacy*. Madison, Wisconsin: University of Wisconsin Press, 1964.

———. *Spheres of Influence: The Great Powers Partition Europe, from Munich to Yalta*. Chicago: Ivan R. Dee, 1993.

Gardner, Richard N. *Sterling Dollar Diplomacy: Anglo-American Collaboration in the Reconstruction of Multilateral Trade*. Madison, Wisconsin: University of Wisconsin Press, 1964.

Gellman, Irving. *Secret Affairs: Franklin Roosevelt, Cordell Hull, and Sumner Welles*. Baltimore: Johns Hopkins Press, 1995.

Gilbert, Martin S. *Churchill and America*. New York: Free Press, 2008.

———, ed. *The Churchill Documents: Testing Times, 1942 (Official Biography of Winston S. Churchill)*. Hillsdale, Michigan: Hillsdale College Press, 2014.

———. *Winston S. Churchill, Finest Hour, 1939–1941*, Volume VI. Boston: Houghton Mifflin, 1983.

———. *Winston S. Churchill, Road to Victory, 1941–1945*, Volume VII. Boston: Houghton Mifflin, 1986.

Gillies, Donald. *Radical Diplomat: The Life of Sir Archibald Clark Kerr, Lord Inverchapel, 1882–1951*. London: I. B. Tauris, 1999.

Goodwin, Doris Kearns. *No Ordinary Time*. New York: Simon & Schuster, 1994.

Gorodetsky, Gabriel, ed. *Maisky Diaries: Red Ambassador to the Court of St. James's 1932–1943*. New Haven, Connecticut: Yale University Press, 2015.

Halifax, Lord. *Fullness of Days*. London: Collins, 1957.

Hamby, Alonzo. *Man of Destiny: FDR and the Making of the American Century*. New York: Basic Books, 2015.

Hamilton, Nigel. *The Mantle of Command*. Boston: Houghton Mifflin Harcourt, 2014.

———. *Montgomery, D-Day Commander*. Washington, D.C.: Potomac Books, Inc., 2007.

Harbutt, Fraser J. "Churchill, Hopkins, and the 'Other' Americans: An Alternative Perspective on Anglo-American Relations, 1941–1945," *The International History Review*, Volume 8, No. 2, May 1986.

———. *Yalta 1945: Europe and America at the Crossroads*. Cambridge: Cambridge University Press, 2010.

Harriman, W. Averell, and Elie Abel. *Special Envoy to Churchill and Stalin, 1941–1946*. New York: Random House Inc., 1975.

Harvey, John, ed. *War Diaries of Oliver Harvey*. London: Collins, 1978.

Hassett, William D. *Off the Record with FDR, 1942–1945*. New Brunswick, New Jersey: Rutgers Press, 1958.

Hastings, Max. *Inferno: The World at War, 1939–1945*. New York: Alfred A. Knopf, 2011.

———. *Overlord: D-Day and the Battle for Normandy*. New York: Simon and Schuster, 1984.

———. *Winston's War: Churchill, 1940–1945*. New York: Vintage, 2011.

Haynes, John Earl, and Harvey Klehr. *Venona: Decoding Soviet Espionage in America*. New Haven, Connecticut: Yale University Press, 1999.

Haynes, John Earl, Harvey Klehr, and Alexander Vassiliev. *Spies: The Rise and Fall of the KGB in America*. New Haven, Connecticut: Yale University Press, 2009.

Heinrichs, Waldo. *Threshold of War: Franklin D. Roosevelt and American Entry into World War* II. New York: Oxford University Press, 1990.

Hickman, Tom. *Churchill's Bodyguard*. London: Headline, 2005.

Hixson, Walter L., ed. *The American Experience in World War II: The United States in the European Theater*. London: Routledge, 2003.

Hodgson, Godfrey. *The Colonel: The Life and Wars of Henry Stimson, 1867–1950*. New York: Alfred A. Knopf, 1990.

Hollis, General Sir Leslie. *One Mariner's Tale*. London: Andre Deutsch, 1956.

Holmes, Richard. *Churchill's Bunker*. New Haven, Connecticut: Yale University Press, 2010.

Hough, Richard. *Winston and Clementine: The Triumphs & Tragedies of the Churchills*. New York: Bantam Books, 1991.

Hull, Cordell. *The Memoirs of Cordell Hull*. New York: Macmillan Co., 1948.

Humes, James C. *Churchill, Speaker of the Century: A Biography*. New York: Stein & Day, 1980.

———. *Eisenhower and Churchill: The Partnership That Saved the World*. New York: Three Rivers Press, 2001.

Ickes, Harold LeClair. *The Secret Diary of Harold L. Ickes: The Lowering Clouds, 1939–1941*. New York: Simon and Schuster, 1954.

Ironside, Edmund. *Time Unguarded: The Ironside Diaries, 1937–1940*. Westport, Connecticut: Greenwood Press, 1974.

Isaacson, Walter, and Evan Thomas. *The Wise Men: Six Friends and the World They Made*. New York: Simon & Schuster, 1986.

Ismay, Lord General Hastings. *The Memoirs of General Lord Ismay*. New York: The Viking Press, 1960.

Israel, Fred L., ed. *The War Diary of Breckinridge Long: Selections from the Years, 1939–1944*. Lincoln, Nebraska: University of Nebraska Press, 1966.

Jablonsky, David. *Churchill and Hitler: Essays on the Political-Military Direction of Total War*. London: Routledge, 1994.

James, Robert Rhodes. *Anthony Eden*. New York: McGraw-Hill, 1987.

———. *Churchill: A Study in Failure, 1900–1939*. New York: Penguin, 1981.

Jeffery, Keith. *The Secret History of MI6*. New York: Penguin Press, 2010.

Jenkins, Roy. *Churchill: A Biography*. New York: Farrar, Straus and Giroux, 2001.

———. *Franklin Delano Roosevelt*. New York: Times Books, 2003.

Jennings, Ivor. *Cabinet Government*. London: Cambridge University Press, 1965.

Johnson, Paul. *Churchill*. New York: Viking, 2009.

Jordan, Jonathan W. *American Warlords: How Roosevelt's High Command Led America to Victory in World War II*. New York: NAL Caliber, 2015.

Kaiser, David. *No End Save Victory: How FDR Led the Nation into War*. New York: Basic Books, 2014.
Keegan, John. *The Second World War*. New York: Penguin Books, 1990.
———. *Winston Churchill: A Life*. New York: Penguin, 2007.
Kemper, R. Crosby, II, ed. *Winston Churchill: Resolution, Defiance, Magnanimity, Good Will.* Columbia, Missouri: University of Missouri Press, 1996.
Kennan, George F. *American Diplomacy, 1900–1950.* New York: New American Library, 1951.
———. *Memoirs, 1925–1950*. Boston: Little, Brown and Company, 1967.
———. *Russia and the West Under Lenin and Stalin*. Boston: Little, Brown and Company, 1961.
Kersaudy, François. *Churchill and De Gaulle*. New York: Atheneum, 1983.
Kessler, Ronald. *The Sins of the Father: Joseph P. Kennedy and the Dynasty He Founded*. New York: Warner Books, 1996.
Kimball, Warren, ed. *Churchill and Roosevelt: The Complete Correspondence*. 3 Volumes. Princeton, New Jersey: Princeton University Press, 1984.
———. *Forged in War: Roosevelt, Churchill, and the Second World War*. New York: William Morrow and Company, 1997.
———. *The Juggler: Franklin Roosevelt as Wartime Statesman*. Princeton, New Jersey: Princeton University Press, 1991.
———. *Swords or Ploughshares? The Morgenthau Plan for Defeated Nazi Germany, 1943–1946.* Philadelphia: Lippincott, 1976.
King, Ernest J., and Walter Muir Whitehill. *Fleet Admiral King: A Naval Record*. New York: W. W. Norton & Co., 1962.
Koskoff, David. *Joseph P. Kennedy: A Life and Times*. New York: Prentice-Hall, 1974.
Krock, Arthur. *Memoirs: Sixty Years on the Firing Line*. New York: Funk & Wagnalls, 1968.
Kubek, Anthony. "The Morgenthau Plan and the Problem of Policy Perversion." *Journal of Historical Review,* Fall, Vol. 9, No. 3, 1989.
Lamb, Richard. *Churchill as War Leader*. New York: Carroll & Graff Publisher, 1991.
Langer, William L., and S. Everett Gleason. *The Undeclared War, 1940–1941*. New York: Harper & Brothers, 1953.
Langworth, Richard M. *Churchill and the Avoidable War: Could World War II Have Been Prevented?* Create Space Independent Publishing Platform, 2015.
———. *Churchill by Himself: The Definitive Collection of Quotations*. New York: Public Affairs, 2008, 2012.
———. *The Churchill Companion: A Concise Guide to the Life & Times of Winston Churchill (Second Edition)*. The Churchill Centre, 2010.
———. *The Patriot's Churchill: An Inspiring Collection of Churchill's Finest Words*. London: Ebury Press, 2010.
Larrabee, Eric. *Commander-in-Chief: Franklin Delano Roosevelt, His Lieutenants and Their War*. New York: Harper and Row, 1987.
Lash, Joseph P. *Roosevelt and Churchill, 1939–1941*. New York: W. W. Norton & Co., Inc., 1976.
Lavery, Brian. *Churchill Goes to War: Winston's Wartime Journeys*. Annapolis, Maryland: Naval Institute Press, 2007.
Lawrence, David. *Diary of a Washington Correspondent*. New York: H. C. Kinsey & Co., 1942.

Leahy, William D. *I Was There: The Personal Story of the Chief of Staff to Presidents Roosevelt and Truman Based on His Notes and Diaries Made at the Time*. New York: Whittlesey House, McGraw-Hill Book Co., 1950.

Leasor, James. *War at the Top: The Experiences of General Sir Leslie Hollis, KCB KBE*. London: Michael Joseph LTD, 1959.

Lee, J. M. *The Churchill Coalition, 1940–1945*. Hamden, Connecticut: Archon Books, 1980.

Levine, Isaac Don. *Eyewitness to History: Memoirs and Reflections of a Foreign Correspondent for Half a Century*. New York: Hawthorn Books, 1973.

Levy, Herbert. *Henry Morgenthau, Jr.: The Remarkable Life of FDR's Secretary of the Treasury*. New York: Skyhorse Publishing, 2010.

Lewin, Ronald. *Churchill as Warlord*. New York: Stein and Day, 1982.

Lewis, Gordon K. "On the Character and Achievement of Sir Winston Churchill." *The Canadian Journal of Economics and Political Science*, Volume XXIII, Number 2, May 1957.

Liddell Hart, Basil H. *German Generals Talk*. New York: Quill, 1979.

———. *History of the Second World War*. New York: G. P. Putnam's Sons, 1970.

Lohbeck, Don. *Patrick J. Hurley*. Chicago: Henry Regnery Company, 1957.

Lukacs, John. *Churchill: Visionary, Statesman, Historian*. New Haven, Connecticut: Yale University Press, 2002.

———. *The Duel: 10 May–31 July 1940: The Eighty-Day Struggle Between Churchill and Hitler*. Boston: Houghton Mifflin, 1991.

———. *Five Days in London*—May 1940. New Haven, Connecticut: Yale University Press, 1999.

Lutze, James. "The Secret of the Churchill-Roosevelt Correspondence: September 1939–May 1940." *Journal of Contemporary History*, Volume 10, No. 3, July 1975.

Lyttelton, Oliver Viscount Chandos. *The Memoirs of Lord Chandos*. London: Readers Union, 1964.

Macdonald, Bill. *The True 'Intrepid': Sir William Stephenson and the Unknown Agents*. Surrey, British Columbia: Timberholme Books LTD, 1998.

Macmillan, Harold. *The Blast of War, 1939–1945*. New York: Harper & Row, 1968.

———. *War Diaries: Politics and War in the Mediterranean: January 1943–May 1945*. London: Macmillan, 1984.

Macrae, Stuart. *Winston Churchill's Toyshop: The Invention and Making of England's Secret Weapons*. New York: Walker and Company, 1971.

Mahl, Thomas E. *Desperate Deception: British Covert Operations in the United States, 1939–44*. Dulles, Virginia: Brasseys, 1999.

Maier, Thomas. *When Lions Roar: The Churchills and the Kennedys*. New York: Crown, 2014.

Maisky, Ivan. *Memoirs of a Soviet Ambassador: The War, 1939–1943*. New York: Charles Scribner's Sons, 1968.

Manchester, William. *The Last Lion: Winston Spencer Churchill: Alone, 1932–1940*. Boston: Little, Brown, 1983.

Manchester, William, and Paul Reid. *The Last Lion: Winston Spencer Churchill, Defender of the Realm, 1940–1965*. Boston: Little, Brown and Company, 2012.

Martin, John. *Downing Street: The War Years*. London: Bloomsbury, 1991.

Matloff, Maurice. *US Army in WW2: War Department, Strategic Planning for Coalition Warfare*. Washington, D.C.: Office of the Chief of Military History, Department of the Army, 1959.

Matloff, Maurice, and Edwin M. Snell, *Strategic Planning for Coalition Warfare, 1941–1942*. Washington, D.C.: Center of Military History, United States Army, 1990.

Mayers, David. *The Ambassadors and America's Soviet Policy.* New York: Oxford University Press 1995.

———. *FDR's Ambassadors and the Diplomacy of Crisis: From the Rise of Hitler to the End of World War II.* New York: Cambridge University Press, 2013.

McClellan, David S., and David C. Acheson. *Among Friends: Personal Letters of Dean Acheson.* New York: Dodd, Mead & Company, 1980.

McIntire, Ross T. *White House Physician.* New York: G. P. Putnam's Sons, 1946.

McJimsey, George. *Harry Hopkins: Ally of the Poor and Defender of Democracy.* Cambridge, Massachusetts: Harvard University Press, 1987.

McNeill, William Hardy. *America, Britain, and Russia: Their Co-operation and Conflict, 1941–1946.* New York: Johnson Reprint Corporation, 1970.

Meacham, Jon. *Franklin and Winston: An Intimate Portrait of an Epic Friendship.* New York: Random House, 2004.

Medvedev, Roy. *Let History Judge: The Origins and Consequences of Stalinism.* New York: Columbia University Press, 1989.

Mikesell, Raymond F. *Foreign Adventures of an Economist.* Eugene, Oregon: University of Oregon Press, 2000.

Miscamble, Wilson D. *From Roosevelt to Truman: Potsdam, Hiroshima, and the Cold War.* Cambridge; New York: Cambridge University Press, 2007.

Moggridge, Donald. *Maynard Keynes: An Economist's Biography.* New York: Routledge, 1995.

Monnet, Jean. *Jean Monnet Memoirs.* New York: Doubleday & Company, 1978.

Montefiore, Simon Sebag. *Stalin: The Court of the Red Tsar.* New York: Alfred A. Knopf, 2004.

Moody, Joanna. *From Churchill's War Rooms: Letters of a Secretary 1943–45.* Gloucestershire, Britain: Tempus Publishing, 2007.

Moran, Baron Charles McMoran Wilson. *Churchill: Taken from the Diaries of Lord Moran: The Struggle for Survival, 1940–1964.* Boston: Houghton Mifflin Company, 1966.

Moreira, Peter. *The Jew Who Defeated Hitler: Henry Morgenthau Jr., FDR, and How We Won the War.* Amherst, New York: Prometheus Books, 2014.

Morgan, Kay Summersby. *Eisenhower was My Boss.* New York: Prentice-Hall, 1948.

———. *Past Forgetting: My Love Affair with Dwight D. Eisenhower.* London: Collins, 1977.

Morgenthau, Henry, III. *Mostly Morgenthaus: A Family History.* New York: Ticknor & Fields, 1991.

Morison, Samuel Eliot. *History of United States Naval Operations in World War II: The Battle of the Atlantic, September 1939–May 1943.* Boston: Little, Brown and Company, 1966.

———. *History of United States Naval Operations in World War II: The Invasion of France and Germany, 1944–1945.* Boston: Little, Brown and Company, 1968.

Morrison, Elting. *Turmoil and Tradition: A Study of the Life and Times of Henry L. Stimson.* New York: Atheneum, 1964.

Morrison, Herbert. *An Autobiography.* London: Odhams Press, 1960.

Moseley, Leonard. *Marshall: Hero for Our Times.* New York: Hearst Books, 1982.

Murphy, Robert. *Diplomat Among Warriors.* Garden City, New York: Doubleday, 1964.

Nasaw, David. *The Patriarch: The Remarkable Life and Turbulent Times of Joseph P. Kennedy.* New York: Penguin Press HC, 2012.

Nicolson, Nigel, ed. *Diaries and Letters of Sir Harold Nicolson.* London: Collins, 1967.

———. *Alex: The Life of Field Marshal Earl Alexander of Tunis.* New York: Atheneum, 1973.

Nisbet, Robert. *Roosevelt and Stalin: The Failed Courtship.* Washington, D.C.: Regnery Gateway, 1988.

Norwich, John Julius, ed. *The Duff Cooper Diaries*. London: Weidenfeld & Nicolson, 2005.

Olmsted, Kathryn S. *Red Spy Queen: A Biography of Elizabeth Bentley*. Chapel Hill, North Carolina: University of North Carolina Press, 2002.

Olson, Lynne. *Citizens of London: The Americans Who Stood with Britain in Its Darkest, Finest Hour*. New York: Random House Trade Paperbacks, 2011.

———. *Those Angry Days*. New York: Random House, 2013.

———. *Troublesome Young Men: The Rebels Who Brought Churchill to Power and Helped Save England.* New York: Farrar, Straus and Giroux, 2007.

Orange, Vincent. *Churchill and His Airmen: Relationships, Intrigue and Policy Making 1914–1945*. London: Grub Street, 2013.

Osborne, John, and Ronald Alport. *Bank of England, Unpublished War History*. London: Bank of England, 1950. http://www.bankofengland.co.uk/archive/Pages/digitalcontent/archivedocs/warhistoryww2.aspx.

O'Sullivan, Christopher D. *Harry Hopkins: FDR's Envoy to Churchill and Stalin*. Lanham, Maryland: Rowman & Littlefield, 2015.

Parrish, Thomas. *Roosevelt and Marshall: Partners in Politics and War, the Personal Story*. New York: W. Morrow, 1989.

———. *To Keep the British Isles Afloat: FDR's Men in Churchill's London, 1941*. New York: Smithsonian Books/Collins; 2009.

Pawle, Gerald. *The War and Colonel Warden*. London: George G. Harrap, 1963.

Perkins, Frances. *The Roosevelt I Knew*. New York: Penguin Books, 2011.

Perry, Mark. *The Most Dangerous Man in America*. New York: Basic Books, 2015.

———. *Partners in Command: George Marshall and Dwight Eisenhower in War and Peace*. New York: Penguin, 2008.

Persico, Joseph. *Franklin and Lucy: Mrs. Rutherfurd and the Other Remarkable Women in Roosevelt's Life*. New York: Random House, 2008.

———. *Roosevelt's Centurions: FDR and the Commanders He Led to Victory in World War II*. New York: Random House, 2013.

———. *Roosevelt's Secret War: FDR and World War II Espionage*. New York: Random House, 2001.

Picknett, Lynn, Clive Prince, and Stephen Prior. *Friendly Fire: The Secret War Between the Allies*. Edinburgh: Mainstream Pub., 2005.

Pilpel, Robert H. *Churchill in America, 1895–1961*. New York: Harcourt Brace Jovanovich, 1976.

Pimlott, Ben, ed. *The Political Diary of Hugh Dalton, 1918–40, 1945–60*. London: Jonathan Cape, 1986.

Pincher, Chapman. *Their Trade Is Treachery*. London: Sidgwick & Jackson, 1981.

Pitt, Barrie. *Churchill and the Generals*. London: Sidgwick & Jackson, 1981.

Plokhy, S. M. *Yalta: The Price of Peace*. New York: Viking, 2010.

Pogue, Forrest C. *George C. Marshall: Ordeal and Hope, 1939–1942*. New York: Viking Press, 1999.

Pottle, Mark, ed. *Champion Redoubtable: The Diaries and Letters of Violet Bonham Carter, 1914–1945*. London: Weidenfeld & Nicolson, 1998.

Probert, Henry. *Bomber Harris: His Life and Times: The Biography of Marshal of the Royal Air Force Sir Arthur Harris*. London: Greenhill Books, 2006.

Radzinsky, Edvard. *Stalin*. New York: Doubleday, 1996.

Rees, David. *Harry Dexter White: A Study in Paradox.* New York: Coward, McCann & Geoghegan, 1973.

Reid, Walter. *Churchill: 1940–1945, Under Friendly Fire*. Edinburgh: Birlinn, Limited, 2008.

Resis, Albert, ed. *Molotov Remembers [Conversations with Felix] Chuev*. Chicago: Ivan R. Dee, 1993.

———. "Spheres of Influence in Soviet Wartime Diplomacy." *Journal of Modern History* 53, No. 3 (September 1981): 417–439.

Reynolds, David. *The Creation of the Anglo-American Alliance 1937–41: A Study in Competitive Co-Operation*. Chapel Hill, North Carolina: University of North Carolina Press, 1988.

———. *From World War to Cold War: Churchill, Roosevelt, and the International History of the 1940s.* Oxford: Oxford University Press, 2007.

———. *In Command of History: Churchill Fighting and Writing the Second World War*. New York: Random House, 2005.

———. "Lord Lothian and Anglo-American Relations, 1939–1940." *Transactions of the American Philosophical Society*, Volume 73, Part 2, 1983.

Rhodes James, Robert. *Anthony Eden: A Biography.* New York: McGraw-Hill Co., 1986.

———. *Churchill: A Study in Failure, 1900–1939*. London: Weidenfeld & Nicolson, 1990.

Roberts, Andrew. *The Art of War: Great Commanders of the Modern World Since 1600.* London: Quercus, 2009.

———. *A History of the English Speaking Peoples Since 1900*. London: Weidenfeld & Nicholson, 2006.

———. *Hitler and Churchill: Secrets of Leadership.* London: Phoenix, 2004.

———. *"The Holy Fox": A Life of Lord Halifax*. London: Papermac, 1992.

———. *Masters and Commanders*. New York: Harper Perennial, 2010.

———. *Salisbury: Victorian Titan*. London: Weidenfeld & Nicholson, 1999.

———. *Storm of War: A New History of the Second World War*. New York: Harper Perennial, 2012.

Robertson, David. *Sly and Able: A Political Biography of James F. Byrnes*. New York: W. W. Norton & Co. Inc., 1994.

Roll, David. *The Hopkins Touch: Harry Hopkins and the Forging of the Alliance to Defeat Hitler*. New York: Oxford University, 2013.

Romerstein, Herbert, and Eric Breindel. *The Venona Secrets: Exposing Soviet Espionage and America's Traitors*. Washington, D.C.: Regnery Publishing, 2000.

Roosevelt, Eleanor. *This I Remember*. New York: Harper & Brothers, 1949.

Roosevelt, Elliott. *As He Saw It*. New York: Duell, Sloan and Pearce, 1946.

Rose, Norman. *Churchill: An Unruly Life*. London: Simon & Schuster, 1994.

Rosenman, Samuel I. *Working with Roosevelt*. New York: Harper, 1952.

Sainsbury, Keith. *Churchill and Roosevelt at War*. London: Macmillan, 1994.

———. *The Turning Point: Roosevelt, Stalin, Churchill, and Chiang-Kai-Shek, 1943.* New York: Oxford University Press, 1986.

Sandilands, Roger James. *The Life and Political Economy of Lauchlin Currie: New Dealer, Presidential Adviser, and Development Economist*. Durham, North Carolina: Duke University Press, 1990.

Saward, Dudley. *Bomber Harris: The Story of Marshal of the Royal Air Force Sir Arthur Harris, Bt, GCB, OBE, AFC, LLD, Air Officer Commanding-in-Chief, Bomber Command, 1942–1945*. Garden City, New York: Doubleday Publishing, 1985.

Schlesinger, Arthur M., Jr. *The Coming of the New Deal: 1933–1935: The Age of Roosevelt*, Volume II. Boston: Houghton Mifflin, 2003.

Schneer, Jonathan. *Ministers at War: Winston Churchill and His War Cabinet*. New York: Basic Books, 2015.

Schoenfeld, Maxwell Philip. *The War Ministry of Winston Churchill*. Ames, Iowa: Iowa State University Press, 1972.

Schwarz, Jordan A. *Liberal: Adolf A. Berle and the Vision of an American Era*. New York: Free Press, 1987.

Service, Robert. *Stalin: A Biography*. Cambridge, Massachusetts: Belknap Press, 2005.

Sherwood, Robert E. *Roosevelt and Hopkins: An Intimate History*. New York: Harper & Brothers, 1948.

Simpson, B. Mitchell, III. *Admiral Harold R. Stark: Architect of Victory, 1939–1945*. Columbia, South Carolina: University of South Carolina Press, 1989.

Singer, Barry. *Churchill Style: The Art of Being Winston Churchill*. New York: Abrams, 2012.

Skidelsky, Robert. *John Maynard Keynes, 1883–1946: Economist, Philosopher, Statesman*. New York: Penguin Books, 2005.

———. *John Maynard Keynes*, Volume *3: Fighting for Freedom, 1937–1946*. New York: Viking Penguin, 2001.

Smith, Amanda. *Hostage to Fortune: The Letters of Joseph P. Kennedy*. New York: Viking Adult, 2001.

Smith, Gaddis. *American Diplomacy During the Second World War, 1941–1945*. New York: John Wiley and Sons, Inc., 1965.

Smith, Jean Edward. *FDR*. New York: Random House, 2007.

Smith, Merriman. *Thank You, Mr. President*. New York: Harper & Brothers, 1946.

Soames, Mary. *Clementine Churchill: The Biography of a Marriage*. Boston: Houghton Mifflin Company, 1979.

———. *A Daughter's Tale*. New York: Random House, 2012.

———, ed. *Winston and Clementine: The Personal Letters of the Churchills*. Boston: Houghton Mifflin Company, 1999.

Spears, Edward. *Assignment to Catastrophe: Prelude to Dunkirk, July 1939–May 1940*. New York: A. A. Wyn, 1954.

Stafford, David. "Intrepid: Myth and Reality." *Journal of Contemporary History*, Volume 22, No. 1, April 1987.

———. *Roosevelt and Churchill: Men of Secrets*. Woodstock, New York: Overlook Press, 2000.

Stalin, Joseph. *The Great Patriotic War of the Soviet Union*. New York: International Publishers, 1945.

Standley, William H., and Arthur A. Ageton. *Admiral Ambassador to Russia*. Chicago: H. Regnery Co., 1955.

Steil, Benn. *The Battle of Bretton Woods*. Princeton, New Jersey: Princeton University Press, 2013.

Stelzer, Cita. *Dinner with Churchill*. New York: Pegasus, 2012.

Stettinius, Edward R., Jr. *Roosevelt and the Russians: The Yalta Conference*. Garden City, New York: Doubleday & Co., 1949.

Stevenson, William. *A Man Called Intrepid*. Guilford, Connecticut: Lyons Press, 2000.

Stimson, Henry L., and McGeorge Bundy. *On Active Service in Peace and War*. New York: Harper & Brothers, 1948.

Stoler, Mark A. *Allies and Adversaries: The Joint Chiefs of Staff, the Grand Alliance, and U.S. Strategy in World War II*. Chapel Hill, North Carolina: University of North Carolina Press, 2000.

———. *George C. Marshall: Soldier-Statesman of the American Century*. London: Twayne Publishers, 1989.

———. *The Politics of the Second Front: American Military Planning and Diplomacy in Coalition Warfare, 1941–1943*. Westport, Connecticut: Greenwood Press, 1977.

Sturrock, Donald. *Storyteller: The Authorized Biography of Roald Dahl*. New York: Simon and Schuster, 2011.

Tanenhaus, Sam. *Whittaker Chambers: A Biography*. New York: Random House, 1997.

Taylor, A. J. P. *Beaverbrook*. New York: Simon and Schuster; 1972.

———. *English History, 1914–1945*. New York: Oxford University Press, 1965.

Tedder, Lord. *With Prejudice: The War Memoirs of Marshal of the Royal Air Force*. Boston: Little, Brown and Company, 1966.

Thompson, R. W. *Winston Churchill: The Yankee Marlborough*. Garden City, New York: Doubleday, 1963.

Thompson, Walter H. *Assignment: Churchill*. New York: Farrar, Strauss & Young, 1955.

———. *Beside the Bulldog*. London: Apollo Publishing, 2003.

———. *I Was Churchill's Shadow*. London: Christopher Johnson, 1951.

———. *Sixty Minutes with Winston Churchill*. London: Christopher Johnson 1957.

Toye, Richard. *Churchill's Empire: The World That Made Him and the World He Made*. New York: Henry Holt and Co., 2010.

Troy, Thomas F. *Wild Bill and Intrepid: Donovan, Stephenson, and the Origins of the CIA*. New Haven, Connecticut: Yale University Press, 1996.

Tully, Grace. *FDR My Boss*. New York: C. Scribner's Sons, 1949.

Tuttle, Dwight William. *Harry L. Hopkins and Anglo-American-Soviet relations, 1941–1945*. New York: Garland Pub., 1983.

Van Dormael, Armand. *Bretton Woods: Birth of a Monetary System*. London: Macmillan, 1978.

Van Minnen, Cornelis A., and John F. Sears, eds. *FDR and His Contemporaries: Foreign Perceptions of an American President*. New York: St. Martin's Press, 1992.

Waller, Douglas. *Wild Bill Donovan: The Spymaster Who Created the OSS and Modern American Espionage*. New York: Free Press, 2010.

Ward, Geoffrey C., ed. *Closest Companion: The Unknown Story of the Intimate Friendship between Franklin Roosevelt and Margaret Suckley*. New York: Simon and Schuster, 2012.

Warner, Oliver. *Admiral of the Fleet: Cunningham of Hyndhope*. New York: Dutton, 1951.

Wedemyer, A. C. *Wedemeyer Reports!* New York: Holt and Company, 1958.

Weisbrode, Kenneth. *Churchill and the King: The Wartime Alliance of Winston Churchill and George VI*. New York: Penguin Books, 2015.

Weinstein, Allen, and Alexander Vassiliev. *The Haunted Wood: Soviet Espionage in America—The Stalin Era*. New York: Modern Library, 1999.

Welles, Benjamin. *Sumner Welles: FDR's Global Strategist*. New York: St. Martin's Press, 1997.

Welles, Sumner. *Seven Major Decisions*. London: Hamish Hamilton, 1951.

———. *Time for Decision*. New York: Harper & Brothers, 1944.

Whalen, Richard J. *The Founding Father: The Story of Joseph P. Kennedy*. New York: New American Library, 1964.

Wheeler-Bennett, John. *Action This Day: Working with Churchill*. London: Macmillan and Co., 1968.

———. *Special Relationships: America in Peace and War*. New York: St. Martin's Press, 1975.

Wheeler-Bennett, John, and Anthony Nicholls. *The Semblance of Peace: The Political Settlement after the Second World War*. New York: W. W. Norton & Co., 1974.

White, Theodore, ed. *The Stilwell Papers*. New York: William Sloane Associates, 1948.

Williams, Francis, ed. *A Prime Minister Remembers: The War and Post-war Memoirs of the Rt. Hon. Earl Attlee*. London: Heinemann, 1961.

Wilson, Theodore A. *The First Summit*. Boston: Houghton Mifflin Company, 1969.

Winant, John Gilbert. *Letter from Governor Square: An Account of a Stewardship*. Boston: Houghton Mifflin Company, 1948.

Winik, Jay. *1944: FDR and the Year That Changed History*. New York: Simon & Schuster, 2015.

Woods, Randall Bennett. *A Changing of the Guard: Anglo-American Relations, 1941–1946*. Chapel Hill, North Carolina: University of North Carolina Press, 1990.

Young, Kenneth. *Churchill and Beaverbrook: A Study in Friendship*. New York: James H. Heineman, Inc., 1966.

Zhukov, Marshal Georgy. *The Memoirs of Marshal Zhukov*. London: Jonathan Cape, 1971.

Zoller, Curt J. *Annotated Bibliography of Works About Sir Winston S. Churchill*. London: Routledge, 2004.

Index

Page numbers in italics indicate illustrations.

About the Author

Lewis E. Lehrman was presented the National Humanities Medal at the White House for his work in American history. Lehrman has written for the *Washington Post, New York Times, Wall Street Journal, Finest Hour, National Review, New York Sun, Harper's, The Churchill Project at Hillsdale College*, and *The Chartwell Bulletin.*

Lehrman authored *Lincoln at Peoria: The Turning Point* (a history of Mr. Lincoln's anti-slavery campaign from 1854 to 1865), *Lincoln "by littles"* (a book of essays about President Lincoln), and *Money, Gold, and History* (essays analyzing the modern history of money and its role in civilization), among other books.

Lehrman, with Richard Gilder and Gabor Boritt, founded the Gilder Lehrman Lincoln Prize, which awards the Lincoln Prize for the best work of the year on the Lincoln era. Lehrman and Gilder established the Gilder Lehrman Center for the Study of Slavery, Resistance and Abolition at Yale University, which awards the Frederick Douglass Prize to the best work of the year on slavery, resistance, and abolition.

Together, Lehrman and Gilder developed the Gilder Lehrman Collection of original historical manuscripts and documents to teach American history from primary sources. The collection is on deposit for public access at the New-York Historical Society.

The Gilder Lehrman Institute of American History has developed a highly acclaimed national program for teaching American history in high schools and colleges throughout America (www.gilderlehrman.org). The Gilder Lehrman Institute, with George Washington's Mount Vernon and Washington College, established the George Washington Prize for the best book of the year on the era of President Washington.

Lehrman received a B.A. from Yale and an M.A. in history from Harvard. He was a Carnegie Teaching Fellow in History at Yale and a Woodrow Wilson Fellow in History at Harvard. He has been awarded honorary degrees from Babson College, Gettysburg College, Lincoln College, Marymount University, and Thomas Aquinas College.